MONEY, BANKING
INTERNATIONAL TRADE AND PUBLIC FINANCE

MONEY, BANKING INTERNATIONAL TRADE AND PUBLIC FINANCE

By

Ne. Thi. Somashekar

ANMOL PUBLICATIONS PVT. LTD.
NEW DELHI - 110 002 (INDIA)

ANMOL PUBLICATIONS PVT. LTD.
4374/4B, Ansari Road, Daryaganj
New Delhi - 110 002
Phones: 23261597, 23278000
Visit us at: www.anmolpublications.com

Money, Banking, International Trade and Public Finance

First Published, 2004

ISBN 81-261-1722-2

PRINTED IN INDIA

Published by J.L. Kumar for Anmol Publications Pvt. Ltd., New Delhi and Printed at Mehra Offset Press, Delhi.

Dedicated
to
The Lotus Feet
of
Sri Shaneshwara Swamy

CONTENTS

PART - A
MONEY

1. The Nature of Barter and Monetary Economy 3
2. Monetary Standards 20
3. Demand for and Supply of Money 46
4. Value of Money 60
5. Inflation, Deflation, Stagflation 84

PART - B
BANKING

1. Commercial Banking 107
2. Central Banking 134
3. Reserve Bank of India 151
4. State Bank of India 178
5. Money Market and Capital Market 182
6. Structure of Banking in India 203
7. Development Banks 230
8. Banker and Customer 247
9. Opening and Operating Bank Accounts 271
10. Pass Book 282
11. Cheques 287

12. The Paying Banker 304
13. Collecting Banker 313
14. Loans and Advances 320
15. Types of Securities 329
16. Modes of Creating Charge 349
17. Guarantees 360
18. Letter of Credit 370
19. Accounts and Audit of Banks 378

PART - C

INTERNATIONAL TRADE

1. Internal and International Trade 389
2. Gains from International Trade 400
3. Terms of Trade 405
4. Balance of Payments 419
5. Trade Policy 434
6. Foreign Investment and Collaborations 452

PART - D

PUBLIC FINANCE

1. Nature and Principle of Public Finance 497
2. Public Revenue 510
3. Public Expenditure 536
4. Public Debt 545
5. Fiscal Policy and Deficit Finance 556
Bibliography 575

PREFACE

There are many excellent text books on **Money, Banking, International Trade and Public Finance** written by well known English and American writers. However, none of these can claim to cover the entire courses of study prescribed by Indian universities. Moreover, most of these books are above the understanding of an average Indian student of Economics. The present book is an humble effort in this direction.

This book is designed to provide a comprehensive introduction to the subject matter of Money, Banking, International Trade and Public Finance. It should prove a useful text to any student embarking upon a course of study in this subject. It covers the syllabi prescribed by all the Indian universities in **Monetary Economics** for the degree and the post graduate classes. In addition, I hope, it will also be of beneficial to candidates appearing for various competitive examinations such as I.A.S., I.E.S., C.A and N.E.T. examinations.

The present volume contains **4** parts devoted mainly to the study of Money, Banking, International Trade and Public Finance. Part **'A'** of the book consisting 5 chapters presents a discussion of the various topics of theoretical and practical importance in the monetary sphere. Part **'B'** of the book covering 19 chapters mainly relating to banking devoted to the study of the development of money market, commercial bank, central bank and other financial institutions and their importance in the economy. Part **'C'** of the book contains 6 chapters that largely concern themselves with the study of the International trade sector of the economy. Part **'D'** of the book consisting of 6 chapters discusses the theory of Public Finance in its various aspects.

The help of many sources of information has been taken in writing this volume. In order to acknowledge these sources, a bibliography has been given at the end of the book. Many of my students and colleagues have read the manuscript and told me that the presentation is clear, logical and systematic. I would now leave the judgement to the other readers and I particularly welcome their comments and constructive criticisms.

I express my gratitude to my honourable guide Shri Dr. A. Ethirajulu Naidu M.A., M. Phil., Ph.D., who has been inspiring me to finish this work timely. My thanks are also due to my wife Smt. Sujatha Somashekar and my son N.S. Swaroop who gave me sufficient time to complete this work. I also extend my thanks to Prof. K. Varaha Murthy, Department of Economics, (A.F.G.C.), Gauribidanur, Prof. R. Venu Gopala, Department of Commerce (GFGC), Koratagere, Prof. Sunanda, Department of Economics (M.E.S. College) Bangalore, Prof. Krishnaveni, Department of Economics (Sheshadripurm College) Bangalore, Prof. Amaranarayana, Department of Economics (SFGC), Thumkur, Prof. V.R. Heggade, Principal (Thunga College), Thirthahalli, Shri Mahalinga (Sapna Book House) Bangalore, and Srinivasamurthy (Anmol Publications Pvt. Ltd.) New Delhi for rendering assistance in various forms in preparing the manuscript of this book.

Thanks are also due to S. Madhusudan and his staff, M/s Data Link, Bangalore for Typesetting with efficiency and patience.

Finally, I like to thank the publishers for undertaking to publish this book.

23.06.2003 **Ne. Thi. Somashekar**

Part - A

MONEY

1. The Nature of Barter and Monetary Economy 3

2. Monetary Standards 20

3. Demand for and Supply of Money 46

4. Value of Money 60

5. Inflation, Deflation, Stagflation 84

Chapter - 1

THE NATURE OF BARTER AND MONETARY ECONOMY

Introduction

In the primitive society man was self sufficient. In the beginning of human existence, wants were simple, limited and direct and every individual produced his own food of animal flesh and vegetables, prepared his own clothing and found his own shelter. But with the passage of time, people settled in different regions which increased their needs. This necessitated them to have transactions in order to get the commodities not available with them. Initially exchange was direct, i.e., exchange of goods for goods. This direct exchange of goods was known as **Barter System**. Barter is exchanging of "the comparatively surplus for the comparatively necessary". For instance, a farmer who had plenty of food but no clothes exchanged a part of his food with the person who had plenty of clothes but no food. In course of time, barter exchange proved to be inconvenient and more time consuming. In this chapter we shall be studying the inconveniences of barter system, evolution of money and its functions.

Inconveniences of the Barter System

A few major inconveniences of the barter system may be traced below :

Inconveniences of the Barter System

1. Lack of double coincidence of wants.
2. Difficulty of Sub-division.
3. Lack of common measure of value.
4. Lack of common store of value.
5. Inconvenience for borrowing and lending.
6. Lack of Portability.

1. Lack of double coincidence of wants

The barter economy lacked double co-incidence of wants. For example, Swaroop had 20 sheep and he wanted one horse. Swaroop must go in search of man who had horse and who wanted sheep. Suppose Swaroop meets Shashanka who had horse, but Shashanka did not want sheep, and he wanted grain then Swaroop cannot exchange his sheep with Shashanka. Here wants of Swaroop and Shashanka do not coincide. Lack of co-incidence of wants of Swaroop and Shashanka will hinder the exchange of sheeps for horse. Thus, the barter system lacked double co-incidence of wants.

2. Difficulty of Sub-division

The second inconvenience or the difficulty of the barter system was the lack of sub-division of many things. Because many things could not be sub-divided, it hindered exchange of goods. To turn to the old example, Swaroop had 20 sheep Shashanka has one horse. If both of them agree to exchange 20 sheep for one horse, the exchange could take place. But if Swaroop wants to give only ten sheep, can Shashanka give Swaroop half horse? Here obviously Shashanka cannot give half horse for ten sheep. So exchange cannot take place. Thus under the barter system many such things as sheep, goat, cow etc., could not be divided and hence exchange of such things became difficult. In the modern world Swaroop can sell his ten sheep for 1000 rupees and with the 1000 rupees he gets, he can purchase any thing. The rupee can be divided into 100 paise and the difficulty of sub-division is solved by the use of money.

3. Lack of Common Measure of Value

The barter economy also lacked common measure of value. This means there was nothing in that old society to measure the value of things. Today we have money. With the help of money we can measure the value or the worth of goods. For example, one goat costs Rs. 800, one sheep costs Rs. 1,000, one hen costs Rs. 150 and one cycle cost Rs. 1,250 and so on. With money we can measure the value of anything in the present-day world. In the ancient society there was no such a common commodity as money to measure the value of goods. Then the people crudely measured the value of things in things only. One sheep costed measured 12 hens; 1 cow costed 8 sheep and so on.

4. Inconvenience for Borrowing and Lending

Barter system is inconvenient as regards borrowing and lending. For instance, if a person borrows a pair of oxen for a year to two, he cannot return the same pair of oxen, because by that time they would either become old, slim or even die. Therefore, it is not possible to return the same pair of oxen in original form after lapse of time. So lending and borrowing become extremely difficult under barter system.

5. Lack of Portability

Under barter system, it is inconvenient to carry bulky goods from one place to another for transaction purposes. But, in the present money economy, any amount of money can be easily carried or transferred without any difficulty.

6. Lack of Common Store of Value

Lastly, the barter system lacked a common store of value. This means people had no proper means to store their wealth. Today we store our wealth in gold or bank savings. In those times people had to store their wealth in cows or sheep or goats etc. Clearly, this was bad, because the cows or the sheep died whenever there was an epidemic among the animals. In this sense the barter system lacked a good store of value.

The barter system therefore was extremely inconvenient. Thus men gave up the barter system. Instead, they used a commonly accepted commodity which was used to buy and sell goods and services. This commonly accepted commodity was known money.

Evolution of Money

How money developed through the various stages from ancient time to the modern times? Answer to this is the evolution of money. The stages in the evolution of money may be divided into

1. Animal money
2. Commodity money
3. Metallic money and
4. Paper money.

1. Animal money

Animals were being used a common medium of exchange in the primitive hunting stage. History records that cattle occupied a place of pride as money in the earliest period of human civilization. In temperate regions of Europe, Asia, and Africa cattle was regarded as the most standard unit of barter for quite a long time in the primitive era. In the Aryavartha, the early Aryans used cows as money. In the fourth century B.C., the Roman State had officially recognised crows and sheep as money to collect fines and taxes.

2. Commodity money

Under barter system different communities have at different times, used different commodities as money. Generally articles of common consumption were used as money, which include tobacco, hides, shells, bullets and nails etc. People living near sea-shore chose shells, fish, or baits as a medium of exchange. Hunting communities adopted, skins, tigers claws, jaws, elephants' tusks, bows, arrows, etc., as money. People living in cold countries used skins, furs, reindeers or dogs as money. Similarly people in villages used cattle, goats, sheep or agricultural commodities as money. Thus different commodities were used as money which were commonly consumed or desired by people. Even now, in some villages rice and wheat are commonly used as money for buying other goods.

3. Metallic money

With the advancement of civilisation, commodity money began to prove inconvenient. The commodities were bulky and difficult to carry from one place to another. They could be lost or easily destroyed by fire and they even lost their value often. Thus the money that satisfied his own people could not satisfy others. This led to discover something that would not satisfy people all over the world. The discovery of metals led him to use them as money. In the beginning several metals like gold, silver, copper, iron, etc., were used as money in their crude form. These metals were durable, scarce, precious and were also superior to commodities as money.

The introduction of coinage was undoubtedly due to private enterprise: but the privilege was soon usurped by the State. Each king tried to introduce his own coins, Sovereignty and independent coinage, so to say, went together. The kings used to issue coins of definite weight, fineness, size and also with their images on the face of the coins.

4. Paper money

Paper currency forms the third stage in the evolution of money. Upto 17th century people used metallic coins alone as money. But metallic money too had its limitations. It would be easily lost or stolen. They were bulky to carry from place to place. When trade and commerce increased in 17th and 18th centuries merchants preferred to carry receipts issued by goldsmiths and money lenders with great reputation which were accepting by others. These receipts were safe and secured like the metallic coins themselves. Moreover, the merchants were also afraid of the highway robbers. That was how paper money was used as a substitute money or as a representative money: it represented gold and silver coins and was also easily convertible into gold and silver coins.

The evolution of money did not stop here. Paper currency has now been replaced by bank money or credit money. This is also due to the needs of the times and requirements of exchange. The rapid expansion of trade and commerce during 18th and 19th centuries increased the transactions between merchants and dealers and the value running to crores of rupees. Naturally, it became difficult to use paper money alone. Besides, the development of banks availed a better media for easy and convenient transactions viz., bank credit. The bank money or credit comprises of cheques, drafts, bills of exchange and other negotiable instruments, which can be issued to any amount and also can be quickly sent to far off distances without risk. There is both safety and convenience. As a result, therefore bank credit, has becomes extremely popular. In all advanced countries like U.K., U.S.A., and others, more than 85 per cent of money is in the form of credit money.

Meaning of Money

The word **Money** is derived from the Latin word **Moneta** which refers to the name of the Goddess Juno, in whose temple at Rome money was coined. Money is the modern oil which lubricates the wheels of all economic activity and organisation.

Money may be any commodity by common consent as a medium of exchange. It is accepted in payment for goods and services and in settlement of debts. It is given and received without preference to the person who is using it. For instance, a rupee note is a rupee note whether it is used by the President of India or by a blind beggar in the street. Anything which is used as money should have the following features:

(a) it should be used a to buy and seli all goods and services.

(b) it should be generally acceptable, that is, it should be accepted in payment for goods and services ;

(c) it should pass from hand to hand, that is, it should be received regularly with the idea of offering it in payment to others ; and

(d) it can be anything-a useful or useless commodity, a metal (like gold or silver), a piece of paper (e.g. currency note). etc.

Money can be defined as follows:

Money is any commodity a metal or even a piece of paper which is generally accepted by people, a medium of exchange and payment.

There is one difference between money and all the other goods, People want goods because of their usefulness. But the commodity serving as money is wanted because it helps in buying all other goods.

Definitions of Money

The concept money has been defined in different ways by different economists. A few important definitions are-

1. Walker

Money is what money does". According to this definition, we can include all those things in money which performs the functions of money. Thus money does not comprise metallic coins and currency notes only. It also includes cheques, hundies, bills of exchange, etc., because they also performs the functions of money.

2. Crowther

Money as "any thing that is generally acceptable as a means of exchange (i.e. as means of settling debts) and at the same time acts, as a measure of value".

3. Robertson

"Money is a commodity which is used to denote anything which is widely accepted in payment for goods or in discharge of other kinds of business obligations".

4. G.D.H. Cole

"Money is purchasing power some thing which buys things".

5. Marshall

"Money includes all those things which are (at any time and place) generally current without doubt or special enquiry as a means of purchasing commodities and of defraying expenses".

Money may be thus any commodity chosen by common consent as a medium of exchange. It is accepted in payment for goods and service and in settlement of debts. It is given and received not with reference to the person who is noting it. e.g., a rupee note is a rupee note whoever uses it, either a common man or the Prime Minister of India.

Qualities of Good Money

Money, to be called good, must have the following qualities or characteristics.

1. General Acceptability

Money to be good, must be generally acceptable by all the people in the country. Gold and silver coins, and currency notes are generally accepted by all the people as money in the country. So they are good money. But the bank cheques are not generally accepted as money, and so the cheques are not good money.

2. Portability

Good money should be portable. It should not be heavy to carry in the pockets. Good money should contain big value in small bulk Gold coins satisfy this condition. Even currency notes are not heavy to carry. So both the gold coins and the currency notes may be called good money. Bricks and tiles very heavy and even if they are made money, they are not good money. This is because they are not portable.

3. Durability

Good money material should also be durable. If the money material is not durable and is perishable, it does not constitute good money. In this sense, paper currency are not good money, because they are easily destroyed. But the torn notes can be exchanged for new notes at the Reserve Bank at no extra cost. In that case we may say that currency notes are also durable, and therefore, they are good money. All coins satisfy this condition of durability.

4. Cognizability

Good money should have cognizability. This means that we should readily recognise money as such. For example we can easily recognize a one -rupee coin as a rupee coin. Even a child can recognise it as a rupee coin. Good money should have cognizability in this sense. If money has no such cognizability, it may be termed as bad money. There should be no doubt in recognizing the money or the coin.

5. Homogeneity

Good money should possess homogeneity. This means each coin should be similar to the other and there should be no difference between the two coins. One rupee coin is exactly similar to the other one-rupee coin. There is no difference between the two. This is called homogeneity.

6. Divisibility

Good money should be divisible. For example, one rupee is divisible into 100 paise. This will help us to purchase even the smallest of the things. If money is not divisible in this way, we call such money as bad money.

7. Stability

Lastly, good money should have stability of Value. Good money should not have changes in its purchasing power quite often. If money undergoes change in this value quite often, it becomes bad money. The purchasing power of money should remain constant, so that the buyers or the sellers may not be put to a loss. Unfortunately, most of the modern currencies have lost their original value since the World War II. This is indeed a bad sign.

Thus good money should have durability, cognizability homogeneity, divisibility, stability, portability and have general acceptability.

Classification of Money

Modern money can be classified as under.

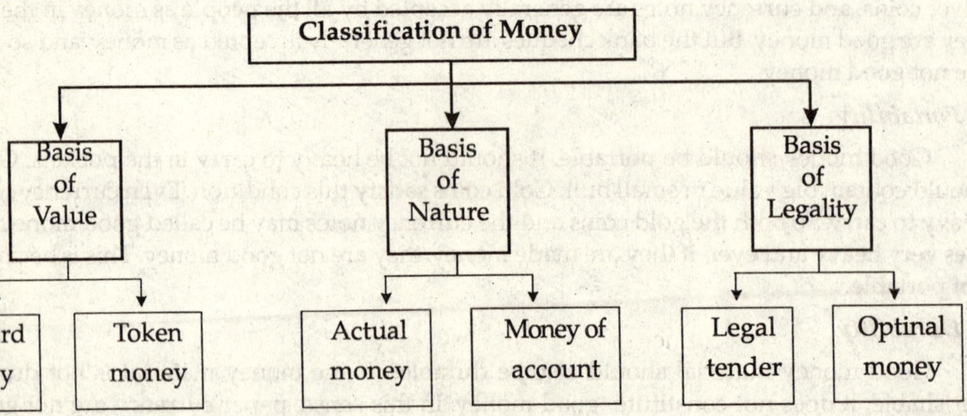

A. Classification on the Basis of Value

1. Standard or full bodied money

Standard money is one which is made of pure metals like gold, silver, and copper etc. Standard money is also known as full bodied money. Full bodied coins are those coins, whose face value and intrinsic (real value) value are equal. In the past gold and silver coins were full bodied coins.

A coin is said to be subject to free coinage when anybody is permitted to bring his metal to the mint and get it changed into coins. If the government does not change any price for minting it will be called a "gratuitous" coinage. If the government charges more than the cost, it is "Seigniorage". If the government charges just the cost of minting it is known as "Brassage".

2. Token Money

Token coins are made out of impure metals. Their official value will be greater than their real value. Generally, token coins are worthless by themselves but are given value by the government. For instance, the present paper currency and metallic coins are of this nature. Their face value is greater than their real value.

B. Classfication on the Basis of Nature of Money

J.M. Keynes classifies money as (a) Actual money and (b) Money of Account.

1. Actual Money

It refers to money used in practice in a country. It serves as a medium of exchange and as well as the basis of deferred payment. Goods and services are brought and sold and wealth is stored in terms of actual money.

2. Money of Account

This refers to that type of money in terms of which accounts are maintained in the country. All loans, prices and values are expressed in terms of the money of account. In India, the types of money had undergone changes i.e.,. India had used gold and silver coins and at a present uses paper currency. However, the account of money is maintained in the form of rupees only.

C. Classification of the Basis of Legality

1. Legal Tender

Legal tender money is one which a creditor is bound by law to accept in discharge of the debt due to him.

The creditor cannot refuse when payment is offered in the legal tender. If he refuses, the payment is deemed to have been made on the day it was offered and the debtor does not incur any interest liability thereafter.

Limited Legal Tender : When money can be offered upto a limited amount , it is called a limited legal tender. A creditor is not bound to accept it when paid beyond this sum.

Unlimited Legal Tender : The money is unlimited legal tender when it can be offered for payment to an unlimited extent till the entire debt is cleared. Our rupee and half-rupee coins are unlimited legal tender, although they are not subject to free coinage and the metal contained in them has not the same value equal to the value given to them by the government. All other coins of smaller denominations are of limited legal tender i.e., they can be paid upto Rs. 25/- only. For instance, if you have to pay the college examination fee of Rs. 50/- you can pay the same on the form of currency notes, rupee coins or half rupee coins as they are of unlimited legal tender. But you cannot pay the entire sum in the form of 10 paise, 5 paise or 25 paise etc.

2. Optional Money

It refers to the bank-money or bank credit which is ordinarily accepted by the people but has no legal sanction behind it. Though it enjoys general acceptability, no one could be forced to accept it against the wishes of the people. However, if the person paying this type of money enjoys high credit in the market everyone will readily accept it. The different instruments used under this system are cheques, hundies and so on.

Functions of Money

Having studied the nature and qualities of money, let us now consider the functions of money. These functions are of the same nature as the remedies that might be employed to overcome the inconveniences of the barter economy. These have been summed up in the following couplet:

Let us describe each one of them briefly.

A. Primary Functions of Money

1. Medium of exchange

It is true that people can directly sell goods and services. But there are many disadvantages of this barter transaction. Barter involves two economic decisions, namely, a sale and a purchase. Merging these two decisions into one complicates the decision-maker's problem. It is generally difficult to have double coincidence of wants of individuals in a modern economy. For example, if a farmer having surplus rice wants to have a cow, then he must search not only for a man who wants his rice, but for one who also have a cow. Also goods are not readily divisible add to the complications under barter. The use of money, as medium of exchange removes all of these problems, since money generalises the purchasing power. The decisions regarding a sale are separated from the decisions regarding purchase. The absence of coincidence of wants of individuals is no longer a problem.

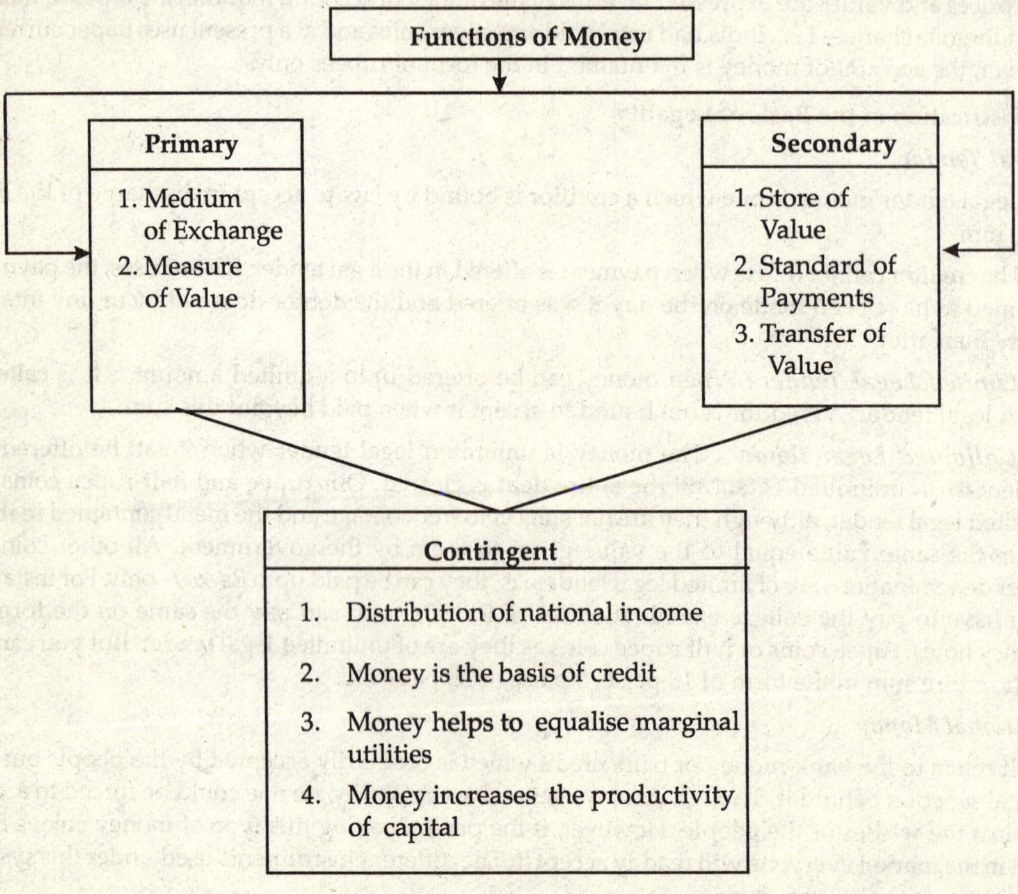

2. Common measure of value

In a modern economy, the values of goods and services are measured in terms of the unit of money just as the unit of measuring length is meter. Such a common unit of account is important for the emergence of price and for rational economic calculation and choice by the individuals. For example, if the price of a chair is Rs. 100 and the price of a table Rs. 800, comparing the money prices it is easy for anyone to say that the value of one table is equivalent to the value of eight chairs. This sort of comparison, in terms of money prices can be made for any number of commodities. Under barter it is difficult to measure/compare the values of goods.

B. Secondary Functions of Money

1. Money acts as a store of value

Without the use of money it would be impossible to build up for the future store of many things. Money, therefore makes it possible for a person to provide for old age. By foregoing current consumption he can accumulate a reserve of purchasing power for use in the future, though there is no certainty that the things he wants will be available when he wants them. Money serves as a store of value or more correctly it enables a person to keep a portion of his assets liquid. Liquid assets are those which can be used for any purpose at any time he likes. Most of the persons in the modern world prefer to keep currency notes in their pockets or at home, or they may keep current accounts with the banks withdrawable by cheques. The necessity arises from the fact that the stream of income and that of expenditure do not keep pace with each other.

2. Money acts as a standard of deferred payments

The use of money makes it possible for payments to be deferred from the present to some future date; it also enables contracts to be made in the present for the future delivery of goods. Credit transactions cannot easily be carried out unless money is used. The vast credit structure of the modern world is based on the use of money and much of production today depends on credit facilities being available. Money by serving as a standard measure of payments over time, makes borrowing and lending much less risky. Thus, money helps to buy and sell or borrow and lend. In other words, money serves as a standard of deferred payments.

3. Money acts as a transfers value

Money transfers value. A person can sell his property in one place, and with the money so obtained, he can purchase the property in another place, value will thus be transferred . Such things have happened in India after the partition of the country.

The following lines sum the primary and secondary functions of money :

> *"Money's a matter of functions four,*
> *A medium, a measure, a standard, a store.*
> *But this does not complete the functions*
> *unless we add transferability more."*

C. Contingent Functions

1. Distribution of national income

Money helps in the distribution of national income between people and various factors of production in the form of remunerations, viz., rent to landlord, wages to labour, interest to capital and profit to entrepreneur.

2. Money is the basis of credit

In recent years, the importance of credit has increased in all countries of the world. Credit instruments are used on an extensive scale. The use of cheques, bills of exchange etc., has gone up particularly in the developed countries of the west. Money becomes the basis of credit and without it credit instruments cannot circulate. The important credit instruments are cheques, bills, promissory notes etc.

3. Money helps to equalise Marginal utilities

Money enables the consumers and producers to maximise their satisfaction. In other words to get optimum satisfaction, the marginal utilities of goods should be equalised with their prices. Beyond this point of equality, the prices will be more and the utilities will decline.

4. Money increases the productivity of Capital

Capital can be found in several forms, but money is the most liquid type of capital. Capital, on account of its liquidity could be put to several productive uses. The mobility of capital is also facilitative on account of the liquidity of money.

From this discussion, one fact clearly emerges i.e., the basic function of money is the medium of exchange. All other functions flow from this.

Significance of Money

Money is the modern oil which lubricates the wheels of all economic activity and organisation. In the absence of money, business would have been at a standstill; the exchange system would not have progressed substantially because of the difficulties of the barter system; production and consumption would have had their own difficulties. All these drawbacks of economic activity and organisation were removed with the introduction of money. It helped the exchange system by providing a means of measuring the value of each commodity and service. This led to price mechanism and monetary transactions. All the factors of production and distribution could now be rewarded in terms of money. In the long run the country also can become prosperous through foreign trade and the accumulation of more money.

Hence money is what money does. It ranks as one of the fundamental discoveries of man and has acquired so much significance that the present-day economy is described as money economy. It has made possible rapid economic progress and man is so accustomed to its use that he can not think of dispensing with it. It has facilitated the realisation of the advantages of the division of labour, the introduction of large-scale production of goods and services, and the extension of various forms of business and financial transactions

We may now enumerate the specific roles of money in the present day world as below.

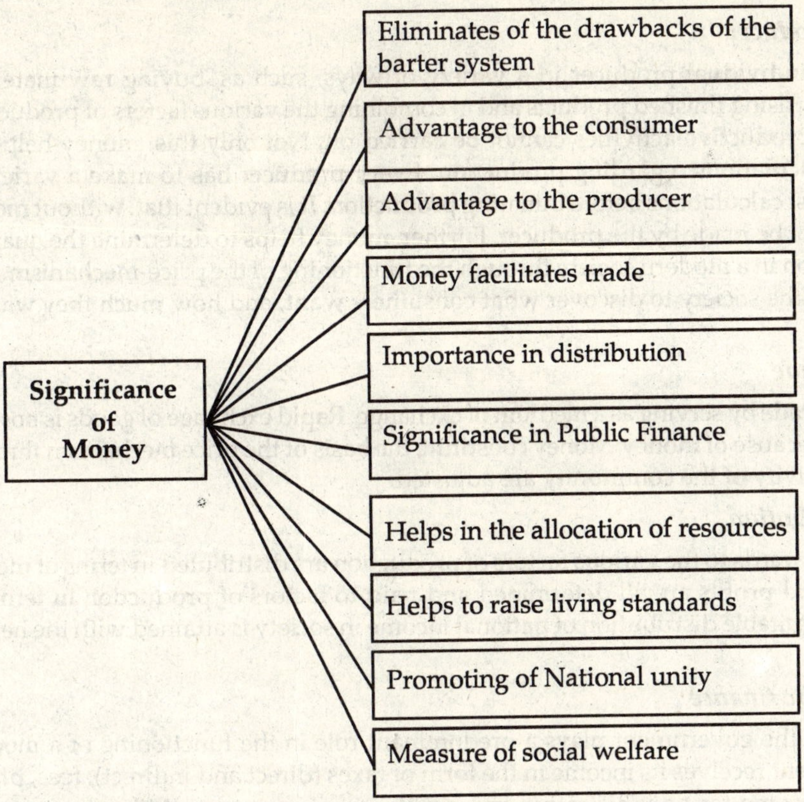

1. Money eliminates the drawbacks of the barter system

The difficulties and drawbacks of the old barter system have now disappeared. The double coincidence of wants between two individuals is no longer necessary. The value can now be measured easily and quickly. There is no difficulty in the exchange of indivisible goods. Nor is there any difficulty in exchanging one commodity for another. No difficulty is experienced in strong purchasing power.

2. Advantage to the consumer

The consumer has greatly benefited with the invention of money. The consumer can postpone his demand today if he so desires. If the consumer finds that the price of a particular commodity is high, he can postpone the purchase of the commodity till its price falls down to a more reasonable level. The purchasing power implicit in money can be utilized by the consumer at his option. It is not necessary for the consumer to spend money as soon as he obtains it. Due to the general acceptability and comparative stability of money, the consumer can utilize it as and when it suits him.

Besides money helps the consumer to equalize the marginal utilities accruing from diverse commodities. As is well-known, every consumer wishes to secure the maximum utility from his expenditure. But this is possible only when the marginal utilities obtainable from the various commodities are equal to each other. Money plays an important role in establishing equality among the marginal utilities of various commodities upon which the consumer incurs expenditure. What is more, money ensures freedom of choice to the consumers who can exercise their choice by comparing the monetary prices of rival products.

3. Advantage to the producer

Money helps the individual producer in a variety of ways, such as, buying raw materials, borrowing capital, advertising finished products and in combining the various factors of production. Without money, these productive activities cannot be carried on. Not only this, money helps the producer in making calculations regarding production. Every producer has to make a variety of calculations, such as, cost calculations before initiating production. It is evident that, without money, these calculations cannot be made by the producer. Further, money helps to determine the quantity and quality of production in a modern society through the functioning of the price-mechanism. This price mechanism helps the society to discover what consumers want, and how much they want of particular goods.

4. Money facilitates trade

Money facilitates trade by serving as a medium of exchange. Rapid exchange of goods is possible in a modern economy because of money. Money constitute the basis of the price mechanism through which the economic activity of the community are adjusted.

5. Importance in distribution

As we know, the rewards to the various factors of production are distributed in terms of money. Rent, interest, wages and profits are all determined and paid to factors of production in terms of money. Furthermore, equitable distribution of national income in society is attained with the help of money.

6. Significance in public finance

As is well-known, the government plays a predominant role in the functioning of a modern economy. The government receives its income in the form of taxes (direct and indirect), fees, prices, etc., and utilizes this income for administrative and development purposes. Without money, the administrative and developmental functions of a modern state would become difficult, if not impossible. Furthermore, the incurring of public debt and deficit financing too would be ruled out in the absence of money. In fact, fiscal management by the government would be an impossible task without money.

7. Money helps in the allocation of resources to different lines of production

The price-mechanism (expressed-in terms of money) allocates economic resources to different industries and lines of production in a capitalist economy. Without this price-mechanism, all economic activity under capitalism would come to an end. Even in a socialist economy. The Planning Commission is guided by the price-mechanism in the allocation of economic resources to individual industries.

8. Money helps to raise living standards

The smooth and uninterrupted functioning of the money-economy helps the society to raise its living standard by increasing overall production and through equitable distribution of wealth.

9. Money is the measure of social welfare

Social welfare can be measured through the medium of money. How much utility is derived by a particular person can only be measured in terms of money. An atmosphere of uncertainty will permeate Economics in the absence of money.

10. Promotion of national unity

Money has served to promote national unity in every country. The invention of money has lessened social isolation in a country. Money has encouraged trade and commerce. People residing in distant regions meet each other for commercial purposes. This serves to strengthen national unity in the country.

Money in a Capitalist Economy

The modern economy is rightly known as the money economy, for money occupies a central position. The influence of money is to be found in every section of the economy. The widespread use of money and credit and the changes in the value of money have profound influence on economic activity. The importance of money can be explained as follows:

(a) Money is the general medium of exchange

Everything is bought and sold, i.e., exchanged through the medium of money. Without it, there can be no trade and, therefore, no large-scale production.

(b) All incomes are in the form of money

This necessarily follows from the fact that money serves as general medium of exchange and of payments in settlement of debts. The firm which sells its goods receives money in payment ; its income, therefore, consists of money. Since every payment is made in money, every income is a money income (payment by one becomes income for another). Thus, in a modern economy, all incomes are money incomes.

(c) Wealth consists mostly of money

Everyone -individuals, institutions, companies and government-wishes to hold some cash to meet current obligations. The amount of cash held by people will naturally differ from individual to individual and from institution to institution. But money constitutes the most important form of wealth.

(d) Importance of money in consumption

A worker in a cloth mill cannot be paid in cloth or an employee in a shoe factory in shoes or a worker in a steel mill in iron. It is impossible for workers to go about exchanging cloth or shoes or iron for rice, wheat, vegetables and hundreds of odd things they require. When payment is made in kind (and not in money) there is a high possibility that the consumer gets too much of some goods and too little of others. The consumer, therefore, does not maximise satisfaction in the absence of money. On the other hand, when a consumer receives his income in the from of money, he can distribute it on the different goods in such a way that his total satisfaction will be the highest.

(e) Importance of money in production

The present day industrial production is based on minute division of labour or specialisation and also the existence of an extensive market to dispose of the commodity. It is money which has made possible extreme specialisation and, therefore, large-scale production. Money helps producers to discover through the price mechanism-what people want and how much they want. The producers use money to purchase materials for the construction of their factories : they use it to buy the supplies and materials necessary for their equipment. They bid comparatively in the markets of the world for the raw materials used in the process of manufacturing. They employ money as a means of attracting to their organisations the requisite labour force and officials.

(f) Significance of money in trade

In a primitive economy, there was very little trade. Naturally, the system of exchange was barter. With extension of trade, the need for money arose. Large scale production and extension of markets to sell the goods produced are impossible without the use of money. In the last two hundred years trade has become very extensive and to facilitate this, new types of money have been evolved. The use of bank cheques and bank drafts facilitates buying and selling of goods as well as payments.

Money, thus, occupies a central position in a capitalist economy. But what is its position in a socialist economy ?

Money in a Socialist Economy

The question is whether money has any role to play in a completely state-controlled, regulated and guided economy which is the socialist system. Marx, the father of communism, believed that money was the major cause for the exploitation of labour by the capitalists. When the communist party came to power in Russian after the Revolution of 1917, it attempted to replace money in selected areas by introducing a system of cards. It also endeavoured to abolish the use of money through extensive direct controls and free distribution of goods. It was hoped to effect a transition to a natural economy in which purchase and sale, and the medium with which they were carried out-that is, money-would have no place. It was soon realised that it was impossible to usher in communism without money and money calculation.

(a) Money is essential as a medium of payment

Even though the price system is given an inferior and subordinate position and does not always serve as a guide to production and consumption, yet the socialist Russian economy depends upon money as a medium of payment and as a standard of value.

(b) Money is essential to guide economic activity

Money will have to exist in order to guide economic activity, as in a capitalist economy.

(c) Money is needed for allocation of resources

The planning authority in a socialist economy has the responsibility of allocating economic resources in different lines of production. This can be done on the basis of social needs, etc., but without the help of a pricing system the process of allocation becomes almost impossible.

(d) Money is needed for distribution of incomes

Even in a socialist economy, the distribution of goods among the millions of consumers in an equitable manner will be difficult in the absence of a monetary mechanism.

Thus, the socialist economy will have to remain a money economy, even if every sector of it is planned and directed by the government.

Dangers of Money

Money, is not, however, an unmixed blessing. Money is a good servant but a bad master.

Money has proved dangerous in several ways.

(1) Economic Instability

Some economists are of the view that money is responsible for economic instability that is to be found in capitalist economies.

When there was no money, saving was not divorced from investment. Those who saved also invested,. But in a monetised economy, saving is done by certain people and investment by some other people. Hence, it does not follow that savings is and investment should be equal. When saving in a community exceeds investment, then national income, output and employment decrease and the economy is engulfed in depression. On the contrary, when investment exceeds savings (i.e., investment financed not by genuine savings but through deficit financing), then national income, output and employment increase and there is a spell of prosperity. But if the process of money creation and investment continues beyond the point of full employment, inflationary situation will be created. Hence, disparity between savings and investment resulting from the creation of money, is said to be the main cause of economic fluctuations.

The main danger of money lies in its liability of being over-issued in the case of inconvertible paper money. The over-issue of money may result in hyper-inflation as in India in 1973-74. Excessive rise in prices hits hard the consuming public and the fixed-incomists. It engenders speculation and inhibits productive enterprises. It also upsets debtor creditor relationship. It adverse affects distribution of income and wealth in the community so that the gulf between the rich and poor widens.

(2) Economic Inequalities

Money has proved to be a very convenient tool for amassing wealth and of the exploitation of the poor by the rich. It has created a yawning gulf between the 'haves' and the 'have-nots'. The misery and degradation of the poor is, thus, to no small measure due to the existence of money.

(3) Moral Depravity

Money has weakened the moral fibre of man. The evils to be found in the affluent society are only too obvious. The wealthy monopolise all the social evils like corruption, the 'wine and the woman'. In their case, money has proved to be a soul-killing weapon. In the words of an eminent German economist Von Mises, "money is regarded as the cause of theft and murder, of deception and betrayal. Money is blamed when the prostitute sells her body and when the bribed judge perverts the law. It is money against which the moralist declaims when he wishes to oppose excessive materialism. Significantly enough, avarice is called the love of money and all evil is attributed to it." Money in itself may not be bad, but its possession no doubt facilitates corruption and crime.

Thus, 'money which is a source of so many blessings to mankind becomes, unless we control it, a source of peril and confusion.'

Essential Features of a Sound and Satisfactory Monetary System

A modern economy uses money and credit extensively. A sound and satisfactory monetary system should, therefore, bring about an efficient and stable system of money and credit. We know that the primary function of money and credit is to facilitate exchange and, through exchange, promote production and distribution of goods services (within a country and between countries). This implies that the monetary authorities, charged with the function of issue of currency notes and creation of credit, should supply a sufficient amount of money to facilitate the easy flow of goods and services. The supply of money should neither be to much (for too much money will lead to an inflationary situation) nor too little (for too little money will result in a business depression). Thus, a sound monetary system will help to promote trade and development.

The use of money and credit facilitates production and distribution of goods. But money had another primary function also-to serve as measure of value. The value of all goods and services in an economy is expressed in terms of money. But unfortunately, the value of money need not be stable-it may rise (when the price level falls) or it may fall (when the price level rises). This instability in the value of money has serious consequences on the different sections of the community, as well as the nature of economic activity. For example, a rise in the value of money (fall in prices) may result in a business depression and unemployment ; a fall in the value of money (rise in prices) may result in inflation and consequent suffering to fixed income groups. Therefore, a satisfactory monetary system should assure not only an adequate supply of money but also establish a stable value to money.

Circular Flow of Money

National income is both a flow of goods and services and a flow of money incomes. On the one side, production units combine capital and labour and turn out goods and services, known as the gross national product. On the other, the production units which produce goods and services distribute money incomes to all the participants in the production process in the form of wages, rent interest and profit ; this is the total earnings of all the factor units and this is also called gross national income. What do people do with their earnings ? They will obviously spend them on getting goods and services produced by the community. The flow of national product is thus circular and one paves the way for the other. In fact, there are two flows-one is physical and the other monetary but both are related and both are completed at the end of each round of production and distribution. We can illustrate this circular flow assuming a two sector economy-viz., business sector and the household sector, the former producing with the help of the latter and the latter receiving income and spending the same on the goods and services produced by the former. We assume away the Government and the external relationship with other countries.

The above circular flow of money model has been prepared taking:

(a) Value of aggregate goods prepared (i.e. GNP) = Rs. 100 crores.

(b) Total income generated (i.e. GNI) = Rs. 100 crores.

The value of aggregate goods and services is the result of the aggregate expenditure of the community. The household sector spends Rs. 100 crores in buying goods and services produced by the business sector ; the expenditure of the household sector (Rs. 100 crores) becomes the income of the business sector (Rs. 100 crores). There is thus a circular and continuous flow of money.

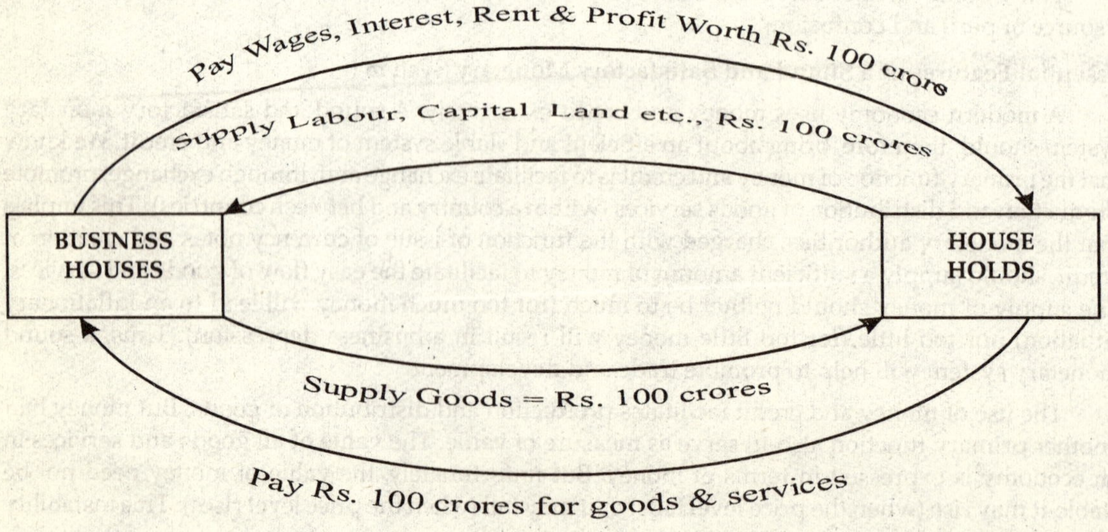

The above model of circular flow of money is too simple. Properly speaking, even in a two-sector model, saving and investment of the community should be taken into consideration. Saving is done both by the households and the business sector ; saving is withdrawal from the circular flow. But investment is undertaken by the business sector and it is injection into the circular flow. So long as saving and investment are equal, the total circular flow of money would be the same. To make the model of circular flow of money, we have to take the Government and the external sector. The Government's expenditure is injection and Government taxation has the effect of withdrawal from the circular flow of money. Likewise, exports are of the nature of injection into the circular flow (a country's exports are like country's investment elsewhere) while imports for which the country has to pay is of the nature of withdrawal from the income stream. The model of a circular flow of money is really useful to understand the working of an economy. The basic point to remember is that any increase in expenditure by the community on consumption (designated as C) or on investment (designated as I) or in Government expenditure (designated as G) or in exports will have the effect of expanding the circular flow of funds. On the other hand, saving (S), taxation and imports have the effect of contraction of the circular flow.

Bonus and Circular Flow of Money

Bonus payments are made by business enterprises of their profit surplus or their savings and are normally spent by the recipients (viz. the workers) on consumption. In our example, however, bonus payments are not used by the working class for their consumption expenditure but are to be used for developmental purpose. In any case bonus payments which are to be invested in development bonds have the effect of increasing investment and , therefore, expanding the circular flow of money.

Compulsory Deposit Instalments

These instalments are paid by the Government out of their savings. The recipients of these instalments may be expected to use these funds in only two ways-on consumption or on investment. In either case the total volume of expenditure increases and the circular flow of money expands.

Conclusion

From the above discussion, it is clear that the money may be any commodity chosen by common consent as a medium of exchange. It is accepted in payment for goods and services and in settlement of debts. It is given and received without reference to the person who is using it. For instance, a rupee note is a rupee note whether it is used by the President of India or by a blind beggar in the street.

Questions for Discussion

1. Define money, Explain the functions and form of money.
2. Discuss the role of money in a modern economy.
3. "Money is a good servant but a bad master" Comment
4. Explain the concept of circular flow of money and show its significance.
5. State the important landmases in the evolution of money.
6. "Money is a human invention to overcome the difficult of barter" Explain the statement bringing out the role of money in the modern economy.

Chapter - 2

MONETARY STANDARDS

Introduction

One of the most important functions of money is to serve as the standard measure of value. Therefore, the value of this monetary unit should not fluctuate too violently. To achieve this objective, the value of its currency unit is fixed in terms of one or two metals; gold and silver. Sometimes a country fixes the value of its currency with the currency of another country and artificially maintains it. This has resulted in the various monetary systems or standards. There is Monometallism, Bi-metallism and Paper Standard.

Meaning of Monetary Standard

The term **Monetary standard** refers to the type of standard money used in a country. The standard money, of course, is that legal money in which the government of the country itself discharges its own obligations. The monetary standard is thus, synonymous with the standard money adopted by a country's monetary authority. If the standard money happens to be made of gold the country is said to be on the gold standard. If the standard money is of paper, the monetary standard is referred to as paper standard.

In short, monetary standard refers to the nature and conditions of the issue of the standard money of a monetary system. In the words of Cathcart, "A monetary standard is the standard that is chosen by a society for its ultimate standard of value and which also, usually, serves as an asset of value promised on demand by debt-money issuers".

Some writers have defined monetary standard in a broader sense to include within its scope not only the selection of a unit of account, but also the laws and practices affecting a country's money. According to Shapiro. "The monetary standard of a nation involves the overall sets of laws and practices which control the quality and quantity of money in the system". Similarly, in the words of Kent, "A monetary standard can be defined as a monetary system built upon a specific standard of value". Such definitions create awkward situations because they imply that every change in the monetary system changes the monetary standard.

Monetary standard has two aspects : national and international. Basically, monetary standard is national in character because it is intended to meet the internal requirements of an economy, i.e., to serve as a medium of exchange and a measure of value. But, the monetary standard also assumes international character since it has to facilitate international payments. Thus, a sound monetary standard should fulfil two objectives :

(i) to maintain stability in the currency's internal value or the price level and

(ii) to maintain stability in the currency's external value, i.e., its value in terms of foreign currencies.

Qualities of a Good Monetary Standard

A sound monetary standard should possess the following qualities :

1. Simplicity

The monetary system should be simple and easily understandable. A simple monetary system inspires public confidence.

2. Elasticity

A good monetary system should be elastic. It should be capable of changing the money supply according to the requirements of the economy.

3. Economy

The monetary system should be economical. It should not require heavy expenditure on its operation. An expensive monetary system is a burden on the country. In this regard, paper money is better than metallic money.

4. Stability

A good monetary system should ensure internal price stability and external exchange rate stability. Stable internal price level is necessary for the economic growth of the country and stability in the foreign exchange rates is essential for the development of foreign trade.

5. Convertibility

A sound monetary system must possess the quality of convertibility of the currency into some expensive metal. Convertible currency system serves to inspire public confidence and facilitate international payments.

6. Legality

A good monetary system must possess legal sanction; it must be backed by the force of law. Legal tender money increases public confidence and ensures general acceptability.

7. Automatic Working

A good monetary system should have built-in-flexibility. It should be capable of operating automatically without government intervention. According to Prof. Cannan, gold standard was "a fool-proof and knave-proof standard". There was no scope for artificial change in gold standard.

8. Economic Development

An ideal monetary system must be helpful for a country to achieve the objectives of economic development and maximisation of employment.

9. Other Qualities

A monetary standard should also possess some other qualities like transferability, portability, cognizability, uniformity, divisibility, etc.

Types of Monetary Standard

Various monetary systems or monetary standards have been adopted in practice from time to time. These are as follows.

I. Metallic Standard

Under metallic standard, the monetary unit is determined in terms of some metal like gold, silver, etc. Standard coins are made out of the metal. Standard coins are full-bodied legal tender and their value is equal to their intrinsic metallic worth. The important thing to note is that to be on a metallic standard, country must keep (i) its monetary unit at a constant value in terms of the selected metal, and (ii) its various types of money convertible into the selected metal at constant values. Metallic standard may be of two types : monometallism and bimetallism.

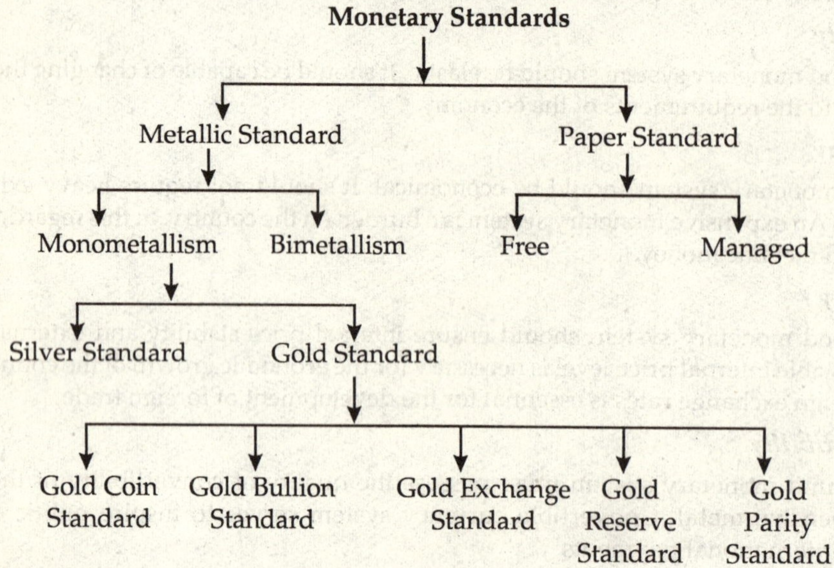

1. Monometallism

When a country makes one precious metal, gold or silver, as its standard of value, then that system is known as monometallism. If the standard metal is gold it is called gold standard. If it is silver, the system is called silver standard. Coins of definite weight and fineness circulate as the standard coins, encouraging exchange and functioning as the measure of value. There will be the free market of the metal, and unlimited free coinage of the coins from the specified metal of standard fineness. So the volume of money as well as the rate of exchange, even on the international level, is regulated.

Features of Monometallism

Essential features of monometallic standard are given below:

(a) Standard coins are defined in terms of only one metal.

(b) These coins are accepted as unlimited legal tender in the discharge of day-to-day obligations.

(c) There is free coinage (i.e., manufacture of coins) of the metal.

(d) There are no restrictions on the export and import of the metal to be used as money.

(e) Paper money also circulates, but it is convertible into standard metallic coins.

Types of Monometallism

Monometallism can be of two types :

1. Silver Standard

Under silver standard, the monetary unit is defined in terms of silver. The standard coins are made of silver and are of a fixed weight and fineness in terms of silver. They are unlimited tender. There is no restriction on the import and export of silver. The silver standard remained in force in many countries for a long period. India remained on silver standard from 1835 to 1893. During this period, Rupee was the standard coin and its weight was fixed at 180 grains and fineness 11/12. The coinage of the Rupee was free and people could get their silver converted into coins at the mint. Similarly, silver coins could be melted into bullion.

Silver standard lacks universal recognition as compared to gold standard. There is greater instability of both internal and external values of money under silver standard because silver price fluctuates more than that of gold. Thus, as far as the metal is concerned, gold is preferred to silver in most of the countries.

2. Gold Standard

Gold standard is the most popular form of monometallic standard. Under gold standard, the monetary unit is expressed in terms of gold. The standard coins possess a fixed weight and fineness of gold. The gold standard remained widely accepted in most of the countries of the world during the last quarter of the 19th century and the fist quarter of the 20th century. The U.K. was the first country to adopt the gold standard in 1816. She was also the first to abandon this standard in 1931. Germany adopted the gold standard in 1873, France in 1878 and the U.S.A., in 1900. Gradually, gold standard disappeared from different countries and finally it was completely abandoned by the world by 1936.

Merits of Monometallism

Monometallic standard has the following advantages :

1. Simplicity

Since only one metal is used as a standard of value, monometallism is simple to operate and easy to understand.

2. Public Confidence

Since the standard money is made of a precious metal (gold or silver), it inspires public confidence.

3. Promotes Foreign Trade

Monometallism facilitates and promotes foreign trade. Gold or silver standard is easily acceptable as an international means of payment.

4. Avoids Gresham's Law

Monometallism avoids the operation of Gresham's law. According to this law, when both good as well as bad money exist in the economy, bad money tends to drive out of circulation good money.

5. Self-Operative

It makes the supply of money self-operative. If there is surplus money supply, the value of money will fall and the people will start converting coins into metal. This will wipe out the surplus money, again creating balance.

Demerits of Monometallism

The following are the demerits of monometallism :

1. Costly Standard

It is a costly standard and all countries, particularly the poor countries, cannot afford to adopt it.

2. Lacks Elasticity

Monometallism lacks elasticity. Money supply depends upon the metallic reserves. Thus, money supply cannot be changed in accordance with the requirements of the economy.

3. Retards Economic Growth

Economic growth requires expansion of money supply to meet the increasing needs of the economy. But, under monometallism, scarcity of metal may create scarcity of money supply which, in turn, may hinder economic growth.

4. Lacks Price Stability

Since the price of the metal cannot remain perfectly stable, the value of money (or the internal price level) under monometallism lacks stability.

2. Bimetallism

When two metals, gold and silver, are recognised as standards of value, and when both circulate freely as legal tender at a fixed ratio of exchange with each other, that system is called Bimetallism. Both metals of standard weight and fineness are also freely minted in this system. The ratio of exchange with each other is maintained by the currency authority. When both the metals are full legal tender but only one is freely minted, then that system is called Limping standard. As one is not freely minted but only the other, there will be a limp, as in walking. France had this standard for some time when both gold and silver were used as under Bimetallism, but silver was not freely minted.

Features of Bimetallism

(a) A bimetallic standard is based on two metals; it is the simultaneous maintenance of both gold and silver standards.

(b) There is free and unlimited coinage of both metals.

(c) The mint ratio or the ratio of the values of gold and silver at the mint is fixed by the government.

(d) Two types of standard coins (i.e., gold coins and silver coins) are in circulation at the same time.

(e) Both the coins are full-bodied coins. In other words, the face value and the intrinsic value of both the coins are equal.

(f) Both the coins are unlimited legal tenders. They are also convertible into each other.

(g) There is free import and export of both the metals.

Merits of Bimetallism

The merits of bimetallism are discussed below:

1. Convenient Full-bodied Currency

Bimetallism provides convenient full-bodied coins for both large and small transactions. It provides portable gold money for large transactions and convenient silver money for smaller payments. This argument has, however, lost its force now when credit money has developed.

2. Price-Stability

Under this monetary system, shortage of one metal can be offset by increasing the output of the other metal. Consequently, stability in the prices of both the metals and hence, in the internal prices can be ensured.

3. Exchange Rate Stability

Bimetallism ensures stability of exchange rate. As long as gold and silver are stabilised in terms of each other, the currencies of all countries with fixed values in gold or in silver would exchange for each other at nearly constant rates.

4. Sufficient Money Supply

Under bimetallism, sufficient money supply is assured to meet the trade requirements of the economy. Since there is no question of both metals becoming scarce simultaneously, money supply is more elastic under this system.

5. Maintenance of Bank Reserves

Under bimetallism, the maintenance of bank reserves becomes easy and economical. Under this system, both gold and silver coins are standard coins and unlimited tender. Therefore, it is easy for the banks to keep their cash reserves either in gold coins or in silver coins or in both.

6. Low Interest Rates

Since, under bimetallism, money is made of two metals, its supply is generally more than its demand. As a result, the interest rate declines. Banks can extend loans at cheaper rates. This would increase investment and hence production in the economy.

7. Stimulates Foreign Trade

Bimetallism stimulates international trade in two ways: (i) A country on bimetallism can have trade relations with both gold standard and silver standard countries. (ii) There are no restrictions on imports and exports due to the free inflow and outflow of both types of coins.

Demerits of Bimetallism

Bimetallism has the following demerits :

1. Operation of Gresham's Law

Bimetallism in a single country is a temporary and not workable monetary standard due to the operation of Gresham's law. According to this law, when there is a disparity between the mint parity rate and the market rate of exchange of the two metals, bad money or the over-valued metal at the mint (whose mint price exceeds market price) tends to drive out of circulation good money or under-valued metal at the mint (whose market price exceeds mint price). Thus, ultimately, single metal money (monometalism) will remain in practice. Thus, national bimetalism is only a temporary phenomenon. Only international bimetallism can prove permanent and practicable.

2. Inequality between Mint and Market Rates

Bimetallism can operate successfully only if the equality between the market rate and the mint rate can be maintained. But, in practice, it is difficult to maintain equality between the two rates, particularly when one metal is oversupplied than the other.

3. No Price Stability

The argument that bimetallism ensures internal price stability and there will be an automatic adjustment between supply and demand for money is illusionary. There can be a possibility of both the metals to become scarce.

4. Payment Difficulties

Bimetallism leads to difficult situation in the settlement of transactions when one partly insists on payment in terms of a particular type of coins.

5. Encourages Speculative Activity

It encourages speculative activity in the two metals when their prices fluctuate in the market.

6. No Stimulus to Foreign Trade

International trade is stimulated if all the countries adopt bimetallism. But, this is a rare possibility in the present circumstances.

7. Costly Monetary Standard

Bimetallism is a costly monetary standard and all nations, particularly the poor nations, cannot afford to adopt it.

Gresham's Law

In connection with coinage there is Gresham's Law. Sir Thomas Gresham was the financial adviser to Queen Elizabeth I (1533-1603). She was anxious to reform English currency. But whenever new coins, freshly minted, were put in circulation she found that they were disappearing. She consulted her financial adviser who, after studying the situation, said, "bad money drives good money out of circulation when both are legal tender". This is called Gresham's law.

Bad money means old coins which are worn out and which have therefore slightly lost their intrinsic value. They also lose their appeal when both good and bad money are in circulation. So they are disposed of, whenever possible, for good money. Good money means coins of full value, of standard weight and fineness. They are brand new being just out of the government mint. This good money is normally hoarded, melted for ornaments and other purposes, or even exported for it may fetch a higher value abroad. The same is the tendency when we have brand new notes as well as soiled notes. We try to preserve the new ones and part with the soiled ones.

The theoretical explanation of this law is in terms of the divergence of the market rate of exchange of the two currencies from mint rate. If the mint rate (i.e., the official rate of exchange between two types of money) differs from the market rate of exchange between the two types of money, then the over-valued money at the mint will tend to drive the under-valued money out of circulation. Suppose, under bimetallism, one gold coin exchanges for 10 silver coins, i.e., the official rate of exchange or the mint rate is 1 : 10. Now, if the market rate is 1 : 12, then gold is under-valued and silver is over-valued at the mint rate (i.e., the market rate of gold exceeds the mint rate and the market rate of silver is less than its mint rate). In this case, gold will become good money and silver a bad money. The bad money (silver) will drive out good money (gold) from circulation.

Operation of the Law

When both good and bad money are together in circulation as legal tender, good money disappears in three ways :

1. Good Money is Hoarded

When both good and bad money circulate simultaneously, people have the tendency to hoard good money and use bad money for making payments.

2. Good Money is Melted

Since, both good coins and bad coins are in circulation and have the same value, people prefer to melt good coins to convert them into ornaments or other itmes of art.

3. Good Money is Exported

In payments to the foreign countries, gold coins are accepted by weight and not by counting. Thus, it would be profitable to pay to the foreigners in terms of new full-weight coins rather than old and light-weight coins.

Gresham's Law a General Form

Gresham's law, in its original form, applies only to debased coins of monometallic system (i.e., gold standard). But, the law can, however, be extended to all forms of monetary standards :

1. Under monometallism (for example gold standard), the old and worn-out coins are regarded as bad coins and full-weight coins are considered good coins. According to Gresham's law, the old and worn-out coins drive new and full-weight coins out of circulation.
2. Under bimetallism (generally a system of gold and silver coins), coins of over-valued metal are considered bad money and coins of undervalued metal as good money. Thus, according to Gresham's law, the over-valued coins will drive under valued coins out of circulation.
3. Under paper standard, if both standard metal coins and inconvertible paper notes are in circulation, metallic coins will be good money and paper notes will be bad money. Thus, paper notes will drive out standard coins from circulation.

Marshall presented a generalised version of the law : "Gresham's law is that an inferior currency, if not limited in amount, will drive out the superior currency".

Limitations of the Law

Gresham's law will operate if the following necessary conditions are satisfied.

1. Intrinsic value of Good Money

An important condition for Gresham's law is that the intrinsically higher value money (i.e., good money) must also be more valuable in other uses than it is as money in circulation. The failure of this condition to apply explains why the coin currency today remains in circulation as fairly as paper currency despite its higher intrinsic value.

2. Fixed Parity Ratio

The applicability of the law requires that the intrinsically more valuable money must be relatively fixed by law in its parity with another money. The law will not hold where one money becomes intrinsically more valuable than another money (at the old parity) if the parity changes.

3. Sufficient Money Supply

The law will operate only if both good money and bad money are in circulation and the total money supply is more than the actual monetary requirements of the economy.

4. Adequate Supply of Bad Money

The applicability of the law requires that there should be sufficient bad money in circulation to meet the transactions requirement of the people. If there is scarcity of bad money, both good and bad money will remain in circulation and the law will not operate.

5. Contents of Pure Metal

The law will not operate if the content of pure metal in coins is less than that in the old ones.

6. Acceptability of Bad Money

The law will operate if people are prepared to accept bad money in transactions.

7. Distinction between Good Money and Bad Money

The law assumes that people can distinguish between bad money and good money.

8. Development of Banking Habit

The law applies in the absence of banking habits. Development of banking habits among the people tend to discourage hoarding and thus restrict the operation of Gresham's law.

9. Convertibility

The law also does not operate if the country is on convertible paper standard.

GOLD STANDARD

Gold standard is the most popular form of monometallic standard. Under gold standard, the monetary unit is expressed in terms of gold. The standard coins possess a fixed weight and fineness of gold. The gold standard remained widely accepted in most of the countries of the world during the last quarter of the 19th century and the first quarter of the 20th century. The U.K. was the first country to adopt the gold standard in 1816. She was also the first to abandon this standard in 1931. Germany adopted the gold standard in 1873, France in 1878 and the U.S.A. in 1900. Gradually, gold standard disappeared from different countries and finally it was completely abandoned by the world by 1936.

Meaning

Gold standard has been defined differently by different monetary economists. According to **D.H. Robertson**, "Gold standard is a state of affairs in which a country keeps the value of its monetary unit and the value of a defined weight of gold at an equality with one another". According to Coulborn, "The gold standard is an arrangement whereby the chief piece of money of a country is exchangeable with a fixed quantity of gold of a specific quality". In the words of **Kemmerer**, "a gold standard is a monetary system in which the unit of value, in which price and wages are customarily expressed, and in which the debts are usually contracted, consists of the value of a fixed quantity of gold in an essentially free gold market".

Features of the Gold Standard

Basic features of the gold standard are :

(a) The monetary unit is defined in terms of certain weight and fineness of gold.

(b) All gold coins are held as standard coins and considered unlimited legal tender.

(c) All other types of money (paper money or token money) are freely convertible into gold or equivalent of gold.

(d) There is unlimited coinage of gold at no cost.

(e) There is free and unlimited melting of gold.

(f) Import and export of gold is freely allowed.

(g) The monetary authority is under legal obligation to buy and sell at the fixed price without limit.

Functions of Gold Standard

There are two main functions of the gold standard :

1. To maintain Stability of the Internal price-level

This is an important function of the gold standard. This standard renders valuable service in maintaining stability of the internal price-level. As is well-known, additional currency under the gold standard cannot be issued unless additional gold reserves are available. As pointed out above, there is a direct relationship between money and gold under this standard. In order to issue additional currency, the monetary authority needs additional gold reserves. Since gold reserves are not found in unlimited quantities, there is no danger of any exclusive issue of money under gold standard. The possibility of inflation is almost non-existent.

2. To maintain Stability in Foreign Exchange Rates

Gold standard renders useful service in maintaining exchange stability which in its turn, stimulates the foreign trade of the country. As pointed out above, the monetary authority under gold standard sells gold to an unlimited extent at a fixed price. The people can buy gold in the desired quantity at that price. If the balance of payments of the country turns unfavorable, the importers would like to make foreign payments in gold instead of in foreign currencies, because the monetary authority is ever ready to sell gold at a fixed price. When importers make foreign payments in gold, the demand for foreign currencies will naturally go down. Consequently, there will be no rise in foreign exchange rate. Gold standard thus helps to maintain exchange stability.

Automatic Working of the Gold Standard

The most important feature of the gold standard is that it is an automatic standard. It can operate automatically without interference from the monetary authority. In other words, under international gold standard, the equilibrium in the balance of payments of the gold standard countries is automatically achieved through gold movements.

The self-adjusting mechanism of gold standard can be explained by the theory of gold movements. According to this theory, the country with relatively high cost-price structures loses gold, while the country with relatively low cost-price structure gains gold. In other worlds, the country with deficit balance of payments (i.e., with excess of imports over exports) will experience gold outflow and the country with surplus balance of payments (i.e., excess of exports over imports) will experience gold inflow.

Suppose two countries A and B are on gold standard. Further suppose that country A experiences a deficit balance of payments while country B has a surplus balance of payments. The disequilibrium between these two countries will be automatically corrected through the mechanism involving the following steps :

1. Gold Movement

Gold will flow out of country A with adverse balance of payments and will flow in to country B with favourable balance of payments.

2. Changes in Money Supply

Given the gold reserve ratio in both the gold standard countries, the outflow of gold will lead to a contraction in the supply of money (i.e., of currency and credit) in country A. On the other hand, the inflow of gold will result in the expansion of money supply in country B.

3. Changes in Prices and Economic Activity

Contraction in money supply will lead to a fall in the prices and the profit margins in country A. This will, in turn, reduce investment, income output and employment in that country. On the other hand, expansion of money supply will raise prices and profit margins and consequently investment, income, output and employment in country B.

4. Changes in Imports and Exports

Fall in prices in country A will encourage foreigners' demand for its products. Moreover, decrease in income in country A will discourage demand for goods from other countries. Thus, exports will increase and imports will decrease in country A. Similarly, rise in prices in country B will lead to a reduction in exports and increase in income will lead to an expansion of imports in that country.

5. Equilibrium in the Balance of Payments

Expansion of exports and contraction of imports would create conditions of favorable balance of payments in country A. On the other hand, contraction of exports and expansion of imports will lead to an adverse balance of payments in country B. As a result, gold will start flowing from country B to country A and this will ultimately remove disequilibrium in the balance of payments in both the countries.

Thus, the movements of gold as a consequence of a disequilibrium in balance of payments will automatically create conditions for removal of the disequilibrium in the balance of payments in the gold-standard countries. The self-adjusting mechanism of the gold standard may be summarised as in the following diagram :

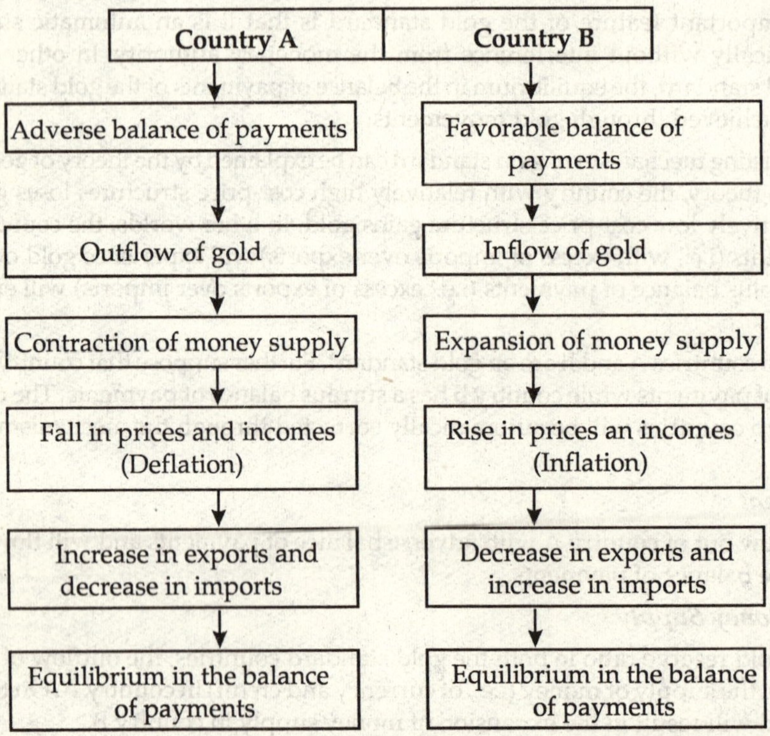

Conditions of the Gold Standard

For the smooth and automatic working of gold standard, certain conditions are to be fulfilled. These conditions are called 'the rules of the gold standard game'. According to Crowther, "The gold standard is a jealous God. It will work provided it is given exclusive devotion".

1. Rules of the gold standard should be observed

Monetary authorities should adopt "the rules of the gold standard game". The observance of these rules is very important for the success of the international gold standard. The rules are :

(i) gold movement should be freely allowed between countries ;

(ii) there should be automatic expansion or contraction of currency and credit with the inflow and outflow of gold ; and

(iii) the monetary authorities in the different countries should co-operate and facilitate the adjustment process.

2. Maintenance of stable exchange rates

The major objective of the international gold standard is to bring about stable exchange rates. Monetary authorities should be willing to follow this primary objective of maintaining stable exchange rates. This will necessitate the monetary authorities following the rules of the gold grame scrupulously, even though it may involve inflationary and deflationary conditions.

3. Flexibility of prices

The efficient working of the international gold standard would require a certain degree of flexibility in the price, wage and income structure of all the gold standard countries. For instance, inflow of gold will lead to expansion of money and credit and hence rise in prices and wages, i.e., an inflation will follow a favourable balance of payments. On the other hand, outflow of gold will lead to contraction of money and credit, fall in price and unemployment. Such price flexibility in prices and costs of production will be essential for the smooth and automatic working of the gold mechanism. The monetary authorities should permit this flexibility.

4. Trade should be free

The use of high import duties has the tendency to restrict imports but promote exports - that is, to bring out the favourable balance of payments. If any one country follows such a policy, it may not matter but if all gold standard countries adopt similar policies, international trade will be considerably reduced. If countries believe that an increase of imports is dangerous and should be avoided at all costs, international gold standard will have no place at and hence it will fail.

5. Absence of large capital movements

An effective functioning of international gold standard will require the absence of large capital movements between countries. Sometimes, large capital movements take place due to political, social and economic disturbances. Such outflow of capital is of the nature of panic movement of capital and if it is of considerable quantity it will break the gold mechanism. Political and financial stability and the absence of panic outflow of capital (i.e., gold) are necessary conditions for the success of the gold standard.

Before 1914 all these conditions were present and hence the international gold standard worked smoothly and successfully. But during 1919-29 these conditions could not be fulfilled and hence some countries like France advocated the return to the international gold standard but these attempts failed as countries did not intend to follow the rules of the gold game.

Advantages of the Gold Standard

The important advantages of the gold standard are as follows :

1. Creates confidence

The gold standard creates confidence in the public mind since the common circulating medium is convertible to gold coins or gold bars or gold drafts.

2. Stability in the rate of exchange

The gold standard fixes the rate of exchange between countries with reference to the gold contents of the respective currencies. There is very little chance for the rate of exchange to fluctuate under gold standard.

3. Automatic working

The gold standard works in an automatic fashion. An adverse or favourable balance or an inflation or deflation is automatically corrected.

4. Stability in internal prices

The gold standard brings about relative stability in internal prices. Import of gold will lead to rise in prices and export of gold will result in contraction of prices. But the rise in prices will not be too high to make it an inflation ; so also contraction of prices will not be so bad as to make it a depression.

5. Medium of payments between countries

Gold serves as the medium of payments between countries. It promotes international trade and facilitates international investments.

Disadvantages of the Gold Standard

The chief demerits of the gold standard are :

1. Not Always Simple

Gold standard in all its forms is not simple. The gold coin standard and, to some extent, gold bullion standard may be regarded as simple to understand. But, the gold exchange standard which relates the currency unit of a country to that of the other is by no means simple to be comprehended by a common man.

2. Lack of Elasticity

Under the gold standard, the monetary system lacks elasticity. Under this standard, money supply depends upon the gold reserves and the gold reserves cannot be easily increased. So money supply is not flexible enough to be changed to meet the changing requirements of the country.

3. Costly and Wasteful

Gold standard is a costly standard because the medium of exchange consists of expensive metal. It is also a wasteful standard because there is a great wear and tear of the precious metal when gold coins are actually in circulation.

4. Fair-weather Standard

The gold standard has been regarded as a fair-weather standard because it works properly in normal or peaceful times but during the periods of war or economic crisis, it invariably fails. During abnormal periods, those who have gold try to hoard it and those who have paper currency dry for its conversion into gold. In order to protect the falling gold reserves, the monetary authority prefers to suspend the gold standard.

5. Sacrifice of Internal Stability

The gold standard sacrifices domestic price stability in order to ensure international exchange rate stability. In fact, under gold standard, inflation and deflation respectively are necessary companions to a favourable and an unfavourable balance of payments. Given the world's total monetary gold stock, and individual country's monetary gold stock, the trading country's money supply and the internal price level changes by the inflow or outflow of gold as a result of international trade. Thus the presence of external trade almost guarantees price instability under gold standard mechanism.

6. Not Automatic

The automatic working of the gold standard requires the mutual cooperation of the participating countries. But, during the World War I, because of the lack of international cooperation, all types of countries, those receiving gold as well as those losing gold, found it necessary to abandon the gold standard to prevent disastrous inflation on the one hand and even more disastrous deflation and unemployment on the other.

7. Deflationary

According to Mrs. Joan Robinson, gold standard generally suffers from an inherent bias towards deflation. Under this standard, the gold losing country is under the compulsion to contract money supply in proportion to the fall in gold reserves. But the gold gaining country, on the other hand, may not increase its money supply in proportion to the increase in gold reserve. Thus, the gold standard, which necessarily produces deflation in the gold losing country, may not generate inflation in gold receiving country.

8. Economic Dependence

Under gold standard, the problems of one country are passed on to the other countries and it is difficult for an individual country to follow independent economic policy.

9. Unsuitable for Developing Countries

Gold standard is particularly not suitable to the developing economies which have adopted a policy of planned economic development with an objective to secure self-sufficiency.

Causes for the Breakdown of the Gold Standard

Before World War I, gold standard worked efficiently and remained widely accepted. It succeeded in ensuring exchange stability among the countries. But with the starting of war in 1914, gold standard was abandoned everywhere mainly because of two reasons : (a) to avoid adverse balance of payments and (b) to prevent gold exports falling into the hands of the enemy.

After the war in 1918, efforts were made to revive gold standard and, by 1925, it was widely established again. But, the great depression of 1929-33 ultimately led to the breakdown of the gold standard which disappeared completely from the world by 1937. The gold standard failed because the rules of the gold standard game were not observed. Following were the main reasons of the decline of the gold standard.

1. Violation of Rules of Gold Standard

The successful working of the gold standard requires the observance of the basic rules of the gold standard : (a) there should be free movement of gold between countries ; (b) there should be automatic expansion or contraction of currency and credit with the inflow and outflow of gold ; (c) the government in different countries should help facilitate the gold movements by keeping their internal price system flexible in their respective economies. After World War I, the governments of gold standard countries did not observe these rules mainly because they did not want their people to experience the inflationary and deflationary tendencies which would result from following the gold standard.

2. Restrictions on Free Trade

The successful working of gold standard requires free and uninterrupted trade of goods between the countries. But during interwar period, most of the gold standard countries abandoned the free trade policy under the impact of narrow nationalism and adopted restrictive policies regarding imports. This resulted in the reduction in international trade and thus followed the breakdown of the gold standard.

3. Inelastic Internal price System

The gold standard aimed at exchange stability at the expense of the internal price stability. But during the interwar period, the monetary authorities sought to maintain both exchange stability as well as price stability. This was impossible because exchange stability is generally accompanied by internal price fluctuations.

4. Unbalanced Distribution of Gold

A necessary condition for the success of gold standard is the availability of adequate gold stocks and their proper distribution among the member countries. But in the inter-war period, countries like the U.S.A. and France accumulated too much gold while countries of Eastern Europe and Germany had very low stocks of gold. This shortage of gold reserves led to the abandonment of the gold standard.

5. External Indebtedness

Smooth working of gold standard requires that gold should be used for trade purposes and not for the movement of capital. But during the inter-war period, excessive international indebtedness led to the decline of gold standard. There were three main reasons for the excessive movement of capital between countries : (a) After World War I, the victor nations forced Germany to pay war reparations in gold, (b) There was movement of large amounts of short-term capital (often called as refugee capital) from one country to another in search of security ; (c) There was plenty of borrowing by the under developed countries from the advanced countries for investment purposes.

6. Excessive Use of Gold Exchange Standard

The excessive use of gold exchange standard was also responsible for the breakdown of gold standard. Many small countries which were on gold exchange standard kept their reserves in London and New York. But rumours of war and abnormal conditions forced the depositing countries to withdraw their gold reserves. This led to the abandonment of the gold standard.

7. Absence of an International Monetary Centre

Movement of gold involves cost. Before 1914, such movement was not needed because London was working as the international monetary centre and the countries having deposit accounts in the London banks adjusted their adverse balance of payments through book entries. But during inter-war period, London was fast losing its position as an international financial centre. In the absence of such a centre every country had to keep large stocks of gold with them and large movements of gold had to take place. This was not proper and easily manageable. Thus, gold standard failed due to the absence of international financial centre after World War I.

8. Lack of Monetary Co-operation

Economic co-operation among the participating countries is a necessary condition for the success of gold standard. But after World War I, there was complete absence of such co-operation among the gold standard countries, which led to the downfall of the gold standard.

9. Political Instability

Political instability among the European countries also was responsible for the failure of gold standard. There were rumours of war, revolutions, political agitations, fear of transfer of funds to other countries. All these factors threatened the safe working of the gold standard and ultimately led to its abandonment.

10. Great Depression

The world-wide depression of 1929-33 probably gave the final blow to the gold standard. Falling prices and wide-spread unemployment were the fundamental features of depression which forced the countries to impose high tariffs to restrict imports and thus international trade. The great depression was also responsible for the flight of capital.

11. Rise of Economic Nationalism

After the World War I, a wave of economic nationalism swept the European countries. With an objective to secure self-sufficiency, each country followed protectionism and thus imposed restrictions on international trade. This was direct interference in the working of the gold standard.

Thus, both endogenous as well as exogenous factors were responsible for the breakdown of the gold standard : (a) Some factors referred to the internal weaknesses of the gold standard ; (b) Others pointed out the failures of the monetary authorities to help the smooth working of the system ; and (c) Still others indicated the adverse external circumstances under which the gold standard had to work. Under the conditions prevailing today, motivated by economic nationalism and dominated by selfish commercial systems, there is little hope of revival of the gold standard in the near future.

Forms of Gold Standard

Historically, there have been different forms of gold standard. They are (a) gold coin standard, (b) gold bullion standard, (c) gold exchange standard, (d) gold reserve standard and (e) gold parity standard.

A. Gold Coin Standard

Gold coin standard or gold currency standard or gold species standard is the oldest form of gold standard. It is also known as orthodox gold standard or traditional gold standard. This standard was prevalent in the U.K., France, Germany and the U.S.A. before the World War I. Gold coin standard is also regarded as full gold standard because under this standard full-bodied standard coins made of gold were circulated. Other forms of money are redeemable into gold. According to Crowther: "A currency system in which gold coins either form the whole circulation or else circulate equally with notes is known as the full-gold standard".

Features of the Gold Coin Standard are:

(a) Monetary unit is defined in terms of gold. For example, before World War I, sovereign was the standard coin in the U.K. Its weight was 123.17447 grains with 11/12 purity.

(b) Other forms of money (e.g. token coins and paper money) are also in circulation. But they are convertible into gold.

(c) Coinage is unlimited and free of cost.

(d) There is free and unlimited melting of gold coins.

(e) The government buys and sells gold at fixed ;prices and thereby maintains parity between the face value and intrinsic value of the standard coin.

(f) There is free import and export of gold.

(g) Gold is unlimited legal tender for all types of payments. All values are expressed in terms of gold.

Merits

The gold coin system had the following advantages :

1. Public Confidence

Since the standard coin is made of gold, it is universally acceptable. Thus, gold coin standard enjoys full confidence of the public.

2. Automatic Working

It is automatic in working and needs no government intervention. Money supply depends upon the volume of gold reserves and money supply can be changed in accordance with the desired changes in the volume of gold reserves.

3. Price Stability

Since there are no frequent changes in the supply of gold, this system ensures reasonable degree of internal price stability.

4. Exchange Stability

Free and unrestricted import and export of gold under gold coin standard ensures stability in foreign exchange rates. This promotes international trade.

5. Simplicity

This is the simplest form of gold standard which can be easily understood by the common people.

B. The Gold Bullion Standard

After the First World War, many countries returned to the gold standard but on the bullion basis. A country is said to be on the gold bullion standard, when is currency system contains the following features :

1. The standard currency unit, expressed as a definite quantity of gold of a certain fineness.
2. Gold is not coined but is kept in the form of bars or bullion as a reserve against the currency notes which are in circulation.
3. All currency units such as the currency notes and subsidiary coins are redeemable at par in gold bullion, in fixed quantities.
4. Gold bars are bought and sold by the Treasury or the central bank in fixed quantities and at fixed prices, without any limit whatsoever. For instance, when England was on the gold bullion basis between 1925 and 1931, the Bank of England redeemed its notes in gold bars of 400 oz, at the rate of £ 3 - 17 - 6 per oz.

5. As in the gold coin standard, gold is freely imported and exported under the bullion basis also.

The gold bullion standard was used by many countries in the inter-war period (1919-39) as a means of economising the use of gold. The basis of this system is that gold is not required for internal circulation and that gold bars are required for settling international payments.

Resemblance with gold currency standard. The gold bullions standard resembles the gold coin basis in two important respects. One, the currency unit is defined in terms of a weight of gold. All currency notes and subsidiary coins are convertible to gold coins or gold bars. Two, in both the systems, gold is used to correct an adverse balance of payments with any other country.

Differences between the two systems. In the gold coin standard, gold coins circulate along with other forms of currency. In the gold bullions basis, on the other hand, gold coins do not circulate and the circulating medium consists of currency notes and subsidiary coins. Secondly, as against the rule of free coinage and free melting under the gold coin basis, the central bank or the monetary authority will sell or buy gold bars in fixed quantity at fixed prices. But the purpose behind free coinage and free melting as well as selling and buying gold bars is the same – viz., to settle payments between countries.

The gold bullion standard is considered superior to the gold currency system on two grounds : In the first place, the entire gold reserve is held by the central bank or the Treasury and gold will be available only for purposes of international payments, i.e., to meet adverse balance of payments and not for internal purposes. Secondly, the gold bullion standard is usually adopted to "economise" on gold by those countries which want all the advantages of the gold standard but without the circulation of gold coins.

In some respects the gold bullion standard is inferior to the gold coin basis. For instance, the common man will easily recognise and understand the working of the gold coin standard, for gold coins actually circulate in the country and paper currency notes are convertible to gold coins. But he does not ordinarily come across gold under the gold bullions version. Besides, it is difficult for him to convert his currency notes into gold bars since he will never be able to command so much resources. Thus, the gold coin standard creates greater public confidence than the gold bullion standard.

C. Gold Exchange Standard

A country is said to be on the gold exchange standard if its currency unit is convertible to another country's currency unit which is on the gold coin or bullion standard. In this system the currency unit is convertible to gold not directly but indirectly through the help of some other currency. The features of the gold exchange standard are :

(a) The standard currency unit of the country is expressed in terms of a definite quantity of gold of certain fineness.

(b) Neither gold coins circulate in the country nor gold bars are kept as a reserve against paper currency notes.

(c) The monetary authorities maintain a reserve or bank account in a foreign country.

(d) All currency notes and subsidiary coins issued by the central bank or the treasury are convertible to or redeemed, in minimum amounts at fixed rates on demand, in a foreign country.

(e) The monetary authorities are prepared to buy or sell foreign drafts against local currency.

Merits of the Gold Exchange System

The gold exchange standard has definite superiority over the other systems – it is very economical in the use of gold.

(a) Like the gold bullion standard, the exchange system gives up the use of gold for internal circulation. As gold coins do not circulate within the country, the monetary authorities need not buy gold for foreign purposes.

(b) The same gold reserves kept in one country (say, England) will serve as the basis of monetary systems in two countries (for England and India).

(c) By keeping a balance or reserve with foreign banks, the Government can earn some interest on its deposits. This is much better than keeping gold in the form of bars or bullion which cannot earn any income for the monetary authorities.

(d) The Government can earn a profit from the margin between the prices at which it buys and sells foreign exchange.

(e) All the advantages of the gold coin or gold bullion standard are made available without the actual use of gold.

(f) It is possible for even small countries to be on this standard since the system can be operated with a small quantity of gold reserve in a foreign country.

Weaknesses of the Gold Exchange System

But the gold exchange standard, in certain respects, is inferior to the other systems.

(a) It does not merit the confidence of the public. For, under the gold exchange standard, people do not use gold at any stage or at any time. It is difficult for the common man to realise and accept the fact that his currency is convertible to gold.

(b) Among all the types of the gold standard, it is this system which requires the maximum degree of monetary management.

(c) Many large countries consider it beneath their national dignity and prestige to link their currencies to some other currencies. They, therefore, do not prefer this system.

(d) No independent country will like to keep its gold reserve in another country for fear that either the foreign country may turn an enemy or it may go off the gold standard. This is responsible for the lack of confidence among nations in this system.

D. Gold Reserve Standard

After the breakdown of gold standard, a new monetary system, called gold reserve standard, was development in 1936 mainly to ensure stability in exchange rates. In 1936, Great Britain, the U.S.A. and France entered into a Tripartite Monetary Agreement according to which free flow of gold or foreign currency was allowed to stabilise exchange rates and promote foreign trade without affecting the internal value of the domestic currency. For this purpose, Exchange Equalisation Funds were created. The gold reserve standard functioned successfully for three years and came to an end with the outbreak of World War II.

Basic Features

The essential features of the gold reserve standard are :

1. No Link with Gold

Under this standard, gold is used neither as a medium of exchange nor as a measure of value. The domestic currency is made of paper money and token coins. The convertibility of domestic currency into gold is not ensured.

2. No Free Movement of Gold

Under this system, private individuals are not allowed to import and export gold. The government monopolises the country's import and export of gold. Gold is imported and exported only for monetary purposes.

3. Exchange Equalisation Fund

Under this standard, the participating countries have to set up Exchange Equalization Fund for the purpose of maintaining stability in exchange rates. The Exchange Equalisation Fund, which is also known as Exchange Equalisation Account, comprises, besides local currency, foreign exchange and gold. If the demand for foreign currency rises, the Fund will increase the supply of that foreign currency in the open market and thus will prevent any rise in the value of that currency in terms of other currencies.

4. Strict Secrecy

The composition and movement of reserves of the Exchange Equalisation Fund are kept strictly confidential from the public

5. Exchange Stability

Under this standard, exchange rate stability is achieved without distributing the internal economy of the member country.

E. Gold Parity Standard

In essence, gold parity standard is the modern version of the gold standard. It came into force with the establishment of the International Monetary Fund (IMF) in 1946. Under this standard, every member country has to define the par value of its currency in terms of gold in order to determine the exchange rate. The gold parity standard aims at maintaining stable exchange rates without interfering into the domestic monetary system of the member countries.

Main Features

The basic features of the gold parity standard are given below.

1. No Link with Gold

Under this standard, gold is neither a medium of exchange nor a measure of value. The domestic currency comprises paper money and token coins of cheaper metals. The domestic currency is incovertible into gold coins or gold bars or foreign currency.

2. Par value of Money

Every member country has to define the par values of its money in-terms of gold. The par values of different currencies further determine the exchange rates for foreign transactions.

3. Exchange Rate Flexibility

This standard allows reasonable flexibility in the exchange rates because the member nations can alter the par values of their currencies under the regulations of the IMF.

4. Provision of Loans

Under this system, the IMF provides loans in foreign currencies to the member countries to ensure stability in foreign exchange rates.

5. Independent Monetary Policy

Under this standard, the member nations can follow independent monetary policies in their domestic affairs. The monetary policy of one country has no direct or indirect link with the monetary policy of another country.

II. THE PAPER STANDARD

Paper standard refers to a monetary standard in which inconvertible paper money circulates as unlimited legal tender. Under paper money standard, although the standard money is made of paper, both currency and metallic token coins serve as standard money for purposes of payment. No gold reserves are required either to back domestic paper currency or to facilitate foreign payments. The paper standard is known as managed standard because the quantity of money in circulation is controlled and managed by the monetary authority with a view to maintain stability in prices and incomes with the country. It is also called flat standard because paper money is inconvertible in gold and still regarded as full standard because paper money is inconvertible in gold and still regarded as full legal tender. After the general breakdown of gold standard in 1931, almost all the countries of the world shifted to the paper standard.

Features of the Paper Standard

The paper standard has the following features:

(a) Paper money (paper notes and token coins) circulates as standard money and is accepted as unlimited legal tender in the discharge of obligations.

(b) The unit of money is not defined in terms of commodity.

(c) The commodity value (or intrinsic value) of the circulating money is particularly nil.

(d) Paper money is not convertible in any commodity or gold.

(e) The purchasing power of the monetary units is not kept at par with any commodity (say gold).

(f) Paper standard is national in character. There is no link between the different paper currency systems.

(g) The foreign rate of exchange is determined on the basis of the parity of purchasing powers of the currencies of different countries.

Merits of the Paper Standard

Various merits of the paper standard are described below :

1. Economical

Since under paper standard no gold coins are in circulation and no gold reserves are required to back paper notes, it is the most economical form of monetary standard. Even the poor countries can adopt it without any difficulty.

2. Proper Use of Gold

Wastage of gold is avoided and this precious metal becomes available for industrial, art and ornamental purposes.

3. Elastic Money Supply

Since paper money is not linked with any metal, the government or the monetary authority can easily change the money supply to meet the industrial and trade requirements of the economy.

4. Ensures Full Employment and Economic Growth

Under paper standard, the government of a country is free to determine its monetary policy. It regulates its money supply in such a way that ensures full employment of the productive resources and promotes economic growth.

5. Avoids Deflation

Under paper standard, a country avoids deflationary fall in prices and incomes which is the direct consequence of gold export. Such type of situation arises under gold standard when a participating country experiences adverse balance of payments. This results in the outflow of gold and contraction of money supply.

6. Useful During Emergency

Paper currency is very useful in times of war when large funds are needed to finance war. It is also best suited to the less developed countries like India. To these economies, it makes available large amounts of financial resources (through deficit financing) for carrying out development schemes.

7. Internal Price Stability

Under this system, the monetary authority of a country can establish stability in the domestic price level by regulating money supply in accordance with the changing requirements of the economy.

8. Regulation of Exchange Rate

Paper standard provides more effective and automatic regulation of exchange rate, whereas under gold standard, the exchange rate is absolutely fixed. Whenever exchange rate fluctuates as a result of disequilibrium between demand and supply and forces, the paper standard works on imports and exports and restores equilibrium. It allows the forces of demand and supply to operate freely to establish equilibrium.

Demerits of the Paper Standard

The paper standard suffers from the following defects.

1. Exchange Instability

Since the currency has no link with any metal under paper currency, there are wide fluctuations in the foreign exchange rates. This adversely affects the country's international trade. Exchange instability arises whenever external prices move more than domestic prices.

2. Internal Price Instability

Even the commonly claimed advantage of paper standard, i.e., domestic price stability, may not be achieved in reality. In fact, the countries now on paper standard experience such violent fluctuations in internal prices as they never experienced under gold standard before.

3. Dangers of Inflation

Paper standard has a definite bias towards inflation because there is always a possibility of over-issue of currency. The government under paper standard generally has a tendency to use managed currency to cover up its budget deficit. This results in inflationary rise in prices with all its evil effects.

4. Dangers of Mismanagement

Paper currency system can serve the country only if it is properly and efficiently managed. Even the minor mistake in the management of paper currency can bring such disastrous results that cannot be conceived of in any other form of monetary standard. If the government issues little more or little less currency than what is required for maintaining price stability, it may lead to cumulative inflation or cumulative deflation.

5. Limited Freedom

In the present day world of economic dependence, it is almost impossible for a particular country to isolate itself and remain unaffected from the international economic fluctuations simply by adopting the paper standard.

6. Absence of Automatic Working

The paper standard does not function automatically. To make it work properly, the government has to interfere from time to time.

Methods of Note Issue

The currency laws of every country lay down certain rules and regulations for the issue of notes by the central bank. In different countries, different principles are followed, but all of them have the same aims and objectives. The chief aim is to secure uniformity. Uniformity is automatically realised when the note-issue function is exercised by a single institution.

The currency laws of every country prohibit the issue of notes by commercial banks and other institutions, and multiplicity is thus avoided. The second aim is to have a currency system which is elastic, a system under which the volume of currency can be finally adjusted to the requirements of trade and business. Lastly, it is essential to have a sound basis for note issue so as to secure convertibility of notes into gold. This, in fact, was very important so long as currency was convertible into gold. But now almost all countries have adopted the system of inconvertible paper money and this aim is not now of any significance. Several systems of note issue have been introduced in several countrics but the following are the chief categories.

1. Partial Fiduciary System

This system of note issue was introduced in England by the Bank Charter Act of 1974. According to this system, notes issued upto a certain limit called the fiduciary limit need not be covered by gold, they need be covered only by government securities. Notes issued over and above fiduciary limit should be backed up cent percent by gold. The Charter Act placed the fiduciary limit at 14 millions and the Bank of England was allowed to issue notes beyond that limit only with cent percent gold backing. At the same time the Bank of England was asked to buy and sell gold at £ 3-17-9 and £ 3-17-19 1/2 per standard ounce. This provision was intended to secure full convertibility of notes into gold as England was on gold standard at that time. This system, it was claimed, ensures convertibility of notes into gold and at the same time checks tendency to over issue.

But the very serious defect of the system is that it lacks elasticity as the supply of currency cannot be varied according to the needs of trade and business as it is tied down to the amount of metallic reserves. It hampers the freedom of the central bank by imposing a rigid limitation upon the issue of the currency and the system cannot control inflations and deflations. The act of 1944 has come in for a good deal of criticism on the ground that it was not able to prevent financial crisis, that it lacked elasticity and at the same time immobilised too much of gold. The weakness of the Act is apparent as it had to be suspended several times to meet financial crisis.

The Acts of 1928 and 1939 authorised the Bank of England to raise the fiduciary limit with the permission of the Treasury and the Parliament. It may be noted that the fiduciary limit has been increased during the war and after and at the end of 1956, the fiduciary limit stood at £ 2,025 million so that the system has practically been abandoned by England. The fiduciary limit is subject to variation with the permission of the treasury and the Parliament.

2. Maximum Issue System

This system was in practice in France from 1870 to 1928. Under this system, a legal maximum is fixed to the note issue and the maximum limit is subject to review from time to time. The important features of this system is that no gold cover is prescribed. This system has been abandoned by France as it was found to be too rigid. The central bank is given a relatively free hand upto a certain limit to vary the amount of note issue and the system did not prescribe any relationship between the gold and the note circulation.

This system of note issue has been praised by Lord Keynes and several other writers as worthy of adoption by all countries. The maximum limit will check the propensity to over issue but at the same time within the limit, the central bank is free to change the supply of money.

3. Proportional Reserve System

Under this system, a certain percentage of the notes issued had to be covered by gold reserves, the rest being covered by specific assets such as trade bills and government securities. The Central Bank will have to maintain a certain percentage of gold reserves against note issue 20% or 40% or some other percent. Just as commercial banks need not maintain cent percent cash reserves against deposits because all depositors do not withdraw cash at one and the same time, in the same manner a central bank need not keep 100% gold reserves to secure full convertibility of notes as all the notes will not be presented for conversion into gold at the same time.

The proportional reserve system has been adopted by US, & U.S.A in 1914. The Federal Reserve Banks in addition to the approved securities; maintain 24 percent of gold reserves against note issue. This system, it is claimed secures elasticity and convertibility of notes into gold. The gold reserves create confidence in the public.

The system has a grave weakness in that it leads to multiple expansion and contraction of currency. If the central bank acquires Rs. 25 worth of gold it can issue notes to the extent of Rs. 100 and this is a thing that the central bank can easily carry out. But when one unit of gold reserve is lost, the bank will have to deflate currency by four times, a policy that involves difficulty in carrying out. This system it is pointed out, merely stabilises the relationship between the volume of gold and the volume of currency but cannot stabilise the value of currency. In times of crisis the system cannot secure full convertibility of all the notes presented for redemption. Thus it has the worst of both the words, it does not secure convertibility, nor can it prevent inflation and deflation from occurring.

4. Minimum Reserve System

Under this system, the central bank has to maintain minimum reserve of gold or foreign securities or both and no maximum limit is placed on the amount of note issue. The central bank is completely trusted and is given a relatively free hand to regulate the volume of currency according to the needs of the money market. The minimum reserves are prescribed as a concession to the feeling that exists in some quarters that they create a sense of confidence in the minds of the people. In India notes were issued under the proportional system till 1956 Act has introduced the minimum Reserve system.

The change has been made to meet the financial requirements of the second plan period. Under the present provision the Reserve Bank should maintain a minimum reserve of Rs. 200 crores worth of gold and foreign securities, of which gold should at least be Rs. 115 crores in value and the rest of the reserves may consist of foreign securities.

Qualities of a Good Currency System

A good currency should have the following characteristics:

1. The currency system must be simple, so that people can easily understand it. If it is complicated, people will not understand its working and will not be able to work it well.
2. The currency unit should have stable value. In other words, the good currency system must ensure a reasonable stability of the prices in the country. This means that the purchasing power of money in terms of goods and services in the country must not fluctuate too violently. Rapid price changes are harmful to trade, industry and the people at large.
3. The good currency system must bring about stable external value of the currency. If the ratio of a country's currency with the foreign currencies is maintained stable, its foreign trade would flourish. Economists have, however, come to hold now that the stability of internal prices is to be preferred to the stability of the foreign exchange ratio.
4. The currency system should receive the confidence of the general public. The currency system must inspire confidence. If the people have no faith in it, they will not accept it. The gold standard commanded the respect and confidence of the general public. But during the interwar period, it came under suspicion and mistrust. That was one of the reasons why it had to be given up. The paper currency system in which the people of the country have full confidence would be ideal.
5. The currency system must be elastic and automatic, so that the currency expands or contracts in response to the requirements of trade and industry. When as a result of rapid economic development trade expands, currency must expand sufficiently. The paper currency system is cheap and elastic.
6. The currency system should be definite and well-defined and should be subject to clear rules and regulations. Nothing should be left vague in the system. Privileges of the people as well as the obligations of the currency authority should be laid down in unmistakable terms so that there is no possibility of any misunderstanding.

The Indian paper currency system, as obtains today on the whole commands the confidence of the people of India. It is cheap since expansion of currency is relatively easy. It permits the Government and the monetary authorities to expand and contract the volume of currency according to the requirements of industry and trade. True, the purchasing power of the rupee is not so stable either internally, or externally. We know that the internal price level had risen to dizzy heights in 1973-74 and the internal purchasing power of the rupee had fallen considerably. Likewise the external value of the rupee has been fluctuating and since 1972 the rupee has been floated (no fixed value for the rupee). But in all these respects, the rupee is not in any way peculiar but resembles other major currencies of the world. For instance, inflation is a worldwide phenomenon ; and floating of currencies was resorted to by other countries too. Given these limitations and weaknesses, the Indian paper currency system has worked well.

Conclusion

To conclude, the term monetary standard refers to the type of standard money used in a monetary system. Standard money is that money through which the monetary authority may ultimately discharge its own obligations. The monetary standard is thus synonymous with standard money.

Questions for Discussion

1. What is a monetary standard ? What are the qualities of a good monetary standard.
2. Explain Bimetalisim as a monetary system. Describe its merits and demerits.
3. What is monometallism. Describe its merits and demerits.
4. State and explain the working of the Gresham's law.
5. What is gold standard ? Give main advantages and disadvantages of gold standard.
6. Account for the breakdown of gold standard.
7. Distinguish between different forms of gold standard. What are their merits and demerits.
8. Discuss the various methods of note issue. Which one is better and why ?

Chapter - 3

DEMAND FOR AND SUPPLY OF MONEY

Introduction

Money is demanded either as a medium of exchange or for the purpose of keeping it as an asset (as cash balance). It may be demanded for the purpose of transactions, as a precaution against unexpected expenditure or for speculative purposes. The supply of money consists of currency notes and coins on the one side and bank deposits on the other. The proportion of currency and bank deposits may differ in developed and developing economies. Before we discuss the value of money in the next chapter, it will be useful to have an idea of the demand for and the supply of money. The modern notion about these aspects of money is different from the traditional one. Let us analyse demand for and supply of money separately.

Demand for Money

People demand money for the functions it performs. Essentially money has two functions–exchange function and asset function. The first function refers to the fact that money is the general medium of exchange; the second function implies that money is held in preference to all other assets. The transactions demand for money depends on the nature and volume of transactions in the country during a given period of time which, in turn, depends upon the volume of national income in the country. The asset demand for money, however, depends upon the people's desire to hold cash at a particular time. But both the exchange and asset functions of money are closely related to each other.

We may classify the above two functions in another way too. The transactions demand for money may be taken as active demand because money is used actively for carrying out transactions. But money can be active only over a period of time. On the other hand, the asset demand for money (i.e., demand for money to be held as an idle balance) is passive and has relevance only at a point of time–at a given point of time, money is not active but passive. The time element is point of time, money is not active but passive. The time element is thus important in the distinction between the two kinds of demand for money.

Since money is demanded for exchange purposes, it has come to be demanded for other purposes also – to meet difficult situations, as a store of value, for speculative purposes, and so on. Cambridge economists gave three important reasons for holding money, viz., transactions motive, precautionary motive and speculative motive. Others have added a few more.

Transactions Motive

This motive can be looked at (a) from the point of consumers who want income to meet the household expenditure which may be termed the income motive and (b) from the point of view of the businessmen, who require money and want to hold it in order to carry on their business, i.e., the business motive.

(a) Income Motive

The transactions motive relates to the demand for money or the need for cash for the current transactions of individual and business exchanges. Individuals hold cash in order "to bridge the interval between the receipt of income and its expenditure". This is called the 'Income Motive'. Most of the people receive their incomes by the week or the month, while the expenditure goes on day by day. A certain amount of ready money, therefore, is kept in hand to make current payments. This amount will depend upon the size of the individual's income, the interval at which the income is received and the methods of payments current in the locality.

(b) Business Motive

The businessmen and the entrepreneurs also have to keep a proportion of their resources in ready cash in order to meet current needs of various kinds. They need money all the time in order to pay for raw materials and transport, to pay wages and salaries and to meet all other current expenses incurred by any business of exchange. Keynes calls it the 'Business Motive' for keeping money. It is clear that the amount of money held, under this business motive, will depend to a very large extent on the turnover (i.e., the volume of trade of the firm in question). The larger the turn-over the larger, in general, will be the amount of money needed to cover current expenses.

Precautionary Motive

Individuals and business firms will keep additional sums of money on hand to provide protection in the event of emergency. Failure to have sufficient amount of money might force an individual or firm into liquidation at certain times. One misfortune may lead to another. For instance, illness reduces income on the one hand and increases expenditure on the other ; it will necessitate emergency borrowing and thus impair the person's credit standing as well as his ability to meet other emergencies. This is the precautionary motive for holding money. The volume of money required to satisfy precautionary motive will differ widely with individuals and business firms, according to the nature of their business, their access to the credit market, the case with which their other securities can be converted into money when an emergency arises, and so on. Keynes lumps together the transactions and precautionary motives.

Speculative Motive

Keynes defines the speculative motive as "the desire of earning profit by knowing better than the market what the future will bring forth". Suppose the rate of interest is expected to decline in the near future. As a result, securities bearing fixed interest can be expected to rise in value. Accordingly, those who have such securities would wish to hold on to those securities so as to secure profits from the higher price of securities. Or, those who have funds may convert them to fixed interest-bearing securities now so as to dispose them of later. Thus, if people anticipate a rise in the price of securities (i.e., fall in the rate of interest), they would hold less money with them but would hold more securities. On the other hand, if people anticipate a fall in the price of securities (i.e., a rise in the rate of interest) they would dispose of their securities now at higher prices, hold money to buy securities when their prices would have fallen. Thus, people who have the option to hold their wealth in the form of money or in securities will be influenced by the rate of interest and their anticipation regarding the future.

The demand for cash for speculative purposes–which is the most important motive according to Keynes–depends upon the rate of interest. Other things being equal, the higher the rate of interest, the less will be the demand for idle cash. In other words, the liquidity preference for speculative purposes is a negative function of the rate of interest, and we can write it as :

$$M_2 = L_2(r), \text{ where}$$

M_2 represents the cash balances needed for speculative motive

r represents the rate of interest.

L_2 represents the function which equalises the two sides of the equation.

Now the total demand for money consists of the demand for cash transactions and precautionary motives (M_1) and the speculative demand for cash (M_2). The total demand for money (M) is, therefore,

$$M = M_1 + M_2$$
$$= L_1(Y) + L_2(r)$$

Thus, by combining the L_1 (Y) and L_2 (r) functions, we can get the L (Y, r) function which shows the total demand for money corresponding to the various income levels and interest rates.

The demand for cash is illustrated in Fig. 1

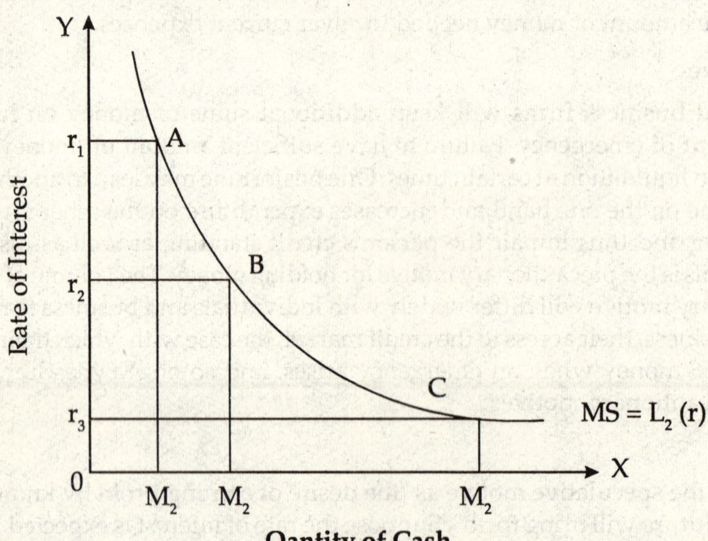

Fig. 1

The liquidity preference curve or the demand curve for cash slopes downward to show that more would be demanded at lower rates of interest. But after a certain stage when the rates os interest fall below a certain minimum (r_3) the demand for cash becomes absolute or infinite. This means that below this minimum rate of interest, the demand for cash for speculative purposes will be perfectly interest elastic or horizontal. Point C is often referred to as the liquidity trap, which tells us that the rate of interest cannot fall below the rate determined by the liquidity trap, even though the monetary authorities might increase the quantity of money.

The Demand for Money Function

From Keynes's General Theory, economists had learnt that the demand for money depends upon the level of real income and the expected rate of interest, that the transactions and precautionary motives depend upon income and the speculative motive is influenced only by the rate of interest. But after the contributions to analysis of demand for money made by Baumol, Tobin and others, it is now clear that all the three motive depend on both income (y) and interest rate (i). So, we write the demand for money function as

$$M_d/P = L(y, i),$$

Where M_d/P denotes real money demand, y real income and i, the real rate of interest. The real amount of money demanded is directly related to real income and inversely related to the interest rate. This is the demand function for money in the short period. In the long period, the demand for money would depend also on the development of near-money substitutes such as the use of bank cheques, credit cards and bills of exchange etc.

The short period demand for money function can be plotted and shown through a diagram as in the fig. 2.

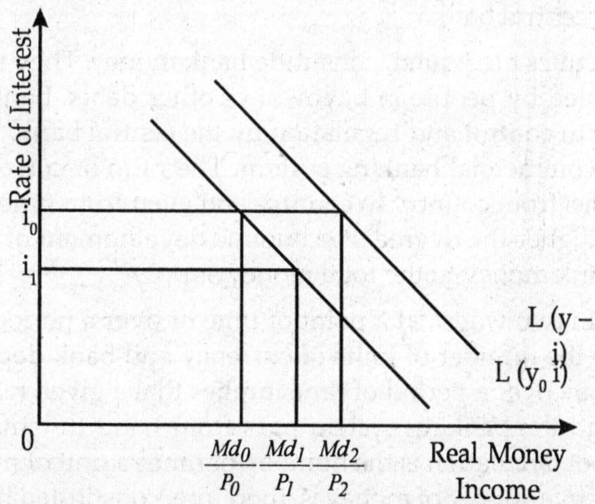

Fig. 2 : The Demand for Money Function

We have three variables – y, i, M_d/P to be shown whereas our diagrams are two-dimensional. So one variable has to be held constant. We choose real income (y) to remain constant. The figure shows the demand for money on the horizontal axis and the associated rate of interest on the vertical axis. The demand-for money function associated with Y_0 level of money income is $L(Y_0\ i)$. It slopes from left down to the right showing the inverse relationship between Y and i. As the interest rate declines from i_0 to i_1, the demand for money rises from M_{d0}/P_0 to M_{d1}/P_0.

What happens to the demand function when the level of real money income in the economy rises ? In that case, we have to draw a new demand function which is to the right of the earlier demand function. It is the new demand function $L(Y_1, i)$. This function shows that at the same rate of interest i_0, more money is demanded than before. The demand for money at i_0 goes up from $M_{d0}/$

P_0 *to* M_{d2}/P_2. This is because the demand for money is income elastic.

Supply of Money

We have described the demand for money as the demand for the stock (not flow) of money to be held. The flow is over a period of time and not at a given moment. In the case of a commodity, it is a flow. Goods are being continually produced and disposed of. This is the essential difference between the demand for money and the demand for a commodity. Similarly, the supply of money conforms on the 'stock' concept and not the 'flow' concern. Just as the demand for money is the demand for money to hold, similarly, the supply of money means the supply of money to hold. Money must always be held by some one, otherwise it cannot exist. Hence, the supply of money means the sum total of all the forms of money which are held by a community at any given moment.

Constituents of Money

The money supply in a modern economy comprises coins, currency notes and bank demand deposits. Coins and currency notes constitute legal tender money, or currency. In these days coins are comparatively a small amount while notes form bulk of the currency. Coins and notes in most countries are issued by the central bank of the country under directions from the Government. The Government may sometimes issue a part of the paper currency supply as, for example, Re. I notes are issued by the Government of India. Thus the supply of currency with the public is the result of decisions by the Government and the central bank.

Bank deposits, against which cheques are issued, constitute bank money. They represent debt of commercial banks which are accepted by people in payment of other debts. Bank deposits are created by commercial banks, subject to control and regulation by the central bank. The supply of bank money is decided upon by the commercial banking system. The ratio of currency and bank money to the total money supply varies from country to country and even from time to time in the same country. Broadly speaking, the higher the degree of economic development of a country, the greater would be the proportion of bank money to the total money supply.

We can consider money supply in two ways : at a point of time or over a period of time. At a point of time, the supply of money is the number of units of currency and bank deposits with the general public. But the supply of money over a period of time implies that a given number of units of money created by Government and the banking system pass from hand to hand many times during the given period. The velocity of circulation is the number of times a unit of money changes hands during a given period. The effective supply of money is, therefore, constituted by the quantity of money multiplied by the average velocity of circulation.

Concepts of Money Supply in India

In India, the Reserve Bank of India employs as many as four measures of money supply, viz., M_1, M_2, M_3 and M_4 for analysis and policy formulations. These measures are based on the recommendations made by the second working group of the Reserve bank of India, the report of which was published in January 1977. Broadly, the main characteristics which separate one pleasure from the other is the varying degree of liquidity. The four measures are defined below and are being arranged in descending order of liquidity.

(i) M_1 measure consists of :

(a) Currency notes and coins with the public ;

(b) Net demand deposits of all commercial and co-operative banks;

(c) Other deposits held with the RBI (e.g., deposits of the IMF, IFCI, IDBI, etc.).

(ii) M_2 measure consists of :

(a) M_1 and

(b) Savings deposits with post office savings banks.

(iii) M_3 measure consists of :

(a) M_1 and

(b) Net time deposits of all commercial and co-operative banks.

(iv) M_4 measure consists of :

(a) M_3 and

(b) Total deposits with the post office savings organisation.

Currency with the public includes paper notes and coins issued by the RBI and put into active circulation. The net demand deposits of banks (commercial and co-operative) include the deposits in the current account and the demand deposit portion of savings deposits, all held by the public. Inter-bank holding of deposits is not included in the net demand deposits. Other deposits with the Reserve Bank include the demand deposits of non-banking financial intermediaries such as IFCI, IDBI, ICICI ; foreign central banks and governments, and international institutions such as IMF and IBRD, etc.

In the advanced countries the total supply of money is defined as the quantity of simple money (M) issued by the central bank and its velocity of circulation (V) and quantity of bank money (M') and its velocity of circulation (V'). Thus MV + M'V' provides the total supply of money.

This measure of money supply may be good for a wider coverage, however, it does not give correct information of money supply at a point of time. Moreover, the velocity of circulation is an exogeneous factor over which central bank has no control.

Monetary Base or High Powered Money

Theory of money supply has been explained in different ways by the economists. The earlier version of money supply dealt with money in an ordinary sense. Money supply defined in narrow sense (M_1) includes C, DD and OD.

High-powered money (H), on the other hand, refers to money produced by the monetary authorities of a country. In case of India, the Reserve Bank of India and the Government of India produce high powered money. The RBI also calls high-powered money as monetary base or reserve money.

High-powered money includes currency held by the public (C), cash reserves of banks (R), and other deposits with the Reserve Bank. Symbolically.

$$H = C + R + OD$$

The basic difference between 'ordinary money' (M_1) and 'high-powered money' (H) is that of the second component, i.e., DD in M_1 and R in H. Banks are the producers of demand deposits (DD) but they do not enjoy unrestricted power in this respect. In fact, the banks have to maintain certain cash reserves in order to produce DD. The monetary authorities have the power to determine cash reserves on the basis of which banks produce demand deposits. Cash reserves lend power to money, therefore, money created out of it called high powered money. In fact, the whole process of multiple creation of credit rests upon high-powered money.

Factors Affecting Stock of High powered Money

The main factors influencing stock of high-powered money are as follows:

(a) Net Reserve Bank credit to government ;

(b) Reserve Bank credit to banks ;

(c) Reserve Bank credit to development banks ;

(d) Net foreign exchange assets of the RBI ; and

(e) Net non-monetary liabilities of the RBI (it has a negative effect on H).

Effect of Money Supply and Monetary Base on Monetary Policy Formulation

Currency is an important component of both money supply and monetary base. The issue of currency is done by the Reserve Bank, and the Government of India. It is subject to certain statutory restrictions. Variations in C are not possible except over comparatively long periods. In such a situation, changes in C do not have an important role to play in monetary policy formulation.

Other deposits of the RBI (OD) constitute a very small proportion of M_1 and H, therefore, changes in OD do not have any significant role in monetary policy formulation.

These are the changes in DD and R which have important policy implications. While banks can influence DD but they do not enjoy unrestricted powers. They have to maintain certain cash reserves (R) to produce demand deposits. If the supply of R is more than its demand, the banks will have excess reserves (ER), which they may invest in marketable securities (government and private) or may use for loans and advances. Changes in R have significant effects on the level of economic activities. The monetary authorities can regulate and control the magnitude and flow of credit by controlling R.

This may, however, be pointed out that the money supply is policy determined but in the ultimate analysis it is governed by the behaviour of people and banks which itself depends upon other variables, such as rates of interest, the spread of banking facilities in the country, banking habits of the people, holding of black money, etc.

In all the components enumerated above, currency is the most liquid asset followed by demand deposit which are fixed in price and redeemable into money on demand. Saving deposits with post office savings banks fall next in terms of liquidity. Likewise, the degree of liquidity is less in case of time deposits for these are not redeemable into money before maturity without loss of time and money.

Trends in Money Supply

Over the past 40 years money supply (M_3) has substantially increased, from Rs. 2,016 crores in 1950-51 to Rs. 2,70, 000 crores in July 1990. It has increased at an annual average rate of about 15 percent. Increasing money supply is indicative of growing monetisation of the economy.

During the same period, composition of money supply has also undergone a change. Thus, whereas in 1950-51, currency formed 69 percent of the total money supply, this proportion has come down to 60 percent presently : conversely, the proportion of deposit money has gone up from 31 percent in 1950-51 to about 40 percent. The growth of deposits may be a reflection of the expansion of banking facilities in the country and their growing popularity with the public. But as a medium of payment, currency notes still hold firm ground for the majority of people. As on March 31, 200 K M_1 was Rs. 379, 791 crores and M_3 was Rs. 1,311,583 crores.

These four concepts of money supply are illustrated in following figure.

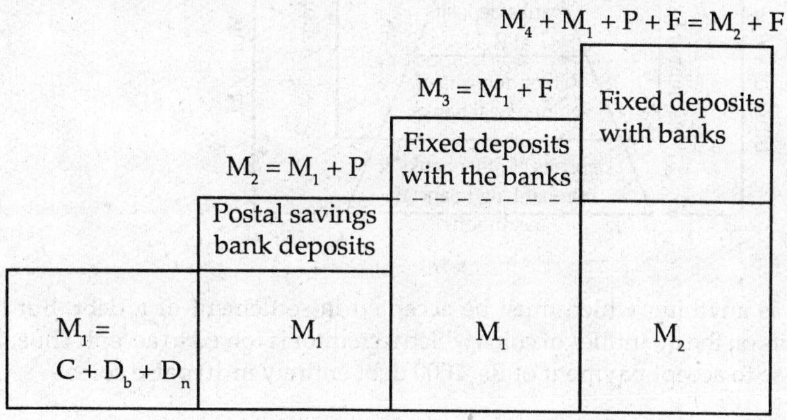

Four Measures of Money Supply in India

Economic Insight : Different Concepts of Money Supply

There have been changes in the concept of money supply from time to time. Changes in the financial world and the efforts to find a 'true' measure of the money supply led to several different measures of the money stock being introduced. There are several measures of money supply mainly because there are different types of bank accounts.

Narrow Money

Most countries of the world have two measures of the money stock : broad money supply and narrow money supply. Narrow money consists of all the purchasing power that is immediately available for spending. Two measures of narrow money are M_1 (or monetary base) and M_2. M_1 consists of notes and coins in circulation and the commercial banks 'deposits of cash at the central bank'. M_2 consists of notes and coins in circulation and the non-interest bearing bank accounts — mainly current accounts. M_2 also includes other interest-bearing deposits of banks. Such deposits are the deposits of the private sector which can be withdrawn easily and quickly (with giving a notice). Since all this money is readily available for spending it is sometimes referred to as the 'transactions balance'. Any bank deposit which can be withdrawn on demand without incurring loss of interest is referred to as a sight deposit.

Despite some differences in definitions from country to country, the above concepts apply to measures of the money stock(s). These are related to the functions of money. This idea is illustrated in figure. Cash, i.e., notes and coins are at the apex of the money supply. Similar relationships exist for all countries. Certain deposits can be moved in definitions of the money supply from time to time.

The various measures of money supply reflect different concepts of money and different definitions may be used for different purposes. The M_4 definition implies that money is the 'temporary abode of purchasing power'.

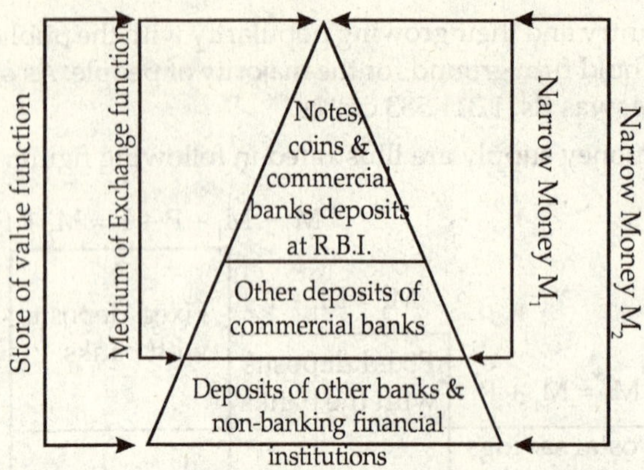

Legal Tender

Legal tender is anything which must be accepted in settlement of a debt. But the law of a country places limits on the quantities of coins which a creditor is forced to accept. Thus, for example, a creditor can refuse to accept payment of Rs. 1000 debt entirely in 10 paise coins.

Fiat Money

The form of money which the government has decreed to be legal tender may also be termed 'fiat money' because it is based solely on the faith of the public in its value. In India this means notes and coins, which may also be termed representative money; this is because their nominal value exceeds the value of metal or paper of which they are made. Bank deposits are not legal tender but, because of their greater security and convenience, they are often more acceptable than cash in settlement of debts.

Quasi-money and Near-money

There are some assets which have some of the attributes of money and fulfil some of its functions, but not well enough to be considered money. Such assets may be termed quasi-money. For example, a postal order may be used as a medium of exchange and perhaps and as a store of value, but its usefulness as such is limited and it is a form of quasi-money. Other examples are plastic tokens and lunch vouchers.

Near-money is an asset which can quickly be turned into money. This consists of things such as Treasury bills (T-bills, in short), certificates of deposit (CD) and commercial bills. Near-money assets provide liquidity for banks.

Creators of Money Supply

The supply of money in a country depends upon three agencies, viz., the central bank, the Government and the commercial banks. The central bank has monopoly of the supply of currency. The issue of currency notes in India is done by the Reserve Bank of India subject to statutes which lay down the denominations, quantity, reserves to be maintained, and other related matters. The system of note issue adopted by the Government will also determine the nature of reserves the Reserve Bank has to keep against note circulation (such as gold, foreign exchange, rupee securities, etc.). Deposit money is created by commercial banks but this is subject to the control and regulation of the central bank of the country. Ultimately, therefore, the currency component depends directly and deposit component depends indirectly on the Reserve Bank of India. But the volume of money supply is influenced not only by the central bank of a country, but also by the monetary and fiscal measures adopted by the government.

The Central Bank and the Money Supply

As mentioned above, the central bank of a country has a direct influence on the volume of currency in the country. The Reserve Bank of India (RBI) issues currency notes of all denominations. Even one-rupee notes and coins are issued by the Government of India through the agency of the RBI. The present system of note-issue in India is known as the minimum reserve system, under which the RBI has to keep a minimum reserve of gold, coin, bullion and foreign securities of not less than Rs. 200 crores, of which the value of gold should at least be Rs. 115 crores. The rest of the reserves should consist of rupee coins and rupee securities ; and the total reserves should be equal to the total volume of paper currency notes in circulation.

So long as the RBI can maintain the minimum amount of gold reserves, it is in a position to expand its note-issue simply by acquiring rupee securities. If the general public require additional paper currency notes, they will withdraw the same from the commercial banks, who, in turn, will get the same from the Banking Department of the RBI which finally will get the amount from the Issue Department. The supply of paper currency in India can be varied easily. During the busy agricultural season, the Indian public are able to get more currency notes from the RBI ; and during the slack season, the surplus cash with the general public is passed on to the RBI (the people pass it on to the commercial banks ; the latter shift it to the Banking Department of the RBI, which, in turn, shifts into the Issue Department).

Commercial Banks and the Money Supply

Commercial banks have the power to create bank deposits. Whenever they make loans and advances to various parties, they are creating deposits in their name. The more loans the banking system gives, the more is the volume of bank deposits. In periods of industrial and business expansion, the demand for bank loans will expand ; and, therefore, the creation of bank deposits will also expand. On the other hand, a decline in business activity will be accompanied by a contraction of bank deposits. The capacity of the banking system to expand the volume of bank deposits. (i.e., bank money) will depend upon :

(a) The volume of cash available to the banking system ;

(b) The ratio of cash to bank deposits ;

(c) The willingness of borrowers to borrow funds from the commercial banks ; and

(d) The control of the central bank over the commercial banks.

The central bank is vested with certain powers to control the volume of bank deposits. These powers are known as quantitative and qualitative (more commonly known as selective) controls. Through these weapons, the central bank influences the volume of cash available to the commercial banks and thus expand or contract bank deposits or the central bank can directly give instructions. In recent years, the RBI has been using direct controls — known as selective controls — through which commercial banks are asked not to give loans to particular parties of limit loans with in certain amounts and so on. Thus the volume of money supply is influenced by the central bank of a country, the currency component directly and deposit component indirectly through control over the loan operations of commercial banks.

The Government and the Money Supply

The Government too has an important influence on the supply of money in a country. In a general way, the taxes imposed by the Government and collected from the public will reduce the volume of money with the people ; likewise, borrowing of the Government from the general public will have the effect of reducing the money supply with the people. On the other hand, Government expenditure has the opposite effect, viz., increasing the supply of money. In the first place, the Government may finance part of its expenditure through creation of money when it finds that its income through taxation and borrowing is not adequate to meet its expenditure. This is known as deficit financing. The normal method of money creation is that the Government, faced with a deficit, provides its own securities (viz., it promises to pay) to the central bank and collect equal amount of IOU from the latter. The Government uses these funds to pay off its creditors. The result is that the volume of cash with the public as well as with the banking system increases. The banking system may expand deposits on the basis of the larger cash resources.

There is another way by which the Government can increase the volume of money supply. It can borrow from the commercial banks against its own securities. In such a case, the commercial banks will created demand deposits in the name of the Government. This is similar to the Government borrowing from the central bank. When the Government spends the deposits provided by the banking system, the volume of money supply with the public is increased. The cash with the banking system too will rise leading to expansion of bank deposits.

If the Government follows a policy of surplus budgeting (more income but less expenditure) there will be a larger transfer of funds from the public to the Government resulting in a reductions of money supply with the people. There will be reduction of cash balances with the banking system too which will result in reduction of bank deposits. On the other hand, if the Government follows a policy of deficit budgeting, the volume of money supply with the people will increase.

The supply of money in a country can, therefore, be increased if –

(a) Commercial banks expand their lending (or credit) operations and thus expand bank deposits ;

(b) Central bank puts in more money in circulation or influences commercial banks to expand credit ; and

(c) The Government borrows from the central bank and the commercial banks and thus is responsible for expansion of currency as well as deposits.

In this connection, the people too can influence the volume of money supply in a country in two ways : First, they may wish to hold more cash with themselves. This will reduce the volume of cash held by the banking system and consequently reduce the volume of bank deposits or bank money with the public. Secondly, the general public may be willing to borrow more or less and thus help the banks to create or contract bank deposits.

The Velocity Circulation of Money

Our discussion of money supply so far was confined to the total money supply at any particular moment of time. But if we have to find out the supply of money over a period of time, say, a year or so, we have to take into account what is known as "the velocity of circulation of money". As we know, the basic function of money is to serve as a medium of payments. A unit of money may be spent several times during a given period of time moving from one person to another. The average number of times money is transferred from one person to another in a given period of time is known as "the velocity of circulation of money". In other words, velocity of circulation is the average number of times that each unit of money is spent for purchases of goods and services during a given period of time.

Thus, if we wish to estimate the total supply of money in a given period, we should multiply the total amount of money in circulation by its velocity of circulation during that period. In algebraic term, the total supply of money during a given period is indicated by MV. (The M here stands for the total amount of money in circulation, while V stands for the velocity of circulation in a given period of time). Thus, the total money supply is affected to a considerable extent by its velocity of circulation. If the velocity of circulation increases, the money supply would also increase, other things remaining the same. On the contrary, if the velocity of circulation decreases, the money supply would also decrease, other things remaining the same. It would, however, be remembered, that it is not only metallic money or paper money which has its velocity of circulation. Credit money has also its velocity of circulation. If the velocity of credit money increases, that will have the same effect on total money supply as an increase in the velocity of circulation of metallic money or paper money. Thus, credit money and the velocity of credit money have also to be taken into account while estimating the total money supply in a given period of time.

Factors Affecting Velocity of Circulation

The velocity of circulation of money depends upon the following factors :

1. Time-unit of Income Receipts

The time interval of receiving income, whether it is per day, per week, per month or so. The more often income is received (say, weekly instead of monthly) the shorter is likely to be the average interval of time for holding the money, so higher will be the velocity of circulation and vice versa.

2. Method and Habits of Payment

The method and habits of payment also govern the velocity of circulation of money. Such practices and instalment payments make possible the use of the same unit of money repeatedly, whereas lump sum payments would necessitate large cash balances, which would lower the velocity of circulation of money.

3. Degree of Regularity of Income Receipts

The degree of regularity of income receipts also affect the velocity of money. If stable income is received by people at regular intervals, they will be inclined to spend money freely in the current period on the basis of assured income in the next period; consequently, the velocity of circulation will be high. However, under conditions of irregularity and uncertainty of income receipts, people will have a tendency to keep more cash balances with them with the result that the velocity of circulation will be lower.

4. Distribution of National Income

The distribution of national income also affects the velocity of circulation of money. The velocity of circulation differs between the wealthy and the poor strata of society. In the case of the rich, the velocity of circulation of money will be lower, because they are inclined to hold cash balances, while it will be higher with the poor, because the latter will spend their money as soon as they receive it on account of their small cash holdings. A high degree of inequality causes lower velocity of money in circulation.

5. Business Conditions

Business conditions may also influence the velocity of circulation of money. In a prosperous, flourishing business situation, transaction will be rapid and naturally, the velocity of circulation of money will be high. In a slack season of business, on the other hand, the velocity of circulation will be low. Under a wave of pessimism about income expectations, however, the velocity of circulation of money will tend to decline. In short, during inflation, the velocity of money increases while during deflation, it decreases.

6. Development of the Banking and Financial System

The state of development of the credit and financial system in an economy greatly influences the rapidity of circulation of money. In a backward society, without well developed financial and banking institutions, the velocity of money is likely to be lower than in an advanced community. Since, in backward societies, thee are no facilities for investment, people are induced to hoard more money in order to meet contingent expenditure.

7. Speed in Transportation of Money

The speed in transportation of money also determines it velocity of circulation. More rapid transportation of cash and cheques in the commercial world, due to quick remittance facilities provided by banks, naturally enhances the velocity of circulation of money. In retail trades, coins of small denominations may circulate speedily, whereas in wholesale trades, notes of large denominations may be more in circulation. Similarly, the velocity of circulation of currency money and deposit money made be different under different circumstances. In that section of the community in which the banking habit is in vogue, the velocity of circulation of deposit money would be very high. In the rural sector, where banking facilities are not adequately available, cash velocity will be very high.

8. Stage of Economic Development

The velocity of circulation is also influenced by the stage of development of the country in question. In a predominantly agricultural country, the wants of the people are limited in number. The barter system may also be in operation. Consequently, the velocity of circulation will be low in such a country. On the contrary, in a developed and industrialized country, the wants of the people are numerous and the people need increasing amounts of money to satisfy them. The velocity of money, thus, goes on rising with the economic development of the country.

9. Size of Propensity to Consume

According to Prof. Keynes, the higher the propensity to consume in a country, other things remaining the same, the higher shall be the velocity of circulation of money in that country. The people in such a country will spend a major portion of their income on consumption. Consequently, the velocity of money will go up. On the contrary, the lower the propensity to consume, other things remaining the same, the lower shall be he velocity of circulation of money. The reason is that in such a country people tend to save a major portion of their income instead of spending it on consumption. This brings the velocity of circulation down.

10. Development of the Means of Transport and communications

With the development of the means of transport ad communications in a country, the field of exchange operations also expands in the same proportion. Goods and services come to be bought and sold much more quickly than before. This results in an increase in the velocity of circulation of money.

11. Mobility of Credit Money

The greater the rapidity with which money is transferred from the account of one person to that of another, the higher shall be the velocity of circulation of credit money. Thus, with economic development and the progress of the banking system, the velocity of circulation of credit money goes on rising to higher and higher levels.

12. People's Liquidity Preference

The liquidity preference of the people is also an important factor which influences the velocity of circulation of money. If the ordinary people as well as the traders and merchants keep large cash balances to meet their requirements, the velocity of circulation of money will go down. If, on the contrary, these sections keep smaller cash balances to meet their day-to-day requirements, the velocity of circulation of money will go up. In other words, the higher the liquidity preference of the people, the lower shall be the velocity of circulation of money.

Conclusion

From the above discussion, it is clear that the demand for money is basically different from the demand for commodities. Money is demanded for two purposes, for transactions in goods and services and for asset-holding. As to the supply of money, economists hold different opinions.

Questions for Discussion

1. Analyse the factors determining (a) the demand for and (b) supply of money.
2. Explain briefly in constituents of money supply in a country.
3. What are the factors affecting money supply ? How do commercial banks affect money supply ? Discuss in terms of these factors.
4. Discuss different definitions of money supply (M_1, M_2, M_3 M_4) as used by the Reserve Bank of India.

Chapter - 4

VALUE OF MONEY

Introduction

The term 'value of money' means the purchasing power of money or the quantity of goods and services a unit of money buys. It is the reciprocal of the general purchasing power. The value of money may rise or fall depending upon the conditions of its demand and supply. When the value of money rises it commands more of other articles in exchange. When its value falls, it commands less goods in exchange.

Economists have laid down certain standards of value of money and we may distinguish three such standards. The first one is the consumption standard which indicates the purchasing power of money in terms of goods and services that enter into the final consumption of people. In formulating such, a standard, two difficulties are involved. Firstly, there is a difficulty of ascertaining the goods and services that an ordinary family buys. The second difficulty is that of ascertaining the price of goods.

The second standard laid down by economists is the labour standard, which aims at measuring the value of money in terms of units of human effort. It is generally determined from the rate of wages paid for a day's work. Any attempt to fix such a standard is beset with the difficulty of finding common labour unit to which different kinds of human effort can be compared.

Thirdly, the wholesale standard indicates the value of money in buying those goods that enter into wholesale markets, whose prices are quoted and recorded regularly. Most of the commodities whose prices are quoted in such markets are raw materials in various stages of production and finished goods which are on their way to reach the ultimate consumers. The quantities dealt with are large and for this reason the value of money is called the wholesale value.

These definitions are arbitrary and are merely intended to reduce the complexity involved in the concept of value of money. It is impossible to measure the value of money in the absolute sense, because, that would involve comparison of the values of all commodities available for sale in the world.

We have to include within the scope of our investigation all transactions employing the medium of our investigation. Even if the value of money were ascertained in this extremely difficult way, it would interest nobody. So it is a more practicable proposition to ascertain the value of money so far as it is concerned with particular types of transactions only. Even if we attempt to find out the value of money in this narrow fashion, we cannot do so satisfactorily. For instance, an attempt to measure the wholesale value of money involves a lengthy list of commodities of various types and to prepare such a list is a complicated task. Reluctantly we must admit that the absolute value of money cannot be measured.

Fortunately, it is not absolute value of money that we are interested, but only in changes in its value over a period of time. Change in the value of money can be measured by means of a statistical device known as "Index Numbers".

Index Numbers

The measurement in the changes of value of money is done by means of index numbers.

The value of money is the general purchasing power of a unit of money in buying goods and services. Now the prices of commodities do not always move in the same direction. While some prices are rising, the others may not, or even fall. This will create confusion regarding the general purchasing power of the rupee. This problem is overcome by the use of index numbers.

Index numbers are therefore devices for measuring the differences in the magnitude of relative price changes. An index number of prices is that which indicates the price level at any given date as compared with the level of prices at some standard date called the base.

Preparation of Index Numbers

The following are the various steps in the construction of such an index number :

1. Choice of the base year

The first step is to choose a year to serve as the base year, i.e., the year with reference to which the price changes in other years are expressed as percentages. Care must be exercised in its selection. It should be an average year, neither a year of boom nor of depression. Sometimes an average (of prices) of a number of years is taken to serve as the base.

2. Selection of commodities

The second step is to select commodities the prices of which have to be taken to represent the general price-level. The commodities should be really representative and should be sufficiently large in number. The selection of commodities also depends on the object with which the index is prepared. For instance, if the object is to study how the cost of living of working class has been affected by price changes, we select those commodities which figure in the consumption of the working class.

3. Price lists are then taken for each commodity

It is better to have an average of wholesale prices of the same commodity from a number of representative markets. These prices are taken for the base year (or years) and also for the subsequent years, the index number for which we want to construct. Retail prices are better because it is the retail prices which consumers actually pay. But retail prices are not taken because they differ widely from locality to locality.

4. The next step is to represent the price of each commodity for the base year as 100 and the price of the same commodity for the subsequent year as a percentage of the price for the base year. For instance, if the price of wheat in the base year is Rs. 70 per quintal and is called 100, a price of Rs. 154 in the subsequent year should be called 220 and so on in the case of all the commodities taken and all the years.

5. The final step is to strike the average of the numbers thus obtained with reference to each year. The average for the base year will of course come to 100. The other average will be higher or lower than 100 according as the general price-level has risen or fallen.

The following table shows how index number is constructed

Commodities	Base year (1961 prices)	Base year index	1972 price	1972 index
Wheat (Qtl.)	Rs. 45.00	100	Rs. 90.00	200
Sugar (Qtl.)	Rs. 70.00	100	Rs. 175.00	250
Milk (Ltr.)	Rs. 0.60	100	Rs. 1.80	300
Cloth (Mtr.)	Rs. 1.50	100	Rs. 3.00	200
Kerosene (Ltr.)	Rs. 0.30	100	Rs. 0.45	150

$$\text{Average} = \frac{500}{5} = 100 \qquad \frac{1100}{5} = 220$$

According to the above table the price index has risen from 100 to 220 or there has been an increase of 120 percent. The model given above is a simple one. However, in actual life the change in prices of sugar or kerosene is not likely to affect the consumer as much as the change in price wheat. Therefore it is necessary to give weightage to the commodities included in the index number according to the percentage of expenditure on these commodities by a consumer. With the weightage given the index number of the above five commodities will be as follows:

Commodities	Weightage	Base year 1961 prices	Base year index	Current year price	Current year index
Wheat	3	Rs. 45.00 (qtl)	100 □ 3	Rs. 90.00	200□ 3– 600
Sugar	1	Rs. 0.70 (qtl)	100 □ 1	Rs. 7.75	250 □ 1–250
Milk	1	Rs. 0.60 (ltr)	100 □ 1	Rs. 1.80	300 □ 1–300
Cloth	2	Rs. 1.50 (mtr)	100 □ 2	Rs. 3.00	200 □ 2–400
Kerosene	1	Rs. 0.30 (ltr)	100 □ 1	Rs. 0.45	150 □ 1–150

$$\text{Average} = \frac{800}{8} = 100 \qquad \frac{1700}{8} = 212.5$$

The cost of living index is normally based on weighted averages as shown above. One should be careful in selecting the weightage for the commodities which should fit in the actual conditions.

Kinds of Index Numbers

There are many types of index numbers. The important types of index numbers are :

1. Consumption Index

For constructing this type of index number of the purchasing power of money, we must take the prices of all goods and services that enter into the final consumption of people. Since it is difficult to construct such a comprehensive index number, one must be content with an index which covers a large and representative part of total consumption.

2. Cost of living index

The cost of living index includes the retail prices of important commodities of consumption entering into the budget of the working class people. It differs from the consumption index in that it does not include personal service.

3. Wholesale price index

The wholesale price index is made up of prices of basic commodities at wholesale rates. It measures the changes in the purchasing power of money over goods whose prices are quoted regularly in the wholesale markets. We take prices of raw materials, partly finished goods and goods which are on their way to the ultimate consumer. The index number is weighted on the basis of the relative importance of different commodities in the national economy as indicated by the census of production.

4. International Index

Each country prepares an index, which we may call international index, made up of commodities that are exported and imported. In preparing such an index, the principal standardised commodities enjoying international markets will be taken into account. A complete index includes both raw materials and manufactured goods which enter into international trade on an important scale. The index is weighed on the basis of the importance of each commodity in the trade of the country concerned. This type of index is used to indicate changes in the terms of trade of a country.

5. Index number of Wages

Many countries construct an index number of wages to show the changes in wages over a period of time. Besides, index number of wages is useful to calculate real wages of labour. This is done by comparing money wages with the working class cost of living index number.

6. Index number of retail prices

The purpose of the index number of retail prices is to measure the value of money with reference to final consumption goods which are dealt with in the retail market. The difficulty with this index number is that retail prices may not be available for the same goods and for continuous periods.

Problems Involved in Construction of Index Numbers

The construction of price index numbers involves a number of problems :

1. Selecting base year

The first problem arises in the selection of the base year. The base year should be normal, i.e., prices of that year should not be subject to a boom or depression or the effect of unusual forces like wars, floods, famines, etc. Otherwise, all the other indices that are related to such base year will present distorted facts and conclusions as a result of the abnormal conditions then prevailing. Further, the base period should not be too far in the past since relative prices tend to change over time ; the more remote in time the base period, the more likely the distortions in the index will appear in the more recent periods.

2. Selection of items

Out of an unwieldy list of commodities required, representative items are to be selected according to the purpose and type of the index number. In selecting items, the following points are to be considered:

(i) items should be representative of the taste, habits and traditions of the people ; *(ii)* they should be cognisable ; *(iii)* they should be such as are not likely to vary in quality over two different periods and places ; *(iv)* the economic and social importance of the various items of consumption should also be considered; and *(v)* the items must be fairly large in number, because reliability greatly depends on the adequacy of the member.

3. Data Collection

A very important difficulty associated with the computation of index numbers is with regard to the collection of the necessary, adequate, representative and continuous data. In most of the cases where adequate and correct information is not available due to the unorganised market and illiterate and indifferent population, the difficulty is enhanced.

4. Weighting

The assignment of different degree of importance to different articles is known as weighting. It is necessary to come to right, unbiased conclusion regarding weights. But the assignment of weights, which is a matter of considerable skill, is arbitrarily done. As there are no strictly logical indicators to choose relative weights, personal judgement is bound to creep into an arbitrary decision. Thus, the result of index numbers based on such weights cannot be regarded as truly correct.

5. Economic dynamism

In a dynamic, economy, there is a continuous change in the nature of consumption and commodities which adds to the difficulties of comparison and construction of index numbers over a period of time.

(a) Many new commodities may come into existence and the old may disappear; thus, long-run comparison may involve difficulties.

(b) The quality and quantity of the commodities may change from time to time, e.g., the quality of a 1960 model motorcar is quite different from that of a 1980 model.

(c) Income, education, fashion and other factors may change the consumption pattern of the people and indices compiled for a period of time may become non-comparable.

6. Selection of Average

Another problem is that of employing a proper method of averaging to get an index figure. There are various methods of averaging and the use of different types of averages gives different results, thereby making comparison difficult. However, the arithmetic mean and sometimes the geometric mean is commonly used for constructing the price indices.

Price indices are, thus, a fair indication of whether our money is buying more or less in one period in relation to another. However, there is no way to measure exactly the changes in the value of money over a period of years, even if we use a much more elaborate technique.

Advantages of Index Numbers

Following are the advantages of index numbers.

1. Measuring Changes in Price Level

The method of index numbers is used for measuring changes in the price-level. This is essential for maintaining price stability. Price stability is conducive to the maintenance of economic activity at the desired level.

2. Measuring Other Economic Changes

We can measure any quantitative change in addition to changes in the value of money and the cost of living. There may be index numbers of wages, imports, exports, industrial activity, employment, change in areas under cultivation, change in population, etc. These measurements indicate social and economic trends and help in farming policies with respect to them.

3. Adjusting Wages and Prices

An index number of cost of living can guide us in the adjustment of wages to changing prices.

4. Exchange Stability

Index number of wholesale prices can guide the currency authority not only in stabilizing price-levels but also in stabilizing foreign exchange.

5. Comparing Economic Conditions

We can compare, with the help of index numbers, economic conditions of a class of people at two different periods.

6. Comparing Purchasing Power of Two Currencies

Index numbers can also be used to compare the purchasing power of two currencies and to fix the purchasing power parity.

7. Equitable Discharge of Debts

Index numbers can be used as a basis for an equitable discharge of contracts, i.e., borrowing and lending. When prices rise, the creditor is a loser, for the same amount returned to him has less purchasing power. It should be more just to ensure that the creditor gets back the same purchasing power. It that is so, then the amount of the principal should be increased in proportion to the increase in prices. Similarly, when the prices fall, the debtor should be asked to pay correspondingly less, otherwise the burden of the debt in terms of commodities and services will be increased in proportion to the fall in prices.

Limitations of Index Numbers

Though index numbers play a very significant role, they suffer from certain limitations. They are :

(i) Index numbers are at best approximations. They cannot be taken as accurate. Their data are open to question and may lead to different interpretations.

(ii) International comparisons are often difficult on account of different bases, different sets of commodities or differences in their quality or quantity.

(iii) Comparisons over time are also difficult. In a dynamic world there is a continuous change in the nature of commodities. Many new commodities come into existence.

(iv) Index numbers only measure changes in the sectional price levels. An Index prepared for a particular purpose may not be useful for another. An index number of workers is useless for middle-class or industrialists. An entirely different set of commodities will have to be selected. The same index numbers cannot throw light on the effect of a price change on all sections of the society.

(v) Weighting is all arbitrary. One set of weights may yield quite a different result from another.

The Quantity Theory of Money

The quantity theory of money is, indeed, a very old theory. It was first propounded in 1588, by an Italian economist, Davanzatti. Later, the classical economists explained the value of money in terms of the quantity theory of money. Classical economists like David Ricardo, David Hume and J.S. Mill not only accepted this theory, but they also sought to introduce improvements and refinements in the body of this theory. The credit for popularizing this theory in recent years rightly belongs to the well-known American economist, Irving Fisher, who, in his book *The Purchasing Power of Money*, published in 1911, gave it a quantitative form in terms of his famous Equation of Exchange.

The Quantity Theory of Money explains the relationship between the quantity of money, i.e., money supply and the general price level. According to this theory, an increase in the supply of money would bring a proportionate increase in the general price level, (i.e., a fall in the value of money).

According to Prof. Taussig, *"Double the quantity of money, and other things being equal, prices, will be twice as high as before ; and the value of money as one-half."* In other words, the value of money, other things being the same, varies inversely as its quantity ; increase of quantity lowers the value and every diminution raising it in a ratio exactly equivalent.

The proportional relationship between the quantity of money and the general price level is illustrated in following diagram.

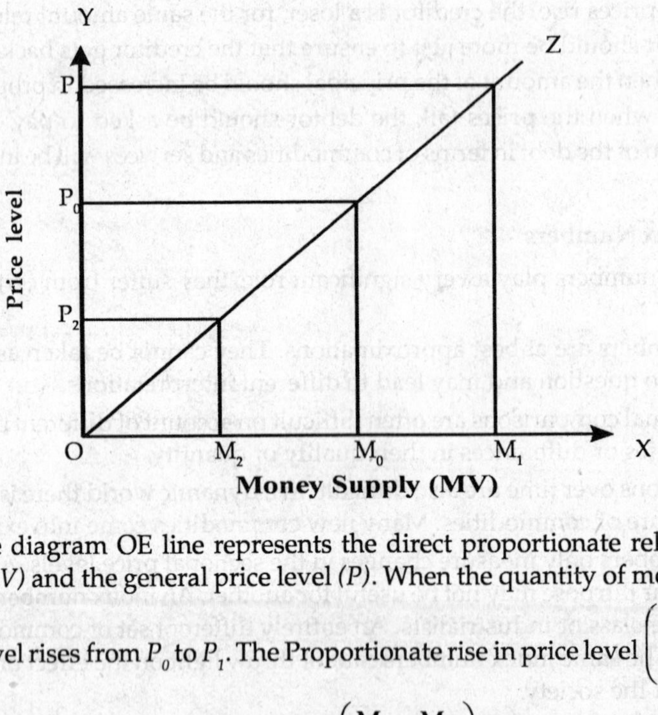

In the above diagram OE line represents the direct proportionate relationship between the money supply *(MV)* and the general price level *(P)*. When the quantity of money increases from M_0 to M_1, the price level rises from P_0 to P_1. The Proportionate rise in price level $\left(\frac{P_1 - P_0}{P_0}\right)$ is equal to the proportionate increase in the quantity of money $\left(\frac{M_1 - M_0}{M_0}\right)$. Similarly, fall in the quantity of money would bring about a proportionate fall in the price level.

In short, the quantity theory implies that the quantity of money brings about a directly proportionate change in the price level and hence an inversely proportionate change in the value of money. Thus, it emphasises a functional relationship between the quantity of money and the value of money. There are two refined approaches to the traditional quantity theory.

1. The cash-transactions approach and
2. The cash-balance approach.

These are discussed in below.

1. The Cash-transactions Approach or Fisher's Quantity Theory of Money

Prof. Irving Fisher, an American Economist has expressed the relationship between the quantity of money and its value in the form of a formula, which is popularly know as **'Quantity Theory of Money'**. According to him money has only one use and that is to help the transaction. Therefore, whatever be the value of money in the country it will have to buy all the available goods and services. The total volume of money during a given period of time will therefore be equal to the total value of all goods and services. The total value of all goods and services is the same as the total demand for money. This formulation of the theory was put in the garb of an equation of exchange by Prof. Fisher. The equation of exchange is,

$$MV = PT$$

Where,

- M is the quantity of money in circulation,
- V is its (transaction) velocity, (that is, the average number of times a unit of money changes hands in effecting business transactions,
- P is the average price level and
- T is the number of transactions affected by money.

MV represents money side or supply side. PT represents goods side or demand side.

Now a days, the greater proportion of money consists of chequable bank deposits. These also, like money, pass from hand to hand in discharge of debts and in payment for goods and commodities. Thus bank deposits add to the supply of money. These deposits have their own velocity of circulation (M 'V'). If equation of exchange can be re-written as,

$$MV + M'V' = PT$$

From the above equation we can ascertain P, the price level

$$P = \frac{MV}{T} \text{ or } P = \frac{MV + M'V'}{T}$$

Assumptions

While using the equation of exchange, Fisher made the following assumptions.

1. Fisher assumed that (P) in the equation is a passive element. It does not change by itself. It is controlled by other elements in the equation.
2. (T) is an independent element; it is not affected by any changes in quantity of money. But it depends on natural resources, technological development, growth of population etc. In short run they are assumed to be constant.
3. (V) is an independent element and is constant in short run. Therefore M has no effect on V.V depends on frequency of receipts and disbursements, regularity of income, facilities of transferring money, development of transport. These are not likely to change in short period.
4. M 'V' is also constant.
5. He also assumed that full employment condition prevails in the economy.

Diagrammatic Explanation

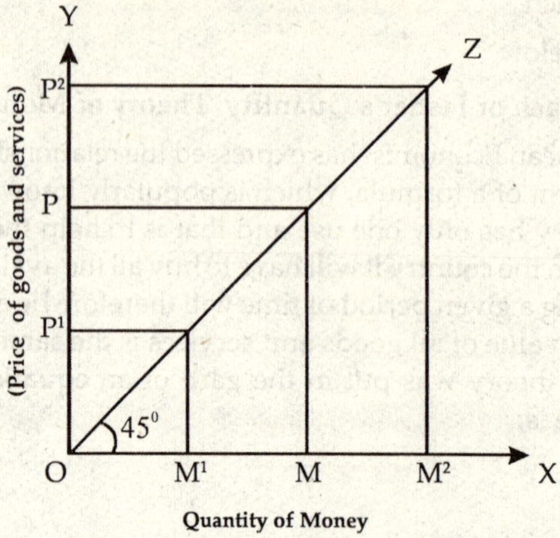

A simple diagram explains Fisher's equation more clearly. *OY* and *OX* will measure price level and quantity of money respectively. When the quantity of money increases from *OM* to OM^2 the price level will increase from *OP* to OP^2 or value of money will become half. When the quantity of money decreases to OM^1 price level will also decrease to OP^1 or value of money will increase two times.

Fisher concludes that since V, V^1, M^1, T are constant. When *M* is doubled the price level will become exactly doubled and the value of money will become half. In other words, other things remaining the same, an increase in quantity of money results in a fall in value of money by same proportion.

Thus P = MV/T.

Criticisms

1. The theory is based on an unrealistic assumption that V and T will not change in short run and they are independent variables. But in practice a change in quantity of money will affect immediately V and T. T changes as business is activised by production and price level change.
2. The theory states that an increase in quantity of money results in an increase in price and not vice-versa. But in reality an increase in price stimulates business which results in an increase in bank deposits. Thus quantity of money will increase due to increase in price level.
3. The theory assumes that changes in quantity of money will lead directly to changes in price level during full employment. But Lord Keynes observes that full employment level does not exist anywhere. Hence it is applicable only to an assumed situation quite unrelated to reality and that is why it fails to apply to realities of life.
4. The theory fails to explain why during depression price level does not increase in spite of an extra pumping in of money. During depression many times prices have the tendency to fail as quantity of money increases.
5. The equation is only a truism : PT = MV is only the other way of writing the obvious fact that the means of payment (MV) must be equal to the total payment actually made (PT).

This does not tell us anything new about money or prices.

6. Here the demand for money is for spending it on goods and services. But keynes feels that money is not demanded for spending alone. It is also demanded for satisfying liquidity preference. The equation ignores this aspect.

2. The Cash-balance Approach or Cambridge Version

As an alternative to Fisher's quantity theory of money, Cambridge economists Marshall, Pigou, Robertson and Keynes formulated the cash balances approach. Like value theory, they regarded the determination of value of money in terms of supply and demand. Robertson wrote in this connection: "Money is only one of the many economic things. Its value, therefore, is primarily determined by exactly the same two factors as determine the value of any other thing, namely, the conditions of demand for it, and the quantity of it available."

The supply of money is exogenously determined at a point of time by the banking system. Therefore, the concept of velocity of circulation is altogether discarded in the cash balances approach because it 'obscures the motives and decisions of people behind it'. On the other hand, the concept of demand for money plays the major role in determining the value of money. The demand for money is the demand to hold cash balance for transactions and precautionary motives. Marshall wrote with regard to the demand for money, "To give definiteness to this notion, let us suppose that the inhabitants of a country... find it just worthwhile to keep by them on the average ready purchasing power to the extent of tenth part of their annual income, together with a fiftieth part of their property, then the aggregate value of currency of the country will tend to be equal to the sum of these amounts."

Thus the cash balances approach considers the demand for money not as a medium of exchange but as a store of value. Robertson expressed this distinction as money "on the wings" and money "sitting". It is "money sitting" that reflects the demand for money in the Cambridge equations. The Cambridge equations show that given the supply of money at a point of time, the value of money is determined by the demand for cash balances. When the demand for money increases, people will reduce their expenditures on goods and services in order to have larger cash holdings. Reduced demand for goods and services will bring down the price level and raise the value of money. On the contrary, fall in the demand for money will raise the price level and lower the value of money.

The Cambridge cash balance equations of Marshall, Pigou, Robertson and Keynes are discussed as under:

(i) ***Marshall's Equation :*** Marshall's equation runs as follows:

Where,

$M = KY$

M = the total supply of money ;

K = the proportion of income which the people want to hold in the form of money (cash-balance) ; and

Y = the aggregate real national income.

Since the value of national income (Y) equals the total output (O) times the prices (P), the Marshallian equation can be represented as follows:

$$M = KPO \qquad \text{or } P = \frac{M}{KO}$$

Marshall argues that the supply of money remaining unchanged, if the magnitude of K changes, then it will certainly influence the price level.

(ii) ***Pigou's Equation :*** While Prof. Marshall expressed his equation in terms of the price level. Prof. Pigou has expressed it in terms of the value of money. Pigou's equation runs as follows :

$$P = \frac{KR}{M}$$

Where,

P = the value of money (i.e., its purchasing power) ;
K = the proportion of total real income to be held in cash ;
R = total real income; and
M = total quantity of money.

In ***Pigou's equation*** it is K and not M which is a more important determinant of the price level.

Since a part of money income people hold in the form of bank deposits, Pigou revised his equation as follows:

$$P = \frac{KR}{M}[c + b(1\text{-}c)]$$

Where,

c = the proportion of cash which the peopie keep in legal tender money;
1–c = the proportion of bank balances held by the people ; and
b = the proportion of legal tender money to deposits held by the banks.

Pigou's equation takes us to the same conclusion that P varies directly with K or R and inversely to M.

(iii) ***Keynes Equation :*** Prof. Keynes also formulated the real-balance quantity equation as follows :

$$P = \frac{n}{K} \quad \text{or} \quad n = PK$$

Where,

P = the general price level or the prices of consumer goods;
n = the total supply of money in circulation ; and
K = the total quantity of consumption units which the people decide to keep in the form of cash.

If K remains unchanged, then changes in **n** will bring about direct proportional changes in P.

(iv) ***D.H. Robertson Equation :*** D.H. Robertson offered a cash balance equation which could be easily compared with Fisher's equation of exchange. He gave the equation

$$M = KPT$$

where M is the supply of money and P is the price level. However, instead of output or income as in Marshall's or Prigou's, he introduced the volume of annual transactions through T in the equation and K refers to the proportion of T which people wish to hold in the form of cash balances. Because of these alterations, his equation compared with Fisher's gives the same direct and proportional relationship between *M* and *P* when *T* and *K* are held as constants. That is, since, according to Fisher $P = MV/T$ and according to Robertson $P = M/KT$, $V = I/K$. Substituting this value of V in Fisher's equation, we obtain.

$$M \cdot I/K = PT \text{ or } M = KPT \text{ as in Robertson's.}$$

Although the relationship suggested between M and P remains the same in both Fisher's and Robertson's, it should be borne in mind that Robertson gave importance to the demand for (or holding of) money whereas Fisher gave importance to the supply of (or spending of) money. Also, the cash balance equations help us to determine the price level at a point of time.

The basic difference between the cash balance equation (s) and Fisher's transactions equation has been explained by Alvin Hansen as follows:

"In the terms of Marshallian approach, sudden and rapid shifts in the desire of public to hold money may profoundly affect prices, even though the monetary authority successfully maintains a high stability in the money supply. The desire of the public to hold cash balance–'liquidity preference' – enters as a powerful factor. Drastic and sudden shifts in the desire to hold money, reflected in a change in *k*, may produce large and quickly moving changes in the level of income and prices. Shifts in the public psychology, in expectations must be taken account of not less than changes in the money supply. In the Marshallian analysis a shift in *k* may start an upward or downward movement. It is *k*, not *M* and holds the stage".

Is Cash Balance Version Superior ?

Although both the cash balance and cash transactions versions of the Quantity Theory apparently look alike, some writers like A.C.L. Day and Kenneth Kurihara treat the cash balance version superior to Fisher's cash transactions version for the following reasons.

1. It brings into analysis income rather than total volume of trade as an explanatory factor, since it is the level of income which determines the demand for cash balances and hence money. For a given known level of income it is easier to estimate the cash balances held by individuals than to know the amount they spent on all the transactions.
2. Marshall with his cash balance approach made the pioneering attempt to integrate Value Theory with Monetary Theory. He determined the value of money interms of supply and demand "by applying conventional value theory to monetary theory."
3. Unlike the cash transactions version which does not explain the casual relationships between money and prices the cash balance version offers explanation as to how the price level can change even when money supply remains constant due to a change in the wishes of the people to hold more or less cash balances.
4. The cash balance approach laid the foundation for the Keynesian liquidity preference theory as well as for the post-Keynesian developments in building the theory of demand for money into a general asset theory.
5. As against Fisher's mechanical concept of velocity of circulation of money, observing the motives and decisions of people behind it, Marshall's "concept of demand for money focuses attention on the process of individual choice among competing alternatives."

Criticism

The cash balance version of the Quantity Theory of Money, however, has been criticised because of its defects and shortcomings.

1. Although it focused attention on the demand for money, one of the important motives for holdings cash, namely, speculative motive, has been completely ignored. As a result, no explicit role has been assigned to the rate of interest in economic activity. As Parinkin observed: "In particular, they cannot serve to validate the classical proposition that a change in the amount of money leaves the rate of interest unaffected. Indeed, not only can they not help, they hinder for the omission of the rate of interest from the cash balance equation, creates the misleading impression that the classical invariance of this rate holds only in the special case where it does not affect the demand for money."
2. The cash balance approach does not explain the role of the real factors such as savings and investment in the price level changes.
3. There is basically no difference between the cash-transactions version and the cash balances version. Both these approaches explain the direct relationship between M and P. If K in the cash balance (Robertson's) version is replaced by I/V then we get $MV = PT$ which is Fisher's equation of exchange. After all, the two versions deal with the two different functions of money– "Money on the wings" in the cash-transaction version and "money-sitting" in the cash balances version. Therefore, the cash balances version also is exposed to most of the major criticisms levelled against the cash transactions version.
4. Unrealistic assumptions such as full employment minimise the policy/empirical significance of this version of the Quantity Theory of Money.

General Evaluation of the Quantity Theory of Money

From the above discussion on cash-transactions and cash-balances approaches to the traditional quantity theory of money, it becomes clear that the theory does not hold much water in explaining the forces causing changes in the values of money.

1. It focuses on immediate rather than ultimate factors

The Quantity Theory equations (both Cambridge and Fisherian) indicate some factors like M,V,T,KR as direct determinants of the value of money. But, actually all these variables are affected by a complexity of economic factors like consumption, savings, investment, income, etc. A number of technical, institutional, psychological factors play their part in the macro-economic drama in a modern economy. Hence, to know the real determinants of the price level and the value of money, one has to beyond the quantity equations.

In short, the quantity theory equations account for only immediate forces affecting the value of money, but furnish little exposition about the ultimate factors behind the factors behind the scene, which are really the villain of the piece.

2. Exogeniety of Money Supply

In quantity equations, the quantity of money M is assumed to be an exogeneous and policy-determined variable. But modern economists say that M is an endogenous variable and likely to respond to P when P, the price level, changes on account of cost-push elements.

3. Lacks analytical approach

In the transactions and cash-balances equations, all kinds of goods are lumped together. No analytical distinctions is made between consumption goods and capital assets to examine their effect upon income, employment, output and prices. Again, the quantity theory pays too much attention to the level of prices, as if the changes in prices are the most critical and significant phenomena in the economic system. Though prices constitute an influential factor in economic operations, it cannot be said that all changes in economic activities are brought about by changes in the price level, but the quantity theory implies that price fluctuations are the cause of trade cycles. However, changes in price level are not the cause but effect of some factors in the economy which are left unconsidered in the equations.

4. Validity in long-run order

Quantity equations are by and large, equilibrium equations for the money market in the long term. They are true only in the long run and not in the short run.

5. No real guidance to policy market

The quantity theory of money furnishes no relevant guidance for an appropriate monetary policy to avoid trade cycles, because they lay emphasis only secular long-run prices, while a trade cycle is relatively a short-term phenomenon.

The theory implies that stability in the value of money can be effectuated through regulation of currency money. But historical evidences do not support this view. In some cases, concentration of money supply has brought about a fall in prices. But there are many cases where even a substantial expansion in the supply of money has failed to bring about a rise in prices during a depression. This is because, it is difficult to induce people to spend more, while they can be easily prevented from spending more. It is like the saying that you can take the horse to the river but you cannot make him drink water if it does not want to. This shows that the quantity of money and prices have no immediate financial relationship.

6. Manipulative Approach

The quantity theory equations trace the result but without explaining the process involved in obtaining it. Equations pose a direct relationship between the changes in the money supply and the price level. But, actually there is no direct and proportionate relationship as depicted.

In short, the quantity theory lacks a chained analysis of causation. It traces the effects of changes in the money supply on the price level. But, actually there is no direct and proportionate relationship as depicted.

7. Consequence rather than causation

The quantity of money is not a causative factor in the state of business and a determinant of value, but it is only a consequence. In fact, the value of money is a consequence of income rather than the quantity of money. For, if people have money income, they would spend it partly or fully. This would increase the velocity of circulation and monetary demand for goods and services and consequently, prices would rise if the supply of goods and services is scarce.

Merits of Quantity Theory

In spite of all these criticisms, the quantity theory of money has certain merits. First of all, the validity of the theory has been brought out in the innumerable instances when large issues of money had pushed up prices to unprecedented levels. Examples are hyper-inflation in Germany and Central European countries in 1923-24 and Kuomintang China in 1947-48. Kemmerer, Gastav Cassel and many others have shown through studies of past events the broad agreement between the rise in prices and the increase in circulation of money which is particularly striking.

Secondly, in the past as well as these days, monetary policy has always aimed at controlling prices through management and regulation of the volume of money in the country. The bank rate policy and open market operations are based on the assumption that large supply of money will lead to higher prices and revival of economic activity and vice versa.

Thirdly, in a broad sense, the quantity theory assets that the rapidity of circulation of money, the volume of bank deposits, issue of paper currency as well as improvements in industries resulting in increased output of goods, should all be emphasised in the determination of the price level. In considering the effect of any one of these influences on price level. It is necessary to watch and determine the effect of other factors which may influence or even outweigh the particular influence under consideration. Thus, in a broader sense, the theory has considerable merit, even though in a strict sense the quantity theory, meaning the every change in the quantity of money will result in an equivalent change in the value of money (or its inverse, the price level), may not be correct.

Keynes's Reformulation of The Quantity Theory

The classical quantity theory of money was not acceptable to Keynes. He found it rather too narrow and unable to explain the general behaviour of prices. To Keynes, the causal relationship is neither direct nor proportional. Keynes's theory of prices, like the rest of his theory, is of a more general nature as compared to the traditional quantity theory of money. Keynes denounced the classical theory on the ground that it is based on unrealistic assumptions of full employment and absence of money illusion. According to Keynes, the theory unnecessarily takes money as neutral and is based on a false division of the economy into the real sector (in which the relative values of the commodities are determined) and the monetary sector (in which these relative values are expressed in terms of money).

Keynes's Version

Keynes contribution lies in removing the old fallacy that prices are directly determined by the quantity of money. His theory of money and prices brings forth the truth that prices are determined primarily by the cost of production. Keynes believes that changes in the quantity of money do not affect the price level (value of money) directly but do so indirectly through the rate of interest, the level of investment, income, output and employment. The initial impact of the changes in the total quantity of money falls on the rate of interest rather than on prices. As the quantity of money is increased (other things remaining the same), the rate of interest is lowered because the quantity of money available to satisfy speculative motive increases. A lowering of the rate of interest (marginal efficiency of capital remaining the same) will raise investment, which in turn, will result in an increase of income, output, employment and prices. The prices rise on account of various factors like the rise in labour costs, bottlenecks in production etc. Thus, in Keynes' view the level of prices is influenced indirectly as a result of the effects of changes in the quantity of money on the rate of interest and hence on investment. It is on account of this reason that Keynes analysis is, at times, spoken of as the contra-quantity 'theory of causation' because it takes rise in prices as a cause of the increase in the quantity of money instead of taking the increase in the quantity of money as a cause of the rise in prices. The process that follows is like this : An increase in the quantity of money... results in the fall in the rate of interest...which encourages investment...which in turn, raises income, output and employment...it results in raising the cost of production...this results in raising prices: The traditional theory ignored the influence of the quantity of money on the rate of interest and thereby on costs and output. It has a direct mechanism as it goes directly from increase in the quantity of money to increase in the level of prices. Keynes substituted in its place the indirect mechanism which explained the rise in the price level as part of the process in which investment, income and employment changes. The figure - shows that when money supply is raised form *M1* to *M2*, output and prices increase in the same proportion: M_F shows the money supply consistent with full employment: aggregate output is the maximum here. Beyond the full employment limit, if money supply is increased from *M3* to *M4* prices rise proportionately with money while output remains the same.

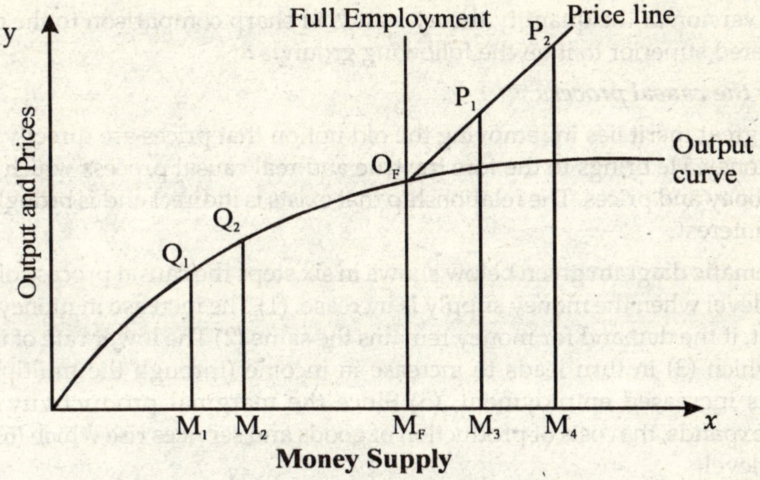

Keynes's reformulated quantity theory

The Reformulated Quantity Theory

It should be clear that Keynes reformulated the Quantity Theory. The pith and substance of the theory of money as reformulated by him is: *"As long as there are human and material unemployed resources in the economy, a rise in the price level will help expansion of income, output and employment. However when the level of full employment has been attained and the supply of the factors of production becomes inelastic, true inflation sets in."* Steps have to be taken to curb it and to keep it within bounds. This reformulated version brings forth the fact that an increase in money becomes a matter of concern only after full employment. Thus, it points out the desirability of resorting to deficit financing in order to fight deflation.

Let us now understand Keyen's theory of money and prices in terms of effective demand with the help of Fig. - Changes in aggregate demand will affect prices according to the effect of such changes on cost and output. It may be noted that effective demand will not change in exact proportion to the variations in the quantity of money nor will prices change in exact proportion to changes in effective demand ; increased effective demand will manifest itself partly in increased employment and partly in increased prices. In the beginning, starting from a period of depression, employment is likely to rise faster than prices; later as full employment is approached, prices are likely to rise faster than employment.

However, the proposition that "so long as there is unemployment, income will change in the same proportion as the quantity of money ; and when there is full employment, price will change in the same proportion as the quantity of money" is mere approximation to the truth. It is a general sort of statement subject to so many qualifications as prices do rise during the transition period (till the level of full employment is reached). A rise in prices during the period may occur on account of the following reasons:

(1) Increased bargaining power of the workers (2) Operation of the law of diminishing returns and (3) Bottlenecks in production.

Merits of Keynes' Version of the Quantity Theory of Money

Keynes' version of the quantity theory stands in sharp comparison to the old classical theory and is considered superior to it on the following grounds :

1. It analyses the causal process

Keyne's great merit lies in removing the old notion that prices are directly determined by the quantity of money. He brings to the fore the true and real causal process which exists between the quantity of money and prices. The relationship that exists is indirect and is brought through changes in the rate of interest.

The schematic diagram given below shows in six steps the causal process of the increase in the general price level when the money supply is increase. (1) The increase in money supply lowers the rate of interest, if the demand for money remains the same (2) The lower rate of interest encourages investment which (3) in turn leads to increase in income (through the multiplier), (4) Increased output means increased employment, (5) Since the marginal productivity of labour falls as employment expands, the costs of production of goods and services rise which (6) leads to rise in the general price level.

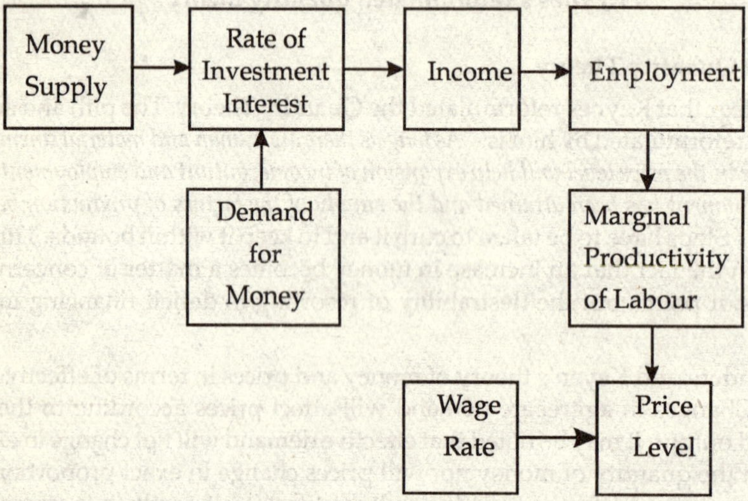

2. It does not assume full employment

The quantity theory of money like all classical doctrines, is based on the assumption of full employment. As long as the human and material resources were taken to be fully employed, it was easy for the classical thinkers to say that an increase in the quantity of money was associated with or followed by a rise in the price level. Since money in the classical scheme could not affect employment, it could raise prices only. According to Prof. Dillard, "this leads to the conclusion that all increases in the quantity of money tend to be inflationary, a conclusion quite valid under the assumption that resources are fully employed, but a nonsense conclusion when this special assumption is dropped." Keynes, on the other hand, does not assume full employment. To him unemployment is the rule and full employment only an exception. He says, "So long as there is unemployment, employment will change in the same proportion as the quantity of money."

3. It tells us when to dread inflation

Keynesian approach to the quantity theory of money helps us to look at inflation entirely from a different perspective. It tells us when to dread inflation and when not to dread it. As long as there is unemployment of resources, inflation is not to be feared as it results in an increase in employment and output. But once the level of full employment is attained, true inflation begins and it becomes a real threat. According to classicals, every increase in money supply results in inflation (as full employment was always presumed). To Keynes, only that increase in money supply results in inflation which takes place beyond the level of full employment. Thus, Keynesian version shows a great advance on the traditional version of the quantity theory of money.

4. It integrates monetary theory with the theory of value

Another great merit of Keynes' theory of money and prices is that it integrates monetary theory with the theory of value. Keynes gave up the traditional division of the economy into the real sector and the monetary sector and pointed out that there could be no monetary economy in which money was neutral. The integration of the theory of money with the theory of value on the one hand and with the theory of output on the other, was achieved through the rate of interest : the missing link in the process (rate of interest) was at last discovered.

According to value theory, the price (which is the value expressed in terms of money) is determined by the forces of demand and supply and the production is carried to the extent of the equality of the marginal cost with marginal revenue. Thus, the concepts of marginal cost, marginal revenue, demand and supply, their elasticities (specially in the short period) become important in the theory of value. When Keynes discusses the theory of prices in general (price level), he emphasises cost of production, elasticity of demand, elasticity of supply and other concepts which are important in the theory of value or individual price determination. Keynes shows that prices rise on account of the rise in costs of production ; costs of production rise because of the inelasticity of short-period supply of output and employment. *From a monetary theory of prices, Keynes, thus, shifted to a monetary theory of output*. This, in itself, turned out to be an important contribution as it resulted in a successful integration of the quantity theory of money with the theory of value.

Further, Keynes also integrated the theory of output with the theory of money. In fact, the integration of monetary theory with the theory of value is accomplished through the theory of output in which the rate of interest, by influencing the volume of investment, plays a vital role. Changes in the quantity of money, by bringing about changes in the rate of interest affect investment and hence output and employment. As the volume of output and employment changes, the costs of production vary and prices are also affected. The traditional theory did not pay any heed to the influence that the quantity of money exerts on the rate of interest and through it on income, output, employment and prices. Thus, in addition to integrating the theory of output with the theory of value, Keynes also integrated the theory of output with the monetary theory (theory of money).

5. It differentiates between the determination of the general price level and individual prices

Keynes' theory differentiates between the determination of the general price level and individual prices. Individual prices of various commodities are determined by the forces of demand and supply with reference to the nature of competition and the type of market, whereas a large number of considerations enter the determination of the general price level. To him, analysis of the fluctuations in the general price level is not so simple and straight as has been assumed by the exponents of the traditional quantity theory of money; that is, an increase in the volume of money will not straightway raise the price level. The whole process is highly complicated and roundabout, certainly not so direct and simple as was claimed by the classical economists.

Assumptions and Limitations

No doubt the reformulated version of the quantity theory of money takes into consideration a large number of factors ignored in the classical quantity theory of money. Yet, the new version has its own shortcomings. They mostly stem from its assumptions.

Firstly, it assumes that productive resources are perfectly elastic in supply before the level of full employment, i.e., there are no shortages of land, labour and capital. It further presumes perfectly inelastic supply of the factors beyond the level of full employment.

Secondly, it assumes that effective demand increases in proportion to an increase in the quantity of money, failing which output will not expand.

Thirdly, the whole relationship between the quantity of money and the price level is set in motion through the so-called missing link–the rate of interest. But whether or not a change in the rate of interest will cause a corresponding change in the whole chain of investment, employment, income, output, cost of production and prices, will depend upon the two other determinants, namely, the marginal efficiency of capital and the propensity to consume. Suppose that marginal efficiency of capital is falling or the propensity to consume is decreasing, a fall in the rate of interest may not be able to generate any increase in income, output, employment and hence prices. Thus, unless these elements are assumed to be given or constant, the whole chain of causation may not work at all. Despite these shortcomings, Keynes' analysis is more acceptable as it takes into consideration the phenomenon of employment in the economy and it is superior to the traditional quantity theory.

Milton Friedman's Quantity Theory of Money

Prof. Milton Friedman, of the University of Chicago, was awarded the Nobel Prize in Economics for the year 1976 for "his achievements in the fields of consumption analysis, monetary history and theory, and for his demonstration of the complexity of stabilization policy." His major contribution, however, lies in the field of monetary economics, particularly the quantity theory of money.

Milton Friedman's "The Quantity Theory of Money–A Restatement marked the resurgence of modern economists interest in the Quantity Theory of Money. In that easy Friedman has asserted that quantity theory of money is primarily a theory of the demand for money. Friedman classifies the holders of money into two groups. The first group is comprised of the ultimate owners of all wealth–individuals who consider money as one of the forms in which to hold their wealth. These are referred to as ultimate wealth holders. The second group is comprised of business enterprises to whom money is a factor of production. These are referred to as business enterprises. Friedman's Theory is essentially set out in respect of the demand for money by wealth holders. This approach views money as an asset and regards it simply as one way of holding wealth. Friedman argues that the demand for money by wealth holders is a function of the following variables.

1. Total Wealth (W)

The Wealth, Friedman refers to, is total wealth, that is, human wealth plus non-human wealth. The concept of wealth in economics generally includes all assets such as bonds, stocks, shares, equities, land, building etc., which can be traded and yield an income. Friedman argues that the income from labour is also amenable to trade and there is a little difference between trade in other assets and trade in future income from labour. It is, therefore, analytically sensible to include human wealth in the concept of wealth. In practice, estimates of total wealth are rarely available. So income is generally used as a surrogate for wealth. Income, as we know, includes both property income and labour income. Friedman rejected the use of current income as a proxy for wealth because in the short run current income is subjected to erratic fluctuations. Instead, Friedman introduced to monetary analysis a longer-term concept of income like permanent income. This is an average of past, present and future income and confirms closely to an individual's expected or normal income. As wealth rises, permanent income will rise which in turn will increase the demand for money.

2. Percentage of total wealth in non-human forms (H)

Friedman's definition of wealth includes human as well as non-human wealth but the substitution of human wealth-for non-human wealth is limited owing to institutional constraints. Since human wealth exhibits much less liquidity than non-human wealth, Friedman argued that as the percentage ratio of non-human to total wealth decreases, there may be an increased demand for money to compensate for the illiquidity of human wealth.

3. The Opportunity cost of holding money $\left(rm, rb, re, \frac{\Delta p}{p}\right)$

The opportunity cost of holding money depends on the rate of interest and the rate of change in the price level.

The opportunity cost of holding money is the income forgone by not holding other assets such as bond, equity, durable goods and also human wealth. According to the Principle of diminishing marginal rate of substitution, Friedman asserted that if the return on other assets increases, the demand for money would decline. Thus, the rate of return on various assets is relevant for determining the demand for money.

When the price level rises, the real value of money holding would fall in proportion to change in price level, when price level rises the return on money balance is negative and it is positive when there is fall in price. Therefore, the expected rate of price change may be taken as the expected change in return for money. When higher the rate of return on money, greater is the demand for holding money balance and less is the return, lower is the demand.

4. Other variables that determine the utility of money (U)

Besides the above, there may be other variables like the over-all economic outlook that can influence the demand for money. One such variable suggested by Friedman is the degree of economic stability expected to prevail in the future. If a war or recession is anticipated then the demand for cash balances will increase. Other factors can influence the utility of money and subsequently affect its demand.

Friedman's demand for money by individual wealth holders is summed up symbolically as below :

$$\frac{\text{Md}}{\text{p}} = f\left(\text{W}, \text{H}, \frac{\Delta\text{p}}{\text{p}}, \text{r}_\text{m}\text{r}_\text{d}, \text{r}_\text{s}\text{U}\right)$$

where *Md* is the demand for money balances, W is total wealth, H is ratio of non-human wealth to human wealth, P is the price level. r_m is the expected rate of return on money, r_o is the rate of return on fixed value securities, including expected changes in their prices; $\frac{\Delta p}{p}$ is the expected rate of change of prices of goods and hence the expected rate of return on real assets, r_s is the expecterd rate of return on equities, including expected changes in their price and U is a symbol for whatever variables other then income that may affect the utility of money.

In practice, it is difficult to find reliable estimates of total wealth, therefore, we use permanent income (Y) as proxy for total wealth (W). Replacing W by Y in the above functional form we get,

This is Friedman's demand for money presented in the form of a function.

$$\frac{Md}{p} = f\left(W, H, \frac{\Delta p}{p}, r_m r_d, r_s U\right)$$

Fig.

Friedman's quantity theory of money is explained in terms of Fig.-where income *(Y)* is measured on the vertical axis and the demand for the supply of money are measured on the horizontal axis. M_D is the demand for money curve which varies with income. *MS* is the money supply curve which is perfectly inelastic to changes in income. The two curves intersect at E and determine the equilibrium income *OY*. If the money supply rises, the *MS* curve shifts to the right to M_1S_1. As a result, the money supply is greater than the demand for money which raises total expenditure until new equilibrium is established at *F* between M_D and M_1S_1 curves. The income rises to OY_1.

Thus Friedman presents the quantity theory as the theory of the demand for money and the demand for money is assumed to depend on asset prices or relative returns and wealth or income.

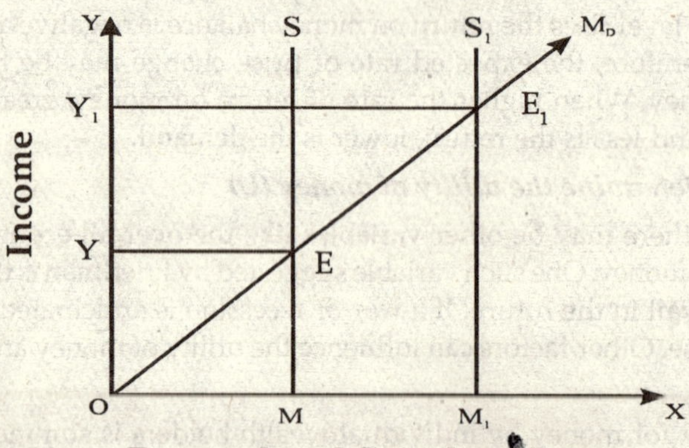

Demand and Supply of Money

He shows how a theory of the stable demand for money becomes a theory of prices and output. A discrepancy between the nominal quantity of money demanded and the nominal quantity of money supplied will be evident primarily in attempted spending. As the demand for money changes in response to changes in its determinants, it follows that substantial changes in prices or nominal income are almost invariably the result of changes in the nominal supply of money.

Its Criticisms

Freidman's reformulation of the quantity theory of money has evoked much controversy and has led to empirical verification on the part of the Keynesians and the Monetarists. Some of the criticisms levelled against the theory are discussed as under.

1. Very Broad Definition of Money

Friedman has been criticised for using the broad definition of money which not only includes currency and demand deposits (M_1), but also time deposits with commercial banks (M_2). This broad definition leads to the obvious conclusion that the interest elasticity of the demand for them (M_2) rises. But the demand for currency and demand deposits (M_1) falls. So the overall effect of the rate of interest will be negligible on the demand for money. But Friedman's analysis is weak in that he does not make a choice between long-term and short-term interest rates. In fact, if demand deposits (M_1) are used a short-term rate is preferable, while a long-term rate is better with time deposits (M_2). Such an interest rate structure is bound to influence the demand for money.

2. Money not a Luxury Good

Friedman regards money as a luxury good because of the inclusion of time deposits in money. This based on his finding that there is higher trend rate of the money supply than income in the United States. But no such 'luxury effect' has been found in the case of England.

3. More Importance to Wealth Variables

In Friedman's demand for money function, wealth variables are preferable to income and the operation of wealth and income variables simultaneously does not seem to be justified. As pointed out by Johnson, income is the return on wealth, and wealth is the present value of income. The presence of the rate of interest and one of these variables in the demand for money function would appear to make the other superfluous.

4. Money Supply not Exogenous

Friedman takes the supply of money to be unstable. The supply of money is varied by the monetary authorities in an exogenous manner in Friedman's system. But the fact is that in the United States the money supply consists of bank deposits created by changes in bank lending. Bank lending, in turn, is based upon bank reserves which expand and contract with *(a)* deposits and withdrawals of currency by non-bank financial intermediaries; *(b)* borrowings by commercial banks from the Federal Reserve System; *(c)* inflows and outflows of money from and to abroad: and *(d)* purchase and sale of securities by the Federal Reserve System. The first three items definitely impart an endogenous element to the money supply. Thus the money supply is not exclusively exogenous, as assumed by Friedman. It is mostly endogenous.

5. Ignores the Effect of Other Variables on Money Supply

Friedman also ignores the effect of prices, output or interest rates on the money supply. But there is considerable empirical evidence that the money supply can be expressed as a function of the above variables.

6. Does not consider Time Factor

Friedman does not tell about the timing and speed of adjustment or the length of time to which his theory applies.

7. No Positive Correlation between Money Supply and Money GNP

Money supply and money GNP have been found to be positively correlated in Friedman's findings. But, according to Kaldor, in Britain the best correlation is to be found between the quarterly variations in the amount of cash held in the form of notes and coins by the public and corresponding variations in personal consumption at market prices, and not between money supply and the GNP.

Despite these criticsms, "Friedman's application to monetary theory of the basic principle of capital theory–that is the yield on capital, and capital the present value of income–is probably the most important development in monetary theory since Keynes's *General Theory*. Its theoretical significance lies in the conceptual integration of wealth and income as influences on behaviour."

Money and Other Forms of Wealth

In a modern economy, since most incomes accrue in the form of money there exists a close relationship between money and income. Similarly, a close relationship between money and wealth may exist in such an economy since a considerable part of the wealth may be held in the form of money. It is useful to distinguish two main forms of wealth, namely, real or tangible wealth and financial or intangible wealth. Real wealth consists of physical assets, such as machines, houses, stocks of raw materials and land. Financial wealth consists of money, bills of exchange, bonds and equity shares. The basic differences between real wealth and financial wealth are as follows:

1. Real wealth is highly specific in form and use whereas financial forms of wealth are predominantly generalised claims against current production.
2. Real wealth is held primarily for the physical services that they yield directly. Financial wealth is held primarily as an attractive income-earning store of purchasing power, representing an indirect claim to the consumption or utilisation of the physical services of economic goods.
3. Real wealth is complementary since it requires the co-operation of other production factors, whereas financial wealth is supplementary in character. The expected yield for the financial wealth, therefore, does not vary with the holder as is the case with real wealth.
4. Real wealth can be increased or decreased only slowly. Financial wealth, however, can be created or destroyed virtually instantaneously by the act of borrowing or repayment.
5. Real wealth is illiquid in the sense that it cannot be easily and quickly converted into money, as in the case of financial wealth.

Money is an important form of financial wealth. It is the most liquid among all the forms of financial wealth. It serves as a medium of exchange in a modern economy and as such it is readily marketable.

The major forms of financial wealth other than money are :

(i) Bills of exchange – a promise to pay a fixed sum of money on a given date in the relatively near future, normally 3 months. These may be issued by governments (Treasury Bills) or traders (Commercial bills).

(ii) Bonds–a method of borrowing for relatively long periods of several years. Bonds issued by firms are commonly known as 'debentures'. A bond consists of a promise to pay a given sum of money annually for a given number of years as interest and to repay the capital sum borrowed at the end of the period. Bonds may also be issued with no maturity date but in the general only governments can borrow in this way (*e.g.*, British government's consols).

(iii) Equity shares do not promise and fixed income to its owner but instead give him a claim to a share in whatever profits are made by the firm which issues the shares.

All these forms of financial wealth are not actually money but these can be easily and quickly converted into money. These are, therefore, called near-money or money substitutes. They add to the spending power of the people by making additional funds available to them through the sale of money substitutes.

Thus, there is a spectrum of liquid assets which can be held by spending units in the economy–the most liquid in this spectrum being money itself.

Role of Financial Intermediaries

If there are no financial assets other than money, then money becomes the only form in which private spending units can save. Investors cannot attract the savings of others by issuing their own financial instruments and they have to restrict their investment to their own savings. Both saving and investment would, therefore, be kept at a relatively low level.

Financial intermediaries assume prominence when institutionali-sation of saving takes place in the economy. Financial institutions are those which collect savings from others issuing in return claims against themselves and use the funds thus acquired to purchase ownership or debt claims. They are placed between ultimate borrowers and lenders. They acquire the primary securities of the borrowers and they create claims which are more liquid than the securities they but and issue them to lenders.

Three important consequences of their activity are :

1. More savings are channelised into investment activity.
2. The liquidity of securities is improved by the lending of financial institutions on them, and
3. An increase in the liquid claims on secondary financial institutions serves to reduce the demand by spending units for money itself and therefore, such an increase in these liquid assets exerts an influence on the interest rate, the price level and the level of income.

Financial intermediaries are of two types : (1) primary, and (2) secondary. The primary financial intermediaries "draw their funds directly from households, business enterprises or government and make them available in turn to the same groups." Commercial banks and life insurance companies are good examples of this type. The secondary financial intermediaries depend for most of their funds on primary financial intermediaries or use their own funds to acquire the securities of primary financial intermediaries." The ICICI and IFCI are good examples of this type.

Conclusion

From the above discussion, undoubtedly we can say that, the term "value of money" is meant the purchasing power of money its buying capacity, i.e., the quantity of goods and services a unit of money can buy obviously, the purchasing power of money depends upon the level of prices of the goods and services to be purchased. Thus, the lower price level, the greater would be the purchasing power of money; and the higher the level of prices, the lower would be the purchasing power. Hence, the purchasing power of money changes inversely with the price level. Thus, the value of money is the reciprocal of the price level general prices.

Questions for Discussion

1. What is meant by the term "Value of Money" ? How is the value of money measured.
2. What is a price index number ? How is it constructed.
3. Critically evaluate the quantity Theory of Money.
4. Explain briefly Militan Friedman's Quantity Theory of Money.

Chapter - 5

INFLATION, DEFLATION, STAGFLATION

Introduction

Inflation and deflation are exactly opposite in character. If inflation is rise in prices accompanied by rise in the volume of employment, deflation is fall in prices accompanied by fall in the volume of employment. Inflation breeds inequalities of income and wealth among the people of the country. Deflation reduces the national income through fall in the production and employment. Therefore inflation is unjust, deflation is inexpedient.

Inflation has been a continuous process in India since the beginning of World War II. But in the last few years, it has become a world wide phenomenon. Every government is making frantic attempts to control it.

Inflation

Broadly speaking, inflation stands for rise in the price level in a country or, which is the same thing, fall in the value of money. Inflation is said to refer to a situation in which "too much money is chasing too few goods or there is too much currency in relation to the physical volume of business being done"; and so on. The implication in all these ideas is that rise in the price level is due to an increase in the volume of money. But the price level may rise due to a rise in the cost of production. Besides, there can be inflationary pressure on prices without the prices actually rising.

According to Keynes inflation stands for rise in price level which comes into existence after the stage of full employment. He talkes of two types of rise in prices ; (a) rise in prices accompanied by increase in production, and (b) rise in prices not accompanied by such an increase in output.

When an economy has a large number of men unemployed and resources unutilized – i.e., the economy is working below full employment – an expansion of money or some other factors leading to an increase in demand, will result not only in a rise in the price level but also a rise in the volume of goods and services in the system. The rise in prices is followed by increased production and employment. This will continue till all unemployed men find employment and other resources are fully utilized, i.e., till the economy reaches full employment. Any rise in the price level after the full employment stage cannot lead to production or employment. The initial rise in price level up to the stage of full employment is advantageous as there is an increase in output and also in employment ; the term reflation is used to refer to such a rise in the price level. The rise in price level after the stage of full employment is bad for the country since there is no corresponding increase in production or employment ; **"inflation"** is used to express such a rise in one price level.

Kinds of Inflation

There are various kinds of inflation. We deal with the major ones below.

1. Cost-Push Inflation and Demand-Pull Inflation

This classification is made on the basis of its origin. Demand-pull inflation originates from the demand side. General price level increases because the demand for goods and services exceeds the supply at existing prices. It is loosely described as "too much money chasing too few goods". This version of inflation is given by the quantity theorists, both traditional and modern, as well as by J.M. Keynes. Traditional quantity theorists assume full-employment in the economy whereas, the modern version lead by Milton Friedman does not assume conditions of full-employment. To both, excessive increase in the quantity of money is the cause of inflation. Whereas, according to Keynes, increase in the level of income causes excessive demand as output remains constant after full-employment. This causes a rise in the general price level.

Cost-push inflation originates from the supply side. Aggregate demand remaining constant, if there is an increase in the cost of production, aggregate supply will decrease, causing a fall in prices. There are two principal causes of cost-push inflation: wage-push and profit-push. Wage-push inflation occurs when trade unions succeed in securing wage-rate increases higher than the marginal productivity of the workers. Due to an increase in the labour-cost per unit of output, prices increase, but at the same time there is unemployment, as output is reduced. Profit-push inflation occurs when monopolists and oligopolists succeed in increasing prices more than the cost. This enables them to earn more profits.

In practice, we find that inflation is neither purely cost-push nor purely demand-pull but combines the elements of both. Demand-pull inflation can be controlled through suitable restrictive monetary and fiscal policies. But in order to curb cost-push inflation, strong anti-trust and anti-union legislations are necessary.

2. Open and Suppressed Inflation

When the price-mechanism is allowed to operate freely without any interference by the government, open inflation results. On the contrary, when the government imposes monetary and fiscal controls, like price control, rationing, licensing etc., to control inflation, suppressed inflation occurs. Once these controls are removed, suppressed inflation is again converted into open inflation.

3. Creeping, Walking, Running and Galloping Inflation

This classification is made on the basis of the speed with which price level rises. A slowly rising price level is referred to as creeping inflation. Sometimes governments deliberately resort to creeping inflation in order to stimulate trade and commerce. Galloping inflation or hyper-inflation is dangerous to an economy. If the rise in prices is allowed to continue unchecked, prices rise to the extreme limit. This situation is called hyper inflation. Here value of money reaches its lowest limit and money begins to lost its importance as a measure of value and medium of exchange. People begin to convert money into goods and services. There is 'flight from currency'. Such a situation had occurred in Germany often the First World War. As stated earlier, creeping inflation, means slowly rising price level. When the rate of increase in price level occurs at a greater speed and rapidity, it becomes walking inflation. And if no control is exercised by the government, walking inflation becomes running inflation and running inflation develops into a galloping inflation.

4. True inflation and Semi-inflation

According to J.M. Keynes, a rise in price level after full-employment is true inflation, where as a rise in price level before the full-employment due to bottlenecks in the economy is semi-inflation.

5. Currency and Credit Inflation

When inflation is caused due to excess supply of money in relation to the available output, it is called currency inflation and when it is caused by excess credit, it is called credit inflation. Sometimes government encourages credit expansion in order to finance the development process, or expand production.

6. Deficit-induced Inflation

When governments resort to printing notes' in order to cover a deficit in their budgets, the consequent rise in prices is called deficit-induced inflation. This kind of inflation is found in developing countries which are forced to resort to deficit financing to meet the expenditure of their development process.

7. War-induced Inflation

Expenditure during war increases tremendously as modern warfare is very costly. To meet this expenditure, supply of money is increased but output remains more or less constant as near full-employment conditions prevail during war.

8. Ratchet Inflation

A ratchet is a wheel which allows motion only in one direction. In the same manner, under ratchet inflation, prices in certain sectors are not allowed to fall by powerful trade unions and monopolists even after a decline in the aggregate demand. Prices move in one direction. In other words, prices have an upward ratchet effect. Such a situations is known as ratchet inflation.

9. Sectorial Inflation

Due to excess demand for the products of certain industries, prices rise in these sectors. In the deficit-demand industries prices do not fall because prices and wages are rigid downwards due to the activities of strong trade unions and monopolists. This kind of inflation is called sectorial inflation. This kind of inflation had occurred in the USA in the fifties of this century.

Theories of Inflation

1. Demand-pull inflation

Demand-pull inflation occurs when the aggregate demand exceeds the level of output at full employment level. The classical writers hold money supply responsible for excess demand conditions, as the Quantity Theory of Money implies. Modern writers, however, point out that a rise in the marginal efficiency of capital or a rise in the propensity to consume can bring in demand-pull inflation.

The essence of demand-pull inflation theory can be explained with the help of a diagram.

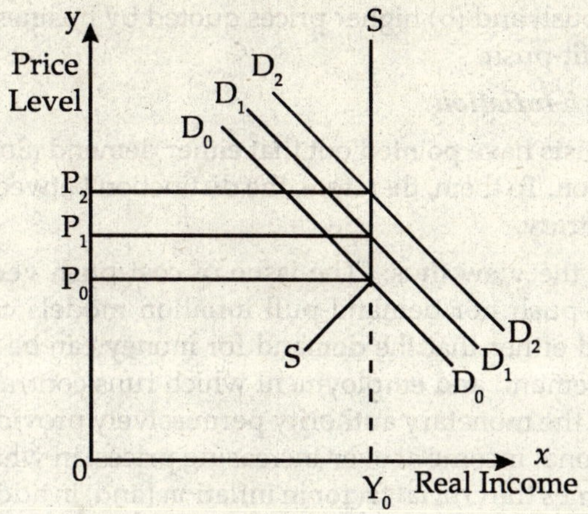

As the diagram shows, at full employment income level (Y_0), the aggregate supply function becomes perfectly (price) inelastic and any increase in demand beyond D_0, therefore, increases the price level from P_0, to P_1 or P_2.

2. Cost-Push Inflation

According to the cost-push inflation theorists prices are pushed up by a rise in the cost of production such as a rise in the cost of raw materials or a rise in wages. Thus, according to this view it is on the supply side that inflation emerges. This may be explained with the help of a diagram.

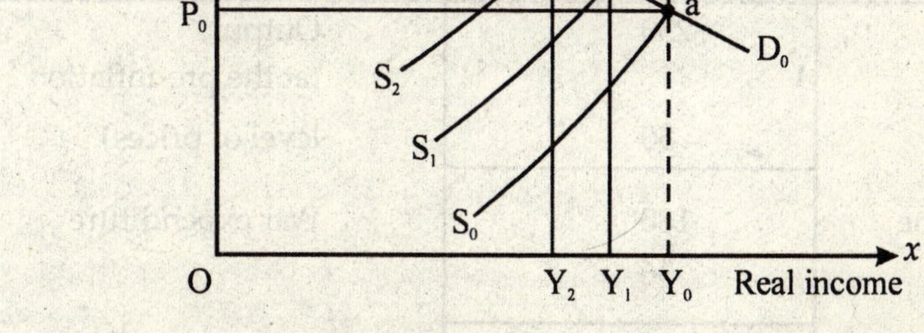

The above diagram shows that as aggregate supply function shifts from full employment (a) level to (b) and (c), real income falls from Y_0 to Y_1 and Y_2, given the aggregate demand function. In order to maintain the full employment level of real income price level must rise (from P_0 to P_1 to P_2).

As may be noted from the diagram, it is the supply shifts that cause inflationary rise in the price level. There are two explanations to the supply shifts : (a) higher money wages due to trade union intervention or wage-push and (b) higher prices quoted by business firms under monopoly or duopoly conditions or profit-push.

3. Demand-pull vs. Cost-push inflation

Several modern economists have pointed out that either demand alone or supply alone could be held responsible for inflation. To them, therefore, the distinction between demand-pull and cost-push is meaningless and arbitrary.

H.G. Johnson sums up the view thus: "The issue of cost-push versus demand-pull was a spurious one... Neither cost-push nor demand-pull inflation models can generate a sustained inflation unless it is assumed either that the demand for money can be compressed indefinitely without adverse effects on demand and employment which runs contrary to the theory and fact of monetary behavior or that the monetary authority permissively provides the additional money required to circulate the national income at ever-increasing prices, in which case the behaviour of the monetary authority becomes the crucial factor in inflation (and, in addition, the question arises for the cost-push theory as to what determines the pace of inflation). The two theories are therefore not independent and self-contained theories of inflation, but rather theories concerning the mechanism of inflation in a monetary environment that permits it".

4. Inflationary Gap Analysis

The concept of inflationary gap has been developed more recently with the help of Keynes' ideas on "true" inflation.

The inflationary gap has been defined as "an excess of anticipated expenditures over available output at base prices". Anticipated expenditures are determined by the consumption (saving) functions and the tax-structure (determining the size of disposable income). Available output, on the other hand, is determined by the degree of employment in the economy and the technological conditions. If there is any excess of anticipated expenditure over the available volume of goods and services, then, the price level will go up. This may be explained with a numerical example :

Anticipated Expenditure	**(Rs. Cr.)**	**Available Output**	**(Rs. Cr.)**
National income	230	Output (at the pre-inflation level of prices)	200
Taxes	50		
Disposable income	180	War expenditure	90
Saving (20%)	36		
∴ Anticipated expenditure :	144	Available output	110

∴ The inflationary gap = Rs. 144 Cr. – Rs. 110 Cr. = **Rs. 34 Crores**

The following diagram explains this :

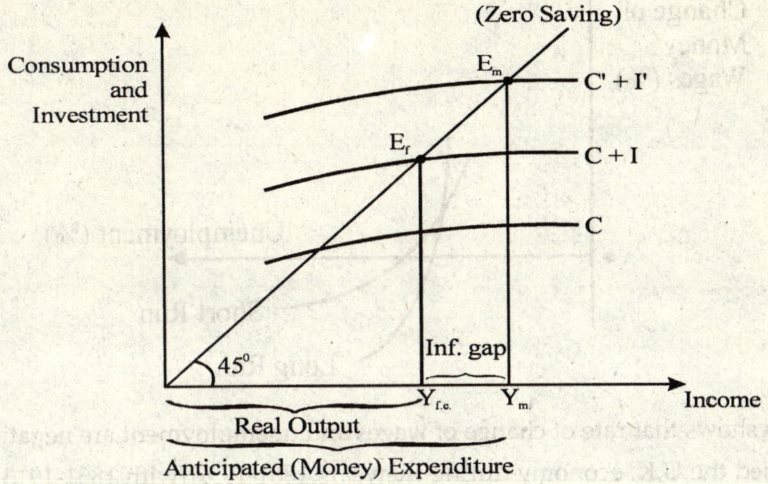

This inflationary gap may be bridged with the help of (a) an increase in the voluntary savings (from Rs. 36 crores to Rs. 70 crores) or (b) an increase in taxes (from Rs. 50 crores to Rs. 84 crores) or (c) an increase in the available output.

Inflation, then, has been made "typically a short-run phenomenon peculiar to a stationary, full employment economy". (Kurihara)

5. Inflation and Unemployment — Phillips Curve Analysis

The assumptions of Classical / Neo-Classical economists such as,

(a) Full employment (implying output rigidity and employment rigidity)

(b) perfect/pure competitive markets (implying a price and no Trade Union activities, etc.)

(c) Wage rigidity (except under shifts in occupations) made their analysis highly restrictive. There was a need for a theoretical analysis to deal with relationships among factors such as unemployment (changes), the wage (money) rate (changes) and price (changes). Also the Keynes–Plgou controversy over the efficiency of price or wage flexibility for general equilibrium made economists think of the necessary tools of analysis to put the controversial points to test theoretically and empirically.

On the policy side also, it was greatly felt, especially in the 1950s with the revival of monetary policy, that the domestic objectives of the (monetary) policy authorities namely full employment, price stability and economic growth are not always compatible and hence conflict was possible among them resulting in inconsistent policy measures. Answers to policy questions like "what, in the existing situation, is the minimum level of employment consistent with the absence of inflation" were sought by the economists.

The phillips curve analysis shows the relationship between changes in the wage rate and the level of unemployment.

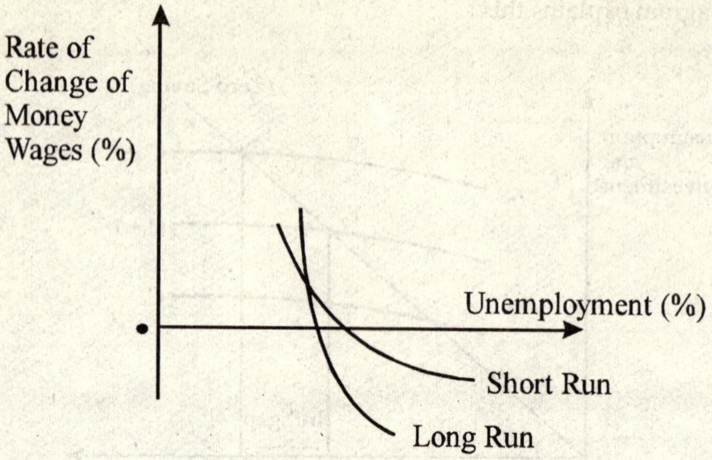

This diagram shows that rate of change of wages and unemployment are negatively related.

Phillips studied the U.K. economy during the years 1861-1957 (with 1861-1913, 1913-48 and 1948-57 as sub-periods). With the help of such an empirical study, Phillips concluded :

1. "...the rate of change of money wage rates can be explained by the level of unemployment, except in, or immediately after, those years in which there is a sufficiently rapid rise in import prices to offset the tendency for increasing productivity to reduce the cost of living".
2. "Ignoring years in which import prices rise rapidly enough to initiate a wage-price spiral, which seem to occur very rarely except as a result of war, and assuming an increase in productivity of 2% per year, it seems from the relation fitted to the data that if aggregate demand were kept at a value which would maintain a stable level of product prices the associated level of unemployment would be a little under 2½%. If, as is sometimes recommended, demand were kept at a value which would maintain stable wage rates the associated level of unemployment would be about 5½%".
3. "There will be a lower average rate of increase of wage rates if unemployment is held constant at a given level than there will be if unemployment is a allowed to fluctuate about that level".

It should be noted, however, that Phillips himself recognised the fact that these conclusions were "or course tentative".

R.G. Lipsey made a similar empirical analysis dealing with the U.K. data relating to the periods 1923-39 and 1948-57 and his analysis explained wages much better.

Samuelson and Solow (AER, May proceedings) applied the Phillips curve analysis to the U.S. Data. Although the observations did not suggest any consistent relationship between wage rate change and unemployment, 'the period between the turn of the century and the first war, the decade between the end of that war and the great depression, and the most recent ten or twelve year–all show a rather consistent pattern. Wage rates do tend to rise when the labour market is tight and tighter the faster. What is most interesting is the strong suggestion that the relation has shifted upward slightly but noticeably in the forties and fifties. This apparent upward shift of Phillips curve in the

USA, was due to the new market power of the Trade Unions in the USA and due to other imperfect characteristics of the American Labour Market.

A comparison between the USA case and the UK case suggests that "anything which will shift the relationship downward decreased the price in unemployment that must be paid when a policy is followed of holding the rate of wage and price increase by pressure on aggregate demand".

"Translating the Phillips' diagram showing the American pattern of wage increase against degree of unemployment into a related diagram showing the different levels of unemployment that would be "needed" for each degree of price level change, Samuelson and Solow came to the following "guesses" :

1. In order to have wages increase at 2½% (equivalent to 2½% of productivity growth) so that price stability can be achieved for the US economy, 5% to 6% unemployment is inevitable. This is the unemployment cost of price stability.
2. To reduce the US unemployment to around 3%, the price level must rise by 4% to 5% per year. This is the inevitable inflation cost of unemployment.

These "guesses" hold good, according to them, only in the short run, as in the longer run, structural and technological changes are possible.

Milton Friedman (AER, March 1968) expressed the view that the conventional Phillips curve "is merely a transitory short-run relationship. According to this view, in the long run, the Phillips curve turns out to be a vertical line drawn at the natural rate of unemployment (which is the rate corresponding to that real wage at which the demand for and supply of labour are equated). The natural rate of unemployment will be different in different countries and may change from time to time in the same country.

Whether the long-run view is used or the short-run view, the Phillips curve analysis points out that price stability can be achieved only at the cost of higher level of unemployment.

6. Charles L. Schultz's Sectorial Inflation Analysis

Charles Schultz has offered a 'demand shifts' hypothesis in which the demand-pull and cost-push theories of inflation have been combined. He developed this hypothesis with the help of the U.S. Data over the 1955-57 (inflation) period. He found out that the 1955-57 U.S. Inflation, with 3% increase in price level per year while money demand rose only about 5% per year, was neither due to excess demand nor due to the active exercise of market power. It was, according to him, mainly due to a substantial change in the composition of demand. It arose initially out of excess demand in particular industries. But it resulted in general price rise only because of the downward rigidities and cost-oriented nature of price and wages. "It is not characterized by an autonomous upward push of costs nor by an aggregate excess demand. Indeed, its basic nature is that it cannot be understood in terms of aggregates alone. Such inflation is the necessary result of sharp changes in the composition of demand, given the structure of prices and wages in our economy".

"The downward rigidities and cost-oriented nature of prices and wages act like a ratchet on the price level".

Thus, according to Schultz.

1. Prices and wages are flexible upward in response to excess demand but they tend to be rigid downwards.

2. Excess demand in particular industries transmits its impact to the rest of the economy through its influence on the price of materials and the wages of labour.

It is clear that such a kind of inflationary process "cannot be neatly labelled".

7. A Model of "Corrective Inflation"

The Brazilian inflationary trends suggest that substantial dampening effects on the rate of inflation would have been possible with a more realistic government policy with regard to the public utility (especially railroads) rates. The subsidies given, if eliminated, should result in an instantaneous rise in the price level and the producers would transfer to the buyers the burden of the subsidy cuts. The increase in the price level caused by the elimination of the subsidies (or any such corrective measure) has been named as "Corrective Inflation", "since it is followed by a substantial reduction of public expenditures on subsidies which will result in a noticeable lowering of the subsequent rate of inflation". That this "corrective inflation" is more advantageous to the public that the original inflation over a longer period of time can be easily seen with the help of the diagram given below.

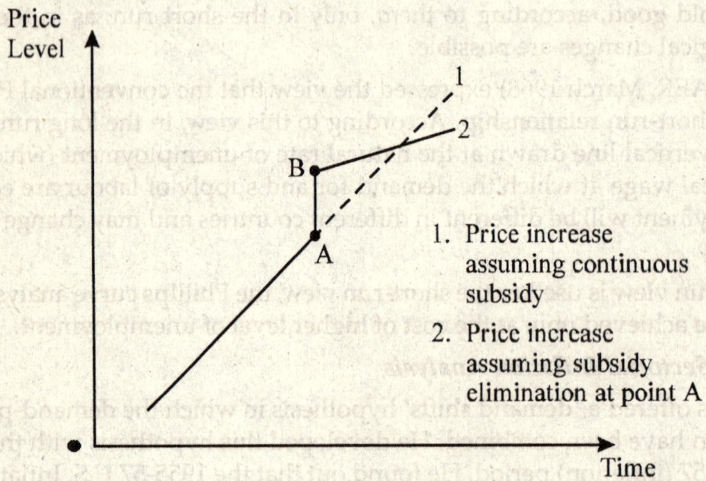

Causes of Inflation

The main factor responsible for inflation is generalised excess demand. The factors that cause excess demand are the factors that result in inflation. Excess demand in turn may be the result of upward shift in demand and or downward shift in supply. Factors working on the demand side and supply side together cause inflation.

Factors Affecting Demand

1. Demand is greatly affected by an increase in the supply of money. An increase in the supply of money leads to an increase in the aggregate demand and so prices rise.
2. Increase in public expenditure also influences demand. The activities of State are increasing day by day as most modern states are welfare states. As a result, there is a tremendous increase in public expenditure. Public expenditure also increases during a war or in the context of developing economy. Both developing as well as developed countries of the

world are spending large quantities of money on social services, improvement of human resources, on public enterprises and public utilities and in laying the infrastructure for their economies. All this causes an increase in the aggregate demand.

3. Deficit financing is yet another important factor affecting demand. If a government's expenditure exceeds its income, it has a deficit budget. It can meet this deficit by borrowing from the banking system. It includes borrowing from the commercial banks as well as from the Central Bank. Borrowing from the Central bank means creation of new money. Such kind of financing is called deficit financing. If the deficit is financed by printing more bank notes, it causes an increase in aggregate demand and prices rise rapidly.
4. A reduction in taxes by the government increases the disposable income and purchasing power. This leads to an increase in the aggregate demand.
5. Increase in private expenditure, both consumption and investment expenditure, causes excess demand for goods and services. Due to increase in investment, employment and income increase, causing an increase in aggregate demand.
6. Rapid growth of population also causes increase in aggregate demand for goods and services.
7. Existence of black money due to corruption also causes an increase in aggregate demand, resulting in a rise in prices.
8. Expectations too play a role here when prices are expected to rise in the near future, people buy more consumer goods. Speculative activities of the business men also causes inflation.
9. Inflation abroad has its influence on the price level within a country. When the country has to import high priced goods from a country in which there is already inflation, the domestic prices also increase.

Factors Affecting Supply

Inflation also in caused by a reduction in the aggregate supply of goods and services.

1. Shortage in the supply of factors of production like labour, capital, raw-materials, power etc., reduces output.
2. Activities of speculators and hoarders create an artificial scarcity of goods, resulting in a rise in their prices.
3. Shortage of food and raw-materials due to continuous drought or floods also causes an increase in their prices which then spreads to the other sectors of the economy.
4. Sometimes the activities of strong trade unions cause strikes or lead to lock-outs resulting in a fall in output. If the trade unions succeed in getting the money wages increased more than the productivity of their workers, prices will be more as cost of production increases. This kind of inflation is called cost-push inflation.
5. An increase in exports causes a further fall in the output available for domestic consumption. This causes a rise in their prices.

Effects of Inflation

Inflation is an economic process whose effects are felt by every citizen and in every corner of the economy. While some members of the society gain from inflation, others get hurt. Those people, whose money incomes do not rise as fast as the price-level, suffer a reduction in their real incomes.

For those whose money incomes rise faster than price level, inflation brings gains in the form of increase in real income. It inflicts more harm on low and fixed income groups than on high and flexible income groups. Effects of inflation on different groups of people can be studied under the following heads.

1. Debtors and Creditors

During inflation prices increase and value of money decreases. So debtors are in a better position to repay their loans. They stand to gain as they borrowed money when it was dear and repay it when it is cheap. But creditors lose as they are paid in terms of depreciated currency (money whose value has fallen).

2. Wage Earners and Salary Earners

Those wage earners who are organised into strong trade unions are able to chase the galloping inflation. But they seldom with the race. There is a time-lag between rise in the cost of living (due to rise in prices) and rise in wages. Even if they succeed in getting higher a wages, it may not be proportionate to the rise in cost of living. As a result, their real wages and standard of living decrease.

Salary-earners are less organised than wage-earners. Their salaries do not increase at all or may not increase proportionately. So they suffer much during inflation.

3. Entrepreneur

Inflation is a great stimulant for the entrepreneur. A seller's market is created during inflation as whatever is produced can be sold. Inflation converts an entrepreneur into a profiteer. He earns abnormal profits due to the time-lag between rising prices and rising costs. They also earn windfall profits as they prices of inventories go up.

4. Investors

There are two kinds of investors : investors in equities and investors in fixed interest yielding bonds. Equity holders are those persons who hold shares and stocks of companies. They earn dividends from them and not fixed interest. During inflation, investors in equities gain as they earn more dividends from the increased profits of companies. Investors in fixed interest yielding bonds, who are generally small investors, suffer during inflation.

5. Agriculturalists

Farmers, as a class, gain most during inflation. They receive high prices for food and raw-materials and prices and costs paid by them lag behind these prices. They are also in a position to repay their old loans and can free themselves from mortgages.

6. Fixed Income Groups

Fixed income earners like pensioners, and holders of fixed deposits, people who live upon rents etc., suffer the most during inflation.

7. Consumers

Consumers, as a class, lose during inflation as they have to pay high prices for essential goods. Their cost of living increases. Sometimes they are forced to buy inferior quality goods at higher prices.

8. Social Effects

As the cost of living increases, the workers realize that they are chasing after the 'money illusion'. So they resort to strikes and other forms of agitation as a means for increasing their wages. Inflation also is a paradise for hoarders, speculators and black marketeers, while the poor working class suffer the most. Inflation redistributes income and wealth in favour of the rich, particularly the businessmen, traders and speculators. It makes the rich richer and that poor poorer.

We can conclude from the above discussions that inflation is unjust in its effects. If it goes on unchecked, the entire economy gets ruined.

Measures for Control

Inflation can be controlled by monetary measures, fiscal measures and other measures.

1. Monetary Measures

These measures aim at reducing money incomes. (a) Monetary policy is one of the important monetary measures. The Central bank can adopt a number of methods to control the quantity and quality of credit. It increases its bank rate, sells securities in the open market, raises the reserve ratio and adopts a number of selective credit control measures. (b) Another monetary measure is to demonetise currency of higher denominations. It is also useful to curb the black money propagation. (c) The most extreme monetary measure is to issue new currency in the place of old currency.

2. Fiscal Measures

Monetary measures must be supplemented with fiscal measures to make them more effective. Some of the fiscal measures are as follows:

(a) The government expenditure on unnecessary and nondevelopment activities should be reduced. This will also put a check on private expenditure. Besides, heavy taxation is also advisable.

(b) The rate of personal and commodity taxes should be raised and new taxes should be levied. But tax rates should not be too high to curb saving and investment.

(c) Savings on the part of people shall be encouraged. It will reduce the disposable income of the people and hence consumption will also decrease.

(d) Besides, the government should adopt anti-inflationary budgetary policy. For this purpose, the government should give up deficit financing and instead have surplus budgets.

3. Other Measures

(a) Production at home must be encouraged.

(b) Imports of goods must be made.

(c) Price control and rationing must also be introduced.

(d) Wages must be frozen.

(e) Speculative activities must be curbed by all means.

(f) Compulsory savings must be enforced on people.

Inflationary Trends in India

The most commonly used measure of the rate of inflation in India is in terms of the variation in Wholesale Price Index (WPI). The WPI is available for almost all tradeable commodities consumed by the bulk of the population. The WPI is available on weekly basis with a gap of about two weeks. This enables us to compute weekly rate of inflation.

In the entire planning period, spanning over the last six decades, India has recorded a moderate rate of inflation with the exception of the first plan when annual inflation rate was – 3.2%.

The average decadal rate of inflation was just 1.7% during the 1950s. The rate fluctuated between – 12.5% to 13.8%. The negative rate of inflation was caused by bumper harvest in 1952-53 and the peak rate of inflation in 1956-57 was due to excess demand conditions created by high rates of private and public investment.

During the 1960s, the average decadal rate of inflation picked up to 6.4%. The inflation rate fluctuated between – 1.1% to 13.9%. The peak rate of inflation was mainly attributed to exogenous supply shocks like Indo-China War, Indo-Pakistan War and shortages of wage goods brought about by harvest failure in the mid-1960s. The negative inflation rate in 1968-69 was due to bumper harvest in 1967-68 and stagnant demand conditions in the industrial sector.

The average inflation rate in the decade of the 1970s rose to 9.0%. The rate fluctuated between – 1.1% to 25.2%. The failure of Kharif crops in 1972-73 and the unprecedented rise in crude oil prices in 1973 led to the peak inflation rate in the year 1974-75. The money supply expansion over and above the growth in money demand also added fuel to inflation. The inflation rate fell to – 1.1% in 1975-76 due to extraordinary demand contractionary policy taken by the Government. But inflationary pressure remained latent in the economy because the cost-push factors were still present.

The decadal average rate of inflation moved down to 8% in the 1980s. The inflation rate fluctuated between 4.4% to 18.2%. The fall in the decadal rate of inflation was mainly due to improvement in the growth performance of the economy.

The inflation rate once again shot up in the first half of the 1990s. The inflationary rise in prices in the 1990s was a result of both demand side and cost-push factors. The high fiscal deficit driven growth of the 1980s stimulated the demand side of the economy. The Gulf crisis of 1991 pushed up the crude oil prices and exerted upward pressure on manufacturing costs. The twin forces of excess demand and cost-push factors pushed the economy to a medium-term path of inflation. The inflation rate fluctuated between 10% to 15%. In 1991-92, inflation rate rose to 12.1%. The price level continued rising at the rate of 10.1% in 1992-93. Despite the introduction of anti-inflationary measures, inflation rate in 1993-94 was 1.4%. During 1994-95, inflation rate again rose to 12.6%. From 1995-96 to 2001-02, there was a reversal of inflationary trend. The inflation rate started declining after September 2001. The inflation rate for the week ended January 19, 2001 has dropped to a low of 1.3% which is the lowest in the last two decades.

Causes of Inflation

We have already seen that inflation can occur due to either demand side factors or cost-push factors. Accordingly, causes of inflation in India is analysed from these two different aspects.

Demand-side Factors

In a developing country like India, supply of output is not so price responsive as in developed countries. Consequently the autonomous increase in demand for output has a greater impact on the price level than on output. The factors that contributed to autonomous growth in aggregate demand for output are :

1. Rapid growth in government expenditure

The rapid growth in government is a relatively recent phenomenon. Though the money value of government expenditure in India has increased during the entire planning period, it was only in late 1970s that real expenditure also started growing rapidly. The share of government expenditure in national income rose from 21.6% in 1970-71 to 33.3% in 1980-81. By this time the trend rate of inflation had also increased, thereby roughly offsetting the growth in monetary expenditure. The share of government expenditure in national income further rose to 42.6% in 1990-91. The period after 1983 witnessed a positive and accelerating rate of growth of real government expenditure. The demand-side stimulus of the growth in real government expenditure was more than the growth in productive capacity of the economy. The growing demand-supply imbalance in 1980s and the first half of the 1990s led to inflationary price rise in the range of 4 to 15%. It should be noted that the share of capital expenditure in total government expenditure has been declining, throughout this period, while the share of non-developmental expenditure like interest payments, subsidies and salaries to government employees has been rising. Thus the increase in government expenditure was concentrated in areas where demand expansion was not accompanied by supply expansion.

2. Large-scale public borrowing

The Government of India had to depend on public borrowing (mainly borrowing from banks and financial institutions) to close the gap between its expenditure and revenue from the beginning of the planning process. But the borrowing requirement of the government sector has been rising at an alarming rate since the early 1980s. The budget of the Central Government has been showing a revenue deficit since 1979-80. So the government had to take resort to borrowed funds not only to finance capital expenditure but also a growing volume of current expenditure. The deficit-driven growth in current expenditure fuelled the growth in aggregate demand for output. At the same time, large-scale government borrowing pushed up the interest rates and crowded out private investment. The slow growth of productive capacity caused by deceleration in public and private investment and the high growth of aggregate demand has set the economy on a path of inflation in the 1980s and the first half of the 1990s.

3. Monetisation of Deficit

The normal capital receipts were never adequate to finance the fiscal deficit. Till the mid-1990s the government had to finance a part of the fiscal deficit by short-term borrowing from the RBI. The RBI, in turn, accommodated the borrowing requirement by creating money. Thus increase in fiscal deficit automatically translated itself into an increase in money supply. This phenomenon, known as monetisation of deficit, grew in the 1980s fuelling deficit-driven growth and inflation.

Supply Side Factors

The supply side shocks are generated by cost-push factors. If the market for products and factors are imperfect, the sellers (producers or factor-owners) can push up the product and factor prices even in the absence of any excess demand. The cost-push factors that contributed to inflationary price rise in India are as follows:

1. Uneven agricultural grow

The level of agricultural production in India still depends on monsoon. In the past, bad monsoon led to harvest failure. This, in turn, caused a contraction in the supply of agricultural goods. The rise in agricultural prices increases the costs of industrial production in two ways. First, rise in costs of materials in agro-based industries. Second, rise in food prices and consequent rise in industrial wages. In either case, industrial sector is subjected to supply shocks. Though the relative importance of agro-based industries has declined in the last decade, supply shocks in agricultural can still cause inflationary price rise via increase in wages.

Moreover, harvest failure encourages big farmers and the traders to hoard agricultural goods in the expectation of further rise in prices. Hoarding causes withdrawal of goods from the market, thereby fuelling further price rise.

2. Agricultural price policy

The government had been pursuing a policy of price support since the early 1970s to provide production incentives to the big farmers. The price support scheme had been instrumental in maintaining the market prices of foodgrains above the market-clearing level. The upward revision of support prices from time to time led to periodic increase in the whole prices of foodgrains. This, in turn, caused periodic upward revision of wages and prices in the organised sector.

3. Slow growth in industrial output

The slow growth of consumer goods sector in an expanding economy was one of the main reasons for inflationary rise in prices of industrial goods during the first three decades of planning. Infrastructural bottlenecks that began to appear from the early 1970s led to widespread dislocation in production and consequent rise in operating costs of industrial units.

4. Administered price hike

The prices of many important commodities are administered by the government. These commodities are used by other sectors as inputs. The prices of these commodities are increased from time to time to cover the increase in costs resulting from inefficiency and corruption. The examples of these commodities are petroleum products, coal, non-ferrous metals, electricity and fertilisers. The administered hike in the prices of these commodities led to increase in costs of production of a wide variety of commodities.

Inflationary price rise in India can be atrributed to many other factors on the supply side of the economy. Indirect taxes on a wide range of commodities including inputs that enter into the production of other commodities have resulted in cascading of taxes. The steady depreciation of rupee in the last two decades led to continuous increase in the prices of essential imports like petroleum products. This had contributed to cost-push inflation.

Effects of Inflation

Inflation affects the economy in many ways. Here, we consider a few adverse consequences of inflation.

1. Inflationary price rise creates uncertainty about future rates of inflation and adversely affect production decisions.
2. Price signals provide important information to economic agents and help them to make right decisions. At times of inflationary price rise, importance of price signals are undermined. The unanticipated movements in prices distorts the price structure and thereby affect resource allocation among the different sectors.
3. Inflation adversely affects the financial system. The increase in inflation uncertainty discourages the firms from undertaking long-term contracts. The uncertainty about future

price encourages savers to move away from financial assets which are not indexed to inflation to real assets. At times of inflation, creditors are unwilling to advance loans at fixed interest rate because inflation decreases the real purchasing power of the principal amount to be repaid by the debtors.

4. Inflation adversely affects the balance of payments. If the domestic rate of inflation is higher than the world rate of inflation, domestic products will be substituted by foreign products (imports) which have become relatively cheaper and foreigners will buy less of own products which have become relatively expensive. The rise in imports and the fall in exports will adversely affect the balance of payment.
5. Inflation hurts the poor because they have no protection against inflation.
6. Inflation diverts resources from productive and innovative activities to hoarding and speculative activities.

Control of Inflation

Anti-inflationary measures are of two types : demand contractionary policies are needed if inflation is caused by excess demand for output and cost-reducing policies are needed to control cost-push inflation. In case of mixed inflation, we have to combine demand reducing measures with cost controlling policies.

Demand Reducing Measures

The contractionary demand management policies are of two types: fiscal policy and monetary policy.

Fiscal contraction aims at reducing the aggregate demand for output. The cut in government spending can be used to directly reduce the aggregate demand for output. Again, taxes can be raised to reduce disposable income or at least to contain the growth of disposable income. This way fiscal policy can discourage private consumption expenditure. The demand inflation is often caused by investment boom in certain sectors. Then fiscal incentives and disincentives can be used to discourage investment in inflation-potent sectors and encourage investment in sectors where output expansion is possible. Thus tax hikes and expenditure cuts are the typical prescriptions of contractionary fiscal policy in an inflationary situation.

The measures available to control the volume of money supply and credit in the economy constitute the crux of monetary policy. The interest policy is an indirect instrument of control as interest rates affect expenditure. At times of inflation, central bank may increase the bank rate to regulate the flow of credit to the consumers and the investors. The monetary authority also control liquidity through open market operations in government securities. An open market sale of government securities mops up excess liquid cash and increases the interest rates, signalling a tight monetary policy. The selective credit control measures can also be used for limiting banks' capacity to expand credit at times of inflation. In India, selective credit control measures have been abandoned following the recommendations of Narasimham Committee.

Cost Reducing Measures

A cost-push inflation can be checked by devising cost reducing measures. The producers and factor-owners are held responsible for cost-push inflation. The monopoly or oligopoly power of the sellers causes frequent hikes in product and factor prices. Such administered price hikes can be checked by improving the working of the market system and by promoting policies which curb the market power of the producers and factor-owners.

The supply side shortages causing inflation can be managed in the short-run by encouraging import of commodities in short supply.

Money Supply and Prices

Money affects both the level of prices and output. The output effect of monetary policy stems from three sources. First, expansionary monetary policy can be used to sustain demand expansion in the economy created by expansionary fiscal policy. But this is only a short-run effect since the growth in money supply over and above the growth in money demand will soon cause prices to rise and real demand to fall. Second, money supply creation is also a process of credit creation provided banks are fully loaned up. The greater availability of credit and its absorption by the firms directly increases the investment demand for output. Third, money supply expansion is expected to reduce short-run interest rate and thereby increase investment demand. The extent by which investment demand rises depends on inflationary expectations of the investors.

In the Indian context, we have not observed a clear relationship between the change in money supply and the change in price level. In the year 1956-57, wholesale prices rose by 13.8% but the money supply increased by 8.5%. Thus money supply and price level were not proportionately related. Again in 1958-59, wholesale prices rose by 4.1% while money supply increased by 2.6%. There are periods when relatively high growth in money supply co-existed with low rates of inflation. For example, during 1996 to 1999, the average growth in money supply was 17.3% per annum but the inflation rate was 6% per annum. The transmission lag of monetary policy can be long and variable and the effect of money supply growth on price level may take long time to realise, so that in the short run price level may not respond to money supply changes.

Deflation

Deflation is the opposite of inflation. It is associated with falling prices. Deflation, according to Prof. Paul Einzing, "is a state of disequilibrium in which a contraction of economic power tends to cause, or is the effect of, a decline of price level." However, each and every fall in prices cannot be described as deflation. For example, a price fall, after inflation has reached its height, is 'disinflationary' and not deflationary. Deflation refers to a situation where prices fall causing substantial increase in unemployment, reduction in output and decrease in the incomes. In order to sharpen the concept of deflation, certain related terms such as Reflation, Disinflation have been coined. We define them below:

1. Reflation

It refers to a situation in which prices are deliberately increased to take out the economy from the depth of depression. In this case, the rising prices will be accompanied by a rise in output and employment.

2. Inflation

True inflation occurs after full-employment. In this case employment remains the same while prices go on increasing.

3. Disinflation

It refers to a situation when prices fall due to well planned anti-inflationary measures. In this case, prices fall without bringing about reduction in output or employment.

4. Deflation

It refers to a state of the economy in which falling prices are accompanied by falling leve'ls of output and employment.

These terms are explained better through the diagram.

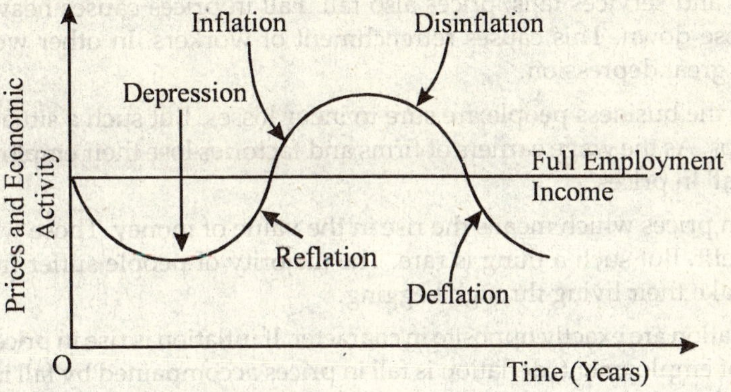

Control of Deflation

Deflation is caused by deficiency in aggregate demand and aggregate spending. Due to low economic activity and unemployment, aggregate income is less and hence aggregate expenditure also is less. Therefore, the anti-deflationary policy should aim at increasing aggregate spending. Since private investment is less due to low profit expectations, government should compensate by spending more on public works like constructions of roads, canals, dams etc. Government should finance its expenditure by borrowing from banks. This will increase employment and incomes which in turn increases aggregate consumption expenditure. Profit expectation will move up encouraging private investment expenditure. The total effect of this would be a slowly raising economic activity from the bottom of depression.

Inflation Vs Deflation

The terminologies like inflation and deflation have become very common nowadays as the whole world has suffered form inflation. Usually the word 'inflation' is referred to mean 'rise in prices, Several economists have defined 'inflation' in several ways. Kemnerev defined it as, 'inflation is too much money and deposit currency- in relation to the physical volume of business being done. Coulbourn defined it as "Too much money chasing too few goods." T.E. Gregory said that "it is abnormal increase in the quantity of money". All the above definitions arrive at unanimous conclusion namely that inflation is due to excess supply of money.

For Keynes inflation means rise in prices not accompanied by rise in output. This happens after the full employment has been reached. When an economy is working with unemployed resources, expansion of money will bring about rise in production and employment. This will go on till all unemployed resources are fully employed. Beyond this stage any increase in money will not bring about any increase in output, but it will cause rise in output.

Deflation is a phenomenon of fall in prices. A fall in prices will be accompained by fall in production and a fall in employment. Mere fall in prices accompanied by increase in production is not inflation. Inflation refers to rise in money incomes, deflation stands for fall in incomes.

Inflation makes the entire economy active. It makes all available unused resources fully employed. Inflation encourages investment. This further causes rise employment and income. But if it goes beyond a stage it will effect the economy. Instead of benefitting it will weaken the economy.

Deflation is the worst thing. It will adversely affect the volume of production and employment. As demand for goods and services falls, prices also fall. Fall in prices causes heavy loss to firms. They are forced to close down. This causes retrenchment of workers. In other words, the whole economy plunges in a great depression.

When prices fall, the business people are sure to incur losses. But such a situation is a gain to the fixed income groups. As the wage earners of firms and factories lose their employment, they fail to take advantage of fall in prices.

Deflation is fall in prices which means the rise in the value of money. Those who do not loose their jobs, get the benefit. But such a thing is rare. The majority of people suffer from misery and thrown to streets to make their living through begging.

Inflation and deflation are exactly opposite in character. If inflation is rise in prices accompained by rise in the volume of employment, deflation is fall in prices accompained by fall in the volume of employment. Inflation breeds inequalities of income and wealth among the people of the country. Deflation reduces the national income through fall in the production and employment. Therefore inflation is unjust, deflation is inexpedient.

Stagflation

The main problem faced by advanced economies like the U.S.A. and U.K. in recent years has been that of 'stagflation'. Stagflation is characterised by declining output and rising unemployment. The term was coined by economists to name the seemingly paradoxical phenomenon of co-existence of inflation and stagnation. The period of 1950s and 1960s was that of accelerated inflation and growing excess capacity in the economy and also increased unemployment.

Stagflation is a problem more serious than inflation because stagflation is associated also with sluggish economic activity and rapidly rising prices. It redistributes income in favour of the rich through its inflationary impact and disrupts society through increased unemployment. In the words of Prof. P.A. Samuelson, "Stagflation involves inflationary rise in price and wages at the same time. The people are unable to find jobs and firms are unable to find customers for what their plants can produce."

The causes of stagflation are manifold and intertwined. It seems to have become a historical trend. The world economy has experienced inflation in varying degrees continuously for the last 30 years. When there has been an all round rise in prices with state revenues and people's income lagging behind, both governments and individuals have been cutting back their expenditures in certain sectors. This meant slackening of demand for the products of certain industries and there was a prolonged recession.

On the other side, due to rising costs of financing such 'committed' items of state expenditure as salaries, dearness allowances and interest burdens, governments have been resorting to methods of inflationary finance such as deficit financing, borrowing from the central bank and raising of administered prices. Not only this, governments also adopted expansionary policies to boost up investment and growth in the industrial sectors under recession. This promoted inflation in the economy further thereby discouraging exports and enlarging the deficits in the balance of payments. The mounting deficits compelled the governments to restrict imports and impose some monetary and fiscal disciplines on consumption and investment. Stripped to this strait-jacket of economic discipline, the economies of both developed and less developed countries started stagnating.

Economists differ in their assessment of the process of stagflation. Many consider it as the result of a continuous and inevitable process in the world economy, the process of gradually changing expectations about inflation. There is a second group of economists who hold that stagflation was the result of specific policies, shock and combinations of circumstances which could perhaps have been avoided through foresight. Monetarists like Professor Milton Friedman claim that stagflation has supported their view that there is no lasting trade-off between a moderate rate of inflation and unemployment as was claimed by the believers in what has come to be known as the Phillips Curve. Monetarists argue that even if unemployment is reduced because the inflation lowers real wages thereby inducing employers to expand employment, we find that when people's price expectations have adjusted to the actual rate of inflation, the natural rate of unemployment must prevail. Their contention is that a continually higher rate of monetary expansion is needed to maintain the same level of unemployment, which will eventually result into higher inflation and higher unemployment. A former Prime Minister of U.K. admitted in 1977, "We used to think that you could just spend your way out of recession and increase employment by cutting taxes and boosting government spending. I tell you in all candour that the option no longer exists, and that in so far as it ever did exist, it worked by injecting inflation into the economy. And each time that happened the average level of unemployment has risen. 'Higher inflation followed by higher unemployment', that is the history of last 20 years."

What is the way out of this dilemma? How to cure inflation without causing stagnation? The answer, according to some economic experts, is to follow a gradualist policy, on a continuous basis, of restricting wage rates and of a tight control over credit and money supply. At the same time, where taxes can be possibly eased slightly to encourage consumer spending, governments can also try to stimulate investment by making investment attractive. These policies should be appropriately timed and rightly emphasised.

There are problems inherent in wage and price controls; government price fixing regulations have to be redrawn to prevent rather than encourage excessive price rises. The labour force problem should be attacked directly by manpower training programmes designed to develop skills needed in modern economics. Transportation ought to be improved to facilitate access to job-producing areas. Tax incentives might be given to business and industries for on-the-job training. The government itself might become the employer of last resort.

Conclusion

From the above discussion, Inflation may be defined as a state in which there is a continuous upward movement of prices. It is a state in which the value of money is falling. Inflation is an economic process whose effects are felt by every citizen and in every corner of the economy. While some members of the society gain from inflation, others get hurt. Those people, whose money incomes do not rise as fast as the price level, suffer a reduction in their real incomes. For those whose money incomes rise faster than price level, inflation brings gains in the form of increase in real income. It inflicts more harm on low and fixed income groups than on high and flexible income groups.

Questions for Discussion

1. What are the different types of inflation?
2. Give a brief review of inflationary trends in India. Explain, in this context, the causes of stagflation in the early 1990's.
3. What are the main causes of inflation in India?
4. How can inflation be controlled?
5. What is deflation? Distinguish between Inflation and Deflation.

Part - B

BANKING

1.	Commercial Banking	107
2.	Central Banking	134
3.	Reserve Bank of India	151
4.	State Bank of India	178
5.	Money Market and Capital Market	182
6.	Structure of Banking in India	203
7.	Development Banks	230
8.	Banker and Customer	247
9.	Opening and Operating Bank Accounts	271
10.	Pass Book	282
11.	Cheques	287
12.	The Paying Banker	304
13.	Collecting Banker	313
14.	Loans and Advances	320
15.	Types of Securities	329
16.	Modes of Creating Charge	349
17.	Guarantees	360
18.	Letter of Credit	370
19.	Accounts and Audit of Banks	378

Chapter - 1

COMMERCIAL BANKING

Introduction

Banking occupies one of the most important positions in the modern economic world. It is necessary for trade and industry. Hence it is one of the great agencies of commerce. Although banking in one form or another has been in existence from very early times, modern banking is of recent origin. It is one of the results of the Industrial Revolution and the child of economic necessity. Its presence is very helpful to the economic activity and industrial progress of a country.

Origin of Banks

The evolution of banking can be traced back to the era when the use of metallic coins as the media of exchange of goods and services began.

Storage of metallic coins was a serious problem for the common people. Because of the danger of theft and robbery, people started leaving gold and silver and metallic coins in the custody of some reputed person a wealthy merchant or a money changer. The custodian had a strong box (safe) and other means of safe-keeping. He offered this service as a favour for his friends or made a charge for it. The depositor had to go personally to the custodian for the withdrawal of his money. But this practice was found to be inconvenient. Gradually, the depositors were allowed to transfer claims against the metallic coins. The custodian used to issue a receipt to the depositor which said in effect, *"I owe you (IOU) so many pounds"* and the depositor could transfer the receipt to the payee. When these IOUs became popular in payments, the bank note was born. *A bank note is simply a bank debt, or promise to pay, evidenced by a piece of paper.*

Another method of payment was developed soon. Instead of receiving a piece of paper representing the debt of the banker or custodian, the depositor received a deposit card which later on took the shape of the Pass Book. The deposit card was nothing, but a copy of the entries in the books of the banker or custodian. Afterwards, the practice of making payments by writing "an order on the banker to pay someone else" began. The payee could collect the number of coins mentioned in that order from the banker.

Upto this stage, all deposits and bank notes were fully backed by metals and metallic coins. But soon the bankers discovered that, to meet their promises to pay money on demand, they did not need to hold metals or metallic coins equal to 100% of their outstanding debts. They started keeping only a specific fraction of their outstanding debts in cash (or coins) and lent the remaining portion to the credit worthy traders. The bankers paid interest on deposit balances and charged interest from the borrowers. The *fractional reserve principle* is the backbone of modern banking. It has given the bank a great power of increasing or decreasing the total money supply by the mechanism of *credit creation or contraction.*

How did the use of word 'bank' become popular? The origin of 'bank' is traced to a Latin word *'bancus'* which means a bench. European money-lenders and money-changers used to transact their business at benches or tables. They followed the practice of receiving gold and other metals as deposits and issuing receipts. The bench or table used by the trader in money was the symbol of the business of banking or dealing in money. The success or failure in trading was associated with his bench. When a banker failed, his bench used to be destroyed by the people.

Some authorities observe that the word bank was originally derived from the German word 'bank' which means a joint stock fund. This word was italianised into *banco* by the Germans when they were the rulers of a major part of Italy. This term was again changed into *'banck'* by the French. Afterwards, the Britishers converted this term into 'bank which has now been universalised. The term bank or banker is used in almost all the countries of the world to denote a financial institution dealing in money.

Evolution of Banks in India

Bank of Venice started in Italy is said to be the oldest banking institution in the world. The Bank of Barcelona was started in 1401 and the Bank of Genoa in 1407. The Bank of Amsterdam was launched in 1609. The Lombards who migrated to Europe and England from Italy were responsible for the development of modern banking. Their business suffered when King Charles II imposed severe restrictions on them. The goldsmiths were gradually replaced by private bankers. The growth of joint stock commercial banking started after the Banking Act was passed in 1833 in England. Thus, seeds were sown for the growth of modern commercial banking during the 19th century.

Ancient Hindu scriptures provide enough evidence of the existence of money lending business in India. Mahajans, Shroffs, Sahukars, etc. were enjoyed in banking business. In the beginning of the 18th century, the East India Company set up a few commercial banks on modern lines. In 1770, first Indian bank known as the Bank of Hindustan was started and was closed down twenty years later. Later, the East India Company started three Presidency banks with Government participation. These were: the Bank of Calcutta, (1806), the Bank of Bombay (1840) and the Bank of Madras (1843). These banks had the financial participation by the Government also.

During the 18th century, some other banks were also opened by Agency Houses in Madras and Calcutta. All these banks failed. Since all the banks emerged due to Agency Houses failed, the need of banking regulation in India was seriously felt. As a result, Companies Act, 1833 was brought into force. The impact of the Agency Houses got slowly reduced.

Allahabad Bank came into existence in 1865 and Alliance Bank of Simla in 1875. The first purely Indian joint stock bank known as the Oudh Commercial Bank was set up in 1880 and the Punjab National Bank was launched in 1894. The Swadeshi movement in the country in 1906 encouraged the Indian entrepreneurs to start many new banks. There were as many as 648 commercial banks in India by the end of 1947. As many as 161 banks failed in quick succession during 1913-1914 and the people's faith in the banking system was shaken. Thus, there was a great need of an institution to control and regulate banking in the country. As a result, the Reserve Bank of India was set up in 1935 for regulating the banks in the country and to act as a banker to the Government.

In 1923, the three Presidency banks were amalgamated into the Imperial Bank of India. This bank played an important role in the economy of the country. After independence, it was nationalised in 1955 and renamed as the State Bank of India. The State Bank of India opened a large number of branches in rural and semi-urban areas.

Banking after Independence

When the country attained independence in 1947, there were 648 commercial banks with 4,819 branches in India. Because of frequent failure of banks in the country, the Government of India decided to regulate and reform the banking system. The Reserve Bank of India was nationalised in 1949 and the *Banking Companies Act* was passed in the same year. The name of this Act was later changed to Banking Regulation Act in 1965. Enactment of the Banking Companies Act was an important landmark for the smooth progress of commercial banks in the country.

As said earlier, State Bank of India was created by nationalisation of the Imperial Bank of India in 1955. The State Bank has opened a large number of branches in rural and semi-urban areas and has launched several schemes for the farmers, artisans and small scale units.

A scheme of *Social Control* on banks was enforced through statutory measures with effect from 1st February, 1969. The banking industry saw a revolution after 14 major commercial banks were nationalised in June, 1969. More than 90% of the bank deposits came under the control of the Government. Preference was given to rural areas while opening branches. Targets of lending were also fixed for agriculture, artisans, unemployed youth, small scale units, etc.

Regional Rural Banks scheme was launched on 2nd October, 1975. Six more leading commercial banks were nationalised in 1980. As a result of the recommendations of Sivaraman Committee, Agricultural Credit Department, Rural Planning and Credit Cell and Agricultural Refinance and Development Corporation were combined together to set up *National Bank for Agriculture and Rural Development* (NABARD) in July 1982. Later, the *Export and Import Bank of India* (Exim Bank) and the National Housing Bank were set up in 1984 and 1988 respectively.

Meaning

A commercial bank is a profit-seeking business firm, dealing in money and credit. It is a financial institution dealing in money in the sense that it accepts deposits of money from the public to keep them in its custody for safety. So also, it deals in credit, i.e., it creates credit by making advances out of the funds received as deposits to needy people. It thus, functions as a mobiliser of saving in the economy. A bank is, therefore like a reservoir into which flow the savings, the idle surplus money of households and from which loans are given on interest to businessmen and others who need them for investment or productive uses.

Definition of a Bank

The term 'Bank' has been defined in different ways by different economists. A few definitions are:

According to Walter Leaf "A bank is a person or corporation which holds itself out to receive from the public, deposits payable on demand by cheque". Horace White has defined a bank, "as a manufacture of credit and a machine for facilitating exchange".

According to Prof. Kinley, "A bank is an establishment which makes to individuals such advances of money as may be required and safely made, and to which individuals entrust money when not required by them for use".

The Banking Companies Act of India defines Bank as: "A Bank is a financial institution which accepts money from the public for the purpose of lending or investment repayable on demand or otherwise withdrawable by cheques, drafts or order or otherwise".

Thus, we can say that a bank is a financial institution which deals in debts and credits. It accepts deposits, lends money and also creates money. It bridges the gap between the savers and borrowers. Banks are not merely traders in money but also in an important sense manufactures of money.

Types of Banks

Broadly speaking, banks can be classified into commercial banks and central bank. Commercial banks are those which provide banking services for profit. The central bank has the function of controlling commercial banks and various other economic activity. There are many types of commercial banks such as deposit banks, industrial banks, savings banks, agricultural banks, exchange banks, and miscellaneous banks.

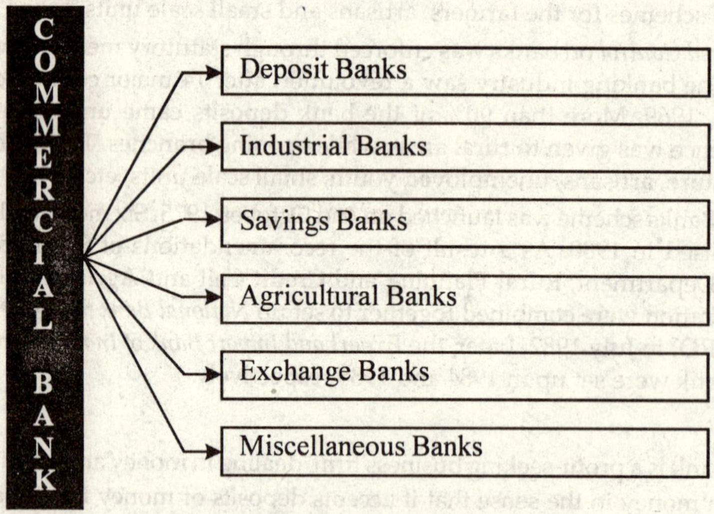

Types of Commercial Banks

1. Deposit Banks

The most important type of deposit banks is the commercial banks. They have connection with the commercial class of people. These banks accept deposits from the public and lend them to needy parties. Since their deposits are for short period only, these banks extend loans only for a short period. Ordinarily these banks lend money for a period between 3 to 6 months. They do not like to lend money for long periods or to invest their funds in any way in long term securities.

2. Industrial Banks

Industries require a huge capital for a long period to buy machinery and equipment. Industrial banks help such industrialists. They provide long term loans to industries. Besides, they buy shares and debentures of companies, and enable them to have fixed capital. Sometimes, they even underwrite the debentures and shares of big industrial concerns. The important functions of industrial banks are:

1. They accept long term deposits.
2. They meet the credit requirements of industries by extending long term loans.

3. These banks advise the industrial firms regarding the sale and purchase of shares and debentures.

The industrial banks play a vital role in accelerating industrial development. In India, after attainment of independence, several industrial banks were started with large paid up capital. They are, The Industrial Finance Corporation (I.F.C.), The State Financial Corporations (S.F.C.), Industrial Credit and Investment Corporation of India (ICICI) and Industrial Development Bank of India (IDBI) etc.

3. Savings Banks

These banks were specially established to encourage thrift among small savers and therefore, they were willing to accept small sums as deposits. They encourage savings of the poor and middle class people. In India we do not have such special institutions, but post offices perform such functions. After nationalisation most of the nationalised banks accept the saving deposits.

4. Agricultural Banks

Agriculture has its own problems and hence there are separate banks to finance it. These banks are organised on co-operative lines and therefore do not work on the principle of maximum profit for the share holders. These banks meet the credit requirements of the farmers through term

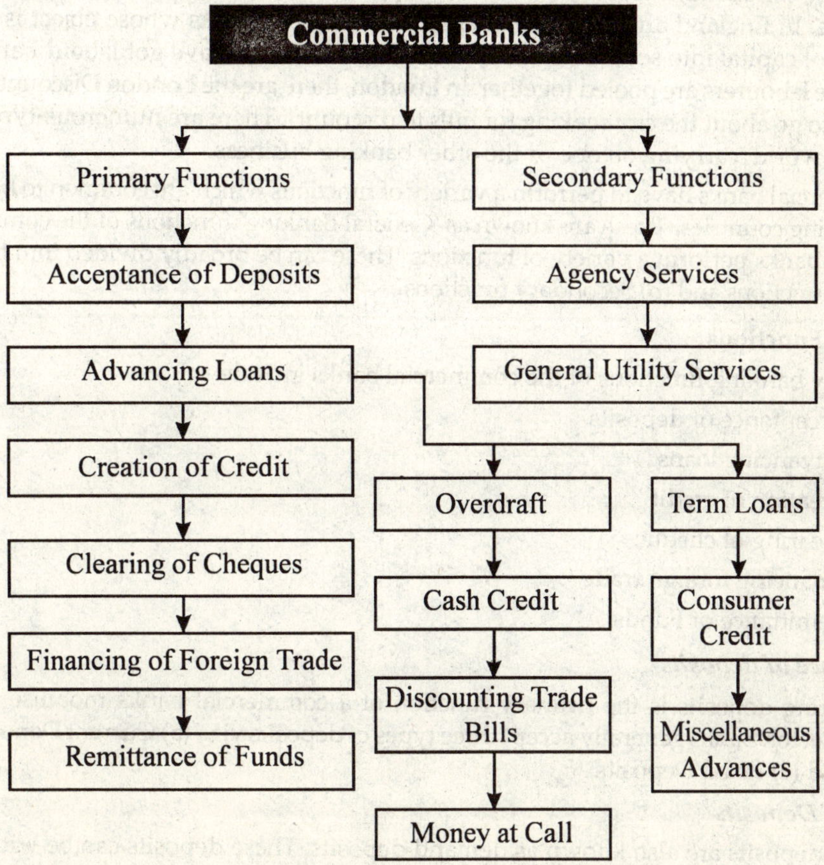

Functions of Commercial Banks

loans. viz., short, medium and long term loans. There are two types of agricultural banks, (a) Agricultural Co-operative Banks and (b) Land Mortgage Banks. Co-operative Banks are mainly for short periods. For long periods there are Land Mortgage Banks. Both these types of banks are performing useful functions in India.

5. Exchange Banks

These banks finance mostly the foreign trade of a country. Their main function is to discount, accept and collect foreign bills of exchange. They buy and sell foreign currency and thus help businessmen in their transactions. They also carry on the ordinary banking business.

In India, there are some commercial banks which are branches of foreign banks. These banks facilitate for the conversion of Indian currency into foreign currency to make payments to foreign exporters. They purchase bills from exporters and sell their proceeds to importers. They purchase and sell "forward exchange" too and thus minimise the difference in exchange rates between different periods, and also protect merchants from losses arising out of exchange fluctuations by bearing the risk. The industrial and commercial development of a country depends these days, largely upon the efficiency of these institutions.

6. Miscellaneous Banks

There are certain kinds of banks which have arisen in due course to meet the specialised needs of the people. In England and America, there are investment banks whose object is to control the distribution of capital into several uses. American Trade Unions have got labour banks, where the savings of the labourers are pooled together. In London, there are the London Discount House whose business is "to go about the city seeking for bills to discount". There are numerous-types of different banks in the world, carrying on one or the other banking business.

Commercial banks have to perform a variety of functions which are common to both developed and developing countries. These are known as 'General Banking' functions of the commercial banks. The modern banks perform a variety of functions. These can be broadly divided into two categories: (a) Primary functions and (b) Secondary functions.

A. Primary Functions

Primary banking functions of the commercial banks include:

1. Acceptance of deposits
2. Advancing loans
3. Creation of credit
4. Clearing of cheques
5. Financing foreign trade
6. Remittance of Funds

1. Acceptance of deposits

Accepting deposits is the primary function of a commercial banks mobilise savings of the household sector. Banks generally accept three types of deposits viz., (a) Current Deposits (b) Savings Deposits and (c) Fixed Deposits.

(a) Current Deposits

These deposits are also known as demand deposits. These deposits can be withdrawn at any time. Generally, no interest is allowed on current deposits, and in case, the customer is required to leave a minimum balance undrawn with the bank. Cheques are used to withdraw the amount. These deposits are kept by businessmen and industrialists who receive and make large payments through banks. The bank levies certain incidental charges on the customer for the services rendered by it.

(b) Savings Deposits

This is meant mainly for professional men and middle class people to help them deposit their small savings. It can be opened without any introduction. Money can be deposited at any time but the maximum cannot go beyond a certain limit. There is a ristriction on the amount that can be withdrawn at a particular time or during a week. If the customer wishes to withdraw more than the specified amount at any one time, he has to give previous notice. Interest is allowed on the credit balance of this account. The rate of interest is greater than the rate of interest on the current deposits and less than that on fixed deposit. This system greatly encourages the habit of thrift or savings.

(c) Fixed Deposits

These deposits are also known as time deposits. These deposits cannot be withdrawn before the expiry of the period for which they are deposited or without giving a prior notice for withdrawal. If the depositor is in need of money, he has to borrow on the security of this account and pay a slightly higher rate of interest to the bank. They are attracted by the payment of interest which is usually higher for longer period. Fixed deposits are liked by depositors both for their safety and as well as for their interest. In India, they are accepted between three months and ten years.

2. Advancing Loans

The second primary function of a commercial bank is to make loans and advances to all types of persons, particularly to businessmen and entrepreneurs. Loans are made against personal security, gold and silver, stocks of goods and other assets. The most common way of lending is by:

(a) Overdraft Facilities

In this case, the depositor in a current account is allowed to draw over and above his account up to a previously agreed limit. Suppose a businessmen has only Rs. 30,000/- in his current account in a bank but requires Rs. 60,000/- to meet his expenses. He may approach his bank and borrow the additional amount of Rs. 30,000/-. The bank allows the customer to overdraw his account through cheques. The bank, however, charges interest only on the amount overdrawn from the account. This type of loan is very popular with the Indian businessmen.

(b) Cash Credit

Under this account, the bank gives loans to the borrowers against certain security. But the entire loan is not given at one particular time, instead the amount is credited into his account in the bank; but under emergency cash will be given. The borrower is required to pay interest only on the amount of credit availed to him. He will be allowed to withdraw small sums of money according to his requirements through cheques, but he cannot exceed the credit limit allowed to him. Besides, the bank can also give specified loan to a person, for a firm against some collateral security. The bank can recall such loans at its option.

(c) Discounting Bills of Exchange

This is another type of lending which is very popular with the modern banks. The holder of a bill can get it discounted by the bank, when he is in need of money. After deducting its commission, the bank pays the present price of the bill to the holder. Such bills form good investment for a bank. They provide a very liquid asset which can be quickly turned into cash. The commercial banks can rediscount, the discounted bills with the central banks when they are in need of money. These bills are safe and secured bills. When the bill matures the bank can secure its payment from the party which had accepted the bill.

(d) Money at Call

Bank also grant loans for a very short period, generally not exceeding 7 days to the borrowers, usually dealers or brokers in stock exchange markets against collateral securities like stock or equity shares, debentures, etc., offered by them. Such advances are repayable immediately at short notice hence, they are described as money at call or call money.

(e) Term Loans

Banks give term loans to traders, industrialists and now to agriculturists also against some collateral securities. Term loans are so-called because their maturity period varies between 1 to 10 years. Term loans, as such provide intermediate or working capital funds to the borrowers. Sometimes, two or more banks may jointly provide large term loans to the borrower against a common security. Such loans are called participation loans or consortium finance.

(f) Consumer Credit

Banks also grant credit to households in a limited amount to buy some durable consumer goods such as television sets, refrigerators, etc., or to meet some personal needs like payment of hospital bills etc. Such consumer credit is made in a lump sum and is repayable in instalments in a short time. Under the 20-point programme, the scope of consumer credit has been extended to cover expenses on marriage, funeral etc., as well.

(g) Miscellaneous Advances

Among other forms of bank advances there are packing credits given to exporters for a short duration, export bills purchased/discounted, import finance-advances against import bills, finance to the self employed, credit to the public sector, credit to the cooperative sector and above all, credit to the weaker sections of the community at concessional rates.

3. Creation of Credit

A unique function of the bank is to create credit. Banks supply money to traders and manufacturer. They also create or manufacture money. Bank deposits are regarded as money. They are as good as cash. The reason is they can be used for the purchase of goods and services and also in payment of debts. When a bank grants a loan to its customer, it does not pay cash. It simply credits the account of the borrower. He can withdraw the amount whenever he wants by a cheque. In this case, bank has created a deposit without receiving cash. That is, banks are said to have created credit. Sayers says "banks are not merely purveyors of money, but also in an important sense, manufacturers of money".

4. Promote the Use of Cheques

The commercial banks render an important service by providing to their customers a cheap medium of exchange like cheques. It is found much more convenient to settle debts through cheques rather than through the use of cash. The cheque is the most developed type of credit instrument in the money market.

5. Financing Internal and Foreign Trade

The bank finances internal and foreign trade through discounting of exchange bills. Sometimes, the bank gives short-term loans to traders on the security of commercial papers. This discounting business greatly facilitates the movement of internal and external trade.

6. Remittance of Funds

Commercial banks, on account of their network of branches throughout the country, also provide facilities to remit funds from one place to another for their customers by issuing bank drafts, mail transfers or telegraphic transfers on nominal commission charges. As compared to the postal money orders or other instruments, bank drafts have proved to be a much cheaper mode of transferring money and has helped the business community considerably.

B. Secondary Functions

Secondary banking functions of the commercial banks include:

1. Agency Services
2. General Utility Services

These are discussed below.

1. Agency Services

Banks also perform certain agency functions for and on behalf of their customers. The agency services are of immense value to the people at large. The various agency services rendered by banks are as follows.

(a) Collection and Payment of Credit Instruments

Banks collect and pay various credit instruments like cheques, bills of exchange, promissory notes etc., on behalf of their customers.

(b) Purchase and Sale of Securities

Banks purchase and sell various securities like shares, stocks, bonds, debentures on behalf of their customers.

(c) Collection of Dividends on Shares

Banks collect dividends and interest on shares and debentures of their customers and credit them to their accounts.

(d) Acts as correspondent

Sometimes banks act as representative and correspondents of their customers. They get passports, traveller's tickets and even secure air and sea passages for their customers.

(e) Income-tax Consultancy

Banks may also employ income tax experts to prepare income tax returns for their customers and to help them to get refund of income tax.

(f) Execution of Standing Orders

Banks execute the standing instructions of their customers for making various periodic payments. They pay subscriptions, rents, insurance premia etc., on behalf of their customers.

(g) Acts as Trustee and Executor

Banks preserve the 'Wills' of their customers and execute them after their death.

2. General Utility Services

In addition to agency services, the modern banks provide many general utility services for the community as given below.

(a) Locker Facility

Bank provide Locker facility to their customers. The customers can keep their valuables, such as gold and silver ornaments, important documents; shares and debentures in these lockers for safe custody.

(b) Traveller's Cheques and Credit Cards

Banks issue traveller's cheques to help their customers to travel without the fear of theft or loss of money. With this facility, the customers need not take the risk of carrying cash with them during their travels.

(c) Letter of Credit

Letters of credit are issued by the banks to their customers certifying their credit worthiness. Letters of credit are very useful in foreign trade.

(d) Collection of Statistics

Banks collect statistics giving important information relating to trade, commerce, industries, money and banking. They also publish valuable Journals and bulletins containing articles on economic and financial matters.

(e) Acting Referee

Banks may act as referees with respect to the financial standing, business reputation and respectability of customers.

(f) Underwriting Securities

Banks underwrite the shares and debentures issued by the Government, public or private companies.

(g) Gift Cheques

Some banks issue cheques of various denominations to be used on auspicious occasions.

(h) Accepting Bills of Exchange on Behalf of Customers

Some times, banks accept bills of exchange, internal as well as foreign, on behalf of their customers. It enables customers to import goods.

(i) Merchant Banking

Some commercial banks have opened merchant banking divisions to provide merchant banking services.

C. Fulfillment of Socio-Economic Objectives

In recent years, commercial banks, particularly in developing countries, have been called upon to help achieve certain socio-economic objectives laid down by the state. For example, the nationalized banks in India have framed special innovative schemes of credit to help small agriculturists, village and cottage industries, retailers, artisans, the self employed persons through loans and advances at concessional rates of interest. Under the Differential Interest Scheme (D.I.S.) the nationalized banks in India advance loans to persons belonging to scheduled tribes, tailors, rickshaw-walas, shoe-makers at the concessional rate of 4 per cent per annum. This does not cover even the cost of the funds made available to these priority sectors. Banking is, thus, being used to subserve the national policy objectives of reducing inequalities of income and wealth, removal of poverty and elimination of unemployment in the country.

It is clear from the above that banks help development of trade and industry in the country. They encourage habits of thrift and saving. They help capital formation in the country. They lend money to traders and manufacturers. In the modern world, banks are to be considered not merely as dealers in money but also the leaders in economic development.

Sources of Bank's Income

A bank is a business organisation engaged in the business of borrowing and lending money. A bank can earn income only if it borrows at a lower rate and lends at a higher rate. The difference between the two rates will represent the costs incurred by the bank and the profit. Bank also provides a number of services to its customers for which it charges commission. etc., This is also an important source of income. The followings are the various sources of a bank's profit :

1. Interest on Loans

The main function of a commercial bank is to borrow money for the purpose of lending at a higher rate of interest. Bank grants various types of loans to the industrialists and traders. The yields from loans constitute the major portion of the income of a bank. The banks grant loans generally for short periods. But now the banks also advance call loans which can be called at a very short notice. Such loans are granted to share brokers and other banks. These assets are highly liquid because they can be called at any time. Moreover, they are source of income to the bank.

2. Interest on Investments

Banks also invest an important portion of their resources in government and other first class industrial securities. The interest and dividend received from time to time on these investments is a sources of income for the banks. Bank also earn some income when the market prices of these securities rise.

3. Discounts

Commercial banks invest a part of their funds in bills of exchange by discounting them. Banks discount both foreign and inland bills of exchange, or in other words, they purchase the bills at discount and receive the full amount at the date of maturity. For instance, if a bill of Rs. 1000 is discounted for Rs. 975, the bank earns a discount of Rs. 25 because bank pays Rs. 975 today, but will get Rs. 1000 on the due date. Discount, as a matter of fact, is the interest on the amount paid for the remaining period of the bill. The rate of discount on bills of exchange is slightly lower than the interest rate charged on loans and advances because bills are considered to be highly liquid assets.

4. Commission, Brokerage, etc.

Banks perform numerous services to their customers and charge commission, etc. for such services. Banks collect cheques, rents, dividends, etc., accepts bills of exchange, issue drafts and letters of credit and collect pensions and salaries on behalf of their customers. They pay insurance premiums, rents, taxes etc. on behalf of their customers. For all these services banks charge their commission. They also earn locker rents for providing safety vaults to their customers. Recently the banks have also started underwriting the shares and debentures issued by the joint stock companies for which they receive underwriting commission.

Commercial banks also deal in foreign exchange. They sell demand drafts, issue letters of credit and help remittance of funds in foreign countries. They also act as brokers in foreign exchange. Banks earn income out of these operations.

Investment Policy of Banks

The financial position of a commercial bank is reflected in its balance sheet. The balance sheet is a statement of the assets and liabilities of the bank. The assets of the bank are distributed in accordance with certain guiding principles. These principles underline the investment policy of the bank. They are discussed below.

1. Liquidity

In the context of the balance sheet of a bank the term liquidity has two interpretations. First, it refers to the ability of the bank to honour the claims of the depositors. Second, it connotes the ability of the bank to convert its non-cash assets into cash easily and without loss.

It is a well known fact that a bank deals in funds belonging to the public. Hence, the bank should always be on its guard in handling these funds. The bank should always have enough cash to meet the demands of the depositors. In fact, the success of a bank depends to a considerable extent upon the degree of confidence it can instill in the minds of its depositors. If the depositors lose confidence in the integrity of their bank, the very existence of the bank will be at stake. So, the bank should always be prepared to meet the claims of the depositors by having enough cash. Among the various items on the assets side of the balance sheet, cash on hand represents the most liquid asset. Next comes cash with other banks and the central bank. The order of liquidity goes on descending.

Liquidity also means the ability of the bank to convert its non-cash assets into cash easily and without loss. The bank cannot have all its assets in the form of cash because each is an idle asset which does not fetch any return to the bank. So some of the assets of the bank, money at call and short notice, bills discounted, etc. could be made liquid easily and without loss.

2. Profitability

A commercial bank by definition, is a profit hunting institution. The bank has to earn profit to earn income to pay salaries to the staff, interest to the depositors, dividend to the shareholders and to meet the day-to-day expenditure. Since cash is the least profitable asset to the bank, there is no point in keeping all the assets in the form of cash on hand. The bank has got to earn income. Hence, some of the items on the assets side are profit yielding assets. They include money at call and short notice, bills discounted, investments, loans and advances, etc. Loans and advances, though the least liquid asset, constitute the most profitable asset to the bank. Much of the income of the bank accrues by way of interest charged on loans and advances. But, the bank has to be highly discreet while advancing loans.

3. Safety or Security

Apart from liquidity and profitability, the bank should look to the principle of safety of its funds also for its smooth working. While advancing loans, it is necessary that the bank should consider the three 'C' 's' of credit character, capacity and the collateral of the borrower. The bank cannot afford to invest its funds recklessly without considering the principle of safety. The loans and investments made by the bank should be adequately secure. For this purpose, the bank should always insist on security of the borrower. Of late, somehow or other the banks have not been paying adequate importance to safety, particularly in India.

4. Diversity

The bank should invest its funds in such a way as to secure for itself an adequate and permanent return. And while investing its funds, the bank should not keep all its eggs in the same basket. Diversification of investment is necessary to avoid the dangerous consequences of investing in one or two channels. If the bank invest its funds in different types of securities or makes loans and advances to different objectives and enterprises, it shall ensure for itself a regular flow of income.

5. Saleability of Securities

Further, the bank should invest its funds in such types of securities as can be easily marketed at a time of emergency. The bank cannot afford to invest its funds in very long term securities or those securities which are unsaleable. It is necessary for the bank to invest its funds in government or in first class securities or in debentures of reputed firms. It should also advance loans against stocks which can be easily sold.

6. Stability in the Value of Investments

The bank should invest its funds in those stocks and securities the prices of which are more or less stable. The bank cannot afford to invest its funds in securities, the prices of which are subject to frequent fluctuations.

7. Principles of Tax-Exemption of Investments

Finally, the investment policy of a bank should be based on the principle of tax exemption of investments. The bank should invest in those government securities which are exempted from income and other taxes. This will help the bank to increase its profits.

Of late, there has been a controversy regarding the relative importance of the various principles influencing the investment policy of a bank particularly between liquidity and profitability. It is interesting to examine this controversy.

Let us examine what happens if the bank sticks to the principle of liquidity only. It is true that if the bank pays importance to liquidity, it can easily meet the demands of the depositors. The bank should have adequate cash to meet the claims of the depositors. It is true that a successful banking business calls for installing confidence in the minds of the depositors. But, it should be noted that accepting deposits is not the only function of a bank. Moreover, the bank cannot afford to forget the fact that it has to earn income to pay salaries to the staff, interest to the depositors, dividend to the shareholders and meet the day-to-day expenditure. If the bank keeps all its resources in liquid form, it will not be able to earn even a rupee. But profitability is a must for the bank. Though cash on hand is the most liquid asset, it is the least profitable asset as well. Cash is an idle asset. Hence, the banker cannot concentrate on liquidity only.

If the bank attaches importance to profitability only, it would be equally disastrous to the very survival of a bank. It is true that a bank needs income to meet its expenditure and pay returns to the depositors and shareholders. The bank cannot undermine the interests of the depositors. If the bank lends out all its funds, it will be left with no cash at all to meet the claims of the depositors. It should be noted that the bank should have cash to honour the obligations of the depositors. Otherwise, there will be a 'run' on the bank. A run on the bank would be suicidal to the very existence of the bank. Loans and advances, though the most profitable asset, constitute the least liquid asset.

It follows from the above that the choice is between liquidity and profitability. The constant tug of war between liquidity and profitability is the feature of the assets side. According to Crowther, liquidity and profitability are opposing or conflicting considerations The secret of successful banking lies in striking a balance between the two.

The balance sheet of a commercial bank is a statement of its assets and liabilities. Assets are what others owe the bank, and what the bank owes others constitutes its liabilities. The business of a bank is reflected in its balance sheet and hence its financial position as well. The balance sheet is issued usually at the end of every financial year of the bank.

Balance Sheet of the Bank

Liabilities	Assets
1. Capital a. Authorised capital b. Issued capital c. Subscribed capital d. Paid-up-capital 2. Reserve Fund 3. Deposits 4. Borrowings from other banks 5. Bills payable 6. Acceptances and endorsements. 7. Contingent liabilities 8. Profit and loss account 9. Bills for collection	1. Cash a. Cash on hand b. Cash with central bank and other bank 2. Money at call and short notice. 3. Bills discounted 4. Bills for collection 5. Investments 6. Loans and advances 7. Acceptances and endorsement 8. Fixed assets

Balance Sheet of the Bank

The balance sheet of the bank comprises of two sides the assets side and the liabilities side. It is customary to record liabilities on the left side and assets on the right side. The following is the proforma of a balance sheet of the bank.

Liabilities

Liabilities are those items on account of which the bank is liable to pay others. They denote other's claims on the bank. Now we have to analyse the various items on the liabilities side.

1. Capital

The bank has to raise capital before commencing its business. Authorised capital is the maximum capital upto which the bank is empowered to raise capital by the Memorandum of Association. Generally, the entire authorised capital is not raised from the public. That part of authorised capital which is issued in the form of shares for public subscription is called the issued capital. Subscribed capital represents that part of issued capital which is actually subscribed by the public. Finally, paid-up capital is that part of the subscribed capital which the subscribers are actually called upon to pay.

2. Reserve Fund

Reserve fund is the accumulated undistributed profits of the bank. The bank maintains reserve fund to tide over any crisis. But, it belongs to the shareholders and hence a liability on the bank. In India, the commercial bank is required by law to transfer 20 per cent of its annual profits to the Reserve fund.

3. Deposits

The deposits of the public like demand deposits, savings deposits and fixed deposits constitute an important item on the liabilities side of the balance sheet. The success of any banking business depends to a large extent upon the degree of confidence it can instill in the minds of the depositors. The bank can never afford to forget the claims of the depositors. Hence, the bank should always have enough cash to honour the obligations of the depositors.

4. Borrowings from other banks

Under this head, the bank shows those loans it has taken from other banks. The bank takes loans from other banks, especially the central bank, in certain extraordinary circumstances.

5. Bills Payable

These include the unpaid bank drafts and telegraphic transfers issued by the bank. These drafts and telegraphic transfers are paid to the holders thereof by the bank's branches, agents and correspondents who are reimbursed by the bank.

6. Acceptances and Endorsements

This item appears as a contra item on both the sides of the balance sheet. It represents the liability of the bank in respect of bills accepted or endorsed on behalf of its customers and also letters of credit issued and guarantees given on their behalf. For rendering this service, a commission is charged and the customers to whom this service is extended are liable to the bank for full payment of the bills. Hence, this item is shown on both sides of the balance sheet.

7. Contingent Liabilities

Contingent liabilities comprise of those liabilities which are not known in advance and are unforeseeable. Every bank makes some provision for contingent liabilities.

8. Profit and Loss Account

The profit earned by the bank in the course of the year is shown under this head. Since the profit is payable to the shareholders it represents a liability on the bank.

9. Bills for Collection

This item also appears on both the side of the balance sheet. It consists of drafts and hundies drawn by sellers of goods on their customers and are sent to the bank for collection, against delivery documents like railway receipt, bill of lading, etc., attached thereto. All such bills in hand at the date of the balance sheet are shown on both the sides of the balance sheet because they form an asset of the bank, since the bank will receive payment in due course, it is also a liability because the bank will have to account for them to its customers.

Assets

According to Crowther, the assets side of the balance sheet is more complicated and interesting. Assets are the claims of the bank on others. In the distribution of its assets, the bank is governed by certain well defined principles. These principles constitute the principles of the investment policy of the bank or the principles underlying the distribution of the assets of the bank. The most important guiding principles of the distribution of assets of the bank are liquidity, profitability and safety or security. In fact, the various items on the assets side are distributed according to the descending order of liquidity and the ascending order of profitability.

Now, we have to analyse the various items on the assets side.

1. Cash

Here we can distinguish cash on hand from cash with central bank and other banks cash on hand refers to cash in the vaults of the bank. It constitutes the most liquid asset which can be immediately used to meet the obligations of the depositors. Cash on hand is called the first line of defence to the bank.

In addition to cash on hand, the bank also keeps some money with the central bank or other commercial banks. This represents the second line of defence to the bank.

2. Money at call and Short Notice

Money at call and short notice includes loans to the brokers in the stock market, dealers in the discount market and to other banks. These loans could be quickly converted into cash and without loss, as and when the bank requires. At the same time, this item yields income to the bank. The significance of money at call and short notice is that it is used by the banks to effect desirable adjustments in the balance sheet. This process is called 'Window Dressing'. This item constitutes the 'third line of defence' to the bank.

3. Bills Discounted

The commercial banks invest in short term bills consisting of bills of exchange and treasury bills which are self-liquidating in character. These short term bills are highly negotiable and they satisfy the twin objectives of liquidity and profitability. If a commercial bank requires additional funds, it can easily rediscount the bills in the bill market and it can also rediscount the bills with the central bank.

4. Bills for Collection

As mentioned earlier, this item appears on both sides of the balance sheet.

5. Investments

This item includes the total amount of the profit yielding assets of the bank. The bank invests a part of its funds in government and non-government securities.

6. Loans and Advances

Loans and advances constitute the most profitable asset to the bank. The very survival of the bank depends upon the extent of income it can earn by advancing loans. But, this item is the least liquid asset as well. The bank earns quite a sizeable interest from the loans and advances it gives to the private individuals and commercial firms.

7. Acceptances and Endorsements

As discussed earlier, this item appears as a contra item on both sides of the balance sheet.

8. Fixed Assets

Fixed assets include building, furniture and other property owned by the bank. This item includes the total volume of the movable and immovable property of the bank. Fixed assets are referred to as 'dead stocks'. The bank generally undervalues this item deliberately in the balance sheet. The intention here is to build up secret reserves which can be used at times of crisis.

Balance sheet of a bank acts as a mirror of its policies, operations and achievements. The liabilities indicate the sources of its funds; the assets are the various kinds of debts incurred by a bank to its customers. Thus, the balance sheet is a complete picture of the size and nature of operations of a bank.

Credit-Creation

An important function performed by the commercial banks is the creation of credit. The process of banking must be considered in terms of monetary flows, that is, continuous depositing and withdrawal of cash from the bank. It is only this activity which has enabled the bank to manufacture money. Therefore the banks are not only the purveyors of money but manufacturers of money.

Basis of Credit Creation

The basis of credit money is the bank deposits. The bank deposits are of two kinds viz, (1) Primary deposits and (2) Derivative deposits.

1. Primary deposits

Primary deposits arise or formed when cash or cheque is deposited by customers. When a person deposits money or cheque, the bank will credit his account. The customer is free to withdraw the amount whenever he wants by cheques. These deposits are called "primary deposits" or "cash deposits". It is out of these primary deposits that the bank makes loans and advances to its customers. The initiative is taken by the customers themselves. In this case, the role of the bank is passive. So these deposits are also called "passive deposits" These deposits merely convert currency money into deposit money. They do not create money. They do not make any net addition to the stock of money. In other words, There is no increase in the supply of money.

2. Derivative deposits.

Bank deposits also arise when a loan is granted or when a bank discounts a bill or purchase government securities. Deposits which arise on account of granting loan or purchase of assets by a bank are called "derivative deposits". Since the bank play an active role in the creation of such deposits, they are also known as "active deposits". When the banker sanctions a loan to a customer, a deposit account is opened in the name of the customer and the sum is credited to his account. The bank does not pay him cash. The customer is free to withdraw the amount whenever he wants by cheques. Thus the banker lends money in the form of deposit credit. The creation of a derivative deposit does result in a net increase in the total supply of money in the economy, Hartly Withers says "every loan creates a deposit". It may also be said "loans make deposits" or "loans create deposits". It is rightly said that "deposits are the children of loans, and credit is the creation of bank clerk's pen".

Granting a loan is not the only method of creating deposit or credit. Deposits also arise when a bank discounts a bill or purchase government securities. When the bank buys government securities, it does not pay the purchase price at once in cash. It simply credits the account of the government with the purchase price. The government is free to withdraw the amount whenever it wants by cheque. Similarly, when a bank purchase a bill of exchange or discounts a bill of exchange, the proceeds of the bill of exchange is credited to the account of the seller and promises to pay the amount whenever he wants. Thus asset acquired by a bank creates an equivalent bank deposit. It is perfectly correct to state that "bank loans create deposits" The derivate deposits are regarded as bank money or credit. Thus the power of commercial banks to expand deposits through loans, advances and investments is known as "credit creation".

Thus credit creation implies multiplication of bank deposits. Credit creation may be defined as "the expansion of bank deposits through the process of more loans and advances and investments".

Process of Credit Creation

An important aspect of the credit creating function of the commercial banks is the process of multiple-expansion of credit. The banking system as a whole can create credit which is several times more than the original increase in the deposits of a bank. This process is called the multiple-expansion or multiple-creation of credit. Similarly, if there is withdrawal from any one bank, it leads to the process of multiple-contraction of credit. The process of multiple credit-expansion can be illustrated by assuming.

a) The existence of a number of banks, A, B, C etc. each with different sets of depositors.

b) Every bank has to keep 10% of cash reserves, according to law, and,

c) A new deposit of Rs. 1,000 has been made with bank A to start with.

Balance Sheet of Bank A

Labilities	Rs.	Assets	Rs.
New deposit	1,000	New Cash	1,000
Total	1,000		1,000

Suppose, a person deposits Rs. 1,000 cash in Bank A. As a result, the deposits of bank A increase by Rs. 1,000 and cash also increases by Rs. 1,000. The balance sheet of the bank is as fallows:

Under the double entry system, the amount of Rs. 1,000 is shown on both sides. The deposit of Rs. 1,000 is a liability for the bank and it is also an asset to the bank. Bank A has to keep only 10% cash reserve, i.e., Rs. 100 against its new deposit and it has a surplus of Rs. 900 which it can profitably employ in the assets like loans. Suppose bank A gives a loan to X, who uses the amount to pay off his creditors. After the loan has been made and the amount so withdrawn by X to pay of his creditors, the balance sheet of bank A will be as follows :

Balance Sheet of Bank A

Labilities	Rs.	Assets	Rs.
Deposit	1,000	New Cash	100
		Loan to X	900
Total	1,000		1,000

Suppose X purchase goods of the value of Rs. 900 from Y and pay cash. Y deposits the amount with Bank B. The deposits of Bank B now increase by Rs. 900 and its cash also increases by Rs. 900. After keeping a cash reserve of Rs. 90, Bank B is free to lend the balance of Rs. 810 to any one. Suppose bank B lends Rs. 810 to Z, who uses the amount to pay off his creditors. The balance sheet of bank B will be as follows :

Suppose Z purchases goods of the value of Rs. 810 from S and pays the amount. S deposits the amount of Rs. 810 in bank C. Bank C now keeps 10% as reserve (Rs. 81) and lends Rs. 729 to a merchant. The balance sheet of bank C will be as follows :

Balance Sheet of Bank B

Labilities	Rs.	Assets Cash	Rs.
Deposit	900	Cash	90
		Loan to Z	810
Total	900		900

Balance Sheet of Bank C

Labilities	Rs.	Assets	Rs.
Deposit	810	Cash	81
		Loan	729
Total	810		810

Thus looking at the banking system as a whole, the position will be as follows :

Name of Bank	Deposits Rs.	Cash reserve Rs.	Loan Rs.
Bank A	1,000	100	900
Bank B	900	90	810
Bank C	810	81	729
Total	2,170	271	2,439

It is clear from the above that out of the initial primary deposit, bank advanced Rs. 900 as a loan. It formed the primary deposit of bank B, which in turn advanced Rs. 810 as loan. This sum again formed, the primary deposit of bank C, which in turn advanced Rs. 729 as loan. Thus the inital primary deposit of Rs. 1,000 resulted in bank credit of Rs. 2439 in the three banks. There will be many banks in the country and the above process of credit expansion will come to an end when no bank has an excess reserve to lend. In the above example, there will be 10 fold increase in credit because the cash ratio is 10%. The total volume of credit created in the banking system depends on the cash ratio. If the cash ratio is 10% there will be 10 fold increase. If it is 20%, there will be 5 fold increase. When the banking system receives an additional primary deposit, there will be multiple expansion of credit. When the banking system loses cash, there will be multiple contraction of credit.

The extent to which the banks can create credit together could be found out with the help of the credit multiplier formula. The formula is :

$$K = \frac{l}{r}$$

Where K is the credit multiplier, and r, the required reserves. If the reserve ratio is 10% the size of credit multiplier will be :

$$K = \frac{1}{r} = \frac{1}{0.1} = 10$$

It means that the banking system can create credit together which is ten times more than the original increase in the deposits. It should be noted here that the size of credit multiplier is inversely related to the percentage of cash reserves the banks have to maintain. If the reserve ratio increases, the size of credit multiplier is reduced and if the reserve ratio is reduced, the size of credit multiplier will increase.

Leaf and Cannon Criticism

Walter Leaf and Edwin Cannon objected to the theory of credit creation. According to them, the commercial bank cannot lend anything more than what it receives as cash from deposits. But the contention of Leaf and Cannon that banks cannot create credit is wrong due to the following reasons:

(a) A single bank may not be able to create derivative deposits in excess of its cash reserves. But the banking system as a whole can do what a single bank cannot do.

(b) As Crowther points out that the total net deposits of commercial banks are for in excess of their cash reserves. It means they can create credit.

Limitation on Credit Creation

The commercial banks do not have unlimited power of credit creation. Their power to create credit is limited by the following factors.

1. Amount of Cash

The power to create credit depends on the cash received by banks. If banks receive more cash, they can create more credit. If they receive less cash they can create less credit. Cash supply is controlled by the central bank of the country.

2. Cash Reserve Ratio

All deposits cannot be used for credit creation. Banks must keep certain percentage of deposits in cash as reserve. The volume of bank credit depends also on the cash reserve ratio the banks have to keep. If the cash reserve ratio is increased, the volume of credit that the banks can create will fall. If the cash reserve ratio is lowered, the bank credit will increase. The Central Bank has the power to prescribe and change the cash reserve ratio to be kept by the commercial banks. Thus the central bank can change the volume of credit by changing the cash reserve ratio.

3. Banking Habits of the People

The loan advanced to a customer should again come back into banks as primary deposit. Then only there can be multiple expansion. This will happen only when the banking habit among the people is well developed. They should keep their money in the banks as deposits and use cheques for the settlement of transactions.

4. Nature of Business Conditions in the Economy

Credit creation will depend upon the nature of business conditions. Credit creation will be large during a period of prosperity, while it will be smaller during a depression. During periods of prosperity, there will be more demand for loans and advances for investment purposes. Many people approach banks for loans and advances. Hence, the volume of bank credit will be high. During periods of business depression, the amount of loans and advances will be small because businessmen and industrialists may not come to borrow. Hence the volume of bank credit will be low.

5. Leakages in Credit-Creation

There may be some leakages in the process of credit creation. The funds may not flow smoothly from one bank to another. Some people may keep a portion of their amount as idle cash.

6. Sound Securities

A bank creates credit in the process of acquiring sound and profitable assets, like bills, and government securities. If people cannot offer sound securities, a bank cannot create credit. Crowther says "a bank cannot create money out of thin air. It transmutes other forms of wealth into money".

7. Liquidity Preference

If people desire to hold more cash, the power of banks to create credit is reduced.

8. Monetary Policy of the Central Bank

The extent of credit creation will largely depend upon the monetary policy of the Central Bank of the country. The Central Bank has the power to influence the volume of money in circulation and through this it can influence the volume of credit created by the banks. The Central Bank has also certain powerful weapons, like the bank rate, open market operations with the help of which it can exercise control on the expansion and contraction of credit by the commercial bank.

Thus, the ability of the bank to create credit is subject to various limitations. Still, one should not undermine the importance of the function of credit creation of the banks. This function has far-reaching effect on the working of the economy, especially on the business activity. Bank credit is the oil which lubricates the wheels of the business machine.

Unit Banking Vs Branch Banking

The banking system in different countries vary substantially from one another, Broadly speaking, however, there are two important types of banking systems, viz, unit banking and branch banking.

A. Unit Banking

'Unit banking' means a system of banking under which banking services are provided by a single banking organisation. Such a bank has a single office or place of work. It has its own governing body or board of directors. It functions independently and is not controlled by any other individual, firm or body corporate. It also does not control any other bank. Such banks can become member of the clearing house and also of the Banker's Association. Unit banking system originated and grew in the U.S.A. Different unit banks in the U.S.A. are linked with each other and with other financial centres in the country through 'correspondent banks".

Advantages of Unit Banking

Following are the main advantages of unit banking.

1. Efficient Management

One of the most important advantages of unit banking system is that it can be managed efficiently because of its size and work. Co-ordination and control becomes effective. There is no communication gap between the persons making decisions and those executing such decisions.

2. Better Service

Unit banks can render efficient service to their customers. Their area of operation being limited, they can concentrate well on that limited area and provide best possible service. Moreover, they can take care of all banking requirements of a particular area.

3. Close Customer-banker Relations

Since the area of operation is limited the customers can have direct contact. Their grievances can be redressed then and there.

4. No evil effects due to Strikes or Closure

In case there is a strike or closure of a unit, it does not have much impact on the trade and industry because of its small size. It does not affect the entire banking system.

5. No Monopolistic Practices

Since the size of the bank and area of its operation are limited, it is difficult for the bank to adopt monopolistic practices. Moreover, there is free competition. It will not be possible for the bank to indulge in monopolistic practices.

6. No Risks of Fraud

Due to small size of the bank, there is stricter and closer control of management. Therefore, the employees will not be able to commit fraud.

7. Closure of Inefficient Banks

Inefficient banks will be automatically closed as they would not be able to satisfy their customers by providing efficient service.

8. Local Development

Unit banking is localised banking. The unit bank has the specialised knowledge of the local problems and serves the requirement of the local people in a better manner than branch banking. The funds of the locality are utilised for the local development and are not transferred to other areas.

9. Promotes Regional Balance

Under unit banking system, there is no transfer of resources from rural and backward areas to the big industrial and commercial centres. This tends to reduce regional imbalance.

Disadvantages of Unit Banking

1. No Economies of Large Scale

Since the size of a unit bank is small, it cannot reap the advantages of large scale viz., division of labour and specialisation.

2. Lack of Uniformity in Interest Rates

In Unit banking system there will be large number of banks in operation. There will be lack of control and therefore their rates of interest would differ widely from place to place. Moreover, transfer of funds will be difficult and costly.

3. Lack of Control

Since the number of unit banks is very large, their co-ordination and control would become very difficult.

4. Risks of Bank's Failure

Unit banks are more exposed to closure risks. Bigger unit can compensate their losses at some branches against profits at the others. This is not possible in case of smaller banks. Hence, they have to face closure sooner or later.

5. Limited Resources

Under unit banking system the size of bank is small. Consequently its resources are also limited.

Hence, they cannot meet the requirements of large scale industries.

6. Unhealthy Competition

A number of unit banks come into existence at an important business centre. In order to attract customers they indulge in unhealthy competition.

7. Wastage of National Resources

Unit banks concentrate in big metropolitan cities whereas they do not have their places of work in rural areas. Consequently there is uneven and unbalanced growth of banking facilities.

8. No Banking Development in Backward Areas

Unit banks, because of their limited resources, cannot afford to open uneconomic branches in smaller towns and rural areas. As such, these areas remain unbanked.

9. Local Pressure

Since unit banks are highly localised in their business, local pressures and interferences generally disrupt their normal functioning.

B. Branch Banking System

It means a system a banking in which a banking organisation works at more than one place. The main place of business is called Head office and the other places of business are called branches. The Head office controls and co-ordinates the work at branches. The day-to-day operations are performed by the branch manager as per the policies and directions issued from time to time by the Head office.

This system of banking is prevalent throughout the world. In India also, all the major banks have been operating under branch banking system.

Advantages of Branch Banking

1. Better Banking Services

Such banks, because of their large size can enjoy the economies of large scale viz., division of work and specialisation. These banks can also afford to have the specialised services of bank personnel which the unit banks can hardly afford.

2. Extensive Service

Branch banking can provide extensive service to cover large area. They can open their branches throughout the country and even in foreign countries.

3. Decentralisation of Risks

In branch banking system branches are not concentrated at one place or in one industry. These are decentralised at different places and in different industries. Hence the risks are also distributed.

4. Uniform Rates of Interest

In branch banking, there is better control and co-ordination of the central bank. Consequently interest rates can be uniform.

5. Better Cash Management

In branch banking there can be better cash management as cash easily be transferred from one branch to another. Therefore, there will be lesser need to keep the cash idle for meeting contingencies.

6. Better Training Facilities to Employees

Under branch banking the size of the bank is quite large. Therefore, such banks can afford to provide better training facilities to their employees. Almost every nationalised bank in India has its separate training college.

7. Easy and Economical Transfer of Funds

Under branch banking, a bank has a wide spread of branches. Therefore, it is easier and economical to transfer funds from one branch to the other.

8. Better Investment of Funds

Such bank can afford the services of specialised and expert staff. Therefore they invest their funds in such industries where they get the highest return and appreciation without sacrificing the safety and liquidity of funds.

9. Effective Central Bank Control

Under branch banking, the central bank has to deal only with a few big banks controlling a large number of branches. It is always easier and more convenient to the central bank to regulate and control the credit policies of a few big banks, than to regulate and control the activities of a large number of small unit banks. This ensures better implementation of monetary policy.

10. Contacts with the Whole Country

Under branch banking, the bank maintains continual contacts with all parts of the country. This helps it to acquire correct and reliable knowledge about economic conditions in various parts of the country. This knowledge enables the bank to make a proper and profitable investment of its surplus funds.

11. Greater Public Confidence

A bank, with huge financial resources and number of branches spread throughout the country, can command greater public confidence than a small unit bank with limited resources and one or a few branches.

Disadvantages of Branch Banking

Following are the disadvantages of branch banking.

1. Difficulties of Management, Supervision and Control

Since there are hundreds of branches of a bank under this system, management, supervision and control became more inconvenient and difficult. There are possibilities of mismanagement in branches. Branch managers may misuse their position and misappropriate funds. There is great scope for fraud. Thus there are possibilities of fraud and irregularities in the financial management of the bank.

2. Lack of Initiative

The branches of the bank under this system suffer from a complete lack of initiative on important banking problems confronting them. No branch of the bank can take decision on important problems without consulting the head office. Consequently, the branches of the bank find themselves unable to carry on banking activities in accordance with the requirements of the local situation. This makes the banking system rigid and inelastic in its functioning. This also leads to "red-tapism" which means "official delay".

3. Monopolistic Tendencies

Branch banking encourages monopolistic tendencies in the banking system. A few big banks dominate and control the whole banking system of the country through their branches. This can lead to the concentration of resources in the hands of a small number of men. Such a monopoly power is a source of danger to the community, whose goal is a socialistic pattern of society.

4. Regional Imbalances

Under the branch banking system, the financial resources collected in the smaller and backward regions are transferred to the bigger industrial centres. This encourages regional imbalances in the country.

5. Continuance of Non-Profitable Branches

Under branch banking, the weak and unprofitable branches continue to operate under the protection cover of the stronger and profitable branches.

6. Unnecessary Competition

Branch banking is delocalised banking, under branch banking system, the branches of different banks get concentrated at certain places, particularly in big towns and cities. This gives rise to unnecessary and unhealthy competition among them. The branches of the competing banks try to tempt customers by offering extra inducements and facilities to them. This naturally increases the banking expenditure.

7. Expensiveness

Branch banking system is much more expensive than the unit banking system. When a bank opens a number of branches at different places, then there arises the problem of co-ordinating their activities with others. This necessitates the employment of expensive staff by the bank.

8. Losses by Some Branches Affect Others

When some branches suffer losses due to certain reasons, this has its repercussions on other branches of the bank.

Thus branch banking system as well as unit banking system suffer from defects and drawbacks. But the branch banking system is, on the whole, better than the unit banking system. In fact, the branch banking system has proved more suitable for backward and developing countries like India. Branch banking is very popular and successful in India. A comparison between unit banking and branch banking is essentially a comparison between small-scale and large-scale operations.

Commercial Banks and Economic Development

Commercial banks are considered not merely as dealers in money but also the leaders in economic development. They are not only the store houses of the country's wealth but also the reservoirs of resources necessary for economic development. They play an important role in the economic development of a country. A well-developed banking system is essential for the economic development of a country. The "industrial revolution" in Europe in the 19th century would not have been possible without a sound system of commercial banking. In case of developing countries like India, the commercial banks are considered to be the back bone of the economy. Commercial banks can contribute to a country's economic development in the following ways :

1. Accelerating the Rate of Capital Formation

Capital formation is the most important determinant of economic development. The basic problem of a developing economy is slow rate of capital formation. Banks promote capital formation. They encourage the habit of saving among people. They mobilise idle resources for production purposes. Economic development depends upon the diversion of economic resources from consumption to capital formation. Banks help in this direction by encouraging saving and mobilising them for productive uses.

2. Provision of Finance and Credit

Commercial banks are a very important source of finance and credit for industry and trade. Credit is a pillar of development. Credit lubricates all commerce and trade. Banks become the nerve centre of all commerce and trade. Banks are instruments for developing internal as well as external trade.

3. Monetisation of Economy

An underdeveloped economy is characterised by the existence of a large non-monetised sector. The existence of this non-monetised sector is a hindrance in the economic development of the country. The banks, by opening branches in rural and backward areas can promote the process of monetisation (conversion of debt into money) in the economy.

4. Innovations

Innovations are an essential pre requisite for economic development. These innovations are mostly financed by bank credit in the developed countries. But in underdeveloped countries, entrepreneurs hesitate to invest in new ventures and undertake innovations largely due to lack of funds. Facilities of bank loans enable the entrepreneurs to step up their investment on innovational activities, adopt new methods of production and increase productive capacity of the economy.

5. Implementation of Monetary Policy

Economic development need an appropriate monetary policy. But a well-developed banking is a necessary pre-condition for the effective implementation of the monetary policy. Control and regulation of credit by the monetary authority is not possible without the active co-operation of the banking system in the country.

6. Encouragement to Right type of Industries

Banks generally provide financial resources to the right type of industries to secure the necessary material, machines and other inputs. In this way they influence the nature and volume of industrial production.

7. Development of Agriculture

Underdeveloped economies are primarily agricultural economies. Majority of the population in these economies live in rural areas. Therefore, economic development in these economies requires the development of agriculture and small scale industries in rural areas. So far banks in underdeveloped countries have been paying more attention to trade and commerce and have almost neglected agriculture and industry. Banks must provide loans to agriculture for development and modernisation of agriculture. In recent years, the State Bank of India and other commercial banks are granting short term, medium-term and long-term loans to agriculture and small-scale industries.

8. Regional Development

Banks can also play an important role in achieving balanced development in different regions of the country. They transfer surplus capital from the developed regions to the less developed regions, where it is scarce and most needed. This reallocation of funds between regions will promote economic development in underdeveloped areas of the country.

9. Promote Industrial Development

Industrial development needs finance. In some countries, commercial banks encouraged industrial development by granting long-term loans also. Loan or credit is a pillar to development. In underdeveloped countries like India, commercial banks are granting short-term and medium-term loans to industries. They are also underwriting the issue of shares and debentures by industrial concerns. This helps industrial concerns to secure adequate capital for their establishment, expansion and modernisation. Commercial banks are also helping manufacturers to secure machinery and equipment from foreign countries under instalment system by guaranteeing deferred payments. Thus, banks promote or encourage industrial development.

10. Promote Commercial Virtues

The business men are more afraid of a banker than a preacher. The businessmen should have certain business qualities like industry, forethought, honesty and punctuality. These qualities are called "commercial virtues" which are essential for rapid economic progress. The banker is in a better position to promote commercial virtues. Banks are called "public conservators of commercial virtues".

11. Fulfillment of Socio-Economic Objectives

In recent years, commercial banks, particularly in developing countries, have been called upon to help achieve certain socio-economic objectives laid down by the state. For example, nationalised bank in India have framed special innovative schemes of credit to help small agriculturists, self-employed persons and retailers through loans and advances at concessionall rates of interest. Banking is thus used to achieve the national policy objectives of reducing inequalities of income and wealth, removal of poverty and elimination of unemployment in the country.

Thus banks in a developing country have to play a dynamic role. Economic development places heavy demand on the resources and ingenuity of the banking system. It has to respond to the multifarious economic needs of a developing country. Traditional views and methods may have to be discarded. "An Institution, such as the banking system, which touches and should touch the lives of millions, has necessarily to be inspired by a larger social purpose and has to subserve national priorities and objectives". A well-developed banking system provides a firm and durable foundation for the economic development of the country.

Conclusion

From the above discussion, undoubtedly, we can say that, commercial banks form the most important part of financial intermediaries. It accepts deposits from the general public and extends loans to the households, firms and the government. Banks form a significant part of the infrastructure essential for breaking vicious circle of poverty and promoting economic growth.

Questions for Discussions

1. What is a commercial bank? What are the main functions performed by commercial banks? How far are they useful for economic development?
2. State the kinds of commercial banks.
3. What do you understand by a commercial bank's balance sheet? What specific information does it convey?
4. What is the investment policy of a commercial bank? Explain the factors that constitute for formulating a suitable investment policy.
5. What is credit creation? How banks create credit? What are the limitations of credit creation?
6. State the advantages and disadvantages of unit banking system.
7. State the advantages and disadvantages of branch banking system.
8. Discuss the role of banks in a developing economy.

Chapter - 2

CENTRAL BANKING

Introduction

A central bank is an 'apex institution' in the banking structure of a country. It supervises, controls and regulates the activities of commercial banks and acts as a banker to them. It also acts as a banker, agent and adviser to the government in all financial and monetary matters. A central bank is also the custodian of the foreign balances of the country and is responsible to maintain the rate of exchange fixed by the government and manages exchange control. The most important function of a central bank is to regulate the volume of currency and credit in a country. It will be no exaggeration to say that a modern central bank is the central arch to the monetary and fiscal framework in almost all the countries developed or developing in the world. In developing economies, the central bank has also to perform certain promotional and developmental functions to accelerate the pace of economic growth.

Meaning of Central Bank

In every country there is one bank which acts as the leader of the money market, supervising, controlling and regulating the activities of commercial banks and other financial institutions. It acts as a bank of issue and is in close touch with the government, as banker, agent and adviser to the latter. Such a bank is known as the **central bank** of the country.

Definition of Central Bank

A banking institution can more easily be identified by the functions that it performs. According to Vera Smith, "the primary definition of central banking is a banking system in which a single bank has either a complete or residuary monopoly in the note issue". Kisch and Elkin believe that "the essential function of a central bank is the maintenance of the stability of the monetary standard". In the statutes of the Bank for International Settlements a central bank is defined as "the bank of the country to which has been entrusted the duty of regulating the volume of currency and credit in that country" De Kock gives a very comprehensive definition of central bank. According to De Kock, a central bank is "a bank which constitutes the pex of the monetary and banking structure of its country and which performs, best it can in the national economic interest, the following functions:

(a) The regulation of currency in accordance with the requirements of business and the general public, for which purpose it is granted either the sole right of note issue or at least a partial monopoly thereof.

(b) The performance of general banking and agency services for the state.

(c) The custody of cash reserves of the commercial banks.

(d) The custody and management of the nation's reserves of international currency.

(e) The granting of accommodation, in the form of rediscounts, or collateral advances, to commercial banks, bill brokers and dealers, or other financial institutions, and the general acceptance of the responsibility of lender of last resort.

(f) The settlement of clearances between the banks.

(g) The control of credit in accordance with the needs of business and with a view to carrying out the broad monetary policy adopted by the state.

The nature of function of a central bank differs in a developed economy as compared to those in a developing economy.

Functions of the Central Bank

The functions of the central bank differ from country to country in accordance with the prevailing economic situation. But there are certain functions which are commonly performed by the central bank in all countries. According to De Kock, there are six functions which are performed by the central bank in almost all countries.

1. Monopoly of Note Issue

The issue of money was always the prerogative of the government. Keeping the minting of coins with itself, the government delegated the right of printing currency notes to the central bank. In fact the right and privilege of note issue was always associated with the origin and development of central banks which were originally called as banks of issue. Nowadays, central banks everywhere enjoy the exclusive monopoly of note issue and the currency notes issued by the central banks are declared unlimited legal tender throughout the country. At one time, even commercial banks could issue currency notes but there were certain evils in such a system such as lack of uniformity in note issue, possibility of over-issue by individual banks and profits of note issue being enjoyed only by a few private shareholders. But concentration of note issue in the central bank brings about uniformity in note issue, which, in turn, facilitates trade and exchange within the country, attaches distinctive prestige to the currency notes, enables the central bank to influence and control the credit creation of commercial banks avoids the over-issue of notes and, lastly, enables the government to appropriate partly or fully the profits of note issue. The central bank keeps three considerations in view as regards issue of notes-uniformity, elasticity (amount according to the need for money), and safety.

2. Custodian of Exchange Reserves

The central bank holds all foreign exchange reserves-key currencies such as U.S. dollars, British pounds and other prominent currencies, gold stock, gold bullion, and other such reserves-in its custody. This right of the central bank enables it to exercise a reasonable control over foreign exchange, for example, to maintain the country's international liquidity position at a safe margin and to maintain the external value of the country's currency in terms of key foreign currencies.

3. Banker to the Government

Central banks everywhere perform the functions of banker, agent and adviser to the government. As a banker to the government, the central bank of the country keeps the banking accounts of the government both of the Centre and of the States performs the same functions as a commercial bank ordinarily does for its customers. As a banker and agent to the government, the central bank makes and receives payments on behalf of the government. It helps the government with short-term loans and advances (known as ways and means advances) to tide over temporary difficulties and also floats public loans for the government. It also manages the public debt (i.e., floats services and redeems government loans). It advises the government on monetary and economic matters.

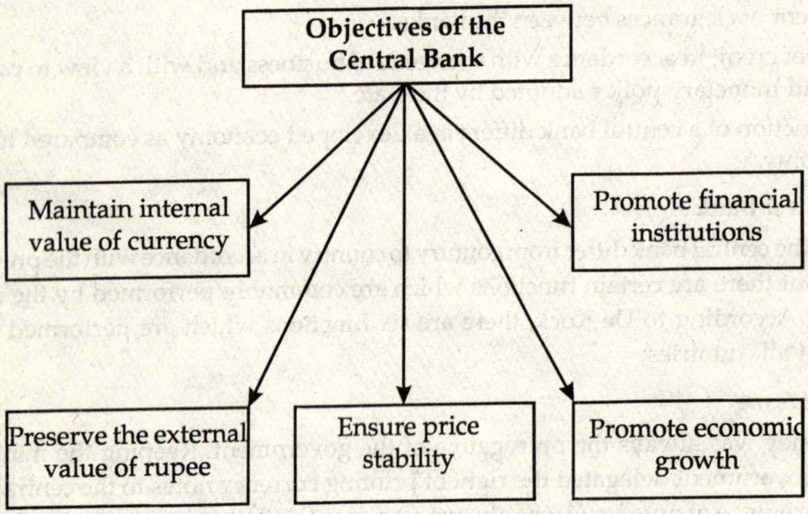

Functions of the Central Bank

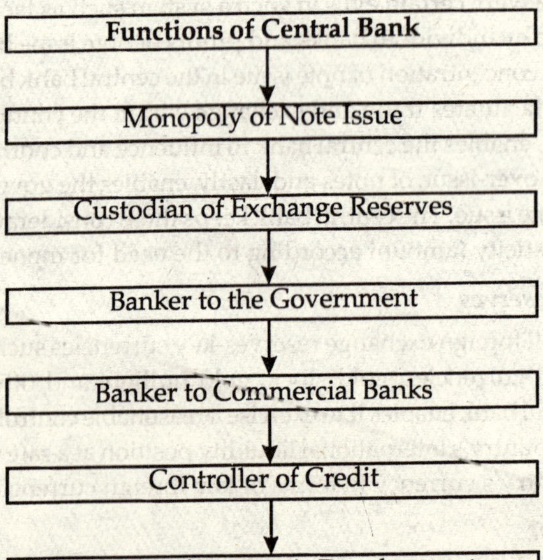

4. Banker to Commercial Banks

Broadly speaking, the central bank acts as the banker's bank in three different capacities : (a) It acts as the custodian of the cash reserves of the commercial banks (b) It acts as the lender of the last resort (c) It is the bank of central clearance, settlement and transfer. We shall now discuss these three functions one by one.

(a) It acts as the custodian of the cash reserves of commercial banks

Commercial banks keep part of their cash balances as deposits with the central bank of a country known as centralisation of cash reserves. Part of these balances are meant for clearing purposes, that is, payment by one bank to another will be simple book entry adjustment in the books of the central bank. There are many advantages when all banks keep part of their cash reserves with the central bank of the country. In the first place, with the same amount of cash reserves, a large amount of credit creation is possible. Secondly, centralised cash reserves will enable commercial banks to meet crises and emergencies. Thirdly, it enables the central bank to provide additional funds to those banking institutions which are in temporary difficulties. Lastly, it enables the central bank to influence and control the credit creation of commercial banks by making the cash reserves of the latter more or less.

(b) Lender of the last resort

As the banker's bank, the central bank can never refuse to accommodate commercial banks. Any commercial bank wanting accommodation from the central bank can do so by rediscounting (selling) eligible securities with the central bank or can borrow from the central bank against eligible securities. By lender of the last resort, it is implied that the latter assumes the responsibility of meeting directly or indirectly all reasonable demands for accommodation by commercial banks in times of difficulties and crisis.

(c) Clearing agent

As the central bank becomes the custodian of cash reserves of commercial banks, it is but logical for it to act as a settlement bank or a clearing house for other banks. As all banks have their accounts with the central bank, the claims of banks against each other are settled by simple transfers from and to their accounts. This method of settling accounts through the central bank, apart from being convenient, is economical as regards the use of cash. Since claims are adjusted through accounts, there is usually no need for cash. It also strengthens the banking system by reducing withdrawals of cash in times of crisis. Furthermore, it keeps the central bank of informed about the state of liquidity of commercial banks in regard to their assets.

5. Controller of Credit

Probably the most important of all the functions performed by a central bank is that of controlling the credit operations of commercial banks. In modern times, bank credit has become the most important source of money in the country, relegating coins and currency notes to a minor position. Moreover, it is possible, as we have pointed out in a previous chapter, for commercial banks to expand credit and thus intensify inflationary pressure or contract credit and thus contribute to a deflationary situation. It is, thus, of great importance that there should be some authority which will control the credit creation by commercial banks. As controller of credit, the central bank attempts to influence and control the volume of bank credit and also to stabilise business conditions in the country.

6. Promoter of Economic Development

In developing economies the central bank has to play a very important part in the economic development of the country. Its monetary policy is carried out with the object of serving as an instrument of planned economic development with stability. The central bank performs the function of developing long-term financial institutions, also known as development banks, to make available adequate investible funds for the development of agriculture, industry, foreign trade, and other sectors of the economy. The central bank has also to develop money and capital markets.

In addition, the central bank may also undertake miscellaneous functions such as providing assistance to farmers through co-operative societies by subscribing to their share capital, promoting finance corporations with a view to providing loans to large-scale and small-scale industries and publishing statistical reports on tends in the money and capital markets. In short, a central bank is an institution which always works in the best economic interests of the nation as a whole. In view of all these functions, as discussed above, it follows that a modern central bank is much more than a Bank of Issue.

Credit Control

It means the regulation of the creation and contraction of credit in the economy. It is an important function of central bank of any country. The importance of credit control has increased because of the growth of bank credit and other forms of credit. Commercial banks increase the total amount of money in circulation in the country through the mechanism of credit creation. In addition, businessmen buy and sell goods and services on credit basis. Because of these developments, most countries of the world are based on credit economy rather than money economy.

Fluctuations in the volume of credit cause fluctuations in the purchasing power of money. This fact has far reaching economic and social consequences. That is why, credit control has become an important function of any central bank. For instance, the preamble to the Bank of Canada Act states that the Bank of Canada will regulate credit in Canada. In India, the Reserve Bank has been given wide powers to control credit creation and contraction by commercial banks. Before we discuss the techniques of credit control, it is desirable to understand the objectives of credit control.

Objectives of Credit Control

The central bank is usually given many weapons to control the volume of credit in the country. The use of these weapons is guided by the following objectives.

(a) Stability of Internal Price-level

The commercial bank can create credit because their main task is borrowing and lending. They create credit without any increase in cash with them. This leads to increase in the purchasing power of many people which may lead to an increase in the prices. The central bank applies its credit control to bring about a proper adjustment between the supply of credit and measures requirements of credit in the country. This will help in keeping the prices stable.

(b) Checking Booms and Depressions

The operation of trade cycles causes instability in the country. So the objective of the credit control should be to reduce the uncertainties caused by these cycles. The central bank adjusts the operation of the trade cycles by increasing and decreasing the volume of credit.

(c) Promotion of Economic Development

The objective of credit control should be to promote economic development and employment in the country. When there is lack of money, its supply should be increased so that there are more and more economic activities and more and more people may get employment. While resorting to credit squeeze, the central bank should see that these objectives are not affected adversely.

(d) Stability of the Money Market

The central bank should operate its weapons of credit control so as to neutralise the seasonal variations in the demand for funds in the country. It should liberalise credit in terms of financial stringencies to bring about stability in the money market.

e) Stability in Exchange Rates

This is also an important objective of credit control. Credit control measures certainly influence the price level in the country. The internal price level affects the volume of exports and imports of the country which may bring fluctuations in the foreign exchange rates. While using any measure of credit control, it should be ensured that there will be no violent fluctuation in the exchange rates.

Methods of Credit Control

The various methods employed by the central bank to control credit creation power of the commercial banks can be classified in two groups. viz., quantitative controls, and qualitative controls.

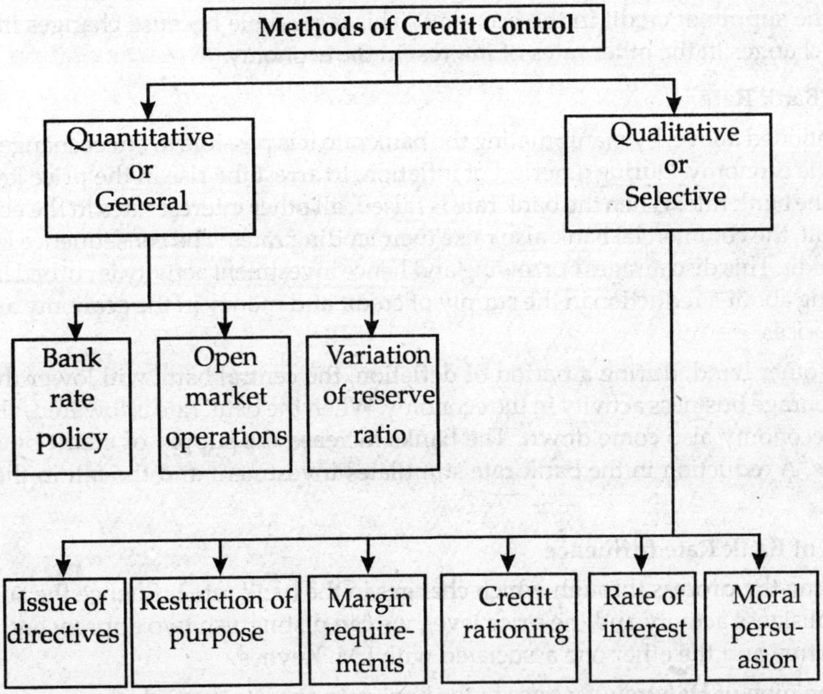

Quantitative controls are designed to regulate the volume of credit created by the banking system. These measures work through influencing the demand and supply of credit. Quanlitative measures, on the other hand, are designed to regulate the flow of credit in specific uses

1. Quantitative Methods

Quantitative methods aim at controlling the total volume of credit in the country. They relate to the volume and cost of bank credit in general, without regard to the particular field of enterprise or economic activity in which the credit is used.

The important quantitative or the general methods of credit control are as follows

A. Bank Rate or Discount Rate Policy

Bank Rate Policy or the Discount Rate Policy has been the earliest instrument of quantitative credit control. It was the bank of England which experimented with the bank rate policy for the first time as a technique of monetary management. Now every central bank has been endowed with this instrument of credit control.

Meaning

Bank Rate refers to the official minimum lending rate of interest of the central bank. It is the rate at which the central bank advances loans to the commercial banks by rediscounting the approved first class bills of exchange of the banks. Hence, bank rate is also called as the discount rate.

Theory of Bank Rate

The theory underlying the operation of bank rate is that by manipulating the bank rate, the central bank is in a position to exercise influence upon the supply of credit in the economy. According to the theory of bank rate an increase or a decrease in the bank rate leads to a reduction or an increase in the supply of credit in the economy. This is possible because changes in the bank rate bring about changes in the other rates of interest in the economy.

Working of Bank Rate

As mentioned above, by manipulating the bank rate it is possible to effect changes in the supply of credit in the economy. During a period of inflation, to arrest the rise in the price level, the central bank raises the bank rate. When the bank rate is raised, all other interest rates in the economy also go up. As a result, the commercial bank also raise their lending rates. The consequence is an increase in the cost of credit. This discourages borrowing and hence investment activity is curbed in the economy. This will bring about a reduction in the supply of credit and money in the economy and therefore in the level of prices.

On the other hand, during a period of deflation, the central bank will lower the bank rate in order to encourage business activity in the economy. When the bank rate is lowered, all other interest rates in the economy also come down. The banks increase the supply of credit by reducing their lending rates. A reduction in the bank rate stimulates investment and the fall in the price level is arrested.

The Process of Bank Rate Influence

Regarding the process through which changes in the bank rate influence the supply of credit, the level of business activity and the price level, we can distinguish two approaches. One put forth by R.G. Hawtrey and the other one associated with J.M. Keynes.

In the opinion of Hawtrey, changes in the bank rate operate through changes in the short term rates of interest. These changes in the short term interest rates, in their turn, influence the cost of borrowing by businessmen and industrialists.

But, according to Lord Keynes, changes in bank rate become effective through changes in the long term interest rates as reflected by changes in the capital value of long term securities.

But, it should be noted that there is not much difference between the two approaches and hence they are complementary to each other.

Bank Rate Under the Gold Standard

Under the gold standard, bank rate was used primarily to set right the disequilibrium in the balance of payments of the country. When there was a déficit in the balance of payments and hence an outflow of gold, bank rate was raised to check the outflow of gold. This was done by attracting the inflow of short term capital in to the country.

Conditions for the Success of the Bank Rate Policy

The efficacy of bank rate as an instrument of monetary management calls for the fulfillment of the following conditions

(a) ***Close relationship between Bank Rate and other Interest Rates :*** It is necessary that the relationship between bank rate and the other interest in the economy should be close and direct. Changes in the rate should bring about similar and appropriate changes in the other interest rates in the economy. Otherwise the efficacy of bank rate will be limited. There is, therefore, the need for the existence of an integrated interest rate structure.

(b) ***Existence of an elastic economic system :*** The success of bank rate requires the existence of an elastic economic structure. That is, the entire economic system should be perfectly flexible to accommodate itself to changes in the bank rate. Changes in the bank rate should bring about similar and desirable changes in prices, costs, wages, output, profits, etc. The existence of a rigid economic structure will reduce the efficacy of bank rate.

(c) ***Existence of short term funds market :*** Another condition required for the success of bank rate policy is the existence of market for short term funds in the country. This will help to handle foreign as well as domestic funds that come up on account of changes in the interest rates, following changes in the bank rate.

Before the First World War, bank rate policy was very effective as an instrument of quantitative credit control because, the conditions necessary for the success of bank rate were there. But, after the war, the significance of bank rate began to wane because the post - war atmosphere was not conducive for the smooth and effective operation of the bank rate policy.

Limitations

The Bank Rate Policy suffers from the following limitations.

(a) It has been argued that bank rate proves ineffective to combat boom and depression. During a period of boom, investment is interest inelastic. Even if the bank rate is raised to any extent, investment activity will not be curbed, because during a period of boom, the marginal efficiency of capital will be very high and the entire business community will be caught in a sweep of optimism. During depression, bank rate becomes ineffective following the general psychology of diffidence and pessimism among the business ...

(b) The growth of non-banking financial intermediaries has proved an effective threat to the effectiveness of bank rate policy. It has been adequately established by the study of the Redcliffe Report and Gurley-shaw, that the mushroom growth of non-banking financial intermediaries has belittled the significance of bank rate. This is because changes in the bank rate immediately affect the rates of interest of the commercial banks only and the non-banking financial institutions are not subject to the direct control of the central bank. Hence, it is said that **"the good boy is punished for the actions of a bad boy"**.

(c) The decline in the use of bills of exchange as credit instruments also has been responsible for the decline in the importance of bank rate.

(d) Further, of late, businessmen have found out alternative methods of business financing, self-financing, ploughing back the profits, public deposits, etc. Indeed, the role of commercial banks as suppliers of loanable funds has been decreasing in importance.

(e) Moreover, the economic structure has not been adequately responding itself to changes in the bank rate. After the war, all kinds of rigidities have crept into the economic system.

(f) The invention of alternative instruments of credit control also has accounted for the decline in the popularity of bank rate.

(g) Further, the dependence of the commercial bank on the central bank for loans also has decreased leading to the decline in getting the bills of exchange rediscounted by the central bank. In addition, there has been an increased liquidity in the assets of banks.

(h) Finally, the increase in the importance of fiscal policy following the Great Depression of 1930's has also reduced the importance of bank take policy as a technique of credit control.

However, in spite of the above limitations that the bank rate policy is subject to, it would be wrong to undermine the significance of bank rate as a tool monetary management. Though, by itself, it may not yield the desirable results, but will certainly prove effective when used with other instruments of credit control. The scope for the use of bank rate by the central bank, therefore, cannot be completely ruled out. The bank rate has undergone a significant revival. Its significance in controlling inflation cannot be undermined.

B. Open Market Operations

After the first world war, bank rate policy as a tool of monetary management began to lose its significance fallowing the invention of alternative techniques of credit control. Among the alternative instruments of quantitative credit control invented in the post-war period, open market operations assumed significance.

Meaning

Open market operations refer to the purchase and sale of securities by the central bank. In its broader sense, the term includes the purchase and sale of both government and private securities. But, in its narrow connotation, open market operations embrace the purchase and sale of government securities only. It was in Germany that open market operations took its birth as an instrument of quantitative credit control.

Theory of Open Market Operations

The theory underlying the operation of open market operations is that by the purchase and sale of securities, the central bank is in a position to increase or decrease the cash reserves of the commercial banks and therefore increase or decrease the supply of credit in the economy.

The modus operandi of open market operations can now be explained. During a period of inflation, the central bank seeks to reduce the supply of credit in the economy. Hence, it sells the securities to the banks, public and others. As a result of the sale of securities by the central bank, there will be a transfer of cash from the buyers to the central bank. This will reduce the cash reserves of the commercial banks. The public has to withdraw money from their accounts in the banks to pay for the securities purchased from the central bank. And the commercial banks themselves will have to transfer some amount to the central bank for having purchased the securities. All this shrinks the volume of cash in the vaults of the banks. As a result the banks will be unable to expand the supply of credit. When the supply of credit is reduced by the banking system, the consequences on the economy will be obvious. Investment activity is discouraged ultimately leading to a fall in the price level.

On the other hand, during a period of deflation, in order to inject more and more credit in to the economy, the central bank purchases the securities. This will have an encouraging effect on investment because the banks supply more credit following an increase in their cash reserves. Thus, the central bank seeks to combat deflation in the economy.

Objectives of Open Market-operations

The main objectives of open market operations are :

(a) To eliminate the effects of exports and imports to gold under the gold standard.
(b) To impose a check on the export of capital.
(c) To remove the shortage of money in the money market.
(d) To make bank rate more effective.
(e) To prevent a 'run on the bank'.

Conditions for the Success of Open Market Operations

The efficacy of open market operations as a tool of quantitative credit control requires the fulfillment of certain conditions discussed below.

1. Institutional Framework

The success of open market operations requires the existence of an institutional framework, that is, the existence of a well-knit and well developed securities market. The absence of a matured money market constitutes a serious impediment to the development of open market operations as an effective instrument of monetary control. In fact, in the under developed countries, the scope for open market operations is limited because of the absence of the institutional framework referred to above.

2. Legal Framework

The effective and meaningful functioning of open market operations calls for a suitable legal setting. The legal setting is that there should be no legal restrictions on the holding of securities by the central bank. It has been found that in some countries the governments have imposed ceilings on the holdings of government securities by central banks. Such legal restrictions obviously circumscribe the efficacy of open market operations.

3. Maintenance of a Definite cash Reserve Ratio

Another condition that should be fulfilled for the success of open market operations is that the cash reserves of the banks should change in accordance with the purchase and sale of securities by the central bank. When the central bank purchases the securities, the cash reserves of the banks should increase and when the central bank sells the securities, the cash reserves of the banks should fall. This means that the banks should maintains a definite cash reserve ratio. But, if the banks keep the cash reserves in excess of the fixed ratio or have other secret reserves, the very purpose of open market operations will be defeated.

4. Non-operation of Extraneous Factors

Due to the operation of certain extraneous factors the cash reserves of the banks may not change in accordance with the requirement of open market operations. For example, when the central bank purchases the securities in order to inject more credit into the economy, this objective may be defeated by an outflow of money due to unfavourable balance of payments or the public may hoard a part of the additional cash put into circulation.

5. Non-existence of Direct Access of Commercial Banks to the Central Bank

Another important condition for the smooth working of the open market operations is that the commercial banks should not have direct access to the central bank for financial accommodation. In case the banks have direct accommodation to the central bank, then the reduction in their cash reserves through open market sale of securities by the central bank may be neutralised by these banks by borrowing from the central bank.

It should be noted here that the above conditions necessary for the success of open market operations constitute by themselves the limitations of the open market operations. In fact, in many countries, particularly in the less developed countries, the success of open market operations is limited because the above conditions are not fulfilled.

Popularity of Open Market Operations

Despite the limitations of open market operations, it has been argued that this technique of credit control is superior to the bank rate policy. The superiority of open market operations stem from the following points.

(a) The discount rate policy seeks to regulate credit in an indirect way, whereas open market operations have a more direct and effective influence on the regulation of credit by the central bank.

(b) The influence of bank rate is on short term interest rates only. The long term interest rates are influenced only indirectly by changes in bank rate. But, the policy of open market operations has a direct bearing on the prices of long term securities and hence on the long term interest rates. It has a direct and immediate effect on the quantity of money and credit and hence on the market interest rates. It is on this score that the policy of open market operations is now increasingly used to influence the interest rates as well as the prices of government securities in the money market.

But, the above two points of the superiority of the policy of open market operations should not make us blind to the fact that the policy of open market operations will itself help to achieve the desired results. It is necessary to combine both bank rate and open market operations judiciously to achieve the desired results. Wherever possible, open market operations will have to be supplemented by the bank rate policy. This will go a long way in producing effective results in regulating the volume of credit in the economy.

C. Variable Cash Reserve Ratio

The traditional instruments of quantitative credit control, bank rate policy and open market operations, suffer from certain inherent defects and have been found unsuitable to serve the interests of underdeveloped countries. Hence, an entirely new and unorthodox instrument of quantitative credit control, in the form of variable reserve ratio, came into vogue, thanks to the Federal Reserve System of the United States. It was, however, Lord Keynes who was responsible for popularising the use of this novel technique of monetary management. The Federal Reserve System became the trend setter by pressing into service variable reserve ratio for the first time in 1933 as a weapon of quantitative credit control.

Meaning

Variable Reserve Ratio refers to the percentage of the deposits of the commercial banks to be maintained with the central bank, being subject to variations by the central bank. In other words, altering the reserve requirements of the commercial banks is called variable reserve ratio.

It is a well known fact that all the commercial banks have to maintain a certain percentage of their deposits as cash reserves with the central bank. The central bank, therefore, acts as the custodian of the cash reserve of the commercial banks. By so doing, the central bank imparts liquidity and confidence into the system. This reserve requirement is subject to changes by the central bank depending upon the monetary needs and conditions of the economy.

In certain countries, like United States and India, there are clear written laws stipulating the banks to maintain the reserve requirements with the central bank. Such a reserve ratio is called the Statutory Reserve Ratio. But, in England, the banks maintain the reserve ratio as a matter of custom. Hence this kind of reserve ratio is called the Customary Reserve Ratio. Anyhow, the central bank has the authority to vary the reserve requirements of the banks.

Theory of Variable Reserve Ratio

The theory underlying the mechanism of variable reserve ratio is that by varying the reserve requirements of the banks, the central bank is in a position to influence the size of credit multiplier of the banks and therefore the supply of credit in the economy. An increase or decrease in the reserve requirements will have a contractionist or expansionary influence respectively on the supply of credit by the banking system.

Working of Variable Reserve Ratio

It is interesting to examine the working of variable reserve ratio as a technique of quantitative credit control. During a period of inflation, the central bank raises the reserve ratio in order to reduce the supply of credit in the economy and therefore to reduce the price level. When the reserve requirements of the banks are raised, the excess reserves of the banks shrink and hence the size of their credit multiplier decreases. It should be noted that the size of credit multiplier is inversely related to the reserve ratio prescribed by the central bank. An increase in the reserve ratio, therefore, discourages the commercial banks from expanding the supply of credit.

On the contrary during a period of deflation, the central bank lowers the reserve requirements of the banks in order to inject more purchasing power into the economy. When the reserve ratio is lowered, the excess reserves with the banks increase and hence the size of credit multiplier increases. This will have an encouraging effect on the ability of the banks to create credit. Thus, the central bank seeks to combat deflation in the economy.

Another variant of Variable Reserve Ratio is the method of Statutory Liquidity Ratio (S.L.R.) which is being used by the Reserve Bank of India. In this case, every scheduled bank in India is required under law to maintain certain liquid assets to meet its liabilities. These liquid assets comprise cash reserves with the central bank, balances with other banks in current account and investment in government securities. By varying the S.L.R., the central bank seeks to influence the credit creating capacity of the commercial banks. This method is known as the method of Secondary Reserve Requirements, and is being extensively used in western countries, like France, the U.S., Sweden, etc.

Other variants of Variable Reserve Ratio include the supplementary Reserve Requirements, Special Accounts System, Special Deposits System, etc.

There is a substantial measure of agreement that variable reserve ratio can be appropriately pressed into service when a country is experiencing large and sudden movements in its gold and foreign exchange assets, especially as a result of speculative international capital movements. The effects of large inflows and outflows of foreign capital can be counteracted smoothly and effectively by changes in the reserve requirements. Again, by varying the reserve ratio, it is possible to meet the minor fluctuations and shifts in the balance of payments position.

Though variable reserve ratio also has been a tool of quantitative credit control. It should be sharply distinguished from the traditional instruments of the bank rate and open market operations which belong to the same group. While the bank rate policy and open market operations alter the volume of free reserves of the banks indirectly by influencing the total amount of reserves, the variable reserve ratio does so directly. "Whereas the other two methods are designed to bring about an actual quantitative change in reserve holdings and thereby in free reserves a change in reserve requirements serves to create or destroy free reserves by a stroke of pen".

Limitations

The following constitute the limittions of variable reserve ratio.

(a) In the first place, variable reserve ratio has been considered to be a blunt and harsh instrument of credit control.

(b) As compared with the open market operations, it is inexact and uncertain as regards changes not only in the amount of reserves, but also the place where these changes can be made effective.

(c) Variable reserve ratio is accused of being discriminatory in its effect. It affects different banks differently. Banks with a large margin of excess reserves would be hardly affected whereas banks with small excess reserves would be hard pressed.

(d) Variable Reserve Ratio is considered to be inflexible. It lacks flexibility in that changes in reserve requirements would not be well adjusted to meet small or localized situations of reserve stringency or superfluity.

(e) This method of credit control is likely to create a panic among the banks and the investors.

(f) Maintaining the reserve ratio with the central bank imposes a burden on the banks because no interest is allowed on these cash reserves by the central bank.

(g) In the event of the commercial banks having huge foreign funds, the method of variable reserve ratio proves ineffective.

In view of the above limitations, according to De Kock, variable reserve ratio should be used "with moderation and discretion and only under abnormal conditions".

Yet, the case for variable reserve ratio is stronger than for bank rate policy and open market operations. Variable reserve ratio has the merit of being applied universally. It is considered to be the battery of the most improved type that the central bank has added to its armoury of the instruments of credit control. The technique of variable reserve ratio has been found extremely popular among the central banks of the less developed and the developing countries. As mentioned earlier, while the success of bank rate and open market operations calls for the fulfillment of certain conditions, in the case of variable reserve ratio, the desired results can be achieved just 'by a stroke of pen'.

From the above, we should not draw the conclusion that any of the three methods is preferable to the others. The right attitude should be not to accept this method or that method but to combine all the three methods in right proportions in order to secure effective results in the field of credit creation. The three methods, as we have seen above, have their own merits and demerits, and hence, no method, taken alone, can be successful in producing the desired results. Therefore, a judicious and skilful combination of all the three methods is essential in order to realize the objectives of credit control. These three methods may be combined in varying proportions to achieve effective results in the field of credit.

2. Selective or Qualitative Methods

The central bank may assume that the inflationary pressure in the country is due to artificial scarcities created by speculators and hoarders who may hoard and black market essential goods through the use of bank credit. Accordingly, the central bank may not regulate and control the volume of credit but central the use of credit or the person's security, etc. Such controls are known as selective or direct controls. The special features of selective or qualitative controls are :

(a) They distinguish between essential and non-essential uses of bank credit.
(b) Only non-essential uses are brought under the scope of central bank controls.
(c) They affect not only the lenders but also the borrowers.

Selective controls attempt to cut down the credit extended for non-essential purposes or uses. Loans extended to speculators to hoard goods or bank credit to consumers to raise their demand for such durable goods as refrigerators, cars, etc., will prove to be inflationary when there is already excessive demand as compared to the limited supply. Essentially, therefore, selective controls are meant to control inflationary pressure in a country.

Objectives

The following are the broad objectives of selective instruments of credit control :

(a) To divert the flow of credit from undesirable and speculative uses to more desirable and economically more productive and urgent uses.
(b) To regulate a particular sector of the economy without affecting the economy as a whole.
(c) To regulate the supply of consumer credit.
(d) To stabilise the prices of those goods very much sensitive to inflation.
(e) To stabilise the value of securities.
(f) To correct an unfavourable balance of payments of the country.
(g) To bring under the control of the central bank credit created by non banking financial intermediaries.
(h) To exercise control upon the lending operations of the commercial banks.

Measures of Selective Credit Control

For the purpose of selective credit control, the central bank generally uses the following forms of control, from time to time.

1. Margin Requirements

Banks are required by law to keep a safety margin against securities on which they lend. The central bank may direct banks to raise or reduce the margin. In the U.S.A. before world war II, the Federal Reserve Board fixed a margin of 40 percent (i.e., a bank could lend up to 60 percent of the value of security). But during the war and later, the margin requirements were raised from 40 per cent to 50 percent, then to 75 percent and in 1946 to 100 per cent in some cases. When the margin was raised to 75 per cent one could borrow only 25 per cent of the value of the security and when the margin requirement was fixed at 100 per cent one could borrow nothing. Thus by raising the margin requirement, the central bank could reduce the volume of bank credit which a commercial bank can grant and a party can borrow. Margin requirement is a good tool to reduce the degree and extent of speculation in commodity market and stock exchanges.

2. Regulation of Consumer Credit

During the II world war an acute scarcity of goods was felt in the U.S.A., and the position was worsened by the system of bank credit to consumers to enable them to buy durable and semi-durable consumer goods through instalment buying. The Federal Reserve Banks of the U.S.A., were authorised to regulate the terms and conditions under which consumer credit was extended by commercial banks. The restraints under these regulations were twofold: (a) They limited the amount of credit that might be granted for the purchase of any article listed in the regulations; and (b) they limited the time that might be agreed upon for repaying the obligation. Suppose a buyer was required to make a down-payment of one-third of the purchase price of a car and the balance to be paid in 15 monthly instalments. Under the regulations restraining consumer credit, the down-payment was made larger and the time allowed was made shorter. The result was a reduction in the amount of credit extended for the purchase of cars and the time it was allowed to run; and the ultimate result was the restriction, in the demand for consumer goods at a time when there was a shortage in supply and when there was a necessity for restriction on consumer spending. This measure was a success in America in controlling inflationary pressures there. In the post-war period, it has been extensively adopted in all those countries where the system of consumer credit is common.

3. Rationing of Credit

Rationing of credit, as a tool of selective credit control, originated in England in the closing years of the 18th century. Rationing of credit implies two things. First, it means that the central bank fixes a limit upon its rediscounting facilities for any particular bank. Second, it means that the central bank fixes the quota of every affiliated bank for financial accommodation from the central bank.

Rationing of credit occupies an important place in Soviet Economic Planning. The central bank of the Soviet Union allocates the available funds among different banks in accordance with a definite credit plan formulated by the Planning Commission.

But the criticism of rationing of credit is that it comes into conflict with the function of the central bank as a lender of the last resort. When the central bank acts as a lender of the last resort it cannot deny accommodation to any bank through it has borrowed in excess of its quota. Moreover, this method proves effective only when the demand for credit exceeds the supply of it.

4. Control through Directives

In the postwar period, most central banks have been vested with the direct power of controlling bank advances either by statute or by mutual consent between the central bank and commercial banks. For instance, the Banking Regulation Act of India in 1949 specifically empowered the Reserve Bank of India to give directions to commercial banks in respect of their lending policies, the purposes for which advances may or may not be made and the margins to be maintained in respect of secured loans. In England, the commercial banks have been asked to submit to the Capital Issue Committee all loan applications in excess of £ 50,000. There is no uniformity in the use of directives to control bank advances. On the one extreme, the central bank may express concern over credit developments; the concern may be combined with mild threat to avoid increase or decrease in the existing level of bank loans. On the extreme, there can be a clear and open threat to the commercial banks financing certain types of activities.

5. Moral Suasion

This is a form of control through directive. In a period of depression, the central bank may persuade commercial banks to expand their loans and advances, to accept inferior types of securities which they may not normally accept, fix lower margins and in general provide favourable conditions to stimulate bank credit and investment. In a period of inflationary pressure, the central bank may persuade commercial banks not to apply for further accommodation or not to use the accommodation already obtained for financing speculative or non-essential activities lest inflationary pressure should be further worsened. The Bank of England has used this method with a fair measure of success. But this has been mainly because of a high degree of co-operation which it always gets from the commercial banks.

6. Direct Action

Direct action or control is one of the extensively used methods of selective control, by almost all banks at some time or the other. In a broad sense, it includes the other methods of selective credit controls. But more specifically, direct action refers to controls and directions which the central bank may enforce on all banks or any bank in particular concerning lending and investment. The Reserve Bank of India issued a directive in 1958 to the entire banking system to refrain from excessive lending against commodities in general and forbidding commercial banks granting loans in excess of Rs. 50,000 to individual parties against paddy and wheat. There is no doubt about the effectiveness of such direct action but then the element of force associated with direct action is resented by the commercial banks.

7. Publicity

Under this method, the central bank gives wide publicity regarding the probable credit control policy it may resort to by publishing facts and figures about the various economic and monetary condition of the economy. The central bank brings out this publicity in its bulletins, periodicals, reports etc.

Limitations of Selective Credit Controls

(a) The selective controls embrace the commercial banks only and hence the non-banking financial institutions are not covered by these controls.

(b) It is very difficult to control the ultimate use of credit by the borrowers.

(c) It is rather difficult to draw a line of distinction between the productive and unproductive uses of credit.

(d) It is quite possible that the banks themselves through manipulations advance loans for unproductive purposes.

(e) Selective controls do not have much scope under a system of unit banking.

(f) Development of alternative methods of business financing has reduced the importance of selective controls.

From the above discussion, we arrive at the conclusion that the two types of credit control measures, quantitative as well as qualitative, are not rivals, but, on the contrary, they supplement each other. For successful monetary management, the central bank should combine the two methods of credit control in appropriate proportions. In fact, a judicious and a skilful combination of general and selective credit control measures is the right policy to follow for the central bank of a country. It must, however, be pointed out that the various methods, whether quantitative or qualitative, cannot ensure perfect credit control in an economy in view of the several limitations form which they suffer, and other complexities involved in the situation.

Conclusion

To conclude, the central bank of a country acts as the leader of the money market, supervising, controlling and regulating the activities of commercial banks and other financial institutions. It acts as a bank of issue and is in close touch with the government, as banker, agent and adviser to the latter.

Questions for Discussions

1. What is a Central Bank? Explain the main functions of the Central Bank?
2. State and explain the various quantitative and qualitative methods of credit control generally adopted by central banks.
3. What do you mean by quantitative controls explain the different methods of quantitative credit controls.
4. What do you understand by selective or qualitative control? Explain fully the various methods of qualitative credit control.
5. Distinguish between bank rate policy and open market operation as methods of credit control.

Chapter - 3

RESERVE BANK OF INDIA

Introduction

Several attempts were made from time to time to set up a Central Bank in India prior to 1934. But unfortunately these attempts failed to bear any fruit. In 1921, the Government of India established the Imperial Bank of India to serve as the Central Bank of the country. But the Imperial Bank did not achieve any appreciable success in its functioning as the Central Bank of the country. In 1925, the Hilton Young Commission was asked by the Government to express its views on the subject. The commission made out a forceful case for the establishment of a brand new Central Bank in the country. According to the Commission, it was not desirable to keep the control of currency and credit in the hands of two separate agencies. The Government of India controlled currency while the Imperial Bank regulated credit prior to the establishment of the Reserve Bank of India in April 1st, 1935. The Hilton Young Commission did not consider this double control on currency and credit as a desirable feature of the Indian monetary system. It was on this account that the Commission recommended the transfer of the control of currency and credit to a new Central Bank to be set up in the country. It was on this account that the Commission recommended the establishment of the Reserve Bank of India as the Central Bank of the country. The Government of India while accepting the recommendations of the Commission brought forward a Bill before the Central Legislature. But the Bill could not be passed on account of differences amongst the members of the legislature. The Government of India, therefore, postponed the idea of a new Central Bank for sometime. In 1929, the Central Banking Enquiry Committee again made a forceful plea for the establishment of the Reserve Bank. Consequently, the Reserve Bank of India Act was passed in 1934, and the Reserve Bank started functioning from 1st April, 1935.

The Reserve Bank of India is the kingpin of the Indian money market. It issues notes, buys and sells government securities, regulates the volume, direction and cost of credit, manages foreign exchange and acts as banker to the government and banking institutions. The Reserve Bank is playing an active role in the development activities by helping the establishment and working of specialised institutions, providing term finance to agriculture, industry, housing and foreign trade. In spite of many criticisms, it has successfully controlled commercial banks in India and has helped in evolving a strong banking system. A study of the Reserve Bank of India will be useful, not only for the examination, but also for understanding the working of the supreme monetary and banking authority in the country.

Capital

Originally, the Reserve Bank was constituted as a shareholders bank, based on the model of leading foreign central banks of those days. The bank's fully paid-up share capital was Rs. 5 crores divided into shares of Rs. 100 each. Of this, Rs. 4,97,80,000 were subscribed by the private shareholders and Rs. 2,20,000 were subscribed by the Central Government for disposal of 2,200 shares at part to the Directors of the Bank (including members of the Local Boards) seeking the minimum share qualification. The share capital of the bank has remained unchanged until today. The Reserve Bank also had a Reserve Fund of Rs. 150 crores in 1982. It was nationalised in January 1949 and since then it is functioning as the State-owned bank and acting as the premier institution in India's banking structure.

Organisation

As per the Reserve Bank of India Act, the organisational structure of the Reserve Bank comprises:

(A) Central Board

(B) Local Boards

(A) Central Board

The Central Board of Directors is the leading governing body of the bank. It is entrusted with the responsibility of general superintendence and direction of the affairs and business of the Reserve Bank.

The Central Board of Directors consists of 20 members as follows.

1. One Governor and four Deputy Governors

They are appointed by the Government of India for a period of five years. Their salaries, allowances and other perquisites are determined by the central Board of Directors in consultation with the Government of India.

2. Four Directors nominated from the Local Boards

There are four local Boards of Directors in addition to the Central Board of Directors. They are located at Bombay, Calcutta, Madras and New Delhi. The Government of India nominates one member each from these local Boards. The tenure of these directors is also for a period of five years.

3. Ten other Directors

The ten other directors of the Central Board of Directors are also nominated by the Government of India. Their tenure is four years.

4. One Government Official

The Government of India also appoints one Government Official to attend the meetings of the Central Board of Directors. This official can continue for any number of years with the consent of the Government, but he does not enjoy the right to vote in the meetings of the Central Board.

The Central Board of Directors exercises all the powers of the bank. The Central Board should meet at least six times in each year and at least once in three months. Usually, the Central Board keeps a meeting in March every year at New Delhi so as to discuss the budget with the Finance Minister after its presentation in parliament. Similarly it keeps a meeting in August at Bombay in order to pass the Bank's annual report and accounts.

For all practical purposes, however, the committee set-up by the Central Board looks after the bank's current affairs. The committee consists of the Governor, the Deputy Governors and such other Directors as may be present. The committee meets once a week. Two sub-committees have also been appointed to assist the committee of the Central Board. Of these, one is called the Building Sub-Committee which deals with matters relating to building projects. The other one is called the

Staff Sub-Committee which is concerned with staff and other matters.

The Governor is the highest official of the Reserve Bank. There are four Deputy Governors to help and advise him. Each Deputy Governor is allotted a particular job to do, and he is fully held responsible for the proper execution of the job.

(B) Local Boards

The Reserve Bank of India is divided into four regions : the Western, the Eastern, the Northern and the Southern areas. For each of these regions, there is a Local Board, with headquarters in Bombay, Calcutta, New Delhi and Chennai.

Each Local Board consists of five members appointed by the Central Government for four years. They represent territorial and economic interests and the interests of co-operative and indigenous banks in their respective areas. In each Local Board, a chairman is elected from amongst their members. Managers in-charge of the Reserve Bank's offices in Bombay, Calcutta, Chennai and New Delhi are ex-officio Secretaries of the respective Local Boards at these places.

The Local Boards carry out the functions of advising the Central Board of Directors on such matters of local importance as may be generally or specifically referred to them or performing such duties which may be assigned to them. Generally, a Local Board deals with the management of regional commercial transactions.

Offices of the Bank

The head quarters of the Reserve Bank is located at Bombay. But for the efficient performance of its functions, the Bank has opened local offices at New Delhi, Calcutta, Chennai, Bangalore, Kanpur, Ahmedabad, Hyderabad, Patna and Nagpur. The Bank can open its office at any other place with the prior consent of the Central Government. The State Bank of India acts as the Agent of the Reserve Bank at those places where the latter does not maintain its own offices. The regional offices of the exchange control department of the Reserve Bank are located at New Delhi, Kanpur, Calcutta and Chennai.

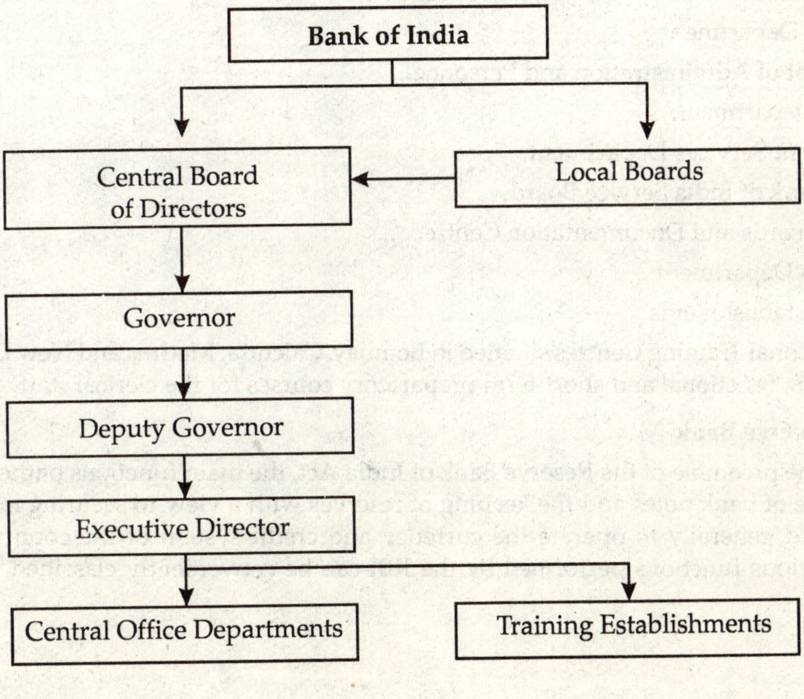

The Reserve Bank has three training establishments viz., (a) Bankers Training College, Bombay, (b) College of Agricultural Banking, Pune and (c) Reserve Bank Staff College, Chennai.

The organisational set-up of the Reserve Bank of India is depicted in above chart.

Departments of the Reserve Bank

To carry out its functions / operations smoothly and efficiently, the Reserve Bank of India has the following departments.

1. Issue Department.
2. Banking Department.
3. Department of Banking Development.
4. Department of Banking Operations.
5. Agricultural Credit Department.
6. Exchange Control Department.
7. Industrial Finance Department.
8. Non-Banking Companies Department.
9. Legal Department.
10. Department of Research and Statistics.
11. Department of Government and Bank Accounts.
12. Department of Currency Management.
13. Department of Expenditure of Budgetary Control.
14. Rural Planning and Credit Department.
15. Credit Planning Cell.
16. Department of Economic Analysis and Policy.
17. Inspection Department.
18. Department of Administration and Personnel.
19. Premises Department.
20. Management Services Department.
21. Reserve Bank of India Service Board.
22. Central Records and Documentation Centre.
23. Secretary's Department.
24. Training Establishments.

There are also Zonal Training Centres situated in Bombay, Calcutta, Madras and New Delhi for conducting induction, functional and short-term preparatory courses for the clerical staff.

Functions of the Reserve Bank

According to the preamble of the Reserve Bank of India Act, the main functions of the bank is "to regulate the issue of bank notes and the keeping of reserves with a view to securing monetary stability in India and generally to operate the currency and credit system of the country to its advantage". The various functions performed by the RBI can be conveniently classified in three parts as follows.

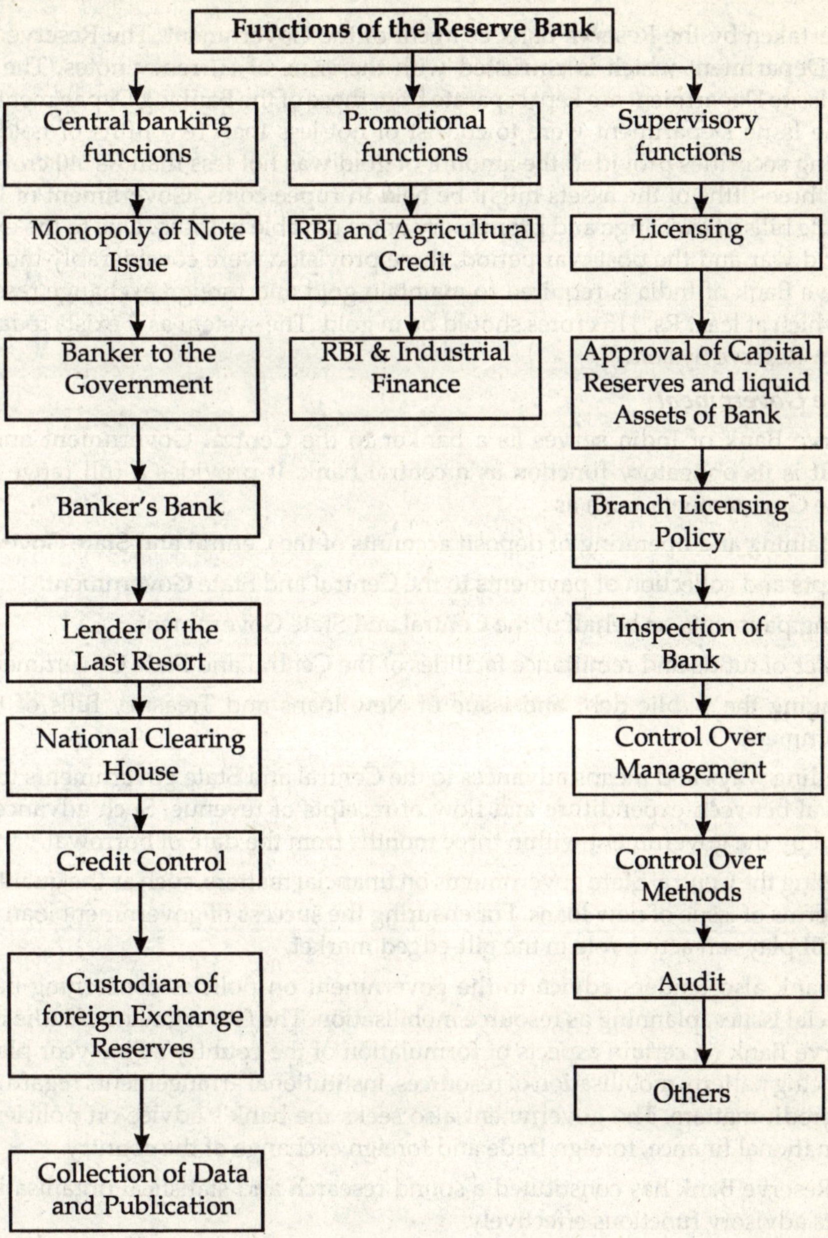

A. Traditional Central Banking Functions

The Reserve Bank of India discharges all those functions which are performed by a central bank. Among these the more important functions are as follows.

1. Monopoly of Note Issue

Under section 22 of the Reserve Bank of India Act, the Bank has the sole right to issue bank notes of all denomination. The distribution of one rupee notes and coins and small coins all over the country is undertaken by the Reserve Bank as agent of the Government. The Reserve Bank has a separate Issue Department which is entrusted with the issue of currency notes. The assets and liabilities of the Issue Department are kept separate from those of the Banking Department, originally, the assets of the Issue Department were to consist of not less than two fifths of gold coin, gold bullion or sterling securities provided the amount of gold was not less than Rs. 40 crores in value. The remaining three-fifths of the assets might be held in rupee coins, Government of India rupee securities, eligible bills of exchange and promissory notes payable in India. Due to the exigencies of the second world war and the post-war period, these provision were considerably modified since 1957, the Reserve Bank of India is required to maintain gold and foreign exchange reserves of Rs. 200 crores, of which at least Rs. 115 crores should be in gold. The system as it exists today is known as the Minimum Reserve System.

2. Banker to the Government

The Reserve Bank of India serves as a banker to the Central Government and the State Governments. It is its obligatory function as a central bank. It provides a full range of banking services to these Governments, such as :

(a) Maintaining and operating of deposit accounts of the Central and State Government.

(b) Receipts and collection of payments to the Central and State Government.

(c) Making payments on behalf of the Central and State Government.

(d) Transfer of funds and remittance facilities of the Central and State Governments.

(e) Managing the public debt and issue of New loans and Treasury Bills of the Central Government.

(f) Providing ways and means advances to the Central and State governments to bridge the interval between expenditure and flow of receipts of revenue. Such advances are to be repaid by the government within three months from the date of borrowal.

(g) Advising the Central State governments on financial matters, such as the quantum, timing and terms of issue of new loans. For ensuring the success of government loan operations, the RBI plays an active role in the gilt-edged market.

(h) The bank also tenders advice to the government on policies concerning banking and financial issues, planning as resource mobilisation. The Government of India consults the Reserve Bank on certain aspects of formulation of the country's Five year plans, such as Financing pattern, mobilisation of resources, institutional arrangements regarding banking and credit matters. The government also seeks the bank's advice on policies regarding international finance, foreign trade and foreign exchange of the country.

The Reserve Bank has constituted a sound research and statistical organisation to carry out its advisory functions effectively.

(i) The Reserve Bank represents the Government of India as member of the International Monetary Fund and World Bank.

3. Banker's Bank

The Reserve Bank has the right of controlling the activities of the banks in the country. All the commercial banks, Co-operative banks and foreign banks in the country have to open accounts with the bank and are required to keep a certain portion of their deposits as reserves with the Reserve Bank. Cash reserves are not to be less than 3% of the demand and time liabilities of the bank. The Reserve Bank has the power to increase this ratio upto 15%. Through this, Reserve Bank is able to regulate and control the credit created by the commercial banks. In addition to this, the scheduled banks are also required to submit to the Reserve Bank a number of returns every Friday.

4. Lender of the Last Resort

The scheduled banks can barrow from the Reserve Bank on the basis of eligible securities. They can also get the bills of exchange rediscounted. The Reserve Bank acts as the clearing house of the all the banks. It adjust the debits and credits of various banks by merely passing the book entries. The Bank also provides free remittance facilities to the banks. Thus, it acts as the banker's bank. The Reserve bank also acts as the lender of the last resort and an emergency bank. It grants short-term loans to scheduled commercial banks against eligible securities in time of need. Similarly, it rediscounts the eligible bills of exchange brought by the commercial banks.

5. National Clearing House

The Reserve Bank acts as the national clearing house and helps the member banks to settle their mutual indebtedness without physically transferring cash from place to place. The Reserve Bank is managing many clearing houses in the country with the help of which cheques worth crores of rupees are cleared every year. The ultimate balances are settled by the banks throught cheques on the Reserve Bank.

6. Credit Control

The Reserve Bank of India is the controller of credit, i.e., it has the power to influence the volume of credit created by bank in India. It can do so through changing the bank rate or through open market operation. According to the Banking Regulation Act of 1949, the Reserve Bank of India can ask any particular bank or the whole banking system not to lend to particular groups or persons on the basis of certain types of securities. Since 1956, selective controls of credit are increasingly being used by the Reserve Bank.

The Reserve Bank of India is armed with many more powers to control the Indian money market. Every bank has to get a licence from the Reserve Bank of India to do banking business within India, the licence can be cancelled by the Reserve Bank if certain stipulated conditions are not fulfilled. Every bank will have to get the permission of the Reserve Bank before it can open a new branch. Each scheduled bank must send a weekly return to the Reserve Bank showing, in detail, its assets and liabilities. This power of the bank to call for information is also intended to give it effective control of the credit system. The Reserve Bank has also the power to inspect the accounts of any commercial bank.

As supreme banking authority in the country, the Reserve Bank of India, therefore, has the following powers.

(a) It holds the cash reserves of all the scheduled bank.

(b) It controls the credit operation of banks through quantitative and qualitative controls.

(c) It controls the banking system through the system of licensing, inspection and calling for information.

(d) It acts as the lender of the last resort by providing rediscount facilities to scheduled banks.

7. Custodian of Foreign Exchange Reserves

The Reserve Bank has the responsibility of maintaining the external value of the rupee. There is centralisation of the entire foreign exchange reserves of the country with the Reserve Bank to avoid fluctuations in the exchange rate.

The RBI has the authority to enter into foreign exchange transactions both on its own account and on behalf of government. The bank is also empowered to buy and sell foreign exchange from and to scheduled bank in amounts of not less than the equivalent of Rs. 1 lakh.

As the custodian of the Nation's foreign exchange reserves, the RBI also administers exchange controls of the country, and enforces the provision of the Foreign Exchange Regulation Act, 1973.

8. Collection of Data and Publications

The Reserve Bank of India collects statistical data and economic information through its research departments. It compiles data on the working of commercial and co-operative banks, on balance of payments, company and government finances, security markets, price tends, and credit measures.

The bank is the principal source of certain financial statistics and banking data. It publish a monthly bulletin, with weekly statistical supplements and annual reports which present a good deal of periodical reviews and comments pertaining to general economic, financial, and banking developments, including the bank's monetary policies and measures, adopted for the qualitative and quantitative monetary management.

The following are the regular publications of the Bank.

(a) Reserve Bank of India Bulletin (monthly) and its weekly statistical supplements.

(b) Report of the Central Board of Directors (Annual)

(c) Report on Trend and progress of Banking in India (Annual)

(d) Report on currency and Finance (Annual)

(e) Review of the Co-operative Movement in India (Published once in two years).

(f) Banking statistics (Basic statistical Returns)

(g) Statistical Tables Relating to Banks in India.

(h) Statistical Statements Relating to the co-operative movement in India.

(i) Adboc Export Committee's Reports and Monographs.

(j) Results of surveys conducted by the bank, such as the survey of India, Foreign Liabilities and Assets, All-India Debt and Investment Survey 1971-72, etc.

(k) History of the Reserve Bank of India (1935-51).

(l) Functions and working of the Reserve Bank of India.

(m) Banking and Monetary Statistics of India and its supplements.

(n) Reserve Bank of India occasional paper (Bi-annual)

B. Promotional Functions

The scope of the functions performed by the Reserve Bank has further widened after the introduction of economic planning in the country. The bank now performs a variety of promotional and developmental functions. The bank's responsibilities include, apart from monetary functions, the institutionalisation of savings through the promotion of banking habit and the expansion of banking system territorially and functionally. The RBI has to provide facilities for agricultural and industrial finance.

(a) Reserve Bank of India and Agricultural credit. The bank's responsibility in this field has been occasioned by the predominantly agricultural basis of the Indian Economy and the urgent need to expand and coordinate the credit facilities available to the rural sector. The RBI has set up a separate Agricultural Department to maintain an expert staff to study all questions of agricultural credit and coordinate the operation of the bank with other agencies providing agricultural finance. The RBI does not provide finance directly to the agriculturists, but through agencies like cooperative banks, land development banks, commercial bank etc. After the establishment of the National Bank for Agriculture and Rural Development (NABARD) on July 12, 1982, all the functions of the RBI relating to rural credit have been transferred to this new agency.

(b) ***Reserve Bank of India and Industrial Finance.*** The Reserve Bank of India has taken initiative in setting up statutory corporations at the all-India and regional levels to function as specialised institutions for term lending. The first of these institutions was the Industrial Finance Corporation of India set up in 1948. Followed by the State Finance corporations in each of the state from 1953 onwards. The RBI has also helped in the establishment of other financial institutions such as the Industrial Development Bank of India, the Industrial Reconstruction Bank of India, Small Industries Development Bank of India. Unit trust of India, etc. For the promotion of foreign trade the Reserve Bank has established the Export and Import Bank of India. Similarly, for the development of the housing industry the RBI has established the National Housing Bank.

Furthermore, the Deposit Insurance and Credit Guarantee Corporation (DICGC), a wholly owned subsidiary of the Reserve Bank, operates credit guarantee schemes with objective of providing cover against defaults in repayment of loans made to small borrowers, including small-scale industrial borrowers, in order that credit flow to them is enlarged.

C. Supervisory Functions

Over the years, extensive powers have been conferred on the Reserve Bank of India for supervision and control of banking institutions. The Banking Regulation Act 1949, provides wide powers to the Reserve Bank to regulate and control the activities of Banks to safeguard the interests of depositors. Amendment Act passed in 1963, and effective from February 1, 1964, provided further powers to the Reserve Bank, particularly to restrain control exercised by particular groups of persons over the affairs of bank and to restrict loans and advances as well as guarantees given by the bank to or on behalf of any one company, firm, association of persons, and gave greater control to the Reserve Bank over the appointment and removal of bank's executive personnel.

The various aspects of the supervisory / regulatory functions exercised by the Reserve Bank may be briefly mentioned as under :

1. Licensing of Banks

There is a statutory provision that a company starting banking business in India has first to obtain a licence from the Reserve Bank. If the Reserve Bank is dissatisfied on account of the defective features of the proposed company, it can refuse to grant the licence. The bank is also empowered to cancel the license of a bank when it will cease to carry on banking business in India.

2. Approval of Capital, Reserves and Liquid Assets of Bank

The Reserve Bank examines whether the minimum requirements of capital, reserve and liquid assets are fulfilled by the banks and approves them.

3. Branch Licensing Policy

The Reserve Bank exercises its control over expansion of branches by the banks through its branch licensing policy.

In September 1978, the RBI formulated a comprehensive branch licensing policy with a view to accelerate the pace of expansion of bank offices in the rural areas. This was meant to correct regional imbalance of the banking coverage in the country.

4. Inspection of Banks

The Reserve Bank is empowered to conduct inspection of banks. The inspection may relate to various aspects such as the bank's organisational structure, branch expansion, mobilisation of deposits, investments, credit portfolio management, credit appraisal profit planning, manpower planning, as well as assessment of the performance of banks in developmental areas such as deployment of credit to the priority sectors, etc. The bank may conduct investigation whenever there are complain about major irregularities or frauds by certain banks. The inspections are basically meant to improve the working of the banks and safeguard the interests of depositors and thereby develop a sound banking system in the country.

5. Control over Management

The Reserve bank also looks into the management side of the banks. The appointments re-appointment or termination of appointment of the chairman and chief executive officer of a private sector bank is to be approved by the Reserve Bank. The bank's approval is also required for the remuneration, perquisites and post retirement benefits given by a bank to its chairman and chief executive officer.

The Boards of the public sector banks are to be constituted by the Central Government in consultation with the Reserve Bank.

6. Control over Methods

The Reserve Bank exercises strict control over the methods of operation of the banks to ensure that no improver investment and injudicious advances made by them.

7. Audit

Banks are required to get their balance sheets and profits and loss accounts duly audited by the auditors approved by the Reserve Bank. In the case of the SBI, the auditors are appointed by the Reserve Bank.

8. Credit Information Service

The Reserve Bank is empowered to collect information about credit facilities granted by individual bank and supply the relevant information in a consolidated manner to the bank and other financial institutions seeking such information.

9. Control over Amalgamation and Liquidation

The banks have to obtain the sanction of the Reserve Bank for any voluntary amalgamation. The Reserve Bank in consultation with the central government can also suggest compulsory reconstruction or amalgamation of a bank. It also supervises banks in liquidation. The liquidation have to submit to the Reserve Bank returns showing their positions. The Reserve Bank keeps a watch on the progress of liquidation proceedings and the expenses of liquidation.

10. Deposit Insurance

To protect the interest of depositors, banks are required to insure their deposits with the Deposit Insurance Corporation. The Reserve Bank of India has promoted such a corporation in 1962, which has been renamed in 1978 as the Deposit Insurance and Credit Guarantee Corporation.

11. Training and Banking Education

The RBI has played an active role in making institutional arrangement for providing training and banking education to the bank personnel, with a view to improve their efficiency.

In brief, the Reserve Bank of India is performing both traditional central banking functions and developmental functions for the steady growth of the Indian economy.

Credit Control

Commercial banks grant loans and advances to merchants and manufacturers. They create credit or bank deposits in the process of granting loans. In modern times, bank deposits are regarded as money. They are as good as cash. They can be used for the purchase of goods or in payment of debts. But excessive creation of credit by commercial bank leads to inflation. Inflation has serious social and economic consequence. For instance, people with fixed incomes, workers and salaried persons suffer greatly on account of rising prices. So a Central Bank must control the credit created by commercial banks in order to maintain the value of money at a stable level. Similarly, excessive contraction of credit leads to deflation. Deflation leads to unemployment and suffering among workers. Under such circumstances the central bank should encourage credit creation. Hence it is essential that the creation of credit is kept with in reasonable limits by the central bank. The central bank has to control and regulate the availability of credit, the cost of cost and the use of credit flow in the economy. Credit control is an important function of the central bank. The central bank is in a position to control credit in its capacity as the bank of issue and the custodian of the cash reserves of the commercial bank.

Weapons of Credit Control

Various weapons or methods or instruments are available to the Reserve Bank of India to control credit creation or contraction by commercial banks. These methods are divided into two categories.

A. Quantitative or general methods or instruments.

B. Quanlitative or selective methods or instruments.

A. Quantitative or General Methods

These are traditional methods of credit control. These methods have only a quantitative effect on the supply of credit. They are use for either increasing or reducing the volume of credit. They cannot control credit for its quality. The important quantitative methods or instruments of credit control are as follows.

1. Bank Rate

The bank rate is the rate of interest at which the Reserve Bank of India makes advances to the commercial banks against approved securities or rediscounts the eligible bills of exchange and other commercial papers. The Reserve Bank of India Act, 1934 defines the bank rate as "the standard rate at which it (the Bank) is prepared to buy or rediscount bills of exchange or other commercial paper eligible for purchase under the Act." The change in the bank rate leads to changes in the market rates of interest i.e., short-term as well as long-term interest rates. If bank rate is raised rates of interest in the money market including the lending rates of commercial banks also rise. So the cost of credit rises. The demand for bank loans generally falls and so the demand for goods will also fall. Thus inflation can be checked or controlled by raising bank rate. Similarly, deflation (i.e., state of falling prices) can be checked by lowering the bank rate. So the bank rate acts as a "pace-setter" in the money market.

The Reserve Bank of India has changed the bank rate from time to time to meet the changing conditions of the economy. The bank rate was raised for the first time, from 3 percent to 3½ percent, in November 1951, with a view to checking an undue expansion of bank credit. The bank rate was further raised to 4 percent on May 16, 1959. In February 1965, the bank rate was further raised to 6 percent. In March 1968, however, the bank rate was reduced to 5 percent with a view to stimulating recovery from the industrial recession of 1967. In January 1971. the bank rate was, however raised to 6 percent as an anti-inflationary device. Subsequently the bank rates was raised to 10 percent in July 1981 and to 12 percent in October 1991. The bank rate was, however, reduced to 10 percent in June 1997. The increases in the bank rate were adopted to reduce bank credit and control inflationary pressures. The Reserve Bank of India has made only a modest use of this instrument.

2. Open Market Operations

Open market operations consist of buying and selling of government securities by the Reserve Bank. Open market operations have a direct effect on the availability and cost of credit. When the central bank purchases securities from the banks, it increases their cash reserve position and hence, their credit creation capacity. On the other hand, when the central bank sells securities to the banks, it reduces their cash reserves and the creidt creation capacity. The Reserve Bank of India did not rely much on open market operations to control credit. It was not used for influencing the availability of credit. Due to under-developed security market, the open market operations of the Reserve Bank are restricted to Government securities. These operations have also been used as a tool of public debt management. They assist the Indian government to raise borrowings. During 1951-52 the sale of securities was more. But in 1961 the purchases were more. This proves that it is not used to credit restraint only.

In India, the open market operations of the Reserve Bank has not been so effective because of the following reasons.

(a) Open market operations are restricted to government securities.

(b) Gift-edged market is narrow.

(c) Most of the open market operations are in the nature of "switch operations" (i.e., purchasing one loan against the other).

3. Cash-Reserve Requirement (CRR)

The central bank of a country can change the cash-reserve requirement of the commercial banks in order to affect their credit creation capacity. An increase in the cash-reserve ratio reduces the excess reserves of the banks and a decrease in the cash-reserve ratio increases their excess reserves. The variability in cash-reserve ratios directly affects the availability and cost of credit. Originally, the Reserve Bank of India Act, 1934 required the commercial banks to keep with the Reserve Bank a minimum cash reserve of 5% of their demand liabilities and 2% of time liabilities. The amendment of the Act in 1962 removes the distinction between demand and time deposits and authorises the Reserve Bank to change cash reserve ratio between 3 and 15%. The method of variable cash-reserve ratio is the most direct, immediate and the most effective method to credit control.

The Reserve Bank of India used the technique of variable cash reserve ratio for the first time in June, 1973. It raised the cash reserve ratio from 3 to 5% in June. 1973. The cash-reserve ratio was further raised to 7% in September 1973. Since then, the Reserve Bank has raised or reduced the cash reserve ratio many times. Recently, the cash reserve ratio was raised to 11% effective from July 30, 1988 and to 15% with effect from July 1989. The present cash-reserve ratio is 13%. This method is mainly intended to control and stabilise the prices of commodities, stocks and shares and prevent speculation and hoarding. The Reserve Bank used the CRR as a drastic measure to curb credit expansion.

4. Statutory Liquidity Ratio (SLR)

Under the Banking Regulation Act, 1949, banks are required to maintain liquid assets in the form of cash, gold and unencumbered approved securities equal to not less than 25% of their total demand and time deposits. This minimum statutory liquidity ratio is in addition to the statutory cash-reserve ratio. Maintenance of adequate liquid assets is a basic principle of sound banking. The Reserve Bank has been empowered to change the minimum liquidity ratio. Accordingly, the liquidity ratio was raised from 25% to 30% in November 1972, to 32% in 1973, to 35% in October 1981, to 38% in January 1988, and to 38.5% in September 1990. There are two reasons for raising the statutory liquidity requirements or ratio by the Reserve Bank of India. They are :

(a) It reduces commercial bank's capacity to create credit and thus helps to check inflationary pressures.

(b) It makes larger resources available to the government.

In view of the Narasimham committee report, the government decided to reduce the statutory liquidity ratio in stages over a 3 year period from 38.5% to 25%. As a first step in this direction, it was reduced to 38% in April 1992. The statutory liquidity ratio was reduced to 37.75% in March 1993 and to 33.75% in September 1994. The statutory liquidity ratio was further reduced to 32.75% in April 1997.

B. Selective Credit Controls

Selective credit controls are qualitative credit control measures undertaken by the central bank to divert the flow of credit from speculative and unproductive activities to productive and more urgent activities. Selective credit controls are better than the quantitative credit controls in many respects. They encourage credit to essential industries and at the same time discourage credit to non-essential industries. Similarly, they encourage productive activities and at the same time discourage speculative activities. In a developing economy like India, qualitative credit controls are mainly intended for the following purposes :

(a) To prevent anti-social use of credit like speculative hoarding of stock.

(b) To divert credit from unproductive activities to productive activities.

(c) To divert credit from non-essential to essential industries.

(d) To encourage credit for certain sectors like priority sector.

Methods of Selective Credit Controls Adopted by Reserve Bank

The Banking Regulation Act, 1949, granted wide powers to the Reserve Bank of India to adopt selective methods of credit control. The Act empowered the Reserve Bank to issue directions to the banks regarding their advances. These directive may relate to the following.

(a) The purpose for which advances may or may not be made.

(b) The margins to be maintained on secured loans.

(c) The maximum amount of advances to any firm or company, and

(d) The rate of interest to be charged.

The Reserve Bank of India has undertaken the following selective credit controls to check speculative and inflationary pressures and extend credit to productive activities.

1. Variation of Margin Requirements

The "margin" is the difference between the "loan value" and the "market value" of securities offered by borrowers against secured loans. By fixing the margin requirements on secured loans, the central bank does not permit the commercial banks to lend to their customers the full value of the securities offered by them, but only a part of their market value. For example, if the central bank prescribes the margin requirements at 40%, that means that the commercial banks can lend only 60% of the market value of the securities of the customers. If the margin is raised to 50%; the banks can lend only 50% of the market value of the securities to the customers. Thus, by changing the margin requirements, the amount of loan made by the banks can be changed in accordance with the policy of the central government. If the central bank raises the margin requirements, the amount of bank advances against securities will be automatically reduced. As a result the bank credit will be diverted from the field of speculative activities to the other fields of productive investments. If, on the contrary, the central bank lowers down the margin requirements, the amount of bank advances to the customers against securities can be automatically increased. Thus by altering margin requirements from time to time, the central bank keeps on changing the volume of bank loans to the borrowers. This method is an effective way of checking the flow of credit to less productive and less desirable uses in the economy.

The Reserve Bank of India has been increasingly using this method in recent years to control bank advances against essential commodities like food-grains, oil-seeds, sugar etc. The main object is to prevent speculative dealings in such commodities. In 1957, the margin against loans on food-grains was increased to 40% and again to 60% in 1970. In March, 1977, the minimum margin was fixed at 85% on advances against stocks of ground-nut oil, castor oil etc. This was done to check undue rise in the price of oil-seeds and vanaspathi. The margin requirements were also increased in the case of pulses, sugar, vanaspathi and oil-seeds in subsequent years. 1984-85 the maximum margins on bank advances against stocks of food-grains was 45% in the case of mills and 60% in the case of others. Reserve Bank has been using this method flexibly according to the needs of the situation. The margin requirements was increased when the prices are going up and decreased when the credit flow has to be increased.

2. Credit Authorisation Scheme (CAS)

Credit Authorisation Scheme is a type of selective credit control introduced by the Reserve Bank in November, 1965. Under the scheme, the Commercial banks had to obtain Reserve Bank's authorisation before sanctioning any fresh credit of Rs, I crore or more to any single party. The limit was later gradually raised to Rs. 6 crores in 1986, in respect of borrowers in private as well as public sector. Under this scheme, the Reserve Bank requires the commercial banks to collect, examine and supply detailed information regarding the borrowing concerns. The main purpose of this scheme is to keep a close watch on the flow of credit to the borrowers. This scheme requires the that the banks should lend to the large borrowing concerns on the basis of credit appraisal and actual requirements of the borrowers. But this scheme was abolished in 1982. Though the scheme has been abolished, the Reserve Bank, however, insists that the banks have to get its approval once the loans have been sanctioned by them to big borrowers. The Reserve Bank would monitor and scrutinise all sanctions of bank loans exceeding Rs. 5 crores to any single party for working capital requirements, and Rs. 2 crores in the case of term loans. This post-sanction scheme has been called "Credit Monitoring Arrangement" (CMA)

3. Control of Bank Advances

This is also used as selective control method. The Reserve Bank has fixed from time to time maximum limits for some kinds of loans and advances. In May 1956, the Reserve Bank issued a directive asking all the commercial banks in the country to restrict their advances against paddy and rice. This directive was issued to check speculative hoarding of paddy and rice. In September 1956, these restrictions were applied to cover food-grains, pulses and cotton textiles. In 1970, the maximum limit for loans against shares and debentures was fixed to Rs. 5 lakhs. This was done to prevent speculation in shares with the help of bank loans.

4. Differential Interest Rates

In 1966, the Reserve Bank announced the policy of "Selective Liberalisation of Credit". According to this policy, the Reserve Bank encouraged credit to defence industries, export industries and food-grains for procurement by government agencies. The Reserve Bank agreed to provide refinance at the bank rate in respect of advances to the above industries. At the same time it made credit dearer for other purposes.

5. Credit Squeeze Policy

Since 1973, the Reserve Bank has adopted a "Credit squeeze policy" or dear money policy as an anti-inflationary measure. This policy aims at curbing overall loanable resources of banks and also enhancing the cost or credit of borrowers from banks.

6. Moral Suasion

This method involves advice, request and persuasion with the commercial banks to co-operate with the central bank in implementing its credit policies. The Reserve Bank has also been using moral suasion as a selective credit control measure from 1956. It has been sending periodic letters to the commercial banks to use restraint over their credit policies in general and in respect of certain commodities and unsecured loans in particular. In June 1957, the banks were advised to reduce advances against agricultural commodities. Regular meetings and discussions are also held by the Reserve Bank with commercial banks to impress upon them the need for their co-operation in the effective implementation of the monetary policy.

Selective credit controls are flexible. They can be tightened, relaxed, withdrawn and re-imposed according to price situation in the market. For influencing the purpose and direction of credit. The Reserve Bank has been using various selective credit controls. It should be noted that qualitative methods are not competitive but complementary to quantitative methods of credit control. Both methods should be employed to control credit created by commercial banks.

Limitations of Selective Controls in India

The Reserve Bank implemented various measures of qualitative control to channelise the flow of credit into productive sectors and restricted the financing of speculative and unproductive activities. The successful operation of selective credit controls, however, suffers from the following limitations:

(a) Traders mostly use their own finance for holding stocks of commodities. This self-financing or private financing reduces the rate of bank finance and its influence.

(b) Traders may manage to get credit from non-controlled sectors and use it in controlled sectors. It is very difficult to ensure that the borrowers use the amount for the purpose for which it is borrowed.

(c) The Reserve Bank has no control over the activities of non-banking financial institutions as well as indigenous bankers. These institutions and bankers play a significant role in financing trade and industry in Indian economy.

(d) The Reserve Bank is not fully equipped with tools and powers to control effectively the inflationary trends in the country. Its general and selective controls are effective only to the extent to which inflationary pressures are the result of bank finance. But the Reserve Bank's credit control measures may not prove effective in case, the inflationary pressures are caused by deficit financing and shortage of goods.

(e) Existence of large quantity of money in the black market also poses a serious limitation to the credit policy of the Reserve Bank. Speculation and hoarding are also carried on with the help of black money. The Reserve Bank could not exercise its effective control over the expansion of black money in the Indian economy.

The methods of selective control are more suitable for under developed countries like India. It is essential to divert credit to more essential industries for speedier economic development. The methods of selective credit control can prove helpful in the achievement of this objective. If the Reserve Bank has not undertaken different selective control methods to check inflationary pressures, the price position in the country might have been some what worse. The selective credit controls, if they are applied along with quantitative credit control methods, have a great role to play in our planned economy.

Monetary Policy of the Reserve Bank of India

Monetary policy, generally refers to those policy measures of the central bank which are adopted to control and regulate the volume of currency and credit in a country. According to Paul Einzig, an ideal monetary policy may be defined "as an effort to reduce to a minimum the disadvantages and increase the advantages resulting from the existence and operation of a monetary system." Broadly speaking, by monetary policy is meant the policy pursued by the central bank of a country for administering and controlling country's money supply including currency and demand deposits and managing the foreign exchange rates.

Reserve Bank of India and Monetary Controls

The main objective of monetary policy pursued by the Reserve Bank of India is that of 'controlled monetary expansion'. In order to achieve this objective the Reserve Bank has at its disposal various instruments, the important among these are as follows.

1. Quantitative requirements and
2. Qualitative or selective controls.

In a developing country like India, the most important objective of monetary policy should be that of 'controlled monetary expansion'. Controlled monetary expansion implies two things.

(a) Expansion in the supply of money and

(b) Restraint on the secondary expansion of credit.

(a) Expansion in the supply of money

In a developing country like India, money supply has to be expanded sufficiently to match the growth of real national income. Although it is difficult to say what relation the rate of increase in money supply should bear to the rate of growth in national income, more generally, the rate of increase in money supply should be somewhat higher than the projected rate of growth of real national income for two reasons.

(i) As incomes grow the demand for money as one of the components of savings tends to increase.

(ii) Increase in money supply is also necessitated by gradual reduction of non-monetised sector of the economy.

In India, the rate of increase in money supply has been far in excess of the rate of growth in real national income. It has resulted, to a large extent, in the creation of consistent inflationary pressures in the economy.

(b) Restraint on the secondary expansion of credit

Government budgetary deficits for financing a part of the investment outlays constitute an important source of monetary expansion in India. It is, therefore essential to restrain the secondary expansion of credit. While exercising restraints, care should be taken that the legitimate requirements of agriculture, industry and trade are not adversely affected. The Reserve Bank has also to channelise credit into the vital sectors of the economy, specially the priority sectors.

In order to achieve the twin gol goals, it is essential to formulate a monetary policy which may regulate the flow of credit to desired sectors. So far as the choice of instruments of the monetary policy is concerned, the Reserve Bank of India has a very limited scope in this respect. The Reserve Bank has at its disposal both quantitative (traditional) and qualitative (selective) methods to control credit. In the past, the Reserve Bank has employed bank rate, open market operations, variable reserves ratio and selective credit controls as the instruments to restrain the secondary expansion of credit.

The progress of the various methods of credit control, contemplated by the Reserve Bank of India suggests that the objective of monetary policy i.e., 'controlled monetary expansion' has been realised to a limited extent. While the supply of money has increased in a greater proportion than the national income, the restraints on the expansion of credit have been rather weak and ineffective. In spite of the various methods employed by the Reserve Bank to contain the inflationary pressures, the general price level has been showing a rising trend. It leads up to this inevitable conclusion that there is something wrong with the monetary policy pursued by the Reserve Bank of India in the recent post. The policy should be that of 'controlled contraction' rather than 'controlled expansion'.

However, if we take into account the nature of the Indian economy and the needs of developmental finance, it would be a folly on our part to adopt a monetary policy of 'controlled contraction'. India is a developing economy, and for the overall development of the various sectors like agriculture, industry, trade, commerce, transport, and foreign trade, availability of huge financial resources is essential. With the concept of developmental planning gaining momentum, the availability of monetary resources in sufficient quantity becomes all the more essential. With limited supply of money the Indian economy will not be able to achieve the objective of self-sustained economic growth. Therefore, the RBI will have to continue with the policy of controlled expansion. The only change that the RBI has to introduce is that it will have to implement the various restraints on the expansion of credit more vigorously and with great authority

Limitations of Monetary Policy

A major failure of the monetary policy in India lies on the price front. The monetary authorities have not been in a position to curb an inflationary rise in price which has often taken violent jumps at intervals. A number of causes account for this failure.

(a) Monetary policy, to be effective, should be able to regulate supply and cost of credit. The Reserve Bank tries to do by controlling the activities of commercial banks and to some extent of co-operative banks. But the proportion of total credit provided by non-banking institutions and other agencies is much higher. The impulses generated by the Reserve Bank have thus a limited impact.

(b) In relation to commercial banks the task of the Reserve Bank is rendered difficult by the limitations inherent in the various instruments of monetary control.

(c) In part the freedom to curtain Reserve Bank accommodation for banks is also constrained by the fact that the device of offering preferential facilities has been used for encouraging banks to lend to such sectors with so many windows opened for refinance as an adjunct to efforts to change the long-term pattern of bank finance, it becomes difficult for the Reserve Bank to close these special windows just when the banks may find it necessary or tempting to use these special facilities.

(d) There is a special consideration that hitherto neglected sectors should be shielded as for as possible from credit curbs. This markes the task of the monetary policy more difficult.

(e) The type of the policy the Reserve Bank has pursued so far requires the presence of a sound statistical and monitoring system. Any defects in this system make it difficult to bring about a speedy and appropriate turn around in credit trends.

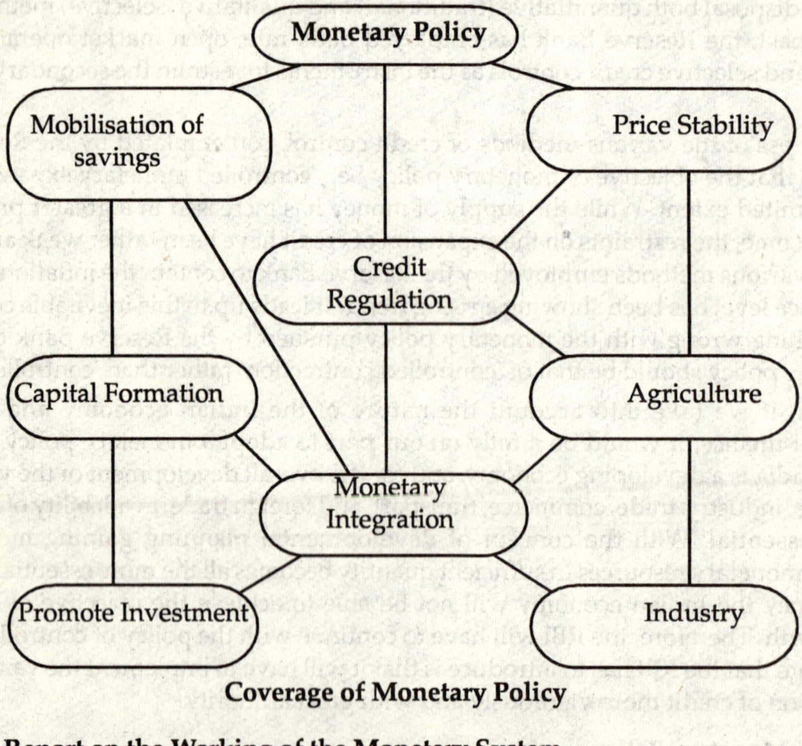

Coverage of Monetary Policy

Chakravarthy Report on the Working of the Monetary System

The committee to review the working of the monetary system headed by S. Chakravarthy submitted its report to the RBI in April 1985. In its terms of reference this committee was required to provide a review of the monetary system and recommend measures for making monetary policy more effective. The committee dealt particularly with the objectives of monetary policy; coordination between monetary policy and fiscal policy; regulation of money supply; maintenance of price stability;

interest rate policy and utilisation of credit. Its main recommendations are as fallows.

(a) The committee had stressed the need to pursue price stability as the primary objective of the monetary policy. However, it suggested that this objective should not come in conflict with the other socio economic goals embodied in the five year plans. The committee pointed out that the major factor that contributed to **colossal** increase in the money supply had been the RBI's credit to the government. The committee thus recommended that an appropriate framework for the regulation of the RBI's credit to the government should be evolved.

(b) The official concept of budgetary deficit did not allow in the past to clearly know the monetary impact of fiscal operations. The committee, therefore, suggested a change in the definition of budgetary deficit. The budgetary deficit of the Central Government was measured in terms of an increase in treasury bills. In the opinion of the committee, this overstated the extent of the monetary impact of fiscal operations because no distinction was made between the absorption of treasury bills and the increase in the holdings of treasury bills by the RBI.

(c) The committee was of the view that banks should have greater freedom in determining their lending rates. This would prevent unnecessary use of credit which presently is possible due to relatively low rates. Further the committee strongly felt that concessional interest rates as a redistributive device should be used in a very selective manner.

(d) The committee did not favour continuance of cash credit as the predominant form of bank credit. In its opinion, certain measures should be undertaken to encourage loans and bills finance forms of bank credit. It also stressed the importance of credit system in the area of priority sector lending. This would enable adequate and timely flow of credit to the priority sectors.

(e) The committee was of the view that the money market in India should be restructured. In its opinion, in the restructured monetary system the treasury bills market, the call money market, the commercial bills market and the inter-corporate funds market should play an important role in the allocation of short term resources. The committee also recommended that the RBI should adopt all the measures which are necessary to develop an efficient money market in this country.

The major recommendations of the Chakravarthy Committee were accepted and have been implemented. The committee had stressed the need for developing aggregate monetary targets to ensure orderly monetary growth. The government has thus on an experimental basis carried out an exercise to evolve such targets in consultation with the RBI. The government has also accepted in principle that increase in entire RBI credit to the government should be reflected in the budget in addition to the narrowly defined figure of the budget deficit. Keeping in view the recommendations of the committee the yields on long-term government securities have been increased and the maturities have been reduced. Moreover, now treasury bills of 364 days maturity are being issued by the RBI. These short-term instruments with flexible rates would enable banks to manage their liquidity better and help in evolving an active secondary market in short term instruments.

The Narasimham Committee Report (1991)

The Government of India set up a nine-member committee under the chairmanship of M. Narasimham, a former Governor of the Reserve Bank of India, to examine all aspects relating to the structure, organisation, functions and procedures of the financial system. This committee on the financial system submitted its report in November 1991. In order to improve the functioning of the financial sector, particularly the banking sector in India, Narasimham Committee has suggested wide-ranging measures.

Recommendations of the Committee

Narasimham Committee made a number of recommendations to improve the productivity, efficiency and profitability of the banking sector. The main recommendations of the committee are :

1. Structural reorganisation of the banking structure

To bring about greater efficiency in banking operations, the Narasimham Committee proposed a substantial reduction in the number of public sector banks through mergers and acquisitions. According to the committee, the broad pattern should consist of :

(a) 3 or 4 large banks (including the State Bank of India) which could became international in character.

(b) 8 to 10 national banks with a network of branches throughout the country engaged in general or universal banking

(c) Local banks whose operations would be generally confined to a specific region; and

(d) Rural banks including Regional Rural Banks mainly engaged in financing agriculture and allied activities in rural areas.

2. Licensing of branches

The committee proposed that the present system of licensing of branches should be discontinued. Banks should have the freedom to open branches purely on profitability considerations.

3. Freedom to foreign banks to open offices

The committee recommended that the Government should allow foreign banks to open offices in India either as branches or as subsidiaries. Foreign banks and Indian banks should be permitted to set up joint ventures in regard to merchant and investment banking, leasing and other forms of financial services.

4. Removal of the duality of control of banks

The committee recommended that the present system of dual control over the banking system between Reserve Bank and the Banking Division of the ministry of Finance should end immediately. Reserve Bank of India should be the primary agency for the regulations of the banking system.

5. Setting up of Assets Reconstruction Fund

Narasimaham committee recommended the setting up of the "Assets Reconstruction Fund" to take over from the nationalised banks and financial institutions, a portion of their bad and doubtful debts at a discount. All bad and doubtful debts of the banks were to be transferred in a phased manner to ensure smooth and effective functioning of the Assets Reconstruction Fund.

6. Special tribunals for recovery of loans

Banks at present face many difficulties in recovering the loans advanced by them. Therefore, the committee recommended that special tribunals should be set up for recovering loans granted by banks.

7. Directed credit programmes

The committee recommended that the system of directed credit programme should be gradually phased out. The concept of priority sector should be redefined to include only the weakest section of the rural community. The directed credit programme for the priority sector should be fixed at 10 percent of the aggregate bank credit. The committee argued that the system of directed credit should be temporary and not a permanent one.

8. Statutory Liquidity Ratio (SLR)

The committee recommended that the statutory liquidity ratio should be gradually reduced from the present 38.5 percent to 25 percent over the next five years.

9. Cash Reserve Ratio (CRR)

The committee recommended that CRR should be progressively reduced from the present high level of 15 percent to 3 to 5 percent.

10. De-regulation of interest rates

The committee recommended that all controls and regulations on interest rates on lending and deposit rates of banks and financial institutions should be removed.

11. Capital adequacy

The committee proposed that banks should achieve 8 percent capital adequacy ratio as recommended by Basle Committee by March 1996.

12. Banks in the private sector

The committee recommended that the Reserve Bank of India should permit the setting up of new banks in the private sector, provided they satisfy all the conditions and norms prescribed by the Reserve Bank. Further, there should be no difference in treatment between public sector banks and private sector banks.

13. Raising capital through the capital market

Profitable banks and banks with good reputation should be permitted to raise capital from the public throught he capital market. Regarding other banks, the government should subscribe to their capital or give a loan. Which should be treated as a subordinate debt, to meet their capital requirements.

14. Proper classification of assets

The committee recommended that the assets of bank should be classified into 4 categories : (a) Standard (b) sub-standard (c) doubtful and (d) loss assets. Full disclosures of assets and liabilities should be made in the balance-sheets of banks and financial institutions as per the International Accounting Standards reflecting he real state of affairs.

15. Free and autonomous banks

The committee recommended that the public sector banks should be free and autonomous.

16. Liberalisation of capital market

The committee recommended liberalisation of the capital market. The office of the "controller of Capital Issues" should be abolished. There should be no need to get prior permission from any agency to issue capital. The capital market should be opened for foreign portfolio investments.

The recommendations of the Narasimham committee (1991) were revolutionary in many respects. Most of the recommendations have been accepted by the government and implemented during the 8th Five year plan.

The Goiporia Committee Report (1991)

Banking in India has made a remarkable progress in its growth and expansion, as well as business. But the quality of customer service has deteriorated day-by-day. To meet the new challenges in the changing environment of liberalised financial system. Indian banks have to be modernised, become more efficient and competitive. The banking sector has to face stiff competition from mutual funds started by various financial institutions and schemes launched by the Unit Trust of India. The saving instruments of non-banking financial institutions, and various small saving schemes of government are more attractive from the investing public point of view. As a result the annual growth rate in deposits has remained almost stagnant in recent years. Improving "customer service' is one of the major steps the banks are required to take for greater deposit mobilisation. The Reserve Bank of India appointed committees from time to time to make necessary recommendations for improvement in customer service. In September, 1990, the Reserve Bank of India set up a committee under the chairmanship of Sri M.N. Goiporia to examine the problem of customer service in banks and suggest measures to improve the situation.

Recommendation of Goiporia Committee

The committee submitted its report on 6th December, 1991. Main recommendations of the committee are as follows :

(a) Extension of banking hours for all transactions, except cash.

(b) Change in the commencement of working hour for bank staff to facilitate timely opening of bank counters.

(c) Immediate credit of outstation cheques upto Rs. 5000/- as against Rs. 2,500/- at present.

(d) Enhancement of interest rate on saving account.

(e) Introduction of tax benefits against bank deposits.

(f) Full use of discretionary powers vested in the bank staff at all levels.

(g) Expeditious despatch of documents lodged for collection.

(h) Extension of teller's duties.

(i) Modernisation of banks.

(j) Opening of specialisation branches for different customer groups.

(k) Introduction of a new instrument in the form of bank order.

(l) Introduction of restricted holidays in banks.

Most of the recommendations were accepted by the Reserve Bank of India, and are being implemented.

The Narasimham Committee Report (1998)

The Finance Ministry of the Government of India set up "Banking Sector Reforms Committee" under the chairmanship of Mr. M. Narsimham in 1998. This committee submitted its report in April, 1998 to the Government of India. Important findings and recommendations of the Narasimham committee (1998) are as fallows.

1. Need for a Stronger Banking System

The Narasimham committee has made out a strong case for a stronger banking system in the country. For this purpose, the committee has recommended the merger of strong banks which will have a "multiplier effect" on industry. The committee has also supported that two or three large strong banks be given international or global character.

2. Experiment with the concept of narrow banking

The committee has suggested the adoption of the concept of "narrow banking" to rehabilitate weak banks.

3. Small, Local banks

The committee has suggested the setting up of small, local banks, which would be confined to states or cluster of districts in order to serve local trade, small industry and agriculture.

4. Capital adequacy ratio

The committee has suggested higher capital adequacy requirements for banks. It has also suggested the setting up of an "Asset Reconstruction Fund" to take over the bad debts of the banks.

5. Review and update banking laws

The Narasimham committee (1998) has suggested the urgent need to review and amend the provisions of Reserve Bank of India Act, Banking regulation Act, State Bank of India Act and Bank Nationalisation Act so as to bring them in line with the current needs of the banking industry.

Role of RBI in Economic Development

The Reserve Bank is India's central bank. It occupies a pivotal position in the monetary and banking structure of our country. It is the apex monetary institution in the country. It supervises, regulates, controls and develops the monetary and financial system of the country. It performs all the typical functions of a good central bank. It also performs a number of developmental and promotional functions. It also assists the government in its economic planning. The bank's credit planning is devised and co-ordinated with the Five year plans. It assists the government in the great task of nation building.

Contribution to Economic Development

Since its inception in 1935, The Reserve Bank of India has functioned with great success, not only as the apex financial institution in the country but also as the promoter of economic development. With the introduction of planning in India since 1951, the Reserve Bank formulated a new monetary policy to aid and speed up economic development. The Reserve Bank has undertaken several new functions to promote economic development in the country. The major contributions of the Reserve Bank to economic development are as follows ;

1. Promotion of Commercial Banking

A well-developed banking system is a pre-condition for economic development. The Reserve Bank has taken several steps to strengthen the banking system. The Banking Regulation Act. 1949 has given the Reserve Bank vast powers of supervision and control of commercial banks in the country. The Reserve Bank has been using these powers :

(a) To strengthen the commercial banking structure through liquidation and amalgamation of banks, and through improvement in their operational standards

(b) To extend the banking facilities in the semi-urban and rural areas and

(c) To promote the allocation of credit in favour of priority sectors, such as agriculture, small-scale industries, exports etc.

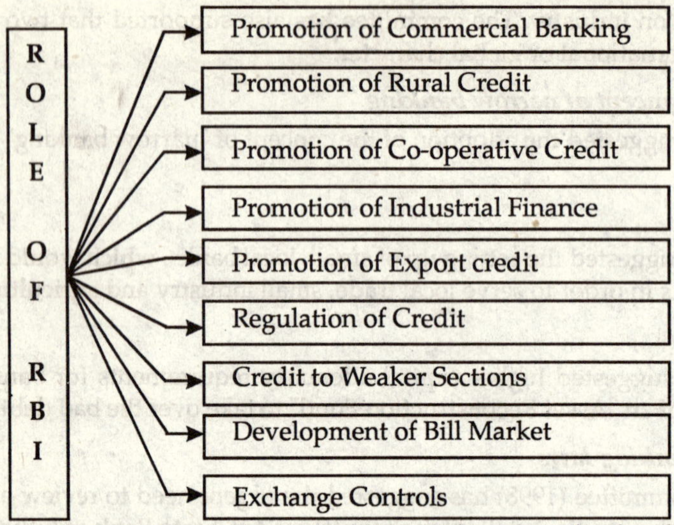

The Reserve Bank is also making valuable contribution to the development of banking system by extending training facilities, to the supervisory staff of the banks through its 'Banker's training colleges.

2. Promotion of Rural Credit

Defective rural credit system and deficient rural credit facilities are one of the major causes of backwardness of Indian agriculture. In view of this, the Reserve Bank, ever since its establishment, has been assigned the responsibility of reforming rural credit system and making provision of adequate institutional finance for agriculture and other rural activities. The Reserve Bank has taken the following steps to promote rural credit :

(a) It has set up Agricultural Credit Department to expand and co-rodinate credit facilities to the rural areas.

(b) It has been taking all necessary measures to strength the co-operative credit system with a view to meet the financial needs of the rural people.

(c) In 1956, the Reserve Bank set-up two funds. Namely, the National Agriculture Credit (long-term operations) Fund, and the National Agricultural Credit (stabilisation) Fund, for providing medium-term and long-term loans to the state co-operative banks.

(d) Regional rural banks have been established to promote agricultural credit.

(e) Some commercial bank have been nationalised mainly to expand bank credit facilities in rural areas.

(f) The National Bank for agriculture and Rural Development has been established in 1982 as the apex institution for agricultural finance.

(g) The Reserve Bank has helped the establishment of many warehouses in the country.

As a result of the efforts made by the Reserve Bank, the institutional finance for agriculture has been increasing considerably over the years. The agricultural output has increased by leaps and bounds. Probably no other central bank in the world is doing so much to help, develop and finance agricultural credit.

3. Promotion of Co-operative Credit

Promotion of co-operative credit movement is also the special function of the Reserve Bank. On the recommendations of the Rural Credit Survey Committee, the Reserve Bank has taken a number of measures to strengthen the structure of co-operative credit institutions throughout the country. The Reserve Bank provides financial assistance to the agriculturists through the co-operative institutions. The Reserve Bank has, thus, infused a new life into the co-operative credit movement of the country.

4. Promotion of Industrial Finance

Credit or finance is the pillar to industrial development. The Reserve Bank has been playing an active role in the field of industrial finance also. In 1957, it has set up a separate Industrial Finance Department which has rendered useful service in extending financial and organisation assistance to the institutions providening long-term finance. It made commendable efforts for broadening the domestic capital market for providing the medium and long-term finance to the industrial sector. In this regard the Reserve Bank took initiative in the establishment of a number of statutory corporations for the purpose of providing finance, especially medium and long-term finance, to industries; Industrial Development Bank of India, Industrial Finance Corporation of India, State Finance Corporations, State Industrial Development Corporations and the Industrial Credit and Investment Corporation of India are some of important corporations established in the country with the initiative of the Reserve Bank. The Reserve Bank has contributed to the share capital of these institutions and providing short-term advances also to some of them. The role of these corporations in providing financial help to industries is commendable. The Reserve Bank has played an active role in the establishment of the Unit Trust of India. The Unit Trust of India mobilises the savings of people belonging to middle and lower income groups and uses these funds for investment in industries. By mobilising the small savings of the people, the Unit Trust has been promoting capital formation which is the most important determinant of economic development. The Reserve Bank also has been encouraging commercial banks to provide credit to the small-scale industries. It has been encouraging credit for small industries through its "Credit Guarantee Scheme". Small-scale industries have been recognised as a priority sector. The Reserve Bank has also been, acting as a "developmental agency" for planning, promoting and developing industries to fill in the gaps in the industrial structure of the country.

5. Promotion of Export credit

"Export or Perish" has become a slogan for the developing economies, including India. In recent years, India is keen on expanding exports. Growth of exports needs liberal and adequate export credit. The Reserve Bank has undertaken a number of measures for increasing credit to the export sector. For promoting export financing by the banks, the Reserve Bank has introduced certain export credit schemes. The Export Bills Credit Scheme, and the Pre-shipment Credit Scheme are the two important schemes introduced by the Reserve Bank. The Reserve Bank has been stipulating concessional interest rates on various types of export credit granted by commercial banks. The Reserve Bank has been instrumental in the establishment of Export-Import Bank. The Exim Bank is to provide financial assistance to exporters and importers. The Reserve Bank has authority to grant loans and advances to the Exim Bank, under certain conditions.

6. Regulation of Credit

The Reserve Bank has been extensively using various credit control weapons to regulate the cost of credit, the amount of credit, and the purpose of credit. For regulating the cost and amount of credit the Reserve Bank has been using the quantitative weapons. For influencing the purpose and direction of credit, it has been using various selective credit controls. By regulating credit, the Reserve Bank has been able.

(a) To promote economic growth in the country.

(b) To check inflationary trends in the country.

(c) To prevent the financial resources from being used for speculative purposes.

(d) To make financial resources available for productive purposes keeping in view the priorities of the plans, and,

(e) To encourage savings in the country.

7. Credit to Weaker Sections

The Reserve Bank has taken certain measures to encourage adequate and cheaper credit to the weaker sections of the society. The "Differential Rate of Interest Scheme" was started in 1972. Under this scheme, concessional credit is provided to economically and socially backward persons engaged in productive activities. The Reserve Bank has been encouraging the commercial banks to give liberal credit to the weaker sections and for self employment schemes. The insurance and credit guarantee corporation of India gives guarantee for loans given to weaker sections.

8. Development of Bill Market

The Reserve Bank introduced the "Bill Market Scheme" in 1952, with a view to extend loans to the commercial banks against their demand promissory notes. The scheme, however, was not based on the genuine trade bills. In 1970, the Reserve Bank introduced "New Bill Market Scheme" which covered the genuine trade bills representing sale or despatch of goods. The bill market scheme has helped a lot in developing the bill market in the country. The bill market scheme has increased the liquidity of the money market in India.

9. Exchange Controls

The Reserve Bank has been able to maintain the stability of the exchange value of the "Rupee" even under heavy strains and pressure. It has also managed "exchange controls" successfully.

Inspite of the limitations under which it has to function in a developing country like India, the over all performance of the Reserve Bank is quite satisfactory. It has been able to develop the financial structure of the country consistent with the national socio-economic objectives and priorities. It has discharged its promotional and developmental functions satisfactorily and acted as the leader in economic development of the country.

Conclusion

From the above discussion, it is made clear that the Reserve Bank of India is the kingpin of the Indian money market. It issues notes, buys and sells government securities, regulates the volume, direction and cost of credit, manages foreign exchange and acts as banker to the government and banking institutions. The RBI is playing an active role in the development activities by helping the establishment and working of specialised institutions, providing term finance to agriculture, industry housing and foreign trade.

Questions for Discussions

1. Discuss the important functions of the Reserve Bank of India.
2. Explain the quantitative method employed by the Reserve Bank of India in order to make its credit policy effective.
3. "Selective credit control is a successful instrument of credit control policy of the Reserve Bank of India" Discuss with special reference to recent trends.
4. Describe briefly the working of the Narasimham Committee Reports.
5. Discuss the view that the right objective of Monetary policy in India currently should be "controlled contraction" and not "controlled expansion" of bank credit.
6. Examine the role of the Reserve Bank of India in economic development of India.

Chapter - 4

STATE BANK OF INDIA

Introduction

The Reserve Bank of India had been attempting to help the villagers through the state-co-operative banks but the extent of its assistance was very limited. At the same time, the need to help the farmers in all possible ways so as to increase agricultural production has been most pressing since Independence. The All India Rural Credit Survey Committee (AIRCSC) recommended the setting up of a State Bank of India, a commercial banking institution, with the special purpose of stimulating banking development in rural areas. The State Bank of India was set up in July 1, 1955, when it took over the assets and liabilities of the former Imperial Bank of India.

Capital

The State Bank of India has authorised share capital of Rs. 20 crores and an issued share capital of Rs. 5,625 crores which has been allotted to the Reserve Bank of India. The shares of the SBI are held by the Reserve Bank of India, insurance companies and the general public who were formerly shareholders of the Imperial Bank of India. The State Bank of India and its associate banks are engaged in the economic development of the country through a wide net work of 13,306 (30-6-2000) branches spread over the country. After 1955, there has been a steady increase in the assets and liabilities of the State Bank of India.

Management

The management of the State Bank vests in a Central Board constituted thus: A chairman and a Vice-chairman appointed by the Central Government in consultation with the Reserve Bank; not more than two Managing Directors appointed by the Central Board with the approval of the Central Government; six Directors elected by the shareholders other than the Reserve Bank; eight Directors nominated by the Central Government in consultation with the Reserve Bank to represent territorial and economic interests, not less than two of whom shall have special knowledge of the working of co-operative institutions and of the rural economy; one Director nominated by the Central Government; and one Director nominated by the Reserve Bank.

Functions

The State Bank of India performs all the functions of a commercial bank and acts as an agent of the Reserve Bank in those places were the latter has no branch offices. Further it is required to play a special role in rural credit, namely, promoting banking habits in the rural areas, mobilising rural savings and catering to their needs. It is expected to look after the banking development in the country. It provides financial assistance to the small scale industries and the co-operative institutions.

We can discuss the functions of the State Bank under the following three sub-heads :

A. Central Banking Functions

Though the State Bank is not the Central Bank of the country, yet it acts as the agent of the Reserve Bank in all those places where the latter does not have its own branches. As agent to the Reserve Bank, the State Bank performs some very important functions :-

(1) It acts as the Bankers Bank

It receives deposits from the commercial banks and also gives loans to them on demand. The State Bank rediscounts the bills of the commercial banks. It also acts as the clearing-house for the other commercial banks. In addition to this the State Bank also provides cheap remittance facilities to the commercial banks.

(2) It acts as the Government's Banker

It collects money from the public on behalf of the government and also makes payments in accordance with its instructions. The bank also manages the public debt of the Central and the State Governments.

B. Ordinary Banking Functions

The ordinary banking functions of the State Bank are as follows :

(1) Receiving deposits from the public

Like other commercial banks, the State Bank also receives different types of deposits from the public. The total deposits of the State Bank stood at Rs. 36,188 crores on 29th June, 1990. Of this amount, Rs. 7,105 crores were demand deposits and Rs. 29,083 crores were time deposits.

(2) Investment in Securities

Like other commercial banks, the State Bank invests its surplus funds in the Securities of Government of India, the State Governments, Railway Securities, Securities of Corporations and Treasury Bills. The total amount invested by the State Bank in these securities stood at Rs. 9,942 crores on 29th June 1990.

(3) Loans and Advances to Businessmen

The State Bank grants loans and advances to businessmen against the security of government papers, exchange bills, approved promissory notes and title deeds. The total advances of the State Bank to businessmen stood at Rs. 24,047 crores on 29th June 1990.

(4) Foreign Banking

In recent years, the State Bank of India has extended its foreign banking business. It has opened its branches in important world banking centres, such as Nassau, Singapore, Hong Kong, London, New York, Frankfurt etc. The Bank's foreign business is expanding every year. It has been able to give a new direction to its foreign business. The State Bank, in collaboration with leading foreign banks, has also been extending loans to foreign governments.

(5) Miscellaneous Work

The miscellaneous functions of the State Bank are as follows :

(a) The State Bank can receive securities, Jewels etc. for safe custody.

(b) Sale and purchase of gold, silver, bullion and coins.

(c) Safe custody of the valuables of its customers.

(d) Issuing of credit certificates to the customers.

(e) Issuing drafts on its own as well as the branches of the subsidiary banks.

(f) Telegraphic remittance of funds from one place to another place.

(g) Acting as the agent of the co-operative banks under certain circumstances.

(h) Working as the liquidator of banking companies and doing other miscellaneous jobs assigned to it by the Reserve Bank.

(i) The State Bank grants special credit facilities to small scale industries and co-operative societies.

C. Prohibited Business of the State Bank

The State Bank of India Act has enumerated certain business which cannot be done by the State Bank.

(a) The State Bank cannot grant loans against stocks and shares for a period exceeding six months. But, according to an amendment of the Act, made in 1957, the State Bank can grant loans to industries against their assets for a period of 7 years.

(b) The State Bank can purchase no immovable property except for its own offices.

(c) The State Bank cannot re-discount those bills which do not carry at least two good signatures.

(d) The State Bank could neither discount bills nor extend credit to individuals or firms above the sanctioned limit.

(e) The State Bank can neither re-discount nor offer loans against the security of those exchange bills whose period of maturity exceeds six months.

Role of the State Bank in Economic Development

Growth of banking facilities is indispensable for speedy economic development. By helping in the encouragement of small savings, mobilisation of savings and development of credit into the priority sectors, the State Bank of India is playing a significant role in India's economic development. The role of the SBI can be studied under the following heads.

1. The SBI and Small-scale Industries

State Bank Group has been the most important single source of institutional finance to small-scale industries in the country. The SBI has set up several pilot centres, to experiment with financing schemes. Through its Instalment Credit Scheme the SBI provides finances for the purchase of equipments and machinery by small and medium size business engaged in approved manufacturing industries. In 1967, the State Bank introduced the "Entrepreneur Scheme", under which credit to the small sector was based on the ability and competence of the entrepreneurs as well as the technical feasibility and economic viability of the project.

2. The SBI and Agricultural Credit

The SBI provides direct advances to farmers for all agricultural operations and indirect loans to Primary Co-operative Credit Societies, Farmers Service Societies, etc. The SBI Group provides agricultural advances for a variety of purposes which include loans to co-operative banks, advances to Land Development Banks, Village Adoption Scheme, Integrated Rural Development, Financial Assistance to marketing and processing societies, development of warehousing facilities, etc.

3. The SBI and Small Road and Water Transport

The development of transport facilities, especially in the rural areas, is very vital for the maximum utilisation of the localised resources. The SBI provides advances to the small road and water transport operators at concessional rates.

4. The SBI and Industrial Estates

The State Bank of India has been playing a significant role in the establishment of industrial estates in the country. The total advances for setting up of industrial estates have increased to over Rs. 2 crores in June 1989.

5. The SBI and Export Promotion

The State Bank of India also helps in the export promotion by providing finances to exporters, maintaining close relationship between exporters and importers, collecting and disseminating information about market etc. About 30 percent of the total export finance of scheduled banks comes from the SBI Group.

6. The SBI and Regional Development

The SBI is also helping in reducing the regional disparities by establishing a major portion of its new branches in the rural and unbanked areas. The Lead Bank Schemes has been very successful in the integrated development of the rural areas.

In brief, the State Bank of India is playing the role of leading public sector commercial bank for the speedy economic development of the Indian economy.

Conclusion

Thus the SBI is truly shaping itself as a national institution of major financial importance. It has helped in making more effective Government control over the country's money market. It has extended appreciably banking facilities to rural and other areas lacking badly in such facilities. The Bank massive resources are made available to the high priority sectors of the economy according to the objectives of planned development. To achieve so much in such a short time is highly creditable indeed.

Questions for Discussions

1. Explain the functions of the State Bank of India.
2. Explain the role of the State Bank of India in economic development of the country.

Chapter - 5

MONEY MARKET AND CAPITAL MARKET

Introduction

The money market concerns trading in money instruments involving borrowing and lending for short periods. It is part of the securities market. The other part is capital market which deals with long-term instruments like equity or shares, debentures and bonds. It provides long-term finance to the government and firms, mostly large ones.

Money Market

Money Market is a short-term credit market. It is the centre in which short-term funds are borrowed and lent. It consists of borrowers and lenders of short-term funds. The borrowers are generally merchants, traders, brokers, manufacturers, speculators and Government. The lenders are commercial banks, insurance companies, finance companies and the central bank. The money market brings together the lenders and the borrowers. It does not deal in cash or money. It deals in trade bills, promissory notes and government papers or bills, which are drawn for short-periods. Dr. S.N. Sen defines money market as "the organisation for the lending of short-term funds, through the use of such instruments as commercial bills of exchange, short-term government securities and banker's acceptances".

The Reserve Bank of India describes money market as "the centre for dealings, mainly of a short-term character, in monetary assets, and it meets the short-term requirements of borrowers and provides liquidity or cash to lenders".

Functions of Money Market

A well-organised and developed money market can help a country to achieve economic growth and stability. It performs a diversity of functions in the banking structure of the economy. They are:

(a) Money market provides outlets to commercial banks, non-banking financial concerns, business corporations and other investors for their short-term funds. It enables them to use their excess reserves in profitable investment.

(b) Money market also provides short-term funds to business men, industrialists, traders etc. to meet their day-to-day requirements of working capital. Money market plays a crucial role in financing both internal as well as international trade.

(c) Money market provides short-term funds not only to private business-men but also to government and its agencies.

(d) Money market enables business-men, with temporary surplus funds, to invest them for a short-period.

(e) Money market serves as a medium through which the central bank of the country exercises control on the creation of credit.

(f) Money market is also of great help to the government.

The functions of the money market are virtually the same in all the countries of the world. But the institutions, instruments and modes of operation are different in different money markets.

Composition of the Money Market

The money market is composed of several financial agencies that deal with different types of short-term credit. We may describe the following important components of the money market.

1. Call Money Market

It is a market for short-period loans. Bill brokers and dealers in stock exchange require financial accommodation for very short periods. Money may be lent for periods not exceeding seven days. Sometimes money is lent only overnight. These loans are called call loans or call money as the banks recall these loans at very short notice. The banks prefer this kind of investment for two reasons. Firstly, call loans can be treated almost like cash and they form the second line of defence for the banks after cash. Secondly unlike cash, the call loans earn some income, in the form of interest, for the banks. The commercial banks are the lenders and the bill brokers and dealers in stock exchange are the borrowers in the call money market. The call money market is an important section of the money market.

2. Collateral Loan Market

When loans are offered against collateral securities like stocks and bonds, they are called 'collateral loans' and the market is known as the collateral loan market. This market is geographically most diversified.

3. Acceptance Market

It refers to the market for bankers acceptances which arise out of trade-both inland and foreign. When goods are sold to anyone on credit, the buyer accepts a bill. Such a bill cannot be discounted anywhere easily. The banker adds his credit to the bill by accepting it on behalf of his customer who has purchased the goods. Such bills can be discounted anywhere. In London, there are specialist firms called acceptance houses which accept bills drawn on them by traders. They are well known all over the world. In the past, the acceptance market was a prominent section of London money market. Its importance has declined considerably in recent years. The function of the acceptance houses in being performed by the commercial banks in several countries.

4. Bill Market or Discount Market

It refers to the market where short-dated bills and other paper is discounted. Before the First World War the most important paper discounted in the London money market was the commercial bill which was used to finance both inland and foreign trade. During the inter-war period the importance of the commercial bills declined. This place has been taken by treasury bills. The treasury bills are promissory note of the government to pay a specified sum after a specified period, generally 90 days. The treasury bills are purchased by the investors and when necessary they are discounted in the discount market.

These markets are not water-tight compartments. They are related to one another. The borrowers in the call money market deal in treasury bills which are discounted with them. Acceptance houses accept bills which are later discounted in the discount market. Thus, the various sections of the money market are intimately related to and are dependent on one another.

Financial Institutions of the Money Market

The money market may also be analysed on the basis of the different institutions engaged in lending and borrowing short-term funds. The nature of these institutions may differ from country to country. The same institutions may also function both as borrower and a lender in the market. The lenders are :

1. The Central Bank

It is the lender of last resort. It lends money to commercial banks when they approach for financial assistance.

2. Commercial banks

They form the most important class of lenders in the money market. They also borrow from the central bank directly or indirectly. The money that they lend comes from the public in the form of deposits repayable on demand. These funds are invested in various forms of assets. These assets which are considered the secondary reserve for the bank are closely linked with the money market.

3. Institutional investors

They include savings banks, insurance companies, trust companies and investment trusts. The portion of their funds kept invested in liquid assets finds its way into the money market.

4. Private individuals, partnerships and companies

Normally this group may not be interested in short-term funds. If the interest rates become attractive, they may divert a portion of their surplus funds to the money market.

The borrowers in the money market must satisfy certain conditions regarding the paper they offer for discounting. "The paper must be absolutely liquid, easily realisable and short of maturity". These conditions are satisfied by bill brokers and dealers in stock exchange.

Characteristics of a Developed Money Market

Professor S.N. Sen has described the characteristics of a developed money market in his well-known study Central Banking in Undeveloped Money Markets. The absence of one or more of these conditions will make a particular money market an undeveloped one. In every country of the world, some type of money market exists. While some of these are very highly developed, a good many are still undeveloped. There are many basic requisites which are necessary for the evolution of a developed money market.

(a) Highly organised commercial banking system

A fully developed money market is characterised by the presence of a highly organised commercial banking system while in an undeveloped money market the banking system is undeveloped. The commercial banks are the most important suppliers of short-term funds and, therefore, any policy they follow regarding loans and advances and investments will have repercussions on the entire money market.

(b) Presence of a central bank

The second essential feature of the organisation of a developed money market is the presence of a central bank. Just as a State cannot exist and function properly without a head, so also a money market cannot function properly without a central bank. The central bank keeps the cash reserves of all commercial banks and comes to their rescue and the money market as a whole in times of difficulties by rediscounting eligible securities. In times of emergency and crisis, the central bank enables the money market to convert near-money into cash. Besides, it performs a valuable service through open-market operations when it absorbs surplus cash during off-seasons and provides additional liquidity in times of financial stringency. Thus the central bank is the leader of the money market, as well as its controller and guide. Without an efficient central bank, a developed money market cannot exist. In an undeveloped money market, either the central bank does not exist or is in its infancy without adequate capacity to influence and control the money market.

(c) Availability of proper credit instruments

An effective money market will require a continuous supply of highly acceptable and, therefore, negotiable securities such as bills of exchange, treasury bills, short-term government bonds, etc. At the same time, there should be a number of dealers in the money market who should buy and sell these securities. Without their presence, there cannot be any competition or "life" in the money market. Thus the availability of adequate short-term assets and the presence of dealers and brokers to deal in them are essential conditions for the evolution of an organised and developed money market. An undeveloped money market, on the other hand, is characterised by the absence of sufficient short-term credit instruments as well as dealers and brokers to deal in them.

(d) Existence of a number of sub-markets

The fourth essential condition for the evolution of a developed money market is the organisation of the money market into a number of sub-markets, each specialising in particular type of short-term assets. Each type of short-term asset-depending upon the nature of the asset and period of maturity involved-is dealt with in a separate market. While a developed money market consists of a number of sub-markets each specialising in a particular type of short-term asset, an undeveloped market does not possess all the important and essential sub-markets particularly the bill market. Besides, there is no coordination between the different sections of the money market in an undeveloped money market.

(e) Availability of ample resources

The fifth essential condition for a developed money market is the availability of ample resources to finance the dealings in the various sub-markets. These resources generally come from within the country but it is also possible that foreign funds may also be attracted. While developed money markets, like London and New Yark, attract funds from all over the world, undeveloped money markets do not attract foreign funds mainly because of political instability and absence of stable exchange rates.

Apart from these above important factors which are responsible for the evolution of a developed money market over a number of years, there should be many other contributory factors also, such as a large volume of international trade leading to the system of bills of exchange, industrial development leading to the emergence of a stock market, stable political conditions, absence of discrimination against foreign concerns, and so on.

It is difficult to come across many developed money markets. London money market is the best example of such a market, for all the characteristics of a developed money market are to be found there. The Indian money market is a good example of an undeveloped money market.

Usefulness of a Developed Money Market

The money market is an important institution in a modern economy and it has influenced profoundly industrial and commercial developments:

(a) In Financing industry and commerce

In the first place, the money market is of very great help in financing industry and commerce. Industries are helped in their working capital requirements through the system of finance bills, commercial paper, and so on. It has played a very important part in the financing of trade and commerce. Both internal as well as international trade is normally financed through the system of bills of exchange which are discounted by the bill market.

(b) Investment of short-term funds

The money market plays a very important role in providing necessary assets for the investment of short-term funds of commercial banks. Commercial banks find such assets in the call money market as well as in the bill market. Thus the money market offers the commercial banks a very good means of temporarily employing their funds in liquid or near-money investments.

(c) Help to the central bank

The money market is of great help to the central bank of the country. For one thing, the money market and short-term rates of interest which prevail there serve as a good barometer of monetary and banking conditions in the country and thus provide a valuable guide to the determination of central banking policy. For another, the developed money market being a highly integrated structure enables the central bank to deal with the most sensitive of the sub-markets so that the influence of the operation of the central bank may spread to other sections also.

(d) Help to the government

Lastly, the money market helps the government. The money market supplies the government with necessary short-term funds through the treasury bills.

Thus, a developed money market is of great assistance to industry and commerce, to the commercial banking system, to the central bank of the country and to the government.

Structure of the Money Market

The Indian money market is composed of two categories of financial agencies : (1) Organised and (2) Unorganised. The organised sector contains, well established, scientifically managed financial institutions comprises : (a) The Reserve Bank of India. (b) The State Bank of India and its associate banks, (c) Joint-stock commercial banks, (d) Exchange banks. (e) Co-operative banks, (f) Development banks. The Reserve Bank of India is the supreme monetary and banking authority in the country. It has the responsibility to control the banking system in the country. It keeps the reserve of all commercial banks and hence is known as the "Reserve Bank". There are joint-stock commercial banks. 91% of the banking institutions are in the public sector. There are foreign exchange banks in the country. There are cooperative banks. There are also post office savings banks which mobilises the savings of small holders. Thus, the organised sector of money market is well developed.

The unorganised sector contains agencies which have diverse policies, lack of uniformity and consistency in the lending business. The unorganised sector includes indigenous bankers, money lenders, nidhis and chitfunds. Money-lenders and indigenous bankers provide about 50 percent of rural finance. There are thousands of chitfunds operating on a big or small scale in many places in

India. This sector is unorganised because its activities are not controlled and co-ordinated by the Reserve Bank of India.

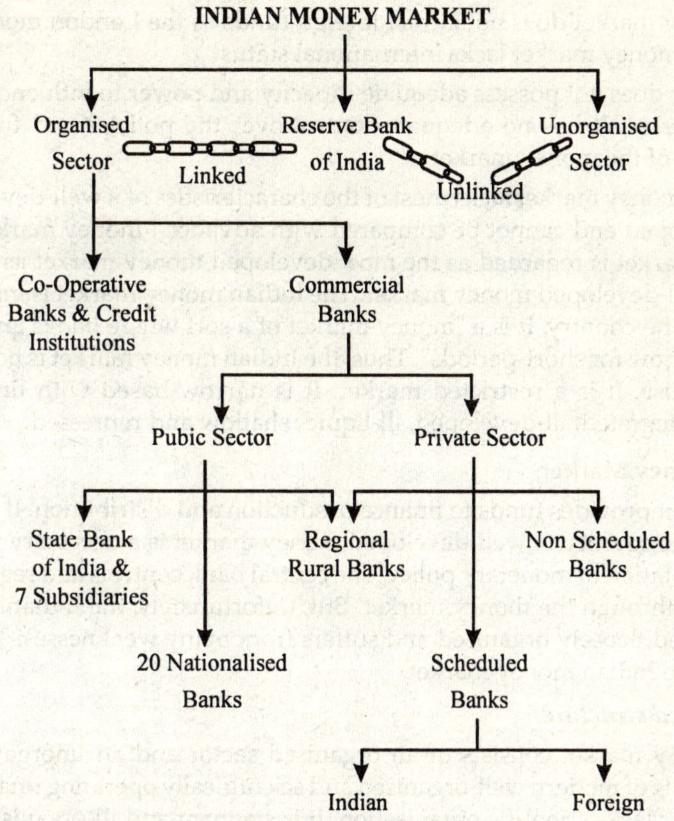

Characteristics of Indian Money Market

The Indian money market is an under-developed money market. It is an under-developed money market. It is loosely organised and suffers from many weaknesses. It is divided into two parts, namely, organised and unorganised sectors. The following are the important characteristics of Indian market:

(a) The Indian money market does not possess a highly organised banking system, necessary for the successful working of a money market.

(b) It does not possess an adequate and continuous supply of short-term assets, such as the bills of exchange, treasury bills or short-term government bonds etc.,

(c) There are no dealers in short-term assets in India, who may act as intermediaries between the government and the banking system.

(d) The Indian money market does not contain the very essential sub-markets such as the acceptance market, commercial bill market etc., A well developed call money market, however, exists in India. But acceptance houses and discount houses are not in existence in India.

(e) There is no proper co-ordination between the different sections of the money market. This is so because the inter-connection between the different sections of the money market is often loose and un-co-ordinated. Thus, the money market structure is unorganised and un-co-ordinated.

(f) There is no uniformity in the interest rates which vary considerably, among the different financial institutions as well as centres. Money-lenders especially charge exorbitant rates of interest.

(g) The Indian money market does not attract foreign funds as the London money market does. Thus, the Indian money market lacks international status.

(h) The Reserve Bank does not possess adequate capacity and power to influence and control the entire money market. It has no adequate control over the policies and functioning of the unorganised part of the money market.

Thus, the Indian money market lacks most of the characteristics of a well-developed market. It is very much undeveloped and cannot be compared with advanced money markets in the world. The London money market is regarded as the most developed money market as it possess all the characteristics of a well-developed money market. The Indian money market is inadequate to meet the financial needs of the country. It is a "money market of a sort where banks and other financial institutions lend or borrow for short-periods". Thus, the Indian money market is not a perfect one. It is unbalanced and loose. It is a restricted market. It is narrow-based with limited number of participants. It is disintegrated, ill-developed, ill-liquid, shallow and repressed.

Defects of Indian Money Market

The money market provides funds to finance production and distribution. It helps to promote economic growth of the country. A well-developed money market is a necessary pre-condition for the effective implementation of monetary policy. The central bank controls and regulates the money supply in the country through the money market. But, unfortunately, the Indian money market is inadequately developed, loosely organised and suffers from many weaknesses. The following are the major defects of the Indian money market.

1. Loose and disjointed structure

The Indian money market consists of an organised sector and an unorganised sector. The organised sector consists of modern well-organised and scientifically operating financial institutions. The unorganised sector lacks scientific organisation. It is stagnant and ill-organised. The existence of unorganised money market is an important weakness of the Indian money market. The unorganised sector consists of indigenous bankers, money-lenders, nidhis, chitfunds etc., This unorganised sector acts independently. It carries on business on traditional lines. It follows its own rules of banking and finance. It does not submit to the control and regulation of the Reserve Bank. There is little contract, co-ordination and co-operation between the unorganised sector and the organised sector. Thus, the Indian money market is unbalanced and loose. In such conditions, it is difficult for the Reserve Bank to ensure uniform and effective implementation of its monetary policy in both the sectors.

2. Wasteful Competition

Wasteful competition exists not only between the organised and unorganised sectors, but also among the members of the two sectors. The relations between the various members of the money market are not cordial. They are loosely connected with each other and generally, follow separatist tendencies. For example, even today, the State Bank of India and other commercial banks looks down upon each other as rivals. Similarly, competition exists between the Indian commercial banks and foreign exchange banks.

3. Absence of All-India money market

Indian money market has not been organised into a single integrated all-India money market.

It is divided into small segments mostly catering to the local financial needs. For example, there is little contact between the money markets in the bigger cities like Mumbai, Chennai and Calcutta, and those in smaller cities.

4. Shortage of Capital

Indian money market, generally suffers from the shortage of capital funds. The availability of capital in the money market is insufficient to meet the needs of trade and industry in the country.

5. Inadequate banking facilities

Indian money market is inadequate to meet the financial needs of the economy. Although there has been rapid expansion of bank branches in recent years, yet vast rural areas still exist without banking facilities. As compared to the size and population of the country, the banking institutions are not enough.

6. Seasonal shortage of funds

India is primarily an agricultural country. There are two seasons in agriculture namely, busy season and slack season. During the busy season, from November to June, there will be excess demand for credit or funds for carrying on the harvesting and marketing operations in agriculture. But there will be scarcity of funds. As a result, the interest rates will rise in this period. But during the slack season, from July to October, the demand for credit will be less. As a result, the interest rates will sharply decline. Thus, there will be wide fluctuations in the interest rates from one period of the year to another.

7. Disparity in interest rates in different centres

There is clear disparity in money rates of interest from place to place and from institution to institution. Different interest rates exist at the same time. Close relationship does not exist between the money market rates and the bank rates. There is also difference in the interest rates of the two principal financial centres, namely, Mumbai and Calcutta. There are several rates of interest and they do not react to a change in Bank Rate. This is due to the fact that funds do not move from one financial centre to another. Disparities in the interest rates adversely affect the smooth and effective functioning of the money market.

8. Undeveloped Bill Market

The existence of a well-organised and well-developed bill market is essential for the proper and efficient working of money market. Unfortunately, inspite of the serious efforts made by the Reserve Bank, the bill market in India has not yet been fully developed. As a result, the short-term bills form a smaller proportion of the bank finance in India. Besides, the absence of developed bill market has reduced the liquidity of the Indian money market.

9. Inelasticity and instability

The Indian money market is inelastic as well as unstable. It is a restricted market. It is narrow-based with a limited number of participants. They are not in a position to effectively mobilise funds. The supply of funds do not increase in proportion to the demand.

10. Absence of sub-markets

Sub-markets like discount houses, acceptance houses, bill brokers etc., do not exist in the Indian money market. Even though a call market exists, it is restricted mainly to inter bank borrowing, and it is not well-developed.

11. Insensitive to International influences

Institutions that carry on foreign exchange business are few in number in our money market. The Indian money market, due to certain limitations, does not attract foreign funds. It has little contacts with foreign money markets. But in recent years, the Indian financial sector has become more global. The flow of foreign exchange has increased. The Indian money market has become more sensitive to international influences.

Measures for Improvement of the Money Market

The Reserve Bank occupies the highest place in the money market. It is the financial or monetary authority and is regarded as an apex institution. The Reserve Bank of India, from time to time, has taken various, measures to remove or correct some of the existing defects and to develop a sound money market in the country. The following are the important measures or steps taken by the Reserve Bank of India :

1. A number of measures have been taken to improve the functioning of the indigenous banks. These measures include : (a) their registration, (b) keeping and auditing of accounts, and (c) providing financial accommodation through banks.
2. The Reserve Bank has taken several steps to remove the differences which existed between the different sections of the money market. All banks in the country have been given equal treatment by the Reserve Bank as regards licensing, opening of branches, the types of loans to be given etc. The discrimination between foreign and Indian banks does not exist now.
3. In order to develop a sound money market, the Reserve Bank has taken measures to amalgamate and merge banks into a few strong banks. Encouragement is also given to the expansion of banking facilities in the country.
4. To develop the bill culture in the money market, the Reserve Bank introduced two schemes : (a) The Bill Market Scheme, 1952 and (b) The New Bill Market Scheme, 1970.
5. The Reserve Bank introduced a "Lead Banking Scheme" in 1969 to eliminate banking deficiencies in rural areas.
6. Steps have been taken to establish relations between indigenous bankers and commercial banks.
7. The Reserve Bank has taken steps to reduce considerably the differences in the interest rates between different sections of the money market as well as different centres of the money market and at different times. The interest rates are deregulated and banking and financial institutions have the freedom to determine and adopt market-related interest rates.
8. Reserve Bank has been able to reduce considerably monetary shortages through open market operations.
9. Steps have been taken to implement the recommendations of working group under the chairmanship of Mr. N. Vaghul and Chakravarty committee.
   (a) Several new money market instruments were introduced to provide suitable instruments to the investors. 182 days and 364 days Treasury Bills were introduced to widening the scope of the short-term money market. In 1992-93, certificate of Deposits, commercial paper were introduced. Certificate of deposits provide and avenue for investment at better rates in the banking sector. Commercial paper introduced in 1989 is a short-term negotiable money market instrument. Reserve Bank introduced two more Treasury Bills in 1997, (i) 14-day Intermediate Treasury Bills and (ii) a new category of 14-day Treasury bills.

(b) In April 1988, the Discount and Financial House of India limited was established with a view to provide liquidity to money market instruments. Discount and Finance House of India is now the apex body in the Indian money market. It has developed a secondary market in government securities by buying and selling them.

10. In 1991, the commercial banks and public sector financial institutions were permitted to set up "Money Market Mutual Funds" (MMMF). The shares or units of money market mutual funds are to be sold only to individuals unlike the other mutual funds. The purpose of this fund is to bring money market instruments, like treasury bills, within the reach of individuals. In 1995, the Reserve Bank permitted private sector institutions to set up Money market mutual funds.
11. The Scheme of Inter-Bank participation (IBP) has been introduced by the Reserve Bank in 1988.
12. Access to bill rediscounting market has been increased by selectively increasing the number of participants in the market.

As a result of various measures taken by the Reserve Bank of India, the Indian money market has shown signs of notable development in many ways. It has become more vibrant and advanced. The present position of the money market is stated below :

1. It is becoming more and more organised and diversified.
2. The government trading in various instruments like 364 - Day Treasury Bills, commercial bills and commercial paper has increased.
3. The volume of inter-bank call money, short notice money and term money transactions has grown significantly.
4. At present Discount and Finance House of India is also participating in the money market, both as a lender and borrower of short-term funds.
5. Banks and non-banking financial institutions are providing "factoring services".

Suggestions to Remove Defects in the Indian Money Market

In view of the various defects in the Indian money market, the following suggestions have been made for its proper development.

1. The activities of the money-lenders, indigenous bankers, and chit funds should be brought under the effective control of the Reserve Bank of India.
2. Hundies used in the money market should be standardised and written in the uniform manner in order to develop an all-India money market.
3. Banking facilities should be expanded, especially in the unbanked and neglected areas.
4. Discounting and rediscounting facilities should be expanded in a big way to develop the bill market in the country.
5. For raising the efficiency of the money market, the number of clearing houses in the country should be increased and their working improved.
6. Adequate and easy remittance facilities should be provided to the businessmen to increase the mobility of capital.
7. As per recommendation of the Narasimham Committee, well-managed non-banking financial institutions, like leasing and Hire-purchase companies, Merchant Banks, Venture capital companies should be allowed to operate in the money market.
8. The Reserve Bank should encourage to open Discount and Acceptance Houses.

9. Harmony between sub-markets and co-ordination of their activities must be achieved.
10. More participants should be allowed into the money market and more instruments should be evolved and introduced in the money market. This will develop the secondary market.

In recent years, the Indian money market has started becoming more deep and wide owing to a number of innovative measures undertaken by the authorities towards its structural reforms and the financial liberalisation. We require a well-developed money market to make our plans a success. A well organised and developed market can help to achieve economic growth and stability.

Recent Innovations in the Money Market

Since a long time the Indian money market has been characterised as disintegrated, ill-developed, ill-liquid, shallow and repressed. The Seventh Plan period, however, witnessed a remarkable improvement in the whole situation and working of the money market in the country. The authorities positively accepted certain major recommendations of the Chakravarty Committee and Vaghul Committee in this context and enthusiastically acted upon in due course of time. In fact, the celebrated reports of these two committees blew the air of financial liberalisation and innovation in the Indian monetary system. Consequently, during the last 3-4 years, the Indian money market has started becoming more deep and wide owing to a number of innovative measures undertaken by the authorities towards its structural reforms and the financial liberalisation.

14-day Intermediate Treasury Bills

With the discontinuance of tap treasury bills, the central government introduced the scheme of 14 day treasury bills to provide the State governments, foreign central banks and specified bodies with an alternative arrangement to invest their surplus funds. The salient features of the scheme are: (i) treasure bills would be sold only to the State governments, foreign central banks and other specified bodies with whom the RBI has an agreement for investing their temporary surplus funds; (ii) these treasury bills would be sold on a non-transferable basis for a minimum amount of Rs. 1,00,000 and in multiples of Rs. 1,00,000; (iii) these treasury bills would be repaid / renewed at par on the expiration of 14 days from the date of their issue, and (iv) the discount rate would be set at quarterly interval such that the effective yield of this instrument would be equivalent to the interest rate on the Ways and Means advances chargeable to the Central government. The total bills outstanding at end-March 2000 was Rs. 2,383 crore of which the share of State governments was 96.18 per cent.

14-Day Auction Treasury Bills

The RBI introduced 14-day auction treasury bills on a weekly basis with effect from June 6, 1997. The dual purpose of introducing these treasury bills is to facilitate the cash management requirements of various segments of the economy and to help in forming a complete yield curve for aiding in the pricing of debt instruments. The 14-day auction treasury bills do not devolve on the RBI unlike the 91-day treasury bills. The total issues of 14 day auction treasury bills during 1999-2000 amounted to Rs. 16,453 crore of which non-competitive bids aggregated Rs. 11,253 crore, representing 68 per cent of the total issues. The subscriptions of the RBI aggregated Rs. 1,134 crore.

91-Day Treasury Bills

Earlier there were two types of 91-day treasury bills - ordinary and ad hoc. With effect from April 1, 1997 ad hoc treasury bills were discontinued. On this day 91 day ad hoc treasury bills amounting to Rs. 38,130 crore were converted into special securities without any specific maturity. The interest on these securities was fixed at 4.6 per cent per annum.

In 1992-93 a scheme for the issue of 91-day treasury bills with the RBI participation was introduced. The cut off yields on these treasury bills were higher than the fixed discount rate of 4.6 per cent per annum on 91-day treasury bills sold on tap.

A gross amount of Rs. 8,155 crore was raised during 1999-2000 in respect of 91-day treasury bills as against Rs. 16,697 crore in the previous year. Out of the total gross amount, non-competitive bids aggregated to Rs. 2,995 crore accounting for about 36 per cent of the value of the total issues.

182-Day Treasury Bills

182-day treasury bills were reintroduced with effect from May 26, 1999. As per the calender, notified amount for 182-day treasury bills remained constant at Rs. 100 at the fortnightly auctions held on Wednesdays preceding the non-reporting Fridays. The cut-off yield has varied within the range of 8.53 - 9.97 per cent.

364-Day Treasury Bills

364-day treasury bills were introduced in April 1992. Since then these treasury bills are auctioned on a fortnightly basis in a regular manner. These treasury bills are not rediscountable with the RBI. However, they offer short-term investment opportunities to banks and other financial institutions. Since 364-day treasury bills constitute a safe avenue for investment, the auctions of these treasury bills have evoked good response. Gross mobilisation through issuance of 364-day treasury bills was Rs. 13,000 crore in 1999-2000 as against Rs. 10,200 crore in 1998-99. The subscription by the RBI was Rs. 2,267 crore or 17.44 per cent of the value of the total issues.

In 1999-2000, there was a relative stability in the yield on both 91-day treasury bills and 364-day treasury bills. The yield spread between these bills was rather small during the year.

The Repo Market

Repo is a money market instrument which helps in collateralised short-term borrowing and lending through sale/purchase operations in debt instruments. Under a repo transaction, securities are sold by their holder to an investor with an agreement to repurchase them at a predetermined rate and date. Under reverse repo transaction, securities are purchased with a simultaneous commitment to resell at a predetermined rate and date.

Initially repos were allowed in the Central government treasury bills and dated securities created by converting some of the treasuries bills. In order to make the repos market an equilibrating force between the money market and the government securities market, the RBI gradually allowed repo transactions in all government securities and treasury bills of all maturities. Lately State government securities, public sector undertakings' bonds and private corporate securities have been made eligible for repos to broaden the repos market.

Explaining the usefulness of repos Report on Currency and Finance 1999-2000 notes that "repos help to manage liquidity conditions at the short-end of the market spectrum. Repos have been used to provide banks an avenue to part funds generated by capital inflows to provide a floor to the call money market. During times of foreign exchange volatility, repos have been used to prevent specualtive activity as the funds tend to flow from the money market to the foreign exchange market".

The Commercial Bill Market

The commercial bill market is the sub-market in which the trade bills or the commercial bills are handled. The commercial bills is a bill drawn by one merchant firm on the other. Generally commercial bills arise out of domestic transactions. The legitimate purpose of a commercial bill is to reimburse the seller while the buyer delays payment. In India, the commercial bill market is highly undeveloped. The two major factors which have arrested the growth of a bill market are: (i) popularity of cash credit system in bank lending, and (ii) the unwillingness of the larger buyer to bind himself to payment discipline associated with the commercial bill. Among other factors which have prevented growth of genuine bill market are lack of uniformity in drawing bills, high stamp duty on usance or time bills and the practice of sales on credit without specified time limit.

Commercial bills as instruments of credit are useful to both business firms and banks. In addition, since the drawees of the bill generally manage to recover the cost of goods from their resale or processing and sale during the time it matures, the bill acquires a self liquidating character. Finally it is easier for the central bank to regulate bill finance. Keeping in view these considerations the RBI has made efforts to develop a bill market in this country and popularise the use of bills. Its two specific bill market schemes, however, had limited success. The old bill market scheme introduced in January 1952 was not correctly designed to develop a bill market. It merely provided for further accommodation to banks in addition to facilities they had already enjoyed. The scheme had, in fact, provided for obtaining loans on the security of bills rather than for their rediscount. In order to encourage use of bills the RBI offered loans at a concessional rate of interest and met half the cost of stamp duty incurred by banks on converting demand bills into usance bills. This scheme, however, failed to make any impact.

Not satisfied with the old Scheme the RBI introduced a new bill market scheme in November 1970. It has been modified from time to time. The two noteworthy features of the new scheme are : (i) The bills covered under the scheme are genuine trade bills; and (ii) the scheme provides for their rediscounting. Even this scheme which really aimed at developing a bill market in the country has not been very successful. The major obstacle to the development of bill finance in this country is the dominant cash credit system of credit delivery where the bonus of cash management rests with banks. Absence of an active secondary market further prevented growth of the market for bills finance.

The success of the bills discounting scheme depends largely upon financial discipline on the part of borrowers. In the absence of such restraints, the RBI, in July 1992, restricted the banks to finance bills to the extent of working capital needs based on credit norms. However, in order to encourage 'bills' culture, the RBI advised banks in October 1997 that at least 25 per cent of inland credit purchases of borrowers should be through bills. Nonetheless the outstanding amount of commercial bills rediscounted by the banks with various financial institutions was only Rs. 235 crore at end - May 2000.

The Certificate of Deposit (CD) Market

A Certificate of Deposit (CD) is a certificate issued by a bank to depositors of funds that remain on deposit at the bank for a specified period. Thus CDs are similar to the traditional term deposits but are negotiable and tradeable in the short-term money markets. In the mid-eighties, the short-term banks deposit rates were much lower than other comparable interest rates. The Vaghul Committee thus felt that the CD as a money market instrument could not be developed in this country until the situation remained unchanged. The Committee stressed that it was necessary for the introduction of the CD that the short-term bank deposit rates were aligned with the other interest rates. In 1988-89, the RBI, as a corrective measure revised upwards the rate of interest on term deposits of 46 to 90 days. Once this was done in March 1989, the RBI introduced CDs with the objective of widening the range of money market instruments and to provide investors greater flexibility in the deployment of their short-term surplus funds. The CDs could initially be issued only by scheduled commercial banks in multiples of Rs. 25 lakh (later lowered to Rs. 10 lakh) subject to the minimum size of an issue being Rs. 1 crore. Their maturity varied between three months and one year. In 1993 six financial institutions, viz., Industrial Development Bank of India, Industrial Credit and Investment Corporation of India, Industrial Finance Corporation of India, the Industrial Reconstruction Bank of India, Small Industries Development Bank of India and Export-Import Bank of India were permitted to issue CDs with a maturity period of more than one year and upto three years. CDs are issued at discount to face value and the discount rate is market determined. They are further freely transferable by endorsement and delivery. Banks pay a high interest rate on CDs. Hence holders of CDs prefer to hold them till maturity and thus secondary activity in CDs has been non-existent. There was also a lack of interest among banks in issuing fresh CDs in 1993-94. The stringent conditions in the money market in 1995-96, however, induced banks to mobilise resources on a large scale through CDs. The outstanding amount of CDs issued by the banks rose from Rs. 8,017 crore as at end-March 1995 to Rs. 21,503 crore as on June 7, 1996 but declined to Rs. 14,296 crore as on March 27, 1998. Thereafter there was a steep fall in outstanding amount of CDs and it was as low as Rs. 872 crore as on May 5, 2000. Due to the tight money market conditions, the discount rates on CDs increased sharply during 1995-96. However, since July 1996 the average discount rate on CDs has steadily declined. On June 2, 2000 effective discount rate range was 8.00 - 11.16 per cent per annum. To bring CDs at par with other instruments such as CPs and term deposits, the minimum maturity of this instrument was reduced to 15 days in April 2000 from 3 months earlier.

The Commercial Paper Market

The Commercial Paper (CP) is a short-term instrument of raising funds by corporates. It is essentially a sort of unsecured promissory note sold by the issuer to a banker or a security house. The issuance of CP is not related to any underlying self-liquidating trade. Therefore, maturity of this instrument is flexible. Usually borrowers and lenders adopt the maturity of a CP to their needs. Highly rated corporates which can obtain funds at a cost lower than the cost of borrowing from banks are particularly interested in issuing CPs. Institutional investors also find CPs as an attractive outlet for their short-term funds. The Vaghul Committee had strongly recommended the introduction of CPs in the Indian money market. In its observations on this instrument, the Committee had stated, "the issue of commercial paper imparts a degree of financial stability to the system as the issuing company has an incentive to remain financially strong. The possibility of raising short-term finance at relatively cheaper cost would provide an adequate incentive for the corporate clients to improve the financial position and in the process the financial health of the corporate sector should show visible improvement".

Following the recommendations of the Veghual Committee, the CP was introduced in the Indian money market in January 1990. The CP can be issued by a listed company which has a working capital of not less than Rs. 5 crore. With maturity ranging from three months to six months they would be issued in multiples of Rs. 25 lakh (later reduced to Rs. 25 lakh) subject to the minimum size of an issue being Rs. 1 crore (later reduced to Rs. 25 lakh). The company wanting to issue CP would have to obtain every six months a specified rating from an agency approved by the RBI. CPs would be freely transferable by endorsement and delivery. According to the RBI's guidelines for the issue of CP, a company will have to obtain P2 rating from Credit Rating Information Services of India Ltd. (CRISIL) or A2 rating from Investment Information and Credit Rating Agency of India Ltd. (ICRA). It has also to maintain the current ratio of 1.33:1 to be eligible to issue CP. Maturity period of CP so far ranged from 3 months to 6 months and the effective interest rates were in the range of 9.35 to 20.9 per cent per annum. Easy liquidity conditions gave fillip to the issue of CPs during 1996-97 and the outstanding stocks of CPs rose from a historical low level of Rs. 71 crore in April 1996 to Rs. 7,127 crore as on July 15,2000 with the typical effective discount rate range being 9.35 - 11.65 per cent annum.

Money Market Mutual Funds

A Scheme of Money Market Mutual Funds (MMMFs) was introduced by the RBI in April 1992. The objective of the scheme was to provide an additional short-term avenue to the individual investors. As the initial guidelines were not attractive, the scheme did not receive a favourable response. Hence, with a view to making the scheme more flexible, the RBI permitted certain relaxations in November 1995. The new guidelines allow banks, public financial institutions and also the institutions in the private sector to set up MMMFs. The ceiling of Rs. 50 crore on the size of MMMFs stipulated earlier, has been withdrawn. The prescription of limits on investments in individual instruments by MMMF has been generally deregulated. Since April 1996, MMMFs are allowed to issue units to corporate enterprises and others. During 1996-97 the scheme of MMMFs was made more flexible by bringing it on par with all other mutual funds by allowing investment by corporates and others. The scheme was later on made more attractive to investors by reducing the lock-in period from 46 days to 15 days. The scheme was further liberalised in 1997-98 and the MMMFs were permitted to make investments in rated corporate bonds and debentures with residual maturity of upto one year. Resources mobilised by the MMMFs could earlier be invested exclusively in call/ notice money, treasury bills, CDs, CPs, commercial bills arising out of genuine trade / commercial transactions and government securities having an unexpired maturity upto one year. The prudential measure that the exposure of MMMFs to CPs issued by an individual company should not exceed 3 per cent of the resources of the MMMF has been retained.

Capital Market

The term "Capital Market" is used to describe the institutional arrangements for facilitating the borrowing and lending of long-term funds. Usually, stress is laid on the markets for long-term debt and equity claims, government securities, bonds, mortgages, and other instruments of long-term debts. Thus, the capital market embraces the system through which the public takes up long-term securities, either directly or through intermediaries. It consists of a series of channels through which the savings of the community are mobilised and made available to the entrepreneurs for undertaking investment activities.

Conventionally, short-tern credit contracts are usually classified as money market instruments, while long-term debt contracts and equities are regarded as capital market instruments. In practice, however, there is a thin line of demarcation between the money market and the capital market, because quite often, the same institutions participate in the activities of both the markets, and there is flow of funds between the two markets.

Classification of Indian Capital Market

The Indian capital market is divided into the gilt-edged market and the industrial securities market. The gilt-edged market refers to the market for government and semi-government securities, backed by the Reserve Bank of India. The securities traded in this market are of stable value. They are mostly demanded by banks and other institutions.

The industrial securities market refers to the market for shares and debentures of old and new companies. This market is further divided into the new issue market and the old market, meaning the stock exchange. The "new issue market" refers to the raising of new capital in the form of shares and debentures. The old capital market deals with securities already issued. Both markets are equally important.

The capital market is also classified into primary capital market and Secondary capital market. The primary market refers to the new issue market. The secondary capital market refers to the market for old or already issued securities. The secondary capital market is composed of industrial security market or the stock exchange.

Importance of Capital Market

An efficient capital market is an essential pre-requisite for industrial and commercial development of a country. An organised and well-developed market operating in a free market economy ensure best possible co-ordination and balance between the flow of savings on the one hand and the flow of investment leading to capital formation on the other. It also directs the flow of savings into most profitable channels and thereby ensures optimum utilisation of financial resources. The importance of capital market in the process of economic development of a country can be described as below.

1. Mobilising savings

The capital market plays a vital role in mobilising savings to put it in productive investment, so that the development of trade, commerce and industry could be facilitated. In this process the capital market helps in the process of capital formation and hence the economic development. The capital market acts as a bridge, between savers and investors.

2. Stability in value

In case of a developed capital market, the experts in banking and non-banking intermediaries put in every effort in stabilising the values of stocks and securities. This process is facilitated by providing capital to the needy at a lower rate of interest and by cutting down the speculative and unproductive activities.

3. Encouragement to economic growth

The process of economic growth is made easier through the capital market. The various institutions of the capital market give quantitative and qualitative direction to the flow of funds. The proper flow of funds leads to the development of commerce, trade and industry.

4. Inducement to savings

Savings are the backbone of any nation's economic development. If capital markets are developed in less developed areas, people will get induced to save more because savings are facilitated by banking and non-banking financial intermediaries.

Thus, it is clear that the capital market is the life-blood of economic development of a country. If the capital market is not developed, it will lead to misuse of financial resources. The capital market plays a significant role in diverting the wrongful use of resources to their rightful use.

Functions of Capital Market

The major functions performed by a capital market are as follows:

(a) Mobilisation of financial resources on a nation-wide scale.

(b) Securing the foreign capital and know how to fill up the deficit in the required resources for economic growth at a faster rate.

(c) Effective allocation of the mobilised financial resources by directing the same to projects yielding highest yield or to the projects needed to promote balanced economic development.

Structure of Indian Capital Market

The capital market in India may be classified into two sectors (a) organised and (b) unorganised sector. In the organised sector of the capital market demand for long-term capital comes from corporate enterprises, public sector enterprises, government and semi-government institutions. The sources of supply of funds comprise individual investors, corporate and institutional investors, investment intermediaries, financial institutions, commercial banks and government. In India, even the organised sector of capital market was ill-developed till recently because of the following reasons.

(a) Agriculture was the main occupation which did not lend itself to the floatation of securities.

(b) The foreign business houses hampered the growth of securities market.

(c) Various restrictions have been imposed on the investment pattern of various financial institutions.

(d) The investment habit of individuals has been very low.

The unorganised sector of the capital market consists of indigenous bankers and private money-lenders. The main demand in the unorganised capital market comes from the agriculturists, private individuals for consumption rather than production and even small traders. The supply of money-capital comes, usually from own resources of money-lenders and falls short of the requirements.

Components of Indian Capital Market

The following are the main components of the Indian capital market:

1. New Issues market.
2. Stock market.
3. Financial institutions.

1. New Issues market

The new issues market represents the primary market where new shares or bonds are offered. Both the new companies and the existing ones can raise capital on the new issue market. The prime function of the new issues market is to facilitate the transfer of funds from the willing investors to the entrepreneurs setting up new corporate enterprises, going in for expansion, diversification, growth or modernisation. Besides, helping the corporate enterprises in securing their funds, the new issues market channelises the savings of individuals and others into investments. The availability of financial resources for corporate enterprises, to a great extent, depends upon the status of the new issues market of the country. Successful issues of new securities is a highly specialised activity and requires both experience and skill. There are a number of methods of marketing new issues of securities.

2. Secondary market or Stock market

Stock market represents the secondary market where existing shares and debentures are traded. Stock exchange provides an organised mechanism of purchase and sale of existing securities. The stock exchanges enable free purchase and sale of existing securities. The stock-exchanges enable free purchase and sale of securities as commodity exchange allow trading in commodities.

3. Financial institutions

Special financial institutions are the most active constitutents of the Indian capital market. Such organisations provide medium and long-term loans repayable on easy instalments to big business houses. Such institutions help in promoting new companies, expansion and development of existing companies and meeting the financial requirements of companies during economic depression. After independence, a number of financial institutions have been set up at all India and regional levels for accelerating the growth of industries by providing financial and other assistance. The following are the main financial institutions that are most active constituents of the Indian capital market

(a) The Industrial Fiance Corporation of India Ltd.
(b) The Industrial Credit and Investment Corporation of India.
(c) State Financial Corporations.
(d) The Industrial Development Bank of India.
(e) National Industrial Development Corporations.
(f) Unit Trust of India.
(g) Life Insurance Corporation of India.
(h) Nationalised Commercial Banks.
(j) Merchant Banking Institutions.
(k) The Credit Guarantee Corporation of India.

Recent Trends in the Capital Market

Capital market is the market for long-term funds, Just as the money market is the market for short-term funds. It refers to all the facilities and the institutional arrangements for borrowing and lending medium-term and long-term funds. It does not deal in capital goods but is concerned with the raising of money capital for purpose of investment. A well-developed capital market is necessary for the economic development of a country. The Indian Capital Market was not properly developed before Independence. But since Independence the Indian capital market has been broadening significantly and the volume of saving and investment has shown steady improvement. Many institutional innovations have been made, liberalisation has been accepted and private sector entered all avenues of trade, commerce and industry. Capital issues control has been abolished. Stock Exchange Board of India has taken the challenge of regulating the capital market. New financial instruments and players entered the market. Leasing companies, hire-purchase companies, venture capital companies were set up in the country.

Recent trends in the capital market : The recent trends in the capital market can be discussed under the following heads :

1. Growth of the Capital Market.
2. New Financial Instruments.
3. New Specialised Financial Institutions.
4. Financial Services.
5. Regulation of Capital Market.

1. Growth of the Capital Market

Since Independence and particularly after 1951, the Indian capital market has grown in size. The volume of saving and investment in the country has shown steady improvement. All types of encouragement and tax relief exist in the country to promote savings. Besides, many steps have been taken to protect the interests of investors. The primary market and secondary market have grown. A very important indicator of the growth of the capital market is the growth of joint-stock companies. In 1951, there were about 28,500 companies, both public and private limited companies, with a paid-up capital of Rs. 775 crores. But in 1997, there were about 64,000 companies, with a paid-up capital of Rs. 1,00,000 crores. In the last two decades, the capital market in India has witnessed significant developments. The volume of capital market transactions have increased sharply and its functioning has been diversified. The number of shareholders runs into several millions, indicating the growth of the cult of equity.

2. New Financial Instruments

The corporate sector has devised new instruments for raising funds from the market. New instruments include Zero interest bonds, equity warrant, secured premium note, deep discount bond and partly convertible debentures. Joint-stock companies could raise more and more finance by the issue of new instruments. These new instrument widened the capital market. The Government of India has introduced into the market. 1) 14-day Intermediate Treasury Bills in April 1997, 2) A new category of 14-day Treasury bills in 1977 3) Commercial Paper, 4) Dated government Securities.

3. New Specialised Financial Institutions

The Government of India has set up a series of financial institutions to provide funds to the large industrial sector. The important financial institutions established are the Industrial Finance Corporation of India, the Industrial Investment and Credit Corporation of India, the Industrial Development Bank of India. The specialised financial institutions are called development banks. They have been underwriting the shares and debentures issued by companies. They have been subscribing to the share capital of companies.

Besides development banks, non-banking finance companies have come into existence all over the country and have been making rapid progress. They advance loans to wholesale and retail traders, small-scale industries and self employed persons. Hire-purchase companies, venture capital companies, fiance corporations are all non-banking finance companies.

Holding Corporation of India, infrastructure Leasing and financial Services Ltd., The Credit Rating Information Services of India, Housing Development Corporation of India have been set up in the country

4. Financial Services

The Entry of service sector in the capital market is adding new dimension in the market. The financial services offered are :

1) Venture Capital, 2) Factoring Services, 3) Leasing, 4) Merchant Banking, 5) Mutual Funds.

5. Regulation of Capital Market

Stock Exchange Board of India has been set up in 1988 to lay guidelines, and supervise and regulate the working of capital market. SEBI in consultation with the Government has taken a number of steps to introduce improved practices and greater transperancy in the capital markets in the interest of the investing public and the healthy development of the capital markets. SEBI has the power to control and regulate the new issue market as well as the old issues market. Since 1992, the Government has allowed Indian companies access to international markets through Euro-equity shares.

Comparison of Money Market and Capital Market

There are important similarities and differences between money market and capital market.

Similarities: The money market and capital market have certain similarities and inter relations. They are :

1. Complementary

The money market and the capital market are complementary to each other and are not competitive. The difference between the two is only of degree rather than of kind.

2. Same Institutions

Certain institutions operate in money as well as capital markets. For example, commercial banks operate in money market as well as in capital market. They have started giving long-term loans also in recent years.

3. Interdependence

Money market and capital market are interdependent. The activities and policies of one market have their impact on those of the other. For example, the increased demand for funds in the capital market also raises the demand and interest rates in the money market. Similarly, the monetary policy also influences the activities of the capital market.

Differences : Money market is distinguished from capital on the basis of the maturity period, credit instruments and the institutions.

1. Maturity period

The money market deals in the lending and borrowing of short-term finance. But the capital market deals in lending and borrowing of long-term finance.

2. Credit instruments

The main credit instruments of the money market are trade bills, promissory notes and Government papers or bills. On the other hand, the main instruments used in the capital market are stocks, shares, debentures, bonds and securities of the Government.

3. Nature of credit instruments

The credit instruments dealt within the capital market are more heterogeneous than those in money market.

4. Institutions

Important institutions operating in the money market are central bank, commercial banks, acceptance houses, non-banking financial institutions, bill brokers etc. Important institutions in the stock market are stock exchanges, commercial banks, development banks and non-banking financial institutions such as insurance companies, mortgage banks and building societies.

5. Purpose of Loans

The money market meets the short-term credit needs of business. It provides working capital to the industrialists. The capital market, on the other hand, meets the long-term needs of the industrialists and provides fixed capital to buy land, machinery etc.,

6. Risk

The degree of risk is small in the money market. The risk is much greater in capital market.

7. Relation with Central Bank

The money market is closely and directly linked with the central bank of the country. The capital market feels Central Bank's influence, but mainly indirectly and through the money market.

8. Market regulation

In the money market, commercial banks are closely regulated. In the capital market, the institutions are not much regulated.

9. Basic role

The basic role of money market is that of liquidity adjustment. The basic role of capital market is that of putting capital to work preferably to long-term and productive employment.

Conclusion

From the above discussion, it is clear that the money and capital markets of a country play an important part, as they control the flow of short-term and long-term funds in the country. The money market determines the volume of working capital available to business and industrial units and also the price level. Likewise, the capital market determines the supply of long-term capital for the industrial units. The study of the monetary system, therefore, is very useful.

Questions for Discussions

1. What is meant by the money market ? Explain its structure and functions.
2. What are the chief characteristics of the Indian money market? Suggest some practical methods of improving its organisation.
3. What are the defects of the Indian money market ? Discuss the efforts made by the Reserve Bank of India to develop the Indian money market.
4. What is Capital Market. Discuss the objectives, importance and functions of capital market.
5. Give main points of distinction between money market and capital market.

Chapter - 6

STRUCTURE OF BANKING IN INDIA

Introduction

At the time of Independence Indian banking system was not sound. There were hundreds of small banks under unscrupulous managements. Hence, in 1949 two major actions were taken which were very important from the point of view of structural reforms in the banking sector. First, the Banking Regulation Act was passed. It gave extensive regulatory powers to Reserve Bank of India over the commercial banks. Another development of no less importance was the nationalisation of the RBI. These two major developments in the immediate Post-Independence period proved to be the turning points in India's commercial banking.

Indian banking system comprises of both organised and unorganised banks. Unorganised banking includes indigenous bankers and village money-lenders. Organised banking includes Reserve Bank of India, Commercial Banks, (including Foreign Banks), Development Banks, Exim Bank, Co-operative Banks, Regional Rural Banks, National Bank for Agriculture and Rural Development, Land Development Banks etc.,.

1. Indigenous Banks

From very ancient days, India has had banking of some type, known as indigenous banking. Indigenous banking peculiar to India had been organised in the form of family or individual business. In different parts of the country the indigenous bankers have been called by different names, such as Shroffs, Sahukars, Mahajans, Chettis, Seths, Kathiwals etc. They vary in size from petty money lenders to substantial shroffs who carry on large and specialised banking business. They are to be found in all parts of the country- in large towns and cities and villages.

Meaning

Indigenous bankers are individuals or private firms which receive deposits and give loans and thereby operate as banks. Since their activities are not regulated, they belong to the unorganised segment of the money market. The indigenous bankers have been engaged in the banking business in both ancient and medieval periods. They received set back with the introduction of modern banking after the arrival of the British. Over the past two and a half decade with the growth of commercial and cooperative banking the area of the operations of the indigenous bankers has contracted further. Still there are a few thousand indigenous bankers particularly in the western and southern parts of the country who are engaged in traditional banking business. The volume of their credit operations is however not known.

Groups

Indigenous bankers do not constitute a homogeneous group. Broadly they may be classified under four main sub-groups. Gujarati shroffs, Multani or Shikarpuri shroffs, chettiars and Marwari Kayas. The Gujarati shroffs operate in Mumbai, Kolkata and the industrial and trading cities of Gujarat. The Marwari Shroffs are active in Kolkata, Mumbai, tea-gardens of Assam and other parts of North-East India. The Multani or Shikarpuri shroffs are to be found mainly in Mumbai and Chennai and the Chettiars are concentrated in the South. Of the four main such groups of the indigenous bankers the Gujarati indigenous bankers are the most important in terms of the volume of business.

Types

There are three types of indigenous bankers : a) those whose main business is banking, b) those who combine their banking business with trading commission business, and c) those who are mainly traders and commission agents but who do a little banking business also. The majority of the indigenous bankers belong to the second group.

Functions of Indigenous Bankers

The main functions of the indigenous bankers are as follows.

1. Accepting Deposits

Indigenous bankers accept deposits from the public. These deposits are of two types : a) the deposits which are repayable on demand, and b) the deposits which are repayable after a fixed period. The indigenous bankers pay higher rate of interest than that paid by the commercial banks.

2. Advancing loans

The indigenous bankers advance loans to their customers against all types of securities, such as land, houses, crops, gold and silver. They also give credit against personal security. They finance inland trade, including the movement of agricultural commodities like sugar, oil seeds etc. But they do not grant direct loans to farmers. They give loans to farmers through money-lenders. They provide loans to small industries which cannot fulfil the necessary loan conditions of commercial banks. In recent years, they are also providing working capital to the small industrialists.

3. Business in Hundies

The indigenous bankers deal in hundies. They write hundies and buy and sell hundies. They also discount hundies and thereby meet the financial needs of the internal traders. They also transfer funds from one place to another through discounting of hundies.

4. Acceptance of valuables for safe custody

Indigenous bankers accept valuables of their clients for safe custody. Some indigenous bankers provide cheque facility. They provide remittance facilities also.

5. Non-Banking Functions

Most of the indigenous banks or bankers also carry on their non-banking business along with the banking activities. They generally have their retail trading business. They also participate in speculative activities. Sometimes, they act as agents to big commercial firms and earn commission.

Defects of Indigenous Bankers

There are, however, certain defects in indigenous banking in India. They are as follows.

1. Mixing banking and Non-banking business

The indigenous bankers, generally combine banking and non-banking business. Many of them undertake speculative activities. Their business is risky as they combine both trading and banking. This is against the principle of sound banking.

2. Unorganised banking system

The indigenous banking system is highly unorganised and segmented. Different indigenous bankers operate separately and independently. They have no coordination with each other. They have no regular contact with the commercial banks. The transfer of funds is not possible in such a system.

3. Insufficient capital

The indigenous bankers largely depend upon their own capital. As a result, their financial resources are insufficient to meet the demand of borrowers.

4. Meagre deposit business

The main business of the indigenous bankers is to give loans and deal in hundies. Their deposit business is meagre or very small. They have failed to tap and mobilise rural savings effectively.

5. Defective lending

The indigenous bankers, generally do not follow the sound banking principles while granting loans. They provide loans against insufficient securities or even against personal securities. They also give loans against immovable properties. They also do not distinguish between short-term and long-term loans.

6. Unproductive loans

The indigenous bankers do not pay attention to the purpose for which the loan is used. They also give money for unproductive and speculative activities or for paying off old debts.

7. Higher interest rates

The indigenous bankers charge very higher interest rates for the loans than those charged by the commercial banks. High rates of interest adversely affect the inducement to produce.

8. Exploitation of customers

The indigenous bankers adopt all types of malpractices and exploit their customers in many ways. For example, they make unauthorised deductions from loans. They overstate the amount of the loan in the document.

9. Discouragement to Bill Market

The indigenous bankers also stand in the way of developing a proper bill market in the country. Bulk of their business is based on cash transactions rather than on hundies.

10. Secrecy of accounts

They adopt a traditional accounting system in vernacular. The indigenous bankers keep secrecy about their accounts and activities. They neither get their accounts audited nor publish annual balance sheets. This raises suspicion in the minds of the people.

11. No Control of Reserve Bank

The indigenous banking business is unregulated. The Reserve Bank of India has no control over these bankers and cannot regulate their activities. In this way the indigenous banks are a great hurdle in the way of developing an organised money market in the country.

Indigenous Bankers and the Reserve Bank

Since its inception in 1935, the Reserve Bank of India has been making sincere efforts : (a) to bring the indigenous bankers under its control, (b) to integrate them with the modern banking system, and (c) to provide various central banking facilities to them. But the Reserve Bank failed to achieve success. It is unable to control the activities of the indigenous bankers. They are outside the control and influence of the Reserve Bank. The policy of the Reserve Bank would become effective only when indigenous banks are directly linked to it.

Suggestions for Reform

Various suggestions have been made to improve the functioning of indigenous banking in the country. They are :

1. The indigenous bankers should be directly linked with the Reserve Bank.
2. The indigenous banks should separate their non-banking business from banking business.
3. They should re-organise their banking business on modern lines. They should maintain proper accounts and get them audited regularly.
4. The wasteful competition between the indigenous bankers and the commercial banks should be ended.
5. The indigenous bankers should stop various malpractices in their business.
6. The benefits of the Banker's Book Evidence Act should be extended to the indigenous bankers also.
7. The indigenous bankers should develop bill - broking business, like bill brokers in the London money market.
8. They should be members of an association.
9. The Reserve Bank should supervise and inspect the conduct of indigenous bankers.
10. The Banking Commission, 1972, in its report suggested that the best way to control the business of indigenous bankers should be through commercial banks. The commercial banks should be encouraged to co-operate with the indigenous bankers. They should provide help to the indigenous bankers. They should provide facilities to indigenous banks to discount their hundies more easily. Thus, commercial banks must take greater responsibility in controlling the activities of indigenous bankers.

In view of the great role played by the indigenous bankers in the Indian economy. It is better to improve indigenous banking than to abolish it altogether. It is also better to reform them rather than replacing them by commercial banks. Legislation should be passed for regulating the activities of indigenous bankers by the Reserve Bank of India. This will help the Reserve Bank to secure effective control over the Indian money market. In the interest of the development of the country, the indigenous bankers should change their attitude and consider organisational and operational changes. Indigenous banking has a positive and perspective role to play in the money market of India.

2. Money Lenders

Money-lenders are those persons whose primary business is money lending. They lend money from their own funds : Broadly, the money-lenders may be classified into two categories : a) the professional money-lenders, and b) the non-professional money lenders. Professional money-lenders are those persons whose business is only lending of money. The Maharajas, Sahukars and Banias are professional money-lenders. They usually hold licences for money lending. Non-professional money lenders are those persons who combine money-lending with other activities. They do not depend entirely on money lending business. They are mainly engaged in other types of activities. They consists of landlords, agriculturists, traders, pensioners, rich windows etc. They have no licence to carry on money-lending business. They give loans to known people within their circle.

Features of Money-lenders

The methods and areas of operations vary from money-lender to money-lender. However, there are certain common features of their activities. They are as follows

(a) Money-lenders mostly lend their own funds.

(b) The borrowers from money-lenders are mainly illiterate and economically weaker sections of the society.

(c) The loans of the money-lenders are highly exploitative in nature.

(d) The credit provided by money-lenders may be secured or unsecured.

(e) The lending operations of money-lenders are prompt, informal and flexible.

Differences between Money-lenders and Indigenous Bankers

The following are the important differences between the money-lenders and the indigenous bankers.

1. The primary business of the money-lenders is money-lending. But the primary business of indigenous bankers is not banking.
2. The money-lenders do not accept deposits from the people. But indigenous bankers accept deposits from the people.
3. The indigenous bankers deal in hundies. But money-lenders do not deal in hundies.
4. The indigenous bankers generally lend for trade or productive purposes. But the money-lenders lend for consumption purposes.
5. Money-lenders operate in a limited area. So the scope of their business is limited. But indigenous bankers have a wider area of operation. So they have a large scale financial operations.
6. The indigenous bankers are largely urban-based, where as money-lenders carry on their business in rural areas.
7. Money-lenders functions in an isolated manner. Generally, they do not have any link with the organised sector of the money market. But indigenous bankers maintain some link with the organised sector because of their hundies business.

Defects of Money-lenders

The working of money-lenders has the following defects.

1. The money-lenders have inadequate resources to meet the needs of the rural people.
2. The loans of money-lenders are exploitative in character. They charge very high interest rates. They adopt all types of malpractices in their business. Some of the malpractices are : a) demanding interest in advance, b) demanding gifts, c) manipulating accounts etc.
3. The loans are mostly provided for consumption and unproductive purposes.
4. The money-lenders give loans against standing crops. In this way, they compel the cultivators to sell their produce at low prices to them.

5. Money-lenders have no uniformity in the matter of rate of interest. Different rates of interest are charged in different parts of the country.

The Government has taken various legislative steps to regulate the activities of money-lenders. There are acts like the Deccan Agriculturist Relief Act and the Money-lenders Act passed by the various states in India.

With the growth of rural banks, co-operative societies and other financial agencies in the rural areas, the importance of money-lenders has considerably declined. In near future, they will at the most, play a marginal role in the matter of rural finance in our country.

3. Co-operative Banks

Co-operative banks, another component of the Indian banking organisation, originated in India with the enactment of the Co-operative Credit Societies Act of 1904 which provided for the formation of co-operative credit societies. Under the Act of 1904, a number of cooperative credit societies were started. Owing to the increasing demand of cooperative credit, a new Act was passed in 1912, which provided for the establishment of cooperative central banks by a union of primary credit societies.

Meaning

Co-operative banks is an institution established on the cooperative basis and dealing in ordinary banking business. Like other banks, the co-operative banks collect funds through shares. They accept deposits and grant loans. They are generally concerned with the rural credit and provide financial assistance for agricultural and rural activities.

Structure of Co-operative Banks

Co-operative banking in India is federal in its structure. It has three sections. At the top there is the State Cooperative Bank which is the apex bank at the state level. At the intermediate level there are the central unions or the central cooperative banks. There is generally one central cooperative bank for each district. At the base of the pyramid there are the primary credit societies which cover the small towns and villages. Each higher level institution is a federation of those below, with membership and loan operations restricted to the affiliated units. This structure of cooperative banks is shown in chart 1 and chart 2.

A. Primary Agricultural Credit Societies

A co-operative credit society, commonly known as the primary agricultural credit society (PACS) is an association of persons residing in a particular locality. It can be started with ten or more persons. The members generally belong to a village. The membership is open to all the residents of the locality or village. Hence people of different status are brought together into the common organisation.

Each member contributes to the share capital of the society. The value of each share is generally nominal so as to enable even the poorest farmers to become a member. The members have unlimited liability, that is, each member is fully responsible for the entire loss of the society, in the event of failure. This will mean that all the members should know each other fully well. The management is honorary, thé only paid member normally being the secretary - treasure. Loans are given for short periods, normally for one harvest season, for carrying on agricultural operations, and the rate of interest is fixed about 6 percent. Dividends are not declared and profits are generally used for the welfare and improvement of the village. The village co-operative society was expected to attract deposits from among the well-to-do members and non-members of the village and thus promote thrift and self-help. It should give loans and advances to needy members mainly out of these deposits. However, the village societies failed to attract deposits and therefore, the Government had to bring into existence two other credit institutions, known as the Central and State Co-operative Banks, whose main function is to provide funds to the primaries which, in turn, will lend to the farmers.

Chart 1

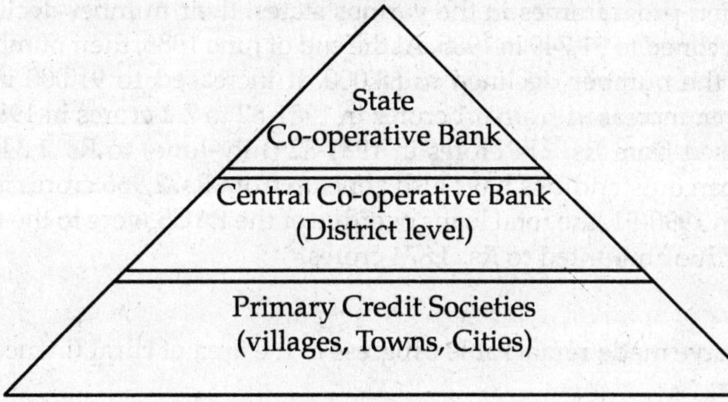

Chart 2

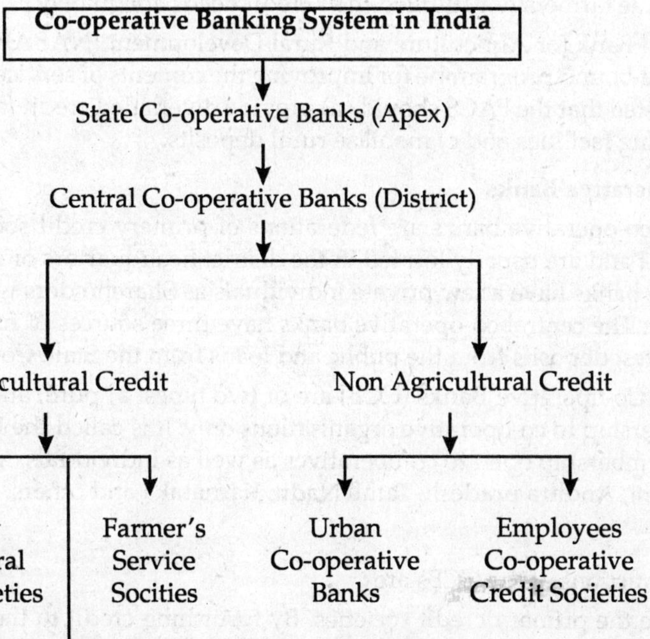

Chart 2 : provides in a nutshell an idea of the co-operative banking system in India.

Progress of PACS

The PACS occupy a strategic position in the co-operative credit structure of the rural economy. In 1951-52, there were 1.08 lakhs PACS. Their number increased to 2.12 lakhs in 1960-61. However, owing to he reorganisation programmes in the various states, their number declined to 94,484 in 1980-81, which further declined to 91,749 in 1985. At the end of June 1986, their number has increased to 92,430. In July 1991, the number declined to 88,000. It increased to 91,000 in 1993-94. Their membership has, however, increased from 6.1 crores in 1981-82 to 7.2 crores in 1985-86. Aggregate deposits of PACS increased from Rs. 314 crores in 1981-82 (July-June) to Rs. 1,349 crores 1990-91 (July-June). Their total loan outstandings have also gone up from Rs. 2,966 crores in 1981-822 to Rs. 4,181 crores in 1990-91. In 1990-91, the total loans overdue of the PACS were to the tune of Rs. 2,784. In 1993-94, the loan overdue amounted to Rs. 3,874 crores.

Shortfalls PACS

Though the PACS have made remarkable progress in the area of rural finance, their shortfalls may be enlisted as under;

1. They have failed to adequately fulfil the credit needs of the small farmers and tenants.
2. A large number of them lacked potential viability.
3. The Banking Commission (1972) observes that PACS neither provided credit for all productive activities of the farmers nor fulfilled their credit needs adequately.

The National Bank for Agriculture and Rural Development (NABARD) has recently stressed the need for a time-bound programme for improving the contents of services rendered by the PACS. It has been suggested that the PACS should : a) provide diversified credit facilities to their members b) extend marketing facilities and c) mobilise rural deposits.

B. Central Co-operative Banks

The central co-operative banks are federations of primary credit societies in a specific area, normally a district and are usually located in the district headquarters or some prominent town of the district. These banks have a few private individuals as Shareholders who provide both finance and management. The central co-operative banks have three sources of fund via., their own share capital and reserves, deposits from the public and loans from the State Co-operative Banks.

The Central Co-operative Banks (CCB) are of two types: a) pure, and b) mixed. A pure CCB confins its membership to co-operative organisations only. It is called the Banking Union. A mixed CCB keeps its membership open to co-operatives as well as individuals. Mixed CCBs are found in the states of Assam, Andhra pradesh, Tamil Nadu, Karnataka and others.

Functions

The major functions of the CCBs are :

1. They finance the primary credit societies. By furnishing credit to the primary socities, CCBs serve as an important link between these societies at the base level and the money market of the country.
2. They accept deposits from the public.
3. They grant credit to their customers on the security of first class gilt edged securities, gold etc.
4. They provide remittance facilities.
5. They act as balancing centres by shifting the excess funds of a surplus primary society to the deficit ones.

6. They keep watch on their debtor primary societies working and progress of recovery of loans.
7. To take up non-credit activities like the supply of seeds, fertilisers and consumer goods necessary to the farmers.
8. To prepare proposals for better utilisation of the financial resources of PACs.

Progress of CCBs

In 1981-82 (July-June) there were 338 central co-operative banks with an aggregate working capital of over Rs. 5,327 crores, or which their total deposits amounted to Rs. 2,768 crores.

In 1993-94 (April-March), their number amounted to 361. Their aggregate working capital has risen to Rs. 27,586 crores, of which deposits amounted to Rs. 16,251 crores.

In 1993-94, CCBs loans outstanding were of the order of Rs. 17,758 crores, of which Rs. 22 percent was loans overdue.

Defects of CCBs

The following are the major defects of the CCBs :

1. They violate the principle of co-operation by working on the lines of commercial banks.
2. They do not appoint experts to examine the creditworthiness of the primary societies. Hence, there has been problems of recovery and overdues.
3. They combine financing and supervisory work together. As a result supervisory work has been a failure in many cases.
4. Some CCBs have been utilising their reserve funds as working capital. This is not a very sound practice.
5. Mixed CCBs vitiate the very purpose of federation of the primary societies.
6. The CCBs charge very high interest rates to meet their high administration costs of small and uneconomic units.
7. Many CCBs are financially and organisationally weak.

To rehabilitate the weak CCBs, the Government of India formulated a scheme called the Central Sector Plan in 1972. Under the Scheme, selected CCBs were to be provided financial assistance for writing off bad debts. But the operation of the scheme has failed to bring about the desired results for two reasons.

(a) Nobody (including the concerned CCBs) took the programme seriously.

(b) There was no effective functioning of the state and district level committees constituted for monitoring the programme.

C. State Co-operative Banks

The state co-operative banks, also known as apex banks, from the apex of the co-operative credit structure in each state. They obtain their funds mainly from the general public by way of deposits, loans and advance from the Reserve Bank and their own share capital and reserves. Any where between 50-90 percent of the working capital of the SCBs are contributed by the Reserve Bank. Like the CCBs, SCBs are also pure or mixed.

Functions

The following are the major functions of SCBs.

1. The SCB acts as a banker to CCBs.

2. They have no power to supervise or control the activities of the affiliated CCBs.
3. A SCB serves as a leader of co-operative movement in a state.
4. In the absence of a district co-operative bank in a state, the SCB may give district financial assistance to the primary credit societies.
5. It co-ordinates the policy of the government with the co-operative principles.
6. It also brings about co-ordination between RBI, money market and co-operative credit societies.
7. It gives a number of subsidies to DCBs for improving co-operative credit societies.
8. It simplifies loan distribution system to enable its member to get loans very easily.
9. It helps the government in framing the schemes for the development of co-operatives in the state.

Defects

SCBs also have the same defects of the CCBs. The following are the major defects of SCBs :

1. They mix up commercial banking activities with co-operative banking.
2. They have insufficient share capital.
3. They utilise their reserve funds as working capital.
4. Some SCBs are not pure federations as they permit individual membership along with affiliation to the CCBs.

Progress

During the year 1980-81, there were 27 state co-operative banks, with an aggregate membership of 12,706 CCBs and primary societies and 12,731 individuals. Their aggregate working capital amounted to Rs. 2,749.6 crores.

In June 1991, there were 28 SCBs, the deposits amounted to Rs. 6,128 crores. Their total loans outstanding were of the order of Rs. 9,660 crores. However, their loans overdues account for 18 percent. In 1993-94 their deposits amounted to Rs. 11,305 crores, and loans outstanding Rs. 9,801 crores.

Present Position of Co-operative Banks

In the real sense, the co-operative movement was from the year 1912, when the defects of the Act 1904 were removed. But the progress has been seen when the Reserve Bank of India has taken keen interest in the growth of the co-operative movement.

The number of primary (urban) co-operative Banks (PCBs) at the end of march 1999 stood higher at 1,501 as against 1,431 a year ago (march 1998). The number of licensed PCBs rose to 1,180 from 1,107 during this period. The number of offices of PCBs moved up to 4,537 from 4,123 at the end of march 1997. Deposits of PCBs aggregated Rs. 23,841 crore at the end of march 1999, rising by 18.6 percent over the year and their outstanding advances were of the order of Rs. 17,675 crore recording an increase of 19.5 percent over the year.

Importance or Benefits of Co-operative Banks

The Co-operative movement has become a powerful instrument for rapid economic growth. It has resulted in several benefits. The expansion of co-operative banks has resulted in several benefits. They are :

1. They have provided cheap credit to farmers. They discouraged unproductive borrowing.

2. They have reduced the importance of money-lenders. More than 60% of the credit needs of agriculturists are now met by co-operative banks. Thus, co-operative banks have protected the rural population from the clutches of money-lenders.
3. Small and marginal farmers are being assisted to increase their income.
4. They have promoted saving and banking habits among the people, especially the rural people. Instead of hoarding money, the rural people tend to deposit their savings in the co-opertative or commercial banks.
5. They have undertaken several welfare activities. They have also taken steps to improve the morals, polity and education.
6. They have played an important part in changing the old customs and traditions of the people which are an obstacle to progress and economic betterment.
7. They have greatly helped in the introduction of better agricultural methods. Co-operative credit is available for purchasing improved seeds, chemical fertilisers and modern implements cheaply and sell their produce at good prices.

Problems or Weaknesses of Co-operative Banks

Various committees and commissions have reviewed the working of the Co-operative banking system. They pointed out a number of weaknesses of the system. Major weaknesses or problems are given below:

1. Excessive overdues

The borrowers from the co-operative banks are not repaying the loans promptly and regularly. There are heavy overdues. Besides overdues at all levels are increasing alarmingly. Lack of will and discipline among the farmers to repay loans is the principal factor responsible for the prevalence of overdues of co-operatives. Large amounts of overdues restrict the recycling of the funds and adversely affect the lending and borrowing capacity of the co-operative societies.

2. Inefficient Societies

The Co-operative credit societies are managed by people who have no knowledge of co-operation. They do not have necessary experience and training. As a result most of the societies are inefficient.

3. Regional disparities

Co-operative benefits are not evenly distributed as between different states. There is the problem of regional disparities in the distribution of co-operative credit. The loans advanced per member varies widely. The farmers of Gujarat, Punjab, Haryana and Tamilnadu are getting much more than those in Orissa, Bihar and West Bengal. Besides, the production loans and investment credit supplied in most of the tribal an hill areas is comparatively very less.

4. Benefits to big land owners

Most of the benefits from Co-operative have been cornered by the big land owners because of their strong socio-economic position. Small farmer are neglected by co-operative societies. Poor farmers are not able to get enough credit.

5. Dependence on outside resources

Co-operative societies or banks depend heavily on outside resources. State Governments and NABARD are the main sources of funds to co-operative societies. This heavy dependence on outside resources will be a great problem in future.

6. Political interference

The co-operative societies are dominated by political parties and politicians. There is favouritism and nepotism in the granting of loans.

7. Inadequate Coverage

Co-operatives have now covered almost all the rural areas of the country. But the membership is only around 45% of the rural families. 55% of rural families are thus still not covered under the co-operative credit system. Agricultural labourers and rural artisans constituted only 10% of the total membership of the co-operative credit system. The weaker sections of the rural community are still not adequately represented in the membership roll.

8. Lack of other facilities

Besides the provision of adequate and timely credit the small and marginal farmers also need other facilities in the form of supply of better seeds, fertilisers, pesticides etc. and marketing services. Very little attention is paid on the provision of such facilities.

9. Dual Control

There is dual control of the co-operatives, on the one side the NABARD and on the other by the State Government under the Co-operative Societies Act. Co-operative societies are treated as part and parcel of the Government has discouraged initiative in management.

10. Competition from private agencies

Co-operative banks are facing stiff competition from money-lenders and traders. Because of this competition, co-operatives could not make much progress.

11. Credit linked to assets

The credit given to a member is based on his assets. Those who do not have assets or those who have small assets do not get enough credit.

Suggestions for the Improvement of the Co-operative Credit Structure

1. The resources of the co-operative banks should be improved. Their dependance on outside resources must be reduced considerably.
2. The Primary Societies should be made more viable and economically strong units.
3. The liability of the members of the primary co-operatives should be made limited.
4. Loans should be given not on the basis of the assets of the member but on the basis of the estimated value of production. Although this method is introduced, it is not functioning properly, and not all societies have implemented it.
5. Loans given should be enough to meet agricultural and other expenses so that the members need not approach the money-lenders.
6. Agricultural inputs like fertilisers, seeds etc., should be supplied by the co-operatives. Credit and marketing should be integrated. Marketing and processing activities should be undertaken by the co-operatives.
7. The co-operatives should be given freedom to adopt management practices, rules and regulations to suit the local needs and conditions.
8. Co-operative training facilities should be expanded and the co-operatives should be manned by well trained personnel. Management should be professionalised.

9. Co-operative movement should become people's movement. They should be made to realise the benefits of co-operations.
10. They should be made agents of commercial banks wherever possible.
11. Steps must be taken for effective audit and inspection.
12. Political interference in the affairs of the co-operatives must be put to an end.
13. Co-operative should take steps to commercialise agriculture to increase the income level to the members and introduce appropriate technologies in agriculture. Members should be encouraged to take up subsidiary occupations.
14. Co-operative banks should diversify their activities and take up banking related services just like commercial banks. The credit societies or banks should be reorganised into multi-purpose societies.

4. Land Development Bank

Already, co-operative credit institutions were started and were working successfully in providing short-period credit to farmers. The Government wanted a special credit institution which would cater to the long-term credit needs of the farmers. Such an institution should be able to assist farmers with long-term loans carrying modest rates of interest and convenient methods of repayment. The Government started the land mortgage banks for this purpose; these banks have now come to be called the land development banks.

The land development banks were setup during the 1920's but their progress has been quite slow. After independence, they have been enjoying a great measure of prosperity, but whatever progress has been achieved is concentrated in only a few states viz., Tamil Nadu, Andhra pradesh, Karnataka, Maharashtra and Gujarat. There are two types of land development banks in the country. At state level, there are Central Land Development Banks, and under each central bank, there are primary land development banks. In some states, there is one Central Land Development Bank for the state which has branches all over the state.

Sources of Funds

There are three important sources of funds of land development banks : a) their own share capital and accumulated reserves b) deposits from the general public, and c) issue of bonds or debentures. The first two sources did not assume any significance and land development banks largely depend upon the third source. They are issued by the Central Land Development Banks and they carry a fixed rate of interest. The period of the debentures varies from 20-25 years. The banks issue two types of debentures, namely ordinary and rural debentures. The period of rural debentures varies between 7 and 15 years. The banks are required to create regular sinking funds to provide for repayment of the debentures. The debentures are generally guaranteed by the State Governments regarding payment of interest and repayment of principal. They are subscribed for by the public, the cooperative banks, commercial banks, the State Bank of India, the LIC and the Reserve Bank of India. These debentures are classified as trustee securities. The Reserve Bank lends on the security of these debentures, if they are guaranteed by the concerned state Government.

The Working of the LDBs

The Land Development Banks provide long-term loans to the agriculturists for permanent improvements on land. They usually charge a percent interest. They grant loans against the security of land or other agricultural property. Loans are usually given on the first mortgage and sometimes even on the second mortgage of land or agricultural property. Generally, they give loans up to 50 percent of the market value of the mortgaged property.

Progress

A remarkable progress has been made by the LDBs in providing long-term finance to the agriculturists. The total number of LDBs (central and primary) increased from 481 in 1960-61 to 920 in 1984-85. In 1984-85 their number of membership had gone up to 10.6 lakhs. In 1984-85, their loan outstanding were to the tune of Rs. 3,643 crores and loan overdues amounted to Rs. 409 crores.

Defects

Several defects have been noticed on the operational side of the Land Development Banks.

1. They charge very high rates of interest.
2. On account of red-tapism, there are the usual delays up to more than a year in granting loans.
3. No second loans is given until the first one is repaid.
4. They give loans only up to 50 percent of the value of the land mortgaged. Thus, a very high margin is kept.
5. They adopt complicated procedures which ultimately force the illiterate farmers to resort to money-lenders to meet their financial requirements.
6. Quite often, loans are granted to discharged prior debts rather than for land improvement.

Suggestions for Improvement

The Reserve Bank of India has made many practical suggestions to tone up the working of the land development banks. First of all, land development banks should not be of the same uniform type as was the case in the past. India, being a large country, exhibits diversity of local conditions. Hence land development banks should reflect these diversities. Secondly, primary land development banks should be set up in large numbers - one for a small group of villages. The purpose is that they are located as near the farmers as possible so as to induce the latter to approach the development bank easily. Thirdly, the land development banks should charge low rates of interest - may be 4 percent or so - to enable the small and marginal farmers to approach them for assistance. Finally, these banks should make efforts to improve their efficiency and work along with other agencies which are also providing credit for farmers.

5. Regional Rural Banks

In spite of the rapid expansion programmes undertaken by the commercial banks in recent years, a large segment of the rural economy was still beyond the reach of the organised commercial banks. To fill this gap it was thought necessary to create a new agency which could combine the advantages of having adequate resources but operating relatively with a lower cost at the village level.

After the declaration of emergency, the then Prime Minister, Smt. Indira Gandhi, announced on July 1, 1975 the 20 point economic programme of the Government of India. One of the points of this programme was the liquidation of rural indebtedness by stages and provide institutional credit to farmers and artisans in rural areas. The Government of India promulgated on September 26, 1975, the Regional Rural Bank Ordinance, to set up regional rural banks throughout the country; the Ordinance was replaced by the Regional Rural Banks Act, 1976. The main objective of the regional rural banks is to provide credit and other facilities particularly to the small and marginal farmers, agricultural labourers, artisans and small entrepreneurs so as to develop agriculture, trade, commerce, industry and other productive activities in rural areas.

Objectives of Regional Rural Banks

The following are the main objectives of regional rural banks :

1. To provide credit and other facilities particularly to the small and marginal farmers, agricultural labourers, artisans, small entrepreneurs and other weaker sections.
2. To develop agriculture, trade, commerce, industry and other productive activities in the rural areas.
3. To provide easy, cheap and sufficient credit to the rural poor and backward classes and save them from the clutches of money lenders.
4. To encourage entrepreneurship.
5. To increase employment opportunities.
6. To reconcile rural business aims and social responsibilities.

Capital Structure

At present, the authorised capital of regional rural banks is Rs. 5 crores, and the issued capital is Rs. 1 crore 50% of the issued capital is to be subscribed by the Central Government, 15% by the concerned State Government, and 35% by the sponsoring commercial banks. The shares of regional rural banks are to treated as "approved securities."

Features of Regional Rural Banks

The following are the features of the regional rural banks :

1. The regional rural bank, like a commercial bank, is a scheduled bank.
2. The RRB is a sponsored bank. It is sponsored by a scheduled commercial bank.
3. It is deemed to be co-operative society for the purposes of Income tax Act, 1961.
4. The area of operations of the RRB is limited to a specified region relating to one or more districts in the concerned state.
5. The RRB charges interest rates as adopted by the co-operative societies in the state.
6. The interest paid by the RRB on its term deposits may be 1% or 2% more than that is paid by the commercial banks.
7. The regional rural bank enjoys many concessions and privileges.

Functions of Regional Rural Banks

The functions of Regional Rural Bank are as follows :

1. Granting of loans and advances to small and marginal farmers and agricultural labourers, either individually or in groups.
2. Granting of loans and advances to co-operative societies agricultural processing societies and co-operative farming societies primarily for agricultural purposes or for agricultural operations and other related purposes.
3. Granting of loans and advances to artisans, small entrepreneurs and persons of small means engaged in trade, commerce and industry or other productive activities within a specified region.
4. Accepting various types of deposits.

The credit policy of regional rural banks is more liberal than co-operative banks. It is not necessary for the borrower to mortgage property or deposit title deeds. It is not necessary to produce "not encumbrance certificate" or get legal opinion.

Progress achieved by Regional Rural Banks

The Regional Rural Banks have achieved significant progress in all directions. The progress achieved is discussed below :

1. Number of Banks

The first, five regional rural banks were started at Moradabad and Gorakhpur in Uttar Pradesh, Bhiwani in Haryana, Jaipur in Rajasthan and Malda in West Bengal. There are now (June 2001) 196 regional rural banks, covering over 400 districts in the country with 14,550 branches. The largest number of offices are started in Uttar Pradesh.

2. Deposits

The deposits of regional rural banks increased substantially over the years. The total deposits were only Rs. 20 lakhs in 1975. They increased to Rs. 25, 430 crores by June 2001.

3. Advances

Total advances granted by all regional banks amounted to Rs. 10 lakhs in 1975. The total advances granted increased to Rs. 11,020 crores in 2000. Over 90% of the advances of regional rural banks are direct advances to small and marginal farmer; landless labourers and rural artisans.

4. Self-employment schemes

The regional rural banks are making notable effort to encourage self-employment schemes.

5. Creation of local employment opportunities

Regional rural banks have been taking active steps to create employment for the local people and achieved good success.

6. Participation in various programmes

During the last 22 years regional rural banks have been active participants in programmes designed to provide credit assistance to weaker sections. For instance, they are providing credit assistance to identified beneficiaries under the New 20 - Point Programme for scheduled castes and tribes.

7. Assistance to physically handicapped persons

Physically handicapped persons are provided finance for purchase of artificial limbs, hearing aids, wheel chains etc.

8. Farmers societies

Regional rural banks have also sponsored and financed about 90 Farmers societies.

9. Integrated Rural Development Programme (IRDP Scheme)

Regional rural banks have been taking active part in the Integrated Rural Development Programme.

Regional rural banks, thus, have achieved notable progress in expanding branch network and extending credit support to weaker sections in rural areas. They exist as rural banks of the rural people.

Problems

The following are the major problems faced by the regional rural banks :

1. Existence of overdues

The most serious problem faced by the regional rural banks is the existence of heavy overdues. Overdues are rising continuously. It is estimated that about 30% of the loans sanctioned still remain due from the borrowers. This has caused innumerable financial problems besides limiting the capacity of regional rural banks to lend and operated as viable units.

2. Losses

Most of the regional rural banks are not economically viable. They have been continuously incurring losses for years together. The accumulated losses are estimated to be Rs. 1200 crores upto March 2000

3. Limited Channels of Investment

Since the regional rural banks have to lend to small and marginal farmers and other weaker sections of the society, the channels of investment are limited. Therefore, their earning capacity is low.

4. Difficulties in deposit mobilisation

Regional rural banks have been facing a number of practical difficulties in deposit mobilisation. Richer sections of the village society show least interest in depositing their money in these banks because they are served by these banks.

5. Procedural rigidities

Regional rural banks follow the procedures of the commercial banks in the matter of deposits and advancing loans. Such procedures are highly complicated and time-consuming from the villagers point of view.

6. Hasty branch expansion

There is haste and lack of coordination in branch expansion. It has resulted in lopsidedness in branch expansion. It has increased infrastructure costs and reduced profitability.

7. High establishment costs

The salary structure of regional rural banks has been revised with the result that establishment costs have gone up. The regional rural banks are unable to cover the increased costs, since their customers are specified weaker sections enjoying concessional interest on loans and advances. The surplus available for meeting interest on deposits, administration costs and other expenses is said to be very low.

8. Multi-agency system of control

Regional rural banks are controlled by many agencies. The present multi-agency control of regional rural banks involves sponsor banks, NABARD, Reserve Bank, State Governments and the central government. This is not conducive to high operational efficiency and viability. So the present multi-agency system of control should be replaced by single agency control.

9. Slow progress in lending activity

The growth in loan business of regional rural banks is low. For this the following reasons may be given :

(a) There has been limited scope for direct lending by regional rural banks in their fields of operation.

(b) It is always difficult to identify the potential small borrowers.

(c) Most of the small borrowers do not like the bank formalities and prefer to borrow from the money - lenders.

(d) There is lack of co-ordination between officials of district credit planning committees and the regional rural banks.

10. Inefficient Staff

As the salary structure of regional rural banks is not attractive when compared to other banks, efficient persons have a tendency to shift to commercial banks to improve their salary and career. Besides, many employees are not willing to work in villages. There is no true local involvement of the bank staff in the villages they serve.

Despite these problems, the regional rural banks have been trying their level best to achieve their social objectives. They have succeeded in projecting their image of "Small Man's Bank." They are in fact, development banks of the rural poor. They have been trying to fill regional and functional gaps in rural finance in our country.

Suggestions for Reorganisation and Improvement

Several expert groups have made a number of suggestions necessary to reorganise the structure and improve the working of regional rural banks. The important suggestions are given below :

1. These banks should continue to work as rural banks of the rural poor.
2. The state governments should also take keen interest in the growth of Regional Rural Banks.
3. Participation of local people in the equity share capital of the regional rural banks should be allowed and encouraged.
4. The regional rural banks should be linked with primary Agricultural co-operative societies and Farmer's service societies.
5. The regional rural banks should be strongly linked with the sponsoring commercial banks and the Reserve Bank of India.
6. A uniform pattern of interest rate structure should be devised for the rural financial agencies.
7. The regional rural banks must strengthen effective credit administration by way of credit appraisal, monitoring the progress of loans and their efficient recovery.
8. The regional rural banks should increase their consumption loans to the villagers and weaker sections. They should be allowed to increase their loans to richer sections of the society.
9. The regional rural banks should be permitted to provide full range of banking services, such as, remittance and other agency services, which would help a lot in developing banking habits among the villagers.
10. The regional rural banks should diversify their loans.
11. The present multi-agency system of control of regional rural banks should be replaced by single agency control.
12. As far as possible, natives should be appointed to work in them. The employees should be given suitable training.

13. Effective steps should be taken to prevent the misuse of funds by borrowers and willful defaulters.
14. Lending procedures should be made easy in order to avoid undue delays.
15. The image of regional rural banks should be improved. They should not be identified as "Second class" banks or an extension of the urban-oriented commercial banks. They must develop their own identity.

Regional rural banks have an important role to play in our rural economy as they have to act as alternative agencies to provide institutional credit in rural areas. They have not been set up to replace co-operative credit societies but supplement them. What the commercial banks have not done in rural areas, regional rural banks are trying to do it now. A such, regional rural banks should be specially assisted to solve their problems and be made real promoters of growth in rural India.

6. NABARD

The National Bank for Agriculture and Rural Development (NABARD) was set-up on 12th July, 1928 under an Act of Parliament. It has been established by merging the Agricultural Credit Department, and Rural Planning and Credit Cell of the Reserve Bank and the entire undertaking of Agricultural Refinance and Development Corporation. Hence, the National Bank has to perform a dual function : a) The function of the Reserve Bank as an apex institution and b) The function of Agricultural Refinance and Development Corporation as a refinance institution.

Objectives

The National Bank for Agricultural and Rural Development (NABARD) is essentially a development bank for promoting agricultural and rural development. The major objectives of NABARD are :

1. To give financial assistance for increasing the agricultural production.
2. To supply the long-term needs of the rural areas.
3. To supply loans by way of refinance.
4. To helps small industries, cottage industries and also artisans.
5. To achieve overall rural development.

NABARD's Financial Resources

The authorised capital of NABARD is Rs. 500 crores and the paid up capital is Rs. 100 crores. The paid-up capital is contributed by the Central Government and the Reserve Bank in equal proportions. At the time of its establishment, loans and advances granted by the Reserve Bank and outstanding against state co-operative banks and regional rural banks were transferred to NABARD. Besides, the Reserve Bank has also sanctioned a credit of Rs. 1200 crores to NABARD. Credits are also received from the U.K., the U.S.A., the Netherlands, Switzerland and West Germany. Besides these, NABARD has been raising funds from the market through the issue of debentures. To meet the loan requirements NABARD draws funds from the Government of India the World Bank and other agencies. NABARD had raised resources to the extent of Rs. 11,000 crores between 1983 and 1999. NABARD has thus sufficient financial resources for financing all agricultural and rural development programmes. At present its paid up capital is Rs. 2000 crores.

Management

NABARD is managed by a Board of Directors, consisting of a Chairman, a managing director and 13 other directors. They are appointed by the Central Government in consultation with the

Reserve Bank. There will be also an Advisory Council.

Functions of NABARD

NABARD does not provide credit directly to the farmers and other rural people. It provides refinance credit to the state co-operative banks, regional rural banks and other financial institutions as may be approved by the Reserve Bank. It is a single integrated agency for meeting the credit needs of all types of agricultural and rural development activities. It performs the following functions.

1. Apex institution for rural finance

NABARD performs all the functions which were previously performed by the Reserve Bank of India. It directs the policy, planning and operations in the field of credit for agriculture and other economic activities in rural areas. It, thus acts as an apex bank in the country for supporting and promoting agriculture and rural development. It is described as "Rural Reserve Banks".

2. Refinance institution

It serves as an apex refinancing agency for the institutions providing production and investment credit for promoting various developmental activities in rural areas. These activities are related to agriculture, small scale industries, village and cottage industries, handi-crafts, small artisans etc. NABARD has taken over the function of refinancing from the Agricultural Refinance Development Corporation. It provides refinance facilities to state co-operative banks, regional rural banks, commercial banks and other financial institutions approved by the Reserve Bank of India. Commercial banks lead in availing of refinance from NABARD.

3. Credit functions

NABARD is empowered to give short-term, medium-term and long term loans in a composite form. It looks after the credit requirements of all types of agricultural and rural development activities.

(a) It provides short-term, medium-term and long-term credits to state co-operative banks, land development banks, regional rural banks and other financial institutions approved by the Reserve Bank of India.

(b) It grants long term loans, upto 20 years, to state governments to enable them to subscribe to the share capital of co-operative credit societies.

(c) It provides medium-term loans to state co-operative banks and regional rural banks for agricultural and rural development.

(d) It gives long-term loans to any institution approved by the Central Government.

4. Contribution of share capital

NABARD contributes to the share capital of any institution concerned with agriculture and rural development.

5. Investment in securities

NABARD can invest in securities of any institution concerned with agriculture and rural development. For promoting innovative investments, NABARD has started "Venture capital fund."

6. Conversion and Rescheduling facilities

NABARD provides refinance to eligible institutions for conversion and rescheduling of loans, under conditions of drought, famine or other natural calamities, military operations etc.

7. Financial help to non-agricultural sector

Besides providing credit to agricultural and allied activities, the NABARD also renders financial help to the non-agricultural sector with the aim of promoting integrated rural development. It provides financial assistance to small scale industries, cottage and village industries and industrial co-operative societies for meeting their working capital and fixed capital needs.

8. Co-ordination of activities

NABARD co-ordinates the activities of central and state governments, planning commission and other institutions concerned with the development of small-scale industries, village and cottage industries, rural crafts and industries in the decentralised sector.

9. Regulatory function

NABARD has the responsibility to inspect regional rural banks, and central and state co-operative banks.

10. Maintenance of Research and Development Fund

NABARD maintains Research and Development Fund : a) to promote research in agriculture and rural development, b) to formulated programmes to suit the requirements of different areas, and to cover special activities.

11. Training programmes

NABARD has to provide comprehensive training programmes to its own staff as well as to the staff of state co-operative banks, regional rural banks etc. The training is to be meant for upgrading the technical skill and competence of the staff.

12. Evaluation of projects

NABARD undertakes monitoring and evaluation of projects refinanced by it. It is responsible for the development, policy, planning operational matters, co-ordination, monitoring, training, consultancy etc., relating to rural credit.

Achievements of NABARD

NABARD is playing a vital role in the reduction of regional imbalances and providing assistance to small farmers, marginal farmers and weaker sections. It has been performing its various functions smoothly. Its performance in extending various types of financial assistance is as follows.

1. Short-term assistance

NABARD sanctioned short-term credit limits worth Rs. 6230 crores during 1997-98 to state co-operative banks for financing seasonal agricultural operations. The credit facility is available at a concessional rate of 3% below the bank rate.

2. Medium-term assistance

NABARD has continued to follow the policy earlier laid down by the Reserve Bank in regard to sanctioning medium-term credit limits for approved agricultural purposes. A major portion of medium-term credit of NABARD went to state co-operative banks and central co-operative banks to convert short-term loans granted to farmers into medium-term loans.

3. Long-term assistance

NABARD grants long-term credit to State Governments for contribution to the share capital of co-operative institutions. During 1997-98, it extended long-term credit worth Rs. 210 crores.

4. Schematic lending

During 1997-98 NABARD sanctioned 6,810 schemes involving its own commitments of Rs. 3930 crores,. Largest number of schemes sanctioned were related to minor irrigation followed by those related to farm mechanisation. Land development, farm mechanisation, plantations and horticulture, poultry, sheep-breeding, piggery, dairy, fisheries etc., are other important schemes which are financed by NABARD.

5. Assistance to less developed states

NABARD like ARDC has continued the policy of promoting agricultural investment in the less developed and unbanked states. Uttar Pradesh, Bihar, Madhya Pradesh, Rajasthan and Orissa have been receiving the largest share of financial benefits from NABARD.

6. Assistance to non-farm sector

NABARD has also provided financial help to non-farm activities with a view to promote integrated rural development. Finance has been provided for production and marketing activities of co-operative sugar mills, handloom weaver's societies, industrial co-operatives, rural artisans etc.

7. Rehabilitation programme

NABARD has been playing an energetic role in strengthening and reorganising the co-operative structure in the country. It has initiated a rehabilitation programme for financially and administratively weak central and state co-operative banks. It has also been providing help in the rehabilitation work of state land development banks and primary land development banks. State Governments have been asked to take effective steps to ensure functional co-ordination between short-term and long-term credit by co-operatives. It has also created a "cell" to monitor the implementation of this directive.

8. Assistance to Research and Development Projects

Every year NABARD has been providing financial help to a number of banks from its Research and Development Fund for setting up or strengthening their "Technical. Monitoring and Evaluation Cell". It has been sanctioning funds for organising research, conferences and seminars on subject having relevance to NABARD.

9. Credit plans under the New strategy

Under the "Service Area Approach", the annual credit plans are prepared by the bank branches. The district level offices of the NABARD would help to improve the quality of credit plans prepared by banks branches and also co-ordiante and effectively monitor the credit plans.

10. Integrated rural development programme

NABARD has helped the implementation of the "integrated rural development programme". Under the 20 point Economic Programme, the NABARD has taken steps to provide adequate financial facilities to the weaker sections of the society.

11. Regional Rural Banks

After the establishment of NABARD, all the refinance facilities earlier available to regional banks have been provided by NABARD.

Thus, NABARD has given a tremendous push to agricultural credit and thus promoted agricultural and rural development. Today, the NABARD has become a king-pin of rural development.

7. Commercial Banks

Commercial banks are very popular almost in every country because of the service they provide to individuals and commerce and industry. A commercial bank may be defined as a financial institution which accepts deposits against which cheques can be drawn, lends money to commerce and industry and renders a number of other useful services to the customers and the society. Commercial banks borrow money from those who have surplus funds and lend to those who need funds for commercial and industrial purposes. Thus, they act as dealers in loanable funds of the society. Commercial banks receive deposits in the form of fixed deposits, savings bank accounts and current accounts and advance money, generally for short periods, in the form of cash credits, overdrafts and loans. They also render a number of service to their customers, such as collection of cheques, safe custody of valuables, remittance facilities and payment of insurance premium, electricity bills, etc.

The commercial banks perform the following major functions :

(a) Receiving deposits from the public and the business firms.
(b) Lending money to various sections of the economy for productive activities.
(c) Issue of demand drafts, traveller's cheques, bank cards, etc, for the smooth remittance of funds.
(d) Provision of locker facility to the customers.
(e) Safe custody of documents, ornaments and other valuables of customers.
(f) Payment of telephone, electricity and water bills on behalf of the customers.
(g) Collection of cheques of the customers.
(h) Issue of letters of credit.
(i) Acting as trustees, executors of wills, etc.

Nationalisation of Banks

The Government of India nationalised 14 major banks in the country in July 1969 and another 6 banks in 1980. The nationalisation of banks was described as "historic", "momentous", "bold" and "timely" by certain sections of the people. The State Bank of India and its seven subsidiaries had already been nationalised. The regional rural banks from their very inception are in the public sector. Thus about 90% of the country's commercial banking system is now in the public sector.

Achievements of Nationalised Banks

A banking revolution occurred in the country during the post-nationalisation era. There has been a great change in the thinking and outlook of commercial banks after nationalisation. There has been a fundamental change in the lending policies of the nationalised banks. Indian banking has become development-oriented. Indian banking has changed from class banking to mass-banking or social banking. Indian banking system has improved and progressed appreciably. Various achievements of banks in the post nationalisation period are explained below.

1. Development-oriented Banking

Historically, Indian banks were mainly concerned with the growth of commerce and some of the traditional industries such as, cotton textile and jute. The banks were concentrated in the big commercial centres. They mostly granted short-term commercial loans. They were unwilling to venture into new fields of financing. But after nationalisation of banks, the concept of banking has widened from acceptance of deposits and mere lending to development oriented banking. Banks are increasingly catering to the needs of industrial and agricultural sectors. From short-term lending, banks have been gradually shifting to medium and even long-term lending. From well-established large industries and business houses, banks are positively shifting to assisting small and weak industrial units, small farmers, artisans and other neglected groups of people in the country. They have adopted the Lead Bank Scheme. Under this scheme, all the districts of the country are allotted to some bank or the other. The lead bank of district is actively engaged in :

(a) Opening bank branches in all important localities.

(b) Providing maximum credit facilities for development in the district, and

(c) Mobilising the savings of the people in the district.

2. Branch Expansion

Rapid economic development pre-supposes rapid expansion of commercial banks. Initially, the banks were conservative and opened branches mainly in cities and big towns. Branch expansion gained momentum after nationalisation of top commercial banks and the introduction of "Lead Bank Scheme". The Lead Bank Scheme has played an important role in the bank expansion programme. The number of branches of all scheduled commercial banks increased from 8,260 in 1969 to 64,240 in 1998. Thus with in 38 years after bank nationalisation, there was over 800 percent increase in the number of branches. There had been a significant increase in bank branches in the rural, underbanked and unbanked areas. The number of branches in rural areas increased from 1860 in 1969 to 32,880 in 1998. With the progress of branch expansion programme, the national average of population per bank office has declined from 63,800 to 15,000. M. Gopalkrishnan says "the single striking feature of the post-nationalisation banking scene is the rapidity with which the branch network has multiplied itself. The rate of branch expansion has been unparalleled any where else in the world." Thus the overall growth of bank branches in the last 30 years has been remarkable in its geographical coverage and removal of regional imbalances in the country.

3. Expansion of Bank Deposits

Since nationalisation of banks, there has been a substantial growth in the deposits of commercial banks. Bank deposits had increased from over Rs. 5,910 crores in 1970-71 to over Rs. 8,10,070 crores in 1999-2000. Thus bank deposits had increased by 150 times. Development of banking habit among people through publicity, extensive branch banking and prompt service to the customers led to increase in bank deposits. To attract deposits, Indian banks have introduced many attractive saving schemes. To attract deposits from widely scattered areas, mobile bank's branches have been introduced by a number of banks. A number of banks have started evening branches, sunday branches for the benefit of their customers. Apart from the quantitative increases in deposits, there has been an impressive qualitative shift. The number of small account holders with the banks has been increasing day-by-day. Aggregate deposits are composed to time deposits and demand deposits. Earlier there was predominance of demand deposits. Now there is predominance of time deposits. The ratio of time deposits to total deposits has been increasing.

4. Credit Expansion

The expansion of bank credit has also been more spectacular in the post-bank nationalisation period. Bank credits had increased from Rs. 4,700 crores in 1970-71 to Rs. 4,43,180 crores in 1999-2000. At present, banks are also meeting the credit requirements of industry, trade and agriculture on a much larger scale than before. Credit is the pillar of development. Bank credit has its crucial importance in the context of development and growth with social Justice.

5. Investment in Government Securities

The nationalised banks are expected to provide finance for economic plans of the country through the purchase of government securities. There has been a significant increase in the investment of the banks in Government and other approved securities in recent years. The investments increased from Rs. 1,727 crores in 1970 to 74,370 crores in 1995.

6. Advances to priority sectors

An important change after the nationalisation of banks is the expansion of advances to the priority sectors. One of the main objectives of nationalisation of banks to extend credit facilities to the borrowers in the so far neglected sectors of the economy. To achieve this, the banks formulated various schemes to provide credit to the small borrowers in the priority sectors, like agriculture, small-scale industry, road and water transport, retail trade and small business. The total credit provided by banks to the priority sectors has increased from Rs. 440 crores in 1969 to Rs. 91,300 crores in March 1998. As a result, advances to priority sectors as percentage of total credit increased from 15% in 1969 to 42% in 1998. The bank lending to priority sector was, however, not uniform in all states. It was quite low in many backward states like U.P., Bihar and Rajasthan. Under the new banking policy stress is laid on the weaker and under-privileged groups in the priority sector "weaker sections" refer to all persons who became suppressed, depressed and oppressed because of socio-political, socio-economic or socio-religious reasons. The concept of profitability has been substituted by "social purposes" with regard to lending to weaker sections of the society. Quantitatively, banks have done well in priority lending. But overdues and bad debts have been a serious problem faced by banks in respect of advances made to the weaker sections of the society. There is always the problem of ensuring the effective end use of the loans given to the priority sectors.

7. Social Banking -Poverty Alleviation programmes

Commercial banks, especially the nationalised banks have been participating in the poverty alleviation programme launched by the government.

(a) Differential interest scheme

With a view to provide bank credit to the weaker sections of the society at a concessional rate the Government introduced the "Differential interest rates scheme" form April 1972. Under this scheme, the public sector banks have been providing loans at 4% rate of interest to the weaker sections of the society. The scheme has shown notable progress. The number of accounts was 2 million and the advances outstanding were Rs. 640 crores at the end of March 1996.

(b) Integrated Rural Development Programme (IRDP)

This is a pioneering and ambitious programme to rectify imbalances in rural economy and also for all-round progress and prosperity of the rural masses. Under this programme banks has assisted nearly 1.8 million beneficiaries during 1997-98 and disbursed a total amount of Rs. 1990 crores as loan. Out of the beneficiaries, over 1 million belonged to scheduled castes and scheduled tribes and 0.7 million were women.

Other important scheme introduced by the government of India and implemented through the banking system includes. a) self-employment scheme for educated youth, b) self-employment programme for urban poor, and c) credit to minority communities.

8. Growing importance of small customers

The importance of small customers to banks has been growing. Most of the deposits in recent years have come from people with small income. Similarly, commercial banks lending to small customers has assumed greater importance. Thus banking system in India has turned from class-banking to mass-banking.

9. Innovative Banking

In recent years, commercial banks in India have been adopting the strategy of "innovative banking in their business operations". Innovative banking implies the application of new techniques, new methods and novel schemes in the areas of deposit mobilisation, deployment or credit and bank management. Mechanisation and computerisation processes are being introduced in the day-to-day working of the banks.

10. Diversification in Banking

The changes which have been taking place in India since 1969 have necessitated banking companies to give up their conservative and traditional system of banking and take to new and progressive functions. The Government had been encouraging commercial banks to diversity their functions. As a result, commercial banks have set up merchant banking divisions and are underwriting new issues, especially preference shares and debentures. There are now eight commercial banks which have set up mutual funds also. Commercial banks have started lending directly or indirectly for housing. Venture capital fund is also started by one public sector bank. State Bank of India and Canara Bank have set-up subsidiaries exclusively for undertaking "factoring services". In future all commercial banks can be expected to diversify their functions and adopt new technologies.

11. Globalisation

The liberalisation of the economy, inflow of considerable foreign investments, frequency in exports etc., have introduced an element of globalisation in the Indian banking system.

8. Credit Cards

Now-a-days some banks are issuing credit cards. The system of issuing credit cards originated in the U.S.A. Credit cards have become very popular in U.S.A. Credit cards are issued in the name of companies to be used by designated executives. They are also issued in the name of individuals to be charged to the company's account or to the personal account.

The credit card system is utilised by big companies, super rich and highly paid executives in our country. But credit cards are not accepted by all establishments in the country. In our country only luxury hotels, airlines, shops and other establishments dealing in costly and luxury goods or providing costly services accept credit cards provided, they have arrangements with the issuing bank.

Advantages of Credit Cards

Credit card holders enjoy certain privileges and advantages. They are :

1. Credit cards enabler persons to purchase goods and services on credit in establishments which accept them. They enjoy credit facility without paying interest for above four to six weeks.
2. Carrying a credit card is more convenient and safer than carrying cash or cheque book.
3. The credit card gives the traveller peace of mind as it takes care of all his needs.
4. Credit card is a safer and convenient method of payment.
5. A credit card holder will be recognised as a man of sound financial standing.
6. The issuing bank or concern will debit the credit card holder or customer's account once in month after receiving details about purchases.

Limitations or Drawbacks of Credit Cards

The following are the limitations or disadvantages :

1. Credit cards cannot be used for making purchases in all business establishments.
2. Issuing bank will place a limit on the expenditure by the credit card holder.
3. Credit card system will increase indebtedness among the card holders. For example, indebtedness has increased tremendously on account of the credit card system in the U.S.A.

Inspite of the limitations, credit cards have become popular instrument in recent years in most of the countries in the world. The future commerce is E-commerce. Credit cards facilitate E-commerce.

Conclusion

It is thus clear that in India, there are different kinds of banks, viz, indigenous bankers, money-lenders, co-operative banks, NABARD, Land development banks, Regional Rural Banks, Commercial banks including the State Bank of India and its subsidiaries and foreign exchange banks. Over all these institutions, there is the Reserve Bank of India which is the central bank of the country.

Questions for Discussions

1. Give an account of the role and significance of indigenous banking.
2. Examine the role of the Money-Lenders in the provision of agricultural finance.
3. What were the objectives of the nationalisation of the major commercial banks in India? How far have these objectives been achieved so far ?
4. Describe the structure of the co-operative bank in India and explain the function of co-operative banks.
5. Evaluate the progress and problems of Land Development Banks.
6. NABARD is described as "Rural Reserve Bank" explain.
7. Critically examine the objectives and achievements of Regional Rural Banks in India.

Chapter - 7

DEVELOPMENT BANKS

Introduction

Since Independence, the Government of India has been responsible for setting up a series of institutions for the development of agriculture, industry, international trade, etc. These institutions have come to be called as development banks. Some of them specialise in industry and some in agriculture. In this chapter we shall be studying the important development banks in India.

Meaning

A development bank is a multipurpose financial institution with a broad developmental objective. It is defined as a financial concern which is concerned with providing financial assistance to business concerns. The financial assistance is provided in the form of loans, underwriting shares and debentures, investment and guarantee activities. It also performs promotional activities in a variety of ways. It renders several services like discovery of investment projects, preparation of project reports, management services etc. Thus, development banks provide capital, technology and entrepreneurship. Development banks are considered to be the backbone of financial market. Industrial development depends on active role played by the development banks.

Features of a Development Bank

Following are the main characteristic features of a development bank:

(a) It is a specialised financial institution.

(b) It provides medium and long term finance to business units.

(c) Unlike commercial banks. It does not accept deposits from the public.

(d) It is not just a term-lending institution. It is a multi-purpose financial institution.

(e) It is essentially a development-oriented bank. Its primary object is to promote economic development by promoting investment and entrepreneurial activity in a developing economy. It encourages new and small entrepreneurs and seeks balanced regional growth.

(f) It provides financial assistance not only to the private sector but also to the public sector undertakings.

(g) It aims at promoting the saving and investment habit in the community.

(h) It does not compete with the normal channels of finance, i.e., finance already made available by the banks and other conventional financial institutions. Its major role is of a gap-filler, i.e., to fill up the deficiencies of the existing financial facilities.

(i) Its motive is to serve public interest rather than to make profits. It works in the general interest of the nation.

Important Development Banks in India

There are about 60 development banks in India. The important development banks functioning in our country are as follows.

1. The Industrial Finance Corporation of India.
2. The Industrial Credit and Investment Corporation of India.
3. The State Financial Corporations.
4. The Industrial Development Bank of India.
5. The Small Industries Development Bank of India.
6. The Industrial Reconstruction Bank of India.
7. The State Industrial Development Corporations.
8. The Unit Trust of India.
9. The Life Insurance Corporation of India.
10. The Export and Import Bank of India.

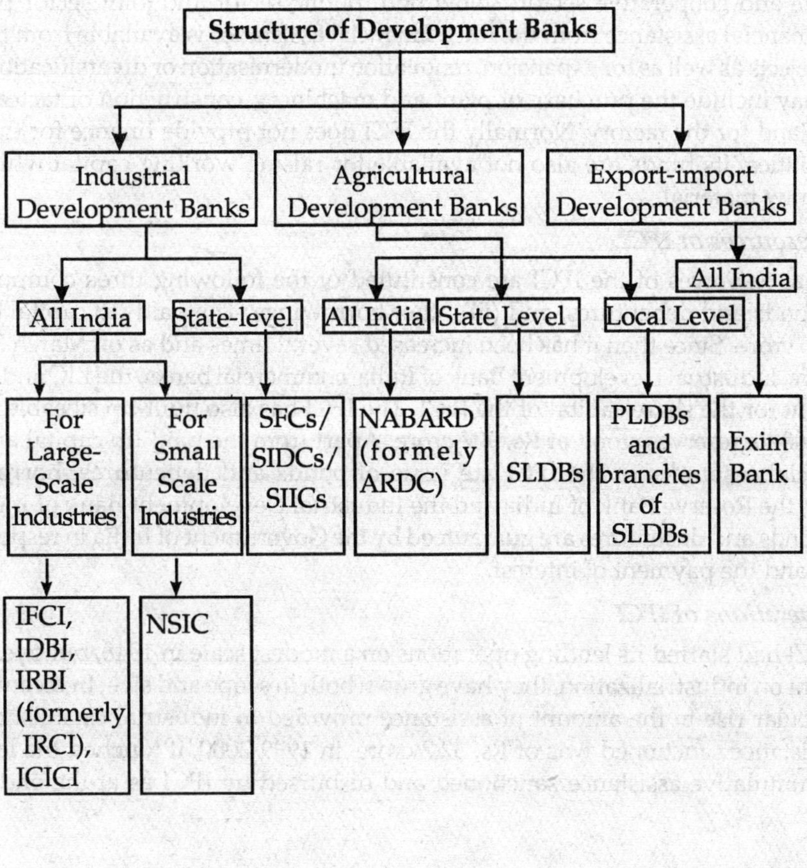

All these banks are being operated at national, state and local levels. They have been providing all types of financial assistance to business units in the form of loans, underwriting, investment and guarantee operations. They have also undertaken promotional activities. They are thus multi-purpose financial institutions. They have done commendable service for the development of industries in our country.

1. Industrial Finance Corporation of India Ltd.

As stated earlier, the Industrial Finance Corporation of India was the first All India Development Bank to be set up in the country. It was set up in 1948 with the object of providing medium and long-term credit to industry. As pointed out earlier, its role was that of a gap filler as it was not expected to compete with the prevailing channels of industrial finance. It was only meant to supplement their efforts. With effect from July 1, 1993, IFCI has been converted into a public limited company and is now known as Industrial Finance Corporation of India Ltd.

Functions of the IFCI.

The industrial Finance corporation of India grants financial assistance in the following forms: (1) Granting loans or advances both in rupees and foreign currencies repayable within 25 years: (2) Guaranteeing rupee loans floated in the open market by industrial concerns: (3) Underwriting of shares and debentures of the industrial concerns: (4) Guaranteeing (a) deferred payments in respect of imports of machinery. (b) foreign currency loans raised from foreign institutions, and (c) rupee loans raised from scheduled banks or State cooperative banks by industrial concerns.

In the beginning, the IFCI was expected to extend financial assistance only to industrial concerns in the private and cooperative sectors. Now both public sector and joint sector projects are also eligible for financial assistance from the IFCI. Financial assistance is available from the IFCI for new industrial projects as well as for expansion, renovation modernisation or diversification of the existing ones. This may include the purchase of plant and machinery, construction of factory building and purchase of land for the factory. Normally the IFCI does not provide finance for the repayment of existing liabilities. Its funds are also not available for raising working capital which includes the purchase of raw material.

Financial Resources of IFCI.

Financial resources of the IFCI are constituted of the following three components: (i) share capital (ii) bonds and debentures, and (iii) other borrowings. The paid-up capital of the IFCI was initially Rs. 5 crore. Since then it has been increased several times and as on March 31.2000 stood at Rs. 1,046 crore, Industrial Development Bank of India, commercial banks, the LIC and the cooperative banks account for the share capital of the IFCI. The IFCI has also built-up sizeable reserves. As on March 31.2000 its reserves stood at Rs. 907 crore. Apart from the paid-up capital and reserves, the major financial resources of the IFCI are issue of bonds and debentures, borrowing from the government, the Reserve Bank of India and the Industrial Development Bank of India, and foreign loans. The bonds and debentures are guaranteed by the Government of India in respect of repayment of principal and the payment of interest.

Lending Operations of IFCI

The IFCI had started its lending operations on a modest scale in 1948, but over the years with greater accent on industrialization, they have grown both in scope and size. In recent years there has been spectacular rise in the amount of assistance provided to industrial establishments. While in 1970-71, assistance sanctioned was of Rs. 32.2 crore, in 1999-2000, it touched the level of Rs. 2,376 crore. The cumulative assistance sanctioned and disbursed by IFCI as at the end of March 2000 stood at Rs. 49,621 crore. Although IFCI provides assistance to all - the private sector, the cooperative sector and the public sector - it is the private sector that is the main recipient of its assistance. For instance, in 1997-98, the private sector accounted for as much as 97.5 per cent of assistance sanctioned followed by joint sector as 2.2 per cent. Public and co-operative sectors accounted for a very negligible amount. However, it is necessary to point out here that IFCI has participated actively in the financing of industrial cooperatives. In fact, it is the financial assistance from the IFCI that has made the experiment of industrial cooperatives successful in this country.

Of the total financial assistance of Rs. 2,376 crore sanctioned in 1999-2000 by IFCI, Rs. 1,721 crore (i.e. 72.4 per cent) was in the form of rupee loans, Rs. 534 crore (i.e. 22.5 per cent) in the form of underwriting and direct subscription and Rs. 121 crore (i.e. 5.1 per cent) in the form of guarantees. Total assistance disbursed in 1999-2000 by IFCI was Rs. 3,262 crore of which the share of rupee loans was as high as 58.4 per cent while that of foreign loans was 7.2 per cent. The share of guarantees was 16.1 per cent.

The IFCI has set up Merchant Banking and Allied Services Department (MBAD) with head office in Delhi and a bureau in Mumbai. MBAD has taken up assignments for capital restructuring, merger and amalgamation, loan syndication with other financial institutions, and trusteeship assignments. It guides entrepreneurs in project formulation and raising resources for meeting project cost, etc.

Appraisal of IFCI's Performance

Opinions differ in respect of the IFCI's working over the past five decades. Looking at the growth of the IFCI's capital financial assistance sanctioned and disbursed and steadily rising profits, its performance seems to be quite impressive. However, an in-depth study reveals certain flaws in its functioning and these have invited criticisms from different quarters. The important criticisms are as follows: (i) As pointed out by the Mahalanobis Committee long ago, the IFCI's lending operations have encouraged concentration of wealth and capital. Even now it is alleged that it pursues a discriminatory policy to the disadvantage of medium and small-sized industrial units: (ii) For a considerable period of time, the IFCI did little to remove regional imbalances. It is difficult to justify why in the past industrial concerns in Maharashtra got as much assistance as the ones located in five backward States of Assam, Orissa, Kerala, Rajasthan and Madhya Pradesh taken together. However, lately IFCI has provided considerable assistance to units established in backward areas: (iii) In sanctioning assistance the IFCI has not always upheld the national priorities as stated in various plan documents: (iv) It has quite often offered assistance to undertakings which could easily raise resources from the capital market: and (v) The IFCI has failed to exercise necessary control over the defaulting borrowers. The borrowing concerns have not in some cases used the loans for the purposes for which they were sanctioned, and yet IFCI has not initiated any action against them.

The performance of IFCI has been extremely unsatisfactory during recent years. The capital adequacy ratio (CAR) fell to 8.80 per cent in 1999-2000 against the minimum stipulated limit of 9 per cent. The ratio of non-performing assets (NPAs) to net assets in 1999-2000 was as high as 20.70 per cent. As a result, profitability has been affected very adversely.

2. The Industrial Credit and Investment Corporation of India Ltd.

The Industrial Credit and Investment Corporation of India (ICICI) was the second all-India development bank to be established in the country. It was set up in January 1955 and it commenced business in March of the same year. The ICICI differs from two other all-India development banks, viz., the IFCI and IDBI in respect of ownership, management and lending operations. Unlike the

IFCI and the IDBI which are public sector development banks, the ICICI is a private sector development bank. Its distinguishing feature is that it provides underwriting facilities which are generally neglected by the other institutions. On April 1, 1996, SCICI Ltd. was merged with ICICI Ltd.

The ICICI provides assistance in various forms, the important ones being: (1) long or medium-term loans or equity participation; (2) guaranteeing loans from other private investment sources; (3) subscription to ordinary or preference capital and underwriting of new issues or securities; and (4) rendering consultancy service to Indian industry in the form of managerial and technical advice.

Financial Resources of ICICI

Initially the resources of the ICICI were rather moderate compared with its present massive resources. Total liabilities and assets of ICICI were Rs. 149 crore in 1971 which rose substantially to Rs. 65,389 crore in 1999-2000. Additional loans from the government and the Industrial Development Bank of India have helped the ICICI in augmenting its resources. The most important source of rupee funds of the ICICI is the issue of bonds and debentures to the public.

Lending Operations of ICICI

In terms of sheer amount of financial assistance provided by the ICICI, its performance has been quite impressive. From Rs. 14.8 crore in 1961-62 and Rs. 43.0 crore in 1970-71, the assistance sanctioned by the ICICI rose to Rs. 44,479 crore in 1999-2000. The ICICI has provided financial assistance in the form of (i) rupee loans including guarantees; (ii) foreign currency loans; (iii) underwriting of shares and debentures; (iv) direct subscription to shares and debentures; and (v) financial services (in the form of deferred credit, leasing, instalment sale and asset credit). Of the total assistance of Rs. 44,479 crore sanctioned by ICICI in 1999-2000. Rs. 18,362 crore (41.3 per cent) went to corporate finance, Rs. 9,448 crore (21.2 per cent) to infrastructure and Rs. 9,376 crore (21.1) per cent to oil, gas and petrochemicals. Assistance disbursed by ICICI in 1999-2000 stood at Rs. 25.836 crore. Of this Rs. 12.216 crore (47.3 per cent) went to corporate finance, Rs. 5,566 crore (21.5 per cent) to oil, gas and petrochemicals. Rs. 3,611 crore (14.0 per cent) to infrastructure and Rs.3.735 crore (14.5 per cent) to other projects.

The ICICI was originally set up to provide finance to industrial concerns in the private sector, and even now they account for the bulk of the loans sanctioned by this institution. The scope of its operations has been enlarged in recent years by including the projects in the joint, public and cooperative sectors. As far as industry wise assistance is concerned, the major recipients of the financial assistance from the ICICI are non-traditional growth-oriented industries such as chemicals, petrochemicals, heavy engineering and metal products.

The ICICI has joined the consortium of the IDBI, the IFCI and other financial institutions for providing loans on soft terms to a number of industries for modernisation. In this country, quite a large number of enterprises in some traditional industries, particularly cotton textiles, jute, sugar, and cement have been facing serious problems for a long time due to obsolescence. Among the new industries some engineering units urgently need modernisation. They all require financial assistance on soft terms to carry out their plans in respect of replacing the outdated plant and machinery. The consortium of all-India development banks now extends assistance to such industrial units for the purpose of modernisation. The ICICI has been assigned the lead responsibility for industrial enterprises in the engineering group.

In 1983, ICICI commenced leasing operations. It provides leasing assistance for computerisation, modernisation/replacement schemes, equipment for energy conservation, export orientation, pollution control, balancing and expansion.

Appraisal of ICICI's Performance.

The ICICI in four and a half decades of its existence has played an important role in providing financial assistance to industrial enterprises in the private sector. Its pioneer work as the underwriting institution in this country has been widely acclaimed. The provision of foreign currency loans is another area where the ICICI has distinguished itself. A large number of growth oriented industries such as chemicals, petrochemicals, heavy engineering and metal products industries are primarily interested in such foreign currency loans for importing capital equipment and it is here that ICICI gives them a helping hand. The ICICI has, however, been rightly criticised for assisting mainly the large units. Moreover, it has done little to promote industrial development in the less developed regions. Its policy of financing the projects in a few relatively industrially advanced states has, in fact, accentuated regional disparities. However, because of this criticism of its functioning, ICICI has increased its assistance to backward areas in recent years. The ICICI has also participated in setting up Technical Consultancy Organisations in a number of backward states.

3. State Financial Corporations

Industrial Finance Corporation of India was set up in 1948 to cater to the needs of large industrial concerns. It can render financial assistance only to limited companies and co-operative societies. After independence the Government of India realised the need for financial institutions at the state level to assist the promotion and expansion of medium and small-scale industries. The State Financial Corporations Act was born out of this need in 1951. The Act was amended in 1956 and 1962. The State Governments were empowered by the Act to establish financial corporation in their respective regions to foster and stimulate the development of medium and small scale industries.

Functions : The state financial corporations are empowered to render financial help in the following forms:

(a) Granting loans and advances to or subscribing to the debentures of industrial concerns repayable within 20 years.

(b) Guaranteeing loans raised by industrial concerns repayable within 20 years.

(c) Underwriting the stocks, shares, debentures, subject to their being disposed off in the market within 7 years.

(d) Guranteeing deferred payments due from industrial concerns on their purchases of capital goods in India.

(e) Granting soft loans to or participating in the equity of the weaker segments of the medium and small-scale sector.

The State Financial Corporations can grant assistance to public limited companies, partnerships and proprietory concerns. The assistance given to a single concern should not exceed 10% of the paid up capital of the corporation or 15 lakhs whichever is less. The limit is raised to 30 lakhs in the case of limited companies and co-operative societies.

Management : The State Finance Corporation is managed by a Board of Directors. The board consists of 10 members of which three are nominated by State Government concerned, one by the Reserve Bank of India, one by the I.F.C. and the remaining four are elected by bank, and insurance companies. One member of the Board is appointed as the Managing Director.

Resources : State Financial Corporations can raise finance by the following methods.

(a) Share Capital

The capital structure of a State Finance Corporations is fixed by the State Government concerned. It is subject to a minimum of Rs. 50 lakhs and a maximum of Rs. 5 crores. Initially the share capital is to be contributed by the State Government concerned, Reserve Bank of India, Co-operative Banks and Insurance companies in a predetermined ratio. Not more than 25% of the share capital may be allotted to the public. The shares are to be guaranteed by the State Government with regard to both principal and interest. With effect from February 1976 the holding of the RBI in SFCs were transferred to IDBI. The rate of dividend should not exceed 5 percent per annum.

(b) Bonds and debentures

The Corporations are empowered to issue bonds and debentures to supplement their resources. The amount raise through this source should not exceed ten times the amount of their paid-up capital and reserve fund.

(c) Public deposits

The corporations are also empowered to accept public deposits for a period of not less than five years. However, the amount of deposits should not exceed the paid up capital of the corporation.

(d) Borrowings

The corporations can also borrow from the Reserve Bank, the IDBI and the State Governments concerned. Borrowings from IDBI account far nearly one third of the total resources.

Working : During the last five decades the SFCs have played a significant role in the development of medium and small-scale industries. The following facts and figure speak of their performance and achievements.

(a) There are at present 18 corporations including the Tamilnadu Industrial Development Corporation. The loans sanctioned from 1971 and 1997 amounted to Rs. 31170 crores. Over 70% of the total assistance sanctioned by all SFC's is provided to small-scale industries. In 1999-2000, the total assistance sanctioned and disbursed by 18 SFCs stood at Rs. 2,231 crore and Rs. 1,730 crore respectively.

(b) The corporations have directly subscribed to the share capital of a number of companies.

(c) The corporations have also provided guarantees for deferred payments by industrial units for purchase of capital goods.

(d) In recent years, there has been some welcome change in the attitude of SFCs towards the small-scale industries and units in backward areas. The assistance sanctioned and disbursed to the units in these areas is gradually increasing.

(e) The corporations have provided financial assistance on very liberal scale to a number of technical entrepreneurs.

(f) The corporations have also advanced loans in foreign currency for import of capital goods.

(g) Some of the corporations have conducted area surveys and prepared project reports to promote industrial development in backward area.

Critical Review of the working of SFCs : The SFCs played a significant role in meeting the medium term financial needs of small and medium-scale industries. Food processing, road transport, chemicals, textiles, metal products, machinery and transport equipment industries have been the major beneficiaries of SFC's assistance.

The following are some of the difficulties and limitations faced by the corporations and the suggestions made to solve them.

(a) A major problem of the SFCs is the magnitude of overdues. The default ratio has been increasing, with the result suits filed for recovery of dues are also increasing. There is need to keep a continuous watch on the assisted units.

(b) The financial position of the assisted units needs periodical review and analysis. Assisted units should be compelled to maintain proper books of accounts and not mix up personal accounts with business accounts.

(c) Many firms are not able to offer adequate security for the loans because of defects in titles to property. Further they do not have the resources to fulfil the conditions for the grant of loans.

(d) The units seeking assistance are not familiar with the procedures and formalities to be gone through to get the loans sanctioned.

(e) The corporations should formulate a sound investment policy and maintain healthy investment portfolio. Loans should be sanctioned only after the economic viability of the projects is proved beyond doubt. However there is dearth of technical personnel to examine the soundness of proposed schemes. This deficiency should be set right.

(f) Paucity of funds is one of the major constraints of these corporations. The public response to capital issues of these corporations is not encouraging on account of the low rate of divided and non-marketability of shares. The corporations should issue shares and bonds with attractive terms and rate of interest.

(g) The corporations should pay more attention for the development of industries in backward areas. They should undertake area surveys for preparation of project for industries having development potentialities.

(h) Steps should be taken to see that assistance given is properly utilised. The corporations should not hesitate to take over the management of defaulting concerns, if it is necessary.

(i) Though the rates of interest charged by the corporations are quite reasonable, the cost of borrowing is high for the industrial units on account of high stamp duty, registration fee etc. The State Government should grant some concession in these charges.

Recently some measures have been taken to streamline these corporations and co-ordinate their activities with other financial institutions engaged in industrial finance. The corporations are acting as agents of their respective State Governments for routing funds under the liberalised scheme of assistance to small-scale industries.

The SFCs are the prime sources of block finance to small and medium scale industries. They should adopt a number of measures, as the commercial banks did to increase their volume of assistance to small scale units. Setting up of separate cell to look after the needs of the small scale units, adoption of some selected districts for intensive operations, conducting surveys to identify industrial potential are some of the measures suggested to make the corporations play a more effective and constructive role in the process of industrial growth.

4. The Industrial Development Bank of India

Prior to the establishment of the Industrial Development Bank of India (IDBI), the country had a number of special industrial financing institutions. They had done commendable work in the field of industrial finance, though in terms of range and magnitude they could not adequately meet the demands of the industry. Furthermore, there was a major lacuna in the system. There was no apex organisation to coordinate the functions of various industrial financing institutions. V.V. Bhatt rightly stated that the country needed a central development banking institution for providing "dynamic leadership in the task of promoting a widely diffused and diversified and yet viable process of industralisation". It was under these circumstances that IDBI was set up in July 1964. The IDBI was initially set up as a wholly owned subsidiary of the Reserve Bank of India. In February 1976 the IDBI was made an autonomous institution and its ownership passed on from the Reserve Bank of India to the Government of India.

The IDBI has rightly been designated as the apex organisation in the field of development banking. It not only has organisational links with other development banks but it also renders some such services to them which only an apex organisation is expected to perform. In the first place, it provides refinance against loans granted to industrial concerns by other development banks like the IFCI, the SFCs and so on and rediscounts their machinery bills. Secondly, it subscribes to the share capital and bond issues of the IFCI, the ICICI, the SFCs and the IIBI. A part from these linkages, the IDBI plays the role of a coordinator at all-India level. For this purpose, a machinery has been evolved and regular meetings of the Heads of various financial institutions are held under its leadership. Thus the IDBI enjoys a unique position in India's development banking system. It occupies the same place in the field of development banking as is occupied by the RBI in the field of commercial banking.

Financial Resources of IDBI

The operations of the IDBI have grown over the years and so have its resources. The main sources of its funds are share capital, reserves, bonds and debentures issues, deposits from companies and Certificates of Deposits, and borrowings from the Reserve Bank of India and Government of India. The total resources of IDBI amounted to Rs. 72.169 crore in 1999-2000. Of this, the share of bonds and debentures was Rs. 43, 976 crore (60.1 per cent). Other sources (inclusive of deposits from companies and Certificates of Deposits) was the second most important source accounting for Rs. 10,096 crore (21.4 per cent) of total resources. The share of reserves and reserve funds was Rs. 8,558 crore (12.8 per cent) while borrowings from the RBI and government stood at Rs. 3.106 crore (6.3 per cent).

Cumulative Assistance by IDBI

The IDBI is the leading development bank in India. Its progress has been spectacular in whole of the period of its existence but particularly so in recent years. The cumulative assistance sanctioned by IDBI till the end of March 2000 aggregated Rs. 2,16,401 crore. Considering the underdeveloped nature of the capital market and the difficulties which a large number of industrial firms encounter in raising funds from the market, this quantum of assistance is not small. In fact, it is almost equal to the amount of financial assistance provided by all other special industrial financing institutions taken together. The amount of assistance disbursed by IDBI till the end of March 2000, from the date of establishment, totalled Rs. 1,38,793 crore. During 1999-2000, assistance sanctioned and disbursed by IDBI stood at Rs. 28,308 crore and Rs. 17,059 crore respectively.

Composition of Financial Assistance

The state pertaining to the IDBI enables it to have considerable flexibility in its operations. It, therefore, can provide financial assistance to all kinds of big, medium and small enterprises. In respect of the size of loans, there are virtually no restrictions on it. Moreover, it is completely free to use its own discretion in respect of the security to be obtained against the loan sanctioned. Its assistance can be broadly classified into the following categories.

1. Direct financial assistance to industrial enterprises

The IDBI provides direct financial assistance to industrial concerns in the form of loans, underwriting and direct subscription to shares and debentures and guarantees. The policy framework of the IDBI in respect of direct financing has been decided by its apex position. It, therefore, generally avoids competing with other special industrial financing institutions. It, in fact, acts as the lender of the last resort. The IDBI's direct assistance to industrial enterprises in the entire period of its existence has accounted for about one-third of its total assistance. Loans as a form of direct finance constitute the major part of the IDBI's financial assistance to the industry.

2. Indirect financial assistance to industries

A major part of the IDBI's assistance is routed through some other financial institutions including the State Financial Corporations. State Industrial Development Corporations and Commercial Banks. This form of assistance is generally characterised as indirect financial assistance. The IDBI's indirect assistance can be broadly classified into four categories: (a) refinance of industrial loans, (b) rediscounting of bills, (c) subscription to shares and bonds of financial institutions and (d) seed capital assistance.

3. Assistance to backward areas

The IDBI has initiated certain financial and non-financial measures to encourage industries in backward areas. Financial measures are mainly of three types: (a) direct financial assistance in the form of loans at concessional rates, longer initial grace period, etc.; (b) concessional refinance assistance to projects in backward areas; and (c) special concessions to projects in North-Eastern area under the bill rediscounting scheme. Non-financial measures aim at helping potential entrepreneurs in identifying and formulating viable projects, technical assistance etc.

Total assistance sanctioned by IDBI in 1999-2000 was Rs. 28,308 crore. Of this, the share of direct assistance was Rs. 26,350 crore (93.1 per cent), refinance of industrial loans Rs. 242 crore (0.9 per cent), and bills finance Rs. 723 crore (2.6 per cent). The share of rupee loans in direct assistance of Rs. 26,350 crore sanctioned by IDBI in 1999-2000 was Rs. 8,914 crore (i.e. as high as 34 per cent).

Industry-wise analysis of IDBI's financial assistance reveals that core and other manufacturing sectors accounted for bulk of the assistance sanctioned and disbursed. Core sector includes industries such as iron and steel, oil exploration and refining, cement and fertilizer. Other major industries that received large sanctions are: chemicals and chemical products, textiles, electronic and electrical products, food manufacturing and artificial fibres.

Promotional Functions of the IDBI

Apart from providing financial assistance to industry, the IDBI performs certain promotional functions as well. These include provision of training in project evaluation and development of entrepreneurship. A special scheme has been initiated for "no industries districts". Under this scheme, IDBI has done surveys to study the industrial potential of no industry districts. The programme is to arrange training for potential entrepreneurs in these districts besides giving financial, technical and administrative assistance to selected projects. It also runs a Technical Consultancy Organisation (TCO). Besides doing feasibility studies, project appraisals, industrial and market potential surveys, etc., TCO has also made considerable progress in training new entrepreneurs. The IDBI is also supporting a number of inter-institutional groups which provide a forum for discussions on industrial development programmes.

Critical Appraisal

The IDBI was set up three and a half decades ago to function as an apex institution in the field of development finance. Judged by its assistance measured in quantitative terms, the performance of the IDBI looks quite impressive. Over the years not only the amount but also the range and pattern of assistance have grown. This is a significant contribution when we view it in the light of the fact that capital market in the country is still not very much developed. However, without undermining the importance of the contributions made by the IDBI, it must be stated that it has failed to develop itself as a true development bank. Its accent on providing loans and treating underwriting of shares and debentures of industrial concerns as a secondary activity is not very appropriate. Secondly, in spite of all its pretensions in providing assistance to projects in backward areas and also to the small-scale sector, the largest beneficiaries of the assistance provided by the IDBI are big industrial concerns. Thus, the distributional consequences of its working are in all probability not very healthy. Finally, the IDBI has mainly concentrated on providing financial assistance. The promotional and consultancy work has not been assigned the same importance as financial assistance. Thus there is need for a change in the approach of the IDBI towards industrial development.

The financial performance of IDBI in recent years has also raised many eyebrows as its profitability has been declining. Moreover, the ratio of its non-performing assets to net assets rose to as high 13.40 per cent in 1999-2000. These are warning signals for IDBI.

5. Small Industries Development Bank of India

With a view to ensuring larger flow of financial and non-financial assistance to the small scale sector, the Government of India announced in the Budget for 1988-89, its decision to establish Small Industries Development Bank of India (SIDBI) as a subsidiary of IDBI. The SIDBI Act was passed by the Parliament on October 1989 and the Bank commenced its operations from April 2, 1990. To equip SIDBI to play its apex role in SSI credit provision more effectively, the Union Budget 1998-99 prossed the delinking of SIDBI from IDBI and transferring of IDBI shareholding in SFCs to SIDBI.

Financial Resources of SIDBI

The SIDBI commenced its operations with an initial paid-up capital of Rs. 250 crore and by taking over the outstanding portfolio of IDBI relating to small-scale sector held under Small Industries Development Fund as on March 31, 1990 amounting to Rs. 4,200 crore. The paid up capital was subsequently raised to Rs. 450 crore. The financial resources of SIDBI aggregated Rs. 16,561 crore in 1999-2000. Of these, borrowings from RBI. Government of India and other sources contributed Rs. 8,012 crore (i.e. 48.4 per cent). Bonds and debentures contributed Rs. 2.437 crore (14.7 per cent).

Financial Assistance by SIDBI.

With a view to ensuring larger flow of assistance to the small-scale units, the immediate thrust of SIDBI was on (a) initiating steps for technological upgradation and modernisation of existing units; (b) expanding the channels for marketing the products of the small-scale sector; and (c) promotion of employment-oriented industries especially in semi-urban areas to create more employment opportunities and thereby checking migration of population to urban areas. SIDBI provides assistance to the small-scale units through the existing credit delivery system comprising State Financial Corporation, State Industrial Development Corporations. Commercial Banks, Co-operative Banks and Regional Rural Banks. The major activities of SIDBI are; (i) refinance of loans and advances; (ii) discounting and re-discounting of bills; (iii) extension of seed capital/soft loans; (iv) granting direct assistance and refinancing of loans; (v) providing services like factoring, leasing etc.; and (vi) extending financial support of State Small Industries Development Corporations. During 1999-2000, SIDBI sanctioned assistance worth Rs. 10,265 crore of which assistance worth Rs. 6,964 crore was disbursed. Till end of March 2000, cumulative sanctions and disbursements by SIDBI were of the order of Rs. 43,886 crore and Rs 33,666 core repsectively.

6. The Industrial Reconstruction Bank of India (IRBI)

To provide financial assistance as well as to revive and revitalise sick industrial units in public/private sectors, an institution called the Industrial Reconstruction Corporation of India (IRCI) was set up in 1971 with a share capital of Rs. 10 crores. In March 1985, it was converted into a statutory corporation called the Industrial Reconstruction Bank of India (IRBI), with an authorised capital of Rs. 200 crores and a paid up capital of Rs. 50 crores.

The following functions were laid down for the IRBI:

(a) to provide financial assistance to sick industrial units,

(b) to provide managerial and technical assistance to sick industrial units,

(c) to secure the assistance of other financial institutions and government agencies for the revival and revitalisation of sick industrial units,

(d) to provide merchant banking services for amalgamation, merger, reconstruction, etc.,

(e) to provide consultancy services to the banks in the matter of sick units, and

(f) to undertake leasing business.

In a similar fashion, the IRBI is to function as the principal credit and reconstruction agency for industrial revival and co-ordinate the activities of other institutions engaged in the revival of industries and also to assist and promote industrial development and rehabilitation of industrial concerns.

The IRBI is empowered to take over the management of assisted sick industrial units, lease them out or sell them as running concerns or to prepare schemes for reconstruction by scaling down the liabilities with the approval of the Government of India.

During 1986-87, the IRBI sanctioned a total assistance of Rs. 148.9 crores and disbursed Rs. 946 crores by way of term loans to industrial units for essential capital expenditure relating to modernisation, diversification, renovation, expansion, etc.

During 1995-96, the sanctions of IRBI amounted to Rs. 897 crore. Its cumulative sanctions amounted to Rs. 3,521 crore and disbursement Rs. 2,404 crore. The sanctions of IRBI amounting to Rs. 1044 crore during 1998-99, indicated a growth of 15.3 percent. The disbursements at Rs. 529 crore registered a growth of 32.9 percent.

7. The State Industrial Development Corporations (SIDCs) and the State Industrial Investment Corporations (SIICs)

Since 1960, the State Industrial Development Corporations and State Industrial Investment Corporations (SIDCs/SIICs) have been set up by state governments as counterparts of the NIDC. Presently, there are 28 such institutions in all.

Besides financial assistance, their main function is to promote industries. They arrange for land, put up industrial estates, construct roads, arrange for the supply of water and electric power, arrange for licences for industrial units and so on in order to promote industries, especially in backward areas.

Organisational deficiencies, insufficient and untrained staff, defaults in payment of dues are the major weaknesses of these institutions.

During 1995-96 their total financial assistance sanctions amounted to Rs. 20,488 crore and disbursement Rs. 1,383 crore.

8. Unit Trust of India

The Unit Trust of India is a statutory public sector investment institution which was set up in February 1964 under the Unit Trust of India Act 1963. This institution began operations in July 1964. UTI was set up with the object of stimulating and pooling the savings of middle and low income groups and to enable them to share the benefits and prosperity of the fast growing industrialisation in the country. This twofold objective has been achieved by three following approaches :

(a) By selling its units under the various schemes of the Trust among as many investors as possible in the different parts of the country.

(b) By investing the sale proceeds of the units in industrial and corporate securities.

(c) By paying dividends to those who have purchased the units of the Trust.

The main source of funds of the Unit Trust of India (UTI) is the sale of units to the public under many schemes. The face value of the 'unit' sold by the Trust is not less than Rs. 10 or more than Rs. 100. There is no limit to the number of units which can be purchased by the unit holders.

At the time of establishment of the Trust, the capital was Rs. 5 crores, divided into 1,000 certificates of the face value of Rs. 50,000 each. These certificates were subscribed by the various institutions in the following way :

Reserve Bank of India	Rs. 2.5 crore
State Bank of India and its subsidiaries	Rs.75 lakhs
Life Insurance Corporation of India	Rs. 75 lakhs
Others (the scheduled commercial banks, the other financial institutions)	Rs. 1 crore.

The UTI which was an associate institution of the RBI up to February 15, 1996, became an associate institution of the Industrial Development Bank of India on February 16, 1966. By doing so, the capital of Rs. 2.5 crore which was held by the Reserve Bank of India earlier, has been transferred to the Industrial Development Bank of India.

The Management of the UTI is vested in a Board of Trustees, comprising a chairman appointed by the Reserve Bank, four trustees also nominated by the Reserve Bank, one trustee nominated by the Life Insurance Corporation of India and two trustees elected by the other contributing financial institutions.

Present Position

As on September 30, 1999, UTI managed 28 equity schemes with unit capital of about Rs. 6155 crore, and market value of investment Rs. 10,816 crore. During the quarter ending September 1999, 21 equity schemes of UTI out-performed the BSE Sensex, which registered an increase of 15.1 per cent. The number of income/debt schemes of UTI stood at 49 and the total investible funds of these schemes amounted to Rs. 35,467 crore as on September 30, 1999. Total investible funds of the UTI stood at Rs. 74,291 crore ad on June 30, 2000. As on June 30, 1999 investments in debt instruments, including money market instruments, was Rs. 23,600 crore (71%) and in equity Rs. 9724 crore (29%). The corresponding figures rose to Rs. 25026 crore (Market Value Rs. 25649 crore) and Rs. 10441 crore (Market value Rs. 11745 crore) as on September 30, 1999. The portfolio restructuring process initiated last year has begun bearing fruits in terms of improved performance of core equity portfolio and the improvement in credit quality of debt.

9. Life Insurance Corporation of India (LIC)

The Life Insurance Corporation of India came into existence on July 1, 1956 and the Corporation began to function on September 1, 1956. The Corporation gets a large amount as insurance premium and has been investing in almost all sectors of the economy, viz., public sector, private corporate sector, co-operative sector, joint sector and now it is one of the biggest term lending institutions in the country.

The paid-up capital of the Corporation is Rs. 5 crore. The Corporation has an accumulated Life Insurance Fund of over Rs. 4,500 crore. The LIC of India plays an important role in the capital market and is the largest institutional investor. Like banks, the LIC is also a captive investor in government bonds. At the end of March 1992, Rs. 27,150 crore was invested by LIC in government securities excluding treasury bills, small savings and other kinds of bonds. Under the law the LIC is required to hold 87.5% of its assets in the form of government and other approved securities and loans to approved authorities for such social schemes as housing, electricity, water supply etc. and remaining 12.5% can be invested in the private sector.

The Corporation subscribes to and underwrites the shares, bonds and debentures of several Financial Corporations and Companies and grants term loans. It maintains close contacts with other financial institutions such as Industrial Development Bank of India, Unit Trust of India, Industrial Finance Corporation of India etc. for co-ordination of its investments.

The LIC is a very powerful factor in the securities market in India. It subscribes to the share capital of companies both preference and equity and also to debentures and bonds. Its share holding extends to a majority of large and medium-sized non-financial companies and is significant in size. There is no doubt, the Corporation acts as a kind of downward stabiliser of the share market, as the continuous inflow of fresh funds enables it to buy even when the share market is weak. About 50% financial assistance is provided by the LIC In the form of rupee loans, about 20% in the underwriting shares (preference and ordinary) and about 25% in underwriting debentures.

Present position

The financial assistance sanctioned by LIC during the year 1998-99 through term loans and underwriting of shares and debentures of corporate sector amounted to Rs. 2730 crore while disbursements aggregated Rs. 2804 crore, registering a significant growth of 43.7 per cent in sanctions and 93.5 per cent in disbursements.

The investment of LIC during 1998-99 at Rs. 7348 crore recorded a rise of 21.8 per cent as compared with an increase of 16.4 per cent during 1997-98.

Investment By LIC

Type of Assistance	As at the end of March		Net Changing during April-March	
	1997	1998	1997-98	1998-99
1. Public Sector	49,416.3	56,063.7	5720.8	6647.4
2. Private Sector	9107.6	9705.4	526.5	597.8
3. Joint Sector	525.8	532.4	18.4	6.6
4. Co-operative Sector	2007.4	2,103.8	92.0	96.4
Total (1 to 4) of which	61057.1	68450.3	6357.7	7348.2
(a) Stock Exchange Securities	43570.4	47913.8	5407.3	5905.7
(b) Loans	16137.9	17088.4	761.8	903.9
(c) Others	1348.8	3403.1	188.6	538.6

Source : LIC of India.

Of the total investments of Rs. 1,39,032 crore made by LIC as at end March 2000, public sector accounted for the major share of Rs. 1,17,059 crore. While private sector got Rs. 19,268 crore. The balance went to co-operative sector and Joint Sector.

Highlights of the Corporation as on 31.3.2002

1. Total Income	Rs. 73,430.95 crore
2. Total Premium Income	Rs. 49,613.28 crore
3. Income from Investment	Rs. 22,807.29 crore
4. Miscellaneous Income	Rs. 1,010.38 crore
5. Total Payments to Policy holders	Rs. 17,480.78 crore
6. Total Life Fund	Rs. 2,33,289.03 crore
7. Total Assets of the Corporation	Rs. 1,93,621.69 crore

Source : LIC of India

10. The Export-Import Bank of India (EXIM Bank)

The Export-Import Bank of India (EXIM Bank) which was established on January 1, 1982 by an Act of Parliament, commenced operation from March 1, 1982. The export loans and guarantee portfolio of the IDBI was transferred on March 1, 1982 to the EXIM Bank, which assumed funded liability of Rs. 169.2 crore and non-funded liability in the form of export guarantees of Rs. 336.4 crore under the General Fund and Rs. 2.5 crore under the Development Assistance Fund, now called Export Development Fund.

Objectives : The Export-Import Bank of India Act 1981 (Act 28 of 1981) defines the objectives as "an Act to establish a corporation to be known as the Export-Import Bank of India for providing financial assistance to exporters and importers, and for functioning as the principal financial institution for co-ordinating the working of institutions engaged in financing export and import of goods and services with a view to promoting the country's international trade and for matters connected therewith or incidental thereto".

Capital : As per section 4 of the Export-Import Bank of India Act, 1981, the authorised capital of the EXIM Bank is Rs. 200 crore. The Government of India may increase the said capital to Rs. 500 crore by notification. The EXIM Bank can raise its resources by issue and sale of bonds and debentures, borrowing from the RBI, borrowing from other institutions approved by the Government of India, acceptance of deposits and loans in foreign currency from any bank or financial institution in any foreign country with the previous approval of the Government of India.

Functions of the EXIM Bank

(a) EXIM Bank provides direct financial assistance to exporters of plant, machinery and related services in the form of medium-term credit.

(b) The bank gives term loans/deferred payment guarantee for project cost financing of units registered as 100 per cent export-oriented units.

(c) The bank provides rediscount of export bills for a period not exceeding 90 days against short-term usance export bills discounted by commercial banks.

(d) The Bank gives facilities for deemed exports in case of specified transactions within India. Consequently, the foreign exchange earnings or foreign exchange savings are determined by Government of India.

(e) The Bank gives overseas Buyers Credit to foreign importers for import of Indian capital goods and related services.

(f) The Bank provides facilities to overseas buyers for Indian consultancy, technology and other related services.

Present Position

Exim Bank sanctioned Rs. 3,055 crore and disbursed P.s. 2,637 crore under various lending projects during 1998-99. At end March 1999 the cumulative outstandings of the Exim Bank aggregated Rs. 3.311 crore, an increase of 13.5 per cent over the year.

Region-wise operations of Export-Import Bank of India

Rs. crore

Regions	*1998-99*			
	Sanctions	*% share*	*Disbursements*	*% Share*
1. South Asia	2.4	0.8	12.6	7.2
2. Americas	15.4	5.0	5.6	3.2
3. West Asia	99.4	32.4	55.8	30.5
4. South-East Asia	34.4	11.2	52.7	29.9
5. Europe and CIS	71.0	23.0	30.9	17.5
6. Sub-Saharan Africa	81.1	26.3	20.6	11.7
7. North Africa	4.6	1.5	-	-
Total	308.1	100.0	176.2	100.0

Source : Export-Import Bank of India.

Region-wise analysis of the operations of Exim Bank showed that West Asia accounted for the largest share of sanctions and disbursements at Rs. 104 crore and Rs. 63 crore respectively during 1998-99.

Exim Bank's resources as on March 31, 1999 aggregated Rs. 4104 crore inclusive of paid-up capital of Rs. 500 crore and resumes of Rs. 400 crore. Exim Bank raised Rs. 173 crore through private placement of bonds for the first time in the Indian Capital Market besides mobilising funds by way of rupee fixed deposits, certificates of deposits etc.

Conclusion

From the above discussion, it is clear that the term development bank broadly includes all types of institutions which provide long-term loans, equity capital and debenture capital to the development of the economy in general. The main objective of a development bank is that of financing development activities in the country.

Questions for Discussions

1. What are Development Banks. Discuss the features of development banks.
2. Explain the role of the IFC in providing funds to industries.
3. Discuss the part played by Industrial Credit and Investment Corporation of India in financing industries in India.
4. Discuss the part played by the IDBI as the apex organisation in the Industrial Finance Structure.
5. What are the functions of the Small Industries Development Bank of India. Discuss its progress and growth.
6. Explain the functions and working of State Financial Corporations.
7. Describe the functions of the Export-Import Bank of India.
8. Describe the functions of the UTI and LIC.

Chapter - 8

BANKER AND CUSTOMER

Introduction

Banking industry occupies an important place in a nation's economy. A bank is an indispensable institution in a modern society. One cannot think of the development of any nation without the active assistance rendered by financial institutions. Banks, in fact, do finance trade, industry and commerce. The modern business and the entrepreneur cannot carry on the commercial activities without the different methods of financing done by the banks. Gone are the days when borrowing was criticised and objected to and the borrower was looked down upon. But today, the time and circumstances have changed. It is natural that every businessman has to change according to the new challenges. Right from small businessman, up to the biggest business tycoon, they invariably depend upon finances of different types given by the banks. Therefore, one has to accept that the banking industry play a vital role in every field and at every juncture of the business.

This chapter deals with the relationship that exists between the banker and customer. All the legal aspects associated with these two vital organs of the banking operations are discussed. The relationship between the customer and the banker is vital. The relationship starts right from the moment an account is opened and it comes to an end immediately on closure of the account. The relationship stands established as soon as the agreement or contract is entered into. The nature of the relationship depends upon the state of the customer's account.

Before we take up the relationship that exists between a banker and his customer, let us understand the meaning of the terms 'banker' and 'customer'.

Meaning and Definition of a Banker

The term 'banker' refers to a person or company carrying on the business of receiving moneys, and collecting drafts, for customers subject to the obligation of honouring cheques drawn upon them from time to time by the customers to the extent of the amounts available on their current accounts.

There are differences of opinion regarding the meaning of the term banker. We have discussed here some of the important ones.

1. Sheldon H.P.

"The function of receiving money from his customers and repaying it by honouring their cheques as and when required is the function above all other functions which distinguishes a banking business from any other kind of business".

2. Sir John Paget

"No person or body corporate or otherwise can be a banker who doesnot take deposit accounts, take current accounts, issue and pay cheques and collect cheques crossed and uncrossed for his customers".

3. G. Crowther

"A banker is a dealer in debt, his own and other people".

4. Macleod

"The essential business of banker is to buy money and debts, by creation of other debts. A banker is therefore essentially a dealer in debts or credit".

5. Dr. H.L. Hart

"A banker or bank is a person or company carrying on the business of receiving moneys, and collecting drafts, for customers subject to the obligation of honouring cheques drawn upon them from time to time by the customers to the extent of the amounts available on their current accounts".

6. Indian Banking Regulation Act

Under section 5(1) (band c) of the Banking Regulation Act 1949, "Banking means the accepting for the purpose of lending or investment of deposits of money from the public, repayable on demand or otherwise and withdrawable by cheque, draft, order or otherwise. Banking company means any company which transacts the business of banking in India".

From the definitions given above, it is clear that if any person or institution fulfils the following conditions, it will satisfy the definition of a banker or a banking company.

(a) Accepting of deposits from the public, repayable on demand or otherwise. The deposits may be of different types, current, savings, fixed etc.

(b) Such deposits must be withdrawable by cheques, drafts, order or otherwise.

(c) Any money accepted as deposits must be for the purpose of lending or investment.

(d) Performance of banking business as the main business.

According to section 6 of the Act, a banker, apart from the usual services, may also engage in any one or more of the following forms of business namely:

1. The borrowing, raising or taking up of money, the lending or advancing of money either upon or without security,
2. The drawing, making, accepting, discounting, buying, selling, collecting and dealing in bills of exchange, hundis, promissory notes, coupons, drafts, bills of lading, railway receipts, warrants, debenture, certificates, scrips, and other instruments.
3. The granting and issuing of the letters of credit, traveller's cheques and circular notes.
4. The buying, selling and dealing in bullion and specie.
5. The buying and selling of foreign exchange including foreign bank notes.
6. The acquiring, holding, issuing on commission, underwriting and dealing in stocks, funds, shares, debentures, bonds, obligations, securities and investments of all kinds.
7. Acting as agents for any government or local authority.

8. The purchasing and selling of bonds, scrips and other forms of securities on behalf of constituents or others.
9. Contracting for public and private loans and negotiating and issuing the same.
10. The receiving of all kinds of bonds, scrips or valuable on deposits or for safe custody or otherwise.
11. The providing of safe deposit vaults.
12. The collecting and transmitting of money and securities.
13. The effecting, insuring, guaranteeing, underwriting, participating in managing and carrying out of any issue, public or private, of state, municipal or other loans or of shares stock, debentures, or debenture stock of any company, corporation or association and the lending of money for the purpose of any such issue.
14. Carrying on and transacting every kind of guarantee and indemnity business.
15. Managing, selling and realising any property which may come into the possession of the company in satisfaction or part satisfaction of any of its claims.
16. Undertaking and executing trusts.
17. Undertaking the administration of estates as executor, trustee or otherwise.
18. The acquisition, construction, maintenance and alternation of any building or works necessary or convenient for the purposes of the company.
19. Doing all such other things as are incidental or conducive to the promotion or advancement of the business of the company.
20. Any other form of business which the Central Government may, by notification in the official Gazette, specify as a form of business in which it is lawful for a banking company to engage.

A banking company is not permitted to engage in any form of business other than those referred to above.

Meaning and Definition of a Customer

The term 'customer' of a bank is not defined by law. In the ordinary language, a person who has an account in a bank is considered as its customer.

There is no statutory definition of the term either in India or in England. However, the legal decisions on the matter throw some light on the meaning of the term.

According to an old view, as expressed by Sir John Paget, "to constitute a customer, there must be some recognizable course or habit of dealing in the nature of regular banking business...... It has been thought difficult to reconcile the idea of a single transaction with that of a customers; that the word predicates, even grammatically, some minimum of custom, antithetic to an isolated act". According to this view, in order to constitute a customer of a bank, two conditions are to be fulfilled;

(a) There must be some recognizable course or habit of dealing between the customer and the banker.

(b) The transactions must be in the form of regular banking business.

Further, for a person to be a customer of a bank, he should have some sort of account with the bank and the initial transaction in opening an account would not constitute the relation of banker and customer; there should be some kind of continuity. The concept of duration does not hold good any longer. At present to constitute a customer, duration is not essential.

According to Dr. Hart "a customer is one who has an account with a banker or for whom a banker habitually undertakes to act as such". Supporting this view point, the Kerala High court observed: (Central Bank of India Ltd., Bombay Vs V. Gopinathan Nair and others - A.I.R., 1970, Kerala 74).

"Broadly speaking, a customer is a person who has the habit of resorting to the same place or person to do business. So far as banking transactions are concerned he is a person whose money has been accepted on the footing that the banker will honour up to the amount standing to his credit, irrespective of his connection being of short or long standing".

Thus a person who has a bank account in his name and for whom the banker undertakes to provide the facilities as a banker is considered to be a customer. It is not essential that the account must have been operated upon for some time.

A more acceptable view is that expressed in Ladbroke Vs Todd (1914, 30, TLR., 433). According to the Learned Judge: "The relation of banker and customer begins as soon as the first cheque is paid in and accepted for collection. It is not essential that the person should have drawn on any money or even that he should be in a position to draw any money". Therefore neither the number of transactions nor the period during which business has been conducted between the parties is material in determining whether or not a person is a customer.

In a later case that took place between official Assignee Vs Natesam Pillai: (Indian case), According to learned judge "the fact that person had no prior banking transaction with the bank would not by itself exclude the possibility of his becoming a customer when he paid in the amount.

All these court decisions lay stress on the fact that the customer need not have continuous transactions with the bank to become a customer. Mere opening, any type of account will satisfy the basic condition to become a customer. His position must be such that transactions are likely to become frequent. When the accounts are opened with the bank, there will be an implication that the person is likely to operate the account frequently.

Thus, in order to constitute a person as a customer, he must satisfy the following conditions.

1. He must have an account with the bank - i.e., Saving bank account, current deposit account, or fixed deposit account.
2. The transactions between the banker and the customer should be of banking nature i.e., a person who approaches the banker for operating Safe Deposit Locker or purchasing travellers cheques is not a customer of the bank since such transactions do not come under the orbit of banking transactions.
3. Frequency of transactions is not quite necessary though anticipated.

Special Types of Customers

Special types of customers are those who are distinguished from other types of ordinary customers by some special features. Hence, they are called special types of customers. They are to be dealt with carefully while operating and opening the accounts. They are:

1. Minors

Under the Indian law, a minor is a person who has not completed 18 years of age. The period of minority is extended to 21 years in case of guardian of his person or property is appointed by a court of law before he completes the age of 18 years.

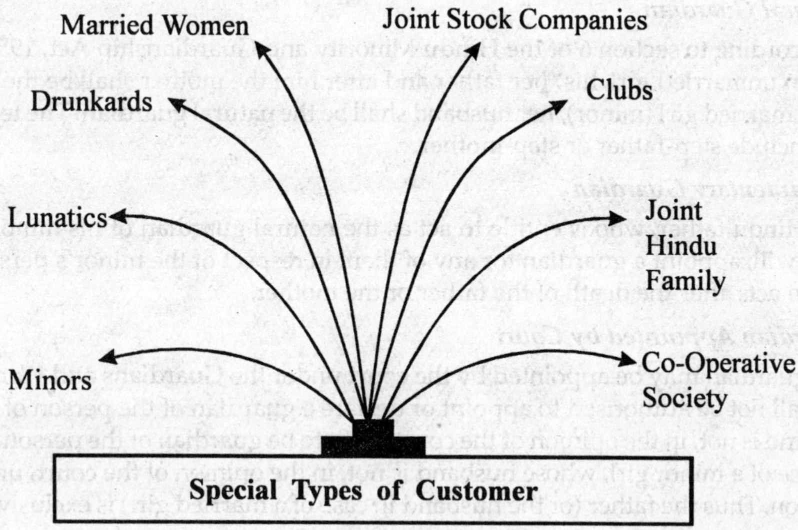

According to Indian Contract Act, a minor is recognised as a highly incompetent party to enter into legal contracts and any contract entered into with a minor is not only invalid but voidable at the option of the minor. The law has specially protected a minor merely because his mental faculty has not fully developed and as such, he is likely to commit mistakes or even blunders which will affect his interests adversely. It is for this reason, the law has come to the rescue of a minor.

A banker can very well open a bank account in the name of a minor. But the banker has to be careful to ensure that he does not open a current account. If a current account is opened and stands overdrawn inadvertently, the banker has no remedy against a minor, as he cannot be taken to a court of law. It is for this reason that the banker should be careful to see that he invariably opens a savings bank account.

The conditions for opening and maintaining accounts in the names of the minors are:

1. The minor should have attained the age of discretion, i.e., he must be about 14 years of age. He must be capable of understanding what he does.
2. The minor should be able to read and write.
3. The minor should be properly introduced. The account opening form should be signed by the minor in the presence of a bank officer who should be able to identify the minor. The date of birth of the minor should be recorded in the account opening form.
4. Banks usually stipulate limits up to which deposits in such accounts can be accepted.
5. Amount tendered by the minor should as for as possible be in cash.
6. In case of time deposits, the amount should be paid in cash on maturity. Prepayment cannot be allowed. Periodical payment of interest on deposits may be made to the minor.

Legal Provisions Regarding Guardianship of a Minor

According to Hindu Minority and Guardianship Act, 1956, a Guardian is one who is recognised by law to be one of the following:

(a) Natural Guardian

According to section 6 of the Hindu Minority and Guardianship Act, 1956, in case of a minor boy or an unmarried girl, his/her father and after him the mother shall be the natural guardian. In case of a married girl (minor), her husband shall be the natural guardian. The terms father or mother do not include step-father or step-mother.

(b) Testamentary Guardian

A Hindu father, who is entitle to act as the natural guardian of his minor legitimate children may, by will, appoint a guardian for any of them in respect of the minor's person or property. Such guardian acts after the death of the father or the mother.

(c) Guardian Appointed by Court

A guardian may be appointed by the court under the Guardians and Wards Act, 1890, but the court shall not be authorised to appoint or declare a guardian of the person of a minor, if his father is alive and is not, in the opinion of the court, unfit to be guardian of the person of the minor. Similar is the case of a minor girl, whose husband is not, in the opinion of the court, unfit to be guardian of her person. Thus the father (or the husband in case of a married girl) is exclusively entitled to be the guardian.

2. Lunatics

A Lunatic or an Insane person is one who, on account of mental derangement, is incapable of understanding his interests and thereby, arriving at rational Judgement.

Since a lunatic does not understand what is right and what is wrong, it is quite likely that the public may exploit the weakness of a lunatic to their advantage and thus deprive him of his legitimate claims. On account of this, the Indian Contract Act recognises that a lunatic is incompetent to enter into any contract and any such contract, if entered into, is not only invalid but voidable at the option of the lunatic.

Since a lunatic customer is an incompetent party, the banker has to be very careful in dealing with such customers. Bankers should not open an account in the name of a person of unsound mind. On coming to know of a customer's insanity, the banker should stop all operations on the account and await a court order appointing a receiver. It would be dangerous to rely on hearsay information. The bank should take sufficient care to verify the information and should not stop the account unless it is fully satisfied about the correctness of the information. In case a person suffers from a temporary mental disorder, the banker must obtain a certificate from two medical officers regarding his mental soundness at the time of operation on the account.

3. Drunkards

A drunkard is a person who on account of consumption of alcoholic drinks get himself intoxicated and thereby, loses the balance over his mental faculty and hence, is incapable of forming rational Judgement.

The law is quite considerable towards a person who is in drunken state. A lawful contract with such a person is invalid. This is for the simple reason that it is quite likely that the public may exploit the weakness of such a person to their advantage and thus, deprive him of his legitimate claims.

A banker has to be very careful in dealing with such customers. There cannot be any objection by a banker to open an account. In case a customer approaches the banker for encashment of his cheque especially when he is drunk, the banker should not make immediate payment. This is because the customer may afterwards argue that the banker has not made payment at all. Therefore, it is better and safer that the banker should insist upon such a customer getting a witness (who is not drunk) to countersign before making any payment against the cheque.

4. Married Women

An account may be opened by the bank in the name of a married woman as she has the power to draw cheques and give valid discharge. At the time of opening an account in the name of a married woman, it is advisable to obtain the name and occupation of her husband and name of his employer, if any, and record the same to enable detection if the account is misused by the husband for crediting therein cheques drawn in favour of his employer.

In case of an unmarried lady, the occupation of her father and name and address of his employer, if any, may be obtained and noted in the account opening form.

If a lady customer requests the bankers to change the name of her account opened in her maiden name to her married name, the banker may do so after obtaining a written request from her. A fresh specimen signature has also to be obtained for records.

While opening an account of a purdah lady, the bank obtains her signature on the account opening form duly attested by a responsible person known to the bank. It is advisable to have withdrawals also similarly attested. In view of practical difficulties involved, it would be better not to open accounts in the names of purdah ladies.

5. Insolvents

When a person is unable to pay his debts in full, his property in certain circumstances is taken possession of by official receiver or official assignee, under orders of the court. He realises the debtor's property and reteably distributes the proceeds amongst his creditors. Such a proceeding is called 'insolvency' and the debtor is known as an 'insolvent'.

If an account holder becomes insolvent, his authority to the bank to pay cheques drawn by him is revoked and the balance in the account vests in the official receiver or official assignee

6. Illiterate Persons

A person is said to be illiterate when he does not know to read and write. No current account should be opened in the name of an illiterate person. However, a savings bank account may be opened in the name of such a person. On the account opening form the bank should obtain his thumb mark in the presence of two persons known to the bank and the depositor. Withdrawal from the account by the account holder should be permitted after proper identification every time. The person who identifies the drawer must be known to the bank and he should preferably not be a member of the bank's staff.

7. Agents

A banker may open an account in the name of a person who is acting as an agent of another person. The account should be considered as the personal account of an agent, and the banker has no authority to question his power to deal with the funds in the account unless it becomes obvious that he is being guilty of breach of trust.

However, if a person is authorised to only act on behalf of the principal, the banker should see that he is properly authorised to do the acts which he claims to do. If he has been appointed by a power of attorney, the banker should carefully pursue the letter-of-attorney to confirm the powers conferred by the document on the agent. In receiving notice of the principal's death, insanity or bankruptcy, the banker must suspend all operations on the account.

8. Joint Stock Company

A joint stock company has been defined as an artificial person, invisible, intangible and existing only in contemplation of law. It has separate legal existence and it has a perpetual succession. The banker must satisfy himself about the following while opening an account in the name of a company:

(a) Memorandum of Association

Memorandum of Association is the main document of the company, which embodies its constitution and is called the charter of the company. It gives details, especially regarding objects and capital of the company. A copy of this document should be insisted upon while opening an account.

(b) Articles of Association

The Articles of Association contain the rules and regulations of the company regarding its internal management. It contains in detail all matters which are concerned with the conduct of day-to-day business of the company. The Articles of Association is also another document that a banker insists upon. It enables the banker to know the details of company's borrowing powers quantum, persons authorised to borrow etc. This will also enable the banker to understand whether the acts of the officers are within the orbit of the Company's Memorandum and Articles.

(c) Certificate of Incorporation

This is another vital document the banker has to verify and insist upon receiving a copy. This document signifies that the company can commence its business activities as soon as it gets this certificate which is not the case with a public company.

(d) Certificate to Commence Business

Only for public companies, the banker insists upon this document for verification. This document gives the clearance to public companies to commence their business activities. A company can borrow funds provided it has obtained this certificate.

(e) Application Form and Copy of the Board's Resolution

A copy of the prescribed application form duly completed in all respects has to be submitted in the beginning and that too duly signed by the company's authorised officers. Along with this, a copy of the resolution passed at the meeting of the board regarding appointment of company's bankers is quite necessary to make every thing lawful. The resolution copy should be signed by the company's Chairman and Secretary in addition, a copy of the specimen signatures of the officers empowered to operate the bank account has to be furnished.

(f) A Written Mandate

This is also another document that a banker insists upon. It contains all the details regarding operation, overdrawing of the account and giving security to the bank by the officers of the company. This document is useful to the bank for opening as well as for operating the account of the company.

(g) Registration of Charges

Whenever a company borrows, it has to give certain assets by way of security and in case the banker accepts them as security, it has to be properly recorded in the company's books, register of charges and duly registered.

9. Any Change in the Company's Constitution or Offices

Whenever there is any change in the constitution like Memorandum or in respect of company's offices, it has to be communicated in writing to the bank and it should not in any way affect the earlier contracts entered into by the company with the bank. To this effect, the bankers usually take an undertaking from the company.

10. Clubs, Associations and Educational Institutions

Clubs, Associations and Educational Institutions are non-trading institutions interested in serving noble causes of education, sports etc. The banker should observe the following precautions in dealing with them.

(a) Incorporation

A sports club, an association or an educational institution must be registered or incorporated according to the Indian Companies Act, 1956, or the Co-operative Societies Acts. If it is not registered, the organisation will not have any legal existence and it has no right to contact with the out-side parties.

(b) Rules and By-laws of the Organisation

A registered association or organisation is governed by the provisions of the Act under which it has been registered. It may have its own Constitution, Charter or Memorandum of Association and rules and by-laws, etc., to carry on its activities. A copy of the same should be furnished by the organisation to the banker to acquaint the latter with the powers and functions of the persons managing its affairs. The banker should ensure that these rules are observed by the persons responsible for managing the organisation.

(c) A Copy of Resolution of Managing Committee

For opening a bank account, the Managing Committee of the organisation must pass a resolution-

(i) appointing the bank concerned as the banker of the organisation.

(ii) mentioning the name/names of the person or persons, who are authorised to operate the account

(iii) giving any other directions for the operation of the said account.

A copy of the resolution must be obtained by the bank for its own record.

(d) An Application Form

An application form duly completed in all respects along with specimen signatures of the office bearers of the Institution is quite essential for operation of the account.

(e) A Written Mandate

It is an important document which contains specific instructions given to the banker regarding operations, over drawing etc.

(f) Transfer of Funds

All funds and cheques which are in the name of the Institution should be invariably credited to the Institution account and not to the personal or private accounts of the office bearers of the Institution.

(g) Death or Resignation

In case the person authorised to operate the account on behalf of a organisation or association dies or resigns, the banker should stop the operations of the organisation's account till the organisation nominates another person to operate its account.

11. Partnership Firm

A partnership is not regarded as an entity separate from the partners. The Indian Partnership Act, 1932, defines partnership as the "relation between persons who have agreed to share the profits of the business, carried on by all or any of them acting for all".

Partnership is formed or constituted on account of agreement between the partners and with the sole intention of earning and sharing profits in a particular ratio. Further, the business is carried on either by all the partners or some partners acting for all. The partners carry joint and several liability and the partnership does not posses any legal entity.

A banker should take the following precautions while opening an account in the name of a partnership firm.

(a) Application Form

A prescribed application form duly completed in all respects along with specimen signatures of the partners of firm is quite essential for operation of the account.

(b) Partnership Deed

The banker should, very carefully examine the partnership deed, which is the charter of the firm, to acquaint himself with the constitution and business of the firm. This will help him to know his position while advancing funds to the firm.

(c) A Mandate

A mandate giving specific instructions to the banker regarding operations, over-drawing etc., is quite necessary. It will enable the banker to handle the accounts according to the needs of the firm.

(d) Transfer of Funds

The banker has to be very careful to see that the funds belonging to the firm should not be credited to the personal or private accounts of the partners.

(e) Sanctioning of Overdraft

While sanctioning funds by way of overdraft, the banker has to check up the partnership deed and examine the borrowing powers of the partners empowered to borrow and he can even ask for the financial statements of the previous years for information and perusal.

12. Joint Accounts

When two or more persons open an account jointly, it is called a joint account. The banker should take the following precautions in opening and dealing with a joint account.

(a) The application for opening a joint account must be signed by all the persons intending to open a joint account.

(b) A mandate containing name or names of persons authorised to operate an account.

(c) The full name of the account must be given in all the documents furnished to the banker, even if the account is to be operated upon by one or a few of the joint account holders.

(d) Banker must stop operating an account as soon as a notice of death, insolvency, insanity etc., of any one account holder is received.

(e) The joint account holder, who is authorised to operate the joint account, himself alone cannot appoint an agent or attorney to operate the account on his behalf. Such attorney or agent may be appointed with the consent of all the joint account holders.

(f) If all the persons are operating the account, then banker must see that any cheque drawn on him is duly signed by all.

(g) Banker must stop making payments as soon as letter of revocation is obtained.

(h) Banker must see that no loan or overdraft is granted without proper security.

13. Joint Hindu Family

Joint Hindu Family is an undivided Hindu family which comprises of all male members descended from a common ancestor. They may be sons, grand sons and great grand sons, their wives and unmarried daughters. "A joint, Hindu family is a family which consists of more than one male member, possesses ancestral property and carries on family business". Therefore, Joint Hindu Family is a legal institution. It is managed and represented in its dealings and transactions with others by the Kartha who is the head of the family. Other members of the family do not have this right to manage unless a particular member is given certain rights and responsibilities with common consent of the Kartha.

The banker has to exercise greater care in dealing with this account.

(a) He must get complete information about the Joint Hindu Family including the names of major and minor coparceners and get a declaration from the Kartha to this effect along with specimen signatures and signatures of all coparceners

(b) The account should be opened either in the personal name of the Kartha or in the name of the family business.

(c) The documents should be signed by the Kartha and major coparceners.

(d) The account should be operated on only by the Kartha and the authorised major coparceners.

(e) While making advances, the banker should ascertain the purpose for which the loan is obtained and whether the loan is really needed by the Joint Hindu Family for business.

14. Trustees

According to the Indian Trusts Act, 1882, "a trust is an obligation annexed to the ownership of property and arising out of a confidence reposed in an accepted by the owner, or declared and accepted by him, for the benefit of another, or of another and the owner". As per this definition, a trustee is a person in whom the author or settlor reposes confidence and entrusts the management of his property for the benefit of a person or an organisation who is called beneficiary. A trust is usually formed by means of document called the "Trust Deed". While opening an account in the names of persons in their capacity as trustees the banker should take the following precautions.

(a) The banker should thoroughly examine the Trust Deed appointing the applicants as the Trustees.

(b) A trust deed which states the powers and functions of trustees must be obtained by the banker.

(c) In case of two or more trustees, the banker should ask for clear instructions regarding the person or persons who shall operate the account.

(d) In case of death or retirement of one or more trustees, banker must see the provision of the trust deed.

(e) The banker should not allow the transfer of funds from trust account to the personal account of trustee.

(f) The banker should take all possible precautions to safeguard the interest of the beneficiaries of a Trust, failing which he shall be liable to compensate the latter for any fraud on the part of the trustee.

(g) The insolvency of a trustee does not affect the Trust property and the creditors of the trustee cannot recover their claims from Trust property.

(h) A copy of the resolution passed in the meeting of trustees open the account should be obtained.

The Banker-Customer Relationship

The relationship between the banker and the customer arises out of the contract entered into between them. This contract is created by mutual consent. A contract that exists between a bank and its customer is a loan contract. This is because if the customers account is in credit, the bank owes him that money and vice versa if the account is overdrawn. This contractual relationship between banker and customer is regulated by the rules contained in the Negotiable Instruments Act, 1881 and the Indian Contract Act 1872. The relationship between the banker and the customer is vital. The relationship starts right from the moment an account is opened and it comes to an end immediately on closure of the account. This relationship is of two types.

A. General relationship.

B. Special relationship.

A. General Relationship

The general relationship between banker and customer can be classified into two types, viz.,

1. Primary relationship and
2. Secondary relationship.

These are discussed below.

1. Primary Relationship

Primary relationship is in the form of a 'Debtor' & 'Creditor' which arises out of a contract between the banker and customer. Banker is neither a bailee nor a trustee nor an agent but only a debtor. Thus the fundamental relationship is that of "Debtor and Creditor". Sometime the banker discharges agency functions like collection of bills, cheques etc., acts as a bailee by keeping valuables in safe custody and acts as trustee by administering the property for the benefit of defined beneficiary. Here the relationship is not that of 'Debtor and Creditor'. The authorities on banking law and many court decisions have said that primary relationship is that of 'Debtor and Creditor'.

Relation of Debtor and Creditor

The true relationship between a banker and his customer is that of a debtor and a creditor. Sir John Paget says: "The relation of banker and customer is primarily that of a debtor and creditor, the respective positions being determined by the existing state of the account. Instead of money being set apart in the safe room, it is replaced by a debt due from the banker. The money deposited with him becomes his property and is absolutely at his disposal". As long as the customer's account shows a credit balance, the banker would be a debtor and in case the customer's account shows a debit balance, the banker would be creditor.

In the case of Joachimson Vs Swiss Banking Corporation, it was held that "the banker undertakes to receive money and collect bills for its customer's account and that money so received is not held in trust for the customer but borrowed from him with a promise to repay it or any part of it".

Even in Indian courts similar opinion is given. By perusing these court decisions and sayings of the authorities on the subject, it is clear that the relationship that exists between the banker and customer is primarily that of debtor and creditor. The mere fact that the banker invites deposits and is prepared to pay interest, and on this condition, the customer deposits his savings, is a clear indication that the customer object to non-payment of interest by the banker so long as the banker is ready and willing to return the deposits, through a legal tender, when demanded in the proper form.

(a) The creditor must demand payment

Although the banker is a debtor and the customer is creditor, it is not at all necessary for the debtor to go to the creditor to pay the amount. This is normally expected in case of commercial transactions where in there are two parties one a debtor and the other a creditor i.e., ordinary debtor-creditor relationship. But, here in case of banker and customer relationship, though the banker is a debtor, he is not expected to approach the creditor for settlement of dues. Here, the relationship is different and has a special feature, namely, demand is necessary from the customer.

Case : Joachimson V/s Swiss Banking Corporation 1921 - It was held that in case of debt due from a bank, an express demand for repayment by the customer is necessary before the debt becomes "actually and accruing due". In case the banker pays the amount on his own accord, he would be indirectly closing the customer's account.

(b) Proper place and time of demand

The demand by the creditor must be made at the proper place and in proper time. It means that the customer should present the cheque for payment at that place of the bank where the customers account is maintained. It is quite clear that at other places, the customer of the state of his account are not known. It is also essential that the customers should demand payment on a working day i.e., not on a holiday or a day which is closed for public. And in addition, it must be presented during business hours i.e., it should not be presented either before or after the business hours.

(c) Demand must be made in proper form

The demand made by the customer must be in the prescribed form as required by the bank. It means that the demand for the refund of money deposited must be made through a cheque or an order as per the common usage amongst the bankers. Otherwise the banker has every right to refuse payment.

So far we have discussed the primary relationship between the banker and the customer. There are other types of relationship called secondary relationship.

2. Secondary Relationship

It will be in the form of :-

(a) Banker as Agent

(b) Banker as Trustee

(c) Banker as Bailee

Let us analyse these three aspects

(a) Banker as Agent

A banker acts as an agent of his customer and performs a number of agency functions for the convenience of his customers. These are as follows;

1. Purchasing or selling of securities.

2. Collection of income
3. Making periodical payments as instructed by his customers.
4. Collecting interest and dividend on securities lodged by his customers.
5. Receiving safe custody valuables and securities lodged by his customers.
6. Collecting cheques, hundies, drafts of the customers.

In this case, the banker and customer relationship is, in the form of an 'Agent' and 'Principal'.

(b) Banker as Trustee

Ordinarily, a banker is a debtor of his customer in respect of the deposits made by the latter, but in certain circumstances he acts as a trustee also. The customer may request the banker to keep his valuables in safe vaults or one may deposit some amount and can request the bank to manage that fund for a specific purpose, which the bank does, or in case of corporate debentures, the bank can become trustee for debenture holders or the bank collects the cheques, hundies of the customers in the capacity of trustee. Thus there are wide varieties of trustee functions discharged by the banker.

(c) Banker as Bailee

Section 2 of the Indian Contract Act defines that bailment as the delivery of goods by one person to another for some purpose upon a contract that they shall, when the purpose is accomplished, be returned or otherwise disposed of according to the direction of the person delivering them.

As a bailee, the banker should protect the valuables in his custody with reasonable care. If the customer suffered any loss due to the negligence of the banker in protecting the valuables, banker is liable to pay such loss. If any loss is incurred due to the situation beyond the control of the banker, he is not liable for penalty.

To conclude, the primary general relationship exists when the account is opened by customer with bank. The relationship is that of debtor and creditor. When the bank acts as Trustee or Agent or Bailee for the valuables, he will be establishing the secondary general relationship.

B. Special Relationship

The special relationship between banker and customer takes the form of rights which the banker can exercise and the obligations which he owes to his customers.

Following are the rights enjoyed by the banker with regard to the customer's account.

1. Right of General Lien
2. Right of Set-off
3. Right to appropriate payments
4. Right to charge Interest, Incidental charges
5. Right not to produce books of accounts
6. Right under Garnishi order
7. Right to close accounts

Some of these rights are discussed below

1. Right of General Lien

One of the important rights enjoyed by a banker is that of general lien. A lien may be defined as the right to retain property belonging to a debtor until he has discharged a debt due to the retainer of the property. In case lien is exercised by a trader on his customer's goods, he has no right to use the goods nor any right to sell them. All that he can do is retain the goods until the obligations are cleared. Once the obligations are cleared by the customer, it is an obligation on the part of the trader to return back his goods immediately. There are two kinds of lien. (a) Particular Lien and (b) General Lien.

(a) Particular Lien

A particular lien confers a right to retain the goods in respect of a particular debt involved in connection with a particular transaction. This lien is enjoyed by the persons who have spent their labour on such properties and have not yet recovered their labour charges or service charges from the debtors. For example, a tailor has the right to retain the cloths made by him for his customer until his tailoring charges are paid by the customer. So is the case with public carriers and the repair shops.

(b) General Lien

A general lien confers a rights to retain goods not only in respect of debts incurred in connection with a particular transaction but also in respect of any general balance arising out of the general dealing between the two parties. This right can be exercised only by persons such as bankers, factors, policy brokers, wharfingers, attorneys of High Court, etc., The basic object of general lien is to have protection for the bank funds. The loans or advances granted to customers can be recovered easily if the general lien is exercised by the bankers.

Banker's lien is a general lien. It has been held in Brandao V/s Barnett·(1864, 3, CB 519) that bankers have general lien on all securities deposited with them as bankers by a customer, unless there be an express contract or circumstances that show an implied contract, inconsistent with the lien.

Further, in the same judgement, a banker's lien has been defined as an implied pledge. Pledge is superior and strengthens the hands of the person who exercises the pledge. In case of pledge, not only the goods will come into the possession of the pledge but in addition, if default is made in complying with the terms of the pledge, the pledgee after giving reasonable notice, can definitely auction the property pledged, recover the proceeds and appropriate the same towards his outstanding arrears. It is because of this reason pledge is said to be much superior and more powerful than lien. But in case of bankers, whenever they exercise their power of lien, it has the effect of pledge. Therefore, it is rightly said that the banker's lien is an implied pledge.

The banker can exercise his power of lien in respect of the following.

(a) Bonds and coupons belonging to the customer deposited for collection.

(b) Customer's securities leftover with the banker after paying the loan.

(c) Any security given by the customer for the purpose of a covering loan.

The banker cannot exercise his power of lien in respect of the following.

(a) Contents of safe deposit lockers belonging to the customer.

(b) Securities and money deposited for specific purpose.

(c) In respect of Trust Accounts wherein his customer (on whom the banker desires to put up his lien) is acting in the capacity of Trustee.

(d) Amounts not due.

(e) In respect of Joint Accounts wherein one of the Joint account holder is a customer on whom the banker desires to exercise his lien.

(f) Documents etc. submitted for getting a loan.

(g) A general lien cannot arise in respect of property of a customer pledged as security for a particular debt.

(h) No lien arises over properties on which the customer has no title.

(i) The banker cannot exercise lien when credit and liability are not in the same rights.

(j) The banker's lien is not affected by the limitation Act.

2. Right of Set-off

The right of set-off is a statutory right which enables a debtor to take into account a debt owed to him by a creditor, before the latter could recover the debt due to him from the debtor. In other words, the mutual claims of debtor and creditor are adjusted together and only the remainder amount is payable by the debtor. A banker, like other debtors, possesses this right of set-off which enables him to combine two accounts in the name of the same customer and to adjust the debit balance in one account with the credit balance in the other. For example, Swaroop has taken an overdraft from his banker to the extent of Rs. 10,000 and he has a credit balance of Rs. 5,000 in his savings bank account, the banker can combine both of these accounts and claim the remainder amount of Rs. 5,000 only. This right of set-off can be exercised by the banker if there is no agreement - express or implied contrary to this right and after a notice is served on the customer intimating the latter about the former's intention to exercise the right of set-off. To be on the safer side the banker takes a letter of set-off from the customer authorising the banker to exercise the right of set-off without giving him any notice.

There are conflicting decisions regarding the application of right of set-off.

In the case of Garnett Vs Mckean (1872, 27, L.T. 560), it was held that in the absence of any special agreement to the contrary, a banker might set-off a customer's credit balance against a debt due to him from the customer and that there was no legal obligation on a bank to give notice to a customer of his intention to combine accounts. But in another subsequent case Greenhalgh and Sons Vs Union Bank of Manchester (1924, 2, K.B. 153), the Learned Judge observed: "If the banker agrees with his customer to open two accounts or more; he has not in my opinion, without the assent of the customer, any right to move either assets or liabilities from one account to the other; the very basis of his agreement with his customer is that the two accounts shall be kept separate".

In view of these conflicting opinions, the banker can be on the safer side by taking an agreement from the customer authorising him to combine the accounts at any time without notice and to return cheques which, as a result of his having taken such action, would overdraw the combined account. However, in such cases as the death or bankruptcy of the customer, the banker can exercise the right of set-off without notice even in the absence of an agreement, in order to ascertain the net amount owing to him.

Conditions Necessary for Exercising the Right of Set-off

The right of set-off can be exercised subject to the fulfillment of the following conditions.

(a) The accounts must be in the same name and in the same right.

(b) By giving notice to customer of banker's intention to combine accounts.

(c) The right can be exercised in respect of debts due and not in respect of future debts or contingent debts.

(d) The amount of debts must be certain.

(e) If there is letter of set-off given by customer.

(f) If the accounts are of dissimilar nature

(g) The right may be exercised in the absence of an agreement to the contrary.

(h) The banker has the right to exercise this right before the Garnishee order is made effective.

Conditions Under which the Right Cannot be Exercised

(a) If the accounts are not in the same right.

(b) The right of set off cannot be extended to a future contingent debt e.g. a bill which will mature in future.

(c) If the amounts of debts are uncertain.

(d) Trust account in which personal account of the customer cannot be combined.

(e) The account balance of an individual cannot be set-off against a joint account balance in which he is one of the account holders.

Automatic Right of Set-off

The banker enjoys the right of "Automatic set-off in following cases.

(a) On the death, insolvency or insanity of customer.

(b) On the insolvency of a partner.

(c) On receipt of garnishee order

(d) On receiving the notice of assignment of a customer's credit balance.

(e) On receiving the notice of second mortgage on the security on which the bank holds first charge.

(f) On the winding up of a company.

Thus the right of set-off a statutory right. But to exercise this right, it is the normal practice of the banker to obtain a letter of set-off from the customer.

3. Right to Appropriate Payments

Whenever the customer deposits funds into his account in the bank, it is his duty to inform the bank to which account they are to be credited (provided the customer has more than one account at the same bank). Once the customer gives specific directions regarding appropriation, the banker has no right to alter them. It is his bounden duty to carry out the instructions of the customer. This right of appropriation is to be exercised by the customer at the time of depositing funds and not later. In case the customer is silent or fails to give instructions, the banker has every right to appropriate in his own way. In case both have not used their powers, the rule given in Clayton's case would be applicable. In this famous case (Davayness V/s Noble, 1816, 1-Merivale 529, 572), the verdict given by the court was as follows; The first item on the debit side is reduced by the first item on the credit side.

Certain conditions have to be fulfilled to apply the rule in Clayton's case. They are:

(a) This rule cannot be applied to the accounts which were stopped in the middle and revived after certain date.

(b) The rule is not applicable to broken accounts.

(c) If two separate accounts are maintained the rule is not applicable.

d) Contrary intentions should not be evidenced by the parties concerned.

4. Right to Charge Interest

As a creditor, a banker has the implied right to charge interest on the advances granted to the customer. The rate of interest is nowadays levied as per the directions of Reserve Bank of India. It is charged on half yearly or quarterly basis and generally compound interest is used. The interest is directly debited, i.e., charged to the customer's account and then the interest is calculated on the principal with interest. Interest may also be fixed by the banker and customer by mutual consent. It may not however be beyond the prescribed limits of Reserve Bank of India. In Konakalla Venkata Satyanarayana and others V/s State Bank of India (AIR, 1975 A.P. 113) the agreement provided that "interest @..... shall be calculated on the daily balance of such account and shall be charged to such account on the last working day of each month". For several years the customer availed the overdraft facilities and periodical statements of accounts were being sent to the customer showing that interest was being changed and debited at compound rate and no objection was raised at any time. The High Court, therefore, held that there was no doubt that the customer had agreed to the compound rate of interest being charged and debited to their account. Banks also charge incidental charges on the current accounts to meet the incidental expenses on such accounts.

5. Right not to Produce Books of Accounts

According to the provisions of the Bankers Book Evidence Act, the banker need not produce the original books of Accounts as an evidence in the cases in which the banker is not a party. He can issue only an attested copy of the required portion of the account which can be utilised as an evidence before the court. When the court is not satisfied with the certified copy, the court can summon the original books. But when a banker is a party to the suit, the court can force the banker to produce the original records in support of his claim.

6. Right under Garnishi Order

The term "Garnishee" is derived from the Latin word "garnire" which means "to warn". This order warns the holder of money of judgement debtor, not to make any payment out of it till the court directs.

It is an order issued by a competent court of law addressed to a banker instructing him to stop or withhold payment of money belonging to a particular person who has committed a default in satisfying the claim of his creditors. Therefore, whenever a bank receives such an order, the banker has to obey the order fully. Let us take an example to clearly explain this procedure.

Chaluvaiah is a contractor and obtains a loan from Eshwarappa a money lender or banker. Chaluvaiah fails to pay the money to Eshwarappa as per the stipulation. Hence Eshwarappa files a suit in the court of law for dues. Eshwarappa also knows that the money is due to Chaluvaiah from the agency (third party) with which he is doing his contract business. Now Eshwarappa can request the court to issue an order directing the Chaluvaiah's agency not to make any payment to Chaluvaiah. If the court issues the order that becomes a garnishee order. In this suit Chaluvaiah is judgement debtor and Eshwarappa is a judgement creditor. The third party is garnishee.

Sheldon defines garnishee order thus, "It is an order obtained by a judgement creditor attaching funds in the hands of a third party, who owes the judgement debtor money, warning the third party, not to release the money attached until directed by court to do so".

Thus garnishee order is a direction given by the court to a third party who is due to the judgement debtor not to make any payment till it gives a verdict regarding the paid money. This order is issued at the request of the judgement creditor.

The garnishee order is issued in two parts.

A. Order - Nisi

It is an order issued by a court on a specific banker ordering him, not to release any funds belonging to a particular customer (judgement debtor) until further orders are issued. In the meantime, the judgement debtor is requested to appear before the court for further proceedings.

B. Order - absolute

This is an order of the court issued to a banker after completion of the hearing of the parties concerned and through this order, the court specifies how much amount is to be kept separate. The banker has to follow these orders after looking at the position of the customer's account.

In the following circumstances the garnishee order would not be applicable.

(a) Where the account of the judgement debtor is a joint account holder with another person;

(b) Where the identity of the judgement debtor is doubtful;

(c) Where the account of the judgement debtor is held by him in the capacity of a Trustee;

(d) Where the judgement debtor has previously made an official assignment of his balance in favour of a third party and the banker is informed about it in writing;

(e) Where the account of the judgement debtor reveals a debit balance.

7. Right to Close Accounts

Banker also enjoys the right to close his customer's account and discontinue operations. This process terminates the relationship between banker and customer. This is done only in situations where the continuation of relationship seems unprofitable to the banker.

These are the rights enjoyed by the banker with regard to the customer's account.

Obligations of Bankers

Bankers are under the obligations to fulfil certain duties while dealing with customers. Such obligations are as under.

1. Obligation to honour the customer's cheques.
2. Obligation to maintain secrecy of customer's account.
3. Obligation to receive the cheques and other instruments for collection.
4. Obligation to honour the cheques of customers across the counter.
5. Obligation to give reasonable notice before closing the customer's accounts.

Some of these obligations are discussed below.

1. Obligation to Honour the Customer's Cheques

Section 31 of the Negotiable Instruments Act, 1881, imposes a statutory obligation upon the banker to honour the cheques of his customer drawn against his current account so long as his balance is sufficient to allow the banker to do so, provided the cheques are presented within a reasonable time after their ostensible date of issue. The section runs as follows.

"The drawee of a cheque having sufficient funds of the drawer in his hands, properly applicable to the payment of such cheque, must pay the cheque when duly required so to do and in default of such payment, must compensate the drawer for any loss or damage, caused by such default".

This provision clearly indicates that the banker should honour the customers demand for payment by cheque on certain conditions which are stated below.

(a) Sufficient Balance

There must be sufficient funds in the account of the drawer. The cheques sent for collection by the customer are not treated as cash in the hands of the banker until the same are realised. The banker credits the amount of such cheques to the account of the customer on their realisation. If the customer draws a cheque on the unrealised amounts, the banker is justified in dishonouring the cheque with the remark "effects not cleared".

(b) Application of the Funds

The funds must be capable of being properly applied to the payment of customer's cheque. This means, the funds maintained for a specific purpose or trust funds or the funds assigned in the name of some other person cannot be applied for honouring the cheques. Thus the funds so sought by the customer by cheque should be unencumbered and must be capable of being properly applied.

(c) Duly Required to Pay

The banker is bound to honour the cheques only when he is duly required to pay. This means that the cheque, is complete and in order, must be presented before the banker at the proper time. Ordinarily a period of six months is considered sufficient within which a cheque must be presented for payment. On the expiry of this period the cheque is treated as state and the banker dishonours the cheque. Similarly, a post-dated cheque is also dishonoured by the banker because the order of the drawer becomes effective only on the date given in the cheque.

(d) The instrument used for drawing the amount should be properly written and fulfil and legal obligations.

(e) The banker should have reasonable time to collect the bill or cheque.

(f) There should not be any legal restriction to pass the cheque for payment say in case of garnishee order, restriction is imposed in the account.

(g) The banker need not honour the cheques presented against domiciled bills.

Thus, the banker should be very careful while honouring a cheque drawn by a customer.

Consequences of Wrongful Dishnour of Cheque

A cheque may be dishnoured by a banker by mistake or by negligence on the part of any of his employees. Even though there is sufficient balance, and the cheque has been drawn in a proper manner. The banker will be held responsible for wrongful dishonour of a cheque because of loss or damage to the customer. The phrase "Loss or damage" in section 31 of the Negotiable Instruments Act 1881 includes (a) The monetary loss suffered by the customer and (b) The loss of credit or reputation in the market. Thus, the banker is liable to compensate the drawer not only for the actual monetary loss suffered by him, but also for the injury top or loss of his reputation, as a result of dishonour of a cheque.

In case the customer happens to be a trader, the loss would be substantial damages. In case the customer is a non-trader, the banker would be liable only for normal damages {(Case: Robin Vs Steward (1854) 146 - B 595) (Case: Gibbs Vs Westminister Bank (1939) 2 K.B. 882)}. In the case of sterling Vs Barclay's Bank Ltd., where the banker had made a mistake in wrongfully dishonouring the customer's cheque, the customer was not entitled to substantial damages but reasonable damages as the customer had two cheques dishonoured earlier and further, people in that trade did not think much of cheques being dishonoured as they just carried on their living with bare necessaries. (Case: Davidson Vs Barday's Bank Ltd., 1940 AII. E.R. 316). The customer had issued a cheque for £ 2-15-

8 and it was dishonoured and the matter was referred to the court and the Court ordered that substantial damages to the tune of £ 250 should be paid.

2. Obligation to Maintain Secrecy of Customer's Account

In every profession, there are certain things to be maintained absolutely in secret; for example, a Doctor is not expected to disclose the details of his patients to others. The profession demands from him that he must maintain those matters in strict confidence. Similarly, a bank's profession also demands that he should maintain the particulars of his customer's accounts in secret.

The banker has an implied obligation to maintain secrecy of the customers account. He should not disclose matters relating to the customer's financial position since it may adversely affect the customer's credit and business. This obligation continues even after the account of the customer is closed.

Only in the following circumstances, disclosure is justified.

(a) To satisfy Statutory Requirements

According to the Income Tax Act, the banker is required to give out information regarding his customers to the Income Tax Department. Similarly, whenever the court needs any information regarding the customers, the banker is required to give the information. According to the Banking Regulation Act, all the banks are required to give in the prescribed forms detailed information regarding the customers to the Reserve Bank of India.

(b) As a common Courtesy

In This case, it is a common practice followed among bankers to exchange information regarding their customers accounts etc., as a matter of common courtesy. Whenever the banker is called upon to give information regarding his customers, he can do so without any difficulty. As far as possible, he should furnish bare facts while expressing his opinion. He should be very careful while expressing his opinion. He should not exaggerate nor underestimate the financial standing of his customers.

(c) Disclosure at the will of Customer

The banker can disclose the state of affairs of the customer's account when the customer gives his consent to disclose the accounts. The auditor of the organisation can fully examine the customer's account when an express consent is given by him. Similarly when a customer gives the name of a guarantor, the guarantor can examine the accounts of the customer which the banker should furnish. When banker acts as a reference, he can disclose the accounts of the customer.

(d) To protect his Own Interest

Whenever the banker is required to protect his own interest, if he discloses the details of a customer's account, it must be a reasonable and proper occasion. For example, if the banker is to recover his own money from a particular customer, he may give the details to his lawyers.

(e) To protect Public Interest

The Banking Commission (1972) opined as follows: When banks are required to give out information regarding their customers in the interest of the public, the information should relate to financial aspect of the customers. The following are instances of such cases:

(i) Where considerable amounts are received from other countries.

(ii) In case the bank thinks that the customer is carrying on such activities which are not congenial in the interest of the nation.

(iii) In case the banker thinks that the customer is trying to break the provisions of the law on the basis of his records.

(vi) When the Government calls upon the bank to give information regarding a particular customer and when the bank feels that a particular customer has committed on offence.

3. Obligation to Receive Cheques and other Instruments for Collection

Basically, the business of banking, as it is known today, comprises acceptance of money on deposit account and payment of cheques. It also includes collection of cheques. It may rightly be contended that anyone who does not perform these essential services is not a banker. Whenever a banker is entrusted with the job of collection of cheques, they must be collected as speedily as possible through the accepted channels. Failure to exercise proper care and employ the recognised route for collection may make the bank liable for any loss which the customer may sustain.

4. Obligation to give Reasonable Notice before Closing the Account

According to law, a debtor and a creditor may terminate the relationship without notice - by the debtor paying off the balance or the creditor recalling the debt. It is not so simple between a banker and a customer for the obvious reason that the banker is under an obligation to houour his customer's cheques. If this obligation could be terminated by the banker without notice, the customer might be faced with an embarrassing situation. Reasonable time must be granted to enable him to make alternative arrangements. Where any customer becomes a nuisance through overdrawing without arrangement or issuing post-dated cheques etc., it is advisable to close his account. But reasonable time has to be given to enable him to make alternative arrangements if he so desires. If a bank abruptly closes the customers account, it might affect his credit, giving cause for an action against the bank for damages.

Obligations of Customers

Customers are under the obligations to fulfil certain duties while dealing with banks. Such obligations are as under:-

(a) Not to draw cheques without sufficient balance.

(b) To draw cheques in such a manner so as to avoid any change of alternation.

(c) To pay reasonable charges for services rendered.

(d) To make a demand on the banker for repayment of deposit.

So far we have discussed the primary and special relationship between the banker and the customer. This relationship starts right from the moment an account is opened and it comes to an end immediately on closure of the account. The relationship stands established as soon as the agreement or contract is entered into. This relationship is shown in the following chart.

Conclusion

To conclude, it is rightly said that the relationship between a banker and its customer is that of a bailee and bailor. As a bailee, the banker is bound to take as much care of the goods bailed to him as a man of ordinary prudence would, under similar circumstances, take of his own goods of the same bulk, quality and value as the goods bailed. However, in the absence of any special contract, the bailee gets protection and is not held responsible for the loss, distruction or deterioration of the thing bailed, if he has taken the amount of care of it.

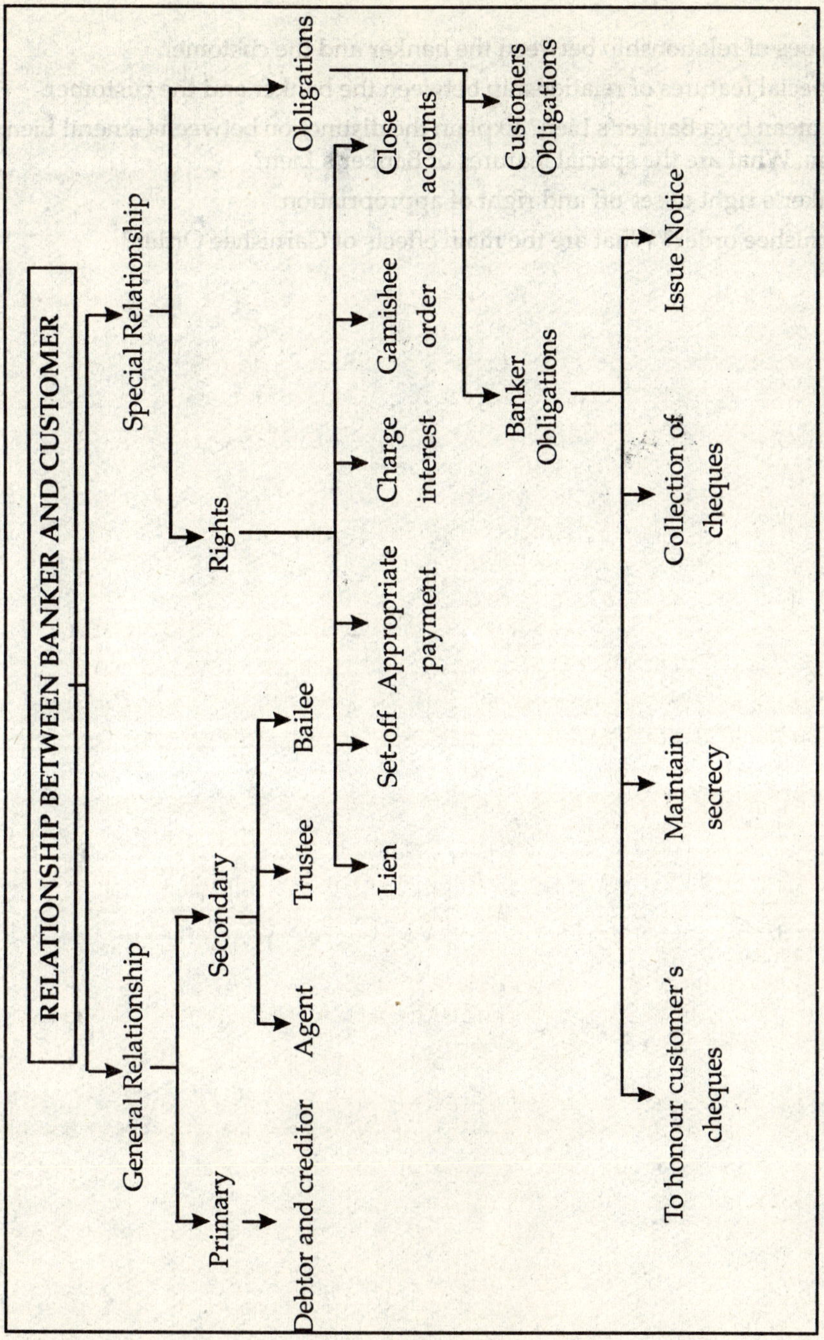
RELATIONSHIP BETWEEN BANKER AND CUSTOMER
General Relationship
Special Relationship
Primary
Secondary
Debtor and creditor
Agent
Trustee
Bailee
Rights
Obligations
Lien
Set-off
Appropriate payment
Charge interest
Gamishee order
Close accounts
Customers Obligations
Banker Obligations
To honour customer's cheques
Maintain secrecy
Collection of cheques
Issue Notice

Questions for Discussions

1. Discuss the types of relationship between the banker and the customer.
2. Discuss the special features of relationship between the banker and the customer.
3. What do you mean by a Banker's Lien? Explain the distinction between General Lien and Particular Lien. What are the special features of Banker's Lien?
4. Discuss a banker's right of set-off and right of appropriation.
5. What is a Garnishee order? What are the main effects of Garnishee Order?

Chapter - 9

OPENING AND OPERATING BANK ACCOUNTS

Introduction

The most important function of a bank is to accept deposits from the public. Customers deposit their savings for safety and earning interest. A bank provides facilities to open various types of accounts keeping in mind the needs of its customers. Generally, the bank accounts are classified into three categories: (a) the current accounts, (b) the fixed deposit accounts and (c) the saving deposit accounts. In recent years, a few new types of accounts have also be introduced by banks. Prominent among them are, the recurring deposit accounts, students deposit accounts, multi-purpose deposit scheme, super savings scheme, janatha deposit scheme, pigmy deposit scheme, loan linked deposits etc. Some banks also issue 'cash certificates' to solicit deposits for a fixed period. It is important to point out that the rates of interest offered by different banks under different schemes do not vary much because these are governed by the directives from the Reserve Bank of India. No bank is allowed to pay higher rate of interest under any scheme as is prescribed by the Reserve Bank. The rates are prescribed by the Reserve Bank taking into consideration the period of deposits.

Types of Accounts

The bank accounts are classified into three categories. These are as follows.

1. Current Account

A Current Account or Demand Deposit Account is a running and active account which may be opened with a bank by a businessman or an organisation by making an initial deposit of Rs. 300 in rural areas and Rs. 500 in urban areas. This account may also be operated upon any number of times during a working day. This account never becomes time barred, because no interest is paid for credit balance in this account.

Before opening a Current Account, banks are required to obtain references from respectable parties, preferably those of a current account-holder. In case, a person or a party opens an account with the bank without satisfactory references, the banker would be inviting unpleasant results.

By accepting deposits on a Current Account, the banker under takes to honour his customer's cheques so long as there is enough money to the credit of the customer. In case of current account, there is no limit on the amount or number of withdrawals. Under Section 129 of the Negotiable Instruments Act, 1881, the banker may have to suffer loss if he pays a forged Cheque or if he pays a Cheque contrary to the instructions given by the customer.

Benefits of Current Accounts

The customers derive the following advantages from current accounts.

(a) Demand deposits are treated at par with cash. They constitute cheque currency. Cheques are readily accepted in business for making and receiving payments.

(b) Businessmen have to receive and make a large number of payments every day. It is difficult to handle cash. The cheque facility removes the difficulty.

(c) There are no restrictions on the number of cheques or on the amount to be drawn at a time by one cheque.

(d) Overdraft facilities are allowed by the banks to the current account holders.

2. Savings Bank Account

Savings deposit account is meant for small businessmen and individuals who wish to save a little out of their current incomes to safeguard their future and also to earn some interest on their savings. A savings account can be opened with as small a sum of Rs. 250. Similarly, small amounts can be withdrawn. A minimum balance of Rs. 250 is to be maintained in the account if cheque book facility is not required. However, if a cheque book has been issued, a minimum balance of Rs. 500 is necessary.

There are restrictions on the maximum amount that can be deposited in this account and also on the withdrawals from this account. The bank may not permit more than one or two withdrawals during a week and may lay down a limit on the amount that can be withdrawn at one time.

Savings account holders are allowed to deposit cheques, drafts, dividend warrants, etc. which stand in their name only. For this facility, it is necessary that account holder must be introduced by a person having a current or savings account in the same bank. However, the banks do not accept cheques or instruments payable to third party for deposit in the savings bank account. Banks allow interest on deposits maintained in savings accounts according to the rates prescribed by the Reserve Bank of India.

Popularity of Savings Accounts

Savings bank accounts is very popular among the general public because of the following advantages.

(a) A savings account can be opened with as little as Rs. 5/- only. It helps the people of small means to save for their future.

(b) The balance lying in the savings bank earns some interest. The customer is benefitted his money grows with the bank.

(c) The money lying with the bank is quite safe. There is no fear of theft.

(d) The money can be withdrawn conveniently from the savings account.

(e) The customer gets the cheque book facility if his account is duly introduced by another account-holder and he keeps a minimum balance of Rs. 100/-. It is quite easy to make payment to third parties by issuing cheques.

3. Fixed Deposit Account

Money in this account is accepted for a fixed period, say one, two or five years. The money so deposited cannot be withdrawn before the expiry of the fixed period. The rate of interest on this account is higher than that on other accounts. The longer the period, the higher is the rate of interest. Fixed deposits are also called "time deposits" or "time liabilities". Fixed deposits have grown in importance and popularity in India during recent years. These deposits constitute more than half of the total bank deposits. The following are the special characteristics of fixed deposits.

(a) Suitability

Fixed deposits are usually chosen by people who have surplus money and do not require it for some time. These deposit accounts are also favoured by the bankers because fixed deposit funds can be utilised by them freely till the due date of the repayment.

(b) Rate of Interest

The rate of interest and other terms and conditions on which the banks accept fixed deposits are regulated by the Reserve Bank of India. The Reserve Bank of India revised the rates of interest on fixed deposits several times. Banks can use fixed deposits for the purpose of lending or investments. So they pay higher rate of interest on fixed deposits. Though interest is payable at the stipulated rate, at the maturity of the fixed deposit, banks usually pay interest quarterly or half-yearly also at the request of the depositor.

(c) Restrictions on Withdrawals

Withdrawal of interest or the principal amount through cheques is not permitted. The depositor is not given a cheque book. At the request of the customer, the banker may credit the amount of interest or the principal to his saving or current account from which he may withdraw the same through cheques.

(d) Payment before due date

Banks also permit the encashment of a fixed deposit even before the due date, if the depositor so desires. But the interest agreed upon on such deposit shall be reduced.

(e) Advances against fixed deposits

The banker may also grant a loan to the depositor on the security of the Fixed Deposit Receipt. Banks are now free to determine the interest rate chargeable on loan advances of over Rs. 2 lakhs.

Opening of Fixed Deposit Account

Fixed deposit account can be opened either with placement of cash or cheque. The depositor has to fill in an "Application Form" requiring the bank to accept deposit of a specified sum of money on deposit account. The application form contains the particulars of the customer, the amount proposed to be deposited, the terms of deposit etc. The specimen signatures of the customer are also to be obtained along with the application. If it is being opened by joint-parties, there should be mandate as to its discharge. A fixed deposit receipt is then issued to the depositor by the bank. The fixed deposit receipt is an acknowledgment of the receipt of the particular amount of money from the person or party named therein.

Contents of Fixed Deposit Receipt

The fixed deposit receipt issued under the seal of the bank has the following contents.

(a) Name and address of the depositor.

(b) Amount deposited, described in words and figures.

(c) The period for which the deposit is made.

(d) The rate of interest allowed on the deposit.

(e) The date of opening the deposit account.

(f) The date on which the deposit will become due for repayment.

(g) The name of the bank, place of its office accepting the deposit.

(h) The words "not transferable" appear prominently across the face of the receipt to indicate its "non-negotiable" character.

(i) Signature of the Manager or other authorised officer of the bank.

(j) On the back of the receipt, particulars of interest accruals, and payment and repayment of deposit on maturity are recorded to be filled in form time to time.

Significance of Fixed Deposit Receipt

1. Fixed deposit receipt is an acknowledgment of the receipt of the particular amount of money from the person or party named therein.
2. The party described therein is entitled to receive the proceeds from the bank on maturity of the period.
3. The depositor is also entitled to the receipt of interest at the stated rate.
4. If the deposit receipt is lost, the depositor has to furnish an "indemnity bond" or stamped paper and thereafter a duplicate receipt may be issued by the bank.
5. It is non-negotiable. Hence, any holder of the receipt under endorsement or delivery has no right to the proceeds of the account.
6. It can be offered as a security for raising the loan. Usually 90% of the deposit is given as an advance at about 1% interest higher than is allowed on the deposit.
7. It does not bear any stamp under the stamp Act applicable to legal documents of claim.
8. But a banker repaying the money to the depositor has to take a stamped receipt as legal acquittance of the payment. Stamped receipt is compulsory when the amount exceeds Rs. 20/-. In case of renewal, simple acknowledgment of the customer is taken and a fresh application for the renewal of deposit is taken from the customer. A new deposit receipt is then issued.

4. Recurring Deposit Account

The Recurring Deposit Account has gained wide popularity these days. Under this, the depositor is required to deposit a fixed amount of money every month for specific period of time. Each instalment may vary from Rs. 5/- to Rs. 500/- or more per month and the total period of account varies from 12 months to 10 years. After the completion of the specified period, the customer gets back all his deposits along with the cumulative interest accured on them.

Recurring deposit account offers the following benefits to the public.

(a) It provides a good way to save in small amounts for use in the future, e.g., education of children, marriage of children, etc.

(b) people having low income may open a recurring deposit account with a commitment to deposit as low as Rs. 5/- every month.

(c) The recurring deposit account can be opened for any period ranging from 12 months to 120 months.

(d) Standing instructions to transfer monthly instalments from the savings account of the depositor are carried out without any charge.

(e) Loan can be taken upto 90% of the deposits if the depositor needs money.

Procedure of Opening Current and Savings Accounts

A bank should be very careful in entertaining a new customer. It will be taking a great risk if it opens an account of a customer without knowing the where-abouts of the latter. As said earlier, the opening of an account involves the honouring of cheques on the part of the bank so long as customer's account has credit balance. The bank will also provide a number of other services to the customer like collection of cheques, dividends, etc. and acting as agent of the customer. When the customer is not adequately known of the bank, it may result in wrong payment or encashment of forged cheques. Hence, it is essential that the bank should make through enquiry regarding the customer before opening an account with him. For this purpose, the bank may follow the procedure given below.

1. Presenting of Application

The applicant should fill in the prescribed form for opening of an account form available from the concerned bank. Banks keep different forms for individuals, Joint Hindu Families, partnership firm, companies, etc. The applicant should fill in the relevant form and mention his name, occupation, full address, specimen signature and other particulars required by the bank. The applicant has also to declare that he will be bound by the bank's rules for the time being in force for the conduct of the concerned account.

2. Introduction

The banks follow the practice of opening the account only when the applicant is properly introduced by an existing customer of the bank. Sometimes, reference is given by the depositor and the bank may seek the opinion of the referees regarding the integrity and financial stability of the applicant. If the bank is satisfied about the identity and standing of the applicant, it will agree to open an account. It is, however, advisable that the person introducing the applicant to the banker or acting as referee must himself be a respectable person.

The idea behind proper introduction, is that the bank should entertain a person only who is honest, reliable and responsible. Such a proper enquiry will prevent fraud and overdrawal of money. The bank should take extraordinary care in accepting the introduction or reference from any person. The signature of the person introducing the applicant should preferably be obtained in the presence of some officer who should tally his signature on record and verify the same.

A question arises as to why bank should not open the account without proper introduction. The answer is that if the introduction is not taken properly, the banker will invite many risks which are as follows.

(a) The bank cannot avail itself of the statutory protection given to the collecting bank by Sec. 131 of the Negoliable Instruments Act. A collecting bank will incur no liability if it has acted in good faith and without any negligence. If the bank does not make proper inquiry and does not get proper introduction, it will be held to be negligent if the customer later on turns to be an undesirable person. The bank will remain liable to the true owners of the cheques, drafts etc., if such instruments are stolen by the customer whose identity cannot be established and process are collected by the bank and withdrawn by the former.

(b) If, overdraft is created by mistake in the account of a customer who is not properly introduced, the bank will not be able to realise the money because the identity of the customer cannot be established.

(c) Undesirable customers may cause annoyance to the public by cheating them. Such a man might defraud the public by issuing cheques on his account without having adequate balance.

(d) If the bank receives deposits from an undischarged insolvent without proper introduction, it will run the risk of attachment of these deposits by the court declaring him insolvent.

3. Specimen Signature

The applicant is required to give his specimen signature on a card meant for this purpose. This will help to protect the bank against forgery because whenever the cheque is presented at the counter of the bank for payment the signature will be tallied with those on the card.

4. Initial Deposit of Cash

When the above formalities are completed, the bank will agree to open an account in the name of the applicant. Before opening the account, the customer must deposit the minimum initial deposit in cash as per rules framed by the Reserve Bank. In case of a savings account, a minimum deposit of Rs. 5/-, if no cheque bank is required, or of Rs. 100/-, if cheque book is required must be made. In case of current accounts, a minimum deposit of Rs. 500, if the branch is in an urban area, or of Rs. 300, if the branch is in any other area, must be made with the bank.

5. Issue of Pass Book

A pass book is issued by the bank to the customer after the account has been opened and an account number has been allotted. The pass book contains the record of transactions between the bank and the customer. It is a copy of the account of the customer in the bank's ledger as on a particular date. It is written by the bank from its records and is meant for the use of the customer. It is called a pass book because it frequently passes between the bank and the customer.

A pass book is very important for a customer because he can know the position of his account and know certain items like interest, incidental charges, dividends collected, bills paid, etc. This will also enable him to prepare a 'Bank Reconciliation Statement'.

Forms Used in Operation of Bank Account

Operating a bank account means that the customer deposits a sum of money in near future and withdraws money from the account according to the needs. The following forms can be used for the operation of the bank account :

1. Pay-in-slip Book.
2. Cheque Book.
3. Pass Book.

1. Pay-in-slip Book

This book contains printed slips with perforated counterfoils. The bank supplies pay-in-slip either in book form or loose to the customer while depositing cash, cheques, drafts. etc. to the credit of his account. Some banks supply slips for depositing (a) Cash, and (b) Cheques/Drafts etc. It is noted that different types of forms are used for the collection of outstation cheques, bills or drafts. The depositor is expected to fill in the amount, nature of account, account number, date, details of currency notes, and coins, signature etc. in the pay-in-slip. After the receipt of the Cash or Cheque and Draft, the bank puts the date-stamp and is signed by the Cashier and counter-signed by the Accountant or Manager and the counterfoil is returned to the depositor, which is used for the record of the customer.

2. Cheque Book

A cheque book contains bank cheque forms with counterfoils which can be used by the customer to withdraw money from his account. The cheque book and the counterfoils are serially numbered and these numbers are entered into the cheque book register of the bank and also recorded in the bank ledger.

3. Pass Book

A pass book is a book in which the banker keeps a full record of the customer's account. It is written by the bank, and hence it is essential for a customer to send it (pass book) periodically to the bank, so that up-to-date entries may be entered by the bank. Same banks, like American Express, Grindlays Bank send a Statement of Account periodically, i.e., fortnightly or monthly to the customer in place of pass book. (It should be noted that a Statement of Account is very popular among Current Account holders.)

Sir John Paget expressed his views on the proper function of the bank's statement and the pass book as : ".................saving negligence or reckless disregard on the part of either the banker or the customer ....to constitute a conclusive, unquestionable record of the transactions between them.............After the full opportunity of examination on the part of the customer, all entries, at least to his debit, ought to be final and not liable to be reopened later, at any rate, to the detriment of the banker".

In support of his view, he cites Devaynes Vs. Noble (1816) Case in which it was decided that on the delivery of the pass book to the customer, he "examines it and if there appears any error or omission, brings or sends it back to the bank to be rectified ; or if not the silence is regarded as an admission that the entries are correct".

Closing of a Bank Account

A bank account may be closed by either party i.e., the customer and the banker. A bank account may be closed in the following cases.

1. At the request of the customer

If the customer requests the bank to close down his account, the bank has to close the account. The customer returns the unused cheques and presents his pass book. The bank closes down the account. The bank completes the pass book and returns it to the customer after writing the words 'Account closed'.

2. Inoperative account

If the customer does not operate an account for a long time (In Punjab National Bank for example, for 3 years), the bank can close down the account. However, the banker is required to give notice to the customer to withdraw his money. In case the customer is not traceable, after a reasonable effort, the amount standing to the credit of the customer is transferred to the 'Unclaimed Deposit Account' and the account is closed. In case the customer claims the amount later on, it is returned to him.

3. At the instance of the banker

The banker is also entitled to close the customer's account when the conduct of the customer is not desirable. For example, when the customer is guilty of forgery or frequently issues cheques without sufficient balance or does not repay the loans and advances etc.

In such circumstances the banker should give a notice to the customer to close his account by a particular date. However, he should not dishonour his cheques in the mean time so long as there is balance in his account. In case the customer does not close the account within the time specified, the banker should close the account and give him a notice that his account has been closed so that he may not issue cheques to his creditors. The bank should return the credit balance standing in his account by a bank draft.

4. On receipt of notice of customer's death.

When the bank receives notice of death of the customer, he must stop operation of the account as death of the customer terminates his authority.

5. On the insanity of the customer

When the bank receives a notice of insanity of his customer, he must stop payment from his account.

6. On insolvency of the customer

When the bank comes to know of insolvency of his customer, he must stop payment. The balance standing to the credit of the customer, he must stop payment. The balance standing to the credit of the customer is transferred to the Official Receiver or Assignee.

7. On receipt of Garnishee Order

The banker should reserve amount specified in the Garnishee Order. He may make payment of the customer's cheques out of the remaining balance, if any.

8. On receiving notice of assignment

When the banker has received notice of assignment of the credit balance in the customer's account, he must stop payment from the account. The bank is liable to pay the balance to the assignee.

Insurance of Bank Deposit

The Bank Deposit Insurance means giving a guarantee to depositors that their deposits will be returned if the bank fails. The need for such a guarantee has arisen after the failure of several banks on account of inadequate capital, unsound banking practices etc. In India, the necessity of Deposit Insurance was felt after the failure of Palai Central Bank, a Scheduled Bank of South India.

Deposit Insurance is regarded as the most powerful competitive edge of banking Industry. However, the application of the Scheme in its present form has shielded the industry from market discipline. Since the depositors have no incentives to favour one bank over another, badly managed banks, even nearing insolvency, have been able to attract deposits as easily as healthy and well-run institutions. It is high time that Deposit Insurance prices the insurance cover on the basis of quality of assets rather than on uniform pricing basis. This would by itself considerably strengthen the banking industry.

Deposit Insurance and Credit Guarantee Corporation (DICGC)

The Deposit Insurance Corporation Act was passed by the Parliament in 1961 which set up the 'Deposit Insurance Corporation' with effect from January 1, 1962. It took over the undertaking of the Credit Guarantee Corporation of India Ltd., with effect from July 15, 1978. Later, by the integration of two organisations the Corporation was renamed as the Deposit Insurance and Credit Guarantee Corporation (DICGC).

Objectives

The DICGC has twin objectives of giving insurance to small depositors in banks and five credit guarantee schemes (four for small borrowers and one for small-scale industries) guaranteeing the priority sector advances granted by participating banks and financial institutions.

Credit Guarantee Function

The DICGC is operating following Schemes : (1) Credit Guarantee Schemes for Small borrowers, e.g., (a) Small Loans Guarantee Scheme, 1971 ; (b) Small Loans (Financial Corporation) Guarantee Scheme, 1971 ; (c) Service Co-operative Societies Guarantee Scheme, 1971 ; (d) Small Loans (Co-operative Banks) Guarantee Scheme, 1984 ; (e) Small Loans (Co-operative Credit Societies) Guarantee Scheme, 1982 ; (2) Credit Guarantee Scheme for small-scale industries, 1981.

Nomination Facility

The Banking Laws (Amendment) Act, 1983, inserted a new part III B in the Banking Regulation Act, 1949 to give effect to some of the recommendations of the Banking Commission. Newly inserted Section 45ZA and the Rules framed thereunder in 1985 provide for the facility of nomination by depositors in banks as follows.

(a) A depositor may nominate, in the prescribed manner, person to whom, in the event of the death of the depositor, the amount to his credit may be paid by the banking company.

(b) In case of a joint account, all the depositors together may nominate a person to whom, in the event of death of all the joint depositors, the amount of their credit may be paid by the banking company. Thus, the nominee's right to receive deposit money arises only after the death of all the depositors. There cannot be more than one nominee in respect of a joint account.

(c) Nomination facility is available to all types of deposit accounts, including the accounts opened for credit of pension.

(d) Nomination can be made in favour of individuals only and not associations, societies, trusts or any organisation or their office-bearers.

(e) In the case of a deposit made in the name of a minor, the nomination shall be made by a person lawfully entitled to act on behalf of the minor.

(f) The nominee can be a minor. The depositor may, while making the nomination, appoint another individual not being a minor, to receive the amount of the deposit on behalf of the nomine in the event of the death of the depositor, or as the case may be, all the depositors during the minority of the nominee.

(g) In case Safe Deposit Lockers in joint names without survivorship benefit, nomination can be made in favour of more than one person. A minor is not accepted as a nominee in case of safe deposit lockers.

(h) In case of death of a sole depositor/all the joint depositors, the name of the nominee can be substituted at his written request in the deposit account/receipts including overdue deposits.

(i) The nomination may be varied or cancelled by the depositor in the prescribed manner. In case of a joint account, variation or cancellation of a subsisting nomination can be made by all the surviving depositors acting together.

On making payment under the provisions of this section, the banking company shall be fully discharged from its liability in respect of the deposit. The right or claim of any other person against the nominee, to whom any payment is made under this section, shall not be affected by such payment. No other person shall be able to get notice of his claim to such deposits to the banking company. Nor shall the banking company be bound by such notice even through expressly given to it.

Non-Resident Account

The non-resident account is defined as "the accounts maintained with banks in India by persons, companies, firms, banks etc., resident or situated outside India". When the account opens in the name of persons, firms, companies or associations it is referred to as 'Private Non-Resident Account'. While in the case of banks such accounts are called as 'Non-Resident Accounts'.

It should be noted that a non-resident means a citizen of India who is living outside India in the following cases.

(a) Taking up employment outside India.

(b) Carrying on business outside India.

Recent Development

There are no major policy changes in the regulations governing Foreign Currency Non-Resident Accounts (FCNRA) and Non-Resident (External) Rupee Accounts [NR (E) RA] except for the conversion rate to be applied for such remittances to NRE A/Cs which is covered under the head of Liberalised Exchange Rate Management System (LERMS), The Budget for 1992-93 has cited two more facilities to Non-Resident Indians (NRIs) which are given below :

1. Gold Import Scheme

The NRIs and returning Indians are permitted to import gold up to 5 kg. On the payment of duty of Rs. 440 per 10 gms in Foreign Exchange. The duty was reduced to Rs. 220 per 10 gms subsequently. Each NRI coming from abroad will be able to bring into India a maximum of 5 kg. of gold provided the person concerned had spent at least six months abroad. NRIs can avail themselves of the facility once in six months.

2. New Deposit Scheme

(With Flexible Deposit Rates) : This Scheme was effective from June 15, 1992. This Scheme covers the following :

(a) Authorised Dealers (ADs) can open these accounts with fresh foreign inward remittances or transfers from existing NRE/FCNR Accounts

(b) The deposit can be accepted for a minimum period of six months and maximum period of three years.

(c) The deposit will not be included in the net demand and time liabilities (NTL) of the Banks and hence these are free from reserve requirements.

(d) Principal and interest are not repatriable.

(e) Once these deposits are withdrawn, these benefits cannot be extended even if the deposit is redeposited in other banks.

3. Home Loan Account Scheme

The Home Loan Account Scheme which has been in operation since July 1, 1989, has now been extended to select housing finance companies and Apex Co-operative Housing Finance Societies. Under this scheme more than 12 lakh accounts have been opened by the end of November 1997. The amount of deposits collected was about Rs. 100 crore.

Conclusion

To conclude, it is rightly said that the relationship between a bank and a customer begins when the customer opens an account with the bank. For the attraction of customers the banks offer different types of facilities. In order to avoid meaning less competition among several banks the Reserve Bank of India has been given the power to fix deposit interest rates. For this purpose, the RBI. issues directives from time to time.

Here, it is made clear that all the accounts are opened with the bank with the cash money by the customer and that is why, in other words, these are known as "Deposit Accounts". Under Section 6 of the Banking Regulation Act 1949, the most important function of a modern bank is to accept deposit of money from the public. The banks have, therefore, introduced different types of accounts with various facilities and privileges.

Questions for Discussions

1. Explain the different types of accounts which a person can open with a bank
2. What is the difference between Current, Savings and Fixed Deposit accounts ? Explain
3. What procedure does a banker follow in opening a new account? Explain.
4. Discuss the various forms used in the operation of a savings or a current account.
5. What is a Recurring Deposit Account?
6. Briefly explain the various types of accounts a bank can open.
7. State the circumstances under which a banker can close the account of a customer.
8. Discuss the role of Deposit Insurance and Credit Guarantee Corporation.
9. Write short note on 'Facility of Nomination'.
10. Discuss the accounts that may be opened by the Non-Resident Indians.

Chapter - 10

PASS BOOK

Introduction

A banker receives deposits on current and savings accounts from his customers. The customers are allowed to withdraw from time to time the amount needed by them through cheques or withdrawal slips from the account. The amounts deposited and withdrawn by each customer from time to time are entered in a separate account opened in the name of the customer in the ledger account of the banker. Similarly, the transactions are entered in a book and handed over to the customer for his reference and information. The entries made in the book also stand as evidence of the transactions between the banker and the customer. This book is known as 'Pass Book'.

Meaning of Pass Book

Pass book is an important book in the operation of a bank account. It contains a copy of the customer's ledger account as it appears in the banker's books. It is an exact extract or copy of the customer's account in the bank's ledger, as on a particular date. It is, in other words, a record of dealings between the customer and the bank. It is written by the bank from its own records. It is supplied by the bank to its customer free of charge. It is meant for the information of the customer. It indicates to him the "state of his account" in the bank. The customer sends it periodically to the bank so that upto date entries may be recorded by the bank. As it passes periodically between the banker and the customer, it is called a "Pass Book". Every entry made in pass book is signed by a responsible official of the bank. Some big banks supply periodical statements of account in place of the pass book. In case of foreign accounts, some banks make use of photography to save the labour of writing statements of accounts. The Photostat copies of the customer's account are sent to the customers for their approval.

Object or Purpose of Pass Book

The object of a pass book is to inform the customer from time to time the condition of his account as it appears on the books of the bank. It supplies evidence in favour of the customer in the event of the litigation or dispute with the bank. In this way, it protects the customer against the carelessness or fraud of the bank. The Pass book also enables the customer to prepare "bank reconciliation statement" for the purpose of finding out the causes of difference between the balance as shown by his cash book and the bank Pass book.

Statement of Account

Some bankers send periodical statements in duplicate to the customers showing the transactions of the banker with the customer. The customer is required to verify the statement and return one copy to the banker for having satisfied of the correctness of the entries. If any discrepancies are found in the statement, the matter is to be referred back to the banker.

Some bankers also maintain loose leaves of the transactions of the banker with the customer. Photo-copies of the entries in the banker's book are sent to the customer as authenticated copies of the accounts of the transactions.

Examination of Entries

A pass book is a replica of the customer's account with the banker. All money deposited by the customer with the banker will find credit in the accounts of the banker and the withdrawals will be debited. When the pass book is handed over to the customer, it amounts to a statement of account rendered by the bank.

Is it necessary for the customer to examine the pass book? Now, in India and United Kingdom, it is not obligatory for the customer to examine the pass book. He need not discover any error or omission and draw the bank's attention. On failure to examine the pass book, he can't be held guilty of negligence. But if the customer agrees to this by signing the form regarding the accuracy of the balance, it becomes an 'account settled' or 'account stated'. It will be implied in such a case that the balance will be paid as a lump sum by the party agreed to be in debt without reference to the individual items.

BANK OF INDIA

Savings Banks Account

Name.............................

A/c No...........................

Date	Particulars	Debit	Credit	Balance	Initials of Bank's Official

Specimen of Folio of Pass Book

Legal Position of Entries in the Pass Book

It is difficult to define precisely the decisive legal effects of entries shown in the pass book. When it is issued to customer and if he does not raise any objection, abviously it becomes "account stated" or "settled account" between him and the banker. But there has been a conflict of opinion regarding conclusiveness of the pass book regarding entries made therein. Sir John Paget is of the view that "the proper function of a pass book is to constitute a conclusive, unquestionable record of the transactions between banker and customer, and it should be recognised as such". He cites Daveyness. Vs. Noble case in support of his view. In this case, it was stated that on delivery of the pass book to the customer, he examines it and if there appears an error or omission, sends it back for rectification or if not, his silence is regarded as on admission that the entries are correct. In Vagliana Brothers., Vs. Bank of England, also it was held that "the return of a balanced pass book by the customer without comments amounts to settlement of account". So, the return of pass book by the customer renders is as a stated and settled account as on the particular date of balancing.

But the legal position both in England and in India is quite different. According to recent judicial decisions in England and India, the entries in the pass book cannot be regard as a conclusive proof of their accuracy and as settled account. Any entry in the pass book is open to comparison and verification by customer. The customer can legitimately question the entries at any time whenever he notices them. The banker is bound to make the suitable corrections. The entries wrongly made or included may be advantages either to the customer or the banker. Both the parties can indicate the mistakes or omissions to get them rectified. So entries made upto date are prima facie evidence and not conclusive evidence. In keptigulla Rubber Estates Co. Vs. National Bank of India, it was held that "When a pass book is returned to the bank by the customer without objection, the account cannot be regarded as settled account and it is not binding on both the banker and customer. In Mowji. Vs. Registrar of Co-operative Societies, Madras, it was stated that "the entries in the pass book can be regarded as prima facie evidence and not conclusive evidence". Thus entries in the pass book are not conclusive evidence of their correctness, in stating the position of customer's account. They are subject to alternation on the basis of real facts.

Effect of Entries in the Pass Book

The entries wrongly made or included in the pass book may be favourable or advantageous either to the customer or to the banker. So the wrong entries can be divided into two types : (1) entries favourable to customer, and (2) entries favourable to banker.

1. Entries Favourable to Customer

The account of a customer may sometimes show a wrong credit balance, which may be due to: (a) duplication of credit entries, or (b) crediting of higher amounts, or (c) omission of any debit entry. or (d) crediting the amount belonging to another customer.

If any entry is made by bank in favour of the customer, the bank can rectify it by due notice to the customer. The customer after such notice cannot withdraw such money. But as long as it is not corrected, the customer acting in good faith can rely on it as the "stated correct account". Entry advantageous to the customer may be used as evidence against the banker. In Akrokeri Mines Ltd. Vs. Economic bank, it was held that "the pass book belongs to the customer and the entries made in it by the bank are statements on which the customer is entitled to act".

When the customer draws a cheque relying on a larger balance shown in the pass book by mistake, the banker has no right to dishonour such a cheque. If he dishonours, he may be held liable to pay damages. In Holland. Vs. Manchester and Liver Pool District Banking Company Ltd., the customer's pass book showed a credit balance of £ 70 and accordingly he drew cheque for £ 65. The banker dishonoured the cheque on the ground of inadequate balance. The court held that "the customer is entitled to act upon the representation contained in the pass book as to the amount of his balance and that he is entitled to recover damages in respect of the dishonour of his cheques".

The banker cannot recover the money wrongly credited if the customer can show that in good faith and relying upon the accuracy of the entry he had been induced to alter his position. This point was decided in Skying. Vs. Greewood. In this case, the bank wrongly credited the account of a Military Officer. The military officer relying on the pass book drew cheques in good faith and spent the amount. When the mistake was detected, the bank saught to recover the amount wrongly credited. It was held that "the bank was not entitled to recover the amount on the ground that the customer relying on the statements sent by the bank altered his position by spending the amount". In this case the customer also acted in good faith. But this favour is not available to business people. The business man is expected to keep regular accounts and know the position of his bank account. So he cannot take advantage of an error, knowingly. This point was decided in Rhind. Vs. Commercial Bank of Scotland.

2. Entries Favourable to Banker

Entries that are favourable to a banker arise when a credit entry has been totally omitted or wrongly stated, or any debit entry has been wrongly made in the customer's account. The legal position in this regard is stated below:

1. The customer can get the mistake rectified as soon as it is detected. This right exists even after he returns the pass book. He can recover the wrongly debited amount or the credit which is omitted.
2. However, the customer will not be entitled to get the mistake rectified if it is proved that :
   (a) The customer was negligent.
   (b) The entries in the pass book constitute a settled account, and
   (c) the position of the banker has been subsequently altered to its prejudice.

It is doubtful as to what act or omissions on the part of the customer amount to settlement of an account or negligence in regard thereto. Entries made in the pass book favouring the bank, under a mistake, cannot be treated as settled account even though customer fails to find out the mistakes. They are liable for correction when forgeries or mistakes are brought to notice. If the customer knowing that some of his cheques are forged does not immediately inform the banker, then he is taken to be guilty of negligence and accordingly he cannot question the correctness of the entries in the pass book. In Greenwood. Vs. Martins Bank, a wife of a customer forged the cheques and drew the amount. The husband kept silent though knowing of the forgeries. On the death of the wife, the husband informed the bank about the forgeries and claimed refund. It was held that he could claim because the banker was guilty of negligence. Silence might not be objectionable. But deliberate silence under circumstances when it was his duty to inform would arise an estoppel.

Now-a-days many banks follow the practice of getting the pass book balance confirmed by the customer in writing. Banks at the end of every half year send letters to customer informing the balance in his account and is requested to confirm in writing the balance stated. Usually a slip is attached to the letter and the customer is required to return it duly signed. It is, however, essential for the banker to be cautious and accurate in posting the entries in the pass book.

Precautions in Writing a Pass Book

While writing the pass book, the bank should take the following precautions:

1. The customer should be requested to present the pass book for completion periodically.
2. All the entries in the pass book must be invariably initialled by a responsible official as a proof of having verified the entries.
3. The pass book must be returned to the customer after it is updated so that he has an opportunity of examining it.

4. When the pass book is sent back or handed over to the customer, the date should be noted in the ledger together with initials of the clerk who writes it.
5. While sending the pass book to the customer, the banker should take steps to ensure the secrecy of its contents.
6. In case of loss of pass book, duplicate copy should be marked with the word "Duplicate" and the fact should be recorded in the ledger also.
7. The banker should indicate to the customer to intimate the objections, if any, from time to time.
8. Confirmation letter should be sent to the customer regarding the balance standing to the credit of his account. A certificate may be enclosed alongwith the statement of account asking for an acknowledgement of the balance as correct. If the account shows a debit balance, it will operate as an acknowledgement of debt and would extend the period of limitation.

Conclusion

To conclude, a pass book is a small book issued by the bank to the customer which contains the record of transactions between the bank and the customer. It is an extract or a copy of the account of the customer in the bank's ledger as on a particular date. It is written by the bank from its records and is meant for the use of the customer. It is called a pass book because it frequently passes between the bank and the customer.

Questions for Discussions

1. Explain pass book with the help of a specimen. Is it necessary for a customer to examine the pass book?
2. State the legal effect of entries made in favour of customer in the pass book.
3. State the legal effect of entries made in favour of banker.
4. List the precautions which a bank should take while writing a pass book.

Chapter - 11

CHEQUES

Introduction

In the olden days, when Goldsmiths were working as bankers, people used to deposit their savings with them with an understanding that whenever they needed funds, the depositors would draw notes. These notes or letters were nothing but small pieces of paper containing a small note addressed to a particular Goldsmith asking him to pay a particular sum of money to the party who presented such a note. It was drawn by the depositor. At a later stage, these notes became cheques.

Every bank has its own printed cheque forms which are supplied to the account holders at the time of opening the accounts. These forms are printed by expert printers on special security paper which is sensitive to chemicals. This is done in order to make chemical alterations, if any, noticeable. Cheques must be drawn on these forms only. The customers may obtain a new cheque book when the old one is finished or is about to finish, by signing the requisition slip provided in the cheque book towards the end. If a customer desires to have more than one cheque book, one to draw cash and another to be issued to his suppliers etc., the bank may have such cheque leaves printed with the crossing as well as superscripts like 'Account Payee' and 'Not negotiable' thereon.

Meaning

A cheque is a negotiable instrument governed by the provisions in the Negotiable Instrument Act. It is an unconditional order, drawn on a specified banker, signed by the drawer, directing the banker, to pay on demand, a certain sum of money only to or to the order of a certain person or to the bearer of the instrument.

Definition

Under Section 6 of the Negotiable Instruments Act, 1881, a cheque is defined as a "bill of exchange drawn on a specified banker and not expressed to be payable otherwise than on demand". To understand this definition, it is necessary to know the definition of a Bill of Exchange.

According to Section 5 of the Indian Negotiable Instruments Act 1881: "A bill of exchange is an instrument in writing containing an unconditional order, signed by the maker, directing a certain person to pay a certain sum of money only to or to the order of a certain person or to the bearer of the instrument".

Essentials

From the above definition it follows that an instrument to be called a cheque must fulfil certain conditions. They are:

1. It is an instrument in writing;
2. It contains unconditional order;
3. It is drawn by the drawer;
4. It is drawn upon a specified banker;
5. To pay a certain sum of money;
6. Payable on demand;
7. Payable to a certain person or his order or to the bearer of the instrument.
8. A cheque should be properly dated
9. It is signed by the maker
10. There are three parties to a cheque viz

    (a) Drawer (b) Drawee and (c) Payee.

These are discussed below.

1. Instrument in Writing

A cheque or a bill of exchange is an instrument in writing. Legally speaking the writing may be done by means of printed characters, type-writer, or by a pen or pencil. But bankers do not generally honour cheques drawn in pencil, unless confirmed by the drawer. This is because, it is easy to make unauthorised alterations when a cheque is drawn in pencil.

2. Contains Unconditional Order

The instrument must contain an unconditional order. For instance, if the banker is ordered to pay a certain sum provided the payee fulfils certain conditions, it cannot be considered a cheques as the order is a conditional one. However, if such instruments are addressed to the payee and not to the banker, the order to pay may be regarded unconditional.

3. Drawn by the Drawer

A cheque is to be drawn or taken out only by the drawer or the account holder. The account holder being a customer of the bank has an account where in he has deposited his funds. He is the rightful or authorised person to draw the cheques for making payments and for that he has to sign the cheques himself.

4. Drawn Upon a Specified Banker

The account holders, whenever they desire to make payments, are expected to draw cheques on a banker and not on an individual. Further, the banker should be specific, i.e., his name and address should be definite.

5. To Pay a Certain sum of Money

The order of the drawer of a cheque must be to pay a certain sum of money and not anything else e.g., securities or goods etc. The amount of money to be paid must be certain and specified both in words and figures.

6. Payable on Demand

According to section 19 of the Negotiable Instruments Act, 1881, when the instrument does not specify for payment, it is always payable on demand. Unless and until a demand is made, the amount in respect of the cheque would not be paid. Demand is necessary to make the banker liable to pay the amount of the cheque.

7. Payable to a certain Person or his Order or to the Bearer of the Instrument

The amount mentioned in the cheque should be paid to a specific person or payee or according to his order. Or it may be made payable to the bearer. Or it may be made payable to the beater of the instrument.

8. It is Signed by the Maker

The maker must sign the instrument. In order to be a valid cheque, the instrument must contain the signature of the drawer. In the case of an illiterate person, his thumb impression will suffice. Though legally permissible, pencil signatures are discouraged by bankers. So also signatures impressed on the cheque by means of a rubber stamp is not permitted generally.

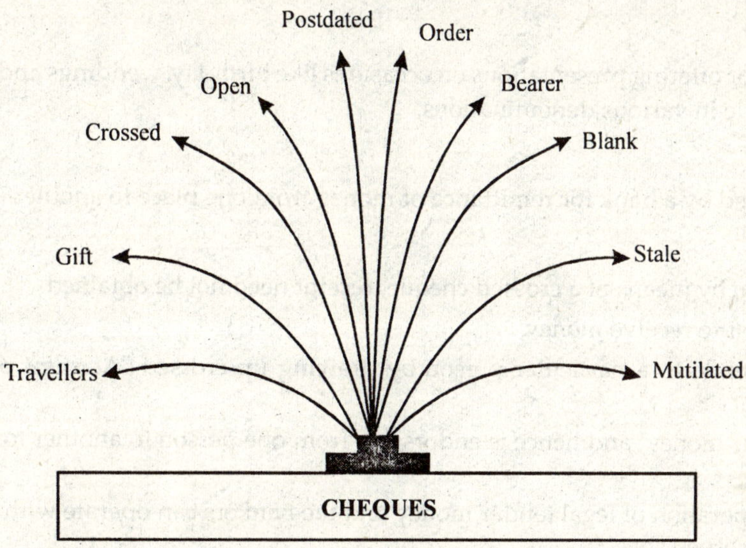

Types of Cheques

Cheques are of the following types

1. Order Cheque

A cheque which is payable to a particular person or his order is called an order cheque.

2. Bearer Cheque

A cheque which is payable to a person who soever bears it is called bearer cheque.

3. Blank Cheque

A cheque on which the drawer puts his signature and leaves all other colums blank is called a blank cheques.

4. Stale Cheque

The cheque which is more than six months old is a stale cheque.

5. Mutilated Cheque

If a cheque is torn into two or more pieces it is termed as mutilated cheque.

6. Post Dated Cheque

If a cheque bears a date later than the date of issue, it is termed as post dated cheque.

7. Open Cheque

A cheque which has not been crossed is called an open cheque. Even if a cheque is crossed and subsequently the drawer has cancelled the crossing at the request of the payee and affixes his full signature with the words "crossing cancelled pay cash", it becomes an open cheque.

8. Crossed Cheque

A cheque which carries too parallel transverse lines across the face of the cheque with or without the words "1 & co", is said to be crossed.

9. Gift Cheques

Gift cheques are used for offering presentations on occasions like birthday, weddings and such other situations. It is available in various denominations.

10. Traveller's Cheques

It is an instrument issued by a bank for remittance of money from one place to another.

Uses of a Cheque

1. If payment is made by means of a crossed cheque, receipt need not be obtained.
2. It is also convenient to receive money.
3. Payment can be made to a particular person by drawing up crossed "Account payee" cheques.
4. The cheque is 'near money' and hence is endorsable from one person to another to settle the effects.
5. It minimises the operation of legal tender money and the bankers can operate with a less amount of cash reserves.
6. No need of counting cash while making payment.
7. If a crossed cheque is lost, only a piece of paper is lost, i.e., the amount remains intact.
8. If payments are made by cheques an automatic record of the account is also maintained in the banker's books.

Advantages of Using Printed Forms

Printed cheques have the following advantages.

1. It is very convenient to the banker as well as to the customer.
2. The customer need not draft the contents of the cheque. He naturally saves time and labour.
3. Printed cheques conform to the definition given in the Negotiable Instruments Act.
4. Any alteration in the cheque can be immediately observed.
5. It helps to identify the drawer as the details of the cheque are recorded in the books of the banker.

6. Only the account holders will be supplied with the printed forms. Others cannot posses it. Hence the forgery has been minimised.
7. Since the cheque forms have serial numbers, it is not only easy to identify the cheque but also, if need be countermanding instructions can be given.
8. Since every cheque leaf has a counter foil, it is very useful to the customer to verify his account and other connected details.

Parties to a Cheque

Basically there are three parties to a cheques viz., (1) Drawer (2) Drawee, and (3) Payee.

1. Drawer

A Drawer is the person who has an account in the bank and who draws a cheque for making payment. He is the customer or account holder.

2. Drawee

A Drawee is the person on whom the cheque is drawn. He is liable to pay the amount. In case of a cheque, the drawee happens to be the banker on whom the cheque is drawn, he is also called the Paying-Banker.

3. Payee

A Payee is the person to whom the amount stated in the cheque is payable. It may be either drawer himself (self cheques) or only other third party states in the cheque.

Material Alterations

Alteration

A cheque may be altered by the drawer or by a third party after it is drawn. For example, the date of cheque may be altered or the amount payable may be altered. Alteration may be made genuinely or fraudulently. Alterations may be material or immaterial.

Material Alteration

An alteration is regarded as material when it alters materially or substantially the operation of the instrument and liabilities of the parties thereto. It is defined as "an alteration which alters the business effects of the instrument if used for any business purpose". So any change in an instrument which causes it to speak a different language in legal effect from that which it originally spoke, or which changes the legal identity or the relation of the parties to it, is a material alteration.

Examples of Material Alterations

Material alterations refer to change of the date, place of payment, amount, payee's name, crossing etc. The following are some of the examples of material alteration.

(a) Alteration of the date of the instrument.

(b) Alteration of the sum payable.

(c) Alteration of the place of the payment.

(d) Alteration of the name of the payee.

(e) Alteration of the crossing marks.

(f) Alteration in the rate of interest.

Examples of Authorised Alterations

Under the Negotiable Instruments Act, 1881, the following do not amount to material alterations.

(a) Filling blanks of the instrument.

(b) Conversion of blank endorsement into an endorsement in full.

(c) Making acceptance conditional.

(d) Altering a general crossing into a special crossing.

(e) Crossing of an uncrossed cheque.

(f) Alteration made with the consent of the parties.

Examples of Non-material Alterations

Immaterial alteration will not affect the validity of the instrument. They do not affect the rights and liabilities of any party. They have insignificant effects. They are as follows.

(a) Alteration made for correcting mistake.

(b) Alteration made to carry out the intention of the original parties.

(c) Alteration made with the consent of the parties.

(d) Alteration which is the result of an accident.

(e) Alteration made before issue or delivery of the instrument.

Effects of Material Alteration

A cheque containing material alteration cannot be regarded as a cheque at all. A cheque with erasers and alterations is not valid against the banker. Under the Indian law such a cheque is void. According to section 87 of the Negotiable Instruments Act "any material alteration renders the instrument void against anyone who is a party thereto, and who has not consented to such alteration". So a banker who finds a cheque materially altered in its contents has to dishonour it, unless it is duly attested by the full signature of the drawer. Such refusal to pay will not amount to wrongful dishonour. Sheldon says "the banker can honour a cheque which bears the drawer's confirmation of any alteration". Material alterations are to be authenticated by the drawer. But the banker cannot refuse to pay a cheque whose alterations are not of material significance, or which are authorised by Act or which are made with the consent of the parties. If a banker pays a cheque bearing unauthorised alterations, he cannot debit the drawer's account and is liable to the true owner. The case illustrating the point is Slingsly and others. Vs. The West Minister Bank Limited.

The banker should take all precautions to see that the cheque is free from material alterations before paying it. The banker should carefully scan the cheque with the help of the magnifying glass or other mechanical appliances of forgery detection to see that the amount is not altered. However, the paying banker gets protection where the alteration is apparently not noticeable and the payment is made in due course. The paying banker is also protected, from wrong payment of an altered cheque if the customer is found to have negligently drawn the cheque. It is the duty of the drawer also to draw the cheques with great care. In Macmillan Arthur. Vs. London Joint Stock Bank it was stated that "the Customer is bound to exercise care in drawing the cheque in such a way as not to give scope for alteration".

From the above discussion, it is clear that in order to discharge the parties liable on the instrument as cheque, an alteration should be a material one and none authorised by the Act and it should also be apparent on the face of the instrument.

Crossing of Cheques

Crossing first originated in England when cheques were sent from one bank to another. There was the possibility that a cheque might fall in the hands of wrong or unauthorised parties and thereby the original holder was likely to be put to a loss or inconvenience. To avoid this disadvantage, the bankers introduced this new system of crossing of cheques. Crossing automatically means that a cheque should be presented for payment through a bank.

Meaning of Crossing

Crossing of cheques means drawing two parallel transverse lines on the left hand top corner of a cheque. Sometimes, it is also done in the centre of the cheque.

The Negotiable Instruments Act 1881, recognises crossing of cheques. A crossing is a direction to the paying banker that the cheques should be paid only to a banker and if the banker is named in the crossing, only to that banker.

This ensures the safety of payment by means of cheques. The holder of the cheque is not allowed to cash it across the counter.

Types of crossing

Cheques can be crossed in two ways (1) General Crossing (2) Special Crossing.

1. General Crossing

Section 123 of the Negotiable Instruments Act 1881, defines a general crossing as follows :

"Where a cheque bears across its face an addition of the words '& company' or any abbreviation thereof, between two parallel transverse lines, or of two parallel transverse lines simply either with or without the words 'not negotiable' that addition shall be deemed a crossing and the cheque shall be deemed to be crossed generally".

Some specimens of general crossings are given below :

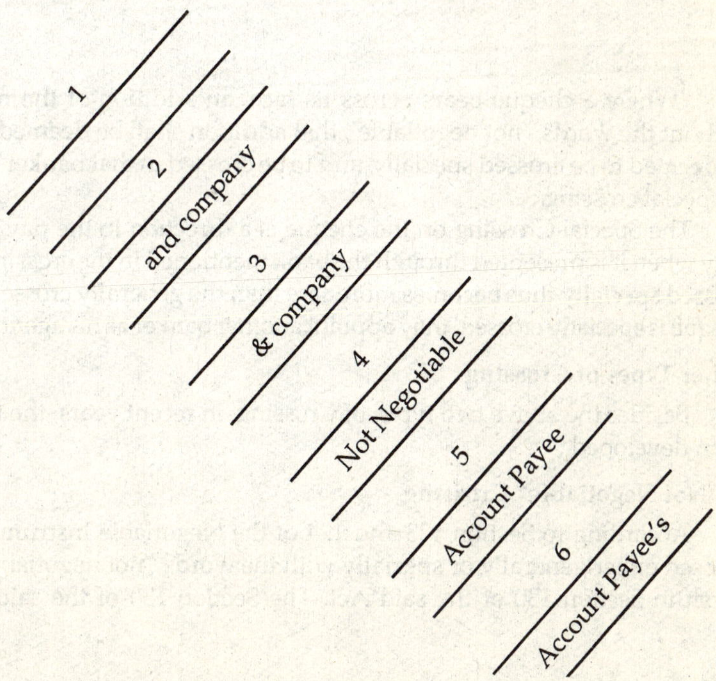

It is to be noted from the above that the drawing of two parallel transverse lines on the face of the cheque constitutes "General Crossing". The lines must be (a) on the face of the cheque, (b) Parallel to each other, and (c) in cross direction (i.e., transverse). Inclusion of words 'and company' is immaterial and of no special consequence.

The effect of general crossing is that the cheque must be presented to the paying banker through any other banker and not by the payee himself at the counter. The collecting banker credits the proceeds to the account of the payee or the holder of the cheque. The latter may thereafter withdraw the money.

2. Special Crossing

Section 124 of the Negotiable Instruments Act 1881, defines a special crossing as follows.

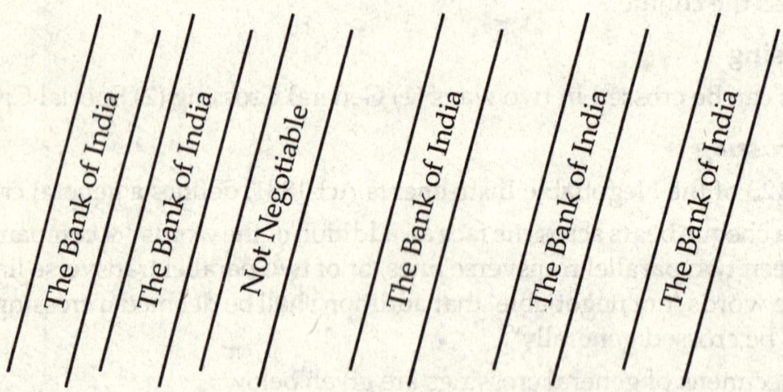

"Where a cheque bears across its face, an addition of the name of a banker, either with or without the words 'not negotiable', that addition shall be deemed a crossing, and the cheque shall be deemed to be crossed specially, and to be crossed to that banker". Following are given specimens of special crossing :

The Special Crossing on the cheque is a direction to the paying banker to honour the cheque only when it is presented through the bank mentioned in the crossing and no other bank. The cheque crossed specially thus becomes more safe than the generally crossed cheque. The banker, to whom a cheque is specially crossed, may appoint another banker as his agent for the collection of such cheques.

Other Types of Crossing

Besides the above two types of Crossing, in recent years, the following types of Crossing have been developed :

1) "Not Negotiable" Crossing

According to Section 123 and 124 of the Negotiable Instruments Act, 1881, a cheque may be crossed either generally or specially with the words "not negotiable". The impact of these words is given in Section 130 of the said Act. The Section 130 of the said Act states, "A person taking a cheque, crossed generally or specially, bearing in either case the words "not negotiable" shall not have and shall not be capable of giving a better title to the cheque than that what the position from whom he took it had". Whereas the cheque is crossed with the words "not negotiable", the bank must be careful in paying such cheques. In such a case, the payment must be made only after the bank is satisfied that the person demanding payment, is the person entitled to get it in reality.

2. Restrictive Crossing or Account Payee Crossing

Restrictive or Account Payee Crossing means a direction to the collecting banker that the proceedings of the cheque are to be credited only to the account of payee named, written or mentioned in the cheque. It is to be noted here that the words "Account Payee" are not recognised by the Negotiable Instruments Act, 1881. The words 'Account Payee Only' constitute an instruction to the collecting banker that he should collect the amount of the cheque for the benefit of the payees only (Nobody can get any benefit except payee). The specimen forms of Restrictive Crossing are shown below :

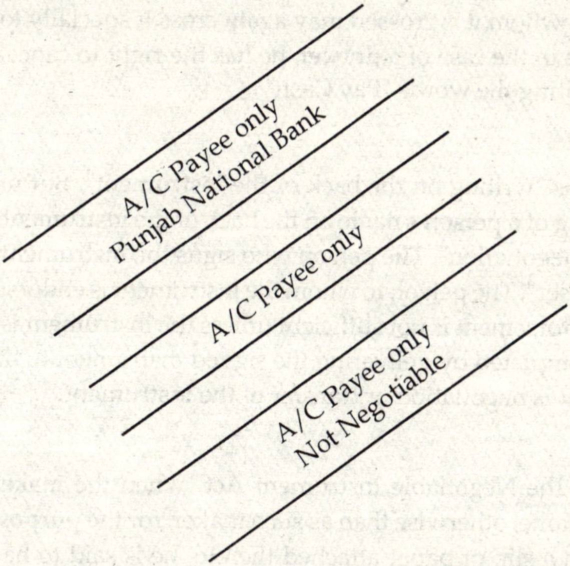

3. Double Crossing

According to Section 127 of the Negotiable Instruments Act, 1881 : "Whereas a Cheque is crossed specially to more than one banker, except when crossed to an agent for the purpose of collection, the banker on whom it is drawn shall refuse payment thereon". This type of crossing may be used only when the banker in whose favour the cheque is specially crossed does not have any branch at the place where the cheque is to be paid. A specimen of such a crossing is given below.

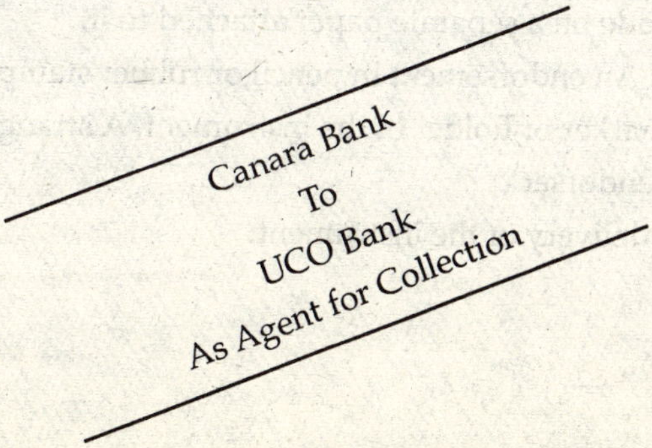

Significance of Crossing

In the case of general crossing, the addition of the words "& Co." does not have any legal significance; but the words "not negotiable" have legal significance. By crossing a cheque generally the person who is not entitled to get its payment, is prevented from getting the cheque cashed at the counter of the paying banker. While in the case of Special Crossing, the name of the banker must be written on the face of the cheque, to whom or to whose collecting agent, payment of cheque is to be made. It is to be noted that the lines are not essential for a Special Crossing. By crossing a Cheque specially, it is quite safer than the generally crossed cheque. In such a case the banker to whom a cheque is crossed specially, may appoint another banker as his agent for the collection of such cheques. Such cheques may be sent through ordinary post.

In short, a cheque can be crossed by the drawer, holder or banker. Section 125 of the Negotiable Instruments Act states, "Whereas a cheque is crossed generally or specially, the holder may add the words "not negotiable". In the case of a banker, the above Section further states: "whereas a cheque is crossed specially, the banker to whom it is crossed may again cross it specially to another banker as his agent for collection". While in the case of a drawer, he has the right to cancel the crossing by putting his full signature and writing the words "Pay Cash".

Endorsement

Endorsement literally means "writing on the back of the instrument". But under Negotiable Instruments Act, it means "writing of a person's name on the back of the instrument or on any paper attached to it for the purpose of negotiation". The person who signs the instrument for the purpose of negotiation is called the "endorser". The person to whom the instrument is endorsed or transferred is called the "endorsee". Mere endorsement is not sufficient unless the instrument is delivered to the endorsee. The endorsement is completed by delivering the signed instrument to the endorsee. The purpose or object of endorsement is negotiation or transfer of the instrument.

Definition of Endorsement

According to section 15 of the Negotiable Instrument Act "when the maker or holder of a negotiable instrument signs his name, otherwise than as such maker, for the purpose of negotiation, on the back or face thereof or on a slip of paper attached thereto, he is said to have endorsed the instrument". Thus a person entitled to get money on a negotiable instrument can transfer his right to another. He may be a maker or holder of the instrument. If he wants to transfer his right to another, he must sign the instrument. The signature is usually made on the bank of the instrument.

Essentials of a Valid Endorsement

The following are the essential of a valid endorsement.

(a) Endorsement must be on the back or face of the Instrument. If no space is left on the instrument, it must be made on a separate paper attached to it.

(b) It should be made in ink. An endorsement in pencil or rubber stamp is invalid.

(c) It must be made by the marker or holder of the instrument. A stranger cannot endorse it.

(d) It must be signed by the endorser.

(e) It must be completed by delivery of the instrument.

(f) It must be an endorsement of the entire bill. A partial endorsement does not operate as a valid endorsement.

Kinds of Endorsement

Endorsement may be of any of the following kinds.

1. Blank endorsement.
2. Special endorsement.
3. Partial endorsement.
4. Restrictive endorsement.
5. Conditional endorsement.

1. Blank endorsement

It is also called "general endorsement". An endorsement is said to be blank if the endorser signs his name only on the face or back of the instrument. Endorsement in blank specifies no endorsee. It simply consists of the signature of the endorser on the endorsement. A negotiable instrument even though payable to order becomes a bearer instruments if endorsed in blank. Thus, a blank endorsement converts an order instrument into a bearer one. It is negotiable by delivery of the instrument.

Example : A bill is payable to the order of Swaroop. Swaroop signs on the back of the bill. This is an endorsement in blank by Swaroop. The bill becomes payable to bearer and is negotiable without any further endorsement.

2. Special endorsement

It is also called "full endorsement". In this type of endorsement, the name of the endorsee is specifically stated. If the endorser adds direction to pay the amount mentioned in the instrument to, or to the order of a specified person, the endorsement is said to be special. In other words it specifies the person to whom or to whose order the cheque is to be payable. A blank endorsement can be easily converted into a special endorsement by any holder of negotiable instrument.

Example

(a) "Pay to x or order", (b) Pay to the order of x

3. Partial endorsement

If an instrument is endorsed for a part of its amount, such an endorsement is said to be partial. Similarly, if an instrument is endorsed to two or more endorsees separately and not jointly, the endorsement becomes partial. Such an endorsement does not operate as a negotiation of the instrument. No right of action arises under a partial endorsement. It is invalid.

Example : The holder of a promissory for Rs. 1,000 writes on it pay B Rs. 500 and endorses the note. The endorsement is invalid for the purpose of negotiation.

4. Restrictive endorsement

An endorsement is said to be restrictive when it prohibits or restricts the further negotiability of the instrument. It merely gives the holder of the instrument the right to receive the amount on the instrument for a specific purpose. It does not give power to him to transfer his rights in endorsement to any one else. "Pay X only" or "pay X for my use" are examples of restrictive types of endorsement.

5. Conditional endorsement

It is also called "qualified endorsement". An endorsement where the endorser limits or negatives his liability by putting some condition in the instrument is called a conditional endorsement. If for instance, the endorser endorses an instrument with the words "pay A or order on his marrying B", the endorsement becomes conditional. A conditional endorsement, unlike the restrictive endorsement, does not affect the negotiability of the instrument. It does not invalidate the instrument. An endorsement may be made conditional in any of the following forms.

(a) 'Sans recourse' endorsement

An endorser may, by express words, exclude his own liability thereon to the endorsee or any subsequent holder in case of dishnour of the instrument. Such an endorsement is called an "endorsement sans recourse" (without recourse). "Pay to A or order without recourse to me" is an example of this type of endorsement. The endorser "sans recourse" is however, liable to the previous endorsers.

(b) Facultative endorsement

An endorsement where the endorser extends his liability or gives up some rights under a negotiable instrument, is called a "facultative endorsement". "Pay A or order, notice of dishonour is waived" is an example of facultative endorsement. Thus, endorser makes himself liable to subsequent endorsees of the cheque even though no notice of dishonour is received by him from the holder. In this type of endorsement, the holders duties towards the endorser are waived.

(c) 'Sans frais' endorsement

Where the endorser, does not want the endorsee or any subsequent holder to incur any expenses on his account, on the instrument, the endorsement is called "sans frais" endorsement.

Legal Effects of an Endorsement

The endorsement of a cheque or bill or exchange has a varied significance. It has following legal effects :

(a) It transfers the property in the negotiable instrument.

(b) It gives the right to sue the acceptor of the bill for recovery of the amount due thereon.

(c) It gives the right to recover from the endorsee and those above him on dishonour.

(d) It gives the holder the right of further negotiation to any one he pleases.

Differences between a Bill of Exchange and Cheque

All cheques are bills of exchange, but all bills of exchange are not cheques. The following are the main differences between a bill and a cheque.

1. Drawee

A cheque is always drawn on a banker. But a bill can be drawn on any person including a banker.

2. Payable on Demand

A cheque is always payable on demand. As a matter of fact, a cheque is meant for immediate payment. But a bill of exchange may be payable on demand or on the expiry of a fixed period.

3. Days of grace

Three days of grace are allowed on bills payable after a certain period of time. No grace days are allowed in the case of a cheque since a cheque is payable on demand.

4. Acceptance

A bill of exchange require acceptance of drawee. But a cheque requires no acceptance and is intended for immediate payment.

5. Payable to bearer on demand

A cheque can be made payable to bearer on demand, but a bill of exchange payable cannot be drawn payable to bearer on demand.

6. Notice of dishonour

Notice of dishonour of a bill is necessary. No such notice is required in the case of a cheque.

7. Stopping the payment

The payment of cheque may be countermanded or stopped by the customer or drawer. But payment of a bill after acceptance cannot be countermanded or stopped by the drawer.

8. Crossing

A cheque can be crossed generally or specially. But a bill of exchange cannot be crossed. There is no provision for "Crossing a bill of exchange".

9. Stamping

A bill of exchange must be properly stamped. But a cheque does not require any stamp.

10. Statutory protection

A banker is given statutory protection with regard to payment of cheques in certain cases. No such protection is available to the drawee or acceptor of a bill of exchange.

11. Noting and protest

A cheque need not be noted or protested when dishonoured. It is generally inland. But a bill may be noted or protested for dishonour. It may be inland or foreign bill.

12. Discounting

A cheque cannot be discounted. But a bill can be discounted and rediscounted with the banks.

13. Sets

Cheques are not issued in sets. But foreign bills are generally drawn in sets of three.

14. Circulation

A cheque is not intended for circulation but for immediate payment. But a bill is circulated by endorsing it.

Distinguish between a Cheque and a Promissory Note

The following are the differences between a Cheque and a Promissory note :

Cheque	Promissory note
1. **Number of parties** A cheque has three parties, namely drawer, drawee and payee.	1. A Promissory note has two parties, namely, maker and payee.
2. **Order and promise** A cheque contains an unconditional order to the banker to pay the money.	2. A Promissory note contains an unconditional undertaking by the debtor to pay the money.
3. **Drawee :** The drawee of a cheque is always a banker.	3. A promissory note may be executed either by a banker or by a non-banker.
4. **Payable on demand** A cheque is always payable on demand.	4. A promissory note may be payable either on demand or after a certain period.
5. **Bearer or order :** A cheque may be payable to order or to bearer.	5. A promissory note cannot be made payable to the bearer on demand.
6. **Crossing :** A cheque can be crossed.	6. There is no practice of crossing a promissory note.
7. **Stamping :** A cheque does not require any stamp.	7. A promissory note must be properly stamped.
8. **Days of grace :** Grace days are not allowed because the cheque is always payable on demand.	8. A grace period of three days is allowed.
9. **Discounting :** A cheque is not discounted.	9. A promissory note can be discounted and rediscounted with banks.

Holder and Holder in Due Course

Holder

According to section 8 of the Negotiable Instruments Act, a holder means "any person entitled in his own name to the possession of the negotiable instrument and to recover or receive the amount due thereon from the parties liable thereto". A holder must, therefore, have the possession of the instrument and also the right to recover money in his own name. In other words, a holder must be in possession of it under a legal title. Holder implies de jure holder and not de facto holder.

Thus, a person who is in possession of the instrument may or may not be a holder. For example, a finder of lost instrument or a thief cannot be a holder. Similarly, a beneficiary or an agent in possession of an instrument will not be a holder. But legal representatives of deceased holder or official assignee or official receiver would be treated as holders of the instruments. It is only the holder and no other person, who can give a valid discharge for the instrument.

Holder in Due Course

In English Law, a holder in due course is know as "bonafide holder for value without notice". A holder in due course is a person who acquires a promissory note, bill or cheque bonafide for value and maturity. Section 9 of the Negotiable Instruments act defines a holder in due course as "any person who for consideration became the possessor of a negotiable instrument if payable to bearer; or the payee or endorsee thereof, if payable to order, before the amount mentioned in it becomes payable, and without having sufficient cause to believe that any defect existed in the title of the person from whom he derived his title". In other words, a holder in due course is a person who takes the instrument in good faith and for value.

Thus, a holder in due course must satisfy the following conditions.

(a) He must have obtained the instrument for valuable consideration or value. Consideration must not be void or illegal. The consideration must be valuable and lawful. So, the donee of a negotiable instrument is not a holder in due course.

(b) He must have become a holder of the instrument before the date of its maturity.

(c) He must have become a holder of the instrument in good faith.

(d) He must have taken the instrument complete and regular on the face of it.

It is thus obvious that every holder is not a holder in due course. A holder of a negotiable instrument will not be a holder in due course, if :

(a) he has obtained the instrument by gift, or

(b) he has obtained the instrument for unlawful consideration, or

(c) he has obtained the instrument after its maturity, or

(d) he has obtained the instrument by some illegal method, or

(e) he has not obtained the instrument in good faith.

Privileges of a Holder in Due Course

A holder in due course occupies a privileged position in the law of negotiable instruments. He has a title free from equities. He enjoys certain rights and privileges which an ordinary holder can never possess. These rights and privileges are as follows :

1. Instrument purged or cured of all defects

The holder in due course gets the instrument free from all the defects in the title. Once a negotiable instrument passes through the hands of a holder in due course, it is purged or cured of defects. It is like a current coin. Anybody who takes a negotiable instrument from a holder in due course can recover the amount from all parties prior to such holder. An instrument once free from defects is always free.

2. Liability of prior parties

All prior parties to the instrument (the drawer, acceptor or endorser) continue to remain liable to the holder in due course until the instrument is duly satisfied. The holder in due course can file a suit against the prior parties liable to pay in his own name. Section 36 of the Act states that 'every prior party to a negotiable instrument is liable thereon to a holder in due course until the instrument is duly satisfied".

3. Rights in case of inchoate instrument

An inchoate instrument is one which is incomplete in some respects. A person who has signed and delivered a stamped but inchoate (incomplete) instrument cannot argue as against a holder in due course that the instrument has not been completed according to the authority given by him.

4. No effect of conditional delivery

Where a negotiable instrument delivered conditionally is negotiated to a holder in due course, the other parties to the instrument cannot escape liability on the ground that the delivery of the instrument was conditional or for a special purpose only.

5. Right in case of fictitious bills

If a bill is drawn on behalf of a fictitious person and is payable to his order, the acceptor is not relieved from his liability to holder in due course because of such fictitious name.

6. No effect of absence of consideration

The plea of absence of consideration or unlawful consideration is not available against the holder in due course. The party responsible is liable to make the payment.

7. Estoppel against denying original validity of the instrument

The plea of original invalidity of the instrument cannot be putforth against the holder in due course by the drawer of a bill of exchange or cheques, or by an acceptor for the honour of the drawer.

8. Estoppel against denying the capacity of the payee to endorse

The maker of a promissory note or the acceptor of a bill is precluded from denying against a holder in due course the existence of the payee and his capacity to endorse.

9. Estoppel against endorser to deny capacity of prior parties

An endorser of the bill by his endorsement guarantees that all previous endorsements are genuine and that all parties had capacity to enter into valid contracts. Therefore, he cannot subsequently deny signature or capacity to contract of any prior party to the instrument.

10. Every holder is a holder in due course

The law presumes that every holder is a holder in due course although the presumption is rebuttable.

Distinction between Holder and Holder in Due Course

The following are the differences between holder and holder in due course.

1. Entitlement

A holder is entitled in his own name to the possession of the instrument. But a holder in due course acquires the possession of the instrument for consideration.

2. Consideration

In case of holder, consideration is not necessary. The instrument may be given as a gift or donation. But consideration is necessary for becoming a holder in due course. A person cannot be a holder in due course if he had obtained the instrument without consideration.

3. Before and after maturity

A holder may get the instrument even after it has become payable. But a holder in due course must get the possession of the instrument before its maturity.

4. Title

A holder does not acquire good title, if the title of any of the prior parties was defective. But a holder in due course acquires good title even though there was defect in the title of any prior parties, provided he had no notice of the defect. His title is free from defects.

5. Presumption

Every holder in due course is a holder, but every holder may not be a holder in due course.

6. Right to recover the amount

All prior parties to a negotiable instrument continue to remain liable to the holder in due course until the instrument is duly satisfied. But a holder of an instrument can recover the amount from maker and the transferor but not all the prior parties.

7. Privileges

A holder does not enjoy any special privileges, but a holder in due course enjoys certain special privileges.

Conclusion

The above discussion clearly shows that, a cheque is a negotiable instrument specified in Negotiable Instruments Act 1881. It is an unconditional order, drawn on a specified banker signed by the drawer, directing the drawee to pay on demand a certain sum of money to or to the order of a specified person or to the bearer of the instrument. The payment of a crossed cheque can be obtained through the bank of the holder. If a cheque is crossed it is easy to trace the person for whose benefit the payment was collected. The crossed cheque is negotiable by mere delivery it is payable to bearer and by endorsement and delivery in case it is payable to order.

Questions for Discussions

1. What is a cheque? What are the essentials of a cheque?
2. What is meant by the term 'crossing of a cheque? Explain the different kinds of crossing of a cheque and their significance?
3. What do you mean by the term endorsement and what are the essentials of a valid endorsement? Explain the different types of endorsements.
4. "Every holder in due course must be a holder, but every holder may not be a holder in due course" - Comment.
5. What is meant by material alteration in cheques? Give examples of alterations which are material and those which are not?

Chapter - 12

THE PAYING BANKER

Introduction

The relationship between a banker and a customer is primarily that of debtor and creditor, the respective positions being determined by the existing state of account. If the customer has a credit balance with the bank, he is the creditor and if he has a debit balance with the bank, he is the debtor of the bank. Thus, bank does not work as a trustee of money deposited with it by the customer because instead of money being set apart in a safe room, it is replaced by a debt due from the bank. When a bank accepts the deposits from a customer, it becomes the debtor of the customer and it will be bound to return the equivalent amount to the customer or his order on demand. In other words, it is the obligation of the bank to honour the cheques issued by the customer if the following conditions are fulfilled :

(a) there is sufficient balance in the account of the customer ;

(b) the cheque is properly drawn and presented; and

(c) there is no legal restriction on payment.

Meaning

The banker who is liable to pay the value of a cheque of a customer as per the contract, when the amount is due from him to the customer is called "Paying Banker" or "Drawee Bank". The payment to b e made by him has arisen due to the contractual obligation. He is also called drawee bank as the cheque is drawn on him.

The payment has to be made by the banker as per the legal obligation also. Section 31 of N.I. Act 1881, says that "the drawee of a cheque, having sufficient funds of the drawer in his hands properly applicable to the payment of such a cheque, must pay the cheque, when duly required to do so, and in default of such payment, must compensate the drawer for any loss or damage caused by such default". According to this provision, the drawee of a cheque, i.e. paying banker has a legal obligations to honour the demand of the drawer or customer. If he fails to pay the money held, he is liable for damages. Thus paying banker has certain obligations to discharge.

While making payment he should be cautious. He cannot honour the cheque when sufficient funds are not available at the credit of the customer. If he pays by oversight he will be running the risk of making good this loss. i.e., making payment without having sufficient funds. At the same time he will also run the risk when he dishonours cheque even when sufficient funds are available at the credit of the customer. He is liable for damages for this wrongful dishonour. Thus in both the cases he runs the risk. However, the customer should present the cheque at the branch where the amount is kept and should not raise any objection if the cheque is dishonoured at branches where the customer does not hold the account. But he is at liberty to open accounts in any number of branches and can draw cheques, when he is having sufficient funds in each account.

Precautions for Payment of Cheques

Honouring of cheques drawn by his customer is a very important obligation of a banker. He should not dishonour his customer's cheques without adequate ground. The customer can claim damages for the injury caused to his credit owing to wrongful dishonour of cheques. Further, if he honours a cheque which is not properly drawn or contrary of the instructions of his customer or against the intention of his customer or when the customer has no adequate balance, he gets into trouble. The paying banker in such a condition is said to be in "between the devil and the deep sea". Tanan says" the banker's position in respect of cheques drawn upon him is not enviable. So the banker has to take care when honouring or dishonouring a cheque drawn by his customer.

Precautions

The banker's duty to pay customer's cheques is delicate and hence, to be handled judiciously as well as cautiously. The banker has to take the following precautions while honouring the cheques of his customers :

1. Proper form

A banker should see whether the cheque is in the proper form. That means the cheque should be in the manner prescribed under the provisions of the Negotiable Instruments Act. It should not contain any condition.

2. Open or crossed cheque

The most important precaution that a banker should take is about crossed cheques. A banker has to verify whether the cheque is open or crossed. He should not pay cash across the counter in respect of crossed cheques. If the cheque is a crossed one, he should see whether it is a general crossing or special crossing. If it is a general crossing, the holder must be asked to present the cheque through some banker. It should be paid to a banker. If the cheque bears a special crossing, the banker should pay only the bank whose name is mentioned in the crossing. If it is a open cheque, a banker can pay cash to the payee or the holder across the counter. If the banker pays against the instructions as indicated above, he is liable to pay the amount to the true owner for any loss sustained. Further, a banker loses statutory protection in case of forged endorsement.

Madras Bank Ltd. Vs. South India Match Factory Ltd., A Cheque was issued by a purchaser in favour of the official liquidator of a company towards the purchase price of certain properties. The bank paid the amount of the crossed cheque to the liquidator across the counter. The Liquidator mis-appropriated the amount. The court held that the "banker committed breach of statutory duty and was negligent in paying direct to the liquidator over the counter and hence, was not entitled to legal protection".

If it is a 'Not Negotiable' crossing, the paying banker has to verify the genuineness of all the endorsements. If it is an 'Account Payee' crossing, the banker can credit the account of the payee named in the cheque and not that of any other person.

3. Place of presentment of cheque

A banker can honour the cheques provided it is presented with that branch of the bank where the drawer has an account. If the cheque is presented at another branch of the same bank, it should not be honoured unless special arrangements are made by the customer in advance. The reasons are:

(a) A banker undertakes to pay cheques only at the branch where the account is kept.

(b) The specimen signature of the customer will be with the office of the bank at which he has an account.

(c) It is not possible for other branches to know that the customer has adequate balance to meet the cheque.

Bank of India. Vs. Official Liquidator : In this case, it was held that "if customer has an account in a bank which has several branches, the branches at which he has no account are justified in refusing to honour his cheques".

4. Date of the cheque

The paying banker has to see the date of the cheque. It must be properly dated. It should not be either a post-dated cheque or a stale-cheque. If a cheque carries a future date, it becomes a post-dated cheque. If the cheque is presented on the date mentioned in the cheque, the banker need not have any objection to honour it. If the banker honours a cheque before the date mentioned in the cheque, he loses statutory protection. If the drawer dies or becomes insolvent or countermands payment before the date of the cheque, he will lose the amount. The undated cheques are usually not honoured.

A Stale cheque is one which has been in circulation for an unreasonably long period. The custom of bankers in this respect varies. Generally a cheque is considered stale when it has been in circulation for more than six months. Banker do not honour such cheques. However, banker, may get confirmation from the drawer and honour cheques which are in circulation for a long time. So verification of date is very important.

5. Mutilated cheque

The banker should be careful when mutilated cheques are presented for payment. A cheque is said to be mutilated when it has been cut or torn, or when a part of it is missing. Mutilation may be either accidental or intentional. If it is accidental, the banker should get the drawer's confirmation before honouring it. If it is intentional, he should refuse payment. The cheques is to be returned with a remark 'Mutilated cheque' or 'Mutilation Requires Confirmation'. In Scholey. Vs. Ramsbottom, the banker was held liable for wrong payment of a cheque which was dirty and bore visible marks of mutilation".

6. Words and figures

The amount of the cheque should be expressed in words, or in words and figures, which should agree with each other. When the amount in words and figures differ, the banker should refuse payment. However, Sec. 18 of the Negotiable Instruments Act provides that, where there is difference between the amount in words and figures, the amount in words is the amount payable. If the banker returns the cheque, he should make a remark 'amount in words and figures differ'.

7. Alterations and overwritings

The banker should see whether there is any alteration or over-writing on the cheque. If there is any alteration, it should be confirmed by the drawer by putting his full signature. The banker should not pay a cheque containing material alteration without confirmation by the drawer. The banker is expected to exercise reasonable care for the detection of such alterations. Otherwise, he has to take risk. Material alterations make a cheque void.

8. Proper endorsements

Cheques must be properly endorsed. In the case of bearer cheque, endorsement is not necessary legally. In the case of an order cheque, endorsement is necessary. A bearer cheque always remains a bearer cheque. The paying banker should examine all the endorsements on the cheque before making payment. They must be regular. But it is not the duty of the paying banker to verify the genuineness of the endorsements, unless the cheque bears 'Not-Negotiable' crossing. He is not expected to know the signatures of all payees. So he gets statutory protection in case of forged endorsements. In India, even in the case of bearer cheques, bankers insist on endorsement though it is not required.

9. Sufficiency of funds

The banker should see whether the credit balance in the customer's Account is sufficient to pay the cheque or not. If there is an overdraft agreement, he should see that the limit is not exceeded. The banker should not make part-payment of the cheque. He should pay either full amount or refuse payment. In case of insufficiency of funds, the banker should return the cheque with the remark 'No Funds' or 'Not Sufficient Funds'.

10. Verification of drawer's signature

The banker takes specimen signatures of his customers' at the time of opening the account. He should compare the drawer's signature on the cheque with the specimen signature of the customer. He should carefully examine the signature to find out whether the drawer's signature is forged or not. If there is any difference or doubt, he should not honour the cheque. He should get the confirmation of the drawer. If there is forgery and there is negligence on the part of the banker to detect the same, there is no protection to the banker, In Prabhu Dayal. Vs. Jwala Bank it was held that "payment of a forged cheque cannot be deemed as payment in due course, though the bank may turn out to be an innocent victim.

Statutory Protection

The legal duty of a paying banker is full of risk because payment of cheques may not be made to the right person. In case a payment is made to a wrong person by bank, the loss will be borne by the banker. In banking practice, the banker honours the cheques of his customers and cannot make enquiries and investigations about the title and status of the person who presents the cheque for payment at the counter of the bank. Regarding the payment of a cheque to a wrong person, Chorley observed, "It is obvious that available routine in a bank and the Clearing House gives no opportunity for investigation of endorsements, except as to their outward regularity. If enquiries were to be made, much expenditure of time and money would be involved and instrument could only be nominally payable on demand and indeed the system which we know, would be impossible".

Protection Available Under the Negotiable Instruments Act

The Negotiable Instruments Act has come to the rescue of the paying banker and provided protection under certain circumstances. These circumstances are given below :

1. Protection in Case of Bearer Cheque.
2. Protection in Case of Order Cheque.
3. Protection in Case of Crossed Cheque.

4. Protection in Case of Obliterated Cheque.
5. Protection in Case of Drafts.

1. Protection in Case of Bearer Cheque

Section 85 (2) of the Negotiable Instruments Act, 1881 states, "Whereas a cheque is originally expressed to be payable to bearer, the drawee is discharged by payment in due course to the bearer thereof, notwithstanding any endorsement whether in full or in blank appearing theron, notwithstanding that any such indorsement purports to restrict or exclude further negotiation".

The above protection is given in the Act on the basis that a bearer cheque always remains a bearer cheque and it bears endorsement in blank or full whether any endorsement restricts further negotiation or not. In case a bearer cheque is stolen or lost and the banker honours the cheque without any knowledge, the banker will be discharged from his duty under the protection given in Section 85 (2) of the said Act. In such a case, the paying banker is not required to verify the endorsement on bearer cheque.

In case a bearer cheque is crossed, the paying banker has no right to pay in across the counter in disregard of the crossing.

2. Protection in Case of Order Cheque

In case the payment is made to a person other than the payee, the paying banker does not get any protection under the Negotiable Instruments Act. It the endorsement is regular and payment is made in due course, the paying banker gets the protection under Section 85 (1) of the Negotiable Instruments Act 1881 : "Whereas a cheque payable to order purports to be endorsed by or on behalf of the payee, the drawee is discharged by payment in due course".

In case, payment is made to a wrong person whose signature is not according to specimen signature, the protection is given to a banker under Section 16 (2) of the Negotiable Instruments Act : "It is not possible for a banker to know each of the endorsers and their signatures". For getting the protection, the banker should note the following :

(a) Regular Endorsement : According to Section 85 (1) of the Act the endorsement should be regular. For example, if a cheque is payable to a right person and signature is bearing same name and the same spellings this is known as regular endorsement. Though this is not a valid endorsement.

(b) Payment in Due Course : According to Section 10 of the Act the cheque should be paid in due course. In case the payment is made on forged signature of the endorser and not that of the drawer, the banker gets statutory protection under Section 10 of the Act.

3. Protection in Case of Crossed Cheque

Regarding payment of Crossed Cheque, the paying banker gets the protection under Section 128 of the Negotiable Instruments Act, 1881 : "Whereas the banker on whom a Crossed Cheque is drawn has paid the same in due course, the banker paying the cheque and the drawer thereof (in case such cheque has come to the hands of the payee) shall be entitled respectively to the same rights and placed in the same position if the amount of the cheque had been paid to and received by the true owner thereof".

In case the payment is made on the instructions of the drawer in good faith without any negligence, the paying banker gets the statutory protection under the Negotiable Instruments Act, 1881: "The payment of crossed cheque in due course makes the drawee banker liable to the true owner of the cheque besides disentitling himself to debit the customer's account".

4. Protection in Case of Obliterated Cheques

According to Section 89 of the Negotiable Instruments Act, 1881, "Whereas a cheque is presented for payment which does not at the time of presentation appear to be crossed or to have had a crossing which has been obliterated, payment thereof by a banker is liable to be paid and paying the same according to the apparent tenor thereof at the time of payment and otherwise in due course, shall discharge such banker from all liability thereon and such payment shall not be questioned by reason of the cheque having been crossed". Thus the above Section is very meaningful where crossing of a cheque is obliterated by dishonest person. Under the above Section the banker gets the protection in the way that the payment is made according to the apparent tenor of the cheque and due course.

5. Protection in Case of Drafts

In case of demand drafts drawn by one branch of a bank upon another branch of the same bank, the banker gets protection under Section 85 of the Negotiable Instruments Act. The Section states : "Whereas any draft, that is, an order to pay money drawn by one office of a bank upon another office of the same bank for a sum of money payable to order on demand, purports to be endorsed by or on behalf of the payee, the bank is discharged by payment in due course".

In short, a banker may get statutory protection under the various Sections of the Negotiable Instruments Act, if he fulfils the terms and conditions of the said Section of the said Act. No protection, however is available, in case the drawer's signature is forged.

Dishonour of Cheques

A paying banker must refuse payment on cheques, issued by his customers, in the following circumstances :

1. When the customer countermands the payment

A banker must refuse to honour cheque when the customer countermands the cheque. Countermands means "the instruction conveyed by the drawer of a cheque to drawee bank not to pay the cheque, when it is presented". The instructions of the customer to stop payment should be in writing. It should be signed by the drawer. The instructions should include the number, the date, the name of the payee and the amount of the cheque. Any one of the partners in partnership accounts or any one of the joint account holders may countermand the cheques. Then the banker has to follow the instructions. Suppose, if there is a request to remove stop order, the banker should get such request signed by all the required signatories. It is better for a banker to suggest the issue of a new cheque. A banker must follow the customer's instructions to stop payment very carefully (Hilton. Vs. Westminister Bank Ltd.). If instructions are given to stop payment by telegram or telephone, the banker should postpone and request the drawer to send a written confirmation. At best he may return the cheque marking 'Payment Countermanded by Telegram 'or' Payment postponed pending confirmation, present again'.

The banker owes no duty to a holder of cheque. Hence, he should not rely on the instructions from a holder on the plea that he had lost the cheque. He should suggest to the holder to obtain written instructions from the drawer. If the cheque is presented in the meanwhile, he may return the cheque in the case of "stop telegram". However, he should see that the customer's credit is not affected or damaged. If the holder of an order cheque has lost it and inform the banker that he has not endorsed it, the banker should stop payment because the presenter must be claiming the amount through a forged endorsement. Otherwise, the banker will be held liable for not acting in good faith and without negligence.

If the banker pays a countermanded cheque, he will not only be required to reverse the entry but also be held liable to pay damages for dishonouring the cheques presented subsequently which would have been honoured otherwise.

2. Notice of the customer's death

The banker should not make payments on cheques presented after the death of the customer. He should return the cheque with the remark 'Drawer Deceased'. However, if the payment is made without knowing the fact of the customer's death, the banker cannot be held liable.

3. Notice of customer's insanity

The banker should stop the payment on cheques drawn and received after the receipt of notice of the customer's insanity. However, the banker should be very careful in this regard. He can believe that the customer is insane only when the latter is sent to the lunatic asylum. Otherwise, he had to obtain the certificate from the competent doctor. Cheques drawn at a time when the customer was rational may be honoured.

4. Notice of the customer's insolvency

A banker should refuse payment on the cheques soon after the customer is adjudicated as insolvent.

5. Receipt of the Garnishee Order

Where Garnishee order is received attaching the whole amount, the banker should stop payment on cheques received after the receipt of such an order. But if the order is for a specific amount, leaving the specified amount, cheques should be honoured if the remaining amount is sufficient to meet them.

6. Notice of assignment

The banker should stop the payment, on receipt of the notice of assignment signed by the customer of the credit balance in his account.

7. Trust accounts

If the banker feels suspicious that the trustee wants to use the amount of the cheque for his personal use, he must stop payment.

8. Suspicion about the title over the cheque

When the banker believes that the person presenting the cheque is not entitled to receive the payment, he should refuse to make payment. Eg. stolen cheque.

When a Banker can Dishonour Cheques

A banker may dishonour a cheque without incurring any liability in the following cases :

1. Post-dated cheques

Refusal to pay post-dated cheque before the date mentioned in the cheque does not amount to dishonour. So, post-dated cheques can be dishonoured.

2. Insufficiency of funds

The banker can refuse to pay the amount if the funds are not sufficient. However, the banker may honour the cheque if he feels that the customer is a trustworthy and long-standing customer.

3. Presentation of Cheque

The banker may refuse the cheque of his customer if it is not duly presented. Presentation of cheque out of business hours, for example, can be dishonoured.

4. Joint accounts

In the case of joint account, the banker can refuse to make payment on the cheque if it is not signed by all the joint account holders.

5. Material alterations

When there is material alteration in the cheque, the banker may refuse payment.

6. Stale cheques

When the cheque is presented after the period of six months from the date it bears, the banker may refuse to make payment.

7. Drawer's signature

If the signature of the drawer on the cheque does not tally with the specimen signature, the banker may refuse to make payment.

8. Difference between words and figures

If there is difference between the amount written in words and figures, the banker may refuse to make payment.

9. Endorsement

If the endorsement is irregular, the banker may refuse payment on the cheque.

10. Proper form of the cheque

If the cheque is not in the proper form i.e., in accordance with the provisions of the Negotiable Instruments Act, and with conditions, the banker should refuse the payment.

11. Drawn on another branch

If the cheque is presented at another branch of the same bank, it should not be honoured unless special arrangements are made by the customer in advance.

Bank's Remarks on Dishonoured Cheques

When a cheque is returned unpaid, the banker should attach a slip containing brief remarks, to convey the reason for dishonouring the cheque. The following remarks are generally made :

(a) R.D. (Refer to Drawer)

This remark is used only when there is reasonable ground to suspect the veracity of the cheque.

(b) N.S. (Not sufficient), N.E. (No. Effects)

These are used where the drawer's balance is inadequate to meet the cheque.

(c) E.I. (Endorsement Irregular)

(d) E.N.C. (Effect is not cleared)

This is used when cheques deposited not yet collected and not available for withdrawal.

Conclusion

In conclusion, it may be observed that the banker must be guided by the recognised practice of bankers. In all cases, the banker must use his own judgement and his knowledge of the general practice of banker.

Questions for Discussions

1. What is paying banker? What precautions should a paying banker take while honouring the cheque of his customer.
2. Under what circumstances can a bank dishonour a cheque of a customer.
3. State and explain the statutory protecting available under the Negotiable Instruments Act to the paying banker.

Chapter - 13

COLLECTING BANKER

Introduction

A banker is not bound to collect cheques and bills on behalf of his customers as it is not a legal duty or obligation. But every modern bank collects cheques and bills on behalf of his customers in order to provide a facility or service to them. This service of collection of cheques on behalf of the customer has become an accepted part of banker's function due to the greater use of the crossed cheques, which are payable through a banker only. In performing this function, he acts as an agent of his customer, and is bound to use reasonable skill, care and diligence.

Meaning

Collecting banker means the banker who collects the cheques and bills on behalf of the customers. In other words, every crossed cheque is necessarily to be collected through any bank, which is known as collecting banker. As Sir John Paget has rightly said "Looking at the restriction on the encashment of crossed cheques, save through a bank and the universal and legally encouraged use of crossed cheques the collection of such cheques must be regarded as an inherent part of banker's business".

While collecting the cheques of a customer, the banker may act in the capacity of either (a) as a holder for value or (b) as an agent of the customer. The legal position of the collecting banker under these two circumstances is discussed below.

Collecting Banker as Holder for Value

A collecting banker is holder for value if he gives the value of the cheque in any form to its customer before collecting the proceeds of the cheque deposited by the latter. He does not remain an agent of the customer, but becomes the owner of the cheque in his own right since he has paid value for it, and has acquired the ownership right in good faith. In such a situation, the banker is called holder for value and he is also the holder in due course.

According to Paget, a banker becomes an holder for value in the following ways:

(a) by lending further on the strength of the cheque ;

(b) by paying the amount of the cheque or part of it in cash or in account before it is cleared ;

(c) by agreeing that the customer may draw before the cheque is cleared ;

(d) by accepting the cheque in avowed reduction of an existing overdraft ;

(e) by giving cash over the counter for the cheque at the time it is deposited in for collection.

In the above circumstances, the banker becomes the holder for value. Further, if he proves that he gave value for a cheque in good faith, he will be able to resist any claim by the true owner provided that (a) the cheque was not tainted with forgery, (b) he had no notice of any previous dishonour or of any defect in the title of his customer, (c) the cheque was not crossed 'not negotiable' (d) the cheque was not overdue for the purpose of negotiation, and (c) the cheque was regular on the face of it in all respects.

If the cheque is dishonoured, the collecting banker can use all the previous parties after giving them the notice of dishonour. The banker undertakes a risk also when he acts as a holder for value. He will be in a difficulty if last, but one endorsement proves to be a forged one. The banker will be liable to the true owner of the cheque. However, he can recover the amount from his customer.

Collecting Banker as an Agent of the Customer

When a collecting banker acts as an agent of the customer, he credits the latter's account with the amount of the cheque after the proceeds of the cheque are actually collected from the drawee banker. The customer can draw the amount after his account is credited with the proceeds. In such a case, banker acts as an agent of his customer and does not get better title to the cheque than that of the customer. If the title of the customer is defective, the banker will run the risk of being liable to the true owner if it collects the cheque. If the cheque collected by the banker does not belong to his customer, the banker will be liable for 'conversion of money' or in other words, for illegally interfering with the rights of the true owner of the cheque.

As an agent of the customer, the collecting banker is a mere "conduit pipe to receive payment of the cheque from the bank on which it is drawn and holds the proceeds at the disposal of the customer". Like any other agent, the banker has to perform his duties diligently for the customer who has paid in his cheques. If he delays or does not exercise the normal skills expected, he will be liable to his customer. It has been held that the reasonable time would be presenting the cheque within one day after the receipt thereof where the cheque is drawn on a bank in the same place, or forwarding or presenting it on the day following the receipt thereof where the cheque is drawn on a bank in another place. After the expiry of reasonable time, the customer paying in the cheque for collection is entitled to presume that it has been collected and the proceeds thereof credited to his account.

Conversion

According to Dictionary of Banking, "Conversion is a legal term signifying wrongful interference with another person's property inconsistent with another's right of possession". Conversion applies only to tangible property and not to debts. Negotiable Instruments are included in the term 'property'. The collecting banker may be charged for conversion if he collects a cheque for a customer having defective title to it. The collecting banker while collecting the payment of a cheque to which his customer has defective title, deprives the true owner of the cheque to receive payment. So he incurs a liability to the true owner of the cheque. The principle which is applied here is that a rightful owner of the cheque can recover the same from anyone who takes it without his authority and in whose hands it can be traced. But the banker has been granted statutory protection in certain circumstances which are discussed later.

In the following cases, the banker is liable for conversion to the true owner of the instrument :

(a) When he collects a cheque, a bill of exchange, or a promissory note bearing a forged endorsement or in respect of which the customer has no title at all ;

(b) when he borrows for his customer the proceeds of a cheque on which the customer has no title or only defective title ;

(c) when he takes as holder for value a cheque marked 'not negotiable; and

(d) when he delivers to the wrong person the goods entrusted with him for safe-custody.

In the following cases, the banker is not liable for conversion to the true owner of a cheque :

(a) where there is no forgery and the instrument comes into the hands of the holder in due course ; and

(b) where there is forgery and the instrument is a cheque, payment whereon has been made in due course by the banker.

Statutory Protection to Collecting Banker

Section 131 of the Negotiable Instruments Act provides protection to a collecting banker who receives payment of a crossed cheque or draft on behalf of his customers. According to section 131 of the Act "a banker who has, in good faith and without negligence, received payment for a customer of a cheque crossed generally or specially to himself shall not, in case the title to the cheque proves defective, incur any liability to the true owner of the cheque by reason only of having received such payment".

The protection provided by section 131 is not absolute but qualified. A collecting banker can claim protection against conversion if the following conditions are fulfilled.

1. Good Faith and Without Negligence

Statutory protection is available to a collecting banker when he receives payment in good faith and without negligence. The phrase in "good faith" means honestly and without notice or interest of deceit or fraud and does necessarily require carefulness. Negligence means failure to exercise reasonable care. It is not for the customer or the true owner to prove negligence on the part of the banker. The burden of proving that he collected in good faith and without negligence is on the banker. The banker should have exercised reasonable care and deligence. What constitutes negligence depends upon facts of each case. Following are a few examples which constitute negligence :

(a) Failure to obtain reference for a new customer at the time of opening the account.

(b) Collection of cheques payable to 'trust accounts" for crediting to personal accounts of a trustee.

(c) Collecting for the private accounts of partners, cheques payable to the partnership firms.

(d) Omission to verify the correctness of endorsements on cheques payable to order.

(e) Failure to pay attention to the crossing particularly the "not negotiable crossing".

2. Collection for a Customer

Statutory protection is available to a collecting banker if he collects on behalf of his customer only. If he collects for a stranger or non-customer, he does not get such protection. As Jones aptly puts if "duly crossed cheques are only protected in their collection, if handled for the customer". A bank cannot get protection when he collects a cheque as holder for value. In Great Western Railway. Vs London and Country Bank it was held that "the bank is entitled for protection as it received collection for an employee of the customer and not for the customer".

3. Acts as an Agent

A collecting banker must act as an agent of the customer in order to get protection. He must receive the payment as an agent of the customer and not as a holder under independent title. The banker as a holder for value is not competent to claim protection from liability in conversion. In case of forgery, the holder for value is liable to the true owner of the cheque.

4. Crossed Cheques

Statutory protection is available only in case of crossed cheques. It is not available in case uncrossed or open cheques because there is no need to collect them through a banker. Cheques, therefore must be crossed prior to their presentment to the collecting banker for clearance. In other words, the crossing must have been made before it reached the hands of the banker for collection. If the cheque is crossed after it is received by the banker, protection is not available. Even drafts are covered by this protection.

To conclude, it is necessary that the collecting banker should have acted without negligence if he wants to claim statutory protection under Section 131 of the said Act. The statutory protection is available to the banker if he collects a cheque marked "Not Negotiable" for a customer, whose name is not used as the payee there-in provided the requirements of the said sections are duly complied with.

Duties and Responsibilities of a Collecting Banker

The duties and responsibilities of a collecting banker are discussed below :

1. Due care and diligence in the collection of cheque.
2. Serving notice of dishonour.
3. Agent for collection.
4. Remittance of proceeds to the customer.
5. Collection of bill of exchange.

1. Due Care and Diligence in the Collection of Cheques

The collecting banker is bound to show due care and diligence in the collection of cheques presented to him. In case a cheque is entrusted with the banker for collection, he is expected to show it to the drawee banker within a reasonable time. According to Section 84 of the Negotiable Instruments Act, 1881, "Whereas a cheque is not presented for payment within a reasonable time of its issue, and the drawer or person in whose account it is drawn had the right, at the time when presentment ought to have been made, as between himself and the banker, to have the cheque paid and suffers actual damage, through the delay, he is discharged to the extent of such damage, that is to say, to the extent to which such drawer or person is a creditor of the banker to a large amount than he would have been if such cheque had been paid".

In case a collecting banker does not present the cheque for collection through proper channel within a reasonable time, the customer may suffer loss. In case the collecting banker and the paying banker are in the same bank or where the collecting branch is also the drawee branch, in such a case the collecting banker should present the cheque by the next day. In case the cheque is drawn on a bank in another place, it should be presented on the day after receipt.

2. Serving Notice of Dishonour

When the cheque is dishonoured, the collecting banker is bound to give notice of the same to his customer within a reasonable time. It may be noted here, when a cheque is returned for confirmation of endorsement, notice must be sent to his customer. If he fails to give such a notice, the collecting banker will be liable to the customer for any loss that the customer may have suffered on account of such failure.

Whereas a cheque is returned by the drawee banker for confirmation of endorsement, it is not called dishonour. But in such a case, notice must be given to the customer. In the absence of such a notice, if the cheque is returned for the second time and the customer suffers a loss, the collecting banker will be liable for the loss.

3. Agent for Collection

In case a Cheque is drawn on a place where the banker is not a member of the 'clearing-house', he may employ another banker who is a member of the clearing-house for the purpose of collecting the cheque. In such a case the banker becomes a substituted agent. According to Section 194 of the Indian Contract Act, 1872, "Whereas an agent, holding an express or implied authority to name another person to act in the business of the agency has accordingly named another person, such a person is a substituted agent. Such an agent shall be taken as the agent of a principal for such part of the work as is entrusted to him".

4. Remittance of Proceeds to the Customer

In case a collecting banker has realised the cheque, he should pay the proceeds to the customer as per his (customer's) direction. Generally, the amount is credited to the account of the customer on the customer's request in writing, the proceeds may be remitted to him by a demand draft. In such circumstances, if the customer gives instructions to his banker, the draft may be forwarded. By doing so, the relationship between principal and agent comes to an end and the new relationship between debtor and creditor will begin.

5. Collection of Bills of Exchange

There is no legal obligation for a banker to collect the bills of exchange for its customer. But, generally, bank gives such facility to its customers. In collection of bills, a banker should examine the title of the depositor as the statutory protection under Section 131 of the Negotiable Instruments Act, 1881. Thus, the collecting banker must examine very carefully the title of his customer towards the bill. In case a new customer comes, the banker should extend this facility to him with a trusted reference.

From the above discussion, there is no doubt to say that the banker is acting as a mere agent for collection and not in the capacity of a banker. If the customer allows his banker to use the collecting money for its own purpose at present and to repay an equivalent amount on a fixed date in future the contract between the banker and the customer will come to an end.

Marking of Cheque

The marking of cheque means 'a cheque which is marked or certified by the drawee banker, to the effect, that it is good for payment". The drawee bank certifies that the drawer of the cheque has sufficient balance in his account and the cheque will not be dishonoured due to lack of funds. Such a certificate is know as "Marking of Cheques".

Generally, the marking of a cheque is done by drawee in writing the words "good for payment" across one corner of the cheque, with the signature of the bank's authorised official and the bank's stamp. The marked cheques are very useful for businessmen as they can purchase the goods required by them, and the sellers will accept the marked cheques like currency-notes. It is to be noted here that marking post-dated cheques is not valid.

When can get the Cheque Marked?

The marking of cheques may be done at the request of :

(a) the drawer

(b) the holder and

(c) another banker.

These have been discussed below

(a) Marking at the request of the drawer

Whereas a cheque is marked by the drawee bank at the request of the drawer, the latter cannot stop payment. In such case, the banker is bound to honour the cheque so marked by it. In case the drawer dies or becomes insane, the banker will have to make the payment because of the cheque having been marked at the request of the drawer. In such case, the banker has statutory protection in refusing other cheques of the customer if there are not sufficient funds in his account.

(b) Marking at the request of the holder

The marking of a cheque at the request of the holder or payee does not virtually place any liability on the paying banker. It simply means that at the time of marking, the drawee banker has sufficient funds to the credit of the drawer to meet the cheque. In such circumstances, there is not guarantee to the holder that the amount of the cheque will be paid to him when he presents it for payment. If a customer has sufficient funds in his account and he presents a cheques for payment, the banker will honour the cheque immediately.

(c) Marking at the request of another banker

When a banker marks a cheque at the request of another banker for clearance purposes, the paying banker is undertaking an obligation to honour it. It actual practice, marking a cheque for clearance purposes entitles the paying banker to earmark the necessary funds to meet the cheque. Sir John Paget expressed his views, "Such marking constitutes a constructive payment or appropriation to a specific person though not directly indicated by the customer".

For the significance of marking of cheque, it is necessary that the sufficient balance of money must be on credit with the drawer on that particular date. It is, however, made clear by the following illustration :

A Cheque drawn on Canara Bank on 21st February, 1987 post-dated to 26th February, 1987, was certified by the Manager of the Bank "Good for Payment on 26th February, 1987". State Bank of India became holder of the cheque in due course, which when presented for payment on 26th February, 1987, was dishonoured on account of lack of funds. In such a case, Canara Bank would not be liable for the cheque.

In short, the practice of marking of cheques at present, has been stopped in India on account of inter-bank agreement.

Conclusion

From the above discussion, there is no doubt to say that, a banker who acts as a collecting banker has certain duties and liabilities, and he is bound to use reasonable care and skill while collecting cheques and other negotiable instruments. Dr. D.L. Hart has observed in connection with the duties of a collecting banker, that, as his customer's agent in the matter, the banker is bound to use reasonable skill, care and diligence in presenting and securing payment of the drafts entrusted to him for collection and placing the proceeds to his customer's account, or in taking such other steps as may be proper to secure the customer's interests.

Questions for Discussions

1. Explain the term "collecting banker". What are his duties and responsibilities in the collection of his customer's cheques?
2. Discuss the position of a collecting banker as :
   (a) a holder for value.
   (b) an agent of his customer.
3. Explain the nature of protection given to the collecting banker under the Negotiable Instruments Act.
4. Give note on the term "Conversion"
5. What is meant by marking of cheques? Bring out the significance of marking with regard to the following.
   (a) Request of the Drawer
   (b) Request of the holder and
   (c) Request of Another Banker.

Chapter - 14

LOANS AND ADVANCES

Introduction

One of the primary functions of a bank is to grant loans. Whatever money the bank receives by way of deposits, it lends a major part of it to its customers by way of loans, advances, cash credit and overdraft. Interest received on such loans and advances is the major source of its income. The banks make a major contribution to the economic development of the country by granting loans to the industrial and agricultural sectors.

The banks make loans and advances out of deposits, received from their customers. Most of these deposits are payable on demand. As such the bank owes a greater responsibility to the depositors. Hence he should be extremely careful while granting loans.

General Rules of Sound Lending

A banker should use his third eye and third ear (although the God has given him only two eyes and two ears) while granting loans. In other words he must be extra careful while granting loans. A banker should take the following precautions.

These are discussed below.

Principles of Sound Lending

1. Safety
2. Liquidity
3. Profitability
4. Diversification
5. Object of loan
6. Security
7. Margin Money
8. National Interest
9. Character of the borrower

1. Safety

The most important golden rule for granting loans is the safety of funds. The main reason for this is that the very existence of the bank is dependent upon the loans granted by him. In case the bank does not get back the loans granted by it, it might fail. A bank cannot and must not sacrifice the safety of its funds to get higher rate of interest. For example, if a reputed credit-worthy businessman offers to pay 10% interest per annum and on the other hand a pauper offers 15% rate of interest per annum. Obviously as per safety rule, the banker should not grant loan to the pauper although paying 5% higher rate of interest.

2. Liquidity

The second important golden rule of granting loan is liquidity. Liquidity means possibility of converting loans into cash without loss of time and money. Needless to say, that the funds with the bank out of which he lends money are payable on demand or short notice. As such a bank cannot afford to block its funds for a long time. Hence the bank should lend only for short-term requirements like working capital. The bank cannot and should not lend for long-term requirements, like fixed capital.

3. Return or Profitability

Return or porfitability is another important principle. The funds of the bank should be invested to earn highest return, so that it may pay a reasonable rate of interest to its customers on their deposits, reasonably good salaries to its employees and a good return to its shareholders. However, a bank should not sacrifice either safety or liquidity to earn a high rate of interest. Of course, if safety and liquidity in a particular case are equal, the banker should lend its funds to a person who offers higher rate of interest.

4. Diversification

'One should not put all his eggs in one basket' is an old proverb which very clearly explains this principle. A bank should not invest all its funds in one industry. In case that industry fails, the banker will not be able to recover his loans. Hence, the bank may also fail. According to the principle of diversification, the bank should diversify its investments in different industries and should give loans to different borrowers in one industry. It is less probable that all the borrowers and industries will fail at one and the same time.

5. Object of Loan

A banker should thoroughly examine the object for which his client is taking loans. This will enable the bank to assess the safety and liquidity of its investment. A banker should not grant loan for unproductive purposes or to buy fixed asset. The bank may grant loan to meet working capital requirements. However, after nationalisation of banks, the banks have started granting loans to meet loan-term requirements. As per prudent banking policy, it is not desirable because of term lending by banks a large number of banks had failed in Germany.

6. Security

A banker should grant secured loans only. In case the borrower fails to return the loan, the banker may recover his loan after realising the security. In case of unsecured loans, the chances of bad debts will be very high. However, the bank may have to relax the condition of security in order to comply with the economic policy of the Government. For example, loans to weaker sections of society may be given without security if so directed by the Government.

7. Margin Money

In case of secured loans, the bank should carefully examine and value the security. There should be sufficient margin between the amount of loan and the value of the security. If adequate margin is not maintained, the loan might become unsecured in case the borrower fails to pay the interest and return the loan. The amount of loan, should not exceed 60 to 70% of the value of the security. If the value of the security is falling, the bank should demand further security without delay. In case he fails to do so, the loan might become unsecured and the bank may have to suffer loss on account of bad debt.

8. National Interest

Banks were nationalised in India to have social control over them. As such, they are required to invest a certain percentage of loans and advances in priority sectors viz., agriculture, small scale and tiny sector, and export oriented industries etc. Again, the Reserve Bank also gives directives in this respect to the scheduled banks from time to time. The banks are under obligations to comply with those directives.

9. Character of the Borrower

Last but not the least, the bank should carefully examine the character of the borrower, Character implies honesty, integrity, credit-worthiness and capacity of the borrower to return the loan. In case he fails to verify the character of the borrower, the loans and advances might become bad debts for the bank.

The above are thus the basic principles of sound lending observed by commercial banks. The ways in which the basic principles are followed, of course, may be modified to suit the need of the hour.

Forms of Lending (Advances)

Banks lend for working capital requirements in the form of :

1. Loans
2. Cash Credit
3. Overdraft
4. Purchase and Discounting of bills of exchange.

1. Loans

This is the oldest and very popular form of lending by the banks. In case of loans, financial assistance is given for a specific purpose and for a fixed period. The customer can withdraw the entire amount of loan in a single instalment. As such, interest is payable on the entire amount. In case he needs the funds again, he has to make a fresh application for a new loan or renewal of the existing one. Ordinarily, the loans is repayable in one instalment. However, a customer may return the loan in more than one instalment also.

Merits of Granting Loans

A. Simplicity

The method is very simple. Interest is payable on the entire amount of the loan.

B. Better recovery of interest and loan

The customer knows in advance the time of return of the loan. Therefore, he makes arrangement for its return. In case he does not return the loan in time, the bank will not grant loans and advances to him in future. It acts as an automatic regulator to discipline the borrower.

C. Profitability

From the point of view of the bank, the method is economical. The customer has to pay interest on the entire amount of the loan even if he has not withdrawn the entire loan. To that extent funds can be used by the bank.

Demerits

A. Inflexibility

The method is simple but inflexible. Borrower has to make a fresh request for the loan every time he requires the loan.

B. Overborrowing

Since the loan method is inflexible a customer takes a loan in excess of his needs to meet any contingency. This results in overborrowing.

C. More formalities

As compared to cash credit and overdraft methods, loan documentation is more complicated.

2. Cash Credit

Cash Credit is the most popular method of lending by the banks in India. It accounts for more than two third of total bank credit. Under cash credit system, a limit, called the credit limit is specified by the bank. A borrower is entitled to borrow upto that limit. It is granted against the security of tangible assets or guarantee. The borrower can withdraw money, any number of times upto that limit. He can also deposit any amount of surplus funds with him from time to time. He is charged interest on the actual amount withdrawn and for the period such amount is drawn.

Commitment charges : To discourage the borrower from keeping large funds idle within the sanctioned limit bank levies commitment charges. This also helps the bank in two ways. Firstly, it compensates him for the loss on idle funds kept by him within the credit limit sanctioned. Secondly, it facilitates better credit funds management. It will be applicable to borrower having a working capital limit of Rs. one crore or more. The rate of commitment charges is 1% per annum on the unutilised portion of cash credit limit sanctioned. However, no such charges will be levied, if the unutilised quarterly operating limit is upto 15%.

Again, it will not be applicable to sick units, export credit or export incentives, inland bills and credit limits granted to commercial banks cooperative banks and financial institutions.

Merits of Cash Credit

A. Flexibility

The greatest advantage of cash credit method is that it is flexible. A customer can withdraw and deposit money any number of times.

B. Economical

The scheme is economical. A borrower has to pay interest only on the amount borrowerd and that too for the period the amount is actually withdrawn. Unlike a loan he is not required to pay interest on the entire amounts of the loan.

C. Less formalities

As compared to the loan method, there are less formalities, and frequent documentation is avoided. Moreover, documentation in this method is less complicated.

Demerits

Cash credit method is not without demerits.

A. Over Borrowing

Credit limits are fixed one in a year. It gives rise to the tendency of fixing higher limits to cover contingencies. Thus it encourages over-borrowing.

B. Division of funds

The bank has control over the amount of credit sanctioned. It does not have any control over the use of such funds. Consequently the borrower diverts the funds, without the knowledge of the bank, for unapproved purposes.

C. Non-utilisation of funds

In practice a large amount of sanctioned cash credit limit remains unutilised. Levy of commitment charges has failed to put an end to this weakness because it is levied on cash credit limit of Rs. one crore or more.

3. Overdraft

One of the main advantages of a current account is that, its holder can avail of the facility of overdraft. An overdraft facility is granted to a customer on a written request. Sometimes, it may be implied where a customer overdraws his account and the bank honours his cheques. [Bank of Maharashtra V/s. M/s United Construction Co. and Others (1985) Bom. 432 A.I.R.]

The bank should obtain a written request from the customer. He should also settle the terms and conditions and the rate of interest chargeable. It is usual to obtain a promissory note from the customer to cover the overdraft.

Distinction between Loan and Cash Credit

(a) Amount

In case of loan a fixed amount is sanctioned, whereas in case of cash credit a limit is fixed.

(b) Period

Loan can be granted for a short, medium and long-term but cash credit is granted only for a short period upto one year only.

(c) Withdrawal

The entire amount of loan is credited to the customer's account. In case of cash credit the customer can withdraw the amount upto the limit as and when he needs.

(d) Interest

In case of loan, interest is payable on the entire loan, whereas in case of cash credit, interest is payable only on the amount actually withdrawn and for the period the amount is withdrawn.

(e) Repayment

Ordinarily a loan is repayable in one lump sum. However, it may be paid in instalments also. On the other hand in case of cash credit, the borrower may repay any surplus amount from time to time.

Distinction between Cash Credit and Overdraft

Ordinarily, in practice no distinction is made between cash credit and overdraft. The reason is that their purpose and nature is almost the same. Inspite of this there are the following points of distinction between them.

(a) Period

The main difference between cash credit and overdraft is that the former is granted comparatively, for a longer period, whereas overdraft is a temporary facility.

(b) Opening separate account

For granting cash credit it is necessary to open a new account. No new account is necessary for overdraft.

(c) Current account

Overdraft facility is granted to a current account holder only. It is not necessary to be a current account holder, to avail of the facility of cash credit.

(d) Control of Central Government

The Central Government exercises strict control over cash credit. There is no such control on overdraft.

(e) Commitment charges

In case of under-utilisation of cash credit a customer has to pay commitment charges. No commitment charges are payable in case of overdraft.

(f) Form of security

Cash credit is ordinarily granted on the security of goods by way of pledge or hypothecation. Overdraft is granted on the personal security of the borrower or financial securities viz., shares, bonds etc.

4. Purchase and Discounting of Bills of Exchange

The bank provides the customers with the facility of purchasing and discounting their bills receivable. This is a method of financial accommodation offered by the banker to the customer. The bank permits the customer to discount his bills receivable and have the value of the bills credited to his account. The bank charges discounting charges on the face value of the bills. It waits till the maturity of the bill and presents it on the due date to the drawee for payment. After collection, the proceeds of the bill are appropriated towards the loan and interest due by the customer. If the bill is discounted, the amount will be recovered from the customer.

Types of Loans and Advances

Loans and advances are of different types. These can mainly be classified on the following bases.

A. On the Basis of Object or Purpose

For which purpose a loan is being taken. It may be for the following purposes.

(a) Commercial loans

This loan is taken to meet short term requirement of capital e.g., working capital.

(b) Consumer loan

This loan is taken to finance household goods like Fridge, T.V., Scooter etc.

(c) Agricultural loan

Such a loan is taken by the farmers to meet their short term requirements like buying seeds, fertilisers, insecticides etc.

B. On the Basis of Time

(a) Short term loan

Such a loan is taken for a period of less than one year. For example, to meet working capital requirements.

(b) Medium term loan

Such a loan is taken for a period ranging from 1 year to 3 years. For example, to purchase equipments for professionals or furniture etc.

(c) Long term loan

Such a loan is taken to meet long term requirements from 3 years to 20 years or more. For example, loans to purchase land, building, plant and machinery etc. However, banks provide long term loans to a very limited extent only.

C. On the Basis of Security

(a) Secured loan

Such a loan is granted on the security of tangible assets, Sec. 5 (a) of the Banking Regulation Act, 1949, defines a 'secured loan or advance' as a loan or advance, made on the security of assets, the market value of which is not at any time less than the amount of such loan or advance.

(b) Unsecured loans

Such a loan is granted without any security. According to Sec. 5 (a) of the above Act an unsecured loan or advance means a loan or advance not so secured.

D. On the Basis of Form

(i) Loan,

(ii) Cash Credit and

(iii) Overdraft.

These have already been discussed earlier in detail. As such these are not being discussed again.

Determining Creditworthiness

A banker has to be very careful while granting loans. There is a greater risk in unsecured loans. Even in the case of secured loans, the banker should carefully examine the creditworthiness of the borrower. The following factors should be kept in mind while determining the creditworthiness of the borrower.

(a) Character

The most important factor to be carefully examined, is the character of the borrower. Character is the sum total of honesty, integrity, credit-worthiness, capacity to repay, sense of responsibility, good habits and reputation enjoyed by the customer. If he possesses these qualities he bears a good character and can be considered crediworthy for the loan.

(b) Ability to run the enterprise

If the borrower is fully capable of running the enterprise and has necessary skill and experience, his chances of success are high. As such there is little or no risk in granting loans.

(c) Adequate capital

An entrepreneur should have an adequate capital of his own. If his capital is inadequate there are greater chances of failure of his business. As such, the banker will not be able to recover his loan in such a situation.

(d) Soundness of the project

The banker should carefully examine the project report to ascertain its viability and soundness. If the project is sound and viable the banker will be able to recover his debt. On the other hand if the project is unsound the project will fail. The banker will not be able to recover his loan.

Sources of Credit Information

A banker needs credit information about a customer, his enterprise, industry etc. in order to assess his creditworthiness. He should cross check the information collected by him from different sources. In India there are no specialised agencies which can provide the necessary information. In western countries there are specialised agencies which supply credit information. However, a beginning has been made by the Reserve Bank of India in the field of credit information collection by establishing a Credit Information Bureau. Therefore, the banks have to make their own arrangement for collecting credit information. Credit information can be collected from the following sources.

1. The Borrower

The starting point is the borrower himself. He is asked to fill up an application form. The form should be carefully devised to elicit full information from the customer. The form should be as detailed as possible. Besides, his account books, pass book and references from his friends and relations should ne carefully examined and cross checked.

2. Credit Information Bureau

As pointed out earlier the Reserve Bank has established a Credit Information Bureau. The Reserve Bank is empowered to collect credit information from the banks under Section 45-C (i) of the Reserve Bank of India Act, 1934. Such credit information is collected in respect of credit limit of Rs. 5 lakhs and over in case of secured advances. Such limit for unsecured advances is Rs. one lakh. This information is available in consolidated form specifying nature of facility, security, charge and outstanding balance.

The information will enable the bank to know the extent of borrowing by the applicant. However, this information is of little or no use. It is available in respect of big customers only and is very scanty.

3. Exchange of Credit Information

This is the most important source of credit information and is based on the customary usage and practice prevalent in the banking industry. However, exchange of credit information amongst banks is of limited use. Because of fear of loosing legal protection, banks are reluctant to exchange free and fair credit information. The Reserve Bank of India (Amendment) Act, 1974 has granted statutory protection to exchange freely credit information by the banks amongst themselves. Moreover, the scope of the term 'credit information' has been enlarged to include information relating to the means, antecedents, history of financial transactions and the creditworthiness of the borrower.

4. Enquiries from Traders and Businessmen in the Same Trade

Credit information can be collected through enquiries made, from the fellow businessmen and traders. However, these too will be of limited use. A businessman will be reluctant to give fair and frank credit information about his fellow trader or businessman. However, such information may be useful, if it is cross-checked.

Conclusion

From the above discussion, the government, the banks and all concerned should seriously consider the situation and necessary steps should be taken before granting loans and advances. The bank dues should be treated at par with any other government dues. Every bank manager should be given adequate powers to take possession of the securities before the borrower has any chance to dispose of the same. The general feeling that one need not repay the bank loan and can get away with it should be erased from the minds of the people.

Questions for Discussions

1. Explain the golden (general) rules of sound lending by the banks.
2. Explain the various forms of lending by the banks.
3. How would you determine the creditworthiness of a borrower?
4. Explain the various sources of credit information. How for credit Information bureau is helpful in this respect?

Chapter - 15

TYPES OF SECURITIES

Introduction

A security is a document that is an evidences of specific claims on a stream of income and/or the particular assets. Debt securities include bonds and mortgages. Ownership securities include common stock certificates and the title to marketable assets. In addition, preferred stock is a hybrid security which entitles its owner to a mixture of both ownership and creditorship privileges.

In this chapter it is proposed to deal with the precautions to be taken by a banker while granting loans against various types of securities.

Characteristics of Good Security

A good security should have the following characteristics.

1. Free from encumbrances
2. Easy marketability
3. Easy storability
4. Durability
5. Free from price fluctuations
6. Easy ascertainment of value
7. Earning of income
8. Free from heavy cost of handling
9. Free from disabilities

These are discussed below.

1. Free from encumbrances

The security must be completely free from prior charges. If the borrower's title is defective, the banker cannot obtain a better title.

2. Easy marketability

The security offered must be such, that it is easily marketable without loss in its value. In other words, it must possess the quality of liquidity.

3. Easy storability

The securities should not pose a problem of storage to a banker. For example, certain goods like timbers, inflamable articles etc., require huge and special storage, which are costly. But some securities like, documents of title to goods, shares, consumer goods etc., can be stored without much difficulties.

4. Durability

A good security must possess the quality of durability. Perishable goods cannot be stored for long. So they are not accepted as good banking securities. Durable goods, alone can be stored for a reasonable period. So they are accepted as good banking securities.

5. Free from price fluctuations

An ideal security is one which is free from wide price fluctuations. When the price of the security falls suddenly, the value of the security becomes lesser than the amount of the loan granted. Hence, there arises a necessity of demanding further securities, or reducing the amount of the loan already sanctioned. It involves additional burden on the part of the banker.

6. Easy ascertainment of value

The security must be capable of being valued without much difficulties. In the case of gold, silver, stock exchange securities, consumer goods, etc., daily market reports are available. So their valuation is not difficult.

7. Earning of income

A good security must be capable of earning income. Such incomes can be appropriated towards the loan amount. For instance, stocks and shares of well established companies earn a steady dividend. Such securities are preferable to a banker.

8. Free from heavy cost of handling

The securities should not involve much handling cost. Bulky materials, which are difficult to store and expensive to handle should not be accepted by a banker.

9. Free from disabilities

Certain securities have some inherent defects in them. For example, partly paid-up shares, a life insurance policy without admission of age, etc., are crippled with certain disabilities. So a banker should avoid such securities.

General Principles of Secured Advances

The following are the general principles or precautions which a banker should observe while granting advances against securities.

1. Validity of the title of the borrower

First of all, the banker must ascertain whether the borrower has a good title to the security. If he is satisfied with the title of the borrower, he must then get the title transferred to him by executing the necessary documents. In any case, a banker cannot obtain a better title than the borrower.

2. Nature of the security

The banker should pay attention to the nature of the security. He must see whether the security possess all the qualities of a good security. A good security must be durable, storable and easily realisable in the market.

3. Free from defects

In the case of secured advances, a banker relies more on the security rather than the credit worthiness of the borrower. Hence, the banker should see that these securities are completely free from defects.

4. Documentation

Documentation is an important step in bank lending. The bank should see that proper documents, such as mortgage deed or pledge or hypothecation arrangement containing all the terms and conditions of the charge are executed. This should be done in order to avoid all future disputes. The documentation procedure differs from bank to bank. Documentation is noting but the process of putting down the terms and conditions of the loan sanctioned in writing.

5. Adequate margin

"Margin" means the excess of the market value of the security over the advance granted against it. The percentage of margin differs from one security to another. A banker must keep adequate margin while granting loans and advances because of the following reasons.

(a) The market value of the security is subject to fluctuations. In case of a fall in the value of the security, the interests of the bank are safe if there is an adequate margin.

(b) The loan amount is going on increasing year after year, since the interest is added to it. But the value of security may remain the same or if may even come down. If the value of security falls, a part of the security becomes unsecured automatically. Hence, adequate margin is needed.

(c) In case of commodities which are subject to Reserve Bank's selective controls, the banker has to keep margin in accordance with the directions of the Reserve Bank.

Form the above discussion, undoubtedly, we can say that all the above principles are very important. But let it not be forgotten that the principles of banking are very dynamic and the banker has to frame his policy in such a way as to suit credit requirements of the economic system of the country.

Types of Securities on which Loans or Advances can be Granted

The following are the important types of securities against which loans or advances are generally granted:

Types of Securities

A. Goods
B. Documents of title to goods
C. Stock exchange securities
D. Real estates
E. Life Insurance policies
F. Fixed Deposits Receipts
G. Book debts

A. Advances against Goods

Banks lend a large part of their funds on the security of goods. The goods may be agricultural products like paddy, rice, wheat, cotton, oil-seeds and raw-jute. They may be manufactured goods like cloth and sugar. They include minerals also. Advances against goods are mainly granted for working capital requirements of business and industries. Lord chorley remarks that 'advances against security of goods are a usual and proper form of banking business". The bankers in India are increasingly lending against goods. Goods are accepted as security by pledge or hypothecation.

Advantages : Goods, as securities are popular among bankers because of their merits. The following are the merits of goods as securities against bank advances.

1. Tangible security

Goods are tangible securities, and so, they are better than guarantees. They can be sold in the market, when the borrower makes a default.

2. Easy realisability

Most of the goods like rice, wheat, sugar, etc., are the necessities of life. So there is always a ready market for them. Hence, they can be easily disposed off in the market, if the borrower makes any default.

3. Easy ascertainment of prices

The prices of goods can be known very easily because daily market reports are published in papers, or announced through radio and television.

4. No price fluctuations

The price of most of the goods are more or less steady.

5. Short-period advances

Advances against goods are always given for short-periods, because most of the goods cannot be stored for a long-period. So, goods satisfy the cannon of liquidity.

6. Easy to create a charge

A charge over goods can be created very easily and with minimum formalities. It does not require any registration of documents, payment of stamp duty, etc., as in the case of real estate.

7. Promotes commerce

Banks promote the development of trade, both internal and international, by lending against goods. Thus they help the people to get necessities of life easily and cheaply. Such advances will be source of strength, stimulation and stability to trade and industry.

Drawbacks or demerits : Goods are safe, sound and dependable securities for a banker. But they are not without risks or demerits. The following are the demerits of goods as securities :

1. Risk of deterioration

Most of the goods are liable to deterioration and damage unless they are properly stored. The quality of some goods will be affected if stored for a long time. For example, fruits and vegetables perish within a short-time. Goods like rice and wheat also lose weight due to evaporation. The colour of cotton will change if stored for a long time. Moisture affects sugar and Jaggery Damages to goods by rats, ants, climatic variations cannot be ignored. As a result, the value of security falls with the passage of time.

2. Risk of fraud

There are greater risks of fraud as regards quantity and quality. Goods of good quality may be mixed up with inferior quality. Again, the contents of packages or bags alleged to contain certain goods may not contain such goods. Moreover, there is a possibility for shortage of goods in each bag. It is humanly impossible for a banker to check each and every bag.

3. Risk of price fluctuations

The prices of some goods fluctuate widely. For example, the prices of luxury goods may fall considerably if they go out of fashion. Industrial goods also subject to very heavy price fluctuations. Bankers are generally reluctant to accept the goods or commodities the prices of which are uncertain and fluctuate too widely and frequently.

4. Risk of storage and verification

The banker is in absolute control of godowns to store the goods, which have been pledged to secure a loan. There are no public warehouses in most of the towns. So the goods given as security have to be kept generally in the godowns of the borrower. The borrower may remove the goods given as security without the knowledge of the banker. Dishonest borrowers may cheat the bank. It is a problem for the banker to verify the physical existence of goods from time to time.

5. Risk of prior charge

Prior charge may exist in respect of the same goods. In such a case, the banker will lose his security. For example, the godown keeper may enjoy a prior lien over the goods in his godown in respect of the godown charges due to him.

6. Heavy transport cost

When the borrower makes a default, these goods have to be brought to the market for sale. It involves transportation of goods. The transport cost is always high in India.

7. Valuation difficult

A banker must have good knowledge of market conditions of various goods. Besides, he must be able to distinguish between various varieties. Otherwise, valuation becomes difficult.

Precautions to be taken by the bankers : In view of the above drawbacks or demerits, a banker should be very cautious while granting advances against goods. He should take the following precautions:

1. Character of the borrower

The banker should take into account the honesty, integrity and trustworthiness of the borrower. It is so because, a man of good character will not indulge in fraudulent activities like adulteration, use of false weights, measures etc.

2. Experience in the business

The banker should also find out whether the customer has sufficient experience in the particular trade in which he has engaged himself. Only experienced persons can know the risks involved in a business, and also the profitable areas of the business. It is always risky to deal with inexperienced persons.

3. Title of the borrower

The banker should ascertain whether the borrower has a genuine title to the goods. This can be done by verifying the invcices or cash receipts.

4. Purpose of the loan

The banker must enquire into the purpose for which the loan is required. The repayment of any loan depends upon the purpose for which it is required. If the loan is required for productive purposes or preparing the goods for resale, loan can be granted without any hesitation. On the other hand, if the loan is asked for speculation, black marketing and hoarding, a banker should refuse it.

5. Proper valuation of goods

Adequate care should be taken to value the goods. It is on the basis of valuation, margin is fixed. Hence, a banker can appoint even experts to value the goods. He should not be carried away by invoice prices, since they might be inflated. So, he should actually compare the prices quoted in the bill with the prices prevailing in the market.

6. Nature of Goods

The banker should pay special attention to the nature of goods as well. Some of the goods cannot be stored for long, since their quality is very much affected. Hence, a banker should prefer only those goods which are not subject to deterioration in quality and which are easily realisable.

7. Proper storage

Necessary care should be taken to see that the pledged goods are properly stored. The banker should also see that proper steps are taken to prevent loss of goods on account of rats and white ants. Besides, he must ask the customer to insure the goods against loss by fire, theft, and all possible risks. He should maintain godown register and record the particulars of goods stored in the godown.

8. Care in a rented godown

If the goods are stored in a rented godown, the banker must establish his prior lien with the owner of the building by means of an agreement. Otherwise, the owner will have a prior lien over the goods in respect of the rent charges due.

9. Take possession of goods

The banker should take delivery of the goods before granting any loan. This delivery may be actual or constructive delivery. The banker should always deal with the owner of goods or agent in possession of goods. When it is possible or practicable to take possession of goods given as security, the banker must ask the customer to enter into a contract of hypothecation.

10. Godown keys

The godown keys must be handled very carefully. They should be kept in a strong room under dual control.

11. Adequate insurance

All goods subject to a charge must be insured upto the full market value of the goods. They must be insured against all possible risks. The policy and the premium receipts should be kept by the bank.

12. Periodical inspection

The godown should be inspected by the banker periodically. The quality and quantity of goods in stock must be tallied with the records maintained by both the banker and the customer. If there is any difference, the customer should be put into task.

13. Strict supervision over the release of goods

Sometimes, the borrowers may be allowed to repay the loan in instalments. In such a case, the banker should ensure that the goods released are only in proportion to the amount of loan repaid. Each release must be directly supervised by a responsible officer of the bank.

14. Short-period advances

Loans against goods must be granted only for short-periods, because the value of goods is likely to fall due to deterioration in their quality.

15. Bank's name board

The godowns containing pledged goods must be locked by the bank's padlock. The bank's name board, reading "Goods pledged to ....Bank" should be affixed permanently outside the godown in a prominent place.

16. Directives of Reserve Bank

The Reserve Bank of India often issues directives prescribing margins on various goods. These margins and other stipulations prescribed by the Reserve Bank should be carefully followed by banks while lending against goods.

B. Advances against Documents of Title to Goods

Documents, which in the ordinary course of trade, are regarded as proof of the possession or control of the goods are called "documents of title to goods". They authorises the possessor or holder to transfer or receive the goods represented by them. Thus the documents of title actually represent goods. They can be transferred by mere delivery or by endorsement and delivery. The delivery of these documents actually amounts to a symbolic delivery of goods represented by them. Banks find it easy to deal with these documents than physically dealing with goods. Hence, these documents are very popular among banks. The following are the important documents of title to goods.

1. Bill of lading
2. Dock warrant
3. Warehouse keeper's certificate
4. Delivery order
5. Railway receipt and lorry receipt

1. Bill of lading

A bill of lading is a document issued and signed by ship owners or captain of the ship, acknowledging that the goods mentioned in the bill have been duly received on board and undertaking to deliver the goods in the like order and condition to the consignee or his order or assignee. The goods will be delivered subject to the payment of freight and other charges specified in the bill of lading.

A bill of lading can be transferred either by endorsement or delivery. The goods mentioned in the bill are to be delivered to the legal-holder. The bill of lading is a proof that the goods have been dispatched by the exporter. The importer cannot claim the goods without the production of the bill of lading.

2. Dock warrant

It is a document issued by a dock company. The document describes the goods, acknowledges the receipt of them and undertakes to deliver them to the order of the depositor.

3. Warehouse keeper's certificate

It is a document given by a warehouse keeper, certifying that he holds certain goods described therein and awaits instruction for their disposal form the person to whom the certificate is addressed.

4. Delivery order

It is a document addressed to the proprietors of the warehouse where the goods are lodged by the owner. It contains his instructions regarding delivery of goods.

5. Railway receipt

A railway receipt is a document of title to goods issued by the railway authorities. It is also a document acknowledging the receipt of goods to be handed over to the payee or his order at the destination.

Merits : Banker advances loans to the customer on the security of documents of title to goods. These documents, as securities, have all the advantages and disadvantages of goods as securities. The reason is that documents of title to goods are symbols of title to goods. The merits are as follows.

(a) These advances are better than guarantees. They have the backing of goods.

(b) The goods have ready and wide market.

(c) Determination of valuation is easy.

(d) Advances are mostly for shorter periods.

(e) The goods have stable prices.

(f) They can be easily disposed off in case of default of payment by the borrower.

(g) These are quasi-negotiable instruments. They can be transferred by mere endorsement and delivery.

Risks or Demerits : Granting of advances against documents of title involve the following risks.

(a) The documents of title to goods give greater scope to commit frauds. In case of goods, the banker can satisfy himself by examining the quality and quantity of the goods. But this is not possible when a document of title is accepted as a security.

(b) The documents of title to goods may be created by sending defective and rejected goods also. There are ample scope for dishonest and unscrupulous persons to indulge in fraudulent activities.

(c) There is scope for forgery of documents of the title to goods. The bankers cannot get any right of ownership to the goods covered by forged documents since the rule is "forgery conveys no title".

(d) There is scope to alter the contents in the documents of title to goods.

(e) The transport companies do not give guarantee about the contents of the bags or packages etc. There may be pilferages in transit.

(f) The unpaid seller has got the right to stop the goods in transit the borrower becomes insolvent before the goods are delivered. In such a case, the banker runs the risk of losing the goods.

(g) There is scope for deterioration or damage of the goods during transit or storage.

(h) In the case of some commodities, there is scope for fluctuation of prices especially in regard to luxury goods.

(i) Sometimes, it becomes difficult to determine the value of certain types of goods.

(j) Some railway receipts are negotiable. In such a case, if the borrower has the defective title, the banker gets no better title.

(k) The railway receipts do not give correct discription of the goods dispatched.

(l) There is a tendency among borrowers to deposit bogus railway receipts or lorry receipts with a view to defraud the banker.

Precautions

The banker has to take the following precautions while accepting the documents of title to goods as securities.

1. Integrity and honesty of the borrower

The banker has to look to the honesty, integrity, capacity, character and credit worthiness of the borrower. The advances are to be made only to trusted and reliable borrowers.

2. Certificate Regarding Packing

The banker has to ask the customer to provide him with the certificate of packing in order to verify the quality and quantity of the goods-in-transit.

3. Depositing of all Copies of Bill of Lading

The banker has to ask the customer to deposit all the copies of bill of lading. Usually the importer is supplied with three copies of bill of lading. If all the copies are not taken over by the banker, the customer may frauduently take delivery of the goods from the shipping company or he may pledge the other copies with another bank by misrepresentation.

4. Documents without Onerous Conditions

The banker should accept only those documents which do not increase the burden or responsibility. For example, the banker may have to pay heavy charges for securing release of goods if there is a qualification in taking the delivery of goods.

5. Blank endorsement

The banker has to take blank endorsement on the document. Otherwise, he is liable to pay all incidental charges of transport.

6. Insurance

The banker has to see that goods are insured to cover the risk of voyage or transport. The banker has to examine whether the insurance policy covers all the risks. Further, he can have an idea of the goods and the value of goods from the insurance policy.

7. Trust Receipt

The banker should not part with the documents until the arrangements are made to secure the loans. He cannot take delivery of goods from steamship company unless the documents are handed over to the customer. So when the bill of lading and other related documents are handed over to the importer (customer) in order to enable him to take delivery of goods, he must obtain a trust receipt from the importer (customer). By executing a trust receipt, the customer agrees to hold goods or sale proceeds of the goods in trust for the banker till the loan amount is rapid. If the customer fails to pay the loan amount, he will be held liable for criminal breach of trust.

8. Clean Documents

The banker should not sanction loans and advances against the documents containing objectionable remarks about packing. At the time of granting loans and advances, the banker should always sanctions loans against the clean documents only.

9. Control

In case the customer fails to get delivery of goods, the banker should take over the goods in its control, store them and later on dispose of them under the instructions of the customers.

From the above discussion, it is made clear that the banker should take precautions carefully before lending money against the security of goods and documents of title to goods. If the banker does so, he will be able to avoid risks in transactions and also utilise his funds in productive purposes.

C. Advances against Stock Exchange Securities

Shares and debentures which are regularly purchased and sold in the stock exchange may be accepted as security by the bank. A stock exchange is an organised market where securities are purchased and old. The securities traded on the floor of a stock exchange include the following.

(a) Bonds issued by the Central and State Governments.

(b) Securities issued by semi-Government authorities like port trusts, electricity boards, improvement trusts, etc. ; and

(c) Shares and debentures issued by the companies.

Merits of Advances against Stock Exchange Securities

Banks made advances against the security of above mentioned securities. The following are the merits of stock exchange securities as cover for bank advances.

(a) Better than Guarantee

Stock exchange securities provide a better security than is provided by a contract of guarantee because securities, even though they are paper documents, are treated as tangible assets. In case of default by the borrower, the bank can sell the securities in the market to recover the loan.

(b) Marketability

Stock exchange securities have a wide and a ready market. They can be sold easily in the stock exchange because they are on the active list of the recognised stock exchange.

(c) Liquidity

Since securities are easily marketable, they are highly liquid. A bank can get cash by selling the securities. Moreover, if a bank does not want to sell the securities, especially the Government ones, it can get accommodation by pledging them with the Reserve Bank of India.

(d) Steady Price

In normal times, the fluctuation in the prices of popular stock exchange securities are less than the changes in the prices of commodities like cotton and oils. More particularly, the fluctuations in the prices of Government securities are very small. So the banks can readily advance loans against the security of Government securities.

(e) Income

The stock exchange securities are not idle assets. They yield income by way of interest or dividend. The amount of income so received can be credited to the loan account of the borrower to reduce his indebtedness.

(f) Convenience

Advancing loans on the basis of stock exchange securities is convenient in many respects. Firstly, it is easy to know the market value of the securities because stock exchange quotations appear in every leading newspaper. Moreover, prices can be known over the phone from the stock exchange. Secondly, it is very easy to ascertain the title of the borrower to the relevant securities by writing to the issuing authority or body. Thirdly, it is easy to transfer stock exchange securities; and lastly it is easy to recover the loan by selling the security in the case of default.

(g) Quick release of Security

The securities can be easily released on discharge of the loan. The securities can again be registered in the name of the borrower without much expenses and formalities.

Risks in Advancing against Securities

The following are the demerits of stock exchange securities as security against advances.

(a) Forfeiture of Securities

If the bank makes advance against partly paid securities and gets them transferred in its name, it may be called upon to pay the remaining balance. If the customer does not pay the calls, the bank will have to pay the calls to avoid the forfeiture of securities.

(b) Non-Negotiability

The stock exchange securities are generally not negotiable instruments. So the bank as a pledgee cannot get a better title than that of the pledger. However, in case of bearer securities, this risk will not be there.

(c) Fluctuation in Prices

The prices of certain securities, particularly shares and debentures of companies, fluctuate widely because of many factors. A bank will suffer loss if it does not keep sufficient margin and the price of a share or a debenture goes down considerably. Wide fluctuations in prices of the securities make them less liquid sometimes, because there are no purchasers and sellers of such securities in the stock exchange.

(d) Company's Lien

The articles of association of most of the companies contain a clause that the company will have a right of lien for the calls or any other amount due by the shareholders. The securities of such companies should not be accepted as security against loans.

(e) Forged Certificates

It is difficult for a bank to distinguish between a genuine share certificate and a forged one. If the bank advances loan against a forged certificate by mistake, it will incur a loss.

Precautions to be Taken in Advancing against Securities

A bank should take the following precautions while making advances against stock exchange securities.

1. Choice of Securities

A bank cannot advance money blindly against each and every security because all the securities are not worth accepting. A bank should continuously examine the approved list of securities dealt with on the stock exchange. It must study the progress and working of various companies whose securities are dealt with on the stock exchange. It must study the audited balance sheets and profit and loss accounts of various companies and the constitution of their boards of directors. On the basis of the study, the bank should prepare a list of securities against which advances may be made. This list must be revised atleast after every quarter. This will reduce risk of making advances on undesirable stock exchange securities.

2. Valuation of Securities

If a customer offers a security against the advance which is in the approved list of the bank, the next step is the valuation of the security. The bank must ascertain the value of the shares and other securities with proper care. Securities cannot, generally, be taken at their face value. Market value is the deciding factor in this case. Generally, the prices of the shares are quoted cum dividend. Bank should deduct the dividend from the current market price. However, a bank should not rely completely on the stock exchange quotations. It should study the economic conditions of the country and the industry concerned. This will help to know the reasons if the price of the security is abnormally high or low.

3. Adequate Margins

The prices of some securities fluctuate widely because of various reasons. A bank should keep adequate margin while lending against the securities so that it may not suffer any loss when there is a heavy fall in the price of the concerned securities.

4. Debentures and Preference Shares

The bank should prefer preference shares and debentures to equity shares because the fluctuations in the prices of debentures and preference shares are small. Similarily, fluctuations in the market prices of the Government and semi-Government securities are small. So they may be preferred by the banks.

5. Partly-paid Securities

When a security or share is offered to a bank, it should examine whether it is partly-paid or fully-paid. Bank should not take the unnecessary risk of advancing against partly-paid shares. Calls may be made against these shares by the company and if the customer fails in paying the calls, the shares are likely to be forfeited. However, if the customer is highly creditworthy, the bank may advance the loan to him against the partly-paid shares. In such a case, it is better to take an undertaking from the customer that he would pay the call, if made by the company.

6. Transfer of Securities

If the securities are bearer and negotiable, the bank can obtain the title by mere delivery. If the securities are registered one, the bank must get the transfer deed signed by the borrower. The bank's charge over the shares will be complete if shares are transferred in its name in the books of the company. When the loan is repaid, the bank may transfer back the shares to the customer.

Alternatively, the bank may secure an equitable charge on the securities. In such a case, the bank should take a 'Memorandum of Deposit' from the customer to make the equitable charge effective. The bank should also obtain a blank transfer deed duly signed by the customer. In case of default, the bank can fill in the transfer deed and get the securities registered in its own name and afterwards sell the securities to realise the loan.

Whenever a bank makes an advance against shares or debentures, it must give a notice to the concerned company stating its interest in the shares deposited with it as security. This will prevent the issue of duplicate certificate by the company

In addition to the above mentioned precautions, the bank should not advance loan against its own shares as it is prohibited by see. 20 of the Banking Regulation Act. The sum total of advances against the stock exchange securities should not exceed 30% of the paid-up capital of the banking company.

D. Advances against Real Estate

By the term 'real estate' is meant "all types of immovable properties including tangible assets like land, building etc. Generally, commercial banks do not favour granting of loans and advances against the security of real estates due to a number of risks and demerits. The commercial banks accept real estate as security in the exceptional cases only, i.e., if the customer has no security to offer except real estate.

Causes of Refusing Real Estate as Security

The commercial banks do not stand in a position to accept real estate as security for their advances on account of a number of difficulties or drawbacks. These difficulties are discussed below.

1. Customer's Title.
2. Heavy Expenses.
3. Valuation.
4. Legal Formalities.
5. Loss of Liquidity.
6. Delay in Realisation.
7. Administration of Properties.
8. Maintenance.

1. Customer's Title

While advancing loans against real estate, customer's title is the major problem. It is very difficult for the banker to find out the customer's interest in the property. When the customers offer property as security particularly in case of agricultural lands etc., the banker has to spend much more time and money to verify the title of the borrower on one side and on the other side, the property may be disputed one.

2. Heavy Expenses

Whereas the bank takes decision to grant loans and advances against the immovable security, the customer has to spend heavy amount in mortgaging the property. In such circumstances, the customer wants to take loan for a long period as legal mortgage is not only expensive but also inconvenient. It is to be noted here that legal mortgage is not a good idea for the customer because it may put an additional burden upon him (customer).

3. Valuation

Another major problem is valuation of property before the bank. A banker cannot rely on its own judgement for this purpose. The value of immovable property depends upon the type of construction, location etc. For such confirmations, the banks have to employ qualified valuers for the purpose.

4. Legal Formalities

While advancing against real estate or property, a number of legal formalities, such as preparation of the mortgage deed, its registration, payment of stamp duty etc. must be completed by the banker and the customer.

5. Loss of Liquidity

When the customers offer immovable property as security, they demand to take loan for a long period because they have to spend much of their time and money on the compliances of papers. In such case if the commercial banks grant loans and advances for a long period, these will affect their liquidity position since, if the customers do not repay loans and advances, it will be very difficult for the bankers to dispose off their immovable properties in the market.

6. Delay in Realisation

In case the mortgager is unable to repay the amount due from him, the banker has to undergo many formalities before the sale of the mortgaged property can be completed. Consequently, the banker has to wait for many months, because it is not possible for the customers to get back banker's moneys.

7. Administration of Properties

As the mortagagee of land and buildings, the banker may be required to administer the land and buildings and also collect rents and keep accounts.

8. Maintenance

In case the customer fails to repay the loan, the banker has to recover the loan by selling its mortgaged property. It is very difficult for the banker to look after the maintenance of the property.

Precautions in Advancing against Real Estate

While lending money against the security of real estate, the banker should take the following precautions.

1. Verification of Title

While advancing money against the real estate as security, the banker should verify the title deeds of the customer very carefully. The banker should also examine the deed through its solicitors. It should be also necessary for the banker to verify if his borrower's property is disputed or not.

2. Tenures of Land

Before accepting real estate as security, the banker should see that the borrower's land must be freehold, leasehold or state-owned. In addition, there may be several changes in the land tenure frequently. While advancing loans, the banker should have knowledge regarding these changes because these are material facts for the bank.

3. Expert Valuation

The valuation of property is a very difficult task. Though the bank is not a valuer but where the loan is granted against real estate as security, the bank should entrust this difficult task to the expert valuers. The value of property depends upon the following.

(a) The location of the property.

(b) Ownership right.

(c) The rental value.

(d) The type of construction

(e) The size and structure of land.

4. Margin

While lending against the real estate, the banker should keep adequate margin. The banker should not grant loans and advances to the extent of more than 50 to 60 percent of the real value of the borrower's property. For instance, where the value of the property is Rs. 5,000/-, the banker should grant loans and advances against the property for less than Rs. 3,000/-. By doing so, the banker may have to avoid involved risks.

5. Insurance

Before granting loans, the banker should examine that the properties of the borrowers are insured against fire and other calamities and the policy should be assigned in favour of the bank.

6. Tax and Rent Payment

Before accepting real estate as security the banker should obtain the receipt for the payment of house-tax and other taxes and must be kept along with title deeds. The banker should also see that all dues are regularly paid or not.

7. Legal Mortgage

According to Section 59 of the Transfer of Property Act, 1882, "Whereas the principal money secured is one hundred rupees or more, a mortgage other than a mortgage by deposit of title deeds (equitable mortgages) can be effected only by a registered instrument signed by the mortgager and attested by at least two witness". Whereas the borrower happens to be a joint stock company, all mortgages must be registered with the Registrar of Companies within 30 days of the date of their creation.

8. Clearance of Income Tax

Before accepting real estate as security, the banker should obtain a certificate from the borrower issued by Income Tax Office about the clearance of the property of the borrower. Under Section 230-A of the Income Tax-Act, 1961, registration of any property (other than agricultural land) is valued at more than Rs. 50,000/- is a must.

From the above discussion, it has been seen that making of advances on the security of real estate is not popular kind of business with commercial banks because commercial banks are not in a position to take their own judgement. These depend upon others both as regards the valuation of the immovable property offered as security as well as the title deeds of the person proposing to mortgage the same.

E. Advances against Life Insurance Policies

A Life Insurance Policy is accepted by bankers as a main security or as a supplementary security. Whereas the banker accepts life insurance policy as a main security, he advances between 85 to 90 per cent of its surrender value. But as a supplementary form, a life insurance policy is more useful because it is advisable to cover the signature by the life of the guaranter.

In India, life insurance business has been nationalised and it is being done by the Life Insurance Corporation of India (LIC). The Corporation has launched several types of insurance policies in the interest and nature of different customers. Some of these policies are the whole-life policy, money-back policy, joint life policy etc.

Merits of Life Insurance Policy as a Security

The life insurance policy is considered good as security due to the following causes.

1. Guarantee of payment

The life insurance policy business is conducted by LIC of India which is a government undertaking and as such the payments, as and when due of all the policies are guaranteed. The risk will be minimised if the banker lends the money against the life insurance policy as security.

2. Legally Assigned

The policy can be legally assigned to the banker and such an assignment is duly registered with the Life Insurance Corporation. Thus, there is no risk in advancing against life insurance policies.

3. Surrender Value

The surrender value of a life insurance policy goes on increasing with the passage of time if the premium is regularly paid. In such circumstances, there is no risk in lending the money against such policy.

4. Easy Supervision

In case the banker advances money against the policy as security, the legal or general duty of a banker is always to keep an eye on the regular premium payments. By taking such steps the risk may be avoided.

5. Self-Liquidating

In the even of the death of the borrower, the loan becomes self-liquidated in nature.

Demerits of Policies as Securities

The life insurance policy has not been very popular with bankers in India. J.W. Gilbert in his book, Logic of Banking observed : "A banker should never make any advances upon the life policies". The shortcoming or demerits of lending money against the life insurance policy are discussed below.

1. Non-disclosure of Material Fact

A contract of life insurance is a contract uberrimae fidei (utmost good faith.) The assured person is bound to make full disclosure of all the material facts within his knowledge to the insurer. In case, there is non-disclosure of any material fact by the assured it may enable there is the insurance company to avoid the claim under the policy. Further, if the assured is found guilty of fraud, the banker shall stand the risk of losing his money.

Section 45 of the Insurance Act, 1938 states : "No insurance policy shall be disputed after it has been in force for two years from the date effecting the policy on the ground of any misrepresentation even as to a material fact, except where the misrepresentation alleged to have been made as to a material fact was knowingly made by the insured in order to defraud the insurance company".

2. Risks in Case of Suicide

The policies issued by the Life Insurance Corporation of India contain a 'suicide clause' stating that if the assured commits suicide within one year from the date of the policy, the security becomes null and void.

3. Irregular Payment of Premia

In case the insured fails to pay the premium regularly, the policy may be lapsed. The surrender value of a policy depends upon the class to which it belongs and the number of years it has been inforce.

4. Unsatisfactory Nature of Law

In India, the bankers do not favour life policies as security for advances on account of unsatisfactory state of law relating to the question of assignment.

Precautions in Advancing against LIC Policies

While accepting life insurance policies as security, the following precautions should be taken by bankers.

1. Endowment Policy Favoured

While lending money against life insurance policy as security, the banker should try to accept endowment policy to whole life policy as there is a definite maturity date in the case of the endownment class. But in the case of the whole-life policy the banker may have to wait for a long time, before the (Banker) may realise his advance from the policy-money.

2. Admission of the Age

Before loan is granted, the banker should examine carefully that the age of the insured has been duly admitted by the Life Insurance Corporation of India. The banker should also obtain a copy of the proof before loan is granted.

3. Restriction of Assignment

Before advancing money against the life insurance policy, the banker should see that there are no restrictions on the assignment of the policy.

4. Margin

Ordinarily the banker should advance only 85 to 90 percent of the surrender value of the policy. But in the case of endowment policy, the banker may exceed this percentage if he is sure that premium of the policy is paid regularly.

5. Insurable Interest

For the validity of life insurance policy, the insurable interest is necessary. This interest is contained in the following cases.

(a) That of a husband in the life of his wife.

(b) That of the wife in her husband's life.

(c) That of a person in his/her own life.

6. Legal Assignment

Before advancing money, the legal assignment of the policy should be taken by the banker. For example, if the policy is taken out by a husband for the benefit of his wife, the husband and wife should sign the assignment. According to Section 38 (1) of the Insurance Act, 1938, "the assignment can be made either by an endorsement on the policy itself or by a separate instrument signed in either case by the transferor or his duly authorised agent and attested by at least one witness specifically setting forth the fact of the transfer or assignment".

7. Precautions Regarding Certain Policies

Some insured policies cannot be legally assigned, e.g., the policy which comes under Section 6 of the Married Women's Property Act which creates a number of profits for the wife and children of the insured. The banker should not grant any advance against such policy.

8. No Prior Encumbrances

While granting loans, the banker should make it clear from the Corporation that the policy does not have any prior encumbrances or charge against it.

In short, before accepting life insurance policy as security the banker should satisfy himself that the insured person has completed all the formalities and the premium also is paid regularly. Thus the banker may avoid his risks or at least minimise his risks.

F. Advance against Fixed Deposits Receipts

The term 'Fixed Deposit' means the money or deposit which is repayable on the expiry of a fixed period of time. This time-period may very from 15 days to 60 months. In case a person deposits his surplus funds or money with the bank for some fixed period, he (customer) is issued 'Fixed Deposit Receipt' by the Bank. The Fixed Deposit Account cannot be withdrawn before the expiry date, as mentioned in the Fixed Deposit Receipt. But sometimes, depositor may require advance-money before the due date of maturity. In such case, ordinarily banks extend advancing facility to their customers, but it should be noted here that banks are not bound to extend such facility. Another option is beneficial for the banker and the customer. Suppose, a Fixed Deposit is made for 36 months and the customer demands money after one or two months, it will be better for the customer to take loan against his Fixed Deposit Receipt. In such case the banker will gain by charging a higher interest rate than allowed on deposits.

Precautions in Advancing against Fixed Deposit Receipt

While granting loans and advances against Fixed Deposit Receipts, the banker should take the following precautions.

1. Receipt must be Issued by Concerned Bank

When the bank grants loans and advances against the Fixed Deposit Receipt, it should be issued by the bank itself. The bank should not grant loans and advances on the Fixed Deposit Receipt which has been issued by another bank. For instance, State Bank of India issued a Fixed Deposit Receipt to Mr. A and in case Mr. A requires money against such receipt, it will be good for State Bank of India to sanction loan against the receipt, as in such case, there will be no risk for the banker.

2. Original Depositor

While advancing money, the banker should see that loan must be granted to the person whose name has been entered in Deposit Receipt. In case the Fixed Deposit Receipt is in favour of two or more than two persons, the loan is sanctioned to one of them, the banker should obtain a letter of authority on which the signatures must be made by depositors.

3. Maintain Ledger and Register

Where the banker grants loans and advances against the Fixed Deposit Receipt, the banker should made a note of its lien across the receipt as well as in the Fixed Deposit Ledger and Register.

4. Margin

The loan must be granted by the banker with the margin of 5 to 10 percent. The bank should not sanction loan exceeding the Fixed Deposit Receipt value. For instance, Mr. A has been issued a Fixed Deposit Receipt of Rs. 10,000/- on January 11, 1993 and in case he demands loan on March 4, 1993, the banker should not sanction loan more than Rs. 9,500/-.

5. Interest Rate

In case the bank advances money against the Fixed Deposit Receipt, the banker should get 2 percent higher interest rate than what is payable by the bank on the deposit, if the deposit is in the name of the borrower only. For example, in case the deposit carries interest at 12 percent per annum, the bank must be charged interest on loan against such a deposit at 14 percent per annum.

6. Others

a) The banker should discourage the loans to a minor against the Fixed Deposit Receipt on account of legal complication. b) The banker should take actual possession of the later signed by the depositor or depositors, in case the customer fails to pay the loan on due date.

G. Advance against Book Debts

Sometimes banks may grant loans and advances to the customers against the security of book-debts. Whereas the bank is fully satisfied with the solvency of the customers, such types of advances may be granted. In terms of Economics, the book-debt means "the amount which the customer of the bank has to get from other persons".

Book-debts are also known as 'actionable claim' and according to Section 130 of the Transfer of Property Act, 1882, the actionable claim means, "a claim to any debt or any beneficial interest in movable property not in the possession of the claimant which the civil courts recognise, as affecting grounds for relief, whether such debt or beneficial interest be existent, accruing, conditional or contingent".

When the bank grants loans and advances against the security of book-debts, it may have to bear many risks on account of any default by the borrower. In such case, it may act as a debt-collector, which he does not like to be placed. Here, it is no doubt to say that book-debts are one of the more risky securities because in case the customer does not repay the loan, the bank may have to serve notice to the customer and if he (customer) does not follow the notice, in such case, the bank will have to start legal proceedings against his customer.

Precautions in Advancing against Book Debts

The banker should take the following precautions while lending money against the security of book-debts.

1. Writing

While lending loans and advances against the book-debts as security, the banker has to act as an assignee of the debts whereas the customer acts as an assigner. The banker should see that the assignment or the agreement between the banker and the customer must be shown in writing.

2. Undertaking

Whereas advancing is granted against the security of book-debts he (banker) should obtain an undertaking from his borrower to pass all payments received by him in respect of the assigned debts to the banker.

3. Solvency and Honesty of the Borrower

Before granting loans and advances against the security of book-debts, the banker should carefully examine the solvency, creditworthiness and honesty of the borrowers. The banker should also check the past experience and market reports of the borrower.

4. Margin

While making advances against the security of book-debts, the banker should keep adequate margins. The basis of the margin must be modified from time to time, and generally it varies from 25 per cent to 40 per cent.

5. Verify the Statement

There should be legal responsibility for the banker to examine the periodical statement of the borrower and also examine the genuineness of the outstandings while lending money against the book-debts.

6. Registration is Must

While advancing against the security of book-debts to limited companies (on the basis of certain conditions), the bank's charges should be duly registered with the Registrar of Companies.

7. Notice of Assignment is Necessary

While lending money against book-debts, the banker should give the notice of assignment to the debtor. It is necessary to prevent the debtor from making payment of the debt to the customer.

From the above discussion, it is clear that the banker should take precautions very carefully while advancing money against the security of Fixed Deposit Receipt and book-debts. If he fails to take precautions, he will have be bear a great loss.

Conclusion

From the above discussion, it is clear that the banker should precautions very carefully while advancing money against the security of goods, documents of title to goods, Life Insurance Policy, real estate, Fixed Deposit Receipt and book-debts. If he fails to take precautions, he will have to bear a great loss.

Questions for Discussions

1. Explain the characteristics of a good security for advancing loan by a banker.
2. What are the principles of secured advances.
3. Mention the precautions which a bank should take in lending against goods and documents of title to goods as collateral.
4. Do you consider a Life Insurance Policy as a good security for an advance and if so, for what reason? In granting an advance against such a policy what are the factors you would specially examine and precautions you would take?
5. What precautions should a banker take while granting a loan against a Fixed Deposit Receipt and Book Debt?
6. Why do commercial banks avoid accepting real estate as security for their advances? What precautions should these take in such transactions?

Chapter - 16

MODES OF CREATING CHARGE

Introduction

Lending is an important function of a commercial bank. While lending, a bank has to keep three important principles in mind, viz, liquidity, profitability and safety. In order to make a safe investment in loans and advances, banks usually insist upon security of some tangible assets. The various types of tangible assets on the security of which banks lend have already been discussed. But a security of tangible asset is of no use unless it is properly charged in favour of the bank. A bank can recover the loan in case of default by the borrower by disposing of the securities only if they are properly charged in favour of the bank. The charge must be registered with the appropriate authorities, wherever required, otherwise the bank may jeopardise its priority therein.

Modes of Creating Charge

The various modes of creating a charge are as follows :

A. Lien,

B. Pledge,

C. Mortgage and

D. Hypothecation.

Each of these types of charges has different legal implications. Rights and obligations of the parties under each of these modes of creating charges are discussed below.

A. Lien

Lien is the right of a creditor to hold possession of the goods of the debtor till he discharges his debt. Right of lien entitles the creditor to retain the security or goods belonging to the debtor till the payment of debt. Lien can be either (a) a general lien, or (b) a particular lien. General lien entitles the creditor in possession to retain the goods till all his claims against the owner of the goods have been met. This is applicable in respect of all amount due from the debtor to the creditor. But a particular lien is a specific lien which confers a right to retain those goods for which the amount is to be paid. These types of lien have been discussed in detail in the chapter entitled 'Banker and Customer Relationship'.

Sec. 171 of the Indian Contract Act confers the right of general lien on the bankers. The bankers have lien not only on the securities like cheques and bills of exchange, but also on goods coming into their possession unless there is a contract to the contrary.

B. Pledge

Pledge is the bailment of movable property to secure the payment of debt or the performance of a promise. Sec. 172 of the Indian Contract Act, 1872 defines pledge as the bailment of goods as security for the payment of a debt or performance of a promise. The person who offers the security is called the pledger or pawner and the creditor or the person who accepts the security is called the pledgee or Pawnee.

Pledge is a special kind of bailment. The term 'bailment' has been defined by Sec. 148 of the Indian Contract Act as the delivery of goods by one person to another for some purpose, upon a contract that they shall, when the purpose is accomplished, be returned or otherwise disposed of according to the directions of the person delivering them. The person who delivers the goods is called the 'bailor' and the person to whom the goods are delivered is called the 'bailee'. Bailment may be made for any purpose like repair, storing, security, etc. But pledge is made only for a specific purpose, i.e., as security for payment of a debt or performance of a promise. Thus, pledge is a kind of bailment having the following essential elements.

(a) Goods must be delivered by the pledger to the pledgee. The delivery to the pledgee may be actual or constructive. Delivery of the key of the warehouse where the pledged goods are stored is a constructive delivery and is sufficient to create a pledge. A pledge involves a transfer of possession of the goods pledged and not of title. The ownership of the goods pledged remains with the pledger.

(b) Pledge can be made only of movable properties. Money cannot be pledged.

(c) A contract of pledge must be supported by a valid consideration. The goods should be offered as security for the payment of a debt or the performance of promise.

Difference between Pledge and Lien

Following are the points of difference between a pledge and a lien

1. Pledge is always created by a contract, whereas no contract is necessary for a right of lien. In most of the cases, lien is created by law.
2. Though in both the cases the possession of the goods is transferred to the creditor, yet in case of a lien, the party in possession of the goods does not have in general any right to sell the goods. In case of pledge, the creditor or the pledgee has right to sell the goods in his possession on the default by the debtor.
3. Right of lien is lost with the loss of the possession of the goods. But pledge is not necessarily terminated by return of goods to the owner. The goods pledged may be redelivered to the pledger for a limited purpose.
4. Lien is purely a passive right. Lien-holder can only hold the goods till the payment is made. Lien holder cannot enforce its claim through a court of law. But a pledgee enjoys the right to sue, right of sale and the right of lien'.

Who can Pledge the Goods?

Generally pledge can be made by a person who is the real owner of the goods. But in the following cases, the non-owners of the goods can also make a valid pledge.

1. Pledge by a mercantile agent

Pledge by a mercantile agent, which is not authorised by the owner of the goods, will be valid if the following conditions are fulfilled.

(a) The mercantile agent is in possession of the goods or documents of title to goods with the consent of the owner,

(b) The mercantile agent acts in the ordinary course of business while making the pledge, and

(c) The pledgee has no notice of the fact that pledger has no authority to pledge and he acts in good faith.

2. Pledge by a person in possession under voidable contract

When the pledger has obtained possession of the goods pledged by him under a contract voidable as per Sec. 19 or 19 A of the Indian contract Act but the contract has not been rescinded at the time of pledge, the pledgee acquires a good title to the goods provided he acts in good faith and without notice of pledger's defect of title. Where goods are obtained by theft, a pledge by a thief will not be valid and the pledgee in this case will acquire no lien over the goods.

3. Pledge where the pledger has only a limited interest

Where a pawner or pledger has only a limited interest in the movable goods, the pledge can be valid only to the extent of that interest. Thus, where a person has only a mortgagee's interest or a mere lien, and he pledges the goods, the pledge will be valid only to the extent of that interest.

4. Pledge by a co-owner in possession

When there are several co-owners of the goods and the goods are in the sole possession of one of the co-owner with the consent of other co-owners, such a co-owner can make valid pledge of the goods.

5. Pledge by seller or buyer in possession after sale

A seller who has got possession of the goods even after sale can make a valid pledge provided the pawnee or the pledgee acts in good faith. Similarly, if the buyer obtains possession of goods with the consent of the seller before payment of price and pledges them, the pledgee will get a good title provided he does not have the notice of seller's right of lien or any other right.

Right and Obligations of Pledger

Section 177 of the Indian Contract Act, 1872 states as under :

"If a time is stipulated for the payment of the debt, or performance of the promise for which the pledge is made and the pawner makes default in payment of the debt or performance of the promise at the stipulated time, he may redeem the goods pledged at any subsequent time, before the actual sale of them; but he must, in that case, pay, in addition, any expenses which have arisen from his default".

Rights

From the above statement, the main rights of the pledger are given below.

(a) The pledger has a right to claim accruals to the goods pledged.

(b) The pledger has a right to receive any surplus from the pledgee in case of sale, that may remain with him after the debt is paid off.

(c) The pledger has a right to claim back the security pledged on repayment of the debt along with interest.

(d) In case the pledgee intends to sell the goods, the pledger has a right to receive a notice in stipulated time.

(e) In case there is any increase in the goods, the pledger has right to such increase.

Obligations (Duties)

(a) It is necessary for a pledger to disclose any fault or risk before the pledgee.

(b) The pledger must repay from the loan and take the delivery of the property from the pledgee within the stipulated time.

(c) The pledger is bound for any loss of the pledgee in case of any defects in pledger's title to the goods.

Right and Obligations of Pledgee or Pawnee

The rights of a pledgee are the following.

1. Right of Retainer

The first and foremost right of the pledgee is to retain the goods till he is paid not only the debt but also interest thereon, all necessary expenses incurred by him in respect of the possession or the preservation of the goods pledged.

2. Right to Extraordinary Expenses

Section 175 of the Indian Contract Act, 1872 states : "The pledgee has right to recover from the pledger extraordinary expenses incurred by him for the preservation of the goods pledged, but it should be noted here that pledgee has no right of lien for extraordinary expenses".

3. Right in Case of Default of the Pledger or Pawner

In case of default by the pledger in the payment of debt or the performance of promise at the stipulated time, the pledgee can exercise the following rights under Section 176 of the Indian Contract Act, 1872.

(a) The pledgee has a right to bring a suit on the debt and can retain the goods pledged as a collateral security.

(b) The pledgee has a right to sell the goods pledged after giving reasonable notice of sale to the pledger.

4. Right of Particular Lien

Under Section 174 of the Indian Contract Act, 1872, "A pledgee has no right to retain the goods for any debt or promise other than the debt for which the pledge was made." In the absence of anything to the contrary, the pledgee may retain the goods pledged for the subsequent advances made by him.

Obligation and Duties of Pledgee

(a) The pledgee is bound to return the goods pledged on the payment of debt. In case he fails to do so, he will be liable to the pledger for any loss.

(b) The pledgee is bound to take care of the goods properly and also keep the goods in proper place. In case he does not do so, he will be responsible for any destruction.

From the above discussion, it has been mentioned that the primary purpose of a pledge, is to put the goods pledged in the power of the pledgee to reimburse himself for the money advanced, when on becoming due, it remains unpaid by selling the goods after serving the pledger with a due notice. It is to be said that the pledgee becomes the owner of the goods pledged as such.

C. Mortgage

Mortgage is a mode of charge created on immovable properties, like land and buildings. It is the transfer of legal or equitable interest in property as security for the debt. Section 58 of the Transfer of Property Act, 1882, defines mortgage as "the transfer of an interest in specific immovable property for the purpose of securing the payment of money advanced or to be advanced by way of loan, an existing or future debt, or the performance of an engagement which may give rise to a pecuniary liability". Mortgage, therefore, is a charge granted by a borrower to a lender on part or whole of his property for the repayment of a debt. The transferor is called "mortgager". The transferee is called "mortgagee". The instrument or deed by which the transfer is made is called the "mortgage deed".

Essential Features of a Mortgage

The following are the essential features of a mortgage.

(a) Immovable property

A mortgage can be effected only in respect of immovable properties. Immovable properties include land and building, trees in the forest, standing crops, and any machinery that is permanently fixed to the earth.

(b) Transfer of interest in the property

Creation of a mortgage requires the transfer of interest in a specific immovable property. Transfer of interest does not mean transfer of ownership. The mortgager transfers some of his rights on the property to the mortgagee. Therefore, a mortgaged property cannot be sold without the consent of the mortgager in the event of any default.

(c) Specific property

The interest to be transferred is always with respect to a "specific property". In other words, the property must be made specific through proper identity like its size, location, boundaries etc.

(d) Possession with the mortgager

The actual possession of the mortgaged property is with the mortgager. He need not always transfer it to the mortgagee.

(e) Object or purpose of mortgage

The object of creating a mortgage is either to secure a loan or to perform an engagement. If the transfer of property is made for any other purpose, it cannot be called a mortgage.

(f) Reconveyance of interest

On repayment of the loan the interest in specific immovable property is reconveyed to the mortgager. Thus, the mortgager gets back all his interest and rights in the property mortgaged as soon as he repays the loan.

(g) Right of sale

In the event of non-payment of the loan, the mortgage has a right to sell the mortgaged property through the intervention of the court. But in case of legal mortgage, the mortgagee can sell the property without the intervention of the court.

(h) Mortgage deed

An agreement in writing between the mortgager and the mortgagee is essential for creating a mortgage. The document which contains this agreement is called "mortgage deed".

Types of Mortgages

Mortgages are governed by the provisions of the "Transfer of Property Act". The Act recognises the following types of mortgages.

A. Simple mortgage
B. Mortgage by conditional sale
C. Usufructuary mortgage
D. English mortgage
E. Mortgage by deposit of title deeds.
F. Anomalous mortgage.

A. Simple mortgage

In case of simple mortgage, the mortgager binds himself personally to pay the mortgage money. The mortgager does not transfer the possession of the property. It he fails to pay according to his contract, the mortgagee cannot directly sell the property. The sale must be through the intervention of the court. In other words, the mortgagee can sell the property through the intervention of the court. As the possession over the property remains with the mortgager, this mortgage is called "non-possessory". A simple mortgage is preferred by banks to other types of mortgages.

B. Mortgage by conditional sale

This type of mortgage is created subject to certain conditions. The mortgager ostensibly sells the mortgaged property with any one of the following conditions:

(a) That the sale shall become absolute if the mortgager fails to pay the mortgage money on a certain date.
(b) That the sale shall become void if the mortgager pays the mortgage money.
(c) That the mortgagee shall re-transfer the property to the mortgager if the mortgager makes payment of mortgage money on a certain date.

The following are the essential features of such a mortgage.

(i) It is an ostensible sale and not a real sale.
(ii) The possession of the property continues with the mortgager.
(iii) The mortgager does not have any personal liability.
(iv) In the event of non-payment, the mortgagee has a right to sue for foreclousure only and not for the sale of property.

Foreclosure means that the mortgager loses his right to redeem the mortgaged property in case of non-payment of the mortgage money. The mortgagee will get this right of foreclosure through the court.

C. Usufructuary mortgage

Under this type of mortgage:

(a) The mortgagee is authorised to retain the possession of property till the loan is repaid.
(b) The mortgagee is also authorised to receive the income, like rents and profits arising from that property. The income so received is to be appropriated towards the loan amount. So the liability of the mortgager is gradually reduced under this type.
(c) In the event of non-payment, the mortgagee can sue neither for the mortgage money nor

for the sale of property. Even the right of foreclosure is not available.

(d) The only remedy available is to retain the possession of property, and receive the income arising therefrom, till the loan is settled.

(e) If the mortgager fails to redeem the property within 60 years, the mortgagee become the absolute owner.

D. English mortgage

Under this types of mortgage :

(a) The mortgager transfers the property absolutely in favour of the mortgagee.

(b) This transfer is subject to a condition that the property will be transferred to the mortgager on repayment of the mortgage money.

(c) In addition to this absolute transfer, the mortgager binds himself personally liable to repay the mortgage money.

E. Mortgage by deposit of title deeds

This type of mortgage is also called "equitable mortgage". Under this type of mortgage :

(a) There is a mere deposit of little deeds to property.

(b) The intention of the deposit is to secure a loan.

This mortgage does not require registration. It is most popular with banks.

F. Anomalous mortgage

A mortgage other than any of the above five mortgages is an anomalous mortgage. It takes various forms depending upon custom, local usage or contract. In real practice, it takes the form of any two mortgages stated above.

Legal and Equitable Mortgage

Legal mortgage may be defined as "the creation by deed of a legal estate or interest inland as a security for the payment of money due, or to become due in favour of the person who takes the security, subject to the mortgager's right to have the estate so created extinguished on repayment of the loan with interest." Thus, in the case of a legal mortgage, the transfer of the legal rights to the person to whom the security is given, is essential.

An equitable mortgage may be created by an agreement, expenses or implied, that an equitable interest in the property, may pass to the mortgagee as security for a debt due. In such case, the mortgager deposits the title deeds with the mortgagee with the intention of giving the mortgagee an equitable interest on the property. In India, equitable mortgages are allowed in Bombay, Calcutta, Madras and Delhi.

Merits of Equitable Mortgage over the Legal Mortgage

An equitable mortgage has the following merits over the legal mortgage.

1. Registration Deed

In case of equitable mortgage, no registered deed is needed as an evidence to the transaction while in the case of legal mortgage it is a must. It is made clear that the borrower may have time and money under equitable mortgage.

2. Creation without Publicity

It is not essential for equitable mortgage to be registered. Generally, it may be created without any publicity and this may not affect the statutes of the borrowers.

3. Less Time Consumed

In case of an equitable mortgage, the time is less required as compared to a legal mortgage. Under equitable mortgage, if a customer wants an advance against his immovable property and can satisfy the bank authorities, the money may be granted to him without any delay.

4. No Need For New Deed

In case of an equitable mortgage the title deed may be returned to the mortgager who can redeposit for raising the new loan. While in the case of legal mortgage, a new deed and registration is always needed.

Demerits of Equitable Mortgage over the Legal Mortgage

Equitable mortgage has a number of demerits due to which legal mortgage is perferred by the banks. The demerits of the equitable mortgage over the legal mortgage have been discussed below.

1. Equitable mortgage is a time-consuming as well as expensive process because property mortgaged can be realised only through the court's order.
2. Equitable title may be affected by the legal mortgage.
3. The borrower may subsequently execute a legal mortgage in favour of another party.
4. An equitable mortgage is full of risk, fraud and negligent dealing. Section 78 of the Transfer of Property Act, 1882 lays down as "Whereas through fraud, misrepresentation or gross neglect of a prior mortgagee, another person has been induced to advance money on the security of the already mortgaged property, the prior mortgagee shall be postponed to the subsequent mortgagee".

From the above discussion, it may be said that although certain demerits are associated with equitable mortgages, the merits far outweigh them. The risks may be avoided if necessary precautions are taken by the banker.

Rights of Mortgager

A mortgager has the following rights.

1. Right to redeem mortgaged property

It is the most important right of the mortgager. After making payment of the debt the mortgager can redeem his property.

2. Right to inspect and copy documents

A mortgager has a right to inspect and copy documents if he has deposited title deeds with the mortgagee.

3. Right to improvement and accretion

In case any improvement or accretion in the mortgaged property happens, the mortgager has a right to receive or enjoy that improvement.

4. Right to get benefit of new lease

If the mortgagee has got the lease of the mortgaged property renewed, the mortgager has a right to get the benefit of such renewal.

5. Right to possession

After making payment of the mortgage debt, the mortgager has a right to take back the possession of the property and return of documents of title to the property duly released.

Rights of Mortgagee (Banker)

A mortgagee has the following rights.

1. Right to foreclosure

In case the mortgager fails to pay the debt after it has become due, the mortgagee can file a suit for foreclosure. Foreclosure means that the mortgager loses his right to redeem the mortgaged property.

2. Right of sale

The mortgagee also has a right to sell the property with or without the permission of the Court (in certain cases under Sec. 69) if the mortgager fails to pay the debt when it has become payable.

3. Right to sue for payment

A mortgagee also has a right in the alternative (of the above two rights) to file a suit for payment when the amount of the debt has become due.

4.Right to re-imbursement of certain expenses

If the mortgagee has to spend some money on maintenance, insurance or payment of lease rent, he has a right of re-imbursement of such expenses from the mortgager. He is also entitled to 9% interest per annum thereon.

5. Right to possession and income from mortgaged property

In case the mortgager fails to pay, the mortgagee has a right to possession of the property till the debt is paid. He also has a right to appropriate any income received from such property.

6. Right to accretion

A mortgagee has a right to hold as security any accretion to the mortgaged property which occurs after the date of the mortgage in the absence of any contract to the contrary.

D. Hypothecation

In layman's language mortgage of movable goods is called hypothecation. According to Hart, "it is a charge on a porperty of which neither ownership nor possession is transferred to the creditor". In simple words it is a pledge without transferring the possession of goods. The salient feature of hypothecation is that neither the ownership nor possession is transferred. Instead a charge is created to give possession of the goods to the lender (banker) whenever he asks him to do so. The banker enjoys the right and powers of a pledgee. Gopal Singh Hira Singh Vs. Punjap National Bank (1976) A.I.R. Delhi 115. "The borrower is in actual physical possession but the constructive possession is still of the bank because, according to the deed of hypothecation, the borrower holds the actual physical possession not in his own right as the owner of the goods but as the agent of the bank". The High Court held, in law there was no difference between pledge and hypothecation with regard to legal possession of the bank. However, to enforce the claim it is essential for the bank to take possession of the hypothecated property on its own or through the Court. In case the banker fails to do so he will be deemed to have waived his right as a hypothecatee. His debt will become unsecured.

Risks in giving loans against hypothecation: Risks in hypothecation are greater as compared to those in pledge because the possession of the goods is with the borrower.

(a) Greater chances of fraud

The borrower may not give possession of the goods or may sell the entire stock. He may also hypothecate the same goods or may sell the entire stock. He may also hypothecate the same goods with another banker.

(b) High legal costs

To recover possession of hypothecated goods, a banker might have to take legal action against the borrower. It will be costly in terms of money and time.

(c) No liquidity

It will take a longer time to recover the possession of goods and realise the debt.

Precautions to be Taken by a Banker in Case of Lending against Hypothecation

A banker should take the following precautions.

(a) Loans to be given to reputed parties only

A banker should sanction loan only to such customers who have good reputation and sound financial position. Such parties should have a clean record of past dealings.

(b) Regular inspection of hypothecated goods

The bank should regularly inspect the stock of the hypothecated goods. It should also verify the stocks with account books.

(c) Periodical statement of stocks

The banker should ask the borrower to submit periodical statement of stock. It should verify those statements with the stocks of the goods.

(d) Signboard of hypothecation in favour of the banker

The banker should ask the borrower to display a signboard on the gate of the godown where the goods are stored indicating that the goods are hypothecated with the banker. The banker should regularly check that such display is being done. It will be a public notice and would avoid the chances of duplicate charge being created on those goods.

(e) Insurance

The banker should ask the borrower to get the goods insured against fire, theft, flood etc. and assign the policy in its favour. The banker should inform the insurer that the goods are hypothecated with him.

(f) Registration of charge

If the borrower is a company, the banker should get the charge registered under Sec. 125 of the Companies Act, 1956. The charge is to be registered with the Registrar of Companies within 30 days of its creation. The banker should obtain a copy of registration of the charge. The banker should also get declaration from the company that it will not create a second charge over those goods. This undertaking should also be registered with the Registrar of Companies along with the registration of charge.

(g) Declaration from the borrower that he is not availing similar facilities from other banks

The banker should obtain a declaration from the borrower to this effect. This undertaking should also be obtained periodically along with periodical statement of stock of hypothecated goods. This declaration should be cross-checked with the information obtained from other banks of the area.

From the above discussion, it is made clear that the banker should give the facility of hypothecation to honest persons only because the goods remain in the possession of the borrower. In case the loan is granted to any unscrupulous person, he may sell the goods hypothecated and pay off other creditors.

Conclusion

To conclude, we have discussed various methods of creating a charge on the security offered for a bank-loan. Now we are in a position to say that every method has its own importance and a few methods are inter-related. The function and achievement of all methods will depend upon the circumstances and financial position of the bank as well as its customer.

Questions for Discussions

1. Discuss the various methods of creating a charge on the security offered for a bank-loan.
2. Define 'pledge' What are its essential ingredients? Who can create a valid pledge? What are the rights and obligations of the pledger and the pledgee?
3. Define mortgage and explain the various types of mortgages.
4. What are legal and equitable mortgages? Explain their relative merits and demerits to the banker.
5. What do you know by hypothecation? What precautions should a bank take while advancing loans against hypothecation of goods?

Chapter - 17

GUARANTEES

Introduction

Guarantee is an important method of securing banker's advances to the customer. It is the personal security of the third party which commands the confidence of the banker. In case the customer is unable to provide the security of tangible asset or the value of such security which is not sufficient to cover the loan amount, the banker may ask the customer to provide a 'guarantee' for the repayment of the amount. J.M. Holden observed, "When a guarantor signs a guarantee in favour of a banker, he is declaring: 'You may advance money to your customer', Mr. X and if he does not repay, I will be responsible".

Meaning

Whenever the borrower does not have sufficient security to offer or if he has exhausted all securities, he can request the banker to accept the surety of the third party. On several occasions the banker agreed to this. However such offer should come from the borrower himself and not by the banker. The person who gives security for the loan raised by the principal debtor is called "GUARANTEE".

Definition

Section 126 of the Indian Contract Act, 1872 defines a contract of guarantee as "a contract to perform the promise or discharge the liability of a third person in case of his default".

According to the Indian Law, guarantee may be either oral or written. But according to English Law, a guarantee is defined as a 'Promise made by one person to another to be collaterally answerable for the debt, default or miscarriage of a third person and must be evidenced in writing".

Three parties are involved in this contract of guarantee. They are as follows.

(a) **Applicant** : The Principal debtor-person at whose request the guarantee is being executed.

(b) **The Beneficiary** : Person to whom the guarantee is being given and who can enforce in case of default.

(c) **The Guarantor** : The person who undertakes to (surety) discharge the obligations of the applicant against his default.

Thus the guarantee is a collateral contract, consequential to a main contract between the applicant and beneficiary.

Example

Suppose Chaluvaiah requests Chandrappa to lend Rs. 50,000/- to Yogananda and guarantees that Yogananda will repay the amount within a stated period, and that on Yogananda is failure to repay the amount he (Chaluvaiah) will himself pay to Chandrappa, it is a contract of guarantee. Hence chaluvaiah is the guarantor, Yogananda is the principal debtor and Chandrappa is the creditor.

Necessity for Bank Guarantee

Applicant Dasarath and Beneficiary Yogananda have a business contract. This is the primary or main contract. Yogananda wants to cover the risk of any possible non-performance of the contract by Dasarath. So Yogananda can ask for a monetary deposit as a cover. Dasarath is not willing to block his money (which he can otherwise profitably use). So Dasarath approaches his bank with a request to issue a Bank Guarantee in favour of Yogananda. Thus here has arisen the need for a Bank Guarantee.

Essentials of a Valid Guarantee

A valid contract of guarantee must satisfy certain essential requirements stated in the definition.

1. Valid contract

The contract of guarantee should have all the essential elements of a valid contract. viz. Consideration, free consent, competence of the parties, legality of object and consideration.

2. Guarantee cannot be obtained by coercion. If there is coercion, there will not be valid contract as consent is not free.

3. Consideration

There need not be a direct consideration between the creditor and guarantee. The money or any other consideration received by the principal debtor is sufficient for the contract of guarantee. Thus there should be some consideration and if consideration is totally absent then the contract of guarantee will be invalid.

4. Competence

The contract of guarantee must be made by the parties who have competence to contract. The creditor and surety must be competent to enter into valid contract. Principal debtor can be a minor. Here surety is regarded as principal debtor and is personally liable to pay the debt.

5. Primary liability

There must be some one primary liable as principal debtor other than surety. The contract of guarantee pre-supposes the existence of liability enforceable by law.

6. Conditional

In a valid contract of guarantee there must be a conditional promise to be liable on the default of the principal debtor. Thus the liability of surety arises only when the principal debtor makes a default.

7. No misrepresentation

While obtaining surety the facts should be revealed to him. The guarantee should not be obtained by misrepresenting the facts to the surety. However, as it is not a contract of absolute good faith, it does not require complete disclosure of material facts to the surety either by principal debtor or by the creditor. But the facts, which are likely to affect the degree of surety's responsibility must be truly revealed to him. Otherwise it is not a valid contract of guarantee.

8. No concealment of facts

The surety should be informed of the facts which are likely to affect the liability. If such facts are conceded the guarantee becomes invalid.

9. The contract of guarantee must be oral or in writing. But as per English law it must be in writing.

Kinds of Guarantees

Under Section 126 of the Indian Contract Act, 1872, a contract of guarantee may be either oral or in writing though a banker shall put it in writing to avoid any dispute. But in oral contract, the existence of the contract is very difficult to prove.

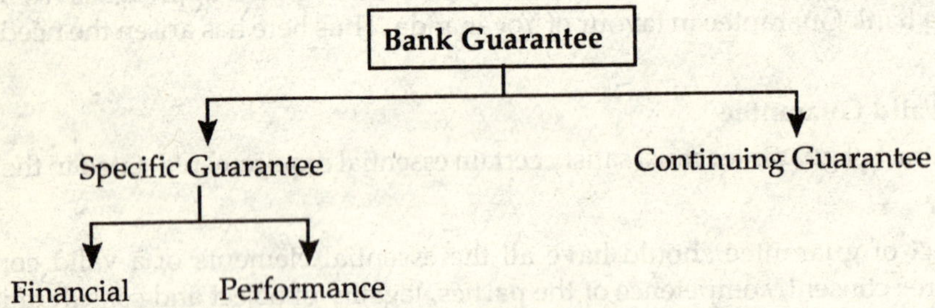

1. Specific or Ordinary Guarantee

Specific or Ordinary Guarantee means a guarantee for the transaction between the debtor and the creditor. Where the advancing money is made against the security of Specific Guarantee, the money should be lent by the banker on a separate loan account. In such case, the liability of the surety extends only to a single transaction.

Illustration

Suppose S stands surety for the repayment of loan of Rs. 20,000/- given by a Bank X to Y. This is a Specific Guarantee. The liability of S will come to an end as soon as Y repays the loan to the Bank X. In case where the Bank X advances another loan to Y, subsequently, S will not be liable.

The Specific Guarantee may be either Financial or Performance :

(a) Financial Guarantee

It means, "to guarantee the customer's (applicant's) financial worth, creditworthiness and his capacity to take up financial risks".

(b) Performance Guarantee

It means, "to guarantee the obligations relating to the technical, managerial, administrative experience and capacity of the customer (applicant)".

However, the liabilities under both these types of bank guarantee are reduced to monetary terms. Bank is not going to be asked to perform the contract in case of default by the applicant of a Performance Guarantee; because what is guaranteed is not the performance but only the financial loss arising out of the non-performance of the commitment made by the applicant. Such Performance Guarantee is issued only on behalf of first-class parties.

2. Continuing Guarantee

According to Section 129 of the Indian Contract Act, 1872, 'a Continuing Guarantee is that which extends to a series of transactions'. It may be remembered here that this guarantee is not confined to single transaction. Under this, the amount of the fluctuating balance on a cash-credit or an overdraft account may be covered by the Continuing Guarantee. But it should be noted here that 'the payment by installments within a stated time is not known as Continuing Guarantee'.

Illustration

If X considers that State Bank of Mysore employs Y in collecting deposits promises State Bank of Mysore to be responsible to the amount of Rs. 20,000/- for the due collection and payment by X of those deposits. This is a Continuing Guarantee.

Revocation of Continuing Guarantee : A continuing guarantee is revoked by the following ways.

(a) By Notice

Section 130 of the Indian Contract Act, 1872, states : "A continuing Guarantee may be revoked any time after giving a notice to the creditor in respect of future transactions. In such a case, the surety would not be responsible for future transactions which may take place between the creditor and the principal debtor after he has revoked the contract of guarantee".

(b) By Death

According to Section 131 of the Indian Contract Act, 1872, "the death of the surety operates as a revocation of the Continuing Guarantee with regard to the future transactions unless the contract provides otherwise. No notice of death need be given to the creditor".

Purpose of the Guarantee : The purpose of the above guarantees is discussed below :

Financial	Performance	Deferred Payment Guarantee
(a) In lieu of earnest money/tender deposit retention money.	For performance of machinery/goods supplied.	Bank guarantees payment of specified amount over a period of one year but less than 10 years.
(b) Issued to Government Departments for releasing disputed claims money like Excise/Customs Duty etc.	For satisfactory performance of Turnkey Projects for a specified period.	

Form the above discussion, it is clear that the banker always prefers to have a continuing guarantee, so that the guarantor's liability may not be limited to the original advance but should also extend to all subsequent debts. Section 38 of the Indian Partnership Act, 1932 lays down that "a Continuing Guarantee given to a firm or a third party in respect of the transactions of a firm, is, in the absence of agreement to the contrary, revoked as to future transactions from the date of any change in the constitution of the firm".

Contract of Guarantee

The contract of guarantee is distinctly different from the contract of indemnity. In terms of Section 126 of the Indian Contract Act, 1872, "a contract of guarantee is a contract to perform the promise or discharge the liability of a third person in case of his default". The same Section further states that "a guarantee may be either oral or written". The above statements of the Act may be made clear by the following example.

If Mr. Eshwarappa applying for a loan of Rs. 12,000/- induces his friend, Mr. Gopikrishnan to promise to Mr. Sreeram to repay the loan in case of Mr. Eshwarappa default, such contract is called a contract of guarantee.

If we analyse the above example, the following points will be seen :

There are three parties in a guarantee and three sub-contracts emerge, i.e.,

(a) the contract between principal debtor and the creditor.

(b) the contract between principal debtor and surety.

(c) the contract between surety and creditor.

Here Mr. Eshwarappa is the principal debtor, Mr. Gopikrishnan is the surety and Mr. Sreeram is the creditor.

Purpose of the Contract

The purpose of the contract of guarantee may be discussed below.

(a) To secure the honesty and fidelity of someone who is to be appointed to some office.

(b) To secure someone from injury arising out of a wrong committed by another.

(c) To secure the performance of something which may be related to a mercantile engagement.

Contract of Indemnity

Section 124 of the Indian Contract Act, 1872, defines indemnity as "a contract by which one party promises to save the other from loss caused to him by the conduct of the promiser himself, or by the conduct of any other person".

According to English Law, "a contract of Indemnity is a promise to save another harmless person from loss caused as a result of a transaction entered into at the instance of the promiser". The scope of the English definition is incomplete because it does not make a distinction between loss caused by the conduct of the promisee, and by the conduct of any other person.

Parties to Indemnity

(a) **Indemnifier :** Person who promises to make good the loss.

(b) **Indemnified :** Person whose loss is to be made good.

Example

If Mr. Swaroop claims to have lost a bank draft for Rs. 3,000 issued by Canara Bank in favour of Mr. Deeraj and agrees to indemnify the Bank against consequence of any proceedings which Mr. Deeraj may take against Canara Bank.

Here Swaroop is the Indemnifier and Canara Bank is the Indemnified.

Analysis of the Definition

If we analyse the above definition given by Section 124 of the Indian Contract Act, 1872, the following points may be included in a contract of indemnity.

(a) The cases where loss is caused by the conduct of the promiser himself or by the conduct of any other person.

(b) The express promise of the indemnifier may be included.

It should be noted here that Indian Courts agree with the English definition of contracts of indemnity. In the case of Gajans Moheshwar Vs. Moheshwar Madan (1942) Bombay 302, Justice observed that ".........Section 124 and 125 of the Contract Act are not exhaustive of the law of indemnity, and that the courts here would apply the same principles that the courts in England do".

Difference between Contract of Guarantee and a Contract of Indemnity

The difference between a contract of guarantee and a contract of indemnity is as follows :

1. Number of Contracts

In a contract of indemnity there are only two parties, viz., the indemnifier and the insured or the promisee or the party indemnified. Whereas in a contract of guarantee, there are three parties, i.e., the creditor, principal debtor, and surety.

2. Nature of Liability

In contract of guarantee, the liability is secondary, the primary liability being that of the principal debtor whereas in the contract of indemnity, the liability of a promiser is primary and independent.

3. Parties' Interest

The person giving the guarantee has no other interest in the transaction apart from his guarantee. But a person giving an indemnity may have some other interest in the contract.

4. Purpose of Contracts

A contract of indemnity is made for the reimbursement of loss but a contract of guarantee may be to provide necessary security to creditor against his advances.

5. Rights of Parties

In a contract of indemnity, the indemnifier can bring the suit against the third party in the name of the indemnified whereas in a contract of guarantee, the surety becomes entitled in law to proceed against the principal debtor in his own right after he has discharged the debt payable by the principal debtor to the creditor.

Rights of the Surety

Right of the surety may classified into the following three heads :

1. Right against the principal debtor.
2. Right against the creditor.
3. Right against the co-sureties.

1. Right Against the Principal Debtor

The surety may exercise the following rights against the principal debtor.

(a) Subrogation

According to Section 140 of the Indian Contract Act, 1872, "When a surety has paid the guaranteed debt on its becoming due or has performed the guaranteed duty, on the default of the principal debtor, he is invested with all the rights which the creditor had against the debtor.

(b) Indemnity

Section 145 of the Indian Contract Act, 1872 lays down that the surety has the right to recover from the principal creditor whatever sum he has rightfully paid under the guarantee.

2. Right Against the Creditor

By Section 141 of the Indian Contract Act, 1872, a surety is entitled to get the benefit of every security which the creditor has against the debtor at the time when the contract of suretyship is entered into, whether the surety knows of the existence of such security or not.

3. Right Against the Co-sureties

The 'co-sureties' means 'when a debt has been granted by more than one person'. Section 146 of the Indian Contract Act, 1872, gives a right of contribution among them. This can be made clear by the following illustration.

Narendra, Nagaraj and Kumar sureties to Central Bank of India for the sum of Rs. 9,000/- lent to Mahalingaih. If Mahalingaiah makes default in payment, Narendra, Nagaraj and Kumar are liable, among themselves, to pay Rs. 3,000/- each.

Liability of the Surety

The liability of the surety is called as secondary, as his liability arises only on default by the principal debtor. Section 128 of the Indian Contract Act, 1872 lays down that "Whereas the parties do not agree to the extent of the liability or the surety does not put up any limit of his liability at the time of entering into the contract, the liability of the surety will be co-extensive with that of the principal debtor".

Example

If Mr. Narayan guarantees to Mr. Venkatesh the payment of the Bill of Exchange by Mr. Muniyappa, the acceptor. In case the Bill is dishonoured by Mr. Muniyappa, in such case Mr. Narayan is liable not only for the amount of the Bill but also for any charges which may become due on him.

Rights of the Banker

Under a contract of guarantee, the rights of the creditor, who may be a banker, are the liabilities of the surety. The banker has a right of general lien on the securities of the surety in his possession. This right may arise when the principal debtor has made default and not before that. If the surety is declared insolvent, the banker is entitled to sue the principal debtor for the recovery of the money.

Liabilities of the Banker (Obligation)

According to Indian Contract Act, 1872, the following are the liabilities on a banker in a contract of guarantee :

1. Not to Discharge the Principal Debtor

Section 134 of the Indian Contract Act states, "The surety is discharged by a contract between the creditor and the principal debtor, by which the principal debtor is released, or by any act or omission of the creditor, the legal consequence of which is the discharge of the principal debtor".

2. Not to give Time to the Principal Debtor

Section 135 of the said Act lays down that "A contract between the creditor and the principal debtor, by which the creditor makes a composition with the promise to give time to, or not to sue the principal debtor, discharge the surety assents to such contract".

3. Not to Conceal Material Facts

Section 140 of the Indian Contract Act provides guarantee which the creditor obtains by means of keeping silence as to material circumstances is not valid.

Example

Swaroop guarantees to Sreenidhi payment for coal to be supplied by him to Preran of the amount of 100 tonnes. Sreenidhi and Preran have agreed that Preran should pay Rs. 20/- per ton beyond the market price, such excess to be applied to liquidation of an old debt. In such example, hereby Swaroop is not liable as surety.

In short, besides the above, the banker should ensure that the guarantee is not obtained by misrepresentation. Any guarantee which has been obtained by means of misrepresentation made by the creditor, concerning a material part of the transaction is invalid.

Merits and Demerits of Guarantee

A contract of guarantee is a direct contract between the creditor and the surety, yet it is necessary that it must be entered into with the knowledge and consent of the principal debtor. In addition, before accepting a guarantee as a security, the banker should see the merits and demerits of the contract of guarantee. Hence the banker should also take precautions while making advances against guarantee as a security. We shall therefore discuss all the points further as follows.

Merits of Guarantee

In practice, the following are the merits of guarantee.

1. Betterment

Where the bank grants loans and advances on the security of guarantee, it (contract of guarantee) may be in a better position than making an unsecured advance. But it should be the legal duty of the banker to see the financial and credit position of the surety in market. In case the debtor fails to repay and if the surety is in sound position, the banker can recover the amount from the surety.

2. Easy

If a person wants to enter into contract of guarantee, there may be no legal and technical formalities before him. In other words he may enter into contract of guarantee without any difficulty. Whereas the bank takes the guarantee in writing, the contract of guarantee will play a positive and sufficient role.

3. No Need for Obligation

Generally, whereas the bank grants loans and advances against several types of securities there may be a number of obligations on the part of the banker. But in contract of guarantee, there may be no need for any obligation on the part of the banker because it is not possible for the banker to take care of any tangible assets of the borrower.

Demerits of Guarantee

Following are the drawbacks or demerits of guarantee.

1. Difficulty in Valuation

It is very difficult for the banker to determine the real value of guarantor. In case the banker does not understand the real position of the guarantor and if loan is granted against his surety and the debtor fails to repay the amount, in such case the banker will not recover the amount from the guarantor.

2. Difficulty in Insolvency

The value of the security given by the guarantor depends upon his solvency. In case the guarantor is declared insolvent, the security will become worthless.

3. Complicated Legal Formalities

In a contract of guarantee the banker has a number of obligations which have to be followed very strictly because the provisions of guarantee are to be made in favour of the guarantor.

4. Difficulty in Drafting

The drafting of the contract of guarantee is very difficult and a number of technical words are to be used. If it is not properly drafted, the guarantor may avoid the liability in case of default by the principal debtor.

Precautions to be Taken by the Banker in a Contract of Guarantee

While granting advances against the security of guarantee, the banker should take the following precautions.

1. Financial Soundness of the Guarantor

Before making advances, the banker should enquire about the integrity, creditworthiness and capacity of the borrower as well as the guarantor or surety. If the proposed guarantor does not have these qualities and the loan is granted on his guarantee, in real practice, such amount is called an unsecured loan. Therefore, it is essential for a banker to accept the guarantee only if the guarantor's financial position is very strong or sound.

2. Careful Drafting

Before granting loans, the banker should see whether the contract of guarantee is drafted properly or not. It should not contain any loophole because in case the principal debtor fails to repay the amount, the bank may not be in a position to recover the amount from the guarantor. So it is necessary for the bank to get the contract drafted by the legal experts of the bank.

3. Contract must be in Writing

Under Section 126 of the Indian Contract Act, 1872, a contract of guarantee may be either oral or written. But in actual practice or on the safe side, the banker should obtain guarantee from the guarantor in writing on the printed form. The banker should also contain the terms and conditions of the contract of guarantee in writing.

4. Powers of the Guarantor

Before making an advance, the banker should examine the powers of the guarantor who gives guarantee to the bank. In case a loan is to be guaranteed by a joint stock company, the banker should properly study company's Memorandum and Articles of Association. For this, the banker should obtain a copy of certificate from the Board's resolution authorising the company to stand surety.

5. Continuing Guarantee

Whereas the loan is granted on a guarantee, the banker should see that the guarantee is going on continually or not. In case the guarantee is given for a specific loan, in such condition, the banker should not sanction loan after the original loan is repaid by the principal debtor.

6. Capacity of the Parties

While advancing money, the banker should examine the capacity of the principal debtor and the guarantor. If the guarantor is a minor, the banker should not accept the guarantee of a minor because he (minor) is not fit to enter into a contract of guarantee.

7. No Modification in Contract

Before granting loan, the banker should satisfy himself about the credit worthiness of the party. He (banker) should not take any step about the modification without the consent of the guarantor. If the banker does so, the liability of the guarantor will come to an end.

Termination of Guarantee

In respect of future transactions taking place, the guarantor may terminate his guarantee due to his insolvency. When the banker receives a notice about the insolvency of his guarantor, he should immediately stop the guaranteed account because if the debtor fails to repay the amount, the banker cannot recover the amount from his guarantor. Under Section 34 (2) of the Provisional and Section 46 (3) of the Presidency Towns Insolvency Acts, the banker has the right to proceed against the estate of such guarantor even if the principal debtor has not defaulted.

The contract of guarantee may terminate under the following points.

(a) On receipt of notice to the creditor of the guarantor's insolvency.

(b) On receipt of notice of principal debtor.

(c) On death of the guarantor, under the Indian Contract, the notice of the death of the guarantor need not be given to the creditor whereas according to English Law, such notice is necessary.

(d) Notice of demand by the creditor on the guarantor.

(e) Change in the constitution of the borrower.

(f) Notice of revocation by the guarantor to the creditor.

From the above one or more events, the contract of guarantee will terminate.

Conclusion

From the above discussion, it is clear that the person who gives security for the loan, raised by the principal debtor is called 'Guarantee'. Banker has to take proper precautions while granting loans and advances on guarantee. If the contract of guarantee is used properly, it may act as a good guide while if it is used wrongly it may act as a master. Therefore, in order to minimise risks and defaults, the banker should take precautions properly.

Questions for Discussions

1. What do you mean by guarantee? Discuss necessity and various kinds of guarantees which are offered to the banks.
2. Explain a contract of guarantee and a contract of indemnity. Distinguish between them. What are the rights and liabilities of the surety and the banker in a contract of guarantee?
3. What are the merits and demerits of granting advances against a guarantee? What precautions should a banker take while making advances on the guarantee on a surety?

Chapter - 18

LETTER OF CREDIT

Introduction

Modern banks facilitate trade and commerce by rendering valuable services to the business community. Apart from providing appropriate mechanism for making payments arising out of trade transactions, the banks gear the machinery of commerce, specially in case of international commerce, by acting as a useful link between the buyer and the seller, who are often too far away from and too unfamiliar with each other. Opening or issuing letters of credit is one of the important services provided by the banks for these purposes. The foundation of the banking business is the confidence reposed in the banking institutions by the people in general and the mercantile community in particular. The standing, reputation and goodwill earned by a banking institution enables it to issue instruments, known as Letters of Credit, in favour of traders and banks to meet the needs of their customers. In fact, a letter of credit carries a promise or an undertaking by the issuing banker which is valued and honoured on a global basis.

In actual practice, a Letter of Credit means "a document issued by a banker authorising the banker to whom it is addressed to honour the Bills of the person named therein to the extent of certain amount".

Definition

A Letter of Credit has been defined by the International Chamber of Commerce as "an arrangement, however, named or described whereby a bank (the issuing bank) acting at the request and in accordance with the instructions of a customer (the applicant of the credit), is to make payment to or to the order of a third party (the beneficiary) or is to pay, accept or negotiate Bills of Exchange (Drafts) Drawn by the beneficiary or authorise such payments to be made or such drafts to be paid, accepted or negotiated by another bank, against stipulated documents and compliance with stipulated terms and conditions".

From the above definition of Letter of Credit, it is clear that there are following parties to a Letter of Credit.

1. The buyer.
2. The beneficiary.
3. The Issuing bank.
4. The notifying bank.

5. The negotiating bank.
6. The confirming bank.
7. The paying bank.

1. The buyer.

The buyer who is the importer, applies to the bank for the opening of a Letter of Credit.

2. The beneficiary.

The seller, who is the exporter, is the beneficiary of the Letter of Credit.

3. The Issuing bank.

The bank which issues the Letter of Credit at the request of the buyer is the issuing bank.

4. The notifying bank.

The notifying bank is the correspondent bank situated in the same place as that of the seller which advises the credit to the beneficiary.

5. The negotiating bank.

It is the bank which negotiates the Bills or Drafts under the Letter of Credit.

6. The confirming bank.

It is the bank the seller insists that the credit must be confirmed by it.

7. The paying bank.

The paying bank is the bank on which the Bill or Draft is drawn. It can be the confirming bank, the issuing bank or the notifying bank.

Types of Letters of Credit

The Letter of Credit can be divided into two broad categories.:

I. Travellers' Letter of Credit.
II. Commercial Letter of Credit.

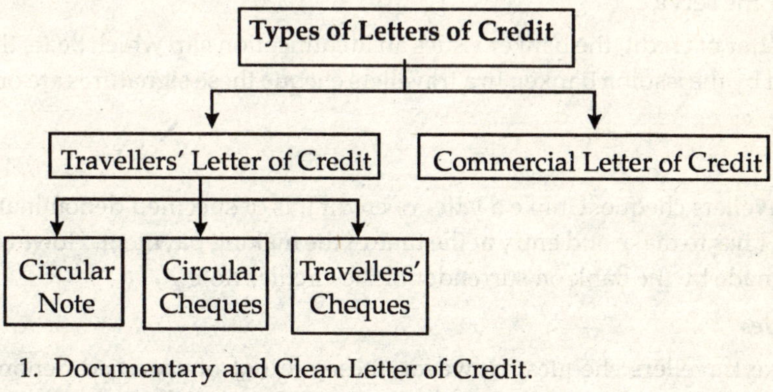

1. Documentary and Clean Letter of Credit.
2. Revocable and Irrevocable Letter of Credit.
3. Circular Letter of Credit.
4. Fixed and Revolving Letter of Credit.

5. Confirmed and Unconfirmed Letter of Credit.
6. Red Clause Letter of Credit.
7. Transferable and Non-transferable Letter of Credit.
8. With or without Recourse Letter of Credit.

These are discussed below.

I. Travellers' Letter of Credit

Such types of Letters of Credit are issued by the banks for the convenience of the travellers. The travellers are saved from the risk of travelling with heavy cash with them. The facility of such Letters of Credit can be available both for travelling in and outside the country. The characteristics of such Letters of Credit are as under.

(a) A Travellers' Letter of Credit is issued by a bank on its own branch/ branches or correspondent bank/banks situated anywhere in the world.

(b) It contains a request by the issuing bank to make payment up to the amount to the person named therein.

(c) The issuing banker may issue a Letter of Identification to the holder of the Letter of Credit. The signature of the holder must be attested therein.

Types of Travellers' Letter of Credit : The Travellers' Letter of Credit can be divided into the following forms.

1. Travellers Cheque

It is issued and drawn by a bank upon its own branch or another bank. It is a request by the issuing bank to the paying bank to pay a specified amount to the holder. It also contains the specimen signature of the holder for the purpose of identification.

2. Circular Letter of Credit

It is addressed to more than one banker. Details of the amount paid by the various bankers are entered in the proforma, printed on the back of the letter of credit. The holder is to deposit the required amount for which he wants a letter of credit with the issuing bank. The issuing bank charges its commission for the service.

In case of a letter of credit, the banker issues an identification slip which bears the signature of the holder attested by the issuing banker. In a travellers cheque these signatures are on the travellers cheque itself.

3. Circular Note

It is like a travellers cheque. Unlike a letter of credit it is of specified denomination. In a letter of credit the banker has to make and entry at the time of the making payment. However, in a circular note, payment is made by the bank on surrender of the circular note.

4. Circular Cheques

These are like travellers cheques. However, these are not of specified denominations. The maximum amount payable is indicated on the circular cheque. No separate identification slip or letter is issued along with it. The holder's signature are on the circular cheques like those on the travellers cheques.

5. Guarantee Letter of Credit

In case of other letters of credit the holder has to pay in advance the required amount of the credit to the banker who issues letter of credit. In case of guarantee letter of credit, the holder is not required to deposit any amount in advance, he is only required to give guarantee of the amount required.

6. Bank Draft or Demand Draft

A bank draft or a demand draft is a bill of exchange drawn by one bank on its own branch or any other bank. The essential features of a bank draft are.

a. It is always drawn by a bank upon its own branch or another bank.

b. It is always payable on demand and it cannot be made payable to bearer.

c. Ordinarily, payment of a demand draft cannot be stopped or countermanded. It is because of this reason payment is demanded through a bank draft.

II. Commercial Letter of Credit

Such letters of credit are issued to facilitate trade and commerce particularly the international trade. An exporter is reluctant to send goods to the importer because he wants to minimise the risk for the payment. Similarly, the importer is also reluctant to send the payment in advance to the exporter. He is afraid that the exporter may not send the goods even after receiving payment in advance. The bank comes to the rescue (help) of both the parties. The documents of goods are sent through the bank with the instructions that the bank should deliver the documents viz., Bill of Lading or Freight Bill to the importer against payment or acceptance of the bill. The importer can get the delivery of the goods by surrendering the bill of lading to the shipping company and the exporter will get the payment from the bank.

However, in the above case a risk is involved. The importer may not pay or accept the bill. The exporter will have to spend unnecessary money in getting the goods back. Such risks can be avoided if a letter of credit is opened by the importer.

A letter of credit issued by the importer's bank guarantees the exporter that the bank will pay or accept the bill accompanying the documents sent through the bank.

The letter of credit specifies what goods have to be despatched and also the date by which the goods must be despatched. The exporter should strictly comply with the terms and conditions of the letter of credit. In case he fails to do so, the bank issuing the letter of credit will not liable to pay or accept the bill drawn by the exporter.

Types of Letters of Commercial Credit

1. Documentary letter of credit

When a clause is inserted in the letter of credit that the document of title to goods viz., bill of lading, insurance policy, invoice etc., must be attached to the bill of exchange drawn under the letter of credit. It is called a documentary letter of credit.

2. Clean letter of credit

If no such clause (as in documentary letter of credit) is inserted in the letter of credit, it is called a clean letter of credit. The documents of title in that case are sent directly to the importer. In a clean letter of credit there is greater risk for the banker. As such a banker issues clean letter of credit only to those customers, who have good reputation and credit in the market.

3. Fixed letter of credit

If the banker specifies in the letter of credit the amount of the bill to be drawn within the time fixed, it is called a fixed letter of credit. Such a letter remains valid until the specified amount is utilised within the specified time.

4. Revolving letter of credit

In case of revolving letter of credit, the banker specifies the total amount upto which the bills drawn may remain outstanding at a time. For example, X opens a letter of credit with City Bank for a total sum of Rs. one lakh valid for a period of 3 months. The beneficiary (exporter) can draw bills under the letter of credit with the condition that the value of such outstanding bills should not exceed Rs. one lakh at any given time.

The main advantage of revolving credit is that the beneficiary may draw a bill for an amount higher, than the one specified in the letter of credit. Again there is no need of renewal again and again. However, it is complicated. It is difficult to ascertain how much amount is outstanding at a particular time.

5. Revocable letter of credit

Unless specified otherwise, a letter of credit will be deemed revocable (Art. 1 Uniform Custom and Practice).

In case of revocable letter of credit, the issuing banker resumes the right to cancel or modify the credit at any time without notice. Therefore, such a letter of credit is hardly of any use. However, as per Art. 2 of Uniform Custom and Practice, in the above case modification or cancellation will become effective only on receipt of the notice by the negotiating banker.

6. Irrevocable letter of credit

Such a letter cannot be modified or cancelled without the consent of the applicant and the beneficiary. As per Art. 3 of Uniform Custom and Practice the issuing banker will be liable in case of irrevocable letter of credit if the exporter strictly complies with the terms and conditions of the letter of credit.

7. Confirmed letter of credit

When the banker issuing the letter of credit requests the advising bank in the exporter's country to signify his confirmation to an irrevocable credit and the advising bank accepts the request, it is called irrevocable and confirmed letter of credit. The advising banker is called confirming banker. He cannot cancel or modify his undertaking without the consent of the parties concerned.

8. Unconfirmed letter of credit

In case the issuing banker does not ask the advising banker to confirm the letter of credit, it remains unconfirmed letter of credit.

9. With recourse letter of credit

You might recall that a bill of exchange may be drawn with recourse to the drawer. If such a bill is drawn under a letter of credit, it is called 'with recourse letter of credit'. In case of such a bill, if the drawee does not honour the bill, the banker as a holder can recover the payment of the bill from the drawer.

10. Without recourse letter of credit

If an exporter wants to avoid his liability (as in the case of with recourse letter of credit) he can ask the importer to open a 'letter of credit without recourse to the drawer'. If the importer fails to honour the bill, the issuing banker cannot hold the drawer liable. He can hold only the drawee liable in such a case. The banker may realise the amount by selling the goods if the documents of title have not been given to the importer.

11. Transferable letter of credit

Where the goods are exported through a middle men, the exporter may ask the importer to open a transferable letter of credit. Under a transferable letter of credit, the beneficiary will be able to transfer his right to draw a bill to a third party.

12. Non-transferable letter of credit

Every letter of credit unless stated otherwise is non-transferable. Hence the beneficiary cannot transfer such a letter of credit to a third party.

13. Back to back letter of credit

A beneficiary of a non-transferable letter of credit may request the bank to open a new letter of credit in favour of some third party on the security of letter of credit issued in his favour, it is called a back to back letter of credit.

14. Red clause letter of credit

If the exporter wants financial assistance in advance against his export for purchase of materials, packing etc., he can ask the importer to arrange a "Packing Credit". This packing credit is made available through the letter of credit by inserting a clause in red ink. Such a clause is called Red Clause. The negotiating banker can advance specified money to the exporter. Such accommodation is of temporary nature and is adjusted at the time of final payment.

Opening a Letter of Credit

A banker runs great risks in opening a letter of credit. Therefore, to protect his interest he must be very careful. He should take the following steps while opening a letter of credit.

1. Application for opening a letter of credit

The applicant is required to fill an application form giving the necessary details viz.,

(a) amount and nature of credit required-documentary or clean, revocable etc.,

(b) goods to be imported along with prices, nature of invoice and other terms.

(c) shipping details and other documents like B/L, Invoice, Insurance policy etc.,

(d) The details about the bill like the amount, name of the drawee, mode of delivery of documents - D/A or D.P,

(e) Other operating instructions.

It will be accompanied with an undertaking by the applicant that he will pay the bill drawn under the letter of credit.

2. Scrutiny of the application

The banker should carefully examine the application and check that all the necessary information has been given by the applicant. He should particularly see that the applicant has signed the undertaking.

3. Taking security

After the banker has examined the application and is satisfied that the necessary information has been submitted, he should ask for necessary security from the applicant in the form of cash and valuables.

4. Fixing margin

The banker should fix the margin to be maintained. This margin is fixed keeping in view the creditworthiness and standing of the applicant.

5. Effective insurance

The banker should ask the applicant to take appropriate insurance policy to cover the risks involved. The policy should be taken in joint names of the applicant and the importer.

Advantages of Letter of Credit

Advantages to the Exporter

(a) Guarantee of payment

In case of foreign trade there is a greater risk as the exporter and importer do not know each other. Moreover, there are other risks as well. With the opening of the letter of credit the exporter is assured of the payment.

(b) No risk of dishonour of bill

Under the letter of credit the bill drawn on the importer is accepted by the negotiating banker. Therefore, there is no risk of its being dishonoured.

(c) No risk of exchange restrictions

The issuing banker examines carefully the restrictions imposed by the importing country before opening letter of credit. The exporter is saved of the botheration and risks of foreign exchange restrictions.

(d) Availability of advance under packing credit facility

An exporter can get advance financial assistance under packing credit to finance purchase of raw materials and its conversion into finished products and other expenses.

(e) No risk of loss due to fluctuation in exchange rates

Under letter of credit the exporter is assured payment in the local currency. Therefore, he does not run the risk of fluctuation in foreign rates.

Advantages to the Importer

(a) It facilitates import

It is very difficult to import goods as the exporter does not know the importer. The issuing banker guarantees the payment to the exporter and he readily agrees to export the goods. In the absence of letter of credit the exporter may be reluctant to export goods.

(b) No risk in import

The risks involved in importing goods directly, is reduced. Under the letter of credit the importer is assured that the bill will be paid or accepted only when documents are received by the negotiating banker.

(c) Assurance of compliance of foreign exchange rules

The issuing banker opens the letter of credit only when it is satisfied that all the requirements of foreign exchange rules of the country of importer have been properly complied with.

(d) Facility of advance payment without any risk

Sometimes an exporter insists for advance payment to buy raw material and meet other costs. In such a case the importer can make advance payment by opening 'Red Clause Packing Credit' letter of credit. The negotiating banker will make advance payment, which will be adjusted while making final payment. Thus the importer is saved of the risks involved, in making advance payment for imports.

Precautions taken by the Bank : While opening a Letter of Credit, the banker should take the following precautions.

(a) Creditworthiness of the Party

Before opening a Letter of Credit, the banker should examine the honesty, integrity and creditworthiness of the importer. The banker should also see the financial position of the importer in the market.

(b) Validity of the Period

When the bank receives an application from the importer, it should examine carefully whether the period of import licence is valid or not. In case the period of import licence is not valid under law, the banker should reject the application immediately.

(c) Terms of Letter of Credit

The terms and conditions of Letter of Credit must be satisfactory. If the negotiating bank fails to satisfy itself with respect to the terms of Letter of Credit, it may have no claim against the bank which issued the Letter of Credit.

Conclusion

To conclude, it is clear that the banker should take precautions and steps properly while opening a Letter of Credit. The prescribed form must be drafted by the legal expert of the bank and it will be the legal duty of the banker to examine all the documents which may be enclosed along with the application.

Questions for Discussions

1. What do you understand by a letter of credit? Explain the various kinds of travellers letter of credit.
2. Explain the various types of letters of credit issued by a bank.
3. Explain the advantages of letter of credit from the point of view of exporter and importer.
4. How is a letter of credit opened? What precautions should a banker take while making payment under a letter of credit.

Chapter - 19

ACCOUNTS AND AUDIT OF BANKS

Introduction

A bank deals in money and the number of transactions is very large. As such there are greater chances of fraud. To check this there should be an efficient system of internal check and internal control. Banks follow continuous audit system. Therefore, there is an imperative need to have foolproof and elaborate accounting system for a bank. The accounting system of a bank has to be devised in such a manner that there is built-in-system of audit of such accounts. The Banking Regulation Act, 1949 has made provisions regarding the accounts and audit of a banking company. An important feature of bank's accounts is that the entry of a transaction must be made on the very (same) day the transaction takes place. It is necessary in order that before closure of the bank on that day the balance in the bank's books may be verified. Moreover, for a bank manager it is necessary to know day to day progress of the bank. This is possible only when the entries relating to deposits and loans are made in the concerned account on the same day.

Salient Features of Bank's Accounts

1. Number of transactions is very large.
2. Bank's account have to be maintained as per Double Entry System of Accounting.
3. Cash transactions and transfer entries occupy an important place in financial transactions of a bank.
4. All the transactions are entered in the books on the same day.
5. The transactions are recorded in the order in which they take place.
6. A bank may maintain separate books of accounts to record transactions with government and non government customers.
7. Regular returns and statements relating to deposits and advance are to be prepared and filed.
8. Final account to be prepared in a very short period of time as such information has to be updated regularly.
9. Elaborate internal check and internal control systems have to be established.
10. An Elaborate system of continuous audit has to be introduced.

Books of Account (Sec. 209)

The companies Act, 1956 requires a banking company to maintain at its registered office proper books of account with respect to

1. all receipts and disbursements of money and the matters in respect of which the receipt and disbursements take place.
2. the assets and liabilities of the bank.

Where a banking company has a branch office, books of accounts relating to the transactions effected at the branch office shall be kept at the branch. At an interval of not more than 3 months, summarised accounts shall be sent to the banking company at its registered office.

Books shall give a True and Fair View

The books of shall give a true and fair view of the state of affairs of the banking company or the branch office as the case may be. The books shall also explain its transactions.

The books shall be kept on accrual basis and according to the double entry system of accounting (Sec. 209 (3)).

Preservation of Books

The book shall be preserved for a period of 8 years. In case of a bank which has been in Existence for a period of less than 8 years, the books shall be preserved for the entire period of its existence.

Persons Responsible to Keep the Books

It is the responsibility of managing director to keep the books of account. If there is no managing director or manager, the directors shall be responsible for keeping the accounts of the bank.

Penalty

If any person fails to take proper steps to ensure compliance of these provision, he shall be punishable with imprisonment which may extend to a 6 months or with fine which may extend to Rs. 1,00 or with both. However, no person shall be liable to imprisonment unless he has committed the default wilfully.

Inspection of Books of Account

The books of account can be inspected by

(a) a director or his duly authorised agent ;

(b) the Registrar of Companies ;

(c) any officer authorised by the Central Government.

Books to be Maintained

The law is silent about the books to be maintained. Therefore, there is no uniformity. The books maintained by a bank differ from bank to bank. Due to lack of space, it is not possible to deal with all the books maintained by a bank. Therefore, only the important books are being discussed. A bank generally maintains the following books.

1. Cash Book or Registers

This is an important book of the bank. Whatever cash is deposited in a bank it is deposited through the cashier. A customer deposits the cash through a pay-in-slip. The cashier makes the entries in his cash book on the basis of a pay-in-slips. At the end of the day cashier tallies his cash balance with cash book.

2. Cash Scroll

To keep a check on the cashier, there is a practice to maintain cash scroll (As a part of internal check). The customer before making payment to the cashier has to get his pay-in-slip (signed) endorsed by some responsible officer of the bank. Such officer records the particulars of the pay-in-slip in the scroll register and returns the pay-in-slip to the customer after putting serial number and his initial. At the end of the day the Bank manager also verifies the cash balance of the cashier with the cash scroll.

Specimen of Cash Scroll

Dr. CR.

Sl.No.	Particulars	Amount Rs. ps.	Sl.No.	Particulars	Amount Rs. ps.

3. Payment Book

Depending upon the volume of transactions, there may be separate cashiers for receiving payment and making payment. Again, most of the banks have introduced teller system for savings bank accounts. As such, the payments up to a certain sum (say upto Rs. 3,000) are made through the officer incharge of the savings bank account counter. However, payments in excess of the above limit are made through the cashier of the bank. Similarly, payment on account of fixed deposit, current accounts are made through the cashier. The concerned officer who has to make the payment issues a token to the payee or holder. The payee or holder presents the token to the cashier who makes the payment and records the token number against the payment. At the end of the day the cashier tallies the amount paid with cash book and concerned departments against the token received.

Specimen of Cash Book Receipt Book

Sl.No.	A/c (savings, current, fixed loan, cash credit etc.)	For credit of	Deposited by	Amount Rs.Ps.

Payment Book

Sl.No.	A/c (savings, current, fixed loan, cash credit etc.)	To Debit of	Paid to	Amount Rs.Ps.

4. Token Book

A token book or register is maintained to make payment through the cashier. The counter clerk who has to make payment gives a token to the payee (customer). He records the token number in the Token Book. Token is a piece of metal (brass) in round, triangular or square shape. The name of the bank and branch and its serial number is engraved on it. It is given to the customer as a token of authority to receive the payment. The cashier can come to know that the person bearing the token is authorised to receive the payment. The cashier takes back the token before making the payment. At the end of the day the tokens are counted and checked. If it is found that any token is missing, the concerned voucher is marked for non-payment on that day and the other payments made are verified.

5. Supplementary Day Book

At the end of the day the receipt and payment vouchers received during the day are entered in the supplementary Day Book. Credit and debit entries are recorded separately. This book is compared with the cash scroll and token book. The total of receipt column of the supplementary day book should tally with the total of the cash scroll. Similarly, the total of the payment side should also tally with the total of the token book.

6. Ledgers

A ledger is an important book as is contains the accounts of the customers opening their accounts with the bank. Separate ledgers are maintained for separate types of accounts, e.g., savings account ledger, current account ledger etc.

These ledgers are maintained in alphabetical order. These ledgers are kept in the form of loose ledgers. The ledger number and the letter of the name starting first and the last name in the ledger are also marked on the ledger. When a customer wants to withdraw money from his account he is to present the cheque to the concerned counter clerk (savings A/c, current A/c etc.) The clerk makes the necessary entry in his account. In case teller system is in operation, he makes the payment also. In case no teller system is maintained, he issues a token to him after making the entry in the token register. The customer gets the payment from the cashier by surrendering his token.

At the end of the day payments made are checked with the entries made in the customer's accounts to see that the payments have been properly debited to the customer accounts.

7. Loan and Advance Register

One of the important functions of a bank is to grant loans. Earlier a bank used to give short-term loans. Now a days a bank also gives medium term and long-term as well as loans for agriculture, small scale and tiny sector industries. Separate sections deal with such loans and therefore separate ledgers are maintained for such loans. Loans are generally secured ones. However, now granting of unsecured loans has also become a common practice.

A loan account of every borrower is opened in this register. The name, address of the borrower, period of loan, nature of advance, amount of loan sanctioned and disbursed, date of loan, security offered if any, rate of interest etc. are entered on the loan register.

8. Bills Receivable and Payable Register

A bank offers the facility of collection of its customer's cheques. Similarly it also makes payment of bills on behalf of its customers. Such bills are entered in separate bills registers. For bills received an Outward Bills Collection Register is maintained. Bills payable are entered in an Inward Bills Collection Register. Date, amount of the bill, the name of the drawer, drawee, payee, place of collection and date of collection are entered in the bill collection register.

In addition a bank maintains bills collection register, bills acceptance register, bills discounting register etc.

9. Transfer Diary / Register

Very often a customer makes a request for transfer of funds from one account to the other. For example, a customer may ask to transfer certain money from his account to the account of his wife in the same bank. In such a case only a transfer entry is made. The book in which such entry is made is called transfer book. At the end of the day the entries in the transfer book are verified with the entries in the accounts of the customer concerned. The relevant vouchers (generally counter foils of pay-in-slips accompanied with cheques) are marked "Transfer" with a rubber stamp.

10. Security Register

In case of secured loans customers deposit securities with the bank. Such securities are recorded in security register. The particulars to be recorded in the security register include, name of the borrower, amount of loan, nature of security, value of security, particulars of charge created, if any, etc.

11. Investment Register

A banker has also to make investment. He enters the particular of the investment made in Investment Register. Such particulars include, name of the institution in which investment made, nature of investment, details of the investment e.g. number of shares or nature of property, period of investment, rate of interest/dividend etc.

12. Branch Ledger

Inter branch transactions are recorded in Branch Ledger. It is kept at the Head office and account of every branch is opened in this ledger.

Final Accounts

The Banking Regulation Act, 1949 has mad provisions for the preparation and audit of Final Accounts. The provisions relating to accounts, as given in the Companies Act, 1956, are also applicable in so far as they are not against the provisions of the Banking Regulation Act, 1949.

Preparation of Balance Sheet and Profit and Loss Account (Sec. 47)

At the expiration of each calender year or at the expiration of 12 months ending with the notified date specified for the purpose by the Central Government, every banking company, in connection with its entire business and every foreign banking company in connection with the business transacted by all its branches in India, is required to prepare for the year or the period, as the case may be, a balance sheet and a profit and loss account on the last working day of the year or the period as the case may.

Form of Balance Sheet and Profit and Loss Account

The balance sheet and profit and loss account shall be prepared in the prescribed form as given in Sch. III or as near thereto as the circumstances permit. In case of a foreign banking company the profit and loss account may be prepared on a date which shall not be earlier than 2 months of the last working day of the year.

Signing of Balance Sheet and Profit and Loss Account

The balance sheet and profit and loss account shall be signed by atleast three directors, where there are more than 3 directors and by all the directors if there are less than 3 directors.

Audit of Bank Accounts

Audit of bank accounts is very important because the number of monetary transactions is very large and there are greater chances of frauds in banks. Therefore, in banks continuous audit is done by the bank staff besides the statutory audit. Again, elaborate and efficient internal check system and internal control system are necessary for efficient audit of bank accounts. The Banking Regulation Act, 1949 has made the following provisions which are supplementary to the audit provisions of the Companies Act, 1956.

Audit of Accounts (Sec. 30)

The balance sheet and profit and loss account of a bank prepared in accordance with Sec. 29 shall be audited by a person duly qualified under the company law for the time being in force to be auditors of companies.

The Reserve bank is also empowered to order special audit if it is satisfied that it is necessary to do so in public interest or in the interest of the company or the depositors.

An auditor is required to report on the following.

(a) Whether or not the information and explanation given were found to be satisfactory.

(b) Whether or not the transactions of the banking company were within its power.

(c) Whether or not the returns received by him from the branches were sufficient for the purpose of his audit.

(d) Whether or not the profit and loss account shows a true balance of profit and loss for the related period.

(e) Any other matter which he considers necessary to report to the shareholders.

Publication and Filing of Accounts (Sec. 30)

The audited balance sheet and profit and loss account alongwith the auditors report shall be published in the prescribed manner. Three such copies shall be filed as returns with the Reserve Bank within 3 months from the end of the period to which they relate.

Precautions and Steps to be Taken by the Auditors

1. An auditor should carefully examine the audit provisions of the Companies Act, 1956 and the Banking Regulation Act, 1949.
2. He should thoroughly examine the Memorandum and Articles Association of the bank to study the rules and regulations of the bank relating to audit and accounts of the bank.
3. The auditor should carefully examine the internal check and internal control systems of the bank.
4. The efficiency of the bank audit is dependent upon the efficiency of the internal check and internal control systems of the bank. In case he finds that the internal check and internal control systems of the bank are not dependable, he should disown his liability.
5. In particular he should thoroughly investigate the following.

A. Assets Side

1. Cash Reserves

He should verify the cash balance with the cash book. He should examine whether or not the bank has deposited the required cash reserve (3% of cash and demand deposit and 6% of time deposit) with the Reserve Bank.

2. Liquid Assets

The auditor should verify whether or not the bank has kept 25% of its time and demand liabilities in the form of liquid assets as required under Sec. 25. In particular the auditor should see that the bank has been maintaining the increased percentage of liquid assets as and when increased by the Reserve Bank.

3. Money at call and short notice

Money at call short notice can only be lent to bank. As such the auditors should verify that it has not been given to non-banking companies.

4. Investments

There are greater chances of fraud in case of investment. The auditor should be very careful in this respect. He should ask for the schedule of investments maintained by the bank. He should see that investments have been made strictly in accordance with the provisions of the Banking Regulation Act, 1949.

He should carefully verify the title deeds of such investments and see that these are in physical or real possession of the bank. He should properly verify their valuation. These have to be valued at the face value or the market value whichever is less. He should see that the securities are free from any charge. In case the charge has been created in favour of the bank, it should be got registered under Sec. 134 with the Registrar.

5. Loans and Advances

He should carefully verify the loans and advances and the securities deposited by the borrower.

The same procedure as applied in the case of verification of investments should be followed in the case of loans and advances also. With the permission of the bank the auditor should confirm the balance from the borrowers. In addition he should examine whether the debts are good. In case they are bad or doubtful, he should see that adequate provision has been made for them. He should see that there is adequate margin between the loan and the security. If it is inadequate he should quality his audit report accordingly.

6. Acceptances and Endorsements

Bills receivable should be examined carefully. He should safeguard against fictitious bills by test checking. These bills should not be overdue and should not have been renewed frequently. In case these have been renewed frequently, such bills may be doubtful. He should see proper provision has been made for rebate on bills and against bad and doubtful bills receivable.

7. Office premises furniture and other assets

The same general principles are also applicable to these assets. However, in the case of these assets, the auditor should see that adequate provision for depreciation has been made by the bank. These have to be valued at historical cost-basis.

B. Liability Side

1. Capital

He should verify the capital with the last balance sheet. He should see that it is as per the provisions of Secs. 11 and 12 of the Banking Regulation Act, 1949.

2. Reserve Fund

He should verify the Reserve Fund with the last Balance Sheet. He should see from the profit and loss accounts that 20% of the profit have been transferred to the Reserve Fund before declaration of dividend by the bank.

3. Deposits and other accounts

He should verify the deposits and other accounts with the help of ledgers maintained by the bank. Test checking with some pass-books may also be done.

4. Acceptances and Endorsements

Bills payable should be examined with the help of Bills Register and the bills of exchange accepted by the bank. Proper provision should have been made for rebate on bills discounted.

5. Profit and Loss Account

He should see that profit and loss account has been prepared in the form set out in Sch. III or near thereto as far as circumstances permit. He should check that profit has not been inflated otherwise, dividend might be paid out of capital.

Necessary explanations as required have also been given 20% of the profits have been transferred to the Reserve Fund as required under. Sec 17 of the Act, adequate provisions should have been made regarding depreciation.

6. Contingent Liabilities

Auditor should examine the contingent liabilities. He should see that adequate provision has been made by the bank for such contingent liabilities.

7. Audit of Branches

The auditor should examine whether or not returns from the branches regarding branch audit have been received. He should incorporate them into his audit report.

Penalty

If the auditor wilfully conceals any fact, he will be punishable with imprisonment which may extend to 3 years or with fine or with both.

Conclusion

From the above discussion, undoubtedly, we can say that, there is an imperative need to have fool proof and elaborate accounting system for a bank. The accounting system of a bank has to be devised in such a manner that there is built in system of audit of such accounts. The Banking Regulating Act, 1949 has made provisions regarding the accounts and audit of a banking company.

Questions for Discussions

1. Explain the various books maintained by a bank.
2. Explain the provisions regarding audit of bank accounts.
3. Write a note on the audit of accounts of a bank.

Part - C

INTERNATIONAL TRADE

1.	Internal and International Trade	389
2.	Gains from International Trade	400
3.	Terms of Trade	405
4.	Balance of Payments	419
5.	Trade Policy	434
6.	Foreign Investment and Collaborations	452

Chapter - 1

INTERNAL AND INTERNATIONAL TRADE

Introduction

The economic development of underdeveloped countries is taking place against the background of the world consisting of countries having close economic relationship with one another. Underdeveloped countries are depending on the import of capital goods for achieving rapid economic development. Foreign capital and Foreign trade are regarded as the **'engine of growth'**. The object of this chapter is to analyse the relationship between Foreign Trade and Economic Development and Balance of payments and Economic Development.

Meaning of International Trade

Foreign trade is an essential element of economic planning for development. It is an instrument to effect the necessary changes in the factor-endowments of these economies. Foreign trade or international trade is the buying and selling of goods between peoples living in different countries. Now this is sponsored by the government of the countries. Every country tries to export manufactured goods and import raw materials, if necessary. Manufactured goods are sold at a higher price; raw materials are bought at a cheaper price. The surplus is favourable to the country that exports the manufactured goods. International trade takes place either because of differences in prices of trade goods or lack of certain commodities.

Differences between Internal Trade and International Trade

Internal trade differs from international trade in many respects. The main differences between the two are :

1. Mobility of Factors of Production

Ricardo advocated a separate theory of international trade on the ground that within the same country, labour and capital are more mobile than they are between different countries. As regards labour, as Adam Smith puts it, "Of all sorts of luggage man is the most difficult to be transported". Several causes are responsible for this; differences of language, tradition, religion, customs, social and political life, etc., or mere inertia may keep labour at home. Capital is more mobile than labour. But even here people prefer to invest their savings in their own country for various reasons. An investor feels a greater sense of security if his capital is invested in his own country.

The result of this comparatively greater immobility of labour and capital between different countries is that competition fails to make costs of production of similar goods equal, as it does in the same country. This gives unequal advantages to different countries in the production of different commodities. The different countries thus constitute noncompeting groups.

There is another consequence of comparative immobility of labour and capital as between one country and another. "Within a country, the price of a commodity, in the long run, tends to approximate to its cost of production. This is so because labour and capital can easily move into or move out of an industry, if the price is respectively more or less than the cost of production. This cannot happen in the case of international trade. Labour and capital being immobile, price and cost of production can seldom approximate.

Also, the consequence of this immobility of factors internationally is that returns to factors tend to equality within, but not between countries.

2. Natural Endowments

Differences in advantages of trade to different countries may arise because of natural causes like geographical and climatic conditions. These lead to territorial division of labour and localization of industries. For instance, some countries may have particular mineral resources like coal, iron ore, copper, etc. Others may have land or climate peculiarly suitable for certain crops, e.g., jute in Bengal, either these advantages cannot be transferred to other countries at all or the cost of moving them is prohibitive.

3. Human Capabilities

Countries differ in human capabilities too. People in some countries are physically more sturdy, whereas in others they are intellectually superior. Some have greater skill and dexterity and others excel in spirit of enterprise and organisational ability.

4. Stock of Capital

Some countries posses large stock of capital goods like the U.K., and the U.S.A. and others like India suffer from capital deficiency. This makes a great difference in the type of goods produced in different countries.

5. Political Sovereignty

In international trade, certain problems arise out of the fact that countries are independent sovereign States and can pursue independent policies with respect to the movement of goods, wages and prices, fiscal matters, banking law, foreign loans, etc., Several kinds of restrictions may be placed on the movement of goods beyond their frontiers by the States.

6. Currency Systems

Different countries have different currency systems. This hampers smooth flow of trade as between one country and another. A number of foreign exchange problems arise in foreign trade which are non-existent in internal trade. To the man in the street this is the main difference between international and domestic trade. Really, it is not the different currencies so much as the possibility of change in their relative values which differentiates between international trade from inter - regional trade.

7. Separate Markets

There are cultural distinctions between markets. The national markets are frequently separate from one another. For instance, the British use right hand drive cars, whereas the French use the left hand drive. Thus, the markets for automobiles are effectively separated. But markets are also separated by language, customs, usage, habits, tastes and host of other causes of difference. Standards differ. Some goods are designed in inches, feet and short tons and others in metric measurements. "Export and import trade must get outside of the culture of the domestic market to become acquainted with different goods, described in different words, using differing measurements, bought and sold on different terms, for different currency units".

8. Economic Nationalism

Different countries have their separate national economic life. "Along with political independence has grown a demand for economic self-reliance, self-esteem expressed largely in plans and hopes for economic development". The national units have been striving for increasing consumption, production, capital formation, etc. Thus, political and economic nationalism is rising especially in newly independent countries widening the differences between international and interregional trade.

9. Trade and Exchange Controls

We find that trade and exchange controls are instituted by almost all modern. States which obstruct the movement of goods and services from one country to another. This also necessitates a separate theory of international trade.

Theories of International Trade

A number of theories have been put forward to explain the basis of trade between nations. This chapter gives an outline of the important theories that explain the basis of international trade.

1. The Comparative Cost Theory

In a nutshell, the Comparative Cost Theory maintains that if trade is free, each country, in the long run, will tend to specialise in the production and export of those commodities in whose production it enjoys a comparative advantage, and to obtain by import those commodities which can be produced at home at a comparative disadvantage ; and that such specialisation is to the mutual advantage of the countries participating in it.

David Ricardo illustrated the Comparative Cost Theory, in 1817, by using a **two country, two-commodity model**. His illustration of the comparative cost theory shows that trade between nations can be profitable even if one of the two nations produces both the commodities more efficiently than the other nation provided that it can produce one of these commodities with a comparatively greater efficiency than the other commodity.

The law of comparative advantage indicates that a country should specialise in the production of that commodity in which it is more efficient and leave the production of the other commodity to the other country. The two nations will then have more of both goods by engaging in trade.

In his celebrated **two country, two commodity model,** Ricardo has taken the production costs of cloth and wine in England and Portugal to illustrate the comparative cost theory.

Country	No. of Units of Labour per Unit of Cloth	No. of Units of Labour per Unit of Wine	Exchange Ratio Between Wine and Cloth
England	100	120	1 wine : 1.2 cloth
Portugal	90	80	1 wine : 0.88 cloth

From the above example, it is evident that Portugal has an absolute superiority in both the branches of production. However, a comparison of the cost of production of wine $\frac{80}{120}$ with the ratio of the cost production of cloth $\frac{90}{100}$ in both the countries reveals that, though Portugal has an absolute superiority in both the branches of production, it will pay her to concentrate on the production of wine, for she has a greater comparative advantage over England in wine relating to cloth $\frac{80}{120} < \frac{90}{100}$, and import cloth form England which has a comparative advantage in cloth production. England and will gain by specialising in producing cloth and selling it in Portugal the change of wine.

In the absence of trade between England and Portugal, one unit of wine commands 1.2 and 0.88 units of cloth in England and Portugal respectively. In the event of trade taking place, on the assumption that, within each country, labour is perfectly mobile between various industries, Portugal will gain if she can get anything more than 0.88 units of cloth in exchange of 1 unit of sine and England will gain if she has to part with less than 1.2 unit of cloth against 1 unit of wine. Hence, any exchange ratio between 0.88 units and 1.2 units of cloth against 1 unit of wine represents a gain to both the countries. The actual rate of exchange will be determined by the reciprocal demand.

Thus, according to Comparative Cost Theory, free and unrestricted trade among nations encourages specialisation on a larger scale. It thereby tends to bring about :

(a) The most efficient allocation of world resources as well as the maximisation of world production ;

(b) A redistribution of relative product demands, resulting in a greater equality of product prices among trading nations ; and

(c) A redistribution of relative resource demands to correspond with relative product demands, resulting in a relatively greater equality of resource prices among trading nations.

The **two country, two commodity model,** of Ricardo is based on the following highly simplifying assumptions :

(a) Labour is the only element of cost ;

(b) Production is subject to the law of constant returns ;

(c) International trade is free from all barriers ;

(d) No transport cost.

Quite naturally, the Comparative Cost Theory has been severely criticised for its unrealistic assumptions.

It should, however, be stated that the Comparative Cost Theory does provide some convincing explanation of the basis of international trade.

2. The Opportunity Cost Theory

The Opportunity Cost Theory, propounded by Professor Gottfried Haberler in 1983, has been applied to the theory of international trade as a substitute for the doctrine of Comparative Cost expressed in terms of labour cost or real cost.

The opportunity cost of anything is the value of the alternatives or other opportunities which have to be foregone in order to obtain that particular thing. For example, assume that a given amount of productive resources can produce either 10 units of cloth or 20 units of wine. Then the opportunity cost of 1 unit of cloth is 2 units of wine.

Thus, the opportunity cost approach defines cost in terms of the value of the alternatives of other opportunities which have to be foregone in order to achieve a particular thing.

According to the opportunity cost theory, the basis of international trade is the differences between nations in the opportunity costs of production of commodities.

As far as the basis of international trade and specialisation are concerned, the logic behind the comparative cost approach and the opportunity cost approach is the same. But there is a notable difference in the treatment. Under the comparative cost approach, we measure the cost of producing wine in terms of labour or in terms of any real cost, but under the opportunity cost approach, we measure, in constant to the comparative cost approach, the cost of producing wine in terms of the amount of cloth foregone in order to produce one more unit of wine.

For illustration of the opportunity cost theory, see appendix 2.1 at the end of the chapter.

3. Heckscher-Ohlin Thesis

Bertil Ohlin and Eli Heckscher have explained the basis of international trade in terms of factor endowments. The classical theory demonstrated that the basis of international trade was the comparative cost difference. However, it did not explain the causes of such comparative cost difference. The alternative formulation of the comparative cost doctrine developed by Heckscher and Ohlin explains why comparative cost differences exist internationally. They attribute international (and inter-regional) differences in comparative costs to :

(a) Different prevailing endowments of the factors of production ; and

(b) The fact that the production of various commodities requires that the factors of production be used with different degrees of intensity.

In short, it is the difference in factor intensities in the production functions of goods along with the actual differences in relative factor endowments of the countries which explains the international differences in the comparative cost of production.

Thus, in a nutshell, the Heckscher-Ohlin theory states that a country will specialise in the production and export of the goods whose production requires a relatively large amount of the factor with which the country is relatively well endowed with capital only if the ratio of capital to other factors is higher than in other countries.

For example, assume that :

(a) **In country A :**

Supply of Labour	=	25 units
Supply of Capital	=	20 units
Capital/labour ratio	=	0.8

(b) **In Country B :**

Supply of Labour	=	12 units
Supply of Capital	=	15 units
Capital/labour ratio	=	1.25

In the above example, even though Country A has more capital in absolute terms, Country B is more richly endowed with capital because the ratio of capital to labour in Country A (0.8) is lower than in Country B (1.25).

The **two country, two commodity model** of Heckscher and Ohlin is based on a number of explicit and implicit assumptions. The important assumptions of the model are :

(a) Both the product and factor markets in both the countries are characterised by perfect competition.

(b) The factors of production are perfectly mobile within each country but immobile between countries.

(c) The factors of production are of identical quality in both the countries.

(d) Factor supplies in each country are fixed.

(e) The factors of production are fully employed in both the countries.

(f) The factor endowments of one country vary from those of the other.

(g) There is free trade between the countries, i.e., there are no artificial barriers to trade.

(h) International trade is casteless, i.e., there is no transport cost.

(i) The techniques of producing indentical goods are the same in both the countries. Because of this act, the same input mix will give the same quantity and quality of output in both the countries.

(j) Factor intensity varies between goods. For instance, some goods are capital intensive (i.e., they require relatively more capital for their production) and some others are labour intensive (i.e., they require relatively more labour for their production.

(k) Production is subject the law of constant returns, i.e., the input/output ratio will remain constant irrespective of the scale of operations.

Most of the above assumptions are, obviously, unrealistic. The Heckscher-Ohlin model has been criticised mainly for its oversimplifying and unrealistic assumptions.

Wassily W. Leontief's study has revealed that the USA, which is a capital rich country, imported capital intensive goods and exported labour intensive goods. This has come to be popularly known as the Leontief Paradox, Which is a negation of the Heckscher-Ohlin thesis. It should, however, be pointed out that Leontief's study has been criticised as unscientific.

Despite its drawbacks ; the Heckscher-Ohlin theory has certain definite merits. These are :

(a) The Heckscher-Ohlin theory rightly points out that the immediate basis of international trade is the differences in the final price of a commodity as between countries, although the actual basis or ultimate cause of trade is the comparative cost differences in production. Thus, it provides a more comprehensive and satisfactory explanation for the existence of international trade.

(b) The Heckscher-Ohlin theory is superior to the Comparative Cost theory in some other respects also. The Ricardian theory points out that comparative cost difference is the basis of international trade; but it does not explain the reasons for the existence of comparative cost differences between nations. The Heckcscher-Ohlin theory explains the reasons for the differences in the cost of production in terms of the differences in factor endowments. This is another aspect of the Heckscher-Ohlin analysis that makes it superior to the Ricardian analysis.

(c) Further, Heckscher and Ohlin made is very clear that "international trade is but a special case of inter-local or inter-regional trade", and hence there is no need for a special theory of international trade. Ohlin states that regions and nations trade with each other for the same reasons that individuals specialise and trade. The comparative cost difference is the basis of all trade-inter-regional as well as international. Nations, according to Ohlin, are only regions distinguished from one another by such obvious marks as national frontiers, tariff barriers and differences in languages, customs and monetary systems.

The modern theory of trade is also called the General Equilibrium Theory of international trade because it points out that the general demand and supply analysis applicable to inter-regional trade may generally be used without substantial changes in dealing with problems of international trade.

(d) Another merit of the Heckscher: Ohlin theory is that it indicates the impact of trade on product and factor prices.

The Heckscher-Ohlin theory indicates that international trade will ultimately have the following results :

(a) Equalisation of commodity Prices

International trade tends to equalise the prices of internationally traded goods in all the regions of the world because trade causes the movement of commodities from areas where they are abundant to areas where they are scarce. This would tend to increase commodity prices where there is abundance and decrease prices where there is scarcity by reason of redistribution of commodity supply between these two regions as a result of trade. International trade tends to expand up to the point where prices in all the regions become equal. But perfect equality of prices can hardly be achieved because of the existence of transport costs and the absence of free trade and perfect competition.

(b) Equalisation of Factor Prices

International trade also tends to equalise factor prices all over the world. It increases the demand for abundant factors (leading to an increase in their prices) and decreases the demand for scarce factors (leading to a fall in their prices) because, when nations are on trade, specialisation takes place on the basis of factor endowments. But, in reality, the presence of a number of imperfections make the achievement of perfect equality in factor prices impossible.

4. The Availability Approach

The availability approach to the theory of international trade seeks to explain the pattern of trade in terms of domestic availability and non-availability of goods. Availability influences operation through both demand and supply forces.

In a nutshell, the availability approach purports that a nation would tend to import those commodities which are not readily available domestically and export those whose domestic supply can be easily expanded beyond the quantity needed to satisfy the domestic demand.

Kravis argues that Leontief's finding that the United States' exports have a higher labour content and a lower capital content than its imports may be explained better and more simply by the availability factor. Goods that happen to have a high capital content are bought abroad because they are not available at home. Some are unavailable in the absolute sense (for example, diamonds) ; others in the sense that an increase in output may be achieved only at much higher costs (that is, the domestic supply is inelastic). When unavailability at home is due to lack of natural resources (relative to demand), the comparative advantage argument is perfectly adequate.

According to Kravis, there are other facts of the availability explanation of commodity trade pattern that cannot be so readily subsumed under the ruberic "comparative advantage". One of these is the effect of technological change. Historical data for the United States indicate that exports have tended to increase most in those industries which have new or improved products that are available only in the United States or in a few other places at the most. Product differentiation and government restrictions are the other factors tending to increase the proportion of international trade that represents purchases by the improving country of goods that are not available at home.

According to Kravis, there are, thus, four bases of the availability factor, namely :

(a) Natural resources ;

(b) Technological progress ;

(c) Product differentiation ; and

(d) Government policy.

The first three of the four bases — natural resources, technological progress and product differentiation — probably tend, on the whole, to increase the volume of international trade. The absence of free competition, a necessary condition for the unfettered operation of the law of comparative advantage, tends to limit trade to goods that cannot be produced by the importing country, argues Kravis. The most important restrictions on international competition are those imposed by the government and by cartels. Those imports that are unavailable or available only at a formidable cost are subject to the least governmental interference. Kravis is of the opinion that the quantitative importance of the availability factor in international trade is considerable. The appears to apply especially to half of world trade that consists of trade between the industrial areas on the one hand and the primary producing areas on the other.

The availability approach has, undoubtedly, considerable merit in its explanation of the pattern of trade.

Role of Foreign Trade in Economic Development

Economic theory gives sufficient support to the view that foreign trade plays a vital role in the economic development of a country. Its contribution to the growth of national income can be quite substantial. As Kindleberger observes: "If a country is pulled into world trade....... the country can and should maximise its real income by specialising along lines of comparative advantage". There is no doubt that the volume and composition of foreign trade as well as the terms of trade have a profound influence on the character and the extent of development of a country. Robertson calls trade an **"engine of growth"**.

Cairncross also highlights the importance of foreign trade in economic development thus: "Over the past century and a half the growth of international trade has continued to open up new opportunities of specialisation and development for the countries engaged in it. These opportunities were particularly apparent in the primary-producing countries overseas that were still in process of settlement, since trade enabled them to bring into use unexploited natural resources and freed them from the limitations of their own domestic markets".

From the point of view of economic development, both imports and exports are important. It is through imports that a country is enabled to obtain plant, machinery and equipment, components, raw materials, technical know-how, which are indispensable for accelerating economic development. If an under-developed country wishes to break the vicious circle of poverty, attain self-sustained growth and transform itself from an agrarian economy to an industrialised one, it will have to import the various requisites of development. Haberler mentions four factors which are essential for economic development and which are made available through foreign trade.

(a) Provision of capital through international investment ;

(b) access to the means of development in the form of raw-materials ;

(c) Semi-finished goods and machinery ;

(d) Access to knowledge, skill, managerial ability and so on and the galvanishing influence of competition.

Thus the economic growth of a country is helped not merely through the exchange of material goods, but also through the exchange of ideas and experience. Both the visible and invisible items are useful in promoting economic development.

International trade helps the economic development of the country in the following ways :

1. It Speeds up the Process of Economic Development

The international trade helps the economic development of an underdeveloped economy by expanding its productive capacity. It encourages the setting up of basic and key industries such as iron and steel industry, heavy electricals and engineering goods industry, the hydro-electric projects etc. Such industries require the imports of plant, machinery, equipment and other appliances as they cannot be produced at home in the initial stages of economic development. Such imports which help expand the productive capacity of the economy are termed as 'developmental imports'. Once these basic and key industries are set up, their capacity must be fully utilised and to do so, the imports of essential raw materials, spare parts and intermediate products become essential. Such imports which help full utilisation of the existing capacity are knows as **'maintenance imports'**. A developing country needs both developmental and maintenance imports for promoting economic development. Besides, international trade facilitates the import of essential consumers' goods such as food-stuffs to meet the rising requirements of the people due to the increase in their incomes generated by the growing investments. The international trade, thus, promotes economic development through expansion of imports and growth of basic industries.

To pay for the imports, exports must also increase proportionately. Of course foreign aid can and does help the developing countries to tide over the difficulties temporarily in their balance of payments but it is not a lasting solution of the problem. Foreign loans create future obligations and increase the burden of debt. Ultimately exports must match the imports, failing which the pace of economic development will slow down. Thus, both imports and exports are essential for the economic development of a country. Hence international trade plays a key role in securing an accelerated rate of economic growth by increasing world output and providing access to scarce resources and world wide markets for products without which poor countries would be unable to grow.

2. It provides Necessary Infra-Structure

The underdeveloped countries generally exchange food-stuffs and raw materials which have low growth potential against machinery and capital goods which have high growth potential. This quickens the pace of economic development by providing social and economic overheads and directly productive activities. As economic development proceeds, the exports of raw materials decline because they are needed to meet the growing requirements of home industries. Consequently, the developing countries have to find new markets for their industrial products to provide for rising imports and cover deficits in their balance of payments. The developed countries can help by liberalising imports from these countries. Foreign trade, therefore, can go a long way in helping the process of economic development of underdeveloped countries.

3. It Widens the Extent of the Market

Foreign trade helps economic development in yet another way also. One of the important factors that hinders economic growth of underdeveloped countries is the small size of their domestic market which in turn leads to low inducement to invest ; low per capita income; low saving and low investment. Thus, these countries are caught in a vicious circle of poverty. Foreign trade can help break this circle by widening the market, stimulating the inducement to invest and thereby raising the volume of saving and investment. Not only this, the expansion of the market results in various types of internal and external economies which lower the costs of production and widen the market still further. This makes the process of economic development cumulative in character. In the words of Meier and Baldwin, "Through the operation of a multiplier-accelerator process the increased income earned in the textile industry induced expansion in the other industries. Part of the growing total income earned in the textile trade was spent on consumption commodities, and this induced an expansion of output in other industries whose factors of production spent, in turn, part of their greater income on consumption goods and thus induced further production and so on, as the multiplier process gradually worked itself out".

4. It Has Great Educative Effect

Besides the direct gains, foreign trade helps economic development in various other ways also. It has great educative effect. It encourages inventions and innovations. It raises labour productivity by increasing the scope of specialisation and size of the market. According to Haberler, foreign trade is, "the means and vehicle for the dissemination of technical knowledge, the transmission of ideas, for the importation of technical know-how, skills, managerial talents and entrepreneurship". The importation of critical skills, technical know-how, ideas and innovations goes a long way in stimulating technological progress in underdeveloped countries and accelerating the pace of their development.

5. It Encourages the Inflow of Capital

The volume of foreign aid depends, among other things, on the volume of foreign trade. The larger the volume of foreign trade, the greater the repaying capacity of foreign capital and hence greater the inflow of foreign capital. Foreign capital not only increases the level of income, output and employment but also helps to tide over balance of payments difficulties and inflationary pressures. It also brings with it entrepreneurship, managerial talents, technical know how, skills and ideas which play a vital role in economic development. International trade thus, serves as the vehicle for the international movements of capital and ideas. Emphasising the importance of foreign capital through trade, J.S. Mill observed, "The foreign capital which renders the increase of production no longer exclusively dependent on the thrift or providence of the inhabitants themselves, while it places before them a stimulating example, and by instilling new ideas and breaking the chain of habit, if not by improving the actual condition of the population, tends to create in them new wants, increased ambition and greater thought for the future".

6. It Brings Efficiency in Production

There exists a vast nonmonetised sector in underdeveloped countries. Agriculture is carried on as a mode of living rather than a business proposition. Foreign trade creates remunerative markets for the agricultural produce and thereby helps to transform the subsistence sector into a commercial sector. The level of income of the peasantry increases and they become development minded and help the process of economic growth.

Foreign trade creates the spirit of healthy competition and brings efficiency in production. There takes place an improvement in production functions both upwards and outwards. The inefficient production units and exploitative monopolies are weeded out. The general improvement in the tone and efficiency of the economic system quickens the pace of economic development. In sum, we may say that foreign trade enlarges a country's consumption capacities, increases world output and provides access to scarce resources and world wide markets for products without which poor countries would be unable to grow. Thus foreign trade is an important stimulator of economic growth.

It promotes greater international and domestic equality by equalizing factor prices, raising real incomes of trading countries and making efficient use of each nation's and the world's resources.

Further, foreign trade helps countries to achieve development by promoting and rewarding those sectors of the economy where individual countries possess a comparative advantage whether in terms of labour, efficiency or factor endowments and thus maximises its national welfare.

Conclusion

From the above analysis, it is clear that foreign trade plays a vital role in the economic development of underdeveloped countries.

Questions for Discussion

1. What is international trade ? Describe the differences between internal trade and international trade ?
2. What is the role of international trade in economic development.
3. Critically examine the Theory of Comparative Cost Advantage.
4. Critically examine Ohlin's theory of international Trade.

Chapter - 2

GAINS FROM INTERNATIONAL TRADE

Introduction

International trade confers a variety of gains and benefits on the participating countries. That is why nations of the world are interested in the promotion of trade and commerce among themselves.

Gains from International Trade

The following gains accrue to the participating nations from international trade :

1. Advantages of Territorial Division of Labour

The biggest gain of international trade relates to the advantages accruing from territorial division of labour and international specialization. International trade enables a country to specialize in the production of those commodities in which it enjoys special advantages. All countries are not equally endowed with natural resources and other facilities for the production of goods and services of various kinds. Some countries are richly endowed with land and forest resources while others happen to have abundant capital resources. Some others have abundant supplies of labour power. Without international trade, a country will have to produce all the goods it requires irrespective of the costs involved. But international trade enables a country to produce only those goods in which it has a comparative or an absolute advantage. This leads to international specialization or division of labour which confers benefits on all the nations participating in trade. Great Britain specializes in capital-intensive goods, India in labour-intensive goods, while Australia concentrates on land-intensive goods like wheat, meat and wool.

2. Increase in Production

International trade leads to an increase in the world output of goods and services on account of the various advantages flowing from international specialization. How international trade leads to an increase in production can be illustrated with the following example :

Country	Labour (Unit)	Cotton (Units)	Jute (Units)
Egypt	1	20	10
India	1	10	20

Egypt can produce with one unit of labour either 20 units of cotton or 10 units of jute. Likewise, India can produce with one unit of labour either 10 units of cotton or 20 units of jute. Egypt enjoys an absolute advantage over India in cotton and suffers an absolute disadvantage in comparison with India in jute. Likewise, India enjoys an absolute advantage in jute and suffers an absolute disadvantage in cotton. Thus, Egypt will produce cotton and export it to India. India, in turn, will specialize in jute and export it to Egypt. This international trade will lead to an expansion in output of the two countries.

Let us suppose that the two countries do not specialize, but produce both the commodities. Then, with 2 units of labour, Egypt's total production would be 20 units of cotton + 10 units of jute. Likewise, India's total output with 2 units of labour would be 10 units of cotton + 20 units of jute. The total combined output of the two goods of the two countries would be 30 units of cotton + 30 units of jute. But if the two countries specialize, then with the application of 2 units each of labour, the total combined output of the two countries would be 40 units of cotton + 40 units of jute. Thus, there would be a net increase of 10 units each in cotton and jute if the two countries decide to go in for specialization. The point to be noted is that free international trade based on specialization always leads to expansion of the world's supply of goods and services.

3. Equitable Distribution of Scarce Resources

There are certain scarce resources which are the exclusive monopoly of a single country or a group of countries. For example, petroleum is the monopoly of certain Middle Eastern countries which have organized themselves into an international cartel. International trade is the only means by which such scarce resources can be equitably distributed among all the nations of the world.

4. Equality in Commodity and Factor Prices

International trade leads to an equalization of the prices of internationally traded goods and productive factors in all the regions of the world. Just how this materializes has been explained at length earlier in the section on "Effects of International Trade".

Broadly speaking, the gains from international trade can be classified under two heads – (a) Gains arising out of international specialization, and (b) Gains arising from exchange values. The gains arising from specialization comprise better utilization of resources, saving of time, improvement in skills and techniques. Gains from exchange include better prices for both countries. The exporting country gets a higher price for its goods while the importing country receives the goods at lower prices, taking into account its domestic costs.

It should however, be remembered that the gains arising from international trade shall be available to the participating countries only if trade is free and unfettered. If the trade is subjected to tariff and non-tariff restrictions by the trading countries, then the gains of international trade shall be nullified in the process. It is also important that the costs of transport should not be unduly high. High transport costs have always the effect of obstructing international trade.

It is clear by now that the gain from international trade arises primarily from two major sources. *First*, international specialization based on the principle of comparative advantage. International specialization has the effect of cutting down costs per unit of the commodities, thus, leading to lower commodity prices. *Second*, the economies of large-scale production further contribute to the lessening of production costs in course of time. It is clear that the size of the market always expands as a consequence of an expansion of foreign trade. An increase in the size of the market inevitably leads to an expansion of output, creating scope for the economies of large-scale production. The economies of large-scale production inevitably result in a reduction in the costs per unit of the output.

Determinants of Gain from International Trade

The size of the gain from international trade is determined by a large variety of factors Some important determinants of the size of gain are as follows :

1. Terms of Trade

The term "Terms of Trade" refers to the *rate* at which country's exports exchange for imports. The terms of trade are determined by the relationship between the prices of exports and the prices of imports. The size of the gain accruing to a country out of international trade is naturally determined by the nature of its terms of trade. The terms of trade of a country can be favourable or unfavourable. Favourable terms of trade imply that the country concerned will get a larger share of the gain out of international trade. Unfavourable terms of trade, on the contrary, means that a relatively smaller share of the gain out of international trade would accrue to the country concerned. It is, however, clear that both the countries cannot have favourable terms of trade. If one country happens to have favourable terms of trade, the other country must, by necessity, have unfavourable terms of trade. Broadly speaking, the terms of trade are favourable to a country when the international exchange ratio (or, exchange ratio between the two countries) settles closer to the domestic exchange ratio of the other country. But they are unfavourable to a country if the international exchange ratio settles closer or coincides with the domestic exchange ratio of that country.

2. Elasticity of Demand

The gain from international trade also depends upon the elasticity of demand for the commodities in the two countries. It has already been pointed out earlier in the preceding section that international trade leads to an expansion in output in both the countries. Real income in both the countries also registers an increase. As a result, the gain from international trade also increases. But the size of this gain also depends upon the elasticity of demand of the commodities of the two countries. Greater the elasticity of demand for the commodities in the two countries, greater would be the volume of international trade. Greater the volume of international trade, greater would be the real income in the two countries. Greater the real income, the larger shall be the size of the aggregate gain.

The distribution of the gain between the two countries will also be governed by the relative elasticity of demand of their products. More inelastic the demand for the product in the importing country, greater would be the share of the gain of the exporting country.

3. Improvement in Productivity

An improvement in productivity in the two countries also increases the size of the gain arising out of international trade. With improvement in productivity, costs and prices fall in both the countries, leading to an expansion of international trade and also an enlargement of the size of the gain. If, however, the productivity increases in one country, the advantage would accrue to the other country because the latter's terms of trade would become more favourable than before.

4. Difference in Cost Ratios

The size of the gain, it is pointed out, also depends upon the relationship between the ratio of the costs of production of the two commodities in the two countries. It is governed by the relationship between the ratio of the cost of production of good. A to good B in one country and the ratio of the cost of production of good. A to good B in the other country. The existence of differences in cost ratios in the two countries is an essential prerequisite for the emergence of gain out of international trade. The greater the difference in cost ratios, larger would be the size of the gain.

5. Stage of Development

The sharing of the gain out of international trade between the two countries is also governed by the stage of development in which a country finds itself. An industrially advanced and capital-rich country generally enjoys a larger share of the gain of trade than an economically backward and labour-abundant country. The reason is obvious. A country exporting capital intensive goods generally enjoys more favourable terms of trade than a country exporting primary or labour-intensive goods.

Measurement of Gain from International Trade

The classical economists adopted the following alternative criteria for measuring the gain arising out of international trade.

1. Reduction in Production Costs

According to the classical economists, the gain arising out of international trade can be measured by the extent to which production costs decline as a consequence of trade among countries. In fact, reduction in production costs is looked upon as a true measure of the gain of international trade. There is no denying the fact that international trade is the result of territorial division of labour or international specialization. Specialization, regional or international, always results in improved productivity which, along with other factors, brings about a reduction in costs. The greater the reduction in costs, the larger the size of gain from international trade.

2. Increase in Real Income

The second alternative criterion, according to the classical economists, is the increase in real income in the participating countries as a result of international trade. The gain, according to this criterion, is measured by the extent to which the net national product (N.N.P) or the real income of a country increases as a consequence of international trade. It need hardly be said that international trade generally increases the net national product of the participating countries ; otherwise, they would not engage themselves in trading activity. The extent to which it increases is the true measure of the gain of trade.

3. Terms of Trade

This represents the most reliable criterion for measuring the share of gain from trade accruing to a country. "Terms of trade" have already been defined as the rate at which country's exports exchange for its imports. The share of gain accruing to a country out of international trade is determined to a very large extent by the nature of its terms of trade. More favourable the terms of trade of a country, the larger shall be its share of total gain out of trade. In other words, a country with favourable terms of trade reaps a larger share of the gain out of trade. Conversely, a country with unfavourable terms of trade will secure for itself a smaller share of the gain.

We may point out here that, whatever the criterion, there cannot be any exact or accurate measurement of the share of gain accruing to a country out of international trade. The "terns of trade", however, provides the most popular and the most scientific basis for measuring the gain out of trade. It is, therefore, to this concept that we turn not for detailed treatment.

Conclusion

It is clear by now that the gain from international trade arises primarily from two major sources i.e., international specialization based on the principle of comparative advantage and the economics of large scale production further contribute to the lessening of production costs in course of time.

Questions for Discussion

1. What are the gains of trade of explain?
2. How can the gains of trade be measured?
3. What factors affect the distribution of gains?

Chapter - 3

TERMS OF TRADE

Introduction

As already pointed out, the term "Terms of Trade" refers to the *rate* at which a country's exports exchange for its imports. Terms of trade are naturally governed by the prices of exports and imports entering into international trade. They indicate the relationship between prices of exports and prices of imports of a country. The terms of trade are said to be favourable to a country when the prices of its exports are high relatively to the prices of its imports. In the same manner, the terms of trade are said to be unfavourable to a country when the prices of its imports are high relatively to the prices of its exports. There are several concepts of terms of trade. Following Gerald M. Meier, we can classify them as follows.

1. Those terms of trade which refer to the rate of exchange between goods :
   (a) Net Barter Terms of Trade,
   (b) Gross Barter Terms of Trade, and
   (c) Income Terms of Trade.
2. Those terms of trade which refer to the exchange between productive factors :
   (a) Single Factoral Terms of Trade, and
   (b) Double Factoral Terms of Trade.
3. Those terms of trade which express the gain arising from international trade in terms of utility :
   (a) Real Cost Terms of Trade, and
   (b) Utility Terms of Trade.

Now we shall discuss each one of them briefly and try to understand their significance.

1. Gross Barter Terms of Trade

The distinction between "gross" and "net" barter terms of trade was introduced by Taussing in 1927. Symbolically, we can express gross barter terms as follow :

$$G = \frac{M_q}{X_q} \times 100$$

Where M_q stands for the import quantity index, X_q for export quantity index and G for gross barter terms. We multiply the whole expression M_q / X_q by 100 in order to get rid of the decimal, and there is no other significance to this number. Let us illustrate the concept with some concrete examples.

The quantity index of imports and exports for the base year (say 1990) will always be equal to 100. The base year will serve as the benchmark period with which we can measure changes in the gross barter terms of trade in any given subsequent year – say 1991, 1992, ..., 2000 etc. Let us look at the following hypothetical sets :

Gross Barter Terms of Trade Index

$$\text{1990 base year} : G = \frac{100}{100} \times 100 = 100 \text{ (base year)}$$

$$\text{1991} \quad G = \frac{120}{100} \times 100 = 120 \text{ (improvement)}$$

$$\text{1992} \quad G = \frac{120}{120} \times 100 = 120 \text{ (no change)}$$

$$\text{1993} \quad G = \frac{100}{120} \times 100 = 83.33 \text{ (deterioration)}$$

For, 1991, the import quantity index is up from 100 to 120 and the export quantity is the same. This means that in 1991 we export the same quantity as in 1990, but we import more in 1991 than in 1990. In other words, the purchasing power of exports has gone up in 1991 compared to the base year 1990. There has been, therefore, a 20 percentage point improvement in the gross barter terms of trade in 1991 as compared to the year 1990. In 1992, compared with the base year 1990, however, there has been no change in gross barter terms. Because both the import and the export quantity index numbers have gone up from 100 to 120 between these two periods. The gross barter terms of trade index is 100 both for 1990 and 1992. In 1993, as compared to the base year 1990, there has been a deterioration in gross barter terms. The import quantity index is constant at 100 both for 1993 and the base year 1990, but the export quantity index for 1993 is 120 as against the base period index of 100. This means that in 1993 we import the same quantity as in 1990 but we are paying more for these imports as indicated by the increase in the export quantity index (from 100 in 1990 to 120 in 1993). Put simply what it means is that we are forced to export more to import the same quantity in 1993 as compared to the year 1990.

In brief, an increase in the import quantity index (the numerator value) tends to improve gross barter terms, while an increase in the export quantity index (the denominator value) would tend to worsen the gross barter terms of trade. The concept of terms of trade used in the theory of reciprocal demand and offer curves or in the neo-classical comparative advantage analysis is in this gross barter terms of trade sense. This concept has its own merits, but it is not the commonly used expression of the terms of trade concept in today's world.

2. Net Barter or commodity Terms of Trade

This is the most commonly (almost universally) used expression for the terms of trade changes in the contemporary world. The gross barter terms concept uses *quantity index* for imports and exports, whereas the net barter or commodity terms concept makes use of the price index for imports and exports. Herein lies the distinction between gross and net barter terms of trade. Symbolically the net barter terms of trade can be written as follows :

$$N = \frac{X_p}{M_p} \times 100$$

Where X_p and M_p stand for price index numbers of exports and imports, respectively, and N stands for net barter or commodity terms. As in the previous case, the expression is multiplied by 100 only to get rid of the decimal.

The price index of imports and exports for the base year (say 1990) will always be equal to 100. We express commodity terms changes in subsequent years always with reference to the base year index. Take a look at the following hypothetical sets of commodity price index numbers of imports and exports.

Commodity Terms of Trade Index

1990 : $N = \frac{100}{100} \times 100 = 100$ (base year)

1991 : $N = \frac{120}{100} \times 100 = 120$ (improvement)

1992 : $N = \frac{100}{120} \times 100 = 83.33$ (deterioration)

1993 : $N = \frac{120}{120} \times 100 = 100$ (no change)

1994 : $N = \frac{96}{80} \times 100 = 120$ (improvement)

1995 : $N = \frac{126}{140} \times 100 = 90$ (deterioration)

In 1991 there is an improvement in commodity terms by 20 percentage points, because we buy our imports at the same price (as in 1990) but sell out exports at a higher price (20 percent higher than in 1990). In 1992, there is a deterioration in commodity terms, because we sell our exports at the same price (as in 1990) but buy our imports at a higher price. In 1993, however, there has been an increase in both the export price index and the import price index by the same percentage point (viz. 20 percent) which leaves the terms of trade unchanged. In 1994 there has been a decrease in both import and export price index, and in 1995, there has been an increase in both index numbers in such a way that commodity terms have turned "favourable" in 1994 but "unfavourable" in 1995 (as compared to the base year 1990). The simple rule is that if there is an increase in our selling price (export price index) there will be an improvement in commodity terms, and if there is an increase in our buying price (import price index) there will be an unfavourable movement in commodity terms of trade.

There is a general belief that improvement in commodity terms would mean an improvement in the economic welfare of the country. Because when the export prices go up we sell our goods at a higher price, and when import prices go down, we will be able to buy foreign goods at a lower price. In either case, commodity terms improve and the country is better off in terms of economic welfare. From this one comes to the conclusion that maximization of commodity terms of trade would mean maximization of economic welfare of a country. But Haberler has, however, argued that the terms of trade should be optimized rather than maximized because the economic welfare of a country will be maximized not when the commodity terms are maximized but when they are optimized. Let us pursue this point and see what Harberler's argument means.

What is important to a country, from welfare viewpoint, is not how high are the export prices but how high are the export earnings. If we are able to sell our export goods at a very high price, (thereby improving commodity terms) it could mean that foreigners buy less of our export goods. In this case we end up with reduced export earnings and thereby reduced economic welfare. What we cannot afford to ignore, is the elasticity of demand for our export goods. Just as the optimum price of a monopolist – the price which maximizes monopoly profits – is not the highest price which the monopolist would be able to charge, the optimum terms of trade which maximize welfare is not the highest price of exports which a country could possibly obtain. Take for instance, the following fig. 20.

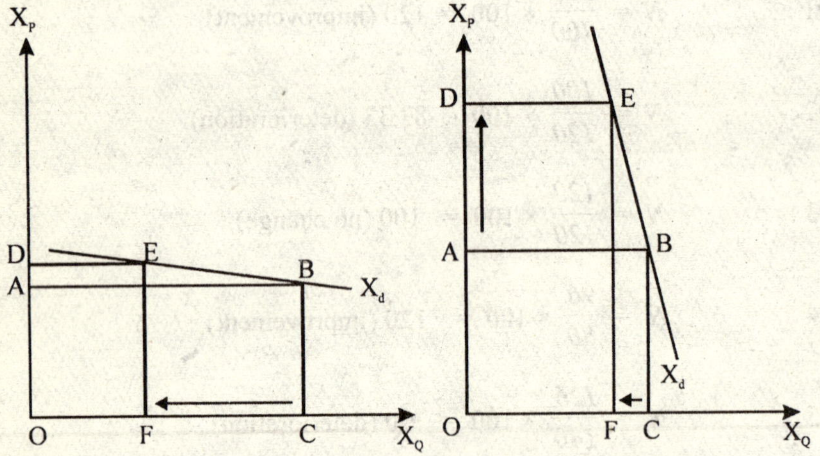

In both the diagrams above, we measure export prices along the vertical axis and export quantities along the horizontal axis. In Diagram. 1A, the export demand curve is very elastic, and in Diagram 1B, it is very inelastic. A slight increase in export prices from *OA* to *OD*, in Diagram 1A, will lead to a substantial fall in the export volume, from *OC* to *OF*. As a result, the export earnings after the export price increase (*ODEF*) are far less than the export earnings before (*OABC*). In such a situation, while commodity terms have improved, export earnings have gone down, reducing the welfare of the country. In Diagram 1B, however, inspite of a very substantial increase in export prices, (from *OA* to *OD*) there is only a very small drop in our export quantities (from *OC* to *OF*) such that the export earnings after the export price increase (*ODEF*) are substantially higher than before (*OABC*). It is, therefore, very important to consider the export demand elasticities before pronouncing a judgement on whether the welfare of the country would go up as a result of an increase in export prices. In other words it is essential to take into account the effect of export price increases on the volume of exports, because we are interested in maximizing export earnings rather than export prices.

The same thing can be said about the import price changes. A decrease in import prices would of course result in an improvement in commodity terms, but it does not necessarily follow from this that the welfare of the country has also improved at the same time. The elasticity of domestic demand for foreign goods will have to be considered. Look at the following two situations for clarification.

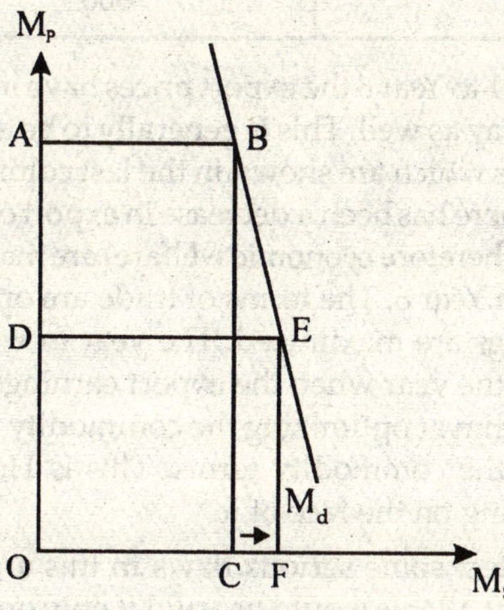

Diagram 2A

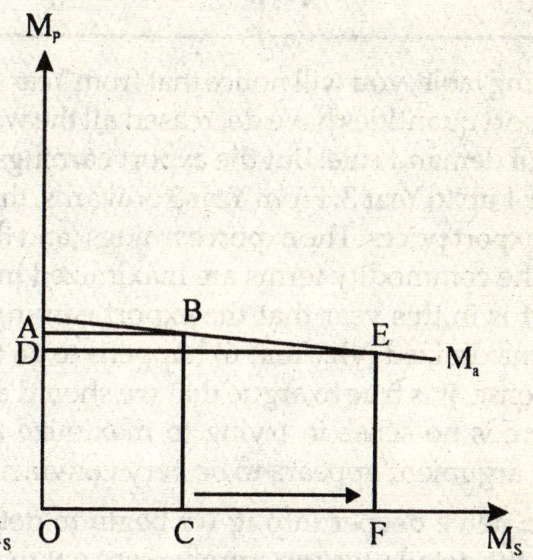

Diagram 2B

Inelastic Import Demand and Elastic Import Demand.

In both the diagrams above, we measure export prices along the vertical axis and import quantities along the horizontal axis. The import demand curve is inelastic in diagram 2A and it is elastic in Diagram 2B. A substantial drop in import prices (from *OA* to *OD*) in Diagram 2A has led to only a small increase in the level of imports (from *OC* to *OF*) such that the import spendings after the import price decrease (*ODEF*) are considerably less than before (*OABC*). In this case, we can say that the improvement in commodity terms brought about by a fall in import prices has led to a reduction in import spendings and therefore to an increase in the welfare of the country. This has happened because the domestic demand for the imported goods is rather inelastic with respect to import prices. In Diagram 2B, however, the situation is the opposite. Here, a small drop in import prices (from *OA* to *OD*) has resulted in a very substantial increase in the level of imports (from *OC* to *OF*) such that the import spendings after the import price decrease (*ODEF*) are substantially more than before (*OABC*). In this situation, the commodity terms have improved due to a fall in import prices but the economic welfare has gone down, since import spendings have gone up.

It is, therefore, not necessarily true to say that maximization of terms of trade will mean maximization of the economic welfare of the country. What necessary is, to optimize the terms of trade rather than maximize the terms of trade. The following table will make this point clear.

Year	Export Price Per Unit ($) (1)	Export Quantity (Units) (2)	Export Earnings ($) (3 = 1 □ 2)
1	8	120	960
2	10	100	1,000
3	15	80	1,200
4	20	50	1,000
5	25	30	750
6	30	20	600

In the succeeding table, you will notice that from Year 1 to Year 6 the export prices have increased all the way; and export quantities have decreased all the way as well. This is generally to be expected because of the law of demand rule. But the export earnings which are shown in the last column have increased from Year 1 up to Year 3. From Year 3 onwards, there has been a decrease in export earnings, despite increase in export prices. The export earnings (and therefore economic welfare) are maximized in Year 3 whereas the commodity terms are maximized in Year 6. The terms of trade are optimized in Year 3 because it is in this year that the export earnings are maximized. The year in which the terms of trade are maximized (viz. Year 6) happens to be the year when the export earnings are the minimum. In this sense, it is true to argue that we should aim at optimizing the commodity terms of trade and that there is no sense in trying to maximize the commodity terms. This is Haberler's contention and the argument appears to be very convincing on the face of it.

If we begin to delve deeper into it, we begin to detect some serious flaws in this argument. Without going into the details, we can simply point out that all this would be valid if only one makes an unrealistic assumption that there is no cost involved in producing export goods. As soon as we begin to argue–and quite realistically so–that export production does involve factor use and factor cost and that marginal costs of producing those goods will be on the rise, the above argument put forth by Haberler tends to be weak. The relation between the terms of trade and economic welfare, as pointed out by Haberler himself, are quite intricate, and therefore one should exercise great care in the interpretation of given changes in the terms of trade in so far as they may affect the welfare of a country.

The commodity terms of trade are the most commonly used measure of terms of trade changes in a country, although it is not so easy to derive immediate welfare implication from those terms of trade changes.

3. Income Terms of Trade

Since it is very important for any country to take into account changes in its volume of exports resulting from export price changes, it is useful to correct the movements in commodity terms for changes in export volume. This is done by the concept of income terms of trade, which was first formulated by G.S. Dorrance in 1948-49. Symbolically we can write it as follows :

$$I = N.X_q \left(or\ I = \frac{X_p}{M_p} \times X_q \ or\ I = \frac{X_p . X_q}{M_p} \right)$$

Where N refers to net barter or commodity terms of trade index (i.e. X_p / M_p), X_q stands for the export quantity index, and *I* stands for income terms of trade. For clarification, let us take a look at the following sets of cases.

Income Terms of Trade Index

$$1990: \quad I = \frac{100 \times 100}{100} \times 100 \text{ (base year)}$$

$$1991: \quad I = \frac{90 \times 120}{100} \times 108 \text{ (improvement)}$$

$$1992: \quad I = \frac{110 \times 80}{100} \times 88 \text{ (deterioration)}$$

For the base year 1990, we assign a value of 100 for all the three variables. viz., export price index, import price index and the export quantity index. Income terms of trade index must, therefore, also be 100 for the base year 1990. Now, in 1991, there has been a fall in the export price index with no change in the import price index suggesting that the commodity terms have worsened. But there has been an increase in the export quantity index from 100 to 120 in 1991. A 10 percentage point decrease in the export price index is, therefore, matched by a 20 percentage point increase in the export quantity index so that in the end, we notice that there has been an 8 percentage point improvement in the income terms of trade in 1991 compared with the base year 1990. In other words, between 1990 and 1991, income terms of trade have improved although the commodity terms of trade have worsened, and the country is better off as reflected by the changes in income terms of trade.

In 1992, as compared with 1990, however, the situation is the opposite; commodity terms have improved by 10 percentage points but income terms have deteriorated by 12 percentage points (from the index of 100 in 1990 to an index of 88 in 1992), and this is because of a 20 percentage point drop in the export quantity index (from an index of 100 in 1990 to an index of 80 in 1992). Income terms of trade have worsened in 1992 even though the commodity terms have improved in that year. The country has been worse off in 1992 (as compared to 1990) due to the worsening of income terms of trade.

What are the welfare implications of the concept of income terms of trade? Practically name. A rise in income terms of trade only indicates that the country can obtain a larger volume of imports from the sale of its exports; its "capacity of import" –based on exports–has increased. A change in the income terms of trade index cannot be interpreted as a measure of the gain from trade or an indicator of welfare. It should be used simply as a measure of the quantity of imports bought by exports.

There is another question. Can we replace commodity terms of trade concept and use, instead, only the income terms of trade concept in its place? In order to answer this question, let us examine the following sets of cases.

Income Terms of Trade Index

$$1990: \quad I = \frac{100 \times 100}{100} \times 100 \text{ (base year)}$$

$$1991: \quad I = \frac{90 \times 120}{100} \times 108 \text{ (improvement)}$$

$$1992: \quad I = \frac{120 \times 90}{100} \times 108 \text{ (improvement)}$$

The income terms of trade are 8 percentage point higher in both 1991 and 1992 as compared with the base year 1990. Can we then say that the situation has been *equally good* in 1991 or in 1992 compared with the year 1990 ? By looking only at income terms of trade index figures, the answer would be "yes". But this would give a misleading picture. For a fuller grasp of the situation, we must know the commodity terms of trade changes. For instance, in 1991, we are selling our exports at a lower price but we are selling more of export quantity. In 1992, we are selling our exports at a higher price but we are selling a smaller export quantity. But in both years 1991 and 1992, our income terms have improved by the same degree. We definitely prefer 1992 situation to 1991 situation and this preference is based on the movement in commodity terms of trade. In 1991, commodity terms have worsened and in 1992, they have improved (compared to 1990 base year), although income terms of trade in both 1991 and 1992 are equally good. Our choice of 1992 as the preferred position has been based on the information, we receive from commodity terms of trade and not income terms of trade. The significance of what is said here is, that the concept of income terms of trade can supplement but by no means replace the concept of commodity terms of trade.

4. Single Factoral Terms of Trade

While income terms of trade correct the commodity terms of trade for changes in the export volume, there is another attempt to correct commodity terms for changes in the productivity in producing export goods. The single factoral terms of trade is an attempt in that direction. It was Jacob Viner who developed the concepts of single and double factoral terms of trade in 1937.

The single factoral terms of trade is the ratio of the export price index and the import price index adjusted for changes in the productivity of the factors used in export production. Symbolically, it can be expressed as :

$$S = N.X_z \left(or\ S = \frac{X_p}{M_p} \times X_z \ or\ S = \frac{X_p . X_z}{M_p} \right)$$

Where N represents commodity terms, X_z stands for the export productivity index, and S stands for single factoral terms of trade. The following sets of cases will make the point clear.

Single Factoral Terms of Trade Index

$$1990: \quad S = \frac{100 \times 100}{100} = 100 \text{ (base year)}$$

$$1991: \quad S = \frac{90 \times 100}{100} = 90 \text{ (deterioration)}$$

$$1992: \quad S = \frac{90 \times 120}{100} = 108 \text{ (improvement)}$$

$$1993: \quad S = \frac{80 \times 125}{100} = 100 \text{ (no change)}$$

For the base year 1990, we give a value of 100 for each of the three variables involved, viz., export price index, import price index and export productivity index. The index of *S*, therefore, must also have a value of 100 for the base year. 1991, there has been a drop in export price index by 10 percentage points which is not offset by any export productivity index, so that single factoral terms have deteriorated by 10 percentage points. In 1992, however, the fall in export price index (by 10 percentage points) is more than offset by a 20 percentage point increase in the export productivity index so that the single factoral terms have improved by 8 percentage points. In other words, in 1991, there has been a worsening of both the commodity terms and the single factoral terms, since there is no change in productivity of export production. In 1992, by contrast, there is worsening of commodity terms but improvement in single factoral terms, which is made possible by increase in productivity of export production.

In 1993, adverse commodity terms have been just neutralized to keep single factoral terms of trade constant. What does this signify ? The 1993 situation clearly shows that the country has suffered a fall in export prices for its export products; and export prices have dropped by 20 percentage points. Commodity terms would clearly reflect this deterioration. But, then the country has been able to absorb this shock of lower export prices by raising productivity in the export sector by 25 percentage points. This is tantamount to saying that the country has brought down the production costs by 25 percent through various measures such as improved technology, labour efficiency etc. Greater productive efficiency has kept the single factoral terms constant in the face of falling commodity terms. Put in a different perspective what it means is, that the country has taken pains to improve its productive efficiency and to cut down production costs, and these productivity gains have been transferred over to the foreign countries in the form of lower prices for exported products. This exporting country in such a situation experiences no productivity gain or improvements in living standards. Productivity increase takes place in the exporting country but the productivity gains go to the importing country.

If the exporting country is a rich country and the improving country is a poor country such a situation as just described above may contribute to an increase in global welfare. Because this would mean income transfer from the rich to the poor countries. It will reduce global inequalities which is in conformity with the spirits of the New International Economic Order enunciated by the United Nations in 1994. This, unfortunately, does not seem to have happened. Because inspite of the remarkable technological progress that has taken place in the industrialized nations like the USA or Japan or Western European countries, their export prices have not come down so as to benefit the Third World countries. On the contrary, the prices which these rich industrialized countries charge for their export products have been rising at a rapid rate. In other words, the rich countries, today, have been enjoying very favourable commodity terms as well as single factoral terms whereas the Third World countries (excluding oil exporting nations) are suffering from both the adverse commodity terms and single factoral terms. No wonder, global inequalities are increasing at such an alarming rate that the rich countries are getting richer and the poor countries are getting relatively poorer and poorer.

Here we are concerned not so much with the question of global inequalities but the significance of single factoral terms of trade as a terms of trade concept. Constant single factoral terms situation in the face of rapidly deteriorating commodity terms (as in 1993 in our example above) could indicate an effort by the country to achieve productivity increases within but losing out that productivity gain to the foreign countries, and thereby helping to increase the standards of living in the foreign countries but not itself. In other words, constant single factoral terms can only console the countries otherwise suffering serious deterioration in commodity terms of trade situation. From a Third World perspective, it is very important to bear this in mind. It is alleged that in respect of manufactured goods produced in the developed countries, the gains from increased productivity have been distributed in the form of higher wagers and profits rather than lower prices to the poor countries, whereas in the case of agriculture production and raw materials produced in the underdeveloped countries, the gains in productivity, although smaller, have been distributed in the form of price reductions benefitting the rich countries. This is a subject of acrimonious debate among scholars in both the international forums and the scholarly journals on the subject. It has generated lot of heat and light, and we will not go into its details because it will lead us off our present track.

Double Factoral Terms of Trade

The most important terms of trade concepts are essentially three, viz., commodity terms, income terms and single factoral terms of trade. We have already discussed these concepts some detail. There are three other terms of trade concepts, viz., double factoral terms, real cost terms and utility terms of trade. These three concepts are somewhat hard to measure, which would therefore reduce their practical utility. For pedagogical purposes as well as to complete the inventory of terms of trade concepts, it is necessary to gain some understanding of what they are. We will discuss them, therefore, only briefly.

When the commodity terms of trade (*N*) are corrected for changes in productivity in producing both exports and imports, the result is the double factoral terms of trade (*D*). This can be symbolically expressed as :

$$D = N.\frac{X_z}{M_z}\left(or\ D = \frac{X_p}{M_p} \times \frac{X_z}{M_z}\right)$$

Where X_z and M_z stand for export productivity index and import productivity index, respectively. *D* will diverge from *S*, single factoral terms, when there is a change in the factor cost of producing imports. This has no significance to the importing country, because it only means that there has been an increase or a decrease in productivity in the country from which it is importing goods. Whether the imports contain more or less foreign imputes in imported goods, is hardly of any interest to the country importing those goods.

The productivity index—of imports or of export—remains an elusive concept. Difficulties of their measurement reduce the practical utility of the factoral terms of trade.

5. Real Cost Terms of Trade

This measure of terms of trade tries to correct the commodity terms (*N*) for changes in export productivity index (X_z) and the "real cost" of producing export goods. The amount of utility lost or sacrificed per unit of resources employed in producing exports constitutes the "real cost" of producing exports, which is expressed as the index of real cost of producing exports (X_r). Symbolically, real cost terms of trade (*R*) can be expressed as:

$$R = N.\frac{X_3}{X_r}\left(or\ R = \frac{X_p}{M_p} \times \frac{X_3}{X_r}\right)$$

A deterioration in commodity terms (*N*) may be offset by a corresponding increase in the export productivity index (X_3) to keep the single factoral terms (S) relatively stable. R would also remain stable with S provided, there is no change in the real cost of producing export goods (X_r). If, however, there is greater loss of satisfaction in raising export productivity it will reflect itself in an increase in real cost index (X_r), and as a result, real cost terms of trade (*R*) will worsen even through single factoral terms (*S*) remain stable.

Real cost of producing exports or the disutility of export productivity increase remains a highly subjective concept, which does not lend itself to measurement in precise quantitative terms. This reduce the practical utility of the real cost terms of trade concept.

6. Utility Terms of Trade

When *R* is corrected for the relative desirability of imports and of the domestic goods whose consumption is foregone because of the use of resources in export production (U_m), we obtain what is called as the utility terms of trade (U). This concept is associated with the name of D.H. Robertson who calls it the "true terms of trade." Symbolically, it can be expressed as.

$$U = N.\frac{X_z}{X_r}.\frac{1}{U_m}$$

An increase in the index of U_m results in a deterioration of utility terms of trade (*U*).

Utility terms of trade, like the real cost terms of trade, involve the use of subjective costs (or disutility) which are very hard to measure. This reduces the practical utility of this concept as well.

Factors on which Terms of Trade Depend

The terms of trade of a country depend on a number of factors. The important factors that influence the terms of trade are:

1. Elasticity of Demand and Supply

The elasticity of demand for exports and imports and the elasticity of supply of exports and imports of a country significantly influence its terms of trade. When the demand for a country's exports is less price elastic than its imports, the terms of trade tend to be favourable because, under such a situation, exports can command a relatively higher price than imports. On the other hand, if the demand for imports is less elastic than that for exports, the terms of trade tend to be unfavourable.

If the supply of country's exports is more elastic than its imports, the terms of trade is likely to be favourable because by contracting and expanding the supply of exports in accordance with market conditions, it may be possible to maintain the export prices.

2. Competitive Conditions

The competitive conditions obtaining in the international market are another important influence on the terms of trade. If a country enjoys a monopoly or oligopoly power in case of the goods, it exports; and if there is a large number of alternative sources of supply of imports, the country would have favourable terms of trade. The absence of close substitutes enables a country to sell her products at high prices. It is the near monopoly power enjoyed by the oil *cartel* that enabled the OPEC countries to improve their terms of trade by hiking the oil prices.

3. Tastes and Preferences

Changes in tastes and preferences may also cause changes in the terms of trade. A change in the tastes and preferences in favour of a country's export goods would help improve its terms of trade and *vice versa*.

4. Rate of Exchange

Changes in the rate of exchange of the currency also affect the terms of trade. For instance, if a country's currency appreciates, the terms of trade of that country will, *ceteris paribus*, improve because the currency appreciation causes an increase in the prices of exports and a decrease in import prices.

5. Tariffs and Quotas

The terms of trade of a country may be affected by tariffs and quotas, Tariffs and quotas, if not maintained in relation by other countries, may have the effect of improving the terms of trade under certain conditions.

6. Economic Development

There are two important effects of economic development to be considered, namely, the *demand effect* and the *supply effect*. The demand effect refers to the increase in demand for imports as a result of increase in income associated with economic development. The supply effect refers to the increase in the supply of import competing goods or import substitutes. The net effect on the terms of trade will obviously depend upon the extent of these effects.

7. Political motives of participating countries

At last in the world full of tension as exists today, it cannot be ignored that the terms of trade are also influenced by the political motives of the government of the countries participating in foreign trade. The terms of trade between friendly nations are favourable while those between the belligerent or countries warring coldly will be unfavourable.

Thus there are many factors which influence the terms of trade between two countries. The list of these factors is not exhaustive and any number of factors can be added to the already indicated ones.

Problems of Measurement of Terms of Trade

The use of price indices to measure the terms of trade suffers from the following limitations :

1. Changes in Quality

Over the years, the quality of internationally traded goods may undergo a change, but the price indices may not reflect this change in quality.

2. Changes in Composition

The changes in the composition of the goods over a period of time may not be reflected in the price indices.

3. Price Differences

The price indices of import and export of goods are usually based on the price declarations made to the customs authorities, which may differ from the actual market selling prices of the imports and exports.

4. Problem of Weightage

Another problem associated with the price index pertains to that of assigning appropriate weights to the various commodities that enter into the international trade of the country.

Terms of Trade and Economic Growth

Terms of trade play an important role in the economy of a country. Improved terms of trade enable a country to import a larger quantity of goods from her trading partners in return for the same quantity of her exports or the same quantity of imports in exchange for a smaller quantity of exports. This greatly influences the income of the countries engaged in trade. Secondly, the terms of trade play a significant role in explaining changes in income differentials among countries. Changes in terms of trade may affect the international distribution of income and unfavourable terms of trade may provide some explanation for the low levels of income in developing countries.

The analysis of terms of trade is very important in the case of developing countries for a number of reasons: Firstly, the volume, of international trade is generally very large in relation to their national income. Secondly, international trade is vital for them because it provides them with technical skills, plant, machinery etc., which are so essential for their economic development. These countries then will naturally be very much concerned with all aspects of their trading relationships, including their terms of trade. Any worsening of their terms of trade (particularly any change in export volume or productivity) other things being equal will reduce their capacity to import and shift income away from them, thus retarding their efforts to promote economic growth.

There are two views. The classical economists believed that the terms of trade would shift in the long run in favour of countries producing primary goods and against those producing manufactured goods. This is so because of the fact that primary products are subject to diminishing returns whereas manufactured goods obey the law of increasing returns. The net effect of this tendency would be an increase in the prices of primary products and a reduction in the prices of manufactured goods. This would in turn make the terms of trade of developing countries favourable.

Recently, however, group of economists, viz., Raul Prebisch, Singer and Myrdal are of the view that the terms of trade of developing countries tend to move against them. Their view, termed secular deterioration hypothesis, was based on the trend in the terms of trade of the U.K., from the latter part of the 19th century to the late 1930's. At the end of this period, a given quantity of primary products exported to the U.K., purchased 40 percent less of manufactured goods than at the beginning. The main reasons for it given by them are as follows :

(a) The developed countries keep most of the gains of the increased productivity in manufactures by increasing wages and profits and not reducing prices. Strong trade union organisations make sure that the gains in productivity are followed by wage-increases. On the other hand, growth in the productivity in primary products results in lower product prices. The result of this is unfavourable terms for the primary product producing countries, where there is practically perfect competition in the factor markets.

(b) There has been a relative increase in the demand for manufactured goods produced by developed economies and decrease in their demand for primary products. This is partly explained by Engel's Law, which states that as income increases a small proportion is spent on food items. Their income elasticity of demand is thus lower for such items which are mainly produced and exported by developing countries, than that of the demand of developing countries for manufactured goods. Secondly, technological progress in manufactures has greatly reduced the demand for raw material used in manufactures. Therefore, Engel's Law coupled with technical progress in manufactured goods have worked together in causing a reduction in the total demand for the primary products, which in turn have shifted the terms of trade to the detriment of the developing countries.

(c) It is argued that the prices of primary products rise and fall sharply in periods of both boom and depression thus losing all the gains of the boom periods. But the prices of manufactured goods do not fall in depression as much as they rise in boom periods, because of the presence of strong trade unions, As a result, there arises a wide gap between the prices of primary products and manufactured goods over successive cycles which in turn make the terms of trade of developing countries unfavourable in the long run.

Raul Prebisch has shown, as pointed out above, that the developing countries are handicapped in their attempts at economic development, since terms of trade are unfavourable to them relative to the developed countries that is why they have to seek loans and grants from the developed countries. The terms of trade are unfavourable to the developing countries since their export earnings are derived from a few commodities only known as the traditional exports, e.g., jute, tea and oilseeds in the case of India. The prices of such commodities do not rise as much as the prices of capital goods and other manufactured goods that they have to purchase. Prices of imported manufactures being relatively high and prices of primary goods exported being relatively low, the terms of trade are unfavourable to the developing countries. There is a secular decline in their terms of trade are unfavourable to the developing countries. There is a secular decline in their terms of trade. Prof. Haberler has questioned this thesis of a secular decline. But Prof. Kindlebeger supports Raul Prebisch and asserts that the terms of trade have been generally favourable to well-developed countries and unfavourable to developing countries.

For economic development, the developing counter is have to purchase from abroad machinery and capital equipment, essential industrial raw materials and technical know-how. But owing to the terms of trade being unfavourable to them they do not have adequate export earnings to be able to purchase their requirements of economic development. This is a great handicap.

In view of the above, we might say that economic development has not benefited the developing countries as much as the well-developed countries.

Conclusion

Thus, fair terms of trade are very important for the economic development of the under-developed countries. Favourable terms of trade enable a country to import a larger quantity of goods for the same quantity of exports or the same quantity of imports for a smaller quantity of exports. This is a potential source of capital formation. In Nurkse's words, "The great advantage of this potential source of capital formation is that it gives rise neither to foreign debt burden nor to the various frictions that may arise from inter-governmental loans and grants." Unfavourable terms of trade accentuate balance of payments and budgetary difficulties. It may, however, be emphasised that unless the additional resources made available by the favourable terms are turned into savings and investment, economic development will not be promoted. Favourable terms by themselves do not accelerate development automatically.

Questions for Discussion

1. What is meant by terms of trade? What factors affect terms of trade.
2. Distinguish between net barter and gross barter terms of trade.
3. How are changes in a country's terms of trade measured? What are the difficulties encountered in this?

Chapter - 4

BALANCE OF PAYMENTS

Introduction

The principal tool for the analysis of the monetary aspects of international trade is the balance of international payments settlement. This statement, also simply known as the **'balance of payments'**, is a systematic record of all international economic transactions, visible and invisible, of a country during a given period, usually a year, In other words, the balance of payments statement is a device for recording all the economic transactions within a given period between the residents of a country and the residents of other countries. Transactions entered on the balance of payments are international transactions - constituting the transfer of assets and liabilities, the creation or the reduction of claims or receipts and payments of funds, which take place between the residents of one country and those of other countries.

Technically speaking, the balance of payments of each of the individual countries always 'balances'. Such equality in the debit and credit side of the balance of payments - known as equilibrium point - has no economic significance. It simply results from the double-entry book keeping procedure which is used to record the transactions.

Kindleberger defines balance of payments as "a systematic record of all economic transactions between the residents of the reporting country and residents of foreign countries during a given period of time" It thus follows that;

1. Balance of payments is a statement of systematic record of all economic transactions between one country and the rest of the world.
2. It is a record pertaining to a period of time. Usually. It is an annual statement.
3. It includes all transactions, current as well as capital.

Other characteristics of the balance of payment account are :

- It is a way of listing receipts and payments in the international transactions of a country.
- It adopts a double-entry book keeping system It has two sides : debit and credit. Payments are recorded on the debit side and receipts on the credit side.
- In the accounting sense, debit and credit will always balance each other. That is to say, debit or the payment side of the balance of payments account of a country represents the total of all the uses made out of the total foreign exchange acquired by the country during a given period, while the credit or receipts side represents the sources from which this foreign exchange was

acquired by this country in the same period. The two sides as such must necessarily balance. If, in the actual balance of payments account the credits and debits do not balance, the balance is usually achieved by adding an item called errors and omissions.

4. It contains two sets of accounts : (a) current account and (b) capital account. Real and short-term transactions are recorded under current account. Capital account records all financial and long-term transactions.

In short, the balance of payments (BOP) is flow statement that records a country's all transactions with the rest of the world of the foreign sector.

Structure of Balance of Payments

A balance of payment statement is a summary of a nation's total economic transactions undertaken on international trade account. It is usually composed of two sections. (1) the current account, and (2) the capital account.

Current Account

Current account mainly consists of two sub-groups : (a) merchandise or the trade account and (b) invisible account.

In the trade or merchandise account, only transactions relating to goods are entered. That is, all goods exported and imported are recorded in the trade account.

The invisible account usually comprises the services account and the gift or charities account. The services account records all the services rendered and received by residents of the nation. It consists of such items as banking and insurance charges, interest on loans, tourist expenditure, transport charges, etc., Similarly, the gifts or charities account consists of all those items which are received or given away free by residents of the nation. It may be in kind or in cash. It goes without saying that these are all referred to as invisible account. It is interesting to note here that the International Monetary Fund (IMF) includes the following items as invisible transactions :

- International transportation of goods including warehousing while in transit and other transit expenses.
- Travel for reasons of business, education, health, international conventions or pleasure.
- Insurance premiums and payments of claims.
- Investment income, including interest, rents, dividends and profits.
- Miscellaneous service items such as advertising, commissions, film rental, pensions, patient fees, royalties, subscriptions to periodicals and membership fees.
- Donations, migrant remittances and legacies
- Repayment of commercial credits.
- Contractual amortisation and depreciation of direct investment.

Capital Account

Capital Account, on the other hand, deals with payments of debts and claims. It consists of all such items as may be employed in financing both imports and exports, namely, private balances, assistance by international institution agencies and specie flow, and balances held on government account. Accordingly, we shall have private capital account, international institutional capital account, specific account and government capital account. Balances in the accounts may rise or fall from year to year, depending upon the movements or fluctuations in other items on capital account.

Items of balance of payments account may, thus be summarised in following Table :

Balance of Payments

Current Account	*Capital Account*
1. Merchandise -Exports & imports	1. Private (non banking) loans:
(a) Private	(a) Long-term
(b) Government	(b) Short-term
2. Non monetary gold movement	2. Banking (excluding central bank)
3. Foreign travel	3. Official (including central bank)
4. Transportation	(a) Loans
5. Government, not included	(b) Amortisation
6. Government, not included elsewhere	(c) Miscellaneous
7. Investment income	(d) Reserves (including changes in the foreign exchange assets of the central bank)
8. Miscellaneous	
9. Transfer payments	
(a) Official	
(b) Private	
Total current Transact Errors and Omissions	Total Capital and Monetary Gold

It should be noted that the two accounts—current, capital—in the balance of payments should necessarily balance. The surplus in the trade or current account must be equal to the deficit in the capital account or the deficit in the current account.

For instance, if India's imports of goods are more than its exports of goods and services to foreigners, it will have a deficit in its current balance of payment. This, she will have to pay either in gold and other assets or by borrowing from other countries. These are credit items in the capital account of the balance of payments. Thus, both the current and capital accounts together will balance each other.

Meaning of Disequilibrium in Balance of Payments

A country's balance of payments is in equilibrium when there is perfect equality between the supply and the demand for foreign exchange. A position of disequilibrium in the balance of payments of a country exists when the demand for foreign exchange exceeds its supply of *vice versa*. When the demand for foreign exchange exceeds its supply, there is said to be a *deficit* in the balance of payments. On the contrary, when the supply of foreign exchange exceeds its demand, there is said to be *surplus* in the balance of payments. Whether the balance of payments is in surplus or in deficit, there exists a disequilibrium which is not desirable in the larger economic interests of the country. It is very seldom that there is a perfect equilibrium in the country's balance of payments. It is either in deficit or in surplus. The disequilibrium in the balance of payments whether it is due to deficit or surplus is undesirable and bad for the country concerned. The surplus disequilibrium may not be so bad for the country as the deficit disequilibrium is. The reason is that the burden of bringing about adjustment in the balance of payments falls more heavily on the deficit than on the surplus countries.

The types of Disequilibrium in the Balance of Payments

The following are the main types of disequilibrium in the balance of payments :

- Cyclical disequilibrium;
- Structural disequilibrium;
- Short-run disequilibrium; and
- Long-run or secular disequilibrium

1.Cyclical Disequilibrium

It occurs on account of trade cycles. Depending upon the different phases of trade cycles like prosperity and depression, demand and other forces vary, causing changes in the terms of trade as well as growth of trade and accordingly a surplus or deficit will result in the balance of payments.

Cyclical disequilibrium in the balance of payments may occur because :

- Trade cycles follow different paths and patterns in different countries. There are no identical timings and periodicity of occurrence of cycles in different countries.
- No identical stabilisation programmes and measures are adopted by different countries.
- Income elasticities of demand for imports in different countries are not identical.
- Price elasticities of demand for imports differ in different countries.

In short, cyclical fluctuations cause disequilibrium in the balance of payments because of cyclical changes in income, employment, output and price variables. When prices rise during prosperity and fall during a depression, a country which has a highly elastic demand for imports experiences a decline in the value of imports and if it continues its exports further, it will show a surplus in the balance of payments.

Since deficit and surplus alternatively take place during the depression and prosperity phase of a cycle, the balance of payments equilibrium is automatically set forth over the complete cycle.

2. Structural Disequilibrium

It emerges on account of structural changes occurring in some sectors of the economy at home or abroad which may alter the demand or supply relations of exports or imports or both. Suppose, the foreign demand for India's jute products declines because of some substitutes, then the resources employed by India in the production of jute goods will have to be shifted to some other commodities of export. If this is not easily possible, India's exports may decline whereas with imports remaining the same, a disequilibrium in the balance of payments will arise. Similarly, if the supply condition of export items is changed, i.e., supply is reduced due to crop failure in prime commodities or shortage or raw materials or labour strikes, etc. in the case of manufactured goods, then also experts may decline to that extent and structural disequilibrium in the balance of payments will arise.

Moreover, a shift in demand occurs with the changes in tastes, fashions, habits, income, economic progress, etc. Propensity to import may change as a result. Demand for some imported goods may increase, while that for certain goods may decline leading to a structural change.

Furthermore, structural changes are also produced by variations in the rate of international capital movements. A rise in the flow of international capital tends to have a direct impact on a country's balance of payments.

3. Short-run Disequilibrium

A short-run disequilibrium in a country's balance of payments will be a temporary one, lasting for a short period, which may occur once in a while. When a country borrows or lends internationally, it will have a short-run disequilibrium in its balance of payments, as these loans are usually for a short period or even if they are for a long duration, they are repayable later on; hence the position will be automatically corrected and poses no serious problem. As such a disequilibrium arising from international lending and borrowing activities is perfectly justified. However, a short-run disequilibrium may also emerge if a country's imports exceed its exports in a given year. This will be a temporary one if it occurs once in a way, because later on, the country will be in a position to correct it easily by creating the required credit surplus by exporting more to offset the deficit. But even this type of disequilibrium in the balance of payments is not justified, because it may pave the way for a long-term disequilibrium. When such disequilibrium (arising from imports exceeding exports or even vice versa) occurs year after year over a long period, it becomes chronic and may seriously affect the country's economy and its international economic relations. A persistent deficit will tend to deplete its foreign exchange reserves and the country may not be able to raise any more loans from foreigners.

4. Long-run Disequilibrium

The long-term disequilibrium thus refers to a deep-rooted, persisted deficit or surplus in the balance of payments of a country. It is secular disequilibrium emerging on account of the chronologically accumulated short-term disequilibria — deficits of surpluses. It endangers the exchange stability of the country concerned. Especially, a long-term deficit in the balance of payments of a country tends to a deplete its foreign exchange reserves and the country may also not be able to raise any more loans from foreigners during such a period of persistent deficits.

In short, true disequilibrium is a long-term phenomenon. It is caused by persistent deep-rooted dynamic changes which slowly take place in the economy over a long period of time. It is caused by changes in dynamic forces/factors such as capital formation, population growth, territorial expansion, technological advancement, innovations, etc. A newly developing economy, for instance, in its initial stages of growth needs huge investment exceeding its savings. In view of its low capital formation, it has also to import a large amount of its capital requirements from foreign countries and its imports thus tend to exceed its exports. These become a chronic phenomenon. And in the absence of a sufficient inflow of foreign capital in such countries, a secular deficit balance of payments may result.

Causes of Disequilibrium in the Balance of Payments

The various causes of disequilibrium in the balance of payments may be classified under the three heads :

1. ***Natural Factors*:** Natural calamities, such as, the failure of rains or the coming of floods may easily cause disequilibrium in the balance of payments by adversely affecting agricultural and industrial production in the country. The exports may decline while the imports may go up causing a discrepancy in the country's balance of payments.

2. ***Economic Factors*:** The economic factors can be further subdivided under the following four sub-heads:

(a) ***Cyclical Fluctuation*** : Business fluctuations induced by the operation of the trade cycle may also cause disequilibrium in a country's balance of payments. For example. If there occurs a business recession in foreign countries it may easily cause a fall in the exports and exchange earnings of the country concerned resulting in a disequilibrium in the balance of payments.

(b) ***Inflationary Spiral at Home*** : An inflationary rise in prices within the country may also produce disequilibrium in the balance of payments. The prices of export items may go up, causing a decline in the volume of exports from the country concerned. The inflationary spiral within the country may also result in an increase in the volume of imports.

(c) ***Capital Movements***: The capital movements (if they happen to be on a large scale) can also cause disequilibrium in the balance of payments of a country. A massive inflow of foreign capital into a country is followed by an unfavourable balance of payments. A large outflow of capital. On the other hand, is accompanied by a favourable balance of payments.

(d) ***Miscellaneous Factors***: The changes in the tastes, habits, fashions of the people; the discovery of new substitutes for exports; the development of alternative sources of supply, etc., may also produce disequilibrium in the country's balance of payments. For example, the invention of synthetic rubber led to a serious decline in the export of natural rubber from countries like Malaysia, Burma, etc., during and after the Second World War.

3. ***Political Factors***: The political factors may also produce serious disequilibrium in the country's balance of payments. For example, the existence of political instability may result in disrupting the productive apparatus within the country, causing a decline in exports and an increase in imports. Likewise, the payment of war reparations of indemnities may also cause serious disequilibrium in the country's balance of payments. The imposition of heavy war reparations on Germany after the First World War produced a serious disequilibrium in its balance of payments.

Measures to Correct Disequilibrium in the Balance of Payments

The various measures to eliminate the disequilibrium in the balance of payments can be classified under two sub-heads :

1. ***Automatic Measures :*** The disequilibrium in the balance of payments may automatically disappear after sometime when certain forces come into operation in the economy. For example, the disequilibrium in the balance of payments of a country under the gold standard was automatically corrected through the inflow and outflow of gold. If the balance of payments was un-favourable, there was an outflow of gold from the country, causing a contraction in the volume of currency and credit, and ultimately a fall in the domestic price level. This encouraged exports while it discouraged imports. The equilibrium in the balance of payments was automatically restored after some time. The opposite process worked when the balance of payments of the country was favourable.

Likewise, the equilibrium in the balance of payments of a country on the paper standard was automatically corrected through fluctuations in its rate of exchange, For example, if the country's balance of payments was unfavourable, the demand for foreign exchange exceeded its supply, and consequently, the exchange value of its currency went down. The fall in its exchange value encouraged exports while it discouraged imports. The equilibrium in the balance of payments was automatically restored after the lapse of some time. The opposite process worked when the balance of payments of the country turned favourable.

The automatic measures discussed above did not produce the desired results in the short period. Nor were they effective in dealing with a serious and fundamental disequilibrium in the balance of payments. The country concerned had, therefore, to resort to certain deliberate measures to bring about an improvement in the balance of payments.

2. ***Deliberate Measures***: The deliberate measures can be discussed under two sub-heads :

(I) Trade Measures : The following trade measures could be undertaken by the country concerned to correct disequilibrium in its balance of payments.

(i) ***Encouragement to Exports***: To remove the deficit in the balance of payments, it is essential to maximize the country's exports. The exports of a country can be pushed up in two ways :

(a) ***Reduction in Export Duties***: The government should either reduce or altogether abolish the export duties so that the export of goods becomes cheaper in foreign countries :

(b) ***Subsidies to Export Industries*** : The government should give subsidies to the export industries within the country to enable them to cut down their production costs and improve their competitive position in the international market.

(ii) ***Reduction in Imports***: It is essential to cut down imports in order to eliminate the deficit in the balance of payments of the country. The imports can be reduced by adopting the following measures :

(a) ***Imposition of New Import Duties and the Enhancement of the Existing Import Duties***: This step will go a long way in making imported goods more expensive within the country. Consequently, the demand for the imported goods will automatically decline in course of time.

(b) ***Import Quota System***:The imports of the country can also be cut down through the adoption of the import quota system. This system can be discussed under the following sub-heads :

(i) ***Licence Quota System*** : Under this system, the importers have to secure import licences from the government and these licences are granted by the government after taking an overall view of the import position of the country.

(ii) ***Unilateral Quota System***: Under this system, the country imposes two types of restrictions on its imports -

(a) ***Global Quota System***: Under this, the government fixes an advance the global quota for every imported item. The country cannot import more than the quota fixed by the government. But to the extent of the quota, the importers can import the commodity concerned from any country.

(b) ***Allocated Quota System***: Under this system, the government not only fixed the global quota of the commodity concerned but also decides in advance how much of the commodity is to be imported from individual countries.

(iii) ***Bilateral Quota System***: Under this system, the government fixes the maximum quota of a commodity which is to be imported from abroad. Up to the extent of this quota, the commodity can be imported at a concessional import duty. If, however, the importers exceed the quota, they have to pay a penal rate of import duty.

(iv) **Import Prohibitions :** This is an extreme measure which is sometimes adopted by the government of a country to eliminate the disequilibrium in the balance of payments. Under this, the government prohibits altogether the import of certain goods which are considered to be non-essential from the national point of view. Developing countries trying to bring about speedy economic development through planning often resort to this method to check the consumption of imported luxury goods by the affluent sections of the community.

(II) Monetary Measures : The following monetary measures are taken either single or in combination by the government to deal with the disequilibrium in the balance of payments :

(i) ***Currency Devaluation***: The government of the country may resort to the devaluation of its currency to eliminate or to reduce the deficit in the balance of payments. Devaluation implies a deliberate reduction in the external value of the currency of the country. Devaluation always encourages exports by cheapening them in foreign countries. On the contrary devaluation has the effect of discouraging imports by making them more expensive within the country. For example, if the currency of a country is devaluated, then its purchasing power in foreign countries automatically goes down. In other words, the imported goods become more expensive than before. Hence, devaluation discourages imports into the country. On the contrary, the purchasing power of the devalued currency increases in terms of foreign currencies as a consequence of devaluation. Consequently, the foreigners start importing more goods from that country. This gives an incentive to the exports of the country. It was to remove the deficit in her balance of payments that India resorted to the devaluation of the Rupee in September, 1949. The Rupee was devalued for the second time on 6th June, 1966. The objective again was to eliminate or reduce the deficit in the country's balance of payments.

(ii) *Money Contraction* : If the Government of a country does not look upon currency devaluation as a proper measure, it may resort to currency contraction to remove the disequilibrium in the balance of payments. The prices of goods and services automatically go down as a result of currency contraction. This gives the much-needed incentive to exports. But the imports are discouraged as a result of the fall in the internal price-level. The increase in exports and the decline in imports helps the country to remove the disequilibrium in the balance of payments. But currency contraction as a method to remove the disequilibrium in the balance of payments is not looked upon with favour by certain economists. If the price-level in the country is deliberately brought down with the help of currency contraction should be used with a good deal of caution to bring about an improvement in the balance of payments.

(iii) *Exchange Control*: Sometimes, the government prefers exchange control to other methods for brining about an equilibrium in the balance of payments. Currency devaluation, it is said, adversely affects the self-respect and reputation of the country. Currency contraction may likewise result in a slump or depression in the economy. Similarly, if the imports are cut down by imposing various types of restrictions by the government, this may lead to retaliation on the part of other countries. They may likewise impose the same restrictions on the exports of the country concerned. Keeping in view the limitations of the above methods, the governments often resort to the system of exchange control to eliminate the deficit in the balance of payments. Under this system, the exporters have to surrender their earnings of foreign exchange to the government in exchange for domestic currency. Likewise, the government allocates foreign exchange to the importers to enable them to make payments for imported goods. Thus, the government comes to have full control over foreign exchange. It utilizes the exchange control system to effect a cut in the volume of imports. Unnecessary imports are altogether stopped by the government by denying foreign exchange to the importers. Many developing countries like India. Kenya, Sudan, Nigeria and others have been restricting imports by not releasing foreign exchange for non-essential goods.

(iv) *Foreign Loans* : The government can also secure loans from foreign banks or foreign governments to reduce the deficit in the balance of payments. Since the repayment of these loans is spread over a long period. This helps the government to remove the deficit in the balance of payments. During the currency of the loans, the government takes steps to improve its foreign exchange position.

(v) *Encouragement to Foreign Investment*: The government induces the foreigners to make investment in the country offering them all sorts of incentives and concessions. This provides the government with extra foreign exchange which is utilized to reduce the deficit in the balance of payments. But while inviting the foreign capitalists to invest their capital within the country, the government sees to it that this does not produce any adverse repercussions on the economy.

(vi) ***Incentives to Foreign Tourists*** **:** The government may also encourage the foreign tourists to visit the country in increasing numbers by offering them various facilities and concessional travel. This increases the foreign exchange earnings of the country with the help of which the deficit in the balance of payments can be reduced.

To *sum up*, the deficit in the balance of payments is not a desirable phenomenon for a country, The methods discussed above aim at reducing imports and stimulating exports. Of these, the first method, trade measures, is obviously the best, and the most effective. It produces immediate results. The government of a country may use this method in combination with other methods to eliminate or reduce a chronic deficit in its balance of payments.

India's BOP During the Plan Period

Throughout the plan period India had to face a deficit in its BOP mainly due to excess of visible exports over visible exports. India's negative BOP has all along offset, at least partly, by positive balance of invisibles (excess of invisible exports over invisible imports). We may now make a brief review of India's BOP during the plan period.

1. First Plan (1951-56)

During the First plan, India had a deficit in BOT of Rs. 542 crores. During this period exports increased by 1% per annum and imports by 3.8%. This was largely offset by a surplus from invisibles equal to Rs. 500 crores, leaving a modest deficit of only Rs. 42 crores in the current account. However, the overall picture of BOP during the plan period was quite satisfactory.

2. Second Plan (1956-61)

In the Second Plan there was a huge deficit in BOT amounting to Rs. 2,339 crores mainly because exports grew at an annual rate of 2.2% but imports increased by 11.8% per annum. This was partly offset by a surplus of Rs. 614 in the invisibles account leaving a deficit of Rs. 1,725 crores in BOT. Two main causes of deficit in BOT were

(a) huge imports of capital goods needed to develop infrastructural (basic and heavy) industries such as iron and steel, heavy chemicals, oil, etc., (which were to supply inputs to a large number of other industries) and

(b) large imports of food-grains needed to feed the ever-growing population (in the face of slow growth of agricultural production).

3. Third Plan (1961-66)

During the Third Plan exports increased at the rate of 4.9% and imports at the rate of 4.7% per annum. In spite of this there was a record trade deficit of Rs. 2,384 crores. Net surplus of invisibles was only rs. 432 crores, leaving a huge deficit of Rs. 1,952 crores in the current account. Four other reasons for adverse BOT position during this period were :

(a) increase in imports of food, fuel and fertiliser to meet domestic shortages ;

(b) imports of capital goods needed for the development of basic and heavy industries in the public sector ;

(c) imports to meet defence needs ; and

(d) slow growth of exports, compared to that of imports.

The deficit was covered in four ways :

(a) borrowing from central banks of other countries ;

(b) withdrawing from PL 480 and PL 665 funds ;

(c) loans from the World Bank ; and

(d) withdrawals from IMF quota.

4. Annual Plans (1966-69)

During these three years of Annual Plans, the deficit in current account was quite large. No doubt exports increased by 13.1% per annum during the three-year period. But imports increased by 19.9% per annum during this period. This was mainly due to huge imports of food-grains caused by fall in domestic production. A major cause of slow growth of exports due to recession in some key sectors of the economy. During this period earnings from et invisibles came down to a very low figure. This was due to the fact that the Government had to pay a huge amount of interest on external debt (i.e., on foreign loan). While trade deficit was Rs. 2,067 crores the surplus from invisibles was only Rs. 52 crores. Thus the deficit in the current account was Rs. 2,015 crores.

5. Fourth Plan (1969-74)

One of the basic objectives of the Fourth Plan was economic self-reliance. During this period exports increased by 13.6% and imports by 11.7% per annum. And the Government succeeded in achieving self reliance to some extent objective by raising exports and restricting imports. Increase in domestic production, due to the Green Revolution, helped reduce import of food-grains. At the same time various export promotion measures were adopted which raised exports of both traditional and non-traditional items. During the five years of the Fourth Plan trade deficit was Rs. 1,564 crores. At the same time the surplus of invisibles increased sharply to Rs. 1,634 crores which generated a small surplus of Rs. 74 crores in the current account. This unprecedented increase in the invisible account was mainly due to disbursement of Rs. 1,680 crores by the USA from PL 480 and other rupee funds.

6. Fifth Plan (1974-79)

during this period exports increased by 18.3% and imports by 19.5% per annum. In spite of this there was a surplus in the current account. The surplus of invisibles of Rs. 6,260 crores far exceeded the deficit on the trade account of Rs. 3,179 crores, creating a net surplus of Rs. 3,082 crores in the current account. Five factors which accounted for the rapid growth of invisibles were :

(a) control of smuggling and illegal transactions in international trade (such as under-invoicing of exports and over-invoicing of imports) ;

(b) reasonable stability in the value of the rupee in the external markets ;

(c) increase in earnings from tourism ;

(d) huge increase in earnings from technical and consultancy services ; and

(e) large remittances by non-resident Indians (mainly emigrants to Gulf countries).

However, the fifth Plan was terminated one year earlier (1978). During the Annual Plan (1979-80), which was the last year of the original Fifth Plan, exports increased by 12.1% and imports by 34.2%.

7. Sixth Plan (1980-85)

During this period exports increased by 13% and imports by 13.9% per annum. The trade deficit of Rs. 30,456 crores was partly offset by a surplus of Rs. 19,072 crores from invisibles, leaving a current account deficit of Rs. 11,384 crores. The deficit was covered in two ways :

(a) withdrawals of special drawing rights (SDRs); and

(b) borrowing from IMF. In 1982 the Government borrowed a huge amount from the IMF by mortgaging its gold reserves.

8. Seventh Plan (1985-90)

During this period trade deficit increased steadily even though exports increased by 19.8% and imports by 16%. During 1985-86 and 1989-90, the total trade deficit amounted to Rs. 52,204 crores. Due to positive balance on invisible account, the deficit in BOP on current account was Rs. 41,047 crores. The trade deficit increased very sharply in 1991. As a result India's foreign exchange in July 1991 was just sufficient to cover only two weeks' worth of imports. The highly adverse BOP position was the cause of serious concern. In such a situation the Government had no other option but adopt a policy of economic liberalisation. The Indian economy was opened up and integrated with the global economy.

9. Annual Plans

During the two annual plans (1990-92) exports increased by 26.5% and imports by 16.6% per annum. For the first time during the last 40 years, net invisibles became negative (Rs. 435 crores) in 1990-91. This was largely the result of a net outflow of investment income of Rs. 6,732 crores in 1990-91 as against Rs. 4,875 crores in 1989-90 — an increase of 38%. This simply means that it was no longer possible to partly neutraise the trade deficit through net invisibles (as was done in the past).

10. Eighth Plan (1992-97)

During this period trade deficit was mounting. By 1996-97 it increased to Rs. 52,561 crores from Rs. 16,934 crores in 1990-91 — an increase of more than 300%. During the Eighth Plan invisibles neutralised the trade deficit to the extent of 58%. This was no doubt a commendable achievement. In spite of this the BOP has shown a deficit in all the years.

11. Ninth Plan (1997-2002)

In 1997-98 the current account deficit reached a record high of Rs. 20,883 crores. But in 1998-99, it fell to Rs. 16,798 crores. In 1999-2000 it again increased to Rs. 17.110 crores. This was largely due to a much greater trade deficit (Rs. 74,119 crores) which could not be neutralised though net invisibles reached an all-time record of rs. 56,120 crores.

India's balance of payments in the year 2000-01 remained largely comfortable. Thought he balance of payments was under pressures during the first six months of 2000 due to hike in oil prices, the sharp fall in share prices in the world market and increases in interest rates in USA and Europe, the situation improved with the mobilisation of funds under the India Millennium Deposits. The balance of payments situation improved further in the second half of the year 2000-01. During the first ten months of the year 2001-02 the foreign currency assets of the RBI have increased by more than $7 billion.

Following table shows India's BOP position (on current account) during the plan period.

India's Balance of Payments on Current Account

[1950-51 to 1999-00]

Year	*Trade Deficit*	*Net Invisibles*	*Balance of Payments*
First Plan (1951-56)	– 542	500	– 42
Second Plan (1956-61)	– 2,339	614	– 1,725
Third Plan (1961-66)	–2,382	431	– 1,951
Annual Plans (1966-69)	– 2,067	52	– 2,015
Forth Plan (1969-74)	– 1,564	1,664	100
Fifth Plan (1974-79)	– 3,179	6,221	3,082
Annual Plan (1979-80)	– 3,374	3,140	– 234
Sixth Plan (198085)	– 30,456	19,072	– 11,384
Seventh Plan (1985-90)	– 54, 204	13,157	– 41,047
Eighth Plan (1992-97)	149,004	86,000	– 62,914
1997-98	– 57,805	36,922	– 20,883
1998-99	– 55,478	38,691	– 16,787
1999-2000	– 74,119	56,120	– 19,119

Causes of BOP Deficit

There were various causes of deficit in India's BOP during the plan period. The main causes were the following :

1. Food problem

Due to food problem which became really serious from 1956 onwards, India had to import huge quantities of food-grains. Therefore a huge amount of foreign exchange had to be spent on food imports.

2. Import of raw materials

After the partition of the country India had to import large quantities of raw materials such as raw jute, raw cotton, hides and skins, etc. Imports of those items also led to continuous outflow of foreign exchange.

3. Oil price hike

In October 1973 the price of crude oil increased by 300%. This was a severe blow to India's BOP on current account. The country had to spend a huge amount of foreign exchange to import crude oil the demand for which was inelastic. Oil price hike has occurred manu times since then.

4. Price inflation

Due to high rate of inflation in India rupee became an overvalued currency. The overvalued currency at fixed rate led to fall in exports and rise in imports. The reason was Indian exporters could not compete with their foreign counterparts in the global market. The main cause of inflation was deficit financing (i.e., covering the budgetary deficit of the Government by printing new currency notes). Due to inflation exports failed to pick up in spite of the adoption of various export promotion measures.

5. Import liberalisation

The policy of import liberalisation, first introduced by Mr. Rajiv Gandhi in 1984 and then Mr. Narasimha Rao in 1991 led to huge increase in imports and large foreign exchange spending. Imports have increased much factor than exports in the last few years and the trend continues unchecked. Even those items which can be produced domestically are not being imported such as ready-made garments or electronic goods.

6. Loan repayment

A large amount of foreign exchange had to be spent to make debt repayment — repay external debt along with interest. As a result India's debt service ratio exceeded 29% in 1990-91. Debt service ratio is a country's repayment obligation of principal and interest for a particular year on its external debt as a percentage of its exports of goods and services (i.e., its current receipts) in that year. Due to ever-increasing external debt burden India's surplus of invisibles has been falling quite sharply in recent years.

Measures to Correct BOP Deficit

Following the recommendation of Rangarajan Panel on BOP, the following measures can be suggested to improve the BOP situation :

1. The current account deficit of 1.6% should be treated as ceiling.
2. The high interest commercial borrowing should be avoided.
3. A quantum jump in exports is required to ensure that exports growth in dollar terms exceed the import growth in dollar terms.
4. A strict policy on short-term external debt with no roll-over beyond six months is to be enforced to avoid East Asian type currency crisis.
5. Maintenance of foreign exchange reserves should be tied to a minimum of three months import bill.
6. The current account deficit should be financed more by foreign direct investment rather than by short-term external loan.
7. A serious effort is necessary to contain the growth of petroleum-based energy consumption.

Currency Depreciation and Devaluation

The foreign exchange market is the cornerstone of international financial system. The rationale for foreign exchange market derives from the fact that cross-border transactions take place as well as from the fact that there exists as many currencies as there are nations. Tourists travelling abroad importers and foreign investors need foreign exchange to make payments.

An Exchange rate of a currency for another is the rate at which one unit of the currency is traded against another. Then the exchange rate of Rs. 48 per dollar means 48 rupees can be exchanged for 1 dollar. The rise in the exchange value of foreign currency, i.e., the fall in the exchange value of domestic currency si called depreciation of the domestic currency. The home currency depreciates (i.e., foreign currency appreciates) in response to excess demand for foreign currency. The currency depreciation is a regular feature in many developing countries due to persistent foreign exchange crisis.

The depreciation is a market-driven adjustment in exchange rate. If the exchange rate of a currency is regulated by the monetary authority, exchange rate will fail to depreciate in response to excess demand in the foreign exchange market. However, the central bank can raise the official exchange value of foreign currency. The central bank engineered depreciation of the currency is called devaluation.

Correction of Balance of Payments Disequilibrium

Automatic Correction

Deliberate Measures

Monetary Measures

1. Monetary contraction/expansion
2. Devaluation/Revaluation
3. Exchange controlment

Trade Measures

Export Promotion

1. Abolition/reduction of export duties
2. Export subsidies
3. Incentives

Import Control

1. Import duties
2. Import quota
3. Import prohibition

Miscellaneous Measures

1. Foreign loans
2. Incentives for foreign investment
3. Tourism development
4. Incentives for inward remittances
5. Import substitution

Conclusion

The main problem faced by India during the plan period has been deficit in the trade account, though not in the current account. The root cause of this had been slow growth of exports in the fact of steadily rising imports. So the long-term solution to India's BOP lies in improving the current account. This can be done by promoting exports as much as possible and, at the same time, by restricting imports to the minimum level.

Questions for Discussion

1. Describe the structure of balance of payments of a country.
2. What are the different types of disequilibrium in the balance of payments? Explain.
3. What are the causes of disequilibrium? Explain the methods of correcting disequilibrium in the balance of payments?

Chapter - 5

TRADE POLICY

Introduction

The commercial policy to be followed by a country with regard to its foreign trade has been the subject or heated controversy centering around whether a country should follow a policy of Free Trade or Protection. A number of arguments have been advanced for and against both the politics. We shall briefly discuss them in the following sections.

Free Trade Policy

Policy of non-interference by government in foreign trade is referred to as "free trade". Free trade policy implies absence of any artificial restriction on or obstacle to the freedom of trade of a country with other nations.

According to Adam Smith, the term **"free trade"** is used to denote "that system of commercial policy which draws no distinction between domestic and foreign commodities and, therefore, neither imposes additional burdens on the latter, nor grants any special favour to the former." In other words, free trade implies complete freedom of international exchange. Under such a policy there are no barriers to the movement of goods among countries and exchange can take its perfectly natural course.

Classical economists like Adam Smith, Ricardo and others pleaded for free trade for the welfare of the world.

Advantages of Free Trade

The following arguments have been advanced in favour of free trade policy

1. ***Comparative cost advantage :*** Free trade is the normal outcome of the comparative cost advantage. It permits an allocation of resources, and manpower in accordance with the principle of comparative advantage, which is just an extension of the principle of division of labour.

   "The fact of free trade establishes an overwhelming presumption that the commodities obtained from abroad in exchange for export are so obtained are lower cost than which the domestic production of their equivalents would entail. If this were not the case, they would not be imported, even under free trade", says Jacob Viner.

   It has been maintained that the gain from free international trade would be the largest due to international specification based on comparative advantage. Free trade leads to the most efficient conduct of economic affairs. In a plea for free trade, they also said that even if some countries do not follow the policy of free trade, an industrial country should follow it unilaterally and it will gain thereby.

2. ***More factor earnings :*** Under free trade, factors of production will also be able to earn more, as they will be employed for better use. Hence, wages, interest and rent will be higher under free trade then otherwise.
3. ***Cheaper imports :*** Free trade procures import at cheap rates. It seems to be an attractive argument in favour of trade at least from the customer's point of view, However, it ignores the question of employment and the interests of producers in the importing country. Here it has been pointed out that under free trade, when consumers gain through lower prices, producers also gain as the factors of production are directed to more gainful and specialised production which gives better earnings.
4. ***Enlarged market :*** Free trade widens the size of the market as a result of which greater specialisation and a more complex division of labour become possible. This brings about optimum production with costs reduced everywhere, benefiting the world as a whole.
5. ***Competition :*** Free trade policy encourages competition from abroad which induces domestic producers to become more alert and improve their efficiency.
6. ***Restricted exploitation :*** Free trade prevents growth of domestic monopolies and consumers exploitation due to competition from abroad.
7. ***Greater Welfare :*** Free trade permits large varieties of consumption goods and improves consumers welfare.

   Haberler concludes that, "International trade has made a tremendous contribution to the development of less developed countries in the nineteenth and twentieth centuries and can be expected to make in the future if it is allowed to proceed freely."

Thus, free trade is the best commercial policy.

Disadvantages of Free Trade

However, the following disadvantages of free trade policy have been mentioned by many critics.

1. Free trade policy runs smoothly if all the countries follow the same. If some countries do not adopt it, the system cannot work gainfully.
2. Free trade may prove advantageous to developed and technologically advanced nations, but less developed countries are certainly at a disadvantage on account of unfavourable terms of trade.
3. Competition induced under free trade is unfair and unhealthy. Backward countries cannot compete with advanced countries.
4. Gains of trade are not equally distributed under free trade due to unequal state of development of different countries.
5. A country with unfavourable balance of payments finds it difficult to overcome this situation under free trade policy.
6. Free trade may encourage interdependence and discourage self-sufficiency but, in the matter of defence each country should have self-reliance and self sufficiency as far as possible.

Despite the clamour of the classical economists about the advantages of the free trade, the policy has either not been adopted by many countries or abandoned by those who had already adopted it. Economic history indicates that for the last two centuries, international trade has developed with protection. Free trade policy has been abandoned by all countries for the following reasons :

(a) Under the system of free trade, the underdeveloped countries suffer very much in competing with the advanced countries. For instance, free trade policy in India adopted by the British Government proved that the one time flourishing industries (handicrafts) of India were completely wiped out due to foreign competition.

(b) Governments under free trade observed political handicaps due to economic interdependence. For political independence due to economic interdependence was inevitable; hence free trade had to go.

(c) Countries cannot allow free import of injurious and harmful products; hence trade restrictions are necessary.

(d) Free trade led to cut-throat competition in the world market, so that exporters, resorted to dumping, which no government can allow beyond a limit; thus, restrictions become inevitable.

(e) Backward countries have to protect their infact industries and hence cannot adopt the policy of free trade.

Policy of Protection

Most government to-day interfere with free flow of international trade. The most common form of such interference is known as *Protectionism*, It is a deliberate policy adopted by the government to help domestic industries to meet foreign competition through imposition of high tariff duties and quotas, besides a large variety of other restrictions on imports.

The idea of protection as an instrument to stimulate economic growth was first mooted by an American economist, Alexander Hamilton, in 1791. Later on, another equally distinguished American economist, Henry Carey, supported this policy of protection. The Government of the U.S.A had accepted the policy of protection by the end of the 19th century. But in Europe, the policy of protection was first suggested by the famous German economist, Frederic List, in the 19th century. Up to the beginning of the First World War, the majority of the countries of the world were following the policy of free trade. But after the end of the war almost all the countries had abandoned free trade in favour of the policy of protection.

Arguments in Favour of Protection

The following arguments have been adduced in favour of protection :

1. ***Infant Industries Argument***: This argument was first presented by Alexander Hamilton. According to this argument, the infant industry in a country must be given protection against foreign competition. The reason is that the infant industries of a country cannot stand the competition of the well organized and well-established foreign industries. Hence, these industries deserve to be protected against the developed industries in foreign countries. This policy of protection has been well-expressed in the following words : **"Nurse the Baby, Protect the Child, and Free the Adult".**

But this argument has been criticized on the following grounds :

(a) Sometimes it becomes difficult to locate the infant industries within the country.

(b) When the infant industry is granted protection ; It becomes difficult to withdraw it even after the industry has fully developed itself. The reason is that during this period certain vested interests come into existence which oppose the withdrawal of protection at a later stage.

(c) When protection is granted to any infant industry, other infant industries also claim it as a matter of right. In such a situation, it becomes rather difficult for the government to accede to the demands of all the infant industries in the country.

As a result of protection, the consumers have not only to pay higher prices but have also to be content with poor quality stuff.

Despite this, the fact remains that the infant industries argument forms an important basis for a policy of tariff protection to domestic industries. The U.S.A., it is pointed out, would have been no more than a supplier of agricultural products like wheat, cotton, timber etc., to industrialised. Europe to-day, had it not beau for the policy of protection adopted by it in the nineteenth century. It is largely due to a policy of protection that the U.S.A is to-day one of the most highly industrialised countries of the world.

2. ***Diversification of Industries Argument*** **:** This argument was first presented by the German economist, Frederic List, According to this argument, every country should, as far as possible, be self-sufficient in all essential commodities. The reason is that a country, which is not self-sufficient, has to face a number of difficulties at a time of war. Even in peacetime, a country depending on few industries may endanger its economy on account of the operation of external factors. Zambia is a classic example. Its exclusive dependence on copper exports landed it in trouble some years back when the international prices of copper suddenly slumped due to external causes. Hence , it is essential that a country should become self-sufficient by going in for a balanced development of all industries in the country. Now this is not possible without following the policy of protection. This argument has been criticized in the ground that the policy of protection deprives the country of all the advantages of division of labour and specialization.

3. ***Home Market Argument*** : According to this argument, when the government cuts down its imports by following a policy of protection, this encourages the sale of home-made goods within the country. Consequently, the volume of employment increases in the country. With increased employment the demand for home-made goods increases still further, resulting in a further development of the home market. But this argument has been criticized on the ground that if imports are reduced through a policy of protection, the exports will also decline in course of time.

4. ***Basic Industries Argument*** : The basic industries are considered to be indispensable for the speedy economic development of a country, because without these industries the economic growth of a country cannot be automatic and self-sustained. The basic industries are those industries which provide the foundation for the development of other industries in the country. For example, iron and steel, heavy chemicals, electric power etc., are basic industries and they should be developed by every country through a policy of protection.

5. ***Employment Argument*:** According to this argument, the volume of employment in a country can be increased by following the policy of protection. The reason is that new industries come into existence as a result of the policy of protection and the people get increasing opportunities of employment within the country. Hence, the policy of protection can play a vital role in solving the problem of unemployment in a country.

   According to the critics, the net volume of employment in a country does not register an increase on account of the policy of protection. If the volume of employment in the protected industries increases, this does not imply that the total volume of employment within the country has gone up. The reason is that if the imports of a country are reduced through the policy of protection, this will have its repercussions in course of time on the exports of the country as well. The exports are bound to go down if the government curtails the imports through the policy of protection. Thus, the policy of protection may lead to an increase in the volume of employment in the export industries. Hence, there is no net increase in total employment within the country on account of the policy of protection. Even knowing this, the developed countries of to-day – the E.C.M., the U.S.A Japan, Canada and Australia have raised in recent years high tariff walls against the entry of goods into their markets from the developing countries on the ground that the existence of recessionary conditions there have seriously reduced employment opportunities for their citizens.

6. ***Proper Utilization of Natural Resources Argument*:** There is always wasteful utilization of a country's natural resources under the policy of free trade. The reason is that when a country acquires specialization in the production of a particular commodity, then this results in a speedy exhaustion of all those resources and materials which enter into the production of that commodity. But there is no such fear under a policy of protection, because under it the natural resources of a country are used to the best possible advantage with in the country. The government can easily control the use of scarce materials and resources in industries with a view to safeguarding them for the future.

7. ***Idle Resources Argument*:** Under the policy of free trade, only those natural resources are utilized which enter into the production of those industries which have been established on the basis of the principle of comparative costs. The remaining resources continue to lie idle and industries connected with them fail to develop under free trade.

8. ***Wages Argument*:** The production costs in a low-wage country and lower than those of a high-wage country. Hence, the low-wage country starts exporting goods and services to the high-wage country. The result is that the industries in the high-wage country gradually start dwindling and ultimately there appears large-scale unemployment within the country. Hence, the high wage country has to adopt the policy of protection in order to protect its industries from ruination. The government of the U.S.A. has given protection to its industries against foreign competition on the basis of this argument. For example, the Government of the U.S.A. has imposed a high import duty on Indian textiles to protect its own textile industry from competition.

   According to some critics, this argument has little or no force behind it. If high wages are given to the workers in a particular country, the level of productivity in that country is also high. And higher productivity reduces the unit cost of the product concerned. Hence, such a country need not fear any competition form the low-wage country.

9. ***To keep Money at Home Argument*:** This argument, it is said, was first advanced by the American President, Abraham Lincoln, in the 19th century. According to this argument,

when a country imports goods, then its money is transferred to the other countries by way of payments for imported goods. Now if that country starts producing those goods itself by following a policy of protection, then the money of that country will remain within the country. But the critics consider this argument as shallow. According to them, the economic satisfaction in the country can be maximized by importing chapter goods from abroad. If a country does not import goods from other countries, its exports are bound to decline in course of time. Further, there is no question of money going out of the country as a result of international trade because ultimately the export and imports of a country always balance against each other.

10. ***Equalization of Cost Argument*:** According to this argument, the difference in the costs of expensive indigenous goods and cheap foreign goods should be wiped out by imposing import duties so that the home industries get stimulus and are able to sell their products in the home market without any difficulty. Thus, the indigenous and the foreign industrials will get equal opportunities of the sale of their products in the market. But the critics consider this argument as a defective one. If this argument is accepted then the inefficient indigenous industries will have to be given greater protection because that is the only way to bring about equality in their comparative costs. Further more, if the difference in comparative costs is wiped out through the imposition of high import duties, their will put an end to all foreign trade of the country.

11. ***Increase in Production of Protected Industries Argument*:** The production of an industry can be increased to a considerable extent by giving protection to it. For example, the German Government had increased agricultural production to a very great extent by giving protection to it before the Second World War. But according to the critics, the expansion of a few protected industries does not imply that the national income of a country will also increase in the same proportion. The reason is that protection to a few industries produces adverse repercussions on export industries, because the exports cannot remain high if the imports are reduced by the government as a result of deliberate policy of protection.

12. ***Improvement in Balance of Trade Argument* :** The policy of protection is sometimes supported on the ground that it leads to a perceptible improvement in the balance of trade of a country. This argument acquires increased importance at a time of inflation when on account of the existence of high internal prices, the imports increase while the exports decline. If the imports are cut down through the imposition of high import duties, there shall be a decided improvement in the balance of trade of the country.

13. ***Dumping Argument*:** Sometimes, the foreign industrialists start dumping their goods in backward and underdeveloped countries. In other words, they start selling their goods at prices which do not cover even, their production costs. The reason is that the foreign industrialists, by dumping their goods, desire to crush the industries of the country concerned. Once the industries of that country are crushed following the policy of dumping, the foreign industrialists raise up their prices again. Such a type of dumping by foreigners proves highly dangerous for the country concerned. In such a situation, the government of the country should protect its industries through the imposition of heavy protective duties on foreign goods. The difficulty here is that it is often difficult do detect dumping because this anti-social practice is generally carried on in a concealed manner.

14. ***Government Revenue Argument*:** The main object of the policy of protection is to given protection to home industries through the imposition of heavy import duties. But when

the government levies protective duties on imported goods it also earns some revenue out of them. Some writers have made this is an argument for supporting the policy of protection. But this argument cannot be considered an important argument, because the objective of the policy of protection is not to earn revenue but to afford protection to the home industries.

15. ***National Self-sufficiency Argument***: According to this argument, every country should, as far as possible, be self-sufficient in the production of all essential commodities. If any country is not fully self-sufficient, it may have to face a lot of difficulties in importing essential goods during war-time. Some critics have severely criticized this argument. According to them, if all the countries of the world become self-sufficient, then international trade would come to a standstill. Moreover, no country can become entirely self-sufficient in the production of essential commodities. Besides, national self-sufficiency invites economic stagnation in the economy. China is a classic example .Under Mao, the Chinese economy had become stagnant due to overemphasis on national self-sufficiency. After Mao, the doors of china have once again been opened to the inflow of capital and technology from the western world.

16. ***National Defence Argument***: According to this argument, it is essential to develop defence industries to maintain the security and independence of the country. Hence, the government should give full protection to enable these industries to develop in the country. In fact, this is the most solid argument advanced in favour of protection.

17. ***Bargaining Power Argument***: If a country adopts the policy of protection, its bargaining power in commercial matters vis-a-vis other countries considerably increases. It is able to get more favourable terms for its exports from other countries.

18. ***National Awakening Argument***: According to this argument, a policy of protection leads to national awakening in the country and the people start, as far as possible, using indigenous goods. This naturally gives encouragement to indigenous industries within the country.

Arguments against Protection

The Following arguments are often adduced against protectionism :

1. ***Low Economic Utilization of Natural Resources*** : It is common knowledge that every country produces goods in accordance with the principle of comparative costs under free trade. Hence, that country comes to enjoy all the advantages and economy of territorial division of labour. But production of the country under the policy of protection is not based on territorial division of labour. In other words, the country under protectionism starts producing even those goods in which it enjoys no natural advantages. Hence, the natural resources of the country are not utilized economically under the policy of protection.

2. ***Encouragement of Inefficient Industries*** : The policy of protection often feeds those industries which are not efficient of economical in the real sense of the term. There is no place for such inefficient and uneconomical industries under free trade. Such industries automatically come to an end in course of time.

3. ***Establishment of Monopolistic Organisations*** : The policy of protection by eliminating foreign competition provides ample opportunities to the indigenous industrialists to set up monopolistic combines to exploit the consumers and the workers.

4. ***Loss of Consumers*** : The consumers suffer losses under the policy of protection because they have to pay higher prices on account of the absence of any foreign competition.

5. ***Tendency to become Permanent*** : When protection is once granted to an industry, it becomes difficult to withdraw it even after the industry fully develops itself. The reason is that during this interval certain vested interests come into existence which oppose any attempt by the government to withdraw protection from the industry.
6. ***Fall in the Efficiency of Industry*** : The level of efficiency in the protected industries invariably goes down on account of the absence of any competition from abroad.
7. ***Inequality in the Distribution of National Income*** : The distribution of national income becomes unequal in the country as a consequence of the policy of protection. The reason is that protection often imposes an unnecessary economic burden on the consumers in the form of higher prices. Moreover, the indigenous industrialists earn increased profits as a consequence of the policy of protection. This increases inequalities in the distribution of national income within the country.
8. ***Reduction in Foreign Trade*** : When a country reduces its imports by levying heavy, import duties, its exports also decline in course of time, because the other countries retaliate by imposing import duties on its exports. Thus, the policy of protection often results in a serious decline in foreign trade.
9. ***Strained Relations among Nations*** : When a country reduces its imports through the policy of protection, the other countries retaliate by levying heavy import duties on that country's exports. This produces unnecessary strain in their mutual economic and political relationship
10. ***Political Corruption*** : The policy of protection often gives birth to political corruption on a large scale. The big industrialists try to secure protection to their industries by offering bribes to political leaders and government officials. The United States of America offers a good illustration of this type of political corruption.

From the above discussion, it appears that the advantages of the policy of protection are several times its disadvantages. In fact, this is the reason why almost all the countries of the world have abandoned the policy of free trade today in favour of the policy of protection. Protectionism has a special significance for backward and underdeveloped countries, because without this policy they cannot accelerate their economic growth.

Methods of Protection

Though there are a number of advocates of free trade, international trade is generally characterised by the existence of various trade barriers. *The main objectives of imposing trade barriers are to protect domestic industries from foreign competition, to guard against dumping, to promote indigenous research and development, to conserve the foreign exchange resources of the country, to make the balance of payments position more favourable, to curb conspicuous consumption to mobilise revenue for the government, and to discriminate against certain countries.*

Trade barriers may be broadly classified into tariff and non-tariff barriers.

Tariffs

Tariffs in *international trade* refer to the duties or taxes imposed on internationally traded commodities when they cross the national borders.

Classification of Tariffs

There are different ways of classifying the tariffs.

1. On the basis of the origin and destination of the goods crossing the national boundary, tariffs may be classified into the following three categories :

(a) Export duties

An export duty is a tax imposed on a commodity originating from the duty-levying country destined for some other country.

(b) Import duties

An import duty is tax imposed on a commodity originating abroad and for the duty-levying country.

(c) Transit duties

An transit duty is a tax imposed on a commodity crossing the national frontier originating form, and destined for, other countries.

2. With reference to the basis for quantification of the tariff, we may have the following three fold classification :

(a) Specific duties

A specific duty is a flat sum per physical unit of the commodity imported or exported. Thus, a specific import duty is a fixed amount of duty levied upon each unit of the commodity imported.

(b) Ad-Valorem duties

Ad-valorem duties are levied as a fixed percentage of the value of commodity imported/exported. Thus, while the specific duty is based on the quantum of commodity imported/exported, the ad-valorem duty is based on the value of the commodity imported/exported.

(c) Compound duties

When a commodity is subject to both specific and ad-valorem duties, the tariff is generally referred to as compound duty.

3. With respect to its application between different countries, the tariff system may be classified into the following three types:

(a) Single Column Tariff

The single-column, also known as the uni-linear, tariff system provides a uniform rate of duty for all like commodities without making any discrimination between countries.

(b) Double Column Tariff

Under the double-column tariff system, there are two rates of duty on some or on all commodities. Thus, the double-column tariff discriminates between countries.

The double-column tariff system may be broadly divided into :

(a) General and conventional tariff;

(b) Maximum and minimum tariff.

The general and conventional tariff system consists of two schedules of tariff–the general and the conventional. The general schedule is fixed by the legislature at the very start and the conventional schedule results from the conclusion of commercial treaties with other countries. The maximum and minimum system consists of two autonomously determined schedules of tariff–the maximum and the minimum. The minimum schedule applies to those countries which have obtained a concession as a result of a treaty or through MFN (most favoured nation) pledge. The maximum schedule applies to all the other countries.

(c) Triple-Column Tariff

The triple-column tariff system consists of three autonomously determined tariff schedules- the general, the intermediate and the preferential. The general and intermediate rates are similar to the maximum and minimum rates mentioned above under the double-column tariff systems. The preferential rate is generally applied in trade between the mother country and the colonies.

4. With reference to the purpose they serve, tariffs may be classified into the following categories:

(a) Revenue Tariff

Sometimes the main intention of the government in imposing a tariff may be to obtain revenue. When raising revenue is the primary motive, the rates of duty are generally low, lest imports should be highly discoveraged, defeating the objective of mobilising revenue for the government. Revenue tariffs tend to fall on articles of mass consumption.

(b) Protective Tariff

Protective tariff is intended primarily, to accord protection on domestic industries from foreign competition. Naturally, the rates of duty tend to be very high in this case because generally, only high rate of duty curtail imports to a significant extent.

(c) Countervailing and Anti-Dumping Duties

Countervailing duties may be imposed on certain imports when they have been subsidised by foreign governments. Anti-dumping duties are applied to imports which are dumper on the domestic market at prices either below their cost of production or substantially lower than their domestic prices. Countervailing and anti-dumping duties are, generally, penalty duties and an addition to the regular rates.

Impact of Tariff

Tariffs affect on economy in different ways. An import duty generally has the following effects:

(i) Protective Effect

An import duty is likely to increase the price of imported goods. This increase in the price of imports is likely to reduce imports and increase the demand for domestic goods. Import duties may also enable domestic industries to absorb higher production costs. Thus, as a result of the protection accorded by tariffs, domestic industries are able to expand their output.

(ii) Consumption Effect

The increase in prices resulting from the levy of import duty usually reduces the consumption capacity of the people.

(iii) Redistribution Effect

If the import duty causes an increase in the price of domestically produced goods, it amount to redistribution of income between the consumers and producers in favour of the producers. Further, a part of the consumer income is transferred to the exchequer by means of the tariff.

(iv) Revenue Effect

As mentioned above, a tariff means increased revenue for the government (unless, of course, the rate of tariff is so prohibitive that it completely stop the import of the commodity subject to the tariff).

(v) Income and Employment Effect

The tariff may causes a switch over from spending on foreign goods to spending on domestic goods. This higher spending within the country may cause an expansion in domestic income and employment.

(vi) Competitive Effect

The competitive effect on the tariff is, in fact, an anti-competitive effect in the sense that the protection of domestic industries against foreign competition may enable the domestic industries to obtain monopoly power with all its associated evils.

(vii) Terms of Trade Effect

In a bid to maintain the previous level of imports to the tariff-imposing country, if the exporter reduces his prices, the tariff-imposing country is able to get imports at a lower price. This will, *ceteris paribus*, improve the terms to trade of the country imposing the tariff.

(viii)Balance of Payments Effect

Tariffs, by reducing the volume of imports, may help the country to improve its balance of payments position.

Nominal Tariff and Effective Tariff

Nominal tariff refers to the actual duty on an imported item. For example, if a commodity X is subject to an import duty of 25 percent *advalorem*, the nominal tariff is 25 percent.

Corden defines the effective protective rate as the percentage increase in value added per unit on an economic activity which is made possible by the tariff structure relative to the situation in the absence of tariffs but the same exchange rates. It depends not only on the tariff on the commodity produced but also on the input coefficients and the tariffs on the inputs.

The effective protective rate of industry j (Ej) may be defined as the difference between the industry's value added under protection (Vj) and under free market condition (Vj) expressed as a percentage of the free market value added.

$$E_j = \frac{Vj - Vj}{Vj}$$

Obviously, the protective effect of a tariff on domestic manufacturing is larger if the import duty on the raw materials used in its manufacture is lower.

Optimum Tariff

If a country raises its tariff (import duty) unilaterally, its terms of trade may improve and its volume of trade may decline. The improvement in the terms of trade initially tends to more than offset the accompanying reduction in the volume of trade, Hence a higher trade indifference curve is reached and community welfare is enhanced. Beyond some point, however it is likely that the detrimental effect of successive reductions in the trade volume begins to outweigh the positive effect of further improvements in the terms off trade; as a result, community welfare begins to fall.

Somewhere in between there must be tariff which optimises a country's welfare level under these conditions.

Thus, the optimum tariff is the rate of tariff beyond which any further gain from an improvement in the terms of trade will be more than offset by the related decline in volume. By raising the rate of tariff beyond the optimum rate, it may still be possible to improve the country's terms of trade; but the gain from this improvement in the terms of trade is more than offset by the related decline in the volume of trade.

Non-Tariff Barriers

Non-tariff barriers (NTBs), many of which are described as *new protectionism measures* (as against tariffs which are regarded as *traditional barriers*), have grown considerably. According to a World Bank study, NTBs in major industrial countries affect more than one-third of imports from developing countries, compared to more than one-fourth from all countries.

NTBs are of two categories. Firstly, there are those which are generally used by developing countries to prevent foreign exchange outflows or result from their chosen strategy of economic development. These include import licencing, foreign exchange regulations, canalisation of imports etc. The second category of NTBs are those which are used by developed economies to protect domestic industries which have lost international competitiveness and or which are politically sensitive for governments of these countries.

The NTBs are less transparent, difficult to identify and their impact on exporting countries are almost impossible to quantify.

As a matter of fact several advanced countries like the U.S.A., who are high priests of free trade, resort to several NTBs, particularly against developing countries. They are even accused of involving in arms-twisting tactics to mend the economic policies of the developing countries. The super 301, of the Omnibus Trade and Competitiveness Act, 1988, of the U.S.A is a case in point.

Jagadish Bhagwati observes that since the late 1970's in the US and the EC, protectionism has increasingly taken the *covert* shape. In those countries which advocated free trade, the U.S. and the West European countries, there has been a growing demand for more protective measured in the wake of the challenge of their trade supremacy, particularly by the pacific rim nations. The growing demand in the EC and US for local content regulation and the controversial super 301 of the US Act are manifestations of these. The super 301 may allegedly be used for convert protectionism, like harassment of successful foreign rivals. First the rivals may be accused of indulging in 'unfair trade' and then they may be taken through time consuming and expensive procedures.

The following are some of the important non-tariff barriers :

Voluntary Export Restraints

Voluntary export restraints (VERs) are bilateral arrangements instituted to restrain the rapid growth of exports of specific manufactured goods. The united States and the European Community have thus regulated the imports of several products. The recent advances in VERs and other new protectionism measures dates from the establishment of the Multi-Fiber Arrangement (MFA) in the mid 1970s. Other bilateral arrangements have involved mainly restraining the growth of specific exports from Japan and the newly industrialising countries (NICs).

Administered Protection

Administered protection encompasses a wide range of bureaucratic government actions, which have grown in absolute as well as relative importance over the last decade or more. Most recent VERs are in fact regarded as the outgrowth of administered protection actions.

Important administrative protection measures include the following:

(a) Health and Product Standards

Several health and product standards imposed by the developed countries hinder the exports of developing countries because of the added costs or technical requirements. The need for maintaining health and product standards is unquestionable. The objection should be to their use with the deliberate intention trade restriction or discrimination.

The Agreement on Technical Barriers to Trade (also known as the Standards Code) evolved by the Tokyo Round of the GATT lays down that when government or other bodies adopt technical regulation or standard for reasons of safety, health, consumer or environmental protection, or for other purposes, these should not create unnecessary obstacles to trade. Exporters from developing countries complain, however, that this code is not respected by developed countries in several cases.

(b) Customs Procedures

Certain customs procedures of many countries become trade barriers. For example, studies point out that frequent changes of Japan's customs regulations are themselves a significant barrier to exporters, especially those not affiliated with Japanese overseas joint ventures.

The Tokyo Round formulated a Customs Valuation Code intended to provide a uniform and neutral system for the valuation of goods for customs purposes which will conform to the commercial realities and to prevent the use of arbitrary or fictitious value.

(c) Consular Formalities

A number of countries insist on certain consular formalities like certification of export documents by the respective consulate, of the importing country, in the exporting country. This becomes a trade barrier when the fees charged for this is very high or the procedure is very cumbersome.

(d) Licensing

Many countries regulate foreign trade, particularly imports, by licensing. In most cases, the purpose of import licensing is to restrict imports.

(e) Government Procurement

Government procurements often tend to hinder free trade. The Tokyo Round has, therefore, formulated an agreement on government procurement with a view to securing greater international competition in government procurements.

(f) State Trading

State trading also hinders free trade many a time because of the counter trade practices, canalisation, etc. State trading was an important feature of the foreign trade of the centrally planned economics and many developing countries. With the economic liberalisations in most of these countries, the role of state trading has declined.

(g) Monetary Controls

In addition to foreign exchange regulations, other monetary controls are sometimes employed to regulate trade, particularly imports. For instance, to tide over the foreign exchange crisis in 1990-

91 and 1991-92, the Reserve Bank of India took several measures which included as 25 percent interest rate surcharge on bank credit for imports subject to a commercial rate of interest of a minimum 17 percent, the requirement of substantially high cash margin requirement on most imports other than capital goods, and restrictions on the opening of letters of credit for imports.

(h) Environmental Protection Laws

The growing concern for environmental protection has led to the extension of environmental protection regulation to the imports. For example, the U.S. Congress was considering a legislation to prohibit the import of shrimp harvested with commercial fishing technology which might adversely affect the endangered or threatened sea turtiles unless the President certified that the supplying country has a turtle conservation programme comparable to that of the U.S.

(i) Foreign Exchange Regulations

Foreign exchange regulations are an important way of regulating imports in a number of countries. This is done by the State monopolising the foreign exchange resources and not releasing foreign exchange for import of items which the government do not approve of for various reasons. Restrictions on currency convertibility can also affect imports.

NTBs and India's Exports

The problem of NTBs for Indian exports has been growing. The ADB study of the effects of NTBs on India's exports to developed countries has come to the following conclusion.

Conventional NTBs generally do not exist in developing country markets at least for Indian exports. Their impact on exports of marine products and leather and leather manufactures to developed economies is somewhat marginal. Their potential adverse effects on India's emerging exports of temperate zone agro-products can be critical. Exports of metal manufactures and readymade garments from India have suffered on account of the NTBs in developed economies. Extension and intensification of NTBs is bound to severely restrict India's export expansion in these two relatively important sectors of the economy. Apart from the actual imposition of these NTBs, the "noise" created is often adequate to drive out exporters and induce a fall in exports. NTBs and their administration bring about undesirable changes in the structure of domestic industry and in the distribution of rewards between rent, profit and wage incomes. The uncertainty they create clearly has an adverse effect on capacity creation and investment in the industry. As a factor responsible for an investment shortage, NTBs prevent the industry from making full use of technological potential and economies of scale. These facts were unambiguously brought out in the findings of our survey of garment firms in India.

The above mentioned study has also pointed out that in the case of NTBs, Indian exporters have not taken full advantage of the scope which exists. Thus, improvements in domestic capability will surely yield export expansion at least in the short run.

The problem of NTBs for Indian exports has increased recently. The threat under the Super 301 and Special 301 is an indication of this. The indications are that India may have to face more problems in future. NTBs are often employed when a country's exports to a country increase considerably, causing problems to the industries in importing countries or when the exporting country does not to the economic or political lines.

Quantitative Restrictions – Quotas

Quantitative restrictions or quotas are an important means of restricting imports and exports. A quota represents a ceiling on the physical volume of the import/export of a commodity.

In this section, we shall confine ourselves to quantitative restrictions on imports, i.e., import quotas.

Types of Import Quota

There are four important types of import quotas, including import licensing. These are :

(a) Tariff Quota

A tariff quota combines the features of the tariff as well as of the quota. Under a tariff quota, the imports of a commodity up to a specified volume are allowed duty free or at a special low rate; but any imports in excess of this limit are subject to duty — a higher rate of duty.

(b) Unilateral Quota

In a unilateral quota, a country unilaterally fixes a ceiling on the quantity of the import of a particular commodity.

(c) Bilateral Quota

A bilateral quota results from negotiations between the importing country and a particular supplier country, or between the importing country and export groups within the supplier country.

(d) Mixing Quota

Under the mixing quota, the producers are obliged to utilise domestic raw materials up to a certain proportion in the production of the finished product.

Import Licensing

Quota regulations are generally administered by means of import licensing. In India, for instance, the import of almost all the items is prohibited except under, and in accordance with, a licence or a customs clearance permit issued under the Imports (Control) Order, 1955, or an *Open General Licence* issued by the Government or under any other provision under the above order.

Under the import licensing system, the prospective importers are obliged to obtain a licence from the licensing authorities: the possession of an import licence is necessary to obtain the foreign exchange to pay for the imports. In a large number of countries, import licensing has become a very powerful device for controlling the quantity of imports – either of particular commodities or aggregate imports.

Impact of Quotas

Like fiscal controls, the quantitative restrictions on imports have a number of effects on the economy. The following are, in general, the important economic effects of quotas:

(a) Balance of Payments Effect

As quotas enable a country to restrict the aggregate imports within specified limits, quotas are helpful in improving its balance of payments position.

(b) Price Effect

As quotas limit the total supply, they may cause an increase in domestic price.

(c) Consumption Effect

If quotas lead to an increase in prices, people may be constrained to reduce their consumption of the commodity subject to quotas or some other commodities.

(d) Protective Effect

By guarding domestic industries against foreign competition to some extent, quotas encourage the expansion of domestic industries.

(e) Redistributive Effect

Quotas also have a redistributive effect if the fall in supply due to important restrictions enables the domestic producers to raise prices. The rise in prices will result in the redistribution of income between the producers and consumers in favour of the producers.

(f) Revenue Effect

Quotas may also have a revenue effect. As quotas are administered by means of licences, the government may obtain some revenue by charging a licence fee.

(g) Terms of Trade Effect

Quotas may affect the terms of trade of the country imposing them. The effect of quotas on the terms of trade depends upon the elasticity of the *foreign offer curves.*

Tariffs Vs. Quotas

Both tariffs and quotas suffer from certain merits and demerits.

Let us first examine the superiority of quotas to tariffs.

(a) As a protective measure, a quota is more effective than the tariff. A tariff seeks to discourage imports by raising the price of imported articles. It, however, fails to restrict imports when the demand for imports is price inelastic. (It may be mentioned here that, in developing countries, the demand for many imports is price inelastic). But a quota is very effective in restricting imports within the required limits.

(b) When compared to tariffs, quotas are much more precise and their effects much more certain. The reactions or responses to tariffs are not clear and accurately predictable; but the effect of quotas on import is certain.

(c) It has been argued that "quotas tend to be more flexible, more easily imposed, and more easily removed instruments of commercial policy than tariffs. Tariffs are often regarded as relatively permanent measures and rapidly build powerful vested interests, which make them all the more difficult to remove. Quotas have many characteristics of a more temporary measures, are designed to deal only with a current problem and are removable as soon as circumstances warrant".

d) It has also been pointed out that quotas may be employed as a measure to prevent the international transmission of severe recessions. A recession usually causes a decline in prices, and this may encourage exports. A country may make use of quotas to guard against such recession induced exports into the country.

Quotas, however, suffer from certain defects. Tariffs, in some respects, are superior to quotas.

(a) The effects of quotas are more rigorous and arbitrary and they tend to distort international trade much more than the tariffs. That is why GATT condemns quotas and prefers tariffs to quotas for controlling imports.

(b) Quotas tend to restrict competition much more than tariffs by helping importers and exporters to acquire monopoly power. If import quotas are allocated only to a few importers, they may enable them to a mass fortunes by exploiting the market. Similarly, quotas tend to promote the concentration of economic power among foreign exporters. Professor Kindleberger points out that "a significant difference between a tariff and a quota is that the conversion of a tariff into a quota which admits the same volume of imports may convert a potential into an actual monopoly and reduce welfare".

(c) Quotas may support inflationary pressures within the country by restricting supply. Tariffs also suffer from the same defect.

(d) Quotas offer greater scope for corruption and nepotism than tariffs.

Advantages of Protectionism

In view of the aforementioned discussion, we may summarise the advantages of protectionism as follows:

1. It has been argued that protection provides greater effective demand to home industries and paves way for their development. To quote Gunnar Myrdal, "one of the difficulties of industrial development in underdeveloped countries, and one of the great hindrances to giving a real momentum to a development policy, is that internal demand must be built up simultaneously with supply".
2. Protection leads to diversified industries. It is necessary, for having self sufficiency on military ground.
3. Protection is essential for the development of defence industries. War goods must be sufficiently produced by the country rather than being imported from abroad.
4. Protection is a retaliation against dumping.
5. Protection is necessary to retaliate protectionary tariffs imposed by other countries.
6. Certain types of protection encourage home industries, investments and increase employment opportunities. This helps in solving the problem of unemployment.
7. Protectionary devices such as tariffs etc., when they restrict imports, terms of trade can be improved.
8. Protectionary devices like customs duties fetch public revenue to the government.
9. Protection policy helps solving the problem of disequilibrium in the balance of payments of the country.
10. Protection can preserve certain classes like agriculturists.
11. Protection promotes patriotic feelings among the people.
12. Protection is essential for the smooth operation of economic planning in a mixed economy.

Role of Protection in Underveloped Countries

Underdeveloped countries like India have just and special reasons to adopt the policy of protection. We may briefly enlist them as under :

1. In these countries the infant industry argument assumes far greater importance than in developed countries. Thus, selective or discriminating protection may be suggested as a remedy for certain economic ills and for the industrial growth of these countries.
2. Again, as these countries are agricultural countries, their economic development cannot be brought about at the desired speed unless due protection is given to a number of prospective enterprises. That is to say, in order to allow backward agricultural countries to

develope their industrial potentialities rapidly, foreign competition should inevitably be minimised through protection.

3. Restrictions by the developing countries are just a traditional step to increase trade; as such, in the long run, foreign trade considerably increases with the increase in income and economic expansion of these countries which helps in strengthening the economy of the world as a whole.
4. From the point of view of practical policies also every nation is forced to have a solid defence, self-sufficiency and full employment. These cannot be achieved without evolving a tariff policy suited to the needs of the country. Most of the developing countries have secured their independence very recently. They must have a strong defence and diversification of their industries through protection.
5. Protection helps in conservingscarce foreign exchange resources. It also helps in a rational allocation of foreign exchange for selected imports.
6. Protection encourages self-reliance and self-sufficiency of the country.
7. Protection is a very important method, among many others, of planned economic development. Planning implies control and regulation of economic activities in the desired directions. Free trade policy is a lassies faire policy, which is ruled out under planning. Since most of the poor countries of the world would have launched upon planning for economic development, protection becomes inevitable for its successful implementation.

Conclusion

In short, developing countries cannot afford to have the luxury of free trade. It is comfortable only under protection. Indeed protection should not be a permanent and blanket protection. Whenever circumstances permit, the way for free trade must not be unnecessarily blocked.

Questions for Discussion

1. What is free trade policy? What are its merits and demerits?
2. What is protection? Give arguments for and against protection.
3. Explain the different effects of tariff and quotas.

Chapter - 6

FOREIGN INVESTMENT AND COLLABORATIONS

Introduction

In today's dynamic world to country, even the most advanced ones, is self-sufficient or up-to-date in all spheres of technology. Technology transfer between nations is, therefore, necessary to accelerate the pace of development.

The recent policy liberalisations in China, Eastern Europe and in a number of other developing countries are a clear indication of the wide acceptance of the positive role of foreign technology and capital in the economic development of the developing countries. There has not been any significant restriction on foreign capital and technology in the developed countries. As a matter of fact for some time now several advanced countries have been actively wooing foreign capital and technology. Indeed the major part of the foreign investments and technology transfers take place between the developed countries. If foreign capital and technology are so much important even for the developed countries, they must be very useful for the developing countries.

Foreign collaboration generally takes two forms, viz. :

(a) Technological collaboration.

(b) Technological and financial collaboration.

Advantages of Foreign Collaboration

The main advantages of foreign collaboration are the following :

1. It enables the Indian firm to upgrade the existing technology or to obtain new technology.
2. Acquisition of new technology enables the firm to enter new business.
3. Foreign equity participation enables the Indian company to take up projects with large outlay than would be possible without such collaboration.
4. Foreign collaboration may make it easier for the Indian company to raise capital through public issue because the public, generally, has a more favourable attitude towards companies with foreign collaboration.
5. Foreign collaboration may help the Indian company to gain managerial expertise.

6. In some cases collaboration with the foreign firm would help to preempt competition.
7. Foreign collaborations in many cases help the Indian company in its exports. The technological upgradation would improve the company's competitiveness not only in the domestic market but also in the foreign market. Similarly, the new technology may also help the company in exports. When the collaboration involves foreign equity participation the foreign collaborator may take an active interest in the exports of the joint venture. A number of Indian companies have been able to increase/start exports because of foreign collaborations.
8. Foreign collaboration may help improve quality, reduce wastages, improve productivity and reduce costs.

Disadvantages of Foreign Collaboration

1. The foreign technology supplied may not be the latest. Particularly when the foreign collaborator does not have equity participation, the collaborator may be reluctant to transfer the latest technology.
2. There are chances of the foreign collaborator over changing. For example, if the foreign company's contribution to the capital takes the form of supply of machinery, the chances of overcharging cannot be ruled out.
3. When there is a tie-up of foreign capital with technology, the Indian party cannot opt for technology of other firms even if that is better.
4. In some cases, the foreign technology may not be the appropriate one for the local conditions.
5. When there is foreign equity participation, there would also be participation in the management by the foreign company. If the foreign company has majority share holding, control of management would be mostly in the hands of the foreign collaborator and the company's policies and future development would be influenced by the foreign company's interests. It is to gain control over the management that several foreign companies have raised their equity holding in their joint ventures in India to 51 percent taking advantage of the policy liberalisation. It may be noted that Mafatal's refusal to permit the Royal Dutch Shell to raise its equity holding in their joint venture, National Organic Chemical Industries Ltd. (Nocil), resulted in Shell pulling out of Nocil. Mafatal turned down Shell's proposal for raising the equity holding to 51 percent because Mafatlal wanted "Nocil to be a proper Indian company".

Types of Foreign Investment

Broadly there are two types of foreign investment, namely, *foreign direct investment* (FDI) and *portfolio investment*.

FDI refers to investment in a foreign country where the investor retains control over the investment. It typically takes the form of starting a subsidiary, acquiring a stake in an existing firm or starting a joint venture in the foreign country. Direct investment and management of the firms concerned normally to together.

If the investor has only a sort of property interest in investing the capital in buying equities, bonds, or other securities abroad, it is referred to as portfolio investment. That is, in the case of portfolio investments, the investor uses his capital in order to get a return on it, but has no much control over the use of the capital.

FDIs are governed by long term consideration because these investments cannot be easily liquidated. Hence factors like long term political stability, government policy, industrial and economic prospects etc., influence the FDI decision. However, portfolio investments, which can be liquidated fairly easily, are influenced by short term gains. Portfolio investments are generally much more sensitive than FDIs. Direct investors have direct responsibility with the promotion and management of the enterprise. Portfolio investors do not have such direct involvement with the promotion and management.

Since the economic liberalisation of 1991, there has been a surge in the FDI and portfolio investments in India.

There are mainly two routes of portfolio investments in India, viz., by Foreign Institutional Investors (FIIs) like mutual funds and through Global Depository Receipts (GDRs), American Depository Receipts (ADRs) and Foreign Currency Convertible Bonds (FCCBs).

GDRs/ADRs and FCCBs are instruments issued by Indian companies in the foreign markets for mobilising foreign capital by facilitating portfolio investment by foreigners in Indian securities. Since 1992, Indian companies, satisfying certain conditions, are allowed to access foreign capital markets by Euro issues.

With reference to foreign investment in India, foreign investment may be classified as follows

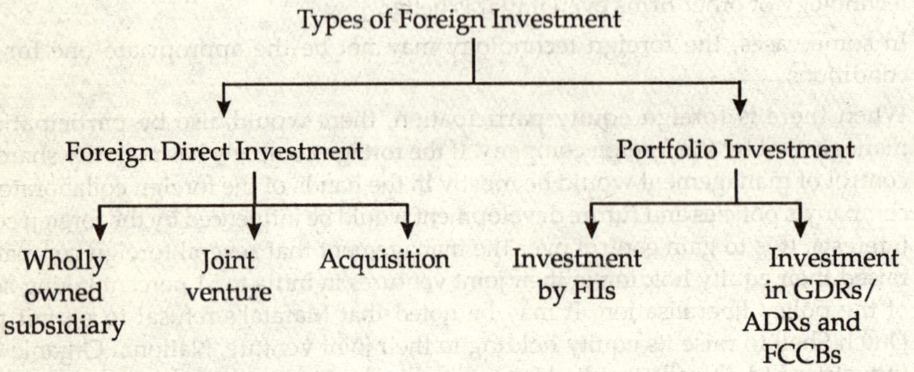

Significance of Foreign Investment

Economic reforms and the far-reaching political changes have resulted in very substantial changes in the international capital flows.

In the 1970s, bank lending was the largest component of capital flows to the developing countries. The most important recipient of this was the public sector. In the 1990s, by contrast, the surge in the capital flows was dominated by bonds, FDI, and portfolio investment, and the private sector did most of the external borrowing. Even in 1990, official flows dominated the international capital flow. FDI as well as private debt flows were much less important. However, by end of the 1990s FDI was about three times the size of the official flows whereas in 1990 FDI was only about half the size of the official flows. Private debt flows also increased substantially.

The belief that **'sovereign lending'** is the safest lending encouraged enormous lending to the government sectors of the developing countries by banks of developed countries and this eventually contributed to the debt crisis of the early 1980s.

The changes in the composition of the capital flows and the substantial increase in the magnitude of some of the flows have remarkably changed the balance of payments and foreign exchange reserves position of several countries. The debt creating flows as a percentage of total flows in the BoP of India averaged as much as 97 percent during the Seventh Plan (1985-90) but declined to less than 20 percent by mid 1990s. Eventually, India began to experience a surplus on the BoP and a very remarkable improvement in the reserves position.

Economic reforms and policy changes encouraging foreign investment in many countries – both the developed and developing (including the erstwhile communist and socialist) – in the 1980s favoured a surge in international investment flows. India was rather a laggard in economic reforms. Privatisation, which was an important element of economic reforms in the market economies too, expanded the scope international capital flows. There have been several other encouraging factors. Declining transport costs and impressive advances in communications technologies and information processing boosted the integration of goods and capital markets. The adoption of common rules to regulate banking and financial reporting decreased information asymmetry and lent further momentum to globalisation, as did the creation of the worldwide web and international coalescence around product standards such as ISO 9000.

As countries began to welcome foreign direct investment and transacting business over long distance grew easier, companies were motivated to reorganise their activities, they sliced up the value–added chain and established production facilities in different markets. This proliferation of production networks has allowed firms to specialise, focus their research efforts, and leverage their core managerial and marketing skills; it has also reinforced the openness resulting from trade liberalisation and the removal of barriers to capital mobility.

Even withe these changes, globalisation might not have taken off were it not for seismic shift in attitudes. Countries worldwide have moved to market based economies and democratic forms of government. This broadening of political participation is feeding centrifugal pressure within nationa.

Foreign investment has assisted and is assisting the economic growth of many countries. As the *World Development Report*, 1991, points out, for the developing countries FDI has several advantages over the official development assistance (ODA): EDI shifts the burden of risk of an investment from domestic to foreign investors. Repayments are linked to profitability of the underlying investment, whereas under debt financing the borrowed finds must be serviced regardless of the project costs. Further, it has also been observed that FDI is the only capital inflow that has been strongly associated with higher GDP growth since 1970.

The contribution of FDI to economic growth is highlighted by the fact that the ratio of FDI flow to domestic investment (gross capital formation) rose for most developed and developing countries during the 1980s. Among the developing countries, since 1970 this ratio has risen in all regions except West Asia, but increases have been most pronounced in Asia and Pacific and, since the mid 1970s, in Africa. The share of FDI in the gross fixed capital formation (GFCF) of developing countries more than doubled between 1986 and 1992, nearing 7.5 percent in 1994.

Although the bulk of the FDI goes to developed countries, its share in their GFCF is only about half of that in developing countries because of the massiveness of their GFCF.

Apart from potential gains through technology transfer, DFI generates employment, accounting for as much as 60 percent of manufacturing employment in some countries such as Singapore.

Given the limitations of domestic savings, many developing countries will have to rely on foreign investment to accelerate economic growth.

Given the incremental capital-output ratio of 4.1., and FDI one percent of GDP will and only about 0.2 percent to the economy's growth rate. It may be noted that China has been able to maintain a GDP growth-rate of over 8 percent for a long time because of a high savings rate and huge inflow of FDI. In this context, it is significant to note the observation of the United Front (UF) Government in its economic policy statement that the nation needs and has the capacity to absorb at least $10 billion a year as foreign investment.

The United Front Government's statement on Common Minimum Programme (CMP) also highlighted the role of foreign investment in the infrastructural development in India. Indeed, a major obstacle to the fast development of the Indian economy has been the infrastructural bottlenecks. As the CMP rightly observes, the economy cannot grow and the needs of the people cannot be met without more capacity is power, oil, telecom, railways, roads and ports. The UF government, which has estimated the cumulative investment requirement of the infrastructure sectors over the next five years to be about $200 billion (Rs. 7,00,000 crore) at the very minimum, stipulates a stepping up of the investment in infrastructures from the present 3.5 - 4 percent of the GDP to at least 6 percent in the next few years. In this context, the CMP proposes a review of the scope, functions and procedures of the Foreign Investment Board in order to make it an effective and credible instrument to foreign investment in India. What a change from the pre-1991 regime of not allowing even the domestic private capital in most of the vital infrastructures! The total power generation capacity of the controversial Enron projects is nearly equivalent to the total additional generation capacity installed in the country during the first two five year plans. The Central Electricity Authority has estimated an additional power generation capacity of 57,000 MW during the Ninth Plan (1997-2002) as the requirement for meeting the demand for power which is expected to grow at the rate of 9 percent year. The investment requirement of this is estimated at $ 47 billion (Rs. 1,64,500 crore). This, obviously, is beyond the domestic resource capability.

Addressing a session on infrastructure at the seminar on 'moving to the market: sustaining reforms in India and Asia' organised by the Confederation of Indian Industry (CII) and Asian Society, in New Delhi on March 9, 1997, Gordon Wu has observed that foreign investment brings for 'E's - efficiency, equity, experience and expertise. In return, there is a fifth 'E' - expatriation of profits.

Factors Affecting International Investment

The important factors affecting international investment are the following.

1. ***Rate of Interest :*** One of the most important stimuli to international capital movements is the difference in the rate of interest prevailing at different places. Capital has a tendency to move from a country with a low rate of interest to a country where it is higher, other things being equal interest rates or foreign exchanges rates.
2. ***Speculation :*** Short term capital movements may be influenced also by speculation pertaining to anticipated changes in the interest rates or foreign exchanges rates.
3. ***Profitability :*** Private foreign capital movement is influenced by the profit motive. Hence, other things being equal, private capital will be attracted to countries where the return on investment is comparatively higher.
4. ***Costs of production :*** Private capital movements are encouraged by lower costs of production in foreign countries. As Kreinin points out, we may distinguish between two types of cost reducing investment. The first arises from the need to obtain raw materials from abroad. Such materials may be either unavailable at home or obtainable only at extremely high costs, but they are essential for the production and sale of final products at

home or abroad. Without them profit opportunities would remain unexploited. Indeed, vast investments in the extractive industries are motivated by the fact that the capital must go where the resources are. The second type of cost-reducing investment pertains to costs of commodities other than materials, primarily labour.

5. ***Economic Conditions :*** Economic conditions, particularly the market potential and infrastructural facilities, influence private foreign investment. The size of the population and the income level of a country have an important bearing on the market opportunities.
6. ***Government Policies :*** Government policies, particularly towards foreign investment, foreign collaboration, remittances, profits, taxation, foreign exchange control, tariffs, and monetary, fiscal and other incentives, are important factors that may influence foreign investment in a country.
7. ***Political Factors :*** Political factors like political stability, nature of important political parties and relations with other countries also influence capital movements.

The United Nations Economic Commission for Asia and the Far East has drawn up the following list of conditions that have to be met if foreign capital is to be attracted to underdeveloped countries.

1. Political stability and freedom from external aggression.
2. Security of life and property.
3. Reasonable opportunities for earning profits.
4. Prompt payment of fair and transferable compensation in case of nationalisation of a foreign owned enterprise.
5. Guarantee of the possibility of remittance of profits, dividends and interest, as well as of a reasonable depreciation allowance on the capital invested.
6. Facilities for immigration and employment of foreign technical and administrative personnel.
7. A system of taxation that does not impose a crushing burden on private enterprise.
8. Freedom from double taxation.
9. Absence of vexatious controls.
10. Non-discriminatory treatment of foreigners in the administration of existing controls.
11. Absence of competition between State-owned enterprises and private foreign capital.
12. A general spirit of friendliness toward foreign investors.

General Agreement on Tariffs and Trade (GATT)

The General Agreement on Tariffs and Trade (GATT), a multilateral treaty between governments, was singed in 1947 and came into force on 1st January 1948.

Objectives

The primary objective of GATT is to expand international trade by liberalising trade so as to bring about all-round economic prosperity. The preamble to the GATT mentions the following as its important objectives.

(a) Raising standard of living.

(b) Ensuring full employment and a large and steadily growing volume of real income and effective demand.

(c) Developing full use of the resources of the world.

(d) Expansion of production and international trade.

Conservations and Principles of GATT

GATT embodies certain conventions and general principles governing international trade among countries that adhere to the agreement. The rules of conventions of GATT require that :

(a) Any proposed change in the tariff, or other type of commercial policy of a member country should not be undertaken without consultation of other parties to the agreement, and

(b) That the countries that adhere to GATT should work towards the reduction of tariffs and other barriers to international trade, which should be negotiated within the framework of GATT.

For the realisation of its objectives, GATT has adopted the following principles :

1. Non-discrimination

The principle of non-discrimination requires that no member country shall discriminate between the members of GATT in the conduct of international trade. To ensure non-discrimination the members of GATT agree to apply the principle of *most favoured nation* (MFN) to all import and export duties. The means that "each nation shall be treated as well as the most favoured nation". As far as quantitative restrictions are permitted, they too, are to be administered without favour.

However, certain exceptions to this principle are allowed. For instance, GATT does not prohibit economic integration such as free trade areas or customs union, provided the purpose of such integration is "to facilitate trade between the constituent territories and not to raise barriers to the trade of other... parties". The GATT also permits the members to adopt measure to counter dumping and export subsidies. However, the application of such measures shall be limit to the offending countries.

2. Prohibition of Quantitative Restrictions

GATT rules seek to prohibit quantitative restrictions as far as possible and limit restrictions on trade to the less rigid tariffs. However, certain exceptions to this prohibition are granted to countries confronted with balance of payments difficulties and to developing countries. Further, import restrictions are allowed to apply to agricultural and fishery products if domestic production of these articles is subject to equally restrictive production or marketing controls.

3. Consultation

By providing a forum for continuing consultation, GATT seeks to resolve disagreements through consultation.

An Evaluation of the GATT

The member countries of GATT account for over 90 percent of the international trade. This indicates that GATT can considerably help in the orderly development of global trade.

One of the principal accomplishments of GATT has been the establishment of a forum for continuing consolations. "Disputes that might otherwise have caused continuing hard feeling, reprisals, and even diplomatic rupture have been brought to the conference table and compromised".

GATT has so far held eight multinational trade negotiations. Through GATT's efforts at getting tariff reductions and other measures aiming at trade liberalisation are not upto expectations, they are in no way insignificant. The average level of tariffs on manufactured goods in industrial countries is about 3 percent now compared to about 40 percent in the immediate post-second War years.

GATT and Developing Countries : Developing countries, however, have been, by and large, dissatisfied with the outcome of GATT's negotiations. This is true of even the Kennedy Round and the Tokyo Round. The Uruguay Round has even frightened them.

The feelings of developing countries was expressed by T. Swaminathan in the following words: "The experience of our participation in the Kennedy Round has not been very different from our experience of the usual, ordinary GATT tariff negotiations. In item-by-item negotiations, for obvious reasons, the main emphasis was, as is customary, placed on products of interest to developed countries. Products of interest to less developed countries generally received a lower priority. The pattern during the Kennedy Round has been by and large the same". Developing countries expressed their sentiments in a joint statement in the following words: "Today, the developing countries participating in the negotiations wish to state that the most important problems of most of them in the field of trade taken up within the framework of these negotiations still remain unresolved. The developing countries deeply regret that they are not in a position to share, to the same extent, the satisfaction of the developed countries at the conclusion and the achievement of the Kennedy Round". This is true of all the Rounds. The developing countries, by and large, are disappointed about the outcome of the Tokyo Round as well, though certain special provisions have been incorporated in their favour. The Uruguay Round has been nerve-testing for the developing countries.

Trade liberalisation has been confined mostly to goods of interest to the developed countries. In case of agricultural commodities not only was that there was no liberalisation, but also there was an increase in protection. Manufactured products of interest to developing countries like textiles and clothing, footwear etc., have been subject to increasing non-tariff barriers. While the developed countries enjoy a more liberalised trading environment, the growing NTBs have been severely affecting the exports of developing countries. The Uruguay Round has been an attempt to clear the way further for the developed countries to the economies of the developing countries. Ironically, the developed countries are increasing the protectionism when the developing countries are liberalising. This is indeed a sad commentary on the GATT and other multilateral organisations.

Uruguay Round Agreement

The eighth and the latest Round of the multilateral trade negotiations held under the auspicious of the GATT is known as the **Uruguay Round** (UR) as it was launched in Punta del Este in Uruguay, a developing country, in September, 1986. Because of the complexities of the issues involved and the conflicts of interests among the participating countries, the Uruguay Round could not be concluded in December, 1990 as was originally scheduled. When the negotiations dragged on, Arther Dunkel, the then Director General of GATT, presented a Draft Act embodying what he thought was the result of the Uruguay Round. This came to be popularly known as the **Dunkel Draft**. This was replaced by an enlarged and modified final text which was approved by delegations from the member countries of the GATT on 15th December, 1993. This Final Act was signed by ministers of 125 governments on 15th April, 1994. The results of the Uruguay Round are to be implemented within ten years since 1995. Different time periods are given for effecting the different agreements.

The first six Rounds of MTNs concentrated almost exclusively on reducing tariffs, while the Seventh Round (Tokyo Round - 1973-79) moved on to tackle Non-Tariff Barriers (NTBs). The UR sought to broaden the scope of MTMs far wider by including new areas such as trade in services, Trade Related aspects of Intellectual Property (TRIPs) and Trade Related Investment Measures (TRIMs).

The most outstanding feature of the UR was the inclusion of the last subject referred to above in the MTNs of GATT. The traditional concerns of the GATT were limited to international trade in goods. The UR went much beyond goods to services, technology, investment and information.

Some of the important features of the Uruguay Round Agreements are given below.

Because of the inclusion of these new aspects in the GATT negotiations, the developing countries had serious apprehensions, about outcome of the Uruguay Round.

The Uruguay Round took up three basic subjects for discussion :

(a) Reducing specific trade barriers and improving market access ;

(b) Strengthening GATT disciplines ;

(c) Problems of liberalisation of trade in services, Trade Related aspects of Intellectual Property rights (TRIPs) and Trade Related Investment Measures (TRIMs).

WTO

Followings the UR agreement, GATT was converted from a provisional agreement into a formal international organisation called **World Trade Organisation (WTO)** with effect from January 1, 1995. WTO will serve as a single institutional framework encompassing GATT and all the results of the Uruguay Round. It will be directed by a Ministerial conference that will meet at least once every two years and its regular business will be overseen by a General Council.

The old GATT system allowed, under what was known as the 'grandfather clause' existing domestic legislation to continue even if it violated a GATT agreement that a member country had accepted by being a signatory to GATT. The WTO, specially rules this out.

The WTO has the following five specific functions.

1. The WTO shall facilitate the implementation, administration and operation and further the objectives of the Multilateral Trade Agreements and shall also provide the framework for the implementation, administration and operation of plurilateral Trade Agreements.
2. The WTO shall provide the forum for negotiations among its members concerning their multilateral trade relations in matters dealt with under the Agreements.
3. The WTO shall administer the 'Understanding on Rules and Procedures Governing the Settlement of Disputes'.
4. The WTO shall administer the "Trade Review Mechanism'.
5. With a view to achieving greater coherence in global economic policy making, the WTO shall co-operate, as appropriate, with the IMF and IBRD and its affiliated agencies.

The General Council will serve four main functions :

1. To supervise on a regular basis the operations of the revised agreements and ministerial declarations relating to (a) goods, (b) services and TRIPs;
2. To act a Dispute Settlement Body
3. To serve as a Trade Review Mechanism; and
4. To establish Goods Council, Services Council and TRIPs Council, as subsidiary bodies.

The WTO is a more powerful body with enlarged functions than the GATT and is envisaged to paly a major role in the world economic affairs. To become a member of the WTO, a country must completely accept the results of the Uruguay Round.

Impact of WTO on Various Aspects of Indian Economy

India, being a founder member of the WTO, has been following the WTO decisions, but as a consequence, certain effects on the Indian economy have become evident.

1. Effects on Indian Industry

WTO has been urging India to lower import duties, remove controls on consumer goods imports, reduce quantitative restrictions, etc. Under the Uruguay Round Agreement, India offered to reduce tariffs on capital goods, components, intermediate goods and industrial raw materials to 40% in case our tariffs were above that percentage; to 25% in case our tariffs were between 25 to 40 percent and to bind the tariff ceiling at 25 percent in case our tariffs were below that percentage. The reduction in tariffs was to be achieved by the year ending 2000.

Since India scrupulously followed the agreement, the tariffs have been reduced year after year to conform with the WTO provisions. As the protection afforded by import duties gradually disappeared, Indian industry had to face increasing competition from foreign goods. Confederation of Indian Industry (CII), the apex body expressed its disapproval against duty-free status of capital goods sector. As a result, CII estimated that indigenous capital goods industry on a conservative estimate lost orders worth Rs. 5,000 crores from foreign countries. Instead of ensuring level playing field, indigenous industry has to pay excise, sales tax, octroi, turnover tax while imported goods are allowed duty-free access to our market. Not only the entire manufacturing industry is faced with a crisis, even machine tools industry, gensets and boiler producers are put at a serious disadvantage. Consequently, imports of finished products are displacing indigenously produced products. As a result, many industrial units are being closed and cheap imports have become an important cause of recession in Indian industry.

India was maintaining quantitative restrictions in the form of quotas, import and export licences on 2,700 agricultural commodities, textile and industrial products. United States along with Australia, New Zealand. Swizerland, European Economic Community and Canada complained to the WTO Dispute Settlement Machinery that these QRs were inconsistent with WTO norms. The dispute settlement panel gave its verdict against India. India went in appeal, but the WTO panel on 23rd August 1999 rejected India's appeal against QRs.

As a result, although India could continue QRs till March 2003, the process was hastened and QRs on all items were removed. This has opened the floodgates for foreign consumer goods to enter the Indian market, thereby seriously damaging Indian industry.

Impact of import of Second Hand Cars in India. The Government of India allowed the import of second hand cars into India. This policy has seriously hit Indian automobile industry. Mr. Rahul Bajaj described this as **"anti-national and anti-India Act"**. In fact, experience the world over has shown that wherever second hand imported cars are allowed, they seriously damage domestic industry. Japanese used cars virtually destroyed New Zealand car industry. Even Mr. Phil Spender. managing Director, Ford India Reacting to thc policy of permitting used cars said: "If the government asks us what to do (about the used cars), I'll be the first to volunteer ways to keep used cars imports out of India". Even other CEOs of MNCs who have invested in the Indian automobile market expressed similar sentiments. Mr. Richard Swano, M.D. General Motors is of the opinion that the import tariff on used cars should be 100% and not 40-50 percent.

Similarly, if India allowed the import of used machine tools, it is likely to have serious repercussions on capital equipment manufactures.

Import of Chinese Goods - In recent years, Chinese goods are flooding the Indian Markets. They include battery cells, cigarette lighters, locks, car stereos, energy saving lamps, VCD players, wrist watches, toys, fans, electric ovens and a large variety of consumer articles. Since China has become a member of the WTO, this is going to create another problem because action against Chinese dumping of goods can be taken only within WTO provisions, Not only that, Chinese goods are coming through normal channels of trade, they are also being smuggled via Nepal at Zero duty. A very porous border from Nepal has increased clandestine imports from China. Both regular and clandestine imports from China. Both regular and clandestine imports from china are making serious forays into the Indian markets, thus hurting quite a large range of consumer goods industries. It is very difficult to prepare an anti-dumping case against China, since it is virtually impossible to obtain information required from Chinese sources due to non-transparent nature of Chinese economy. Dr. B.R Sabade is of the view. "It is extremely difficult to make a case about dumping of Chinese goods. Government can impose a preliminary duty, introduce a trigger price mechanism or declare China is a non-market economy".

2. Impact of WTO on SSI Units

WTO agreements do not discriminate on the basis of size of industries or enterprises. In the WTO regime, reservations may have to be withdrawn, preferential purchase and other support measures may not be available and thus SSIs have to complete not only with the large units within the country, but also the cheap imported products. SSIs are thus losing their markets to cheap imported products. Consequently, a very large number of SSI units are becoming sick or have closed down. Thus the SSI Sector which accounts for 40 percent of manufacturing output, 50 percent of employment and over 33 percent of exports is in jeopardy. Next to agriculture, this sector is the principal source of employment accommodating 18 million persons. The rule of survival of the fittest is being applied to this sector and in their game, only a few able ones will be able to survive. Dumping of Chinese goods has seriously affected SSI sector. The real difficulty with the SSI sector is that it does not have adequate resources to prepare the case for anti-dumping duties in view of the prohibitive costs of anti-dumping investigation. The SSIs cannot collect detailed information on individual products required by the anti-dumping directorate to establish a complete case. Consequently, small industries continue to suffer due to such dumping policy.

Not only that, the entry of multinationals in ordinary consumer goods like ice cream, agarbatti manufacture, food processing, mineral water etc., is also adversely affecting the SSI sector since these were the traditional areas of this sector. In soft drinks, the entry of powerful Coca Cola and Pepsi have eliminated practically all small units engaged in the manufacture of aerated water. MNCs are not interested in hi-tech products. Rather they prefer low technology, quick profit yielding and large volume products with regular demand throughout the year. In the name of consumer interests, MNCs continue to Swallow SSIs and eliminate them from the market.

3. Double Standards of Developed Countries

The basic question is : Developed countries demand so many concessions and reduction of tariffs from the developing countries, but are they encouraging free flow of trade, capital and technology across states; or are they using globalisation to their advantage ? It would be of interest to consider certain issues :

Unfair Game in Agreements on Textiles - India is quite competitive in textiles. But developed countries through various protectionist measures deny access to cost efficient textiles producers. These measures take the form of anti-dumping duties, unilateral change in the rule of origin and unjustifiable foisting of environmental issues. All these measures are taken to protect domestic industry in developed countries and thus, these measures hamper free flow of Indian textile exports.

Developed countries have proposed ten long years to reduce quotas in their domestic textile industries, but they pressurise the developing countries to reduce their tariffs, remove quantitative restrictions, introduce Intellectual Property Rights (IPRs) etc. Immediately. Obvious developed countries play an unfair game so far as textile agreements are concerned.

The United States has signed WTO agreements with the proviso that all such agreements will have to be passed by the US Congress, being a sovereign body. There is another assurance given by the US President to the Congress. In case, the decisions of Dispute Settlement Machinery of WTO go against the United States, they will be reviewed by US justices. If they find the decisions unfair, the US has unilaterally reserved for itself right to walk out of the WTO.

Criticising this big brother like attitude, some commentators believe that the rule makers are not going to tolerate being over-ruled. Many of the US laws like Section 301 of US Trade Act is clearly a violation of WTO agreement. This matter was considered by the Dispute Settlement Panel of WTO which gave its verdict that those laws are WTO compliant. This has emboldened the US to continue to use unilateral action against countries that are not considered by US administration as compliant with US trading interests. It passes one's comprehension how the US Congress should be considered as a super-body over the WTO, while the parliaments of other members of the WTO, especially the developing countries, are denied this right. Although sixteen countries petitioned against the US, but since WTO has supported the US position, all these countries which include besides India, Agrentina, Egypt, Greece, Poland, Korea, Russia can do very little against the US unilateral action since it has the WTO in its pocket. Though patently unjustified, yet Section 107 of Uruguay Round Agreement "Provides that nothing in the Uruguay Round Agreement shall be construed to limit any authority conferred under any law of the United States including sections 301-310 of the Trade Act of 1974".

Child Labour — When imports from developing countries hurt the interests of United, States, a number of environmental and human rights issues were raised with the objective of imposing a ban on the import of Indian carpets, chemicals, handicrafts, ready made garments on the plea that in their manufacture child labour was involved. The United States banned imports of several products from India on the plea of child labour. But the hypocrisy of the US attitude has been blown up by Mr. B.R. Sabade when he writes : "Many American companies have shifted their factories to remote areas in Mexico, Indonesia and some other countries. Children are employed in these factories in large numbers and they have to work for more than 12 hours. Recently, a study conducted by Rugar University has revealed that 290,200 child workers are sweating in shopping malls, factories and farms in the United States". With such double standards, the US uses the child labour stick to punish India.

US Antidumping Act and copy Right Act against WTO Principles–Recently, Japan complained against the US Anti-dumping Act as a violation of WTO principles. A series of investigations carried out regarding Japan's steel exports to United States revealed that the US Anti-dumping Act was inconsistent with WTO principles. The decision of the WTO favouring Japan was delivered on 29th May 2000.

Similarly, European Economic Community complained against the US Copy Right Act since a militated against the WTO principles as provided for under Berne Convention for the protection of litecracy and artistic works. The WTO decision delivered on 15th June 2000 also went against the United States.

4. Agreement on Agriculture

The agreement on Agriculture has only in theory favoured agriculture in developing countries, but in practice, its implementation has seriously affected agriculture in developing countries. According to the Agreement, developed countries agreed to reduce these subsidies by 20 per cent over six years and developing countries by 13 percent over 10 years. However, developed countries under Green Box and Blue Box subsidies continue to support agriculture.

Green Box Subsidies include amounts spent on government services such as research disease control, infrastructure and food security. They also include payments made directly to farmers that do not stimulate production, such as certain forms of direct income support assistance to help farmers restructure agriculture, and direct payments under environmental and regular assistance programmes. This definition is very wide and includes all types of Government subsidies.

Blue Box Subsidies are certain direct payments made to farmers where the farmers are to limit production, certain government assistance programmes to encourage agriculture and rural development in developing countries, and other support on a small scale when compared with the total value of the products supported 15 per cent or less in the case of developed countries and 10 per cent or less for developing countries.

Similar to domestic support subsidies, developing countries are not allowed to increase their negligible level of export subsidies while developed countries are allowed to maintain 64 per cent of their subsidy outlays on the base level. Consequently, agricultural imports from developed countries are available at much below the market price in the domestic economy. *Human Development Report* (1997) reviewing this problem mentions. According to the OECD, the per capita transfer to US farmers amounted to $ 29,000 in 1995. In the main maize producing areas of Mindanao and Cagayan Valley, the average per capita incomes amount to less than $ 300. So each US farmer receives in subsidies roughly 100 times the income of a maize farmer in the Philippines.

"In the real world, as distinct from imaginary or inhabited by free traders, survival in agricultural markets depends less on comparative cost advantage than on comparative access to subsidies. Liberalising local food markets in the face of unequal competition is not a prescription for improving efficiency, but a recipe for the destruction of livelihood".

"Implementation of the Uruguay Round agriculture agreement over the next five years will not materially change the picture........ Agriculture remains the only area of international trade in which export dumping is accepted as a legitimate trade practice".

Earlier, Indian agricultural prices were lower than international prices mostly. But as a result of heavy subsidization of agricultural exports by developed countries, the situation is fast changing. Since international agricultural prices have become lower than Indian agricultural prices, Indian farmers have been put to a serious disadvantage. The phenomenon of farmers' suicides and growing unrest in several states because of the distress of farmers specialising in agricultural commodities and their exports is a very severe human problem. Some economists have, therefore, drawn the attention of the government to the sad plight of Indian farmers due to WTO obligations. Professor P.R. Brahmananda has gone so far as to assert: "We have to think of domestic interests as paramount. If we have to leave WTO for the interests of our farmers, I would not mind it".

India' Role At Doha Ministerial Conference (2001)

The Doha ministerial under the auspices of the WTO in November 2001 had a draft prepared by its director General Mr. Mike Moore, which intended to raise new issues such as investment, competition policy and transparency in Government procurement. The developed countries headed by USA were keen on discussing these issues, but the developing nations wanted the 142-members to consider issues related with the implementation of the early decisions taken after the Uruguay Round in 1994.

The major cause of complaint of the developing countries was that whereas the developed nations in principle agreed to reduction of tariff and non-tariff barriers which were a hindrance to the free trade, but in practice used a number of non-tariff barriers to obstruct the much-intended free flow of trade. US had been able to influence a number of small developing nations to agree to the new agenda, but India spearheaded the attack with Mr. Murasoli Maran, Commerce and Industry Minister by asserting : "We want implementation issues addressed. We want further progress on the built-in agenda of the Uruguay Round, especially on trade in services and agriculture. We will not accept any discussion on non-trade issues like labour standards". Mr. Maran Said : "WTO is not a global government and it should not seek to appropriate to itself responsibilities that legitimately belong to national Governments and legislatures". Although it was feared at an earlier stage the India may be isolated, but the logical stand taken by India to further the interests of developing nations, a number of countries came to support the strong stand taken by India. As a matter of convention, all WTO decisions are taken by the entire membership, typically by concensus. Though a majority vote can be taken, but is hasn't happened so far since the WTO replaced GATT.

As consequence of the pressure from the developing nations, USA and the European Union relented and adopted a number of issues, which had been strong irritants for developing nations.

First of all, it was agreed that developing countries need not source their essential medicines and drugs at high cost from western multinational companies, which hold patents. South Asian, african and Caribbean countries will benefit from this decision. Since China, India and Brazil posses the capacity and technology to manufacture these drugs, they will be entitled to export these medicines without having to secure compulsory licences from licence holders. Brazil representative very candidly put forward the case of developing countries: "We need a political signal that we can do what the US and Canada have just done in providing low-priced doses of antibiotics to combat the anthrax scare". In this way, the fear that the health cover to about 30 per cent of the population available will be eroded significantly as a consequence of the apprehended rise in their prices, will be significantly taken care of.

Secondly, the poor countries will be able to better look after their food security concerns. This would become possible with the start of negotiations on reduction of domestic support and elimination of export subsidies being provided by US and European Union to their farmers. Now that the developed countries are relenting on this issue as a consequence of the strong line taken by India and other developing countries, consequently poorer nations in need of food will be able to get food cheaper and countries intending to export their surplus grains would be able to stand competition from developed countries.

Thirdly, with regard to services and the related removal of restrictions on the natural movement of people, developed countries are going to be tied down for negotiations. The real argument put forth in this regard was that flexibility may be left to different members for bilateral pacts. In this way, it is hoped that India would gain by increasing access for banking, insurance and other companies and increasing opportunities for people to work in other countries.

Fourthly, reduction and elimination of tariffs in non-agricultural goods and other barriers, particularly on products that are important to developing countries, is another major gain for India.

Fifthly, WTO ministerial declaration has stressed the need for establishing a system of registration for wines and spirits known by the region where they are made like champagne. Extension of this geographical indication to other items like basmati rice will also be looked into.

Lastly, US agreed to review anti-dumping rules, but there is a fear that this may not be achieved unless the developing countries build up strong pressure on the US to do so.

The International Monetary Fund

The International Monetary Fund (IMF) is an international monetary organisation which came into existence in December, 1945. The decision to set up the IMF was taken at the United Nations Monetary and Financial Conference of 44 World Nations held at Brettonwoods in July 1944. The establishment of the IMF indeed is a great landmark in the sphere of international economic co-operation.

This fund started functioning on the 1st March 1947, with the following objectives :

1. ***International Monetary Cooperation*** : The most important objective of the Fund was to establish monetary cooperation amongst the various member countries. As already pointed out above, one of the major causes of the Second World War was the absence of monetary cooperation amongst the countries of the world. Hence, it was now considered necessary to establish international monetary cooperation to prevent the outbreak of war in future.
2. ***To Ensure Stability in Foreign Exchange Rates*** : As already said above, there used to be a good deal of instability in foreign exchange rates before the Second World War. This instability of foreign exchange rates had produced adverse repercussions on international trade. Hence, the I.M.F. was established to eliminate this instability of foreign exchange.
3. ***To Eliminate Exchange Control*** : Before the Second World War, almost every country had resorted to exchange control as a device to fix its exchange rate at a particular level. This produced adverse effects on international trade. Hence, it was now considered necessary to remove or relax these exchange controls with a view to giving encouragement to the flow of international trade.
4. ***To Establish a System of Multilateral Trade and Payments System*** : Another objective of the I.M.F. was to establish a multilateral trade and payments system in place of the old bilateral trade agreements, because the latter obstructed the free flow of international trade.
5. ***To Promote International Trade*** : Still another objective of the I.M.F. was to promote international trade by removing all obstacles which had the effect of restricting it.
6. ***To Help Member—Nations to Achieve Balanced Economic Growth*** : The I.M.F. helps the member-nations, particularly the backward nations, to achieve balanced economic growth. To attain this objective, it helps the member-nations to secure a rising level of employment.
7. ***To Eliminate or to Reduce the Disequilibrium in the Balance of Payments*** : The I.M.F. helps the member-nations to eliminate or to reduce the disequilibrium in their balance of payments. To achieve this objective, it sells or lends foreign currencies to the member nations.
8. ***To Promote Investment of Capital in Backward and Underdeveloped Countries*** : The I.M.F. helps to promote the export of capital from the richer to the poorer countries so that the latter could develop their economic resources for achieving higher living standards.

Organisation of the Fund

The International Monetary Fund (I.M.F.) was constituted by subscriptions from members agreeing to participate in the Fund amounting to 8.5 billion dollars out of which India's contribution was 400 million dollars. The subscription was to be partly in the form of gold and partly in domestic currency. A member-country is required to pay 25 percent of its quota or 10 percent of its holdings of gold, whichever is smaller, in the form of gold. The resources of the I.M.F. are thus partly gold and partly currencies of the member-countries, the later being kept in the central banks of the countries concerned. Members' liability to pay a part of its quota in gold has been now (1976) abrogated under the New Articles.

In 1958, there was made a general increase of 50 percent in members' quotas and a specially higher increase for Canada, Germany and Japan. In 1965 and in 1970, quotas were again raised by 25 percent each time. India's quotas, which was originally equal to $400 million, was raised to $600 million in 1958 and $750 million in 1965 and subsequently to $940 million.

A substantial increase in Fund quotas was made in 1979 from SDR 40 billion to SDR 60 billion and subsequently in February 1983 making a 47 percent increase in member quotas raising the Funds' resources from about $ 66,000 million to $ 98,000 million.

It may, however, be added that the above increase in the Fund quotas has not meant a corresponding increase in their borrowing facility. For instance, in 1979 when. Fund quotas were raised, the ceiling, on borrowing was reduced from 6 times a member's quota to 4.5 times. Thus India's ceiling rose only from SDR 7.2 billion to SDR 7.6 billion, though its quota had been increased by 50 percent, Now when quotas were increased in 1983, the controlling group demanded that the ceiling on borrowing should be reduced from 4.5 times to 3 times the quota. The maximum that India could borrow would, in that case instead of rising, come down from SDR 7.6 billion to SDR 6.6 billion, but it might be allowed to retain its old ceiling of SDR 7.6. billion.

The Fund can purchase and sell currencies of member countries for one another subject to the condition that the holding of no member-country's currency should exceed 200 percent of its quota. Raised later to 600 per cent but reduced in 1979 to 450 percent. Thus, a debtor country is saved from gold exports and consequent deflation (as happened under gold standard) through the help of the Fund.

The creditor countries, whose export surplus exceeds 75 percent of their quota, will have their currencies declared scarce. Such currencies are rationed among countries needing them. The I.M.F., however, can increase the supply of scarce currencies by borrowing them or by purchasing them against gold. If even then these currencies are not enough, debtor-countries must restrict their imports from credit-countries and thus achieve equilibrium in their balance of payments.

Thus, a member's quota has four-fold significance: It determines (a) a member's subscription to the Fund, (b) its access to Fund's resources through drawings from the Fund, (c) its relative voting power in the Fund management, and (d) its share of any allocation of SDR's among participants in the Special Drawing Account.

As regards the rates of exchange, member countries are required to fix parties of their currencies with gold. But these parities need not be fixed for all time. An all-round uniform change in them can be brought about by the consent of the member-countries contributing individually more than 10 percent of the aggregate quota. Apart from this, the member-countries can alter exchange value of their currencies by 10 per cent. Another 10 percent change can be brought about with the consent of the Fund. Changes beyond this can be brought about with the consent of the Fund, only to correct fundamental disequilibria.

"Thus, exchange depreciation, which may be necessary for a country, whose money is overvalued, can be accomplished without inviting retaliation. In this way, the Fund not only provides temporary assistance in tiding a country over a period when it cannot acquire an adequate supply of foreign exchange; it also sponsors measures to remedy more fundamental difficulties. And by holding member-countries to their agreement not to engage in competitive exchange depreciation, it introduces a measure of disarmament into the field of international economic relations".

The Fund does not interfere in the internal economy of member-countries in order to restore equilibrium in their balance of payments. The members can withdraw from the Fund by a simple notice in writing.

The IMF is managed by an Executive Board of 20 directors—5 assigned to the largest quota holders (U.S.A., U.K., West Germany, France and Japan), 3 elected by the South African countries, 3 by Latin American countries, 5 by Far East Pacific countries and 4 by Continental Europe.

This is a system analogous to exchange stabilization account evolved by individual countries during the depression years of the thirties. The same principles have been carried to the international plane. It seeks to achieve the purpose of international gold standard without its shortcomings.

Structure and Management

The work of the Fund is carried out through a Board of Governors, and Executive Board, a Managing Director, and staff. Each member country is represented by a Governor and an Alternate Governor on the Board of Governors, which is the Fund's highest authority and which meets annually and may cast ballots by mail or cable between meetings. A member country's voting power primarily reflects its contribution to the Fund's financial resources, which, in turn, is related to its relative size in the world economy.

The highest authority of the Fund is the Board of Governors, in which each of the member countries is represented by a Governor and an alternate Governor. In most cases, the Fund's Governors are ministers of finance or central bank governors in their countries or held comparable rank. The Board of Governors meet once a year but may vote by mail at other times.

The Board of Governors had delegated most of its powers to the Executive Board, which is responsible for conducting the business of the Fund and is, therefore, in permanent session at the Fund headquarters in Washington. The Executive Board is chaired by the Managing Director. Among other duties, the Executive Board acts on requests by members for financial assistance, conducts consultations with members, takes decisions on general Fund policies, and makes recommendations to the Board of Governors on matters requiring a vote of the Governors, such as the admission of new members and increases in the Fund's resources.

The Executive Board appoints the Fund's Managing Director, who serves both as its Chairman and as Chief of the operating staff of the Fund, with a five-year term of office.

The professional and administrative staff of the Fund is comprised of international civil servants, appointed by an owing their duty exclusively to the Fund. The Fund's professional staff consists primarily of economists, but there are, among others, accountants and legal experts. They are recruited on a wide geographical basis from the Fund's members countries. The staff numbers about 1,500, located mainly at the Washington headquarters.

The staff is organized in five area departments (for Africa, Asia, Europe, the Middle East, and the Western Hemisphere) and a number of other departments (Administration, Central Banking Service, exchange and Trade Relations, Fiscal Affairs, IMF Institute, Legal Research, Secretary's and Treasurer's). In addition, there is a Bureau of Language Services and a Bureau of statistics. The Fund also maintains small permanent offices in Paris and Geneva and at the United Nations in New York.

Functions of the Fund

From the brief account of the International Monetary Fund given above, it can be seen that the Fund performs five major functions:

1. ***It serves as a short-term credit institution*** : If any country is in a temporary difficulty in liquidating an adverse balance of payments, the Fund will come to its aid. It does not, however, undertake to supply all the foreign exchange that a country may need. All countries are supposed to have their separate monetary and foreign exchange reserves to meet their normal requirements. The Fund is not intended to supplant them but to provide only a second line of defence in case of emergency. The borrowing country has to pay interest and maintain its quota intact. Should a country borrow unnecessarily, the rate of interest rises as the amount of loan increases. Lower rates are charged if a loan is taken for a short period. If the amount of the loan and its duration are such as to raise the rate of interest to 5 percent, the Fund can then raise the rate to any level by way of penalty, for this is regarded as an abuse of the privilege of membership.

   Thus, it is clear that the credit operations of the Fund are not only conducted on sound business principles but they also ensure that the object of the Fund, viz., to provide short-term loan only, is not defeated.

2. ***The Fund provides a mechanism for improving short-term balance of payments position:*** For this purpose, its rules provide for orderly adjustment of exchange. No member-country can indulge in irresponsible and competitive exchange depreciation thus introducing the law of the jungle in international monetary relations. Whenever a country feels that its rate of exchange is out of line with its economy, the rate can be altered but only after due deliberation between the country and the authorities of the Fund. There is thus provision for the careful determination of the initial rate and its orderly adjustment subsequently. This procedure at once reconciles the claims to internal stability and full employment on the one hand and to international stability and high level of world trade on the other. Every country must now rely on its own productive efficiency rather than on artificial stimulus of exchange depreciation to hold its own in the world markets.

3. ***The Fund provides machinery for international consultations***: It brings together representatives of the principal countries of the words and affords an excellent opportunity for reconciling their conflicting claims. This constructive approach and the measure of international co-operation have had not only a stabilising influence on world economy but they have also led to the expansion and balanced development of world trade and world production. The Fund has thus contributed to the promotion and maintenance of high levels of employment and real income and to the development of the productive resources of the member-countries. For this purpose, the Fund is engaged in constant study and research relating to the important and urgent economic problems of the world.

4. It provides a reservoir of the currencies of the member-countries and enables members to borrow one another's currency.

5. It promotes orderly adjustment of exchange rates to promote exchange stability.

The I.M.F. and the Gold Standard

Sometimes, it is said that the establishment of the I.M.F. constitutes a return to the Gold standard. This, however, is a debatable issue. Prof. John H. Williams considers the I.M.F. as essentially a Gold Standard Plan or a modified version of the traditional Gold Standard. Lord Keynes, on the contrary, believed that there was no similarity between the I.M.F. and the Gold Standard. In fact, according to Lord Keynes, the I.M.F. "is the exact opposite of the Gold Standard".

There is no doubt that the I.M.F. does posses certain characteristics of the Gold Standard. Hence, it is often referred to as the shadow of the Gold Standard. But, at the same time, the I.M.F. has also certain dissimilarities with the Gold Standard, or what comes to the same thing, it has certain similarities with the paper Standard. The Fund can, therefore, be described in the worlds of Prof. Kurihara, "As a mixed Standard embodying within itself some features of the Gold Standard and the Paper Standard, it is the substitute for the old Gold Standard and an alternative to both, a system of completely free exchange rates and a system of extreme exchange control". It represents, in the words of Lord Keynes, "an attempt at an improved system of international currency".

The I.M.F. has certain resemblances with the Gold Standard. They are as follows :

1. ***Link with Gold***: The currency of a country under the Gold Standard has a direct link with gold. Its external value is expressed in terms of a fixed quantity of gold. Under the I.M.F. also, every member-country has to define the par value of its currency in terms of gold, and the external exchange value of the currency in question is determined on the basis of this par value expressed in gold.
2. ***Importance of Gold***: The gold was given an important place in the economy of the country under the Gold Standard. Likewise, gold occupies a position of importance in the economies of the member-countries under the provisions of the Fund. *Firstly,* every member-country has to express the initial par value of its currency in terms of gold. *Secondly,* every member-country has to deposit with the Fund, in gold, 25 percent of its quota or 10 percent of its total holdings of gold and dollars, whichever is less. *Thirdly,* every member-country has to buy and sell gold at prices fixed by the Fund.
3. ***Multilateral Trade and Payments System***: The multilateral trade and payments system was in force under the Gold Standard. In other words the country on the Gold Standard instead of balancing its accounts individually with every other country, balanced them jointly with other countries on the Gold Standard. In the same manner, the I.M.F. also encourages multilateral trade and payments system amongst its different member-countries.
4. ***Exchange Rate Stability***: The main objective of the Gold Standard was that of maintaining stable exchange rates among different countries. The I.M.F. also aims at maintaining stable exchange rates in the same manner as the Gold Standard did. This is an important point of resemblance between the Fund and Gold standard. But there is an important difference as well between the Gold Standard and the I.M.F. The rates of exchange under the Gold Standard were practically rigid. Though this rigidity of the exchange rates was good from the point of view of international trade, it was bad from the point of view of internal economic stability. The Paper Standard, on the other hand, formed another extreme case where the rates of exchange widely fluctuated depending upon the fluctuations in the exchange market conditions of demand and supply. A fluctuating exchange rate was good

from the point of view of the domestic economy, but was harmful from the point of view of international trade. The I.M.F. tries to avoid both extremes (i.e., the gold standard and the paper standard) by following a middle course. The I.M.F. tries to realize the advantages of both the systems at the same time avoiding their disadvantages. Under the I.M.F. rate of exchange is neither completely rigid as under the Gold Standard nor is allowed to fluctuate violently as it did under the Paper Standard. Under the I.M.F. a country can change its exchange rate in order to correct a fundamental disequilibrium in its balance of payments. But the country concerned has to secure the prior consent of the I.M.F. before effecting any change in the rate of exchange. The objective of the I.M.F. is to establish a system of *stable, flexible* exchange rates, a combination, of the gold features of both the Gold Standard as well as the Paper Standard. The I.M.F. thus, resembles the Gold Standard in as much as it aims at maintaining stable exchange rates, but differs from the Gold Standard in as much as it rules out complete rigidity in the exchange rates.

5. ***Mechanism of Expansion and Contraction of Currency*** : The I.M.F. has still another resemblance with the Gold Standard with regard to the reciprocal contraction and expansion of currency which take place due to changes in the balance of payments. Under the Gold Standard, if a country has an unfavourable balance of payments with another country, gold begins to flow out and this outflow of gold causes a contraction in the volume of currency in the country, leading to a fall in the general level of prices. The inflow of gold into the country with a favourable balance of payments leads to an expansion of currency giving rise to an increase in the general price-level. The process of adjustment under the I.M.F. is more or less similar to this. Whenever a member-country has an unfavourable balance of payment with another country, the Central Bank of that country purchases the required foreign currency from the I.M.F. by depositing an equal amount of its own currency with the Fund. The Central Bank then sells they foreign exchange to the commercial banks which, in turn, sell the same to the importers. But during this process the cash reserves of the commercial banks decline with the result that their ability to create credit is correspondingly curtailed, giving rise to a fall in the general price-level.

   On the contrary, when the country with a favourable balance of payments receives the payments from the other country, the cash reserves of its commercial banks will increase, giving rise to a multiple expansion of bank credit within the country. This will have the ultimate effect of raising the price-level in the country. Thus, an unfavourable balance of payments tends to give rise to deflation while a favourable balance of payments tends to promote inflation as under the Gold Standard.

   A country losing gold under the Gold Standard was required by the "rules of the game" to resort to deflation to correct the disequilibrium in its balance of payments. But a country with an unfavourable balance of payments under the dispensation of the I.M.F. need not resort to a policy of deflation because there is no compelling pressure on it to do so. The I.M.F. allows sufficient freedom to its member-countries to formulate their domestic monetary policies in accordance with local needs. The country with an unfavourable balance of payments will, therefore, adopt all possible measures to prevent a fall in its internal price level. Thus, deflation of currency is not an inevitable occurrence in a country confronted with an unfavourable balance of payment under the I.M.F. as it was under the Gold Standard.

   The I.M.F. therefore, rules out the rigid discipline of the Gold Standard, giving to its members a certain amount of freedom to mould their monetary policies in accordance with their changing domestic economic conditions. At the same time, the I.M.F. avoids the disadvantages resulting from freely fluctuating exchange rates as under the Paper Standard.

6. ***Non-imposition of Exchange Control***: Under the Gold Standard, no country could resort to exchange control of any type so far as payments for international trade transactions were concerned. The reason was that international trade under the Gold Standard was allowed to take place in accordance with the principle of comparative costs. The I.M.F. also forbids the member countries to practise exchange control on trade transactions. The member countries have, however, been allowed to resort to exchange control during the transitional period. After this transitional period, all the member-countries will have to eliminate all exchange controls on international trade.

There are also certain dissimilarities between the Gold Standard and the I.M.F. They are as follows :

1. The par values of national currencies are not rigidly fixed in terms of gold under the I.M.F. as it happened under the Gold Standard. The par values of national currencies under the Gold Standard were held equivalent to fixed quantities of gold. No change was allowed in them. Though the par values are fixed in terms of gold under I.M.F. as well, yet there is no rigidity about them. The par values can be changed if the circumstances so warrant.
2. Under the Gold Standard, gold was the basis of the expansion and contraction of currency in the country. If there were fluctuations in gold productions, they had their repercussions on currency expansion or contraction. But under the I.M.F. dispensation, the expansion or contraction of currency is not based upon gold. Consequently, fluctuations in gold production do not have their repercussions on the volume of currency in the country.
3. Under the Gold Standard, there was complete rigidity in the foreign exchange rates. As against this, there is no such rigidity in the foreign exchange rates under the I.M.F. dispensation. If the I.M.F. is convinced that there has been a fundamental change in the economic situation in a country, it can allow it to alter the par value of its currency. Thus, there is certain amount of flexibility, in the I.M.F. which was totally lacking under the Gold Standard.
4. The Gold Standard was automatic in its functioning. It required no conscious efforts on any one's part to make it work. The I.M.F., on the contrary, represents a conscious international monetary management by an international institution.
5. As already pointed out, a country under the Gold Standard resorted to deflation when it lost gold on account of a deficit in its balance of payments. But, under the I.M.F. it is not necessary for a member-country confronted with a deficit in its balance of payments to suffer the evil consequences of deflation. There is no provision in the I.M.F.'s Articles of Agreement which suggests that the country with a deficit in its balance of payments will be required to follow a policy of deflation.
6. Under the Gold Standard, the internal economic situation of a country was affected by foreign influences. This does not happen under the I.M.F. Every country, according to the regulations of the I.M.F., is completely free to determine its internal economic policies. The Fund does not interfere in the internal economy of the member-countries.

   Thus, we find that the I.M.F. has all advantages of the Gold Standard, without its disadvantages. The I.M.F., therefore, does not represent a 'return' of the Gold Standard because there are certain important differences between the Gold Standard and the I.M.F.

Working and Evaluation of the Fund

It is clear that the Fund can play a vital role in achieving international economic stability and in promoting healthy international monetary relations. However, the I.M.F. failed to achieve its objectives in the early years of its operations.

(a) For Many years, the Fund was not able to achieve its fundamental objective of pulling down trade barriers. Agricultural protection dominates fiscal policies in Europe and the U.S.A. It is a pity that the U.S.A. still clings to the protectionist policy in spite of her tremendous competitive strength. These policies are repugnant to the underlying objectives of the Fund. Lack of international coordination of monetary, import and stockpiling policies has aggravated the difficulties.

(b) The Fund is helpless in restraining inflationary pressures in a country and in maintaining monetary stability. The seventh report of the Fund emphasized internal monetary stability as the primary need and it issued a warning to the member-countries to end inflation or the world will move further towards restrictions on trade and currency convertibility. But the warning went unheeded.

(c) The I.M.F. was unable to promote exchange stability in the member-countries. Perhaps the postwar dislocation proved a little too much for the I.M.F. In 1948. France carried 44.4 percent devaluation and established a free market in gold and U.S. Dollars in Paris which was incompatible with the principles of the Fund. But still the Fund treated France in distress with sympathy and enhanced its reputation for its principles, and for its management. Up to September, 1949, there was no general devaluation; but Great Britain devalued her pound at that time by 30.5 percent and the British example was followed not only by the Commonwealth nations (except Pakistan) but also by 13 other countries. India devalued her currency by 36.5 percent in June, 1966 and England again devalued the £ in November, 1967 by 143 percent. The Fund could object to this big change in the par value of the currencies involved, but did not. It felt that the action was necessary to correct a fundamental disequilibrium. The change, though not agreeable was inescapable.

(d) The Fund was unable to prevent dollar shortage in the late forties. It should have declared dollar as a scarce currency and adopted measures to make the dollar freely available. But it did nothing of the kind.

(e) The Fund has suffered all along from inadequacy of funds. Funds of the I.M.F. may not be sufficient to cope with the sudden movements of hot money when there are no exchange controls to stop them. Then there are national sovereignties to be reckoned with. "The I.M.F. agreement is a transparent piece of paper stretched across the cracks which exist in the world polity of every national character".

An apt picture of the working of the Fund is given by Coulborn: "There are fifty (1952) countries trying to play the semi-gold standard game, whereas there used to be six principal players and few lesser ones. Yet it is the same game (because I.M.F. is essentially an amalgamation of the Exchange Equalisation Accounts of gold standard days put under international control), and the chief players are the same, as the voting strengths show. It remains to be seen whether it is a better game played somewhat publicly in Washington, with fairly precise rules codified for it and a large number of amateur players taking a small part, or whether it was between when six starts played with skill and without distraction, making the rules as they went along. It may be a reasonable guess that the best game of all will prove to be a combination of the present form with the earlier one. There might be added both strength and flexibility to the I.M.F. System if the Exchange Equalisation Accounts, provided anew with resources in some cases, came into the exchange market again in the more important financial centres".

Gradually, however, the Fund improved its performance, The annual report of the Fund presented at its annual meeting held in October 1958 in New Delhi said that considerable headway had been made towards the achievement of its objectives. To an increasing extent, the world had been moving towards exchange stability with orderly exchange arrangements, among the Fund's members, the avoidance of competitive depreciation, the elimination of exchange restrictions and establishment of a multilateral system of payments. The Managing Director of the Fund declared at the opening of the annual conference in September 1962 that there were indications that the world was approaching a state of economic equilibrium solid enough to withstand monetary tension. The improvement has continued since then.

A plan for a new international asset, known as the **'special drawing rights'**, was approved by the I.M.F.'s Board of Governors in September, 1967. It is like a normal account in a bank except that no deposits are required to build up the account. Once the allocation is made, participating country automatically receives a share corresponding to its quota in the I.M.F.'s general account. They are treated as part of the monetary reserves to finance their international trade. The special drawing rights supplement the gold, the dollars and pounds sterling most countries now use as money reserves.

In order to mitigate the hardship of the developing countries arising from the unprecedented oil price hike, the I.M.F. set up a three-billion **"Oil facility"**. Fund in 1974 in the form of special drawing rights. The developing countries get a credit out of this fund at a low rate of interest (2.5 percent) to enable them to pay their enhanced oil bills and meet balance of payments difficulties caused thereby. It was decided to keep the **"oil window"** open for another year and to raise the oil facility fund from $3 billion to $6 billion. Interest is subsidized from a fund contributed by oil exporting and industrial countries. The Oil Facility was would up in 1976.

Another facility provided by the Fund to its members is the **Compensatory Financing Facility** Established in February 1963, it is designed to extend the Fund's balance of payments short-term support to such member countries—particularly primary producting countries as suffer from fluctuations in their export receipts due to circumstances beyond their control. Except in the case of natural disasters or other major emergencies, the drawings under this facility cannot exceed in any one year, more than 50% (previously 25%) of the member's quota and the total drawings more than 75% (previously 50%) of the quota. Drawings under the compensatory financing facility are additional to those under the Fund's regular tranche policies.

Mention may also be made of the **Extended Facility** which was established by the Fund in October, 1974. The object of this facility is to provide medium–term assistance for member countries that need to make structural adjustments to correct balance of payments difficulties. This facility represents an important development in Fund practice. Which the usual duration of stand-by agreement is not more than one year, the extended arrangement provides an assurance of Fund support for a period up to three years, as well as providing larger amounts and on longer repurchases terms than are available under the Fund's other facilities. This facility is designed to benefit largely the developing countries.

It was also agreed on August 31, 1975 to establish a Trust Fund out of the profits derived from the sale of the Fund's good. This fund is used to provide balance of payments assistance on concessionary terms to members with low per capita income, initially those with 1973 per capital income not exceeding SDR 300. It was estimated that the trust fund could provide assistance between $ 400 million and $ 500 million a year.

We may summarise the achievements and shortcomings of the I.M.F. thus:-

Achievements

(a) The I.M.F. has provided an excellent forum for the discussion and solution of the economic, fiscal and financial problems having an international aspect.

(b) It has promoted the expansion of international trade in a variety of ways to the mutual benefit of the member countries.

(c) It has promoted exchange stability while at the same proving for an orderly adjustment of exchange rates.

(d) It has simplified to some extent the multiple exchange system.

(e) The Fund has been instrumental in promoting steady progress towards the establishment of a multilateral system of payments in respect of current transactions.

(f) It has liberalised the use of its resources by members in a number of ways.

(g) By promoting economic stability of the member countries, it has accelerated the pace of economic development of the under-developed countries.

(h) The Fund has shown great interest in the economic growth of less-development countries.

Shortcomings

(a) The Fund was unable to tackle the immediate post-war economic problems affecting its members.

(b) The insistence on devaluation in some cases as a cure of disequilibrium in balance of payments was not well-advised.

(c) The Fund followed a passive and weakened policy in the fixation of exchange rates both initially and subsequently.

(d) Inspite of persistent shortage of dollars, it did not declare it as a 'scarce currency' and take steps to ensure its ready availability.

(e) It is said to have granted undue credit to certain countries without making sure of their credit-worthiness.

(f) The Fund has been charged as being partial to the developed countries and not helping adequately the developing countries.

(g) The domination of American administration over the Fund's operations has lid it open to severe criticism by other member countries.

In spite of the shortcomings pointed out above, it must be conceded that the Fund has been a striking success. Considering the growth of the Fund in size, composition and resources and the important role it has played in solving international monetary problems and in formulating international monetary policies, the Fund must be pronounced a great success. There is no doubt that the Fund has remarkably succeeded in the achievement of its main objectives, viz., expansion of international trade, elimination of restrictive practices, stabilising exchange rates and ensuring easy convertibility of currencies. In its operations, it has shown imagination and dynamism.

I.M.F. and Less Developed Countries

From the point of view of the L.D.C.'s (less developed countries), the working of the I.M.F. has not been satisfactory. It did not pay sufficient attention to the problems of the L.D.C.'s. It was supposed that the domestic economic considerations of the L.D.C.'s and the world objectives of international co-operation were not really incompatible, but even mutually reinforcing. That is, the expansion of world trade depended virtually on the monetary stability of the developed countries and that economic development and full employment in the L.D.C.'s would automatically follow. It was not realised that, in economic theory as well as in practice, consideration of full employment and economic development in L.D.C.'s require policies which would usually run counter to the principles of international economic co-operation, free trade and exchange stability.

Thus, a major drawback of the Fund's rules, in principle as well as in practice, has been the asymmetry of its adjustment mechanism as between the high reserve countries and low reserve countries, that is, the well-developed and the developing countries. The Fund expects normal adjustment of the balance of payments through changes in domestic expenditure and change in the exchange rate is to be made as a last resort, when the Fund is convinced that there is a fundamental disequilibrium. This adjustment is very easy for the rich countries because, they have huge stocks of international reserve and abundant provision of international liquidity. They were able, therefore, to avoid going through painful process of adjustment by domestic measures. The L.D.C.'s, on the other hand, had to curtail their domestic investments and slow down their development programmes to adjust their exchange rates. Mr. Pierre-Paul Schweitzer, the Managing Director of the Fund, in his address in April, 1973 observed, "a system in which the burden of adjustment is not equitably shared between surplus and deficit countries, produces strains and frictions which may be political as well as economic".

The funds of the I.M.F. have been largely flowing to the rich countries. The use of the Fund resources by L.D.C.'s during 1966-72 fell to 25% of the total world use. In the sixties, however, the attitude of the Fund improved under the leadership of Mr. Schweitzer. The Fund set up its compensatory finance in order to give assistance to primary producing countries experiencing temporary shortfalls in their export earnings. In 1964, the Fund introduced a facility to finance buffer stocks. The annual reports of the Fund are not more sympatheric to the requirements of the L.D.C.'s.

It may be mentioned that an over-whelming majority of members of the Fund are developing countries and should be able to take care of their special needs. The compensatory financing facility for example, is specially designed to benefit them. Mr. Writteveen, the Managing Director of a Fund, estimated that the value to the developing countries of the trust fund, increased access of fund's resources and the recent liberalisation of the Fund's compensatory financing facility could be of the order of 3 billion a year, in addition to the normal use of the Fund's credit facilities.

It may also be pointed out that it is not the function of the I.M.F. to transfer real resources for development (that is the function of the World Bank). The proper function of the Fund is to supervise the international monetary system and to give members **temporary** assistance to overcome their balance of payments problems. That is why the Fund has always emphasised three aspects of its policies regarding the use of its resources: (a) non-discrimination among its members, (b) the temporary nature of use of its resources, and (c) its conditionality.

IMF and International Liquidity

The IMF duly recognised that the international monetary system cannot consist of fixed arrangements expected to be suitable for ever. Accordingly, suitable changes in the policies and operations of the Fund are directed towards meeting the financial requirements of the dynamic world economy.

The IMF provides short-term financial assistance to its members to meet seasonal balance of payments deficits, as well as emergency situations.

With a view to enable the Fund to achieve its objectives more effectively, the Executive Directors of the IMF recommended in 1958 an increase of 50 percent in the quotas of the members, with additional increases for certain members. As a result of the increase in the quotas of the member countries, the resources of the Fund were increased considerably. Thus, the ability of the Fund to meet the increasing liquidity requirements of its members was enhanced. Hence, at present there seems to be no "inadequacy" problems as such.

In order to make the Fund resources readily available to its members, the following important changes have been made in its procedures for giving accommodation to member countries:

(a) ***Gold tranche policy*** : In 1952, the fund laid down this policy under which a member could draw on the Fund virtually at will to the extent of the gold tranche position with the Fund.

(b) ***Waivers***: Since 1952, in order to promote greater use of its facilities, the Fund has in practice increasingly waived the limitation of drawing in excess of 22 percent of a member's quota in any 12-month duration.

(c) ***Stand-by arrangements*** : Since 1952, a new procedure of drawing called stand-by arrangement was devised by the Fund. Under this scheme, once a request for assistance had been approved, a member is authorised to draw the specified limit of foreign exchange from the Fund within a specified period without further application to the Fund.

(d) ***Liberal credit policy***: In its credit policy also the Fund shows a liberal attitude to member's requests for transactions within the first tranche if they make reasonable efforts to solve their problems. However, requests for drawings beyond the first credit tranche substantial justification.

In December, 1961, the Fund took a decision on a General Arrangement to Borrow (G.A.B.), according to which the Fund has been authorised to borrow supplementary resources under Article VII of the Agreement. The object of the Agreement is to "enable the IMF to fulfil more effectively its role in the international monetary system in the new conditions of widespread convertibility, including greater freedom for short-term capital movement". The total amount of such supplementary resources is equivalent to $ 6.2 billion. The Agreement provides that the request for drawing by participant countries for which supplementary resources are required will be dealt with according to the Fund's established policies and operational practice with respect to the use of its resources.

In short, the Agreement enables the Fund to mobilise quickly large additional resources in defence of the international monetary system. It has increased both international liquidity and the resiliency of the monetary system for the benefit of all.

All these changes are made in order to increase the ability of the Fund to meet the increasing meet of international reserve requirements of the world. No doubt, because of these changes in the policies and procedure of the Fund's working, the "adequacy" of international liquidity has been maintained satisfactorily in the present period. The IMF has tried its best to adapt itself to the dynamic requirements of the world economy. However, from the viewpoint of a long-term perspective and with the growing needs of the newly-developing countries for long-term foreign capital for developmental purpose, many are of the opinion that the present international monetary system cannot provide adequate liquidity in the future, and that it needs substantial reforms and reorganisation in this respect.

Special Drawing Rights

The Special Drawing Right (SDR) is an international reserve asset created by the Fund, taking into account of the global need to supplement existing reserves and it represents a major innovation of the IMF to help alleviate the problem of international liquidity. It is the declared intention of member countries that the SDR should eventually become the principal reserve asset in the international monetary system.

The IMF has two accounts of operation. First, there is *General Account* of the Fund through which all its business in national currencies is conducted. This reflects the currency holdings coming from its members; quota contributions and the purchase and sale of these currencies under the arrangements in force since the Fund's inception. Second, there is the *Special Drawing Account* through which all operations and truncations in SDRs are conducted. The SDR is essentially only an entry in this account at the Fund. Moreover, it is an entry which may be held only by — (a) national monetary authorities (who must be members of the Fund), and (b) by the General Account of the Fund to which participant countries are permitted to transfer SDRs for certain specified purposes, for example, to pay charge levied by the Fund or to repay drawings from the General Account. It is apparent, then, that the SDR is really a created deposit of the Fund—created in the sense that it is defined equivalent in foreign exchange from other members, and that it discharges specified obligations of members towards the Fund's General Account.

Every member of the IMF has the right to become a participant of the SDR facility, but every member is not obliged to join the facility. Obviously, only members of the IMF can participate in SDR facility.

The Special Drawing Right, as mentioned above, is only a book entry in the "Special Drawing Account" of the IMF. The allocation of SDR takes the form of a credit entry in the name of the participating countries in the Special Drawing Account. The total SDRs created by the IMF are allocated to the participating countries in proportion to their quotas in the IMF.

The allocation of SDR to a participant does not involve any payment by it to the IMF. The recipient of SDRs also does not have to give any collateral security to the IMF. SDRs allocated and credited to a participant's account are owned by it and they can be freely used by the said country for meeting payments deficits. One distinct characteristic of SDR is its unconditional use. A participant using SDRs is not called upon to adopt any particular economic policy or seek the prior approval of the IMF.

The possession of SDRs in its account entitled a participating country to an equivalent amount in the currency of other participating countries. The foreign exchange so obtained can be freely used for meeting payments deficits.

Use of SDRs

Participating countries may use the SDRs unconditionally, transferring them in the books of the Fund to another participant (chosen by the Fund), who will be required to supply its own or another currency in exchange. To provide against maldistribution of the SDRs such as would occur if SDRs are drained away from the deficit to the surplus countries, members are required to hold on the average of a five year period Drawing Rights to the amount of at least 30% of the average of their net cumulative allocations over that period.

Members with a balance of payments need may use SDRs to acquire foreign exchange in a transaction with designation—that is, where another member, designated by the Fund, provides currency in exchange for SDRs. The Fund designates members to provide currency in exchange for SDRs on the basis of the strength of their balance of payments and reserve positions. However, a member's obligation to provide currency does not extend beyond the point at which its holdings are three times its total allocations.

Fund members may also use SDRs in a variety of voluntary transactions and operations by agreement among themselves and with prescribed holders :

(a) To obtain currency in transactions by agreement with other members, without any requirement of balance of payments need. Any currency may be exchanged for SDRs, provided that the transaction is made at the "equal value" exchange rate against the SDR determined by the Fund, in turn derived from the representative exchange rate for that currency against its intervention currency.

(b) In swap arrangements, in which a member may transfer SDRs to another member in exchange for an equivalent amount of currency or another monetary asset, other than gold, with an agreement to reverse the exchange at a specified future date and at an exchange rate agreed to by the participants.

(c) In forward operations, in which members can buy or sell SDRs for delivery at a future date against currency or another monetary asset, other than gold, at an exchange rate agreed to by the members.

(d) To make loans of SDRs, at interest rates and maturities agreed to by the parties. Repayment of loans and payment of interest may be made with SDRs.

(e) To settle financial obligations.

(f) As security for the performance of financial obligations, in either of two ways: (1) members may pledge SDRs, which can be earmarked for the duration of the pledge by being recorded in a special register kept by the Fund, or (2) members can agree that SDRs would be transferred as security for the performance of an obligations and that the SDRs would be returned to the transferor when its obligation under the agreement had been fulfilled.

(g) In donations (grants).

Prescribed Holders of SDRs

The fund has the authority to extend the range of official holders of SDRs beyond its member countries and the Fund's General Resources Account. It has prescribed, as of July 31, 1984, the following 14 organizations as prescribed holders: the Andean Reserve Fund, Bogata; the Arb Monetary Fund, Abu Dhabi; the Asian Development bank, Manila; the Bank for International Settlements, Basle; the Bank of Central African States, Yaounde; the Central Bank of West African States, Dakan the East African Development Bank, Kampala; the Eastern Caribbean Central Bank, St. Kitts; the International Bank for Reconstruction and Development and the International Development Association, Washington; the International Fund for Agricultural Development, Rome; the Islamic Development Bank, Jeddah; the Nordic Investment Bank, Helsinki; and the Swiss National Bank, Zurich. Each of these institutions can acquire and use SDRs in transactions and operations with each other and with any of the Funds 147 member countries. Prescribed holders have the same degree of freedom as Fund members to buy and sell SDRs both spot and forward; to borrow. Loan, or pledge SDRs; to use SDRs in swaps and in settlement of financial obligations; or to make donations (grants) with SDRs.

Valuation of SDR

When the first allocation of SDR was made on 1.1.1970, the SDR was valued at par value of the US Dollar. Thus on January 1970 SDR 1 = $ 1 and the value of SDR against other currencies was the same as the exchange rate of these currencies against the US $.

The system of determining the rate of SDRs against each other currencies through the exchange rate of the US $ came under severe criticism with the decision of the United States in August 1971 to revoke the convertibility of the dollar and the subsequent widespread floating of major currencies. Therefore, on 1st July 1974 the Fund put into operation a new SDR valuation technique known as the "*standard basket valuation*". Under the new system of valuation, SDRs were valued in terms of 16 currencies which were assigned specific weights. The currencies included in the basket belonged to the countries whose share in the world exports of goods and services averaged more than one percent. This system of determination of the SDR value in terms of the US dollar as the sum of the dollar values, based on market exchange rates of specified quantum of 16 currencies continued until December 31. 1980. Beginning 1981, the value of SDRs in terms of US dollar was determined as the sum of the dollar values based on market exchange rates of specified quantities of 5 currencies. The currencies in the basket remained same from 1981 to 1998.

The currencies in the basket were assigned certain weights which broadly reflect the relative importance of the currencies in trade and payments, based on the value of the exports of goods and services of the member countries issuing these currencies and the balances of these currencies held as reserves by members of the Fund over a specified period.

With effect from January 1, 1999, the value of SDRs was the sum of values of specified amounts of Euro (France), Euro (Germany), Yen, Pound Sterling and US dollar. The next revision is likely to effect on January 1, 2001.

Allocations of SDRs

The IMF allocates SDRs to its members in proportion to their quotas at the time of allocation. In deciding on the timing and amount of SDR allocations, the Fund considers whether there exists a global need to supplement existing reserve assets and it takes into account the objectives of the Fund's Articles of Agreement, which call upon the members to collaborate with each other and with the Fund with a view to making the SDR the principal reserve asset of the international monetary system.

SDR as a Unit of Account

The SDR is the unit of account for Fund transactions, and it is finding increasing acceptance as a unit of account (or as the basis for a unit of account) for private contracts and international and regional organizations. The use of the SDR as a unit of account is explained, in part, by the fact that the value of the SDR tends to be more stable than that of any single currency in the basket, since it is a weighted average of the exchange rates of the five major currencies in which the prices of goods and services in international trade are denominated.

Since the reduction in the number of currencies in the valuation basket from 16 to 5 in January 1981, there has been growing interest in private financial obligations denominated in SDRs (private

SDRs). However, the activity in private SDRs seems to have diminished recently, reflecting the continued strength of the US dollar in 1983 and 1984.

SDR as a Currency Peg

Some member countries of the IMF have pegged their currencies to the SDR. The value of the member's currency under such arrangements is fixed in terms of the SDR and then set in terms of other currencies by reference to the SDR value of the other currencies as published by the Fund.

A Critical Appraisal of the SDR Scheme

The SDR scheme has been welcomed by many for the following merits :

1. The SDRs are a form of reserve assets which are suitable for incorporation into a country's reserves. These are also a form of international credit creation on the analogy of domestic credit creation by the monetary authority. Moreover, the scheme envisages a pure fiduciary reserve creation, and, therefore, is quite flexible.
2. The scheme would permit the Fund to increase unconditionally the amount of world liquidity as per requirements, i.e., without depending upon the tenuous supply of monetary gold or increasing the obligation of the reserve currency countries.

   Drawing against SDRs would be unconditional in the sense that no change would be required to be made in the domestic economic policies (to restore balance of payments equilibrium) by the country using SDRs.
3. The significance of the scheme, however, lies in the fact that it represents the first serious effort in the set up of international monetary system to move away from gold as a pivot by providing for creation of a fiduciary reserve. No doubt, through the SDRs – "paper gold" – may not completely replace the "yellow metal", it will be a useful and flexible supplement to the existing reserve instrument and credit facilities. Further, it (paper gold) relieves the world monetary authorities from maintaining an open market value of gold. As such, the SDRs scheme implies a partial demonstration of gold.
4. Another merit of the SDRs is that unlike the present Ordinary Drawing Right in the IMF which gives rise to only to a temporary increase in international liquidity, the SDRs are intended to make a permanent addition to it.

However, the SDRs scheme in the form proposed and accepted by the world's apex monetary authority, is subjected to many justifiable criticisms. We shall list some of the important ones below:

1. The scheme is purely fiduciary in nature. Thus, there is all probability of distrust in the new reserve assets (SDRs).

   No Doubt, the moneyness of SDRs do not require any banking once its general acceptability is assured. However, assurance of general acceptability is assured. However, assurance of general acceptability of SDRs in international payments call forth a very clear and efficient management of the world's apex monetary authority, the IMF. Many critics feel that in the prevailing international monetary situation, this is a very difficult task for the IMF. So, if once people's confidence in the SDR is shaken, there is no other alternative but to switch over to some other currency or gold and the scheme will be a flop.
2. Thus, the scheme does not seek to cure the basic problems of international monetary relations such as the international movements of short-term funds arising out of disturbance in the international monetary equilibrium and the currency-gold switches. The scheme is

helpless in the prevention of SDR-gold switches.

3. It has been observed that through SDR "Paper Gold" is a useful and flexible reserve instrument of international liquidity it cannot be used to finance persistent payment deficits without leading to a pervasive and massive intranational inflation.
4. To some critics, the entire scheme of SDRs seems to be a rescue operation for the dollar. The scheme contains a disguised attempt to rehabilitate the dollar by means of a collective international action, because the value of SDR is prescribed to be equal to the present official gold value of the dollar. It still seeks to maintain the pre-war dollar parity in international monetary transactions which has assisted the United States in exporting inflation in the international money market through the artificially over-valued dollar. The scheme smacks of saving today's over-valued dollar from the logical consequence of devaluation.
5. Thus, the scheme is definitely in favour of the U.S.A. but greatly disadvantageous to the rest of the world and especially to the poor nations. Critics feel that the scheme should have been ratified only if the revised peg, i.e., value of SDRs, is kept in parity with the international money market, and not in parity with the artificially, over-valued dollar (in terms of the pre-war gold-dollar parity).
6. There is no established formula to estimate a country's need for reserves. Further, the scheme also contains seeds of inequality and injustice. The distribution of SDRs on the basis of IMF quotas fails to satisfy the canons of equity and efficiency, because according to this scheme, a major part of SDRs has been allocated to rich nations already having enough liquidity. The poor countries lacking enough intranational exchange reserves will have to suffer further.

The World Bank

International Bank for Reconstruction and development (World Bank) is a sister institution of the I.M.F. Both the institutions came into existence simultaneously as a result of the Bretton Woods Conference held in 1944. Though there are several common points between the two institutions, yet there are some fundamental differences in their objective and functions. The objective of the I.M.F. is to remove the short-term disequilibrium in the balance of payments of the member-countries by lending to them foreign currencies out of its own stock. The objective of the World Bank, on the other hand, is to eliminate the long-term disequilibrium in the balance of payments of member-countries by advancing long-term loans to them for development purposes. The aim of the Bank is the reconstruction and the development of the economies of the member countries. According to Prof. John H. Williams, the World Bank is even more important than the I.M.F. In his view, there would hardly be any need for the Fund if the World Bank were to perform its functions well.

Objective of the World Bank

The various objectives of the World Bank, as incorporated in the Articles of Agreement are as follows :

1. To help in the reconstruction and development of member countries by facilitating the investment of capital for the productive purposes including the restoration and reconstruction of economies devastated by war.
2. To encourage the development of productive resources in developing countries by supplying them investment capital.

3. To promote private foreign investment through guarantees and participation in loans and other investments made by private investors.
4 To supplement private foreign investments by direct loans out of its own capital for productive purposes.
5. To promote long-term balanced growth of international trade and the maintenance of equilibrium in the balance of payments of member countries by encouraging long-term international investments.
6. To bring about an easy transition from a war economy to a peace-time economy.
7. To help in raising productivity, the standard of living and the conditions of labour in member-countries.

The World Bank advances loans to member-countries primarily to help them lay down the foundations of sound economic growth. The loans made by the Bank either directly or through guarantees are intended for certain specific projects of reconstruction and development in member-countries.

Organisation

Like the Fund's, the Bank's structure is organised on a three-tier basis; a Board of Governors, Executive Directors and a President. The Board of Governors is the supreme governing authority. It consists of one governor (usually the Finance Minister) and one alternate governor (usually the governor of a central bank), appointed for five years by each member. The Board is required to meet once every year It reserves to itself the power to decide important matters such as new admissions, changes in the bank's stock of capital, ways and means of distributing the net income, its ultimate liquidation, etc. For all technical purposes, however, the Board delegates its powers to the Executive Directors in the day-to-day administration.

At present, the Executive Director are 19 in number, of which five are nominated by the five largest shareholders – the U.S.A., the U.K., Germany, France and India. The rest are elected by the other members.

The Executive Directors elect the President who becomes their ex-officio Chairman holding office during their pleasure. He is the chief of the operating staff of the Bank and is subject to the direction of the Executive Directors on questions of policy and is responsible for the conduct of the ordinary business of the Bank and its organisation.

Capital Resources

The World Bank, like any other corporation, has authorised capital of $ 21 billion divided into 210,000 shares, each having a par value $ 1,00,000. Initially, however, its authorised capital was $ 10 billion. Of the present authorised capital, $ 20.48 billion are subscribed by the issue of 204,848 shares. However, only 10 percent of the par value, viz., $ 2.04 billion, have so far been called in as paid-up capital. The capital stock of the Bank can be increased if a three-fourths majority of the total voting power is cast in its favour. Of the paid-up capital, 2 percent has to be subscribed in gold or U.S. dollars, the remaining 98 percent to be paid in the currency of the member.

Lending Operations

Loans are granted to member countries only after the Bank is fully satisfied about the economic position of the borrowing country as well as the soundness of the specified projects for which assistance is sought. In granting loans, the Bank is prepared to take reasonable risks but insists that funds obtained from it should be used for purposes which are constructive and practical. The Bank has powers of supervision and control to ensure that funds are used for the purposes for which the loan is granted. Normally, the Bank makes medium or long-term loans, the term being related to the estimated useful life of the equipment or plant being financed.

The Bank makes or facilitates loans in any one or more out of its own following ways :

(a) By making or participating in direct loans out of its own funds; or

(b) Out of the funds raised in the market of a member, or otherwise borrowed by the Bank; or

(c) By guaranteeing, in whole or in part, loans made by private investors through the investment channels.

The total outstanding amount of the loans made or guaranteed by the Bank is not to exceed 100 percent of its total unimpaired subscribed capital resources and surplus. The interest rate charged by the Bank on its loans is the estimated cost to the Bank of borrowing money for a comparable term in the market and is uniform without distinction among borrowers. In addition to the rate of interest, the Bank charges on all loans a commission of 1 percent for the purpose of creating a special reserve against losses and profit percent for administrative expenses.

In recent years, the Bank has made loans mainly for specific development projects in the field of agriculture, power, transport and industry. Most of the loans have been made to the underdeveloped countries. India is the Banks's largest individual borrower.

Technical and Advisory Assistance

In addition to providing financial assistance to member countries, the Bank has been rendering signal service to its members by providing them suitable technical assistance to assess their total economic resources and to set up priorities to be followed in their development programmes. Technical assistance on a boarder scale has been provided, for instance, in development programming through Survey Missions, which make intensive studies of national resources and formulate recommendations to serve as the basis of long-term development programmes.

In addition to the training programme, the Bank, with financial assistance form the Rockefeller and Ford Foundations, has set up in Washington an Economic Development Institute to provide an opportunity to selected groups of senior officials from the less developed countries to participate annually in an international course of studies designed to give them a broad perspective of the problems of economic development and to increase their efficiency.

Criticism

The modus operandi of the Bank has been critised on various counts from different quarters :

1. It is alleged that the Bank charges a very high rate of interest on loans. For example, some of the loans which India has received in recent years bean an interest of 53.4 percent including the commission at 1 percent which is credited to the Bank's special reserves.

2. The Bank's insistence, prior to the actual grant of loan, on the country having the capacity to transfer or repay, is open to criticism. The Bank should not apply orthodox standards to judge the transfer capacity of any borrowing country. Transfer capacity follows rather than precedes the loan.

3. The Financial help given by the Bank does not amount to more than a drop in the big ocean of financial requirement to essential for various development projects.

It may be said that the World Bank has not come up to the expectations of many nations. Nevertheless, it has been instrumental to a very large extent in initiating and accelerating the work of economic reconstruction and development in different countries. No doubt, India has derived immense benefit from the World Bank. The Bank may have failed to finance most of the development projects, but it should be remembered that it has financed quite a large number of them which have proved a notable success. The Bank has also played a significant role outside financial matters by serving as a mediator between different countries on major economic and political issues. For instance, its help in the solution and Indus Waters between Indian and Pakistan and the Suez Canal dispute between the U.K. and the U.A.R. has been invaluable.

International Development Association (IDA)

The IDA was set up in 1960 as a subsidiary of the World Bank to provide "soft loans" to the member countries. Thus, the object of the IDA is to provide loans to member countries on liberal terms with regard to the rate of interest and the period of repayment. Another attraction of the IDA loans is that they can be repaid in the currency of the member country.

The developing countries can avail of IDA loans on very liberal terms for projects which are not eligible for assistance from the World Bank either because loans for such projects do not carry the guarantee of the government of the borrowing country or because such project do not contribute directly and immediately to the productive capacity of the borrowing country. Examples of such projects are water supply, urban development, housing, slum clearance, education, sanitation and health facilities, etc.

In approving an IDA credit, three criteria are observed.

1. ***Poverty Test:*** IDA's assistance is limited to the poorest of those countries classified as Part II countries, and which continue to fact such severe handicaps as excessive dependence on volatile primary, products markets, heavy debt servicing burdens, and, often rates of population growth, that outweight the gains of production.
2. ***Performance Test*:** Within the range of difficulties of establishing objective standards of performance, these factors serve as the yardstick for an adequate performance test; satisfactory overall economic policies and past success in project execution.
3. ***Project Test*:** The purpose of the IDA is soft loans, not soft projects. IDA projects are appraised according to the same standard as that applied to the Bank projects – the test essentially requires that proposed projects promised to yield financial and economic returns adequate to justify the use of scarce capital.

A World Bank study on the IDA's assistance points out that the Association has made commendable contribution to the development of many poor countries. The IDA projects in these countries have earned an impressive 18 percent economic rate of return compared to 17 percent even for World Bank projects. In south Asia it has been a sensational 123 percent. **The average has been brought down to 18 percent only because Africa has yielded only 14 percent return.**

In the 4 decades of its operation, a good number of nations have made enough gains to be able to graduate out of IDA. One of them, South Korea, has become a donor.

Asian Development Bank (ADB)

The Asian Development Bank (ADB) is a regional finance institution set up in December 1966 under the auspices of the United Nations Economic Commissions for Asia and the Far East (ECAFE) quarters of the Bank is at Manila, Philippines.

Objects

(1) To promote investment in the ESCAP region of Public and Private capital for development.

(2) To utilities the available resources for financing development giving priority to those regional and sub-regional as well as national projects and programmes which contribute more effectively to the harmonious economic growth of the region as a whole.

(3) To help regional member countries in the co-ordination of their plans and policies for development with a view to actively better utilisation of resources.

(4) To provide technical assistance for preparation ad execution of development projects and programmes including the formulation of specific project proposals.

(5) To co-operative with UN, its organs and subsidiaries including, in particular, the ESCAP and the national entities concerned with investment of the development funds in the region.

Functions

(a) ***Provision of Financial Assistance*:** The ADB is empowered to provide financial assistance in the form of guarantee and loans. Loans are provided by the Bank from out of its ordinary funds and special funds, the former is popularly knows as "*hard loan*" and the latter "*soft loan*".

So far as the grant of financial assistance to various types of projects is concerned, the Charter of the ADB does not impose any restrictions on it. Similarly, the minimum and maximum limits in respect of the loans which the ADB is empowered to provide are left open.

Regarding the criteria for the grant of financial assistance, the approach of the ADB is to evaluate the projects on merit. In evaluating the projects that it proposes to finance, the Bank has regard to aspects such as their economic, technical and financial feasibility, their effect on the general activity of the country concerned; their contribution to the removal of economic bottlenecks and capacity of the country to service additional debts.

(b) ***Provision of Technical Assistance*:** Provision of Technical Assistance constitute an integral function of the Bank. The Bank provides advisory services from its headquarters. It can as well send its own experts or hired consultants on short or long missions for project implementation or for setting up or reorganizing some institutions. The *Technical Assistance Special Fund* was set up by the Bank with a view to providing technical assistance on a large scale.

(c) ***Other Functions* :** Other functions of the ADB pertain to the conduct of surveys and research. The purpose of such surveying and research is to develop a course of action for future and promote regional economic integrations.

Multinational Corporations

Large corporations having investment and business in a number of countries, known by various names such as multinational corporation, transnational corporation, international corporation and global corporation (or firm, company or enterprise) have become very powerful driving force in the world evonomy. Although the multinational corporation took birth in the early 1860s, it was after the Second World War that the multinationals have grown rapidly.

In 1862-63, the U.S. based Singer Sewing Machines established production facility in England. A year or two before Singer did this this, an English company set-up local production facilities in Australia. The first MNC came to India in 1921.

In the early days, the United States was the home of the most of the MNCs. Now there are a number of European and Japanese multinational. Multionationals have been emerging from the developing countries too.

The multinational corporation has been regarded as "the most important and most visible innovation of the post-war period in the economic field"[1]. The relevance of MNCs to the subject of international trade is expressed in the following statement: "All the issues we have examined — trade theory, commercial policy, foreign exchange and the balance of payments, and the international economics of development – are profoundly influenced by the MNCs, which actually does on a transnational basis all of the things that concern the international economic and financial position of national states. It does them quickly, efficiently and this is where many of the MNCs' costs and benefits to the international economy lie".

Definitions

There is, however, no universally accepted definition of the term multinational corporation. As a ILO report observes, "the essential nature of the multinational enterprises lies in the fact that its managerial headquarters are located in one country (referred to for convenience as the "home country") while the enterprise carries our operations in a number of other countries as well ("host countries")". Obviously, what is meant is "a corporation that controls production facilities in more than one country, such facilities having been acquired through the process of foreign direct investment. Firms that participate in international business, however, large they may be, solely by exporting or by licensing technology are not multinational enterprises".

Jacques Maisonrouge, president of IBM World Trade Corporation, defines an MNC as a company that meets five criteria:

(*i*) It operates in many countries at different levels of economic development.

(*ii*) Its local subsidiaries are managed by nationals.

(*iii*) It maintains complete industrial organisations, including R and D and manufacturing facilities, in several countries.

(*iv*) It has a multinational central management.

(*v*) It has multinational stock ownership.

Jame C. Baker defines the multinational corporation as a company[6]:

(*a*) Which has a direct the multinational corporation as a company[6]:

(*b*) Which generally derives from 20 percent to 50 percent or more of its net profits from foreign operations; and

(*c*) Whose management makes policy decisions based on the alternatives available anywhere in the world.

Terms such as international corporation, multinational corporation, transnational corporation and global corporation are often used as synonyms. However, several multinational have evolved into certain advanced stage to transnational organisation and operations that it becomes necessary to draw some distinction between these terms.

A company with manufacturing investment (or service operation) in at least one foreign country may be regarded as an *International corporation.* However, multinational implies international operations of more significance, than this, as indicated in the definition of the MNC given above, such as direct investment several countries and a considerable share of the total business being in foreign countries. A multinational corporation is, obviously, an international corporation. Only those international corporations which satisfy certain criteria, as described above, may be regarded as multinationals.

It would be useful to draw a distinctions between the multinational corporation and transnational corporation.

"Multinational companies are usually organised around a national headquarters, from which international control is exercised —they still have a national identity, even though their subsidiaries may not always care to allow that identity to obtrude in the markets they serve"[7]. A *transactional* company is a multinational" in which both ownership and control are so dispersed internationally. There is no principal domicile and no one central source of power"[8]. Examples include Royal Dutch-Shell and Unilever.

The term *global corporation* is also often used to mean more less the same thing as the transnational corporation.

It may also be pointed out here that some marketing and management experts and some essential dimension to the term global corporation, although it is not agreed upon by many others. According to them, a global corporation is one which views the entire world as a single homogeneous, market which should be catered to by globally standardised products. Theodore Levitt, the world renowned professor of marketing who has championed this line of thinking observes that while "the multinational corporation operates in a number of countries and adjusts its products and practices in each – at a high relative cost", "the global corporation operates with resolute consultancy – a low relative cost – as if the entire world (or major region of it) were a single entity; it sells the same thing the same way everywhere". According to Levitt, "the world is becoming a common market place in which people no matter where they live – desire the same products and life styles. Global companies must forget the idiosyncratic differences between countries and cultures and instead concentrate on satisfying universal drives"[10]. Levitt who says that "the world's needs and desires have been irrevocably homogenized" argues that this "makes the multinational corporation absolute and the global corporation absolute". Levitt's theory has been strongly criticised by several experts.

As pointed out above, many of the multinationals have transformed themselves to transnational/global corporations.

The corporations which have become transnational/global. "Stop thinking of themselves as national marketers who venture abroad and start thinking of themselves as global marketers. The top management and staff are involved in the planning of worldwide manufacturing facilities, marketing policies. Financial flows and logistical systems. The global operating units report directly the chief executive or executive committee, not to the head of an international division. Executives are trained in worldwide operations, not just domestic or international. Management is recruited from many countries; components and supplies are purchased where they can be obtained at the least cost; and investments are made where the anticipated returns are the greatest".

Dominance of the MNCs

The economic dominance of the multinationals is manifested by the fact that the MNCs control between a quarter and a third of all world production and the total sales of their foreign affiliates is about the same as the gross national product of all developing countries excluding oil exporting developing countries.

The economic clout of the MNCs is indicated by the fact that the GDP of most of the countries smaller than the value of the annual sales turnover of the multinational giants. In 1997, the value of the sales of the U.S. MNC General Motors, the biggest multinational in terms of sales turnover, was $ 178 billion. Only a small number of developing countries like India, China, Mexico, Brazil, Republic of Korea, Russia, Indonesia and Argentina, had a GDP which was more than this figure. There were also several developed countries whose value of GDP was less than this. It may be noted that in 1997, India's GDP was only $ 360 billion.

Because of the differences in the definition adopted, the estimates of the number of MNCs also vary. According to the United Nations' World Investment Report 1999, there are now more than 60,000 TNCs, which have more than 500,000 affiliates having sales in excess of $ 11 trillion.

The United States and Europe were the homes for most of the MNCs. Their shares have, however, been declining because of the growth of MNCs in other regions. Japanese MNCs have made rapid strides in the 1970s and 1980s. In 1997, majority of the 20 largest multinationals (in terms or sales) were Japanese. Multinationals from developing countries such as S. Korea and Taiwan have also been making their presence increasingly felt.

Investment pattern

The major part of the business of the MNCs is in the developed economies. The share of the developed countries in the total overseas investment was, in fact, increasing. According to Professors Dunning and Stopford, developing countries' share of foreign direct investment slipped to 27 percent by 1980 from 31 percent in 1971. It dropped further to 17 percent during 1986-90. However, there was a substantial increase in the FDI flows to the developing countries in the 1990s. The economic reforms ushered in the developing countries, particularly the liberalisation of foreign investment and privatisation, have given a boost to the FDI in these countries.

In the case of the LDCs, the investment and employment created by the MNCs have been chiefly concentrated in about a dozen of the nations, China, Brazil, Mexico, Hong Kong, the Philippines, Singapore and South Korea accounting for a major share.

As the Brandt Commission observes, foreign investment has moved to a limited number of developing countries, mainly those which could offer political stability and a convenient economic environment, including tax incentives, large markets, cheap labour and easy access to oil or other natural resources. In poor countries foreign investment is mainly a plantations and minerals, or in countries with large internal markets — like India. The Brandt Commission had also observed that private investment can supplement and complement aid, but it cannot substitute for it; it tends not to move to the countries or sectors which most need aid.

Investment Motives

There are a variety of motives for international investments. They include the following :

(1) To circumvent the tariff walls. For example, getting behind the EEC's common external tariff was certainly a major consideration for U.S. companies during the last many years. Recently, there has been a spurt of such investment in the E.E.C. by companies from Japan and some other countries.

(2) To reduce the production costs by making use of the cheap labour and factors in the home countries and by avoiding/reducing transport costs.

(3) To gain dominance in the foreign market and to effectively fight competition.

(4) To adjust to the government regulation in the host country. For example, some countries prefer foreign investment and domestic production out of it to import of goods.

(5) To mitigate the impact of home country regulations, like anti-trust regulations, regulations against industries causing ecological problem, etc.

(6) To exploit the natural resources of the hose countries.

(7) To enjoy the benefits of tax-havens.

MNCs and International Trade

Peter Druckier, the well-known writer on Management, remarks that multinationalism and expanding world trade are two sides of the same coin. He points out that the period of most rapid growth of multinationals – the fifties and sixties – was the period of most rapid growth of multinational trade. Indeed, during this period the world trading economy grew faster — at an annual rate of 15 percent or so in most years – than even the fastest growing domestic economy, that of Japan.

There seems to be a misconception that the growth of the MNCs has to do with trade restrictions. Peter Drucker points out that far from being a cause of multinationalism, protectionism is incompatible with it; indeed an emergence of protectionism would be the greatest threat to the MNCs. The best proof that protectionism is not at the bottom of the multinational trend is the European development. The rise of the multinationals began when continental Europe abolished protection and joined in a common market. Further, it is not in the most heavily protected industries where multinationalism has forged ahead the fastest. It came late, for instance, in the chemical industry which is very heavily protected. But pharmaceuticals where protectin plays a minor role, was a leader from the start. And there has been almost no multinationalism in heavily protected steel industry.

It is estimated that between one-fourth and one-third of manufactured goods now moving in world trade are being shipped from one branch to another of the MNCs; that is, they are intra-company shipments. The sale of foreign subsidiaries in the host countries in which they are located are three to four times as large as total world exports. Apart from trade in commodities, other transactions also take place extensively between the different parts of these enterprises, for example the granting of loans, the licensing of technology and the provision of services. In all such transactions, transfer prices may be settled which are different from the price which would have been the case between independent parties operating at arms length. Such differences may reflect the legitimate business concerns of the companies but are also capable of being used in order to shift profits from high to low tax countries or to get around exchange or price controls or customs duties. As the Brandt Commission observes, the ability of multinationals to manipulate financial flows by the use of artificial transfer prices is bound to be a matter of concern to governments. The monitoring and control of transfer prices involves inter-governments. The monitoring and control of transfer prices involves inter-governmental co-operation and measures to secure due disclosure of relevant information by companies. This is necessary to make effective tax laws covering transfer prices which exist in many countries., Intra-firm trade also opens up the possibility for corporations to impose restrictive business practices within their own organisation; they can limit the exports of their affiliates, allocate their markets between nations or restrict the use of their technology or that developed by their affiliates. Such practices, although best pursued in the best business interests of the companies, may conflict with the developmental objectives and national interests of host countries.

Merits of MNCs

As the Preface to the ILO report on Multinational Enterprises and Social Policy observes, "for some, the multinational companies are an invaluable dynamic force and instrument for wider distribution of capital, technology and employment; for others, they are monsters which our present institutions, national or international cannot adequately control, a law to themselves with no reasonable concept, the public interest or social policy can accept".

There are a number of arguments in favour of and against the MNCs. MNCs, it is claimed, help the host countries in the following ways :

1. MNCs help increase the investment level and thereby the income and employment in the host country.
2. The transnational corporations have become vehicles for the transfer technology, especially to the developing countries.
3. They also kindly a managerial revolution in the host countries through professional management and the employment of highly sophisticated management techniques.
4. The MNCs enable the host countries to increase their exports and decrease their import requirements.
5. They work to equalise the cost of factors of production around the world.
6. MNCs provide an efficient means of integrating national economies.
7. the enormous resources of the multinational enterprises enable them to have very efficient research and development systems. Thus, they make a commendable contribution to inventions and innovations.
8. MNCs also stimulate domestic enterprise because to support their own operations, the MNCs may encourage and assist domestic suppliers.
9. MNCs help increase competition and break domestic monopolies.

Demerits

MNCs have, however, been subject to a number of criticisms, like those mentioned below :

1. As Leonard Gomes points out, the MNC's technology is designed for world-wide profit maximization, not the development needs of poor countries, in particular employment needs and relative factor scarcities in these countries. In general, it is asserted, the imported technologies are not adapted to : (a) the consumption needs, (b) the size of domestic markets, (c) resource availabilities, and (d) stage of development of many of the LDCs.
2. Through their power and flexibility, MNCs can evade or under mine national economic autonomy and control, and their activities may be inimical to the national interests of particular countries.
3. MNCs can have unfavourable effect on the Balance of payments of a country. For instance, the Coca-Cola, until 1978, had remitted abroad nearly Rs. 6 crores on an initial investment of Rs. 6.6 lakhs in India.
4. MNCs may destroy competition and acquire monopoly powers.
5. The tremendous power of the global corporations poses the risk that they may threaten the sovereignty of the nations in which they do business.
6. MNCs retard growth of employment in the home country.
7. The transnational corporations cause fast depletion of some of the non-renewable natural resources in the host country.
8. The transfer pricing enables MNCs to avoid taxes by manipulating prices on intra-company transactions.

Recent Trends

There has been a considerable change in the attitude towards the multinationals. They are not subject to as severe criticisms as in the past. Even communist have wide opened their doors for the MNCs.

Streeten points out that the following trends suggest that the role of the MNCs has to be reassed.

(i) Many more nations are now competing with U.S. multinational in setting up foreign activities, which means that the controversy is no longer dominated by nationalistic considerations. Japanese and European firms figure prominently among the new multination.

(ii) Developing countries themselves are now establishing multinationals. In addition to companies from the Organisation of Petroleum Exporting Countries (OPEC), and firms established in tax-haven countries, the leading countries where multinationals are being established are Argentina, Brazil, Colombia, Hong Kong, India, the Republid of Korea, Peru, the Philippines, Singapore, and Taiwan.

(iii) Not only do host countries deal with a greater variety of foreign companies, comparing their political and economic attractions, weighing them against their costs, and playing them off against one another, but also the large multinationals are being replaced by smaller and more flexible firms. An increasingly alternative organizations to the traditional form of multinational enterprise are becoming available: banks retailers consulting firms and trading companies are acting as instruments of technology transfer.

(iv) Some multinationals from developed countries have accommodated themselves more to the needs of the developing countries.

Perspective

Future holds out an enormous scope for the growth of MNCs. The changes in the economic environment in a large number of countries indicate this. For instance, the number of bilateral treaties that promote and/or protect FDI has increased markedly, with some 64 such treaties signed in the first 18 months of the 1990s compared with 199 such treaties during 1980-89. Further, of the 82 changes made in FDI policy by 35 countries during 1991, 80 were in the direction of increased liberalisation. Privatisation programmes in more than 70 countries offer new opportunities for foreign investors, especially in the service sector.

The *World Investment Report 1992* describes several developments that point to a rapidly changing context for economic growth, along with a growing role for transnational corporations in that process. These include.

(a) increasing emphasis on market forces and a growing role for the private sector in nearly all developing countries;

(b) rapidly changing technologies that are transforming the nature of organisation and location of international production;

(c) the globalisation of firms and industries;

(d) the rise of services to constitute the largest single sector in the world economy; and

(e) regional economic integration, which has involved both the world's largest economies as well as selected developing countries.

Code of Conduct

As the Brandt Commission observes, there is now much interest in trying to formulate international codes of conduct for the transfer of technology, for restrictive business practices and transnational corporations. Definite progress has been made in some of these negotiations. Any code, of course, will only work if it can influence the actual behaviour home and host governments and of investors. The major elements of any effective code should be capable of being eventually translated into agreements between governments. Such an overall regime will have to have elements of both persuasion and effective implementation, with flexible approaches and attitudes on all sides. The participating governments will have to consult with labour and business to find the means to reconcile interests and to monitor and implement the arguments. The ILO has created a committee for consultation and monitoring the Code of Conduct relating to multinational enterprises. This offers one model. According to the Brandt Commission, the principal elements of an international regime for investment should include :

(1) A framework to allow developing countries as well as trasnational corporations to benefit from direct investment on terms contractually agreed upon. Home countries should not restrict investment or the transfer of technology abroad, and should desist from other restrictive practices such as export controls or market allocation arrangements. Host countries in turn should not restrict current transfers such as profits, royalties and dividends, or the repatriation of capital, so long as they are on terms which were agreed when the investment was originally approved or subsequently negotiated.

(2) Legislation promoted and co-ordinated in home and host countries, to regulate the activities of transnational corporations in such matters as ethical behaviour, disclosure of information, restrictive business practices, cartels, anti-competitive practices and labour standards. International codes and guidelines are a useful step in that direction.

(3) Co-operation by governments in their tax policies to monitor transfer pricing and to eliminate the resort to tax havens.

(4) Fiscal and other incentives and policies towards foreign investment to be harmonized among host developing countries, particularly at regional and sub-regional levels to avoid the undermining of the tax base and competitive positions of host countries.

(5) An international procedure for discussions and consultations on measures affecting direct investment and the activities of transnational corporations.

Foreign Investment by Indian Companies

Although some developing countries like S. Korea and Taiwan, whose economic position had not been better than that of India when India started planned development, have made substantial DFI in other countries, Indian companies have not made any significant foreign investment so far. Although government of India's policy has been one of encouraging foreign investment by Indian companies subject to certain conditions, several factors like the domestic economic policy and the domestic economic situation have been deterrents to foreign investment by Indian companies.

By restricting the areas of operation and growth, the government policy seriously constrained the potential of Indian companies to make a foray into the foreign countries through investment. Added to this was the attraction of the protected domestic market which was, in many cases, a sellers' market which made the Indian companies to ignore the foreign markets.

The new economic policy of India is expected to encourage foreign investments by Indian companies. The curbs on growth, even by mergers and acquisitions, have been removed, financing restrictions have been eased, areas of business opened to the private sector companies have been substantially enlarged and foreign tie up policies have been liberalised. Further, domestic market is becoming increasingly competitive. All these factors should encourage the Indian companies to invest in other countries and take advantage of the economic liberalisation in many foreign countries.

Several Indian companies have established subsidiaries or joint ventures abroad.

Conclusion

We can, thus, conclude that there was complete lack of monetary co-operation amongst the countries of the world after the First World War. Infact, there was an acute commercial rivalry amongst the majority of the countries of the world at that time. Every country was trying to maximize its exports and to minimize its imports. To achieve this objective, several countries resorted to competitive currency devaluation. Thus, there was a sort of economic war going on amongst the majority of the countries of the world. Hence, Monetary policy and Fiscal policy plays a crucial role in moulding the economic character of a country because money and credit in modern economy exercise a vital influence upon the course, nature and volume of economic activities.

Questions for Discussion

1. What is foreign collaboration? Explain the advantage and disadvantages of foreign collaboration.
2. Explain the objectives and achievements of GATT.
3. Explain the functions of IMF and IBRD.
4. What is the role of Multinational Corporations in economic development?
5. Briefly discuss the impact of WTO on various aspects of Indian economy.

Part - D

PUBLIC FINANCE

1. Nature and Principle of Public Finance 497
2. Public Revenue 510
3. Public Expenditure 536
4. Public Debt 545
5. Fiscal Policy and Deficit Finance 556

Bibliography 575

Chapter - 1

NATURE AND PRINCIPLE OF PUBLIC FINANCE

Introduction

The financing of Government is a matter of universal concern for practically everyone enjoys some advantages from the services of government and also contributes to their support. Government business is the largest single business in every advanced modern state. The methods of public finance have certain effects on economic life and can, therefore, be used as instruments or means for bringing about desired social and economic changes.

Meaning

Public Finance is composed of two words — 'public' and 'finance'. The word 'public' is just the opposite of the word 'private'. The latter usually concerns an individual and is generally used in a singular sense whereas the former is a collective term and signifies and association or group of two or more than two people. In its widest sense it refers to all the members of a community. In public finance, however, the word 'public' is used in the narrow sense and it implies government or state.

The word 'finance' ordinarily means money i.e., coins and notes of a country. But here it signifies anything that can perform the functions of money. Thus in public finance, the word 'public', is used in the narrow sense while the word 'finance' is used in its widest sense.

Public finance deals with the income and expenditure of public authorities. Dalton defined Public Finance as "concerned with the income and expenditure of public authorities and with the adjustment of one to another". Hence, fiscal problems and fiscal policies are integral parts of public finance. The fiscal operations and fiscal policies have effects upon the national production and income, the national standard of living, distribution of wealth and income, the money markets, etc., which in turn effect the economic life of the nation.

Definition

The definition of Public Finance can be divided under the following three categories : (I) Very Wide Definitions, (II) wide Definitions, and (III) Narrow Definitions. Definition of Public Finance given by different eminent scholars are as follows :

I. Very Wide Definitions of Public Finance

Under this category, some eminent-scholars have defined Public Finance as follows :

H. Dalton, "Public Finance is concerned with income and expenditure of public authorities and with the adjustment of the one to the other".

C.F. Bastable, "Public Finance deals with the expenditure and income of public authorities of the state, and their mutual relation as also with the financial administration and control".

Findley Shirrats, "The science of Public Finance may be said to be concerned with the manner in which public authorities obtain their income and spend it".

These definitions are defective definitions of public finance on the following points :

1. The study of public finance includes public authorities while educational institution, government hospitals have got no real relationship with public finance.
2. All types of monetary and non-monetary transactions have been included in the study of public finance while as a matter of fact, public finance should include only the monetary and credit resources of the state.
3. The use of the word 'resources' in definition of public finance is ambiguous.

II. Wide Definitions of Public Finance

Under this category, some eminent-scholars have defined Public Finance as below :

Harley L Lutz, "Public finance deals with provision, custody and disbursement of resources needed for the conduct of public or government functions".

Mrs. Hicks, "The main content of public finance consists of examination and appraisal of the methods by which governing bodies provide for the collective satisfaction of wants and secure the necessary funds to carry out their purposes".

Carl C. Plehn, "Public finance is the science that deals with the activities of statesman in obtaining and applying the material means necessary for fulfilling the proper functions of the state".

These definitions are defective definitions of public finance in the sense that they on the one hand include monetary and nonmonetary expenses and gains which is not proper while in the other hand, they do not clarify exactly what the terms Expenditure' and 'Revenue' mean in reality.

III. Narrow Definitions of Public Finance

We can include in this category the definition of public finance as given by Mr. Mehta and Agarwal. According to them; "Public finance constitutes a study of monetary and credit resources of the state".

A Suitable Definition of Public Finance. On the basis of study of the above definitions of public finance, it can be defined as, "Public Finance is a special branch of economics and deals with the principles, problems, policies and processes of different governments' financial system. The financial management means adjustment of income and expenditure of debt of the government".

Scope of Public Finance

The scope of public finance may be divided into (1) Public Expenditure ; (2) Public Revenue ; (3) Public Debt, and (4) Financial Administration, which may be discussed below.

1. Public Expenditure

Public expenditure is the end and aim of the collection of state revenues. Under public expenditure as a sub-division of public finance, we study the principles and problems relating to the expenditure of public funds. We study the fundamental principles governing the flow of government funds into different spending streams and the method of incurring the actual expenditure of state funds on the various items. We also study the classification of public expenditure on different criteria, theoretical setup, and the recent trends in public expenditure. We also investigate the phenomena responsible for these recent trends. In other words, we study the changes in the pattern of public expenditure over time. At times, we also discuss the normative aspect of the problem and evaluate the performance of public expenditure on the basis of certain value judgements and make suggestions for making improvements in the funds spending policies of the government.

2. Public Revenue

In its wider sense, public revenue includes all incomes irrespective of their sources. Consequently, we may broadly include in government or public revenue income, all kinds of taxes, fees and receipts from borrowings. However, for a clear understanding, the scope of the term 'public revenue' is narrowed down by including in it only those incomes which do not carry with them the obligation of repayment on the part of government.

We classify the various sources of public revenue into taxes, fees, assessment, etc., and study the principles which should govern the public revenue and the various methods of raising it. In short, we study the different canons of taxation. Taxation is the main body of this division of public finance, and we mainly analyse the problems of raising the public revenue through taxation. We also study the problem of incidence and impact of taxation, whom the government wants to tax and who is actually taxed etc. We also discuss the important related problems of tax evasion and tax avoidance and examine the causes of these problems and suggest remedial measures.

3. Public Debt

A government or public authority can also obtain income through raising loans in order to finance the shortfall in its traditional income. In modern times, public borrowings constitute an important source of raising funds by public authorities. In fact, governments in developing countries have relied on borrowings much beyond the expediency limits determined by their capacity to service these borrowings. The loans raised in a particular year constitute the receipts of the public authority for that year. It is an income of a capital nature, while the provision of repayment of the capital sum for the year constitutes expenditure of a capital nature. Thus, the problems related to the raising and repayment of loans are studied under this part of public finance. The purpose for which the loan is raised, the different sources from where the loan is raised, the different methods by which the loan is raised, and the payment of interest and repayment of principal amount of loan which are promised, all taken together constitute the subject-matter of public debt. We also examine the borrowing policy of the government and indicate the directions in which improvements could be made.

4. Financial Administration

The scope of public finance is not confined only to public expenditure, public revenue, and public debt. We also have to examine the mechanism by which these processes are carried on. Thus, we are faced with the problem of financial organisation and administration. Under the fiscal or financial administration we are concerned with the government machinery that is responsible for performing the various financial functions of the state. The budget is the master financial plan of the government. It brings together the estimates of anticipated annual revenues and expenditures, implying the schedule of different activities to be undertaken and the means of financing these activities. Execution of the budget is another important function or task related with the financial administration. Varied statistics and estimates have to be collected, processed and prepared. The entire work starting with the procedure of preparation of the budget, presentation of the budget before the parliament or assembly, passing of the budget by the parliament or state legislatures execution of the budget by the government after it has been passed by the parliament and evaluation of the budget etc., constitute the subject-matter of this part of the public finance.

Importance of Public Finance

Public finance had little importance in the 19th century. The reason was that the government did not intervene in those days in economic affairs. But, during the 20th century, public finance has come into the forefront on account of the new concept of 'welfare state'. Modern governments do not confine themselves to law and order only. On the contrary, they actively intervene in economic matters. Hence, the importance of public finance has vastly increased in recent years. The importance of public finance is evident from the following :

1. Helpful in Government Increasing Activities

Today, the government does not confine itself only with the three function of defending the country from foreign aggression, maintaining law and order in the country and giving justice to the public but also has become concerned with the management of transport, electricity, social security, insurance and banking. It requires finance for all these activities the management of which can be done my with the help of the principles of public finance.

2. Helpful in Capital Formation

The main object of the government is to maximise the savings and to invest the same for productive purposes by modifying properly its tax policies. The government these days gives subsidies and grants to different industries to enable them to increase the production of essential goods in the country. These subsidies and grants have special place in the government expenditure of under-developed and backward countries.

3. Importance in Economic Planning

Today, every country is launching its policy of planning to have rapid, balanced and more and more economic development and no doubt, public finance plays a significant role to meet this end. The success of financial planning depends on the fiscal policy of the government.

4. Helpful in Reducing Economic Inequalities

Public finance also plays a vital role in reducing economic inequalities in capitalist countries. For example, the government can levy heavy taxes on the richer sections and spend the income so received on providing cheap food, cheap housing, free medical aid etc., for the poorer sections of the community.

5. Improvement in Employment

Public finance occupies a special place in the modern theory of employment. For example, the government obtains long-term loan and invest it in trade and industries of short-gestation period which give employment to many persons in the country.

6. Helpful in Raising National Income

The income of the people and their standard of living is low in economically backward countries. Public finance serves as a tool of economic upliftment of such countries by raising the level of national income.

7. Helpful in Running Public Enterprises

Huge amount of capital is required for running public enterprises and maintaining essential services, like—water, electricity, health and education etc. Public finance plays a vital role in arranging this huge amount of capital.

Public Finance and Private Finance

The word 'finance' is used for both public finance and private finance. By private finance is meant the financial problems and policies of an individual economic unit (which does not form part of state organs) as compared with those of public authorities. Some people believe that the principles of public finance are same as the principles of family budget while others believe that the principles of public finance and private finance are different. Both these views are justified to some extent because of the existence of similarities and dissimilarities between the principles of public finance and private finance.

Similarities

1. Both public finance and private finance are based on rationality. The individual is tempted by circumstances to act foolishly and irrationally; the government is also subject to whims and caprices in regard to its expenditure. Like the financial decisions of an individual, the decisions of government may also be unwise leading to waste.
2. Just as an individual cannot indefinitely indulge in financing his expenses with the borrowed funds so also a government cannot for ever pursue a policy of deficit financing without risking its own existence. Like an individual, the government has also to repay its loans. The state and individual both have to borrow within the safe limit of their borrowing capacity. The borrowing capacity of the government, although larger than that of an individual, is not limitless. Impecunious governments who have borrowed recklessly have brought ruin on the country marring its political and economic stability.
3. Like an individual or private corporation, the financial policies of the government may not be sound and suffer from many loopholes. Both public and private funds may be misused and may be used to serve the selfish and vested interests of the few individuals.
4. Both the private and the public sectors are engaged in satisfying the wants of the society. The overall economic activities are divided between the two sectors and in some respects their problems and decisions are similar.
5. Both the private and the public sectors have limited resources at their disposal and both the sectors always endeavour to make optimum use of these resources.
6. Both the sectors are engaged in those activities that involve large purchases, sales and other-transactions. They are also engaged in production, exchange, saving, capital accumulation, investment, etc.
7. Both the government and the individual have income. Both may earn their income, obtain it from others in the form of loan or borrow money to be returned as some later date. Their sources of income are therefore, identical.

The above-mentioned facts suggest the similarities between the public finance and private finance. In spite of these similarities, there are, however, following glaring differences between the two forms of finances.

Dissimilarities

Following are the important differences between Public Finance and Private Finance :

1. Adjustment of Income and Expenditure

Every individual tries as far as possible to adjust his expenditure to his income because his expenditure is governed by his income. But this may not be applicable to the government. A government first determines its expenditure and then devises ways and means to raise the necessary revenues to meet the expenditure.

2. Difference in Credit Status

The credit of private individual is limited. He can borrow a limited sum of money for a limited period. As against this, the government can borrow large amounts not only from its own citizens, but also from the foreigners.

3. Nature of Borrowing

In the case of individual there can be no internal borrowing. An individual cannot borrow from himself. He can borrow only from an external agency. The state however, can borrow both from internal as well as external agency. It borrows not only from its own citizens, but also from foreigners.

4. Right to Print Currency

The government has a source of income which is not available to private individual. The government can print notes which are legal tender within the country. The private individual enjoys no such right.

5. Law of Equai-Marginal Utility

The private individual spends his income on various items in such a manner as to secure equal marginal utilities from them. It is only by equalising the various marginal utilities that he can secure maximum utility out of his expenditure. The government, on the contrary, does not given as much importance to this law as a private individual does. Modern governments sometimes incur certain types of expenditure from which they do not derive any advantage. But they do incur this expenditure to satisfy certain sections of the community.

6. Nature of the Budget

A surplus budget is always good for a private individual. But a surplus budget may not be good for the government. J.M. Keynes supported a deficit budget to meet the situation created by depression.

7. Secrecy of the Budget

In a democratic country, the government presents its budget before parliament where it is widely discussed and subjected to criticism. But the budget of a private individual is shrouded in mystery.

8. Difference in Objective

There is a fundamental difference in the objective of private and public finance. The motive of private expenditure is personal benefit whereas the objective of public expenditure is social benefit.

9. Elasticity of Finance

Public Finance is more elastic than private finance. There is not much scope for changes in private finance while drastic changes can be made in government finance. A government can increase its income by imposing fresh taxes on the people which an individual cannot do.

It is clear that there are important difference between private and public finance. Naturally the principles and rules which govern private finance cannot apply to public finance. We have a whole set of principles which govern income expenditure and public debt of government.

Principles of Public Finance

The classical economists have always condemned the imposition of tax as they thought it to be an evil. They advocated the public finance to be kept at the minimum possible level as it is improductive in character. They were of the view that the state should confine itself only to maintain peace, security law and order in the country. Different economists have propounded the following principles of public finance :

1. Principle of Minimum Taxation

According to Prof. J.B. Say, the best of the taxes is one which is minimum in its quantity. It is quite meaningless to talk of minimum expenditure. Secondly, it is of no use to levy a tax which produces minimum return.

2. Principle of Minimum Collective Sacrifice

Some thinkers are of the view that the object of public finance should be minimum collective sacrifice. The load of public expenditure should be so distributed on the public that it has to sacrifice the minimum. According to this theory also, all taxes are necessarily bad. But this cannot be supported with facts which are quite to the contrary. The tax on intoxicants is not bad but is in the benefit of the country as it promotes social welfare. The duty on imports only encourages the indigenous industries. The expenditure by the government on health, education, employment and pension etc., is not of unproductive character as it promotes public welfare.

3. Principle of Economy

This principle states that the government should exercise economy in public expenditure. But as we know that the main object of modern state is to establish a welfare state in view of which it has to perform a number of functions. So, it is not possible for the state to implement this principle of economy in reality.

4. Principle of Maximum Social Advantage

This principle was put forward by the British Economist, Hugh Dalton. According to him, that system of public finance is the best which secures maximum social advantage to the community. The fiscal operations of the state should, therefore, be determined by the principle of maximum social advantage. They should always keep this principle in view while raising revenues or incurring expenditure in various heads.

The imposition of taxation inevitably involves loss of utility to those on whom it is levied, the reason being that taxation leads to some loss of purchasing power by the taxed people. This is the social sacrifice of taxation. Likewise, the spending of money by the state leads to gain of utility by those sections who are benefited by it. This is the social benefit of public expenditure. The state will secure maximum social advantage when its fiscal operations maximise the surplus of social benefit flowing from public expenditure over the social sacrifice resulting from taxation. The state is, therefore, required to continuously compare the social sacrifice with the social benefit in tis fiscal operations.

The state should continue with its fiscal operations so long as the social benefit exceeds the social sacrifice because thereby the community shall be the net gainer. The state shall maximise the net social advantage by continuing with its fiscal operations. But the state should not proceed beyond the points where the social sacrifice equals the social benefit. In case it does so, the net social advantage shall be less than the maximum. The net social advantage shall be maximum only at the point where the social sacrifice equals the social benefits.

As more and more revenue is raised through taxation the social sacrifice involved will go on increasing at an increasing rate, the reason being that there would be increasing loss of purchasing power with additional doses of taxation. On the contrary, the social benefit goes on diminishing with every increase in public expenditure on account of the operation of the law of diminishing utility. Introducing the concept of margin on both sides, the state could secure maximum social advantage by equalising the marginal social sacrifice (involved in taxation) with the marginal benefit (flowing from public expenditure). The point of equality between the marginal social sacrifice and the marginal social benefit is known as the point of maximum social advantage or the point of least aggregate social sacrifice.

Diagrammatic Presentation of the Principle of Maximum Social Advantage

The point of maximum social advantage can also be illustrated by means of a diagram based on the table given below :

Table

(in Units)

No. of Units of Money Taxed and Spent	*Marginal Social Sacrifice (MSS)*	*Marginal Social Benefit (MSB)*
1	5	40
2	8	32
3	12	28
4	16	26
5	23	23
6	30	15
7	38	10

From the table above, it is clear that as the state expands its fiscal operations i.e., raises more revenue through taxation and spends additional amounts for public benefit, the marginal social sacrifice increases while the marginal social benefit declines.

In the diagram below, MSS is the marginal social sacrifice curve sloping upwards from the left to the right. This rising curve indicates that the marginal social sacrifice goes on increasing with every dose of taxation. MSB is the marginal social benefit curve sloping downwards from the left to the right. This falling curve indicates that the marginal social benefit diminishes with every additional dose of public expenditure. The two curves MSS and MSB intersect each other at the point P. PM represents both marginal sacrifice as well as marginal social benefit. Both are equal at OM which represents the optimum limit of the fiscal operations of the state. So long as the MSB curve lies above the MSS curve the fiscal operations of the state add to the net social advantage of the community.

The net social advantage goes on increasing till the MSB becomes equal to the MSS. If the state carries on its fiscal operations beyond OM the MSS will exceed the MSB causing a fall in the net social advantage of the community. The net social advantage can be maximum only at the point where the MSS equals MSB. The equality, thus of the MSS and MSB is an essential pre-requisite for the maximisation of the net social advantage. The marginal social benefit of the last money unit spend should be equal to the marginal social sacrifice of the last money unit raised by taxation if the net social advantage is to be maximised.

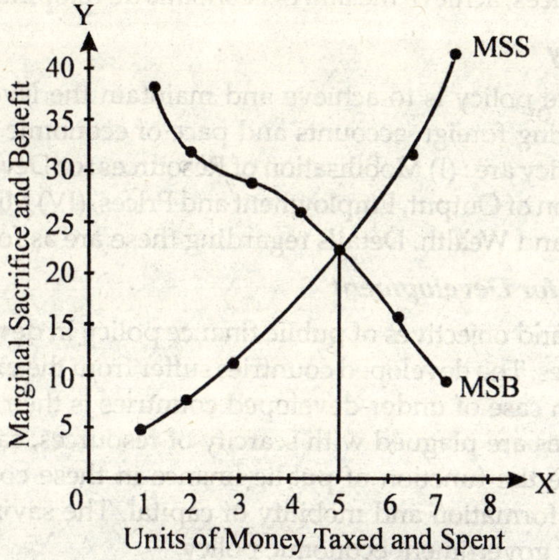

Criticisms of the Principle of Maximum Social Advantage

Although the principle of maximum social advantage is of great theoretical significance. But several difficulties crop up when this principle is translated in practice. Following are the main difficulties :

1. It is difficult to measure Tax Burden

When taxes are levied on the people, they have to undergo sacrifice but it is very difficult to measure this amount of sacrifice.

2. It is difficult to measure Social Benefit

When government incurs expenditure, the people are benefitted. But it is very difficult to measure the benefit.

3. Non-applicability of the Law of Equi-marginal Utility to Public Expenditure

The law of equi-marginal utility may be applicable to private expenditure but certainly not to public expenditure. As is well known, public expenditure is never incurred for the individual benefit but for social or group benefit. Hence it is not possible to equalise marginal benefits accruing to individuals from public expenditure.

4. Public Finance – an Instrument for Economic Stabilisation

The concept of functional finance has come to the forefront. The policy of functional finance permits no such consideration as the equalisation of marginal social benefit with marginal social sacrifice.

Despite the above limitations of the principle of maximum social advantage is of basic importance in the field of public finance. Modern governments keep this principle in mind while planning their public expenditure even though the costs and benefits involved in the implementation of this principle cannot be accurately quantified and measured.

Role of Public Finance Policy in National Economy

Public Finance Policy is one which determines tax structure, public expenditure and public debt with a view to stabilise prices, achieve the aim of economic development and full employment.

Aims of Public Finance Policy

The aim of public finance policy is to achieve and maintain the level of employment, price stability, adjustment or balancing foreign accounts and pace of economic development. The main objectives of public finance policy are : (I) Mobilisation of Resources for Development, (II) Allocation of Resources, (III) Determination of Output, Employment and Prices, (IV) Minimising the Inequalities in the Distribution of Income and Wealth. Details regarding these are as follows :

I. Mobilisation of Resources for Development

There are different aims and objectives of public finance policy in developed countries as well as in under-developed countries. The developed countries suffer from the main problem of economic stability. While the problem in case of under-developed countries is their economic development. The under-developed countries are plagued with scarcity of resources, capital formation and low level of investment. Therefore the function of public finance in these countries becomes to help accelerate the pace of capital formation and mobility of capital. The savings and investments are thus encouraged as a result of government economic policy.

The economic development of under-developed countries can be encouraged in the following ways and means :

1. ***Promotion to Capital Formation :*** The main problem in under-developed countries is the paucity of capital due to low rate of capital formation. Domestic savings and investments are very low. According to Nurksey, "I believe that Public Finance assumes a new significance in the face of problem of capital formation in under-developed countries". The government can take the following measures to increase the rate of capital formation:

   (a) The government should itself invest in social capital.

   (b) It can arrange for advancing loans by its banking and financial institutions.

   (c) private investors should be encouraged to invest their money.

   (d) In this way, the government can curtail consumption through its fiscal policy.

2. ***To Encourage Production :*** The main objective of government in under-developed countries is to maximise the aggregate savings on the one hand and invest the same on the other. It can offer facilities, like-tax holiday, development rebate, investment allowance etc. It can boost exports of the country by giving economic assistance to export industries and can give production to its industries by levy protection tax.

3. ***To Initiate Economic activities :*** Today's age is an age of planning. The government of under-developed countries, therefore, make planning to accelerate the pace of economic progress and have to make provision for implementing the plans.

II. Allocation of Resources

In case of developing and under-developed countries, it is not only sufficient to provide resources for their economic development but also to allocate effectively these resources is essential so that no resource can remain idle. Public finance plays a crucial role in this respect.

Classical economists were of the opinion that allocation of resources becomes an automatic mechanism in perfect competition but the great depression of 1929 falsified this opinion and now it has been firmly believed that it is only through fiscal policy of the government that the best use of the economic resources can be made possible. The government can take the following measures to direct the flow of investment in the desired directions :

1. ***By Strengthening Basic Structure of the Economy :*** The government can strengthen the basic structure of the economy by developing irrigation facilities, means of transport and communication and establishment of technical education centres.
2. ***By Granting Tax Relaxation :*** The government can grant tax relaxations to new industries in order to develop backward areas and to increase production.
3. ***By Expanding Social Security Measures :*** government can expend its income through progressive taxation on social security measure for the poor which affect the economy as a whole directly and indirectly.
4. ***By Discouraging Luxurious Consumption :*** The government can curtail consumption of luxurious goods by imposing heavy dose of taxation and increase healthy consumption of the goods on the other hand.

III. Determination of Output, Employment and Prices

The effect of public finance on output, employment and prices can be studied under the following three heads :

1. ***To Effect Output :*** The government can do the following in this respect :

(a) It can increase production by establishing its own industries.

(b) It can encourage production by allowing subsidies, tax relaxation or tax exemption.

(c) It can impose protection cess to protect its domestic industries from foreign competition.

(d) It can given economic assistance to industries to promote exports.

(e) It can discourage production of luxurious goods by imposing heavy tax.

(f) It can increase production by restraining monopotistic tendencies.

2. ***To Effect Employment :*** In every country there are persons who are able to work but do not want to do work at prevailing rates of wages. No country can have full employment in the sense that all the persons who are able to do work are engaged in one or the other type of work.

(i) ***To Promote Propensity to Consume :*** The main reason of reduced effective demand is the reduction in the quantity of consumption. The government should therefore try to increase the propensity to consume by reducing the amount of tax and economically helping the poor. The people get increased purchasing power as a result of reduced amount of taxes. The government can also increase propensity to consume by spending its income as result of progressive taxation.

(ii) ***To Promote Investment :*** There are two types of investments : (a) Private Investment, and (b) Public Investment. The private investment can be encouraged by reducing interest rates, increasing quantity of money and allowing tax relaxations, while as the government should itself come forward for investment in public construction works to give employment to the public in times of depression. It will increase purchasing power of the public thereby resulting in increase in effective demand.

(iii) ***To Effect Prices :*** Fluctuating prices register a marked feature in modern economy. Depression follows inflation and Vice-Versa. Prices rise in times of inflation and they fall in times of depression with the result that the level of production, demand and employment also comes down.

During Inflation Period : Four measures can be taken by the Government during Inflation Period :

(a) By reducing unproductive expenditure.

(b) Withdrawing purchasing power of the public by increasing old taxes and leaving new taxes.

(c) Heavy borrowing from the public.

(d) By preparing surplus budgets.

During Depression Period : Three measures can be taken by the Government during Depression period :

(a) ***Change in Tax and Public Expenditure :*** Efforts should be made at government level to increase the purchasing power of the people by allowing tax rebate and increase in public expenditure.

(b) ***To Spend on Public Welfare Works :*** The government should increase its expenditure on construction of roads, bridges and dams. This will provide employment to people and increase their purchasing power.

(c) ***Purchase by the Government :*** The government should start purchase of goods-at approved prices in times of depression to let the aggregate demand increase.

(d) ***Deficit Budgets :*** The government should resort to prepare deficit budgets.

IV. Minimising the Inequalities in the Distribution of Income and Wealth

The level of income in under-developed countries is not only low but is associated with marked degree of inequality in the distribution of wealth as well. It is a common experience that rich becomes riches and poor becomes poorer as a result of such state of affair. Public finance plays a significant role in this respect by redistribution of income and wealth from the richer sections of society to the poorer ones by imposing progressive and direct taxes on the richer and spending the revenue on education, medical treatment, house construction, community development projects, development cottage and small-scale industries and other labour welfare projects. The poor will thus get its real income increased and the effective demand will also increase.

It should be pointed out here that the government should not adopt the practice of levying commodity taxes as it only increases burden on the poor section of the society. Secondly the luxurious commodities should be heavily taxed as they are consumed by the rich sections of the society more than the poor.

Conclusion

The conclude, public finance deals with the problems connected with the raising and spending of money by public authorities like the Central and State Governments, the Municipality or the

Panchayat. These public authorities perform certain functions. The carry out these functions money is needed. The methods adopted by the public authorities for raising the necessary funds, and the manner in which such funds are spent, form the subject matter of public finance.

Questions for Discussion

1. Discuss the meaning, scope and importance of Public Finance.
2. Define Public Finance and Distinguish between Public Finance and Private Finance.
3. Explain the Theory of Maximum Social Advantage in Public Finance.
4. What part does Public Finance play in promoting economic development of a country.

Chapter - 2

PUBLIC REVENUE

Introduction

Public revenue occupies the same important place in the study of public finance which production occupies in the study of economics. If production is the means for consumption, public revenue is the means for public expenditure. Like every act of production, it also causes irksomeness and is undesirable in itself. As the irrational and narrow-minded capitalists have taught the workers that 'work is a painful and unpleasant thing', in the same way superfluous and unscrupulous government in the past, by imposing avoidable and heavy burden of unproductive revenue on the people, have taught them that paying of revenue to the government is an undesirable act. Fortunately, the modern democratic government, like modern rational and enlightened capitalists, have assumed the responsibility of recognising the paying attention to peoples' grievances and have tried to extract revenue from the pocket of the public in such a manner that the tax-payer feels the least burden (pain) in paying the tax to the government.

The necessity of raising the public revenue follows from the necessity of incurring public expenditure. As the modern government has to perform several functions for the welfare of the public and as these functions cannot be performed free of cost, they involve substantial amount of public expenditure, which can be financed only through public revenue. If the government wants to provide and ever increasing welfare facilities to its citizens, an ever increasing amount of funds raised through public revenue will be required. The government, therefore, has to think of how and from where and how much revenue should be raised from the public. The amount of public revenue to be raised is a function of the necessity to incurring public expenditure and peoples' ability to pay.

Meaning of Public Revenue

The term 'Public revenue' can be explained both in a narrow and a broad sense. In the broad sense it includes all the income and receipts, irrespective of their sources and nature, which the government obtains during any given period of time. In the narrow sense, it includes only those source of income of the government which are described as 'revenue resources'. In the broad sense of the term, we also include loans which the government raises under the term "public revenue" or more properly public income. The distinction, however, is that in the narrow sense in which the term 'public revenue' is used in public finance includes only those sources of government income which are not subject to repayment while in the broad sense of the term, it includes all the receipts of a government irrespective of the fact whether these are subject to future repayment.

Sources of Public Revenue

Generally speaking, by public revenue is meant the income raised by the government through taxes from the public. Taxes are not, however, the only source of public revenue. There are also various other sources of revenue like fees, price, special assessment, fines and penalties, gift and profit from government enterprises. It is of no use to blend all these sources into a single name of **'taxation'** because all these sources have fundamental difference of one kind or another from each other. Their relative comparison itself is of some significance for the purpose of the study of public revenue. The difference between these various sources may also be of the amount which is raised through any one of them. But this is not so much significant for the purpose of study as the fundamental difference in their nature, method of raising them and their respective effects on the persons from whom these are collected. The following are the important sources of public revenue.

1. Taxation

It constitutes the most important sources of revenue for the modern governments. Following are the main characteristics :

(a) ***Compulsory Payment :*** It is a compulsory payment and every citizen is legally bound to pay the tax imposed upon him.

(b) ***Common Interest of Society :*** The tax is paid by the tax payer to enable the government to incur certain expenses in the common interest of society.

(c) ***No Return for the Tax :*** The payment of a tax by a person does not entitle him to receive any direct benefits from the government in return for the tax.

(d) ***No Relationship between Tax and Benefits :*** There is no direct relationship between the tax paid by the person and the benefits that he may receive as a result of government expenditure.

2. Fee

It is a compulsory payment which is made by those citizens who receive special benefit from the services rendered by the government. For instance, licence fee is charged from those citizens who are given licences by the government.

3. Price

The price is a payment made by the citizens to government for the goods and services to them. As a matter of fact the fee and the price are both paid in exchange for services rendered by the government.

4. Special Assessment

The payment made by the citizens of a particular locality in exchange for certain special facilities given to them by the authorities is known as special assessment.

5. Fines

The government also imposes fines from time to time on those persons who violate the laws of the country. But this source of revenue yields very small income to the government.

6. Gifts and Grants

The government of a country may receive grants from foreign governments for the general or specific purposes.

7. Duties

The excise duties are generally levied on those commodities, the consumption of which does harm to the health and well-being of the citizens. For example, the duties levied on wine, opium and other intoxicants belong to this category. The object in such a case is not so much to earn income as to discourage the consumption of harmful commodities by the citizens.

8. Government Properties

The income from forests and royalty from mines come under this category.

9. Commerce and Industry

Government establishes industries and banks. The profit of state enterprises and banks become one of the sources of revenue to the government.

Classification of Public Revenue

The modern financial literature lays a great stress on the classification of public revenue because this helps to know in what ways the various sources of public revenue resemble one another and in what respects they differ. Besides, the classification of public revenue is important from the point of view of studying the effects and incidence of the various kinds of revenue. Not only that. If we want to have a comparative view of the revenue structure of different states, the classification of public revenue becomes necessary because comparisons are useful only when like are compared with likes. Thus the classification of public revenue is of great practical importance.

We explain below some of the important classifications of public revenue as given by different writers.

1. Seligman's Classification

Seligman classifies public revenue into three broad categories of (a) Gratuitous Revenue, (b) Contractual Revenue and (c) Compulsory Revenue.

(a) Gratuitous Revenue

It is that revenue which the state gets free of cost. This includes gifts, donations etc. In modern times, this source of revenue is of little importance.

(b) Contractual Revenue

This category of public revenue consists of income derived from public property and industry. The state owns land and buildings and earns rent by letting them out to the people. Similarly, government runs various types of enterprises and earns income by selling their products and services in the market. All such incomes constitute contractual revenue because these result from a contract between the state and the people. Seligman calls all contractual incomes as prices because these partake of the prices charged by private producers for the goods and services they sell in the market.

(c) Compulsory Revenue

This category comprises income derived from state's authority for taxation, justice and administration. Taxes, fees, special assessments, fines, penalties etc., are the main sources of income under this head. Thus, according to Seligman, there are three major sources of revenue namely, taxes, fees and prices.

This classification of public revenue suffers from two major defects. The first objection refers to the difference made between prices, on the one hand and taxes and fees, on the other hand. This difference is based on the fact that the former is contractual, while the latter are compulsory but such a notion seems to be superficial. In the words of Prof. J.K. Mehta, "A fee-payer or a tax-payer is compelled to pay the fee or the tax only under certain circumstances. A passenger who travels on government railways pays the price only when he travels. A fee-payer pays the fee only when he uses the services of the court ; and like wise a tax-payer pays the tax only when he has an income above a certain figure. Or again he pays a tax at a certain rate only when he earns an income above a certain amount. There is option in every case. If you want to avoid paying the price do not travel, if you want to avoid paying the income tax do not earn income above a certain limit".

The second objection refers to the object of the government in rendering services. It is said that taxes are imposed to finance services which confer a common benefit on all whereas prices are charged for services which are performed primarily for the benefit of the individuals who pay them. But such a view is erroneous. The ultimate motive of the state is always to serve the community. The individuals who pay the prices are an integral part of the whole community and not an isolated group of persons with an independent existence of their own. Thus this classification suffers from various drawbacks and is not considered as satisfactory.

2. Adam Smith's Classification

Adam Smith classified public revenue under the following two heads :

(a) Revenue from Public

(b) Revenue from State Property

Revenue from public includes all those sources which are commonly known as the sources of revenue of the state from the public. However, Adam Smith emphasised only taxes in this category.

Revenue from state property refers to revenue which is derived by the state from the property it owns. He regarded income from this source as more or less fixed and limited.

Adam Smith's classification of public revenue is too narrow and it does not serve the purpose of modern finance. His entire approach was based on the Laissez faire philosophy which was the order of the day and as such he could not foresee the growth of the public sector and its role as a source of public revenue. Besides, Adam Smith attached no importance to loans as source of revenue and they were regarded as an extra-ordinary source of revenue.

3. Dalton's Classification

Dalton classifies the sources of public revenue into two main classes—taxes and prices. Taxes are a compulsory payment whereas prices are contractual payments. He sub-divided the taxes as

(a) Taxes ordinarily so called

(b) Tributes and indemnities whether arising out of war or otherwise

(c) Compulsory loans

(d) Pecuniary penalties for offences, imposed by court of justice

Prices are Sub-divided as :

(a) Receipts from public property passively held, e.g., rents received from the tenants of public lands.

(b) Receipts from enterprises carried on by a public authority charging only competitive prices and not monopoly prices.

(c) Fees or payments made for services performed by public officials, such as, the registration of births etc.

(d) Receipts from voluntary public loans.

Dalton includes four other sources of public income which do not fall completely under these two main classes. They are as follows :

(a) Receipts from enterprises carried on by a public authority which does use monopoly power to raise its prices above the competitive level.

(b) Receipts from special assessments.

(c) Receipts from the use of the printing press, for the purpose of meeting public expenditure by the issue of new paper money.

(d) Voluntary gifts

This classification may be considered satisfactory as it is broad-based and comprehensive. However, such a classification does not appear to be suitable for making economic interpretations and comparative study of different sources of revenue, as well as, between income and expenditure of the state which are very important in modern days.

4. Taylor's Classification

Prof. Philip E. Taylor classifies public revenue into four parts.

(a) Grants and Gifts

(b) Administrative Revenues

(c) Commercial Revenues

(d) Taxes

(a) Grants and Gifts

Grants-in-aid are a help means by which one government provides financial help to another, usually in the performance of a specified function in a specified manner. Education and health grants from the centre to the states or from the states to the local governments can be cited as examples of grants-in-aid.

Gifts are voluntary contributions from non-governmental donors generally for specified purposes. Gifts, however, do not constitute any significant amount. Grants and gifts as a category of public receipts are voluntary in nature and there is no expectation of direct benefit to the donor.

(b) Administrative Revenues

The revenues in this category include fees, licenses, fines, forfeitures, escheats and special assessment.

(c) Commercial Revenues

The receipts placed in the category of commercial revenues include prices paid for government produced commodities and services. They include payment for postage, tools, tuition fee of public educational institutions, electricity distributed by publicly owned utilities, and the like. Commercial revenues differ from other categories of revenues in that there is direct receipt of a commodity or service in return for payment, and adjustment of the amount of payment at least roughly to cost or benefit.

(d) Taxes

Taxes constitute the most important source of public revenue in modern times. The essential characteristic of a tax is that it is a compulsory payment for which there is no direct quid pro quo.

Taylor's classification of public revenues is more comprehensive and logical.

5. Economic Classification

The various classifications of public revenue discussed so far, suffer from one defect or the other. Moreover, the classifications do not seem to be suitable for making economic interpretations and comparative study of income and expenditure of the state and for analysing their various aspects. Besides, they do not appear to be appropriate for the purpose of accountability and control. The development of the techniques of social accounting, however, has made it necessary to classify the budgetary transactions of the government in a manner that may help the economic interpretation of the fiscal operations of the government. This objective has been achieved through the economic classification of the government budget which is a "classification of government expenditure and receipt by economic categories that are of significance for analysing the short-run effects of government transactions in the working of the economy".

The United Nations have taken an initiative in emphasising on the developing countries to adopt the economic classification of their budget with a view to assess the extent to which the budgetary policy of the government in these countries is contributing to the attainment of the objectives of economic policy, such as acceleration of the rate of economic growth and promotion of economic stability and social justice.

With this end in view, the economic classification of the budgetary transactions of the Central Government in India has been made and published since 1957. According to this classification, the revenue receipts of the Government have been classified into Revenue Account and Capital Account. Revenue Account includes revenue from taxes where as Capital Account includes market loans, foreign aid, income from repayment and other receipts such as, income from public undertakings.

Economic classification enables us to make economic interpretations and is regarded suitable for ensuring sound accountability and control. In other words, it ensures that the funds are spent strictly in the manner and to the extent as sanctioned by the parliament.

In our country, the classification suffers from the defect that there is no correlation between budget heads and plan heads—the reason being that the heads of development plans are prescribed by the Planning Commission whereas the heads of expenditure in the budget are laid down on the basis of recommendations of the Comptroller and Auditor General. Thus there is lack of correspondence between the heads or items in the budget and the development heads under the plan. This drawback stands in the way of the achievement of the goals of performance budgeting where a relationship is established between financial expenditure on the one hand, and the achievement of physical results on the other.

Taxation

Taxes constitute the most important source of public revenue and their effects on the working of the economy are far-reaching. They serve as an important tool of economic growth and stability. But they can realise their wider social and economic objectives only if a judicious choice is made between different possible taxes and their rate schedules. Since all taxes are not alike in their effects, it becomes imperative to study their merits and demerits in terms of the objectives of equity, productivity, efficiency, resource allocation and so on. Such a study enables the authorities to make a right choice between various types of taxes and design the tax structure in such a way as to produce the best or having the least bad economic effects.

The Main Definitions of Tax are as follows :

Seligman, "A tax is a compulsory contribution from the person to the government to defray the expenses incurred in the common interest of all without reference to special benefits conferred".

Prof. Findley Shirras, "Taxes are compulsory contributions to public authorities to meet the general expenses of government which have been incurred for the public good and without reference to special benefits.

Prof. F.W. Taussing, "The essence of a tax as distinguished from other charges by the government is the absence of a direct quid-pro-quo between the tax-payer and the public authority".

Dr. H. Dalton, "A tax is a compulsory contribution imposed by the public authority, irrespective of exact amount of service rendered to the tax payer in return and not imposed as a penalty for any legal offence".

C.F. Bastable, "Tax is a compulsory contribution of the wealth of a person or body of persons for the service of the public powers".

Carl C. Plehn, "Taxes are generally compulsory contributions of wealth levied upon persons natural or corporate to defray the expenses incurred on conferring a common benefit upon the residents of the state".

Characteristics of Tax

Following are the main characteristics of Tax

1. Tax is a Compulsory Contribution

Tax is a compulsory contribution of wealth levied upon persons. The person cannot evade payment of tax simply because he does not want to pay. But there is a limit also to this payment of tax. For example, he can refrain himself from consuming the product and thus will not pay the tax included in the price of the commodity.

2. Tax Income is Spent on Public Welfare Activities

The income received by the government from tax is not spent for the benefits of a particular section of society. As a matter of fact, the non-tax payers get comparatively more benefits than the tax-payers.

3. Tax is not a Payment for Specific Benefit

According to Prof. Pigou, "The essence of tax is the absence of a direct quid-pro-quo between the Tax payer and the public authority".

4. Other Characteristics

Other characteristics of tax are as follows :

(a) It is the personal duty of the tax payer to pay the tax.

(b) Tax is not cost of service.

(c) The assessment and realisation of tax depends on the constitutional authority.

(d) The payment of tax is done out of income.

Objectives of Taxation

One of the objectives of taxation is to raise income to the government to regulate specific activities. The objectives of taxation can be described as follows :

1. To Raise Revenue

The government requires revenue for discharging various types of functions. Tax constitutes major part of this revenue to the government.

2. Regulation of Income

Regulation of economy is considered to be the primary objective of taxation while as raising of revenue as the secondary objective of taxation. The government can curb the consumption of intoxicants through taxation.

3. To Equalise the Distribution of Wealth

The third important objective of taxation is to reduce inequality in the distribution of income and wealth in the society. The purchasing power of the people is reduced as a result of taxation while public expenditure increases the real income of the people. From this point of view, the government levies tax at progressive rate on wealthy sections of society and spends the income received there from on the benefits to the poor section of society.

4. To Main National Income at Proper Level

According to Prof. Lerner, the objective of taxation is not to raise revenue as it can be obtained by other sources as well but the real objective is to maintain national income at proper level.

5. To control Inflation

The additional purchasing power is withdrawn by the government by either increasing the rate of old taxes or levying fresh taxes to safeguard the public from effects in inflation.

Canons or Principles of Taxation

A well managed tax system should be based on certain fundamental principles of taxation. Adam Smith, the father of Economics, has described four principles of taxation which are as follows:

1. Canon of Equity

In the words of Adam Smith, "The subjects of every state ought to contribute towards the support of the government as nearly as possible, in proportion to their respective abilities as in proportion of the revenue which they respectively enjoy under the protection of the state". In other words, every person will pay the taxes to the government in proportion to his ability to pay.

2. Canon of Certainty

According to Adam Smith, the tax which an individual has to pay should be certain, not arbitrary. The tax payer should known in advance how much tax he has to pay, at what time he has to pay the tax and in what form the tax is to be paid to the government. If the tax is certain, the tax official cannot exploit the tax payers in any manner. The time of payment and manner of payment should also be pre-determined. The tax payer as well as the government is benefitted if the tax satisfies the Canon of Certainty.

3. Canon of Convenience

According to this Canon, every tax should be levied in such a manner and at such a time that it affords the maximum of convenience to the tax payer. The reason is that the tax payer makes a sacrifice at the time of payment of the tax. Hence, the government should see to it that the tax payer suffers no inconvenience on account of the payment of tax.

4. Canon of Economy

According to this canon, the tax should be such as to bring the maximum part of the collected revenue into the government treasury. In other words, the cost of tax collection should be the minimum.

Other Canons of Taxation

Some economists have propounded other canons of taxation in addition to the above four canons put forward by Adam Smith.

1. Canon of Elasticity

According to this canon, every tax imposed by the government should be elastic in nature. In other words, the income should be capable of increase or decrease according to the requirements of the country.

2. Canon of Productivity

According to this canon, the tax should be of such a nature as to yield sufficient income to the government. If a tax yields poor income, it cannot be considered as a productive tax. According to this canon it is better to go in for a few productive taxes rather than to impose a large number of unproductive taxes on the people.

3. Canon of Variety

According to this canon, the tax system should contain a large variety of taxes on persons as well as commodities. The reason is that if the government levies a single tax, it will become easier for the tax payer to evade it.

4. Canon of Simplicity

According to this canon, every tax should be simple so that the tax payer can understand its implications without the help of experts. If the tax is complex and complicated, the tax payers will have to seek the assistance of tax experts to understand its implications.

5. Canon of Diversity

This cannon of taxation is based on the principle that all sections of the society should be brought under the network of taxation and therefore it favours the multiple tax system. But it should be borne in mind that too much diversity will be undesirable as it contains the cost of collection of tax being proportionately too high.

6. Canon of Uniformity

Nitti and Conard the well known economists, have propounded this canon of taxation and this means uniformity in the procedure of imposing tax and in the aims in fixing their rates.

7. Canon of Expendiency or Desirability

It is the tax payer who pays the tax and this conon of taxation implies that the tax payer should also be brought into confidence that he is to be taxed. Therefore, any tax should be imposed only after thoughtful consideration of its plus and minus points.

8. Canon of Co-ordination

The conon of Co-ordination dictates that the tax collecting authorities should be well co-ordinated and should not enter into the jurisdiction of another tax collecting authority.

It is, therefore, now clear that no tax system in the world over satisfies all the canons of taxation discussed above. As a matter of fact no tax is fully good or bad. While designing a tax system, efforts should be made to attach more importance to more important canon of taxation in comparison to less important canon. Moreover, attention should be paid to the tax structure as a whole rather than on a particular tax.

Direct and Indirect Taxes

The taxes can be classified on the basis of their forms, nature, aims and methods. The distinction between the direct and indirect taxes is the traditional method. Direct taxes are defined as to indicate those taxes which are paid by individuals on whom it is imposed. While, indirect taxes are paid by the producer or importer and are passed on to consumers. Dalton says that a direct tax is really paid by a person on whom it is legally imposed, while an indirect tax is imposed on one person but paid partly or wholly by another. J.S. Mill says that the intention of a direct tax is that payer himself must bear it while the intention of Indirect tax is that it should be passed on. According to Bastable, taxes levied on permanent and recurring occasions are direct; but those levied on occasional and particular events are indirect. In other words, a tax is a direct one where the impact and incidence are on the same person. Whereas the incidence and the impact are on different persons in case of indirect taxes. To sum up direct taxes are non-shiftable whereas indirect taxes are shiftable. Examples of direct taxes are income tax, death tax, property tax, land tax, etc. Examples of indirect taxes are sales tax, excise tax, custom duty etc.

Merits of Direct Taxes

Following are the main advantages of direct taxes

1. Equitable

Direct taxes are levied in proportion to the income or paying capacity of the tax-payer and hence they are just and equitable. In their case, the ability to pay is judged directly and not indirectly as is the case with indirect taxes. They can easily be graduated and made to conform to the principle of justice in taxation.

2. Elastic

Direct taxes are revenue elastic as the yield from them can be increased easily by changing the rates of taxation, without incurring extra-expenditure. Income tax responded remarkably to meet the growing financial requirements of the governments during the second World War.

3. No Distortion is Caused

It is claimed that direct taxes do not cause distortion in the resource allocation of the economy. For example, a general income tax would leave the relative profitability of different industries unchanged and would not leave any effect on resource allocation.

4. Certainty

Direct taxes are certain. The tax-payer is fully aware of the amount of the tax to pay and the manner of payment and the time of the payment are clearly known to him. This enables him to make provision for the payment of the tax by suitably adjusting his income to expenditure. The public authorities can also calculate their yield with a fair degree of precision and plan outlay with greater certainty and exactness.

5. Economical

Direct taxes can be collected at the source of income and as such they are economical. The administrative cost of collecting these taxes is also low because the same personnel who assess small incomes or properties can assess larger incomes and properties without involving extra cost. Besides, the tax-payers make the payment of these taxes direct to the state and hence every paise that is paid by the tax-payers is deposited in the treasury.

6. Civic Consciousness

The payers of direct taxes feel the pinch and realist the sacrifice when they pay taxes in lump sum and, consequently take keen interest in the affairs of the state. The tax-payers take intelligent and keen interest in the fiscal operations of the government and see whether the revenue raised is properly spent or not. Thus direct taxes create civic sense and responsibility among the tax-payers.

7. Reduce Inequalities

Direct taxes go a long way in reducing the inequalities in incomes as they are progressive in nature and therefore, the rich are subjected to steeply higher rates of taxation, while the poor are exempted from direct taxes.

Demerits of Direct Taxes

The following demerits of direct taxes may be mentioned.

1. Unpopular

Direct taxes are to be paid in lump sum and with the increase in the tax rate, they impose increasing burden on the tax-payer. Besides, they are painful to the tax-payer as they are generally not shifted. Hence such taxes are unpopular and are resisted by the tax payers.

2. Possibility of Evasion

Evasion of direct taxes is easier than those of indirect taxes. The tax-payer is always under the temptation to evade them through fraudulent practices. That is why it is said that a direct tax is a tax on honesty.

3. Inconvenience

Direct taxes impose extra trouble and inconvenience on the tax-payers in the form of filling of forms and disclosing family circumstances and the source of income from which it is derived. Besides, the payment of these taxes in lump sum is not as convenient to the tax-payer as the payment of indirect taxes in small amounts.

4. Arbitrary

Direct taxes are generally imposed on income and property. In their case, it is not possible to determine a precise degree of progressions on account of the difficulties of measuring the ability to pay and the subjective nature of the marginal utility of income. Hence the state ends up with either too much or too little progression and thus direct taxes become just arbitrary.

5. Hindrance in Capital Formation

If the rates of direct taxes are heavy and steeply progressive, they adversely affect the people's desire and ability to work, save and invest and thus prove a hindrance in capital formation.

6. Exemption of Low Income Group

Direct taxes cannot make the low income groups contribute their share to the finances of the state as they are normally exempted from such taxes on the basis of ability and equity. Hence direct taxes lack universal application.

Merits of Indirect Taxes

Following are the main advantages of indirect taxes

1. Indirect taxes are convenient

An important merit of indirect taxes is that they are less inconvenient and less burden some than are the direct taxes. The tax-payers generally pay these taxes in bits and mostly when they buy goods and services in the market. The amount of tax is included in the price of the commodity and the consumer pays the tax without experiencing its pinch. Some time the consumer is not even aware of the fact that he is paying the tax in the form of the higher price of the commodity. Besides, the indirect taxes are paid by the tax-payers at a time when they have the means to pay these taxes.

2. Indirect taxes cannot be evaded

No individual can evade the payment of indirect taxes because they are collected in the form of higher prices of goods sold to the buyers in the market. Consequently, there is no possibility of the evasion of indirect taxes.

3. Indirect taxes are productive and elastic

The indirect taxes can prove to be highly productive and elastic, particularly when they are imposed on essential goods and services like sugar, edible oils and salt whose demand is inelastic. By increasing the rate of tax, the government can secure adequate tax income from these taxes.

4. Indirect taxes lead to social welfare

Indirect taxes imposed on intoxicants like wine, opium etc., serve a great social purpose by curtailing and limiting the consumption of such harmful commodities. Curtailment of consumption of harmful goods indirectly increases social welfare.

5. Indirect taxes are just

Indirect taxes are just and equitable. They are paid by all the individuals when they purchase the goods and services.

6. Indirect taxes help production and investment

Another advantage of indirect taxes is that they serve as a powerful tool in moulding the production and investment activities of the economy, i.e., they can guide the economy in its resource allocation. A proper structuring of indirect taxes can enable the authorities to twist the demand and supply forces in such a way as to yield the desirable results by encouraging the development of the high priority industries and discouraging the development of the low priority ones.

Demerits of Indirect Taxes

Following are the important disadvantages of indirect taxes :

1. Indirect Taxes Promote Economic Inequality

Indirect taxes are generally imposed on the consumption goods. The poor people have to pay as much by way of the indirect taxes levied on commodities as the right people. Obviously, this is unjust and inequitable. Indirect taxes are a type of regressive taxes which promote economic inequality in society by imposing heavier burden on poorer sections of society.

2. Indirect Taxes are Uneconomical

Indirect taxes involve high costs of collecting them. Generally, the traders charge more than the actual amount of commodity tax levied by the authorities by increasing the prices of the taxes goods and services higher than the rate of tax.

3. Indirect Taxes are Uncertain

The revenue accruing to the government from indirect taxes cannot be estimated accurately. As soon as a tax is imposed on a commodity, its price rises in the market. Consequently, its demand falls. It cannot be said with certainty as to what extent the demand of the commodity has fallen consequent upon the imposition of the tax. Consequently, an element of uncertainty is always involved in the case of indirect taxes.

4. Indirect taxes do not create civic consciousness

As indirect taxes are paid only when the consumers buy the goods they pay the amount of tax only in terms of the prices of these goods. They, therefore, do not feel an extra burden of tax. Consequently, they are not conscious about them. The tax-payers generally become indifferent towards their responsibilities and fail to keep a watch on the financial irregularities committed by the authorities.

5. Indirect Taxes are Inflationary

Another weakness of indirect taxes is that they feed inflationary forces. Indirect taxes begin by adding to the sale prices of the taxed goods without touching the purchasing power in the first place as in the case of direct tax (direct taxes take away a part of the purchasing power of the tax-payer which has the effect of reducing demand and prices). Consequently, in the case of indirect taxes inflationary forces are fed through an unending spiral of higher prices, higher costs, higher wages and again higher prices.

Above are the advantages and disadvantages of direct and indirect taxes. Now the question arises as to which one of these two types of taxes is better ? Some economists have answered this question in the following manner.

Comparison of Direct and Indirect Taxes

Direct and indirect taxes may be compared on the basis of their (i) welfare aspect, (ii) administrative aspect and (iii) distribute aspect.

A. Welfare Aspect

It is pointed out that direct taxes are superior to indirect taxes from the point of view of welfare effects. It implies that an indirect tax causes excess burden on the individual, that is, indirect tax reduces the individual's welfare more than the direct tax, when an equal amount of revenue is raised through them. This can be explained with the help of the following diagram.

In the diagram, X-axis represents commodity X, and Y-axis represents the income of an individual. OP is the given income and PL is the price line which is tangent to the indifference curve IC_3 on point E_3 where the individual is in equilibrium position.

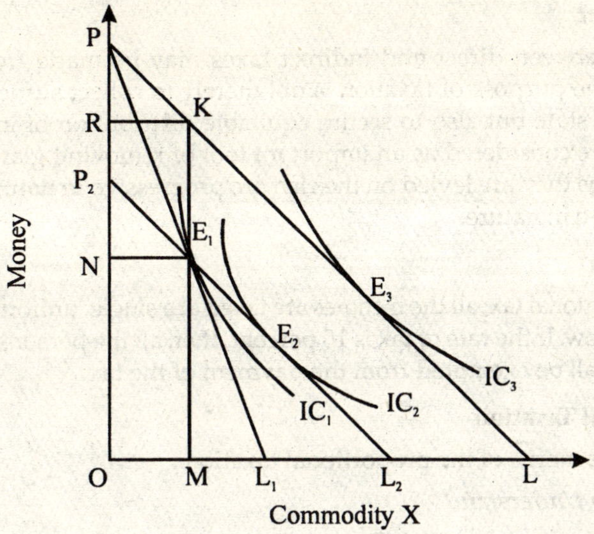

Now suppose an excise duty (an indirect tax) is levied on commodity X and it is included in the price so that the increase in price is equal to the amount of tax imposed. As a result of the rise in price of good X, the new price line will be PL_1 which is tangent to indifference curve IC_1 at point E_1. It shows that as a result of the imposition of excise duty, the individual has shifted from a higher indifference curve IC_3 to a lower one IC_1, that is, his level of satisfaction has decreased. Now the consumer can buy only OM quantity of commodity X and spends PN amount of money to buy it. At the old price (before the imposition of the excise duty), he could purchase OM quantity for PR amount of money. Thus the difference RN or KE_1 is the excise duty which the individual is paying.

Now suppose the same amount of revenue RN or KE_1 is collected by the government through a direct tax, say income-tax. In this case, the consumer's disposable income is reduced by the amount of tax RN and as such the new price line P_2L_2 is drawn at such a distance that it passes through the point E_1 and is parallel to the price line PL (because the income has been reduced by cost difference). In this situation, the consumer is in equilibrium at point E_2 on indifference curve IC_2 which lies at a higher level than IC_1. It means at point E_2 the consumer's level of welfare is higher than that at E_1. In other words, income-tax has reduced the individual's welfare less than that by the excise duty. Hence, an indirect tax imposes an excess burden on the consumer.

B. Administrative Aspect

From the point of view of administrative cost and efficiency, indirect taxes are considered superior to those of direct taxes because the latter are not imposed on low incomes because of their unpleasant nature and administrative cost. Thus it is not possible to make every body contribute to the finances of the state through direct taxes. Prof. Prest asserts that in an economy where there are large number of small, independent producers or illiterate people who are incapable of maintaining accounts and where majority of the people may be living at subsistence level, indirect taxation is more desirable than direct taxation on administrative grounds.

C. Distributive Aspect

A comparison between direct and indirect taxes may be made from the point of view of distribution effects. The purpose of taxation is not merely to collect sufficient revenue to meet the financial needs of the state but also to secure equitable distribution of income and wealth in the society. Direct taxes are considered as an important tool of removing glaring inequalities between the rich and the poor as they are levied on the rich are progressive in nature whereas indirect taxes are generally regressive in nature.

Proportional Taxation

Under the proportional tax, all the incomes are taxed at a single, uniform rate, no matter whether the income is high or low. If the rate of tax is 10 percent, then all the persons shall have to pay the tax at this rate. No one shall be exempted from the payment of the tax.

Merits of Proportional Taxation

Following are the merits of the proportional taxation :

1. Simple and Easy to Understand

It is simple and easy to understand. Even a person with an ordinary intelligence can understand its implication without any difficulty.

2. Easy to Estimate the Amount of Tax

Under the proportional tax, the tax payers can easily estimate the amount of tax which they will have to pay the government.

3. No structural Change in the Socio-economic Set-up

There is no change in the existing distribution of wealth in society as a result of proportional tax, because all the tax payers pay the tax at a single, uniform rate. This involves no structural change in socio-economic set-up of the country.

Demerits of Proportional Taxation

Following are the demerits of proportional taxation :

1. Greater Sacrifices on the Part of the Poor

The burden of taxation falls more heavily on the poor sections of the society as a result of proportional tax because as the income of an individual increases, his marginal utility from money diminishes. If the rich and the poor are taxed at the same rate, then it is clear that the poorer sections will be making greater sacrifices than the richer sections.

2. Social Equality is a Myth

The proportional taxes do not reduce the current inequalities of income in society. Rather they continue status quo in society.

Progressive Taxation

Under progressive tax, an exemption limit is fixed and all those persons whose income is less than that limit, are granted exemption from the payment of the tax. Moreover, the rate of tax goes on increasing with the increase in income. For example, Rates of Income-tax applicable to individuals are as follows :

Slabs of Net Income	*Rates of Income-tax*
Upto Rs. 50,000	Nil
Rs. 50,001 to Rs. 60,000	10%
Rs. 60,001 to Rs. 1,50,000	20%
Above 1,50,000	30%

Merits of Progressive Taxation

Following are the merits of a progressive taxation :

1. Based on 'Ability to Pay'

The tax payer does not oppose this type of tax as this takes into account of the ability to pay.

2. Equality in Wealth Distribution

The distribution of wealth in society can be made more equitable under progressive taxation because the richer persons are required to pay the tax at higher rates than the poorer persons.

3. Productive in Nature

The government can effect a substantial increase in its income through progressive taxation. It can bring about a sizable increase in its revenue through increase in tax rates during a period of crisis.

4. It is Less Expensive

It is economical in the sense that the government can bring about a sizable increase in its income through increases in rates without any increase in cost of collection.

5. Elastic

It is elastic in the sense that with minor changes in the rates, substantial changes can be brought about in the income of the government.

6. Morally Just

It is justified on moral grounds that the richer section should bear a heavier burden of taxation than the poorer section.

Demerits of Progressive Taxation

Following are the demerits of progressive taxation :

1. Rates of Tax

The rates are fixed by the government in an arbitrary manner under progressive taxation.

2. Discourage to Savings

Discouraged savings is another point of drawback of this system.

3. Evasion of Tax

There is always a considerable scope for tax evasion under a system of progressive taxation. The tax payer invariably tries to evade the payment of the tax by presenting false statement of accounts before the taxation authorities.

Difference between Proportional and Progressive Taxation

Under the proportional tax all the incomes are taxed at a single rate which is uniform, no matter whether the income is high or low. For example if the rate of tax is 10% then all the persons shall have to pay the tax at this rate. No one shall be exempted from the payment of the tax.

Under the progressive tax, the rate goes on increasing with the increase in income. This tax has two important characteristics, Firstly, an exemption limit is fixed under a progressive tax. All those persons whose income is less than that limit are granted exemption from the payment of the tax. Secondly, the rate of the tax goes on increasing with increase in income. The progressive tax is sometimes also referred to as graduated tax.

Regressive Tax and Digressive Tax

A regressive tax is first the opposite of progressive tax. It imposes a heavier burden on the poor than on the rich. For example, a regressive tax is one in which the rate of tax decreases as the income of the tax payer increases. This type of tax is very rare these days.

A digressive tax also imposes like the progressive tax, heavier burden on the poor than the rich. This tax is a mixture of progressive and proportional taxation. The tax is progressive up to a certain extent but becomes proportional after that limit. Digressive taxation is also very rare these days.

Simple Tax System and Multiple Tax System

Single Tax System

Under this system, only one tax is levied which can be on agricultural production, income of individuals or any commodity.

Single Tax on Agriculture. Physiocrates believed that it is only agriculture which can be a remunerative source of income and therefore it should be taxed but this has the following drawbacks:

1. Insufficient Income

Only agricultural income tax may not be sufficient to the government in view of its ever increasing functions not a days.

2. Against the Point of Justice

This type of tax brings only the farmers within the network of taxation while capitalist remain outside. Since agricultural commodities are mostly consumed by the poor, they become the sufferers and therefore, the single tax on only agricultural income is unjust.

Single Tax on Income. Some thinkers have advocated only income tax in the form of single tax. They opine that tax is paid out of income and therefore, the individuals should be taxed only with regard to their level of income. Prof. H. Dalton however preferred income tax to land revenue but yet he did not take it as sufficient in the form of revenue to the government.

In view of the above defects, single tax is not looked upon as a practical proposition and all the countries have adopted multiple tax system in place of single tax system.

Multiple Tax System

Modern governments impose more than one tax, like — income tax, property tax, wealth tax, gift tax, death duty, production cess, import duty etc., as a source earning revenue. Multiple tax system is very popular now-a-days and one characteristic present in such type of tax system is that they can be made progressive.

Merits of Multiple System. Following are the merits of multiple tax system :

(a) The government gets adequate income as per its requirement.

(b) The tax system can be made progressive.

(c) Tax evasion can be prevented by following suitable measures.

It is due to the above merits of multiple tax system that its importance is increasing day-by-day.

Specific Tax and Ad Valorem Tax

Indirect taxes can be broadly classified into two categories :

1. Specific Tax

Specific tax is levied on the basis of number, size or weight of the commodity. If a tax is collected at the rate of Rs. 50/- per metric ton weight of commodity, it will be an example of specific tax.

2. AD Valorem Tax

Such type of tax is levied according to the price of the commodity. Sales tax is a tax of this type which keeps the price of the commodity in its consideration.

It is be noted that both these taxes are complementary to each other.

Incidence of Taxation

The theory of incidence of taxation studies the conditions and the process of shifting of taxes. It also studies the proportion in which the direct money burden of a tax is shared between different persons. For a clear-cut understanding of the theory it is necessary to know the definition of impact, shifting and incidence of a tax.

The impact of a tax is on the person who pays it in the first instance. The impact of an import duty is on the importer of that commodity. The impact of an excise duty is on the producer. The impact of house tax is on the landlord. Through these people pay the tax to the government they try to shift as much of it as possible to others.

Shifting

It is the Process by which a tax is passed from one person to another. The shifting of a tax can be done only through the changes in the prices of goods and services. Shifting may be forward or backward. For example, the importer who pays the import duty might shift a part of it to the retailers by increasing the prices of imported goods. It is called forward shifting. If the importer however succeeds in shifting the tax to the manufactures in foreign countries by paying them a lower price of goods, it will be called backward shifting. Similarly a producer paying an excise duty might shift a part of it to the consumers (forward shifting) and other part of it to the supplier of raw materials, machineries and other factors of production (backward shifting).

Incidence

It is the final money burden of a tax on a person who is not able to shift it any further to anyone else. In other words, it is always on the person who ultimately pays a tax, that is, who finally bears the burden of tax. A consumer paying a higher price for the imported goods on account of impor duty is not able to shift the burden to someone else. Therefore, the incidence of tax falls on him and the burden of money, he himself should bear. A labourer has to bear the final money burden of that portion of excise duty, which falls on him through a reduction in his money wages and which he is not able to shift anywhere.

Factors Determining Incidence of a Tax

1. Nature of demand and supply

By far the most important factor effecting incidence is the nature of demand and supply of commodities. So far as this factor is concerned two most important principles can be laid down. (a) Other things remaining the same, greater the elasticity of demand for the commodity taxed, greater are the chances of incidence being on the seller. (b) Other things being equal, greater the elasticity of supply it is more likely that the incidence will be on the consumers.

2. Nature of Tax

Taxes may be either direct or indirect. Direct taxes cannot be shifted. So incidence and the impact are on one and the same person. Indirect taxes on the other hand are those which can be easily shifted, the impact and the incidence of indirect taxes are on two different persons. Hence it can be said that direct taxes cannot be easily shifted while indirect taxes can be easily shifted.

3. Size of Tax

Whether a tax can be shifted or not depends on the size of the tax. If the tax is a very small amount, the seller may bear the tax himself, instead of passing it on to the customers. If, on the other hand, the amount of tax is big the seller may pass it on either wholly or partially to the consumers.

4. Presence of substitutes

The presence of substitutes also affect the incidence of a tax. If a taxed commodity is to compete with a rival untaxed commodity (substituted) it may lead to a diversion of demand from the taxed to the untaxed commodity. As a result the seller of taxed commodity (substituted) it may lead to a diversion of demand from the taxed to the untaxed commodity. As a result the seller of taxed commodity may have to beat the burden of tax. Therefore, the presence of more substitutes reduces the possibility of incidence of taxation being shifted from one to another. But it must be admitted that of the factors discussed above, elasticity of demand and supply is very influential.

Incidence of Direct Taxes : Direct taxes cannot be easily shifted.

1. Income Tax

Prof. Dalton maintains that income tax in general cannot be shifted. It is also felt that a part of the income tax could be shifted in the long run. But it is not true.

2. Direct Tax on Profit

This tax cannot be shifted. If the seller could increase his profit by increasing the price of commodity or any other means he would have already done it, such a tax is not a part of cost of production, but a tax on the success in enterprise.

3. Tax on Unearned Income

Even this tax cannot be shifted because by definition no effort has been made to earn that income.

4. Expenditure Tax

Since this tax is on expenditure and not on buying particular commodity it cannot be avoided by shifting the expenditure from one direction to another. The only way of avoiding it is by not increasing that expenditure.

Incidence of Indirect taxes

1. Import duties

They are paid in the first instance by the importers. Therefore the impact of tax is on importer. But the incidence of import duties may be either on domestic consumer or on the foreign seller. Therefore, import duties may be shifted, either forward or backward. Usually incidence of such duties is on the local buyer and only in exceptional circumstances it will be shifted backward to the foreign exporters. Backward shifting may take place under certain conditions. They are : (a) If the demand for foreign goods in the local market is elastic. (b) If the supply of foreign goods in the local market is inelastic, (c) If the local market is the only market where foreigner sells his goods. (d) If the imported goods have to compete with the rival untaxed substitutes.

2. Excise Duties

It is a tax levied as a specified amount per unit upon a product which is produced at home. It is collected from the producers in the first instance. The shifting of the tax depends on the degree of elasticity of demand and supply. An excise tax will increase they price of a product. And hence at least a part of a tax will be shifted forward to the consumers. To a certain extent there can be a backward shifting, that is, a part of a tax may be shifted to the factors of production.

Incidence under perfect competition : If the perfect competition is present in the industry the tax will be considered as a part of normal cost of production. Therefore it will be shifted in full to the consumers. Under perfect competition in the long rum profits will be normal. Therefore, no producer will bear the burden of tax though he does it in the short run. This is because in the short run some firms will earn super normal profit, some normal profit, and some others minimum loss. But in the long run, if any producer is not able to cover the cost, including the tax he will leave the industry. If this tendency continues and more producer leave the market, because they will not be able to cover the loss, the supply will decrease. Ultimately price will rise to such an extent where the producers are able to cover the cost and earn only normal profits.

Incidence under Monopoly : Whether a tax should be shifted to consumers or it will be borne by the monopolist himself depends on the nature of tax. If a tax is a lumpsum on the monopolist profit the incidence of tax will be on the producer himself. Since a monopolist gets maximum profit, he will not alter the price and output equilibrium even when he has to pay lumpsum tax. But more often a tax on production under monopoly will be conveniently shifted to the consumers. Of course, this depends upon elasticity of demand for the goods.

Taxable Capacity

In simple words, taxable capacity means the maximum capacity of the people of a country to bear the burden of the tax and if the government exceeds this limit, it shall result in over taxation, which besides being injurious to the long-term interests of the community, may pose a serious threat to the political stability of the country concerned.

The concept of taxable capacity has been so loosely used that Prof. H. Dalton has called it a concept of illusory and ambiguous nature.

According to the opinion of Mr. Josiah Stamp, "Taxable capacity is the maximum amount which the citizens can pay to the public authorities without having a really unhappy and downtrodden existence and without dislocating the economic organization too much".

Now, so far as this definition of taxable capacity is concerned, the clause 'without dislocating economic organisation too much' and 'without having a really, unhappy and down-trodden existence' are very much confusing. In simple words, taxable capacity can be defined as follows :

Taxable capacity of a country is that quantity of tax which can be realised without adversely affecting the production and economic stability and interrupting the desired pace of economic development.

Different Concepts of Taxable Capacity

There are three concepts of taxable capacity in vogue which are as follows :

(a) Absolute and Relative Taxable Capacity.

(b) Minimum Optimum and Maximum Taxable Capacity.

(c) National Sacrifice Capacity.

Absolute and Relative Taxable Capacity

The concept of relative taxable capacity is of greater practical importance than the concept of absolute taxable capacity.

The absolute taxable capacity is represented by the difference between total production and total consumption. According to Josiah Stamp, there are two limits to the taxable capacity of the country —

(a) Check to total production, and

(b) Check to total revenue yield as a result of the imposition of the higher ratio of taxation. If an increase in taxation results in a lower production and does not bring an additional revenue to the government, then it should be presumed that the taxable capacity of the country has been reached.

The relative taxable capacity refers to the proportion in which two or more than two communities can contribute, in the form of taxes, in order to meet some common expenditure. Thus, the richer community of the country will be called upon to contribute more than the weaker sections.

Factors Influencing Taxable Capacity

The taxable capacity of a country is influenced by the following factors :

1. Total Wealth of a Country

The taxable capacity of a country is directly related with its total wealth. If the total wealth of a country is more, its people will have corresponding greater taxable capacity and vice versa.

2. Distribution of Income and Wealth

Other things remaining the same, the unequal distribution of wealth does have its positive effect on the taxable capacity of a country. If there is equal distribution of wealth resulting in small amount of wealth with the people of a country, it will be then impossible to realise desired amount of tax from them.

3. Size of Population

The taxable capacity of the country will be affected adversely if the national income of a country does not increase in proportion to the increase in population.

4. From and Nature of Tax System

The taxable capacity of a country will be more if the burden of tax is distributed equitably in the country.

5. Psychology of the Tax Payers

The taxable capacity of a country is influenced to a large extent by the psychology of the tax payer. For example, the taxable capacity of the Indian people went up during the Chinese Aggression on India in October 1962, because the people of India being inspired by partition, were themselves prepared to pay more taxes to the government in order to enable it to prosecute was successfully.

6. Stage of Economic Development

Ordinarily, the taxable capacity in industrially advanced countries is higher than that of the backward and under-developed countries.

7. Nature of the Government

A democratically elected government, by winning public sympathy and co-operation, is in a position to raise more revenues from the people.

8. Inflation

The prices of goods and services invariably rise on account of the inflationary forces but the money income of the people remains more or less unchanged. So, their real income declines and thus the taxable capacity of the people declines in that proportion.

9. Nature of Government Expenditure

If the government incurs a major portion of its expenditure on encouraging production and increasing the level of efficiency of the workers, this will raise the taxable capacity of the country.

10. Standard of Living

If the standard of living of the people is high, their productive power shall also be high. Hence, their income shall be high and consequently, their capacity to pay taxes will also increase to the same proportion.

Effects of Taxation

Taxation has far-reaching effects on the economic organisation. The effects may be either good or bad, depending on the intensity and nature of taxes. Therefore a taxing authority must give importance not only to revenue aspects but also to the economic aspects. According to Dalton, the best system of taxation from the economic point of view, is that which has the best or the least bad economic effects.

A. Effects of Production

According to Dalton the effects of taxation on production can be studied under :

(1) Effects on ability to work, save and invest

All taxes reduce the net income of individuals. If the tax reduces standard of life of a worker, it reduces his efficiency as well as the efficiency of his children. Hence production will also suffer. E.g. a tax on necessaries and comforts will reduce the standard of living of the poor and his ability to work hard and save more. Therefore low income groups should not be taxed heavily. However all taxes on liquor and opium will reduce the consumption of those goods but will increase the ability to work and save most. Ability to invest depends on resources avfailable for investment. i.e., savings. The ability to invest will increase through the increased savings which is the result of hard work and higher efficiency.

(2) Effects on desire to work, save and invest

(a) With regard to effects of taxation on desire to work, save and invest, no general rule can be laid down. Everything depends on the individual's nature and circumstances.

(b) In case of some men, taxation will discourage them from working hard, and save and invest more. In case of others, especially those who have dependents to maintain, taxation will encourage them to put forth greater efforts to earn extra money to pay taxes.

(c) But certain extra taxes do not damage the desire to work and save. It is because the burden of tax may not be much. E.g., A tax on capital gains may not discourage the people to save and work.

(d) The effects of tax on desire to invest depends on the nature of tax, i.e. If a tax is an indirect one, it can be passed on to consumers and thus producers will not feel discouraged to invest. However the desire to save and invest also depends on the elasticity of demand for the goods taxed. If the demand for goods is very elastic, a tax cannot be shifted and it will be borne by producers themselves. The corporate income tax will increase the desire to save and invest.

(3) Effects on Division of Trade and Capital

A tax will also divert the resources from one trade to another. A protective duty on cotton mill industry, develops that industry far and wide as people are encouraged to invest their capital on it. A tax on harmful drugs will raise their price or thus their demand will be curtailed much. As a result all resources including employment will be diverted from that industry to another. In a developing economy decrease in tax on consumer goods and a heavy tax on luxuries will ultimately divert the trade and capital from luxuries to consumer goods industries. A tax concession in backward areas will attract new industries in these areas.

Taxation may also result in the diversion of capital from one country to another. Heavy taxation at home may drive capital to neighbouring countries where taxation is less heavy. Prof. Dalton points out that the effects of taxation on production depends on a wise policy of public expenditure. If the proceeds of taxation are wisely spent, the incentive to produce due to this expenditure may be greater than the check to production due to taxation.

B. Effects of Taxation on Distribution

One of the aims of taxation in modern economy is to reduce the inequalities of income. It was Prof. Wangner of Germany who pointed out that taxation should be used to reduce the inequalities. Therefore progressive taxes like income tax, inheritance tax, etc., tend to remove the inequalities in wealth. The effect of taxation on the rich is to raise the standard of the poor and thereby increase their efficiency. In this regard, though the gain of the community goes up, the ability of the rich to save more will go down. As a result it may entail in a fall in capital formation and employment. Therefore, heavy tax on the rich in the long run ultimately proves dangerous to the community. But all direct taxes that fall heavily on all higher income groups can have favourable distribution effects. But it may also lead to evasion and avoidance of taxes.

The indirect taxes more often fall heavily on lower income groups that spend on larger portion of their income on those goods. Therefore indirect taxes are generally regressive in nature. To avoid a heavy fall of tax (burden) on lower income groups, certain commodities may be exempted from taxes and some others may be taxed heavily. E.g., luxuries may be taxed heavily, while necessaries may be taxed lightly. Precisely it can be said that the direct taxes will serve the purpose of removing the inequalities of income better than the lower income group.

C. Other Effects

(a) ***Taxes should also effect the economic stability :*** Economic stability refers to the maintenance of equilibrium level in trade, employment through their influence on consumption and investment. Thus an adverse tax badly hampers consumption and investment leading to unemployment and instability.

(b) ***Effects of tax on inflation and deflation :*** A heavy tax on income will lead to inflation as people will become extravagant. However taxation on expenditure and sales on the other hand will lead to deflation or depression. The burden of tax must be lighter. Besides, tax concessions will lead to an increase in investment and production. The aims of a tax during these periods are either to increase or decrease the level of consumption through the changes in income and to increase or decrease the supply of money.

Characteristics of a Goods Tax System

The study of a tax system is to be done as a whole. A goods tax system should have the following characteristics

1. Equity

The burden of a tax in a good taxation system should be the minimum. A long with that, it should be distributed amongst the different sections of the community in a just and equitable manner. Heaviest burden should be borne by the broadest shoulders.

From the point of equity, the Indian tax system leaves much to be desired. Predominance of indirect taxes in the Indian tax system reflects the inequitable nature of this system.

2. Inclusive of all the Canons of Taxation

A good tax system should contain all the principles of taxation, like – equity, flexibility, productivity, simplicity, diversity etc.

3. Productivity

The tax system should be such as to provide adequate income to the government to meet its expenditure. From the point of productivity, the Indian tax system leaves much to be desired. The Indian income tax system for example, produces adverse reaction of the citizens on the incentive to work.

4. Elasticity

Two things are essential to bring about elasticity in the tax system. Firstly, there should be proper blending of direct and indirect taxes. Secondly, certain sources of income should be exclusively reserved for emergencies such as, war, etc.

The Indian tax system satisfies the canon of elasticity in a sufficient measure in sofar as the income of the government keeps on increasing in accordance with its requirements.

5. Convenience

While devising the tax system of the country, the government should also keep in mind the convenience of the tax payer because the tax payers make sacrifices when they pay the tax.

6. Absence of Tax Evasion

To achieve this objective, there should be proper blending of all sorts of commodity and personal taxes and this will reduce the scope for tax evasion to the minimum. There is at present a large-scale evasion of the income tax going on in the country, especially by the business classes.

7. Maximum Social Advantage

The tax system should satisfy the objective of Maximum Social Advantage. It should not adversely affect trade and industry of the country. According to H. Dalton, "That system of taxation is the best which is based on principle of maximum social advantage". The objective of every tax system should be to promote the greatest good of the greatest number. It is doubtful if the Indian tax system satisfies this canon of maximum social advantage.

Indian Tax System

A number of characteristics of a good tax system are found in Indian tax system. Both types of taxes, direct and indirect taxes, are levied in our country. Income tax is of progressive nature and tax collection charges are also not very high. Land revenue is paid after harvesting season is off and that too in installments. It thus contains merit of convenience also but at the same time following drawbacks are also found in Indian Tax System

1. More Burden of Indirect Taxes

The burden of indirect taxes which is especially borne by the poor strata of society is growing day-by-day such a pace that this class is very much concerned to meet its requirements of minimum level of standard of living.

2. Adverse Effects on Production and Distribution

The people in India have to pay tax on entertainment then they have also pay tax on the death. The traders and manufacturers are adversely affected by the burden of tax.

3. Uncertainty about Government Revenue

The revenue of government is not certain as 41% of the total revenue is derived from agriculture which is still a gamble in monsoon.

4. Faulty Distribution of Revenue Resources

The distribution of the sources of income between centre, state and local government is defective.

5. Lack of Progressivity

Indian tax system is not progressive. Only income tax is progressive but here is sounds ludicrous that two individuals with the same income are taxed at the same rate irrespective of the fact that one of them has six children and the other has none.

6. Not Administratively Good

The government employees are very much involved in corruption. The people mostly resort the malpractice of tax evasion.

7. Lack of Desirable Flexibility

The Indian tax system is not elastic. The increase in national income should be accompanied by economic property also which is not the case at present in India.

8. Inactive

The tax system should be as such as can boost investment and production both but Indian tax system does not meet this test.

Conclusion

From the above discussion, undoubtedly, we can say that, Public Revenue occupies the same important place in the study of public finance which production occupies in the study of economics. Public revenue include public debt as well along with all types of receipts by the government. But this interpretation of public revenue is not acceptable now-a-days.

Questions for Discussion

1. What is meant by Public Revenue ? Mention the main sources of Public Revenue.
2. Mention the various classifications of Public Revenue.
3. Define Tax. Discuss the aims of imposing taxes in modern times.
4. Discuss critically the various Canons of Taxation.
5. Distinguish between Direct and Indirect Taxes. Discuss their relative merits.
6. Explain proportional and progressive taxation and consider their merits and demerits.
7. Discuss the effects of taxation on production and distribution.
8. Define Incidence of Taxation. Describe the factors which govern the incidence of Taxation.
9. What is Taxable capacity ? How is it measured.
10. Discuss the Chief characteristics of a good tax system.

Chapter - 3

PUBLIC EXPENDITURE

Introduction

The study of public expenditure occupies the same important place in the study of public finance which the study of consumption occupies in the study of the macro-economics. As consumption is the end of all economic activities so also public expenditure is the end of all financial activities of the state. Thus, public expenditure is the most important part of the study of public finance.

Meaning

Public expenditure is the beginning as well as end of all state functions. The scope of state functions was very limited in olden times. Public expenditure, therefore, assumed no such importance in those days as it is today. The modern governments not only perform such primary functions as the civil administration as well as defence of the country, but also take considerable interest in promoting the economic development of their respective countries.

Differences between Public Expenditure and Private Expenditure

Following are the differences between public expenditure and private expenditure :

1. Difference in Income Expenditure Adjustment

The government gets an estimate of its expenditure on various projects and then it finds out sources of revenue to meet out the estimated expenditure as against the individual who is engaged in cutting his coat according to his cloth.

2. Difference on Objectives

The object of private expenditure is to increase its own welfare including that of its family while public expenditure is done for the welfare of society and the nation as a whole.

3. Difference in Flexibility

Private expenditure is flexible and can be curtailed at case but the public expenditure is inflexible the departments of administration give priority to their own demands first.

4. Difference in Control

In case of private expenditure, an individual is free to exercise control while in case of public expenditure, the government is not free to do so.

5. Difference in Area

The items of expenditure are not so wide as those of the government which takes resort to liberal policy in order to meet its liabilities.

6. Difference in Effect

Public expenditure affects the whole of the nation and society as against the individual who himself is affected by his own expenditure.

7. Difference in Economy

Public expenditure is not economical as public servants do not feel much concerned while spendings on behalf of the government. An individual applies equi-marginal utility law in getting maximum satisfaction from his limited resources which defies application in public expenditure.

Causes of Increase in Public Expenditure

Public expenditure has increase manifold in recent times and it continues to be increasing with the passage of time due to the following factors.

1. Democratic Governments

Twentieth century is an age of democracy and democratic governments are for the people. They have to perform an increasing number of functions to satisfy the diverse needs of the people. In democracy, there are a number of political parties in the country and each party is anxious to win the support and sympathy of the people. The supporters of each party clamour for more and more facilities and benefits in the form of more education, more schools and colleges, more hospitals, more roads, greater transport facilities etc. All this has led to a phenomenal increase in public expenditure.

2. Welfare States

Modern states are not police states but welfare states, The days of lassez-faire are gone and dead. The belief of the classical economists that economic system can function smoothly without state intervention and is capable of creating conditions of full employment of human and economic resources has been falsified. On the other hand, Keynes and others with their penetrating analysis have shown beyond any --- of doubt that the state must intervene in the economic system --- secure economic stabilisation in the developed countries and accelerated rate of economic growth in the under-developed countries. This has necessitated the adoption of the strategy of planned economic development involving huge expenditure.

3. War and prevention of War

This is another factor which has increased public expenditure to astronomical heights. Modern wars are very expensive. The nature of warfare has fundamentally changed. The weapons of mass destructions costing crores and crores of rupees are being manufactured. The conventional weapons have lost their importance. Even if there is no war, the constant fear of war and the measures to prevent it have obliged the government to maintain large armies and spend the major portion of their national income on the manufacture of war weapons. This has obviously led tq a huge increase in public expenditure.

4. Collective Satisfaction of Wants

Many wants which were formerly satisfied through private expenditure are not satisfied collectively through public expenditure with a view to reap the advantages of large scale production and avoiding exploitation, wastefulness and duplication. This has led to a phenomenal increase in public expenditure.

5. Increase in the Price Level

Under the impact of the factors, discussed above the prices of all goods and services have increased very considerably in recent times. Consequently, the governments have to pay more of the goods and services it purchases in the market to meet its requirements and hence an increase in public expenditure.

6. Increase in Territory and Population

The physical boundaries of modern states have expanded and small states of the old Greek times have disappeared through the process of unification. Only big states can survive these days and make economic progress. The increase in area of the state has resulted in an increase in the cost of administration. Even if the area has remained the same, the increase in population has contributed to the increase in public expenditure as the governments have to came to the needs of every-increasing population.

7. Urbanisation

With economic development, there is urbanisation of population on a large scale which implies larger per capita expenditure on civic amenities and hence an increase in public expenditure.

8. Nationalisation of Industries and Trade

There is a manifest tendency on the part of modern governments to provide goods and services to the people on a more or less commercial basis. The government are doing so with a view to prevent the exploitation of consumers by private monopoles ; to secure equitable distribution of wealth ; to provide a yard stick for private operation ad to earn profit for the treasury. But the setting up and the management of these enterprises and the payment of compensation has resulted in a tremendous increase in public expenditure.

9. Public Debt

Inherent deficiencies of the free market economy have resulted in economic instability and wide-spread unemployment and under-employment. Consequently the state is called upon to undertake various regulatory and anti-cyclical measures which have lead to enormous increaser in public expenditure. To meet this expenditure, the governments are obliged to borrow on a large scale and this has led to an increase in public expenditure in the form of increasing cost of debt servicing and repayment of the debts.

10. Increase in National Income

With economic development, the national income of the countries has increased many times. Consequently public revenue by way of taxation has also increased and this has led to an increase in public expenditure.

11. Defective Financial Administration

The government are known for extravagance and waste. More often than no, there is duplication and unnecessary multiplicity in government agencies which results in an increase in public expenditure.

Wagner's Views on Public Expenditure

A German economist, Adolph Wagner (1835-1917) writing in 1883, gave a law called the **"law of ever increosing state activity"** on historical facts, primarily of Germany. He based his law on "pressure for social progress" and pointed out that there is a persistent tendency for the activities of different layers of a government—central and states to increase both intensively and extensively. This is because the traditional functions of the state are expanding and are being performed more satisfactorily and efficiently than before and new functions particularly in the sphere of public goods are being undertaken on an increasing scale.

Wagner divided public expenditure into two categories

(a) expenditure for internal and external security and

(b) that for "culture and welfare" which implies education, health, transport, recreation, banking etc. With the change in the nature of the 'use' of force by the state from simple aggression to the prevention of attack and use of more sophisticated weapons, the expenditure for external security would increase. Similarly, according to Wanger, the expenditure on internal security would also increase due to greater friction between economic units and people as urbanisation would progress.

Recently Wiseman and Peacock in their study of public expenditure in U.K. for the period 1890–1955 have revealed that Wagner's Law is still operating but according to their study, the expenditure grows with the growth of revenue. Further, the cost of providing public services increases with economic growth.

Classification of Public Expenditure

By classification of public expenditure, we mean an arrangement of public expenditure in a way which can give us an idea of the nature and objectives of public activities. Classification of Public Expenditure can be explained as follows :

I. Classification Based on Benefits

Plehn and *canon* of 19th century have given this classification in view of the benefits received by the different sections of the society. Plehn has given the following four fold classification of public expenditure :

(a) The expenditure affecting the society in general such as expenditure on health and education of society.

(b) The expenditure done specifically to benefit the particular class of people who cannot help themselves such as medical insurance, old age pension unemployment allowance.

(c) The expenditure which affects only a particular section of the society like expenditure on state enterprises.

(d) The expenditure affecting not only a particular section of society but the society as a whole.

Criticism : It is not easy to separate different sections mentioned in this classification from each other.

II. Classification Based on Expenditure

Prof. Nicklson has classified public expenditure on the basis of revenue accruing from public expenditure as follows :

(a) The expenditure which does not give any revenue to the government such as was expenditure, assistance given by the state to the poor.

(b) The expenditure which does not directly give any revenue to the government directly but indirectly affects public revenue such as free-education etc.

(c) The expenditure which affects partially the public revenue such as expenditures on judiciary etc.

(d) The expenditure which affects public revenue such as expenditure done on railways, post offices, roads etc.

Criticism : This classification does not describe the peculiar characteristics of public expenditure. As a matter of fact, there is no item of public expenditure which does not directly increase public revenue.

III. Classification Based on Functions

Prof. Adam's has distributed public expenditure in the following three heads :

(a) The expenditure by the government to provide safety to the life and property of the people of the country such as police, military, courts and water etc.

(b) The expenditure done to promote trade industry and commerce of the country such as railways, telegraph, transportation etc.

(c) The expenditure done by the government for the development of the country and public welfare such as education, entertainment, social insurance etc.

IV. Mill's Classification

J.S.Mill has criticised the classification of public expenditure made by Prof Adam's and has given the following classification of public expenditure :

(a) Indispensable Expenditure : Such type of expenditure is indispensable as per the legal restrictions such as defence, justice etc.

(b) Voluntary Expenditure : Such type of expenditure depends upon the will of the government such as expenditure on railways and state enterprises.

Criticism : Such type of public expenditure classification is not scientific as it is not simple and easy to classify public expenditure into voluntary and non-voluntary types.

V. Shirras' Classification

Findley Shirras has distributed public expenditure in the following heads :

(a) Primary public expenditure which is done primarily for defence and establishment of peace in the country.

(b) Secondary public expenditure done for the upliftment of society forms this category of expenditure.

VI. Pigou's Classification

A.C. Pigou has distributed public expenditure in the following heads :

(a) Transferable Expenditure : Which is done for the benefit of the people of the country such as unemployment benefits.

(b) Non-transferable Expenditure : Which is done exclusively for its own benefit such as administrative expenditure.

VII. Public Expenditure Based on Administration Unit

Some experts have classified public expenditure as follows :

(a) Central Government Expenditure : This is the expenditure done by the Central Government of India like expenditure on defence of the country.

(b) State Government Expenditure : Such expenditure is done by state government like expenditure on police, agriculture, education etc.

(c) Local Government Expenditure : The expenditure done by Municipality, Zila Parishad or panchayats is local government expenditure.

VIII. American Classification

In America expenditure by the government has been classified on functional basis. The expenditure has been classified as follows :

(a) National Security.

(b) Labour Welfare.

(c) Agriculture.

(d) Commerce and Housing.

(e) International Power.

(f) Natural Resources.

(g) Interest.

(h) Essential Services.

(i) General Administration.

Principles or Canons of Public Expenditure

Every Government keeps the following principles or canons in mind while arranging its expenditure :

1. Cannot of Maximum Social Benefit

The government should incur its expenditure in a manner as to promote the greatest good of the greatest number. There should be maximum increase in production as a consequence of public expenditure. The government should follow the law of equi-marginal utilities in the same manner as an individual does to attain maximum satisfaction out of its expenditure.

2. Canon of Economy

The expenditure of the government should involve no wastage of any kind. Besides, it should produce no adverse effects on production. Along with that it is also essential for the government to see that its expenditure does not produce adverse reactions on the will and power of the people to save.

3. Canon of Sanction

This canon implies that before incurring any expenditure, the government department concerned should take proper sanction from the competent authority.

4. Canon of Elasticity

The canon implies that there should be as much elasticity in public expenditure as possible. In other words, there should be scope for changes in public expenditure according to the requirements of the country.

5. Canon of Productivity

This canon implies that public expenditure should encourage production and productivity both in the economy. As such, a sizeable part of the public expenditure in an economy should be incurred for developmental purposes.

6. Canon of Equality

The public expenditure should bring about maximum equality in the distribution of wealth. If the increased wealth is allowed to swell the pocket of the already rich, the canon of equality would stand defeated.

7. Canon of Balanced Income and Expenditure

According to this canon, the government budget should neither be a surplus budget nor a deficit budget. It should be a balanced budget. But the supporters of functional finance, however, do not agree with this canon. They advocate an unbalanced budget i.e., surplus budget at a time of boom and deficit budget at a time of slump.

Effects of Public Expenditure

The effect of public expenditure is increasing day by day in modern times. Public expenditure affects the economy of any nation significantly. It can bring about the desired changes in the economy of a country by affecting employment, distribution of wealth and production. The effects of public expenditure can be studied under the following three heads :

I. Effects of Public Expenditure on Production.

II. Effects of Public expenditure on Distribution.

III. Effects of Public Expenditure on Economic Stability. Details regarding these are as follows :

I. Effects of Public Expenditure on Production

H. Dalton has discussed the effects of public expenditure on production under the following three sub-heads.

1. ***Effects on the Power to Work and to Save :*** A part of the public expenditure invariably increase the power to work and to save of the people. For example, the government incurs expenditure on the provision of education, medical facilities, cheap housing etc., to the people. This inevitably increases the efficiency of the people. Consequently, their power to work increases and this results in an increase in their income. Thus, there comes about an improvement in the power to save of the people. Likewise, when the government incurs expenditure on agriculture, industry etc., this increases the productive capacity of the country concerned.
2. ***Effects on the will to Work and Save :*** A part of the public expenditure is invariably incurred on the provision of social security services to the people. Under the social insurance schemes, the workers are paid old-age pensions, unemployment allowances and provided free medical aid in case of sickness. This type of public expenditure produces an unfavourable effect on the will, to work and to save, of the workers. When the government provides this type of social security to the workers, they invariably become indifferent towards their future and start saving less than what they would have done otherwise.
3. ***Effects on the Distribution of Resources among Different Industries and Trades :*** The government can also influence the distribution of productive resources among different

industries and traders through the medium of public expenditure. For example, if the government wishes to attract productive resources to a particular industry, it will start giving financial assistance from its own funds to such an industry. Likewise, if the government wishes to attract productive resources to a particular are a or region of the country, it can offer a variety of incentives to the industries to achieve this objective.

II. Effects of Public Expenditure on Distribution

The objective of maximum social advantage can be fulfilled only if the current income inequalities are either eliminated or reduced to the minimum. Hence, it becomes necessary to minimise the income inequalities current in society. In fact, public expenditure is looked upon as an ideal medium to fulfil this objective. The government should levy maximum amount of taxation on richer sections of the community because their taxable capacity is undoubtedly high. The income so earned through taxation should be spent on providing various types of facilities and amenities to the poorer sections.

III. Effects of Public Expenditure on Economic Stability

Following are the Effects of Public Expenditure on Economic Stability :

1. ***Public Expenditure and Depression :*** The government should make a substantial increase in its expenditure at a time of depression, because this will help to bring about an automatic increase in the volume of employment. If, on the contrary, the level of economic activity is high, as it is at the time of boom, public expenditure should be curtailed to deal with the problem of hyper-inflation.
2. ***Public Expenditure and Employment :*** Public Expenditure plays a vital role in influencing the level of employment in an economy. According to J.M. Keynes, the government should step up its expenditure on public works such as roads, buildings, canals etc., at the time of depression and unemployment. This will add to the volume of employment in the economy. Likewise, the government should cut down its expenditure at a time of inflation and overful employment to deal with the problem of the shortage of human resources.
3. ***Public Expenditure and Consumption :*** The government can increase the real savings of the public by providing free housing facility, medical aid, education, old age pension, family allowance etc. This type of expenditure raises the standard of living of the poor.

Conclusion

To conclude, it can now be said that public expenditure increases public welfare. It is true that the expenditure which increases the real income of the poor without cutting the base of national income of the country, increases the economic welfare of the country. The public expenditure has also some anti-welfare effects. The expenditure on defence by the government does not affect the poor. Sometimes the government provides protection to such industries which have nothing to do with the development of the economy. The ruling party in a democratic country sometimes spends money simply to get public vote in its favour and this expenditure does not prove its worth from economic development point of view.

Public expenditure is therefore a double-edged weapon. It can do much good to the community but if it is unwisely made, it can do much harm.

Questions for Discussion

1. Distinguish between Public Expenditure and Private Expenditure. Explain the causes of increase in Public Expenditure.
2. Discuss critically the various Principle of Public Expenditure.
3. Discuss the Effects of Public Expenditure on the economy of a country.
4. Clearly explain how the different economists have classified Public Expenditure.

Chapter - 4

PUBLIC DEBT

Introduction

Public debt means the debt which a government ones to its subjects or to the nationals of other countries. These days, government revenues from taxation and fees are not enough to meet the rising costs of government. Since, governments are also taking achieve part in the economy's development, they borrow on a long-term basis from banks, business organisations and individuals. The public borrowing is known as public debt. Public debt is the obligation on the part of the government to pay the money back to the individuals from whom it has been obtained. According to Prof. J.K. Mehta, "public debt is comparatively modern phenomenon and has come into existence with the development of democratic form of government in the world".

Differences between Public Debt and Private Debt

Just as a person resorts to borrowing to meet out his expenditure in excess of income, the government has also to do the same when its expenditure goes beyond the income. But yet there are differences in public borrowing and private borrowing, which are as follows :

1. Aim

An individual borrows money to, meet his private benefits and family interest while the government does it for the welfare of the country or sometimes to contain the inflationary pressures in the country.

2. Redemption of Loan

The government repays the public debt by taxing the people. The creditors also make their contribution in this task. As against this, the burden of private debt is never born by the creditors.

3. Source of the Loan

The government can borrow from internal as well as from external sources. In other words, it not only borrows from others, it can borrow from itself. But an individual can borrow from external sources only.

4. Secrecy

An indebted person is not looked upon good by other. It is said that a man is rich if he is indebted to none but in case of government, unlike an individual, a secrecy cannot be maintained.

5. Term of Loan

The government can contract loans from the public for a very long-time. A private individual on the contrary, can secure loans, at best, for a short-period only.

6. Use of loan

The loans taken by the government are generally spent to promote the welfare of the people, including the creditors. For example, when the government spends the loan money on development projects, it benefits almost all sections of the community including creditors. On the contrary, private loans are not spent in the interest of the creditors.

7. Credit Differences

Since the government's credit is high, it is able to secure loans at cheaper interest rates than the private borrowers.

8. Impact of Loan

Public debt produces a deep impact on production of wealth in the country. As against this, private debt produces no such impact.

Role of Public Debt

The Gear Depression of 1929-33 and the publication of Keynes' General Theory gave a death blow to the policy of non-intervention of the state in the economic system and the myth of balanced budgeting was explooer. On the other hand, public borrowing came to occupy an important place as an instrument of fiscal policy to iron out business fluctuations and help economic development of under-developed countries. In this connection, we may discuss the role of public debt as under :

1. Depression

The aggregate effective demand falls during depressions which results in involuntary unemployment of economic and human resources. Even in the face of complementary resources being available, here is mass unemployment. Factories are there and labourers are prepared to work but still they do not get jobs. In fact, there is poverty in the midst of plenty. The fall in the aggregate effective demand leads to the fall in prices ; profits disappear and private investment comes to a stand still. To increase the effective demand, government must undertake a programme of public works financed by borrowing, especially from the banking system because if the additional funds are collected through taxes, the private sector production would fall still further. In fact, there is a strong case for reducing the tax rates during depression to stimulate private investment and increasing the government expenditure, financed by borrowing. This will have a stimulating effect on the private sector and pull the economy out of the depth of depression.

As a result of the public works programmes financed by borrowing, the unemployed would be employed on the public works and the aggregate income in the hands of the people will increase. This will lead to manifold increase in consumption and effective demand of the people through the combined operation of the multiplier and acceleration will set the economy on the road to progress and prosperity. Thus public borrowing has a vital role to play during depression.

2. Inflation

Inflation is a phenomenon where too much money chases too few goods. To control inflation, surplus purchasing power must be taken away from the hands of the people. This can be done through taxation and/or borrowing from the public. Greater reliance has to be placed on taxation as an anti-inflationary measure but there is a limit to which taxes can be raised. If the burden of taxes is already very heavy, public borrowing can be resorted to with advantage to control inflation. But such a reasoning is misleading. It is pointed out, on the other hand, that public borrowing may add to the inflationary pressures because it will divert resources from the production of consumption goods to those of capital goods. Since investment goods have longer gestation periods, the demand for consumption goods tends to exceed their supply in the intervening period and as such public debt is bound to be inflationary. Not only this. In under-developed countries, a sizable portion of the public debt is held by the commercial banks as they regard their holding of government securities as a good investment because of their assured liquidity position. This tempts them to use these securities as the basis for credit expansion and thus add to the effective supply of money and hence to the inflationary pressures.

If the government borrows directly from the Central Bank of the country, it surely makes a net addition to the supply of currency and, therefore, contributes to inflation.

However, if public borrowings are used for increasing the productive capacity of the economy, and output increase over a long period, it will check the inflationary forces to that extent. In such situations, other methods of controlling inflation such a price controls, rationing etc., may be followed to check prices from rising.

3. Economic Development

The basic problem of the under developed countries is to secure an accelerated rate of their economic growth and for that they have to tap and mobilise all possible financial resources for the implementation of the schemes of economic development. They have to borrow from foreign countries, impose new taxes, raise the raise of existing taxes and borrow from the people as well.

Public borrowing in under-developed countries has a double role to play : (i) as a source of capital formulation and (ii) as an anti-inflationary measure.

(a) In under- developed countries, borrowing can be used as a means to raise additional resources for under-taking schemes of economic development and for building up social and economic overheads. Moreover public borrowing should be resorted to for financing undertakings of commercial nature which are helpful for the economy and are expected to yield sufficient revenue in future to repay the borrowed funds. Since their benefits extend to future generations, it is all the more desirable that their investment funds are raised through market borrowing and the debt retired by taxing the future generations.

According to Gurley and Shaw, the rising volume of public debt makes the financial structure of the economy strong and healthy which in turn is essential for the economic growth of a country. With economic growth, the non-monetised sector of the economy gets monetised and as such financial requirements of the economy increase greatly and the composition of financial structure undergoes radical changes. Consequently, a need for credit system grows and a variety of credit instruments comes up. The variegated structure of government loans with different maturities provides an ample opportunity for the financial institutions and financial markets of the economy to grow which in turn help in quickening the pace of economic growth.

(b) As a result of huge investment programmes, the income of the people increases and they are anxious to spend it to satisfy their pent up demands but the supply of goods does not keep pace with it on account of the shortage of complementary resources in under-developed economies. Consequently, the prices start rising which pave way for inflation. To curb inflationary tendencies, borrowing becomes necessary to take away the surplus purchasing power from the hands of the people.

4. Wars

Modern wars are very expensive and borrowing becomes a necessary to wage war successfully. Reliance cannot be placed on taxes alone to mobilise resources for war because in that case the burden of taxes would be too heavy and its effects on production disastrous. Even when new taxes are levied and the rates of existing taxes are raised, it takes time to collect the resources through taxation. Besides, taxes cannot be raised beyond a limit without jeopardising the entire economic system. Hence it becomes necessary and desirable to raise additional resources by way of borrowing and transfer resources from the civilian sector to the military sector.

Similarly to meet other emergencies created by famines, floods, earthquakes etc., borrowing becomes a necessity. However, loans for meeting normal governmental expenditure are not desirable.

5. International Co-operation

A system of international loans has many economic and non-economic advantages. It provides safe and remunerative channels of investments for the surplus funds of the lending countries in the borrowing countries. Besides, the lending countries become interested in the economic advancement of the debtor countries and it paves way for international understanding, cooperation and good will which goes a long way in promoting international peace and harmony.

Dangers of Public Borrowing : Public credit is not an unmixed blessing. Some of its dangers are given below :

1. ***Extravagance :*** Public borrowing has sometimes led to reckless borrowing and extravagance. This has burdened posterity with interest payments without any corresponding return. Borrowing by Germany in the inter-war period illustrates the point. Besides, public borrowing offers dangerous facility to the governments and they may be tempted to over-borrow and thus land the states into bankruptcy or repudiation of debts.
2. ***Frictions and Conflicts :*** Foreign loans, instead of promoting international peace and understanding, have led to frictions and conflicts and also loss of political independence by the borrowing countries. The example of Egypt can be cited in this connection. Besides foreign loans result in the drain of wealth out the country, the burden of which becomes too excessive.
3. ***Increase in Future Budgetary Commitments :*** Public debt has to be services. Interest has to be paid on it and the principal amount has to be paid back. This increases future budgetary commitments of the government.
4. ***Adverse Effects on Production and Distribution :*** Unproductive public debts become a permanent burden on the economy of the country and lead to adverse effects on production and distribution by raising the burden of taxation.

Ordinarily, it is the rich sections only which subscribe to the public debt and through debt servicing, wealth is transferred from the poor to the rich.

In view of these disadvantages of public debt, it is sometimes suggested that public borrowing should not be resorted to and public expenditure should be met primarily through taxation. But as said earlier, there is a limit to taxation also and it cannot be raised beyond the limit of taxable capacity without producing undesirable effects upon people's desire and ability to work, save and invest. However, every care must be taken to see that public borrowing is resorted to only when it is in the best interest of the country and all other sources of raising funds have been fully exhausted.

Limits to Public Debt

There has been phenomenal increase in public debt in most countries of the world during the last few decades due to various reasons. The questions arises as to whether there is any limit to public borrowing. Debts after all have to be repaid and therefore a state cannot go on borrowing endlessly without endangering the safety of the state or without impairing the productive capacity of the nation. Let us consider the various sources of raising public debt and the limit in each case.

1. Inflationary Financing

Inflationary financing cannot be carried beyond a certain limit. Inflation is a very dangerous weapon and if it goes out of control, the entire economic life of the country is jeopardised. The example of German inflation in the inter-war period is quite revealing on this point.

2. External Borrowing

No country can borrow from other countries without a limit. The limit is determined by the financial stability and credit of the country which, in turn, depends on the size of the national income and per capita income of its people. But in no case, a foreign government can lend beyond a definite limit.

3. Internal Borrowing

Here again the borrowing power of the government is not unlimited. The maximum limit is set by the savings of the community but actually this would seldom happen because if the government borrows the entire savings of the people, nothing will be left for financing trade and industry. Thus, generally speaking, the government can borrow only the surplus funds i.e., funds over and above those normally required for financing trade and industry.

However, it must be remembered that modern democratic welfare states do not borrow aimlessly; they borrow when it is absolutely essential for economic growth and stabilisation.

In the short run, if the government resorts to excessive borrowing, the supply of funds available to the private sector will be reduced to that extent and therefore a higher rate of interest will come to prevail on account of the general shortage of funds. The interest offered on government loans will have to be raised and this will prevent the authorities from borrowing too much.

In the long-run, however, the total volume of public debt can increase gradually in harmony with the increase in national income and credit structure unless the law of the land puts a limitation on public borrowing. Moreover, in modern times, the technique of refunding the debt comes to the rescue of the government and it can go on borrowing without actually paying the existing debt. Thus there is no limit to raising of public debt in the strict sense of the term. If at all there is a limit, it is not rigid and fixed, as it depends on the growth of national income and credit structure.

Classification of Public Debt

Government loans differ from one another in various respects. The differences arise mainly in regard to the market in which the loans are floated, or the conditions of repayment or the purpose for which they are raised etc. and as such public debts can be classified in many ways. We give below some of the important classifications.

Public debt can be classified as follows :

I. From the Point of View of Time

Following are the types of public debt from the point of view of time :

(a) ***Funded Debt :*** Funded debts are those that are paid after a year or are not redeemable at all. The government sets up a fund for the redemption of the debt and hence called funded debt.

(b) ***Unfunded Debt :*** Unfunded debts are those that are paid within a year like treasure bonds which are for three to six months are never for a longer period than a year.

II. From the Point of View of Redemption

According to Prof. J.K. Mehta, "Redeemable loans are those that the government promises to pay off on some future date. Those for which no such promise is made are called irredeemable loans". Public Debts are mostly redeemable debt. Thus, Public Debts are redeemable and irredeemable from the point of view of redemption.

III. From the Point of View of Production

Following are the types of public debt from the point to view of production :

(a) ***Productive Debt :*** Productive debts are those which are used for those projects which a yield an income to the government.

(b) ***Unproductive Debt :*** Unproductive debts are incurred on those projects which do not yield income to the government. They are considered as dead weight upon the government.

IV. From the Point of View of Voluntariness

Following are the types of public debt from the point of view of voluntariness :

(a) ***Voluntary Debt :*** Generally, government debt is of a voluntary nature. The individuals and the institutions are invited to purchase government bonds.

(b) ***Compulsory or Forced Debt :*** Generally, government debt are of voluntary nature but sometimes the government may have to exercise its influence in times of emergency such as war to raise loan from the public. However, compulsory debts are not common in modern times.

V. From the Point of View of Area

Following are the types of public debt from the point of view of area :

(a) ***Internal Debt :*** A debt is internal if it is subscribed by persons or institutions within the area controlled by the public authority which raises the loans.

(b) ***External Debt :*** A loan is external if subscribed by persons or institutions outside the area controlled by the public authority which raises the loans.

VI. From the Point of View of Productivity

Following are the types of public debt from the point of view of productivity :

(a) ***Productive Debt :*** Productive debts are those which are used for those projects which yield income to the government. For instance, the debts may be used for the construction of railways irrigation and power projects etc.

(b) ***Unproductive Debt :*** As against productive debts these debts are not used on projects which yield income to the government and therefore, they are known as unproductive debt. The special characteristic of unproductive debt is that they have no existing assets and hence they are considered as dead weight upon the government.

Sources of Public Borrowings

There are two important sources of public borrowing, viz., internal sources and external sources. Internally, the government may borrow funds from individuals, charitable trusts, financial institutions, commercial banks and other financial intermediaries and the central bank in the country. Externally, the government may borrow from individuals, international financial institutions and foreign governments. We shall discuss the important sources of public borrowing in the following manner. It may be mentioned at the outset that the exact effects of public borrowing will depend in a large measure on the sources of the borrowed funds.

1. Borrowing from Individuals

If an individual purchases government bonds, some adjustment in his consumption pattern or in the use of his accumulated savings must occur. When government bonds are sold to individuals, there will be very little direct in curtailing either consumption or business investment. The government bonds will be bought largely from funds that would have been used buy other securities and perhaps in part from idle cash balances. This diversion from other securities may indirectly have some contractionary effects which will be considered after the review of the other sources of funds since the effect is common to all of them. The net benefit here is that although individually people possess a very small amount to be spent on any small project but the government may use the whole collective amount successfully in building a big project.

2. Borrowing from Non-Banking Financial Institutions

Another sources of government borrowing is the borrowing from the non-banking financial institutions. When the non-banking financial institutions such as insurance companies, investment trusts, mutual savings banks, chit funds etc., buy government bonds, they reduce their idle cash balances by making investment in the government bonds. However, these institutions prefer to invest their funds in government bonds on account of these bonds being perfectly free from credit-risk and also due to their high negotiability and liquidity. The rate of interest paid on government bonds is, however, relatively low. Consequently, in many cases financial institutions prefer to invest in the high-risk high-return giving securities, particularly in the equity shares of companies under the management of known and experienced industrialists. When the non-banking financial institutions purchase government bonds, they do so in order to reduce their cash holdings.

3. Borrowing from Commercial Banks

As we know, both the individuals and the non-banking financial institutions purchase the government bonds out of their own cash funds. Commercial banks can do so by creating additional purchasing power. The commercial banking system can make additional loans up to an amount determined by the credit multiplier which is determined by their excess cash reserves and the required reserves ratio. The credit creation is made possible by the fact that money loaned by a bank is typically added to the borrowers' account and is, in turn, paid to persons having accounts with other banks.

4. Borrowing from Central Bank

The central bank of the country subscribes, at times substantially, to government loans by supporting these loans in the money and capital markets. This action creates purchasing power in the same manner as the commercial banks do. By purchasing governments bonds, the central bank credits the account of the government. The latter pays to its creditors by drawing cheques on its account maintained with the central bank. Those who have received cheques from the government deposit these cheques with their banks. As a consequence, these banks find themselves with large reserves which become the basis for additional loans and advances.

5. Borrowing from External Sources

Apart from borrowing from different individual and institutional sources in the country, the government may also borrow from other countries. These borrowings can be used to finance was expenditure or to buy the much needed defence equipments or to pay for the import of capital goods required for the various development projects etc. In recent years, the two important external sources of government borrowings are firstly, the international financial institutions like the International Monetary Fund, World Bank, International Development Association and International Finance Corporation. These financial institutions provide loan to member countries for shot term for overcoming the temporary balance of payments of difficulties and for long-term for the development purposes. The second external source of borrowing is the government assistance from friendly nations which is generally received for development projects. In modern times, for the less developed countries, like India, external sources of government borrowings have become considerably important. Up to the end of June, 1987. India had received massive long-term loan assistance of $ 27,325 millions in the form of 106 World Bank loans and 74 IDA credits. She has also received massive assistance from the "Aid India Club", a consortium of friendly aid-giving countries for her economic development.

Methods of Redemption of Public Debt

Following are the main methods of repaying public debt :

1. Repudiation

Repudiation means refusal to pay a debt by the government as was done by Soviet Government in 1917 which repudiated Czarist Debts. Repudiation shakes the confidence of the people and banks in the government and hence, it may find it difficult to raise new loans in the near future.

2. Refunding

If a government sells its bonds to pay its floating obligations, the debt is said to be funded. Refunding is the process by which the maturing bonds are replaced by new bonds.

A major drawback of this method is that the government would be tempted to postpone its obligation of debt redemption and hence the total burden of the debt would continue to increase in future.

3. Conversion

It means exchange of new debt for the old ones. In this scheme of public debt redemption, only the form of debt is changed, and the actual loan is not repaid.

Conversion can be successfully carried out if the credit of the government is good.

4. Actual Repayment

The following measures may be taken for the repayment of public debt :

(a) ***Sinking Fund :*** The government establishes a separate fund known as the 'Sinking Fund' for the repayment of the public debt. The Government goes on crediting every year a fixed some of money to this fund. By the time the debt matures, the fund accumulates enough amount to pay off not only the principal but the interest charges as well.

The sinking fund is looked upon as a systematic method of debt redemption. The burden of the debt is spread over evenly over a number of years. Moreover, it also increases the credit worthiness of the government.

(b) ***Surplus Revenues :*** A policy of surplus budget may be followed annually for clearing off public debt gradually instead of creating a fund for the repayment on maturity.

(c) ***Terminal Annuities :*** A government may issue terminal annuities a part of which matures every year according to serial order announced or decided by lottery system so that the debt can be cleared every year and consequently the burden of interest to that extent every year.

(d) ***Capital Levy :*** Capital levy refers to a heavy tax on property and wealth. It is a once-for-all tax imposed on capital assets above a certain value.

Repayment of External Debt

The redemption of external debt is possible through the earnings of foreign exchanges to pay it. It can be done by creating export surpluses. If foreign loans are invested in those industries which increase the supply of those commodities which are exported, the loans may easily be repaid. If, however, the loans are utilised for unproductive purposes, the export surplus is possible at the cost of home consumption. The burden of debt may be very much felt by the people.

Effects of Public Debt

The effects of public debt may be discussed as under :

1. Public Debt and Consumption

The possession of government bonds gives the bond-holders an additional feeling of security and they can afford to spend a larger percentage of their current income and indulge in excess spending. This raises the level of consumption.

When public debt is rapid, the government has to impose additional taxes and this reduces the aggregate consumption because a part of the extra taxes imposed will be met by curtailing the consumption expenditure. On the other hand, the consumption expenditure of those who receive funds from the government does not increase as they reinvest in other forms of investment. But at the same time, it exercises an healthy effect in controlling inflationary situation.

2. Public Debt and Production

The existence of public debt is likely to affect adversely the level of production through its effects on the people's desire to work and save. The receipt of regular income by way of interest by the bond-holders may reduce their desire to work and save. Similarly, higher rates of taxation to pay off the interest obligations and also the principal amount may serve as a check in the same direction. Besides, the existence of huge debts may generate the fear of the imposition of capital levy or even repudiation of debt. All this will unfavourably affect the people's desire to work and save and hence the production.

If debt is repaid in times of depression or when resources are idle, it will reduce national income and output because the imposition of additional taxation will adversely affect the desire and ability to work and save.

However, the effects of public debt must include the effects of the expenditure of borrowed money. The state is guided by the larger interest of the society as a whole and seeks to promote the greatest good of the greatest numbers and as such produces for the more needy and spends on projects which add to the productive capacity of the economy. The public debt thus viewed exercises whole-some effects on production.

3. Public Debt and Distribution

The government has to pay interest and the principal amount to the bond-holders and this involves transfers of real income from the tax-payers to the bond-holders unless the bond-holders and the tax-payers are identical which is not possible because the rate of taxation cannot be so high as to make the former pay out of their own tax proceeds. The bond holders are generally the rich people and the tax-payers include both the rich and the poor tax-payers. Hence public debt results in the redistribution of income in favour of the rich.

4. Public Debt and Investment

The effects of public debt on investment are not so certain. The existence of large public debt and the consequent high rates of taxation to service the debt may adversely affect the inducement to invest. On the other hand, the existence of huge debt obligations will force the government to follow a cheap money policy and keep the rate of interest at the minimum possible level. Other things remaining the same, this will encourage borrowing and investment. Hence it is not possible to say whether public debt will favourably affect investment or otherwise.

Can Public Debt Lead to National Bankruptcy ? The analogy between private and public debts is not tenable. While there can be a real possibility of an individual to go bankrupt, such a thing is unlikely to happen with a government. The government can always pay off currently maturing debt by the sale of new issues of bonds either to the same or other individuals. Should the need arise, the government can resort to the printing press and get hold of sufficient amount of money to repay her liabilities. It may, however, be conceded that the recourse to the printing of money during inflationary times will be clearly an irresponsible act. This simple emphasises upon the need for caution and does not prove even indirectly the possibility of national bankruptcy.

Public Debt and Liquidity

Public debt is represented by bonds which are highly liquid form of assets as they can be easily got converted into cash. Besides, it adds to the liquidity position of the commercial banks as they can increase their cash reserves by disposing of their government bonds. Thus public debt gives rise to highly negotiable form of assets which has far-reaching effects on monetary management and control and this necessitates a sound debt management policy.

Burden of Public Debt

Public debt represents state borrowings from the public. It has been classified under two heads–internal debt and external debt. We shall now discuss the incidence of internal as well as external debt as follows :

I. Incidence of Internal Debt

This can be discussed under the following four heads :

1. ***Direct Money Burden :*** When the government borrows money from the public, the purchasing power gets transferred from the lenders to the government. The government in its turn spends the loan-money on productive works as a result of which the purchasing power again gets transferred from the government to the producers, contractors, workers etc. Thus, it has little or no money burden.
2. ***Indirect Money Burden :*** This results when the government spends the loan-money on developmental projects, this results in the creation of demand for several commodities and services. As a consequences, the prices of these goods and services goes up imposing

additional burden on the community. This represents indirect money burden of internal debt.

3. ***Direct Real Burden :*** The government repays the principal and interest in the case of internal loans by imposing new taxes on the people. Ordinarily, the tax payers are poor people while the lenders are comparatively better off. When the government repays principal and interest to the people, it results in the transfer of purchasing power from the poorer to the richer sections.
4. ***Indirect Real Burden :*** The government has to levy additional taxes on the people to repay the public debt. As a result, the economic inequalities get further increased. Sometimes, it has to apply cuts in socially desirable expenditure which may have adverse repercussions on the people's capacity to work and save. This, in fact, is the indirect real burden of internal debt.

II. Incidence of External Debt

This can be discussed under the following four heads :

1. ***Direct Money Burden :*** The direct money burden of an external debt is represented by the aggregate of money payments in the form of interest and the principal repayable to the external creditor.
2. ***Indirect Money Burden :*** Sometimes, the interest on external debt is paid in terms of goods and services resulting inevitable in the decline of these goods and services within the country. This represents the indirect money burden of external debt.
3. ***Direct Real Burden :*** The government very soon levies new taxes on the people to pay off the external debt. As a matter of fact, the burden of these taxes falls more on poor people than the rich people and this represents the direct real burden of external debt.
4. ***Indirect Real Burden :*** With the imposition of taxes on people to pay off the external debt, the capacity of people to work and save declines and the productive capacity of the people is also consequently affected. This represents the indirect real burden of the external debt.

Conclusion

From the above discussion, it is clear that the public debt is regarded as an instrument of economic development or of economic stability. During times of inflation, the Government withdraws purchasing power from the people through borrowing so that prices are prevented from rising. During times of depression, the Government encourages credit expansion through the Central Bank to place additional purchasing power in the hands of the public. The government itself raises loans and spends the amount on public works.

Questions for Discussion

1. What is Public debt ? Is there any economic limit to the size of public debt.
2. What are the different kinds of public debt ? What are the principal methods of repaying the public debt with special reference to India.
3. Explain the economic effects of a rising public debt.
4. How far is public debt a burden on future generations ?

Chapter - 5

FISCAL POLICY AND DEFICIT FINANCE

Introduction

Fiscal policy, broadly speaking, consists of

(a) Taxes

(b) Public borrowing and

(c) Public spending.

It is related to public finance and it means the use of taxation public borrowing and public expenditure by government for securing economic stabilisation in developed countries and economic growth in underdeveloped countries. According to Arthur Smithies, fiscal policy means, "a policy under which the government uses its expenditure and revenue programmes to produce desirable effects and to avoid undesirable effects on the national income, production and employment". G.K. Shaw has defined fiscal policy in these words, "We define fiscal policy to encompass any decision to change the level, composition or timing of government expenditure or to vary the burden structure or frequency of the tax payment". The means and instruments employed by the state to influence the general level of economic activity constitute the core of fiscal policy. They include a nation's budget, taxes, spending and borrowing. They also include relief expenditures, subsidies, social security benefits and transfer payments. A skillful management of a nation's budget can go a long way in maintaining economic stability and ensuring higher rates of economic growth.

Meaning of Fiscal Policy

Fiscal Policy may be defined as that part of governmental economic policy which deals with taxation, expenditure, borrowing and the management of public debt in an economy. It is an indispensable instrument of modern public finance. The importance of fiscal policy has greatly increased in modern times, both in the developed as well as the underdeveloped countries of the world. In developed countries, fiscal policy is being increasingly used as an instrument to achieve full employment and economic stability. In under developed countries, on the contrary, fiscal policy is more and more being used as a means to step up the rate of economic growth. Fiscal policy primarily concerns itself with the flow of funds in the economy. Taxation, as it were, diverts the funds from the private sector to the governmental sector, public expenditure, on the contrary, diverts funds from the governmental sector back to the economy. Public borrowing, like taxation, also diverts funds from the private sector to the governmental sector, but the two diversions influence the private sector in different ways,. Management of public debt includes functions, such as, floating of governmental loans, payment of interest thereon and retirement of matured debts. Fiscal policy, thus, exerts a very powerful influence on the working of the national economy. It directly affects the volume of output, income and employment in the economy. The greater the percentage of national income and expenditure represented by the governmental budget, the greater would be the influence of fiscal policy on aggregate economic activity.

Evolution of Fiscal Policy

The evolution of fiscal policy has passed through three well-marked stages which may be described below :

1. Classical View

According to the classical economists, the fiscal policy should have a limited range of operations and the governmental budget should be a small, but a balanced budget. The main pillar of classicism is that famous Say's Law of Markets, according to which every supply creates its own demand. Whatever is produced in the economy is soon sold off, according to J.B. Say. There is, therefore, no surplus or unsold stock. This implies that there can never be overproduction and unemployment in the economy. The fact of the matter is that the classical economists assumed away any possibility of unemployment arising in an unregulated capitalistic economy. They assumed that full employment was already existing in society. The assumption of full employment, in fact, underlies all classical theories and principles of economics. With full employment already existing in society, there was no need for the State to intervene in economic matters, according to the classicists. The State should, therefore, pursue a policy of non-intervention or *laissez-faire* in society.

The State, it was pointed out, should perform the minimum number of functions essential to the existence of society. The classical economists prescribed only three principal functions for the State, namely, (a) the State should ensure the maintenance of internal security, (b) the State should establish and maintain law courts for the settlement of disputes among citizens. According to the classical economists, that government was the best which governed the least. In view of the limited functions prescribed for the State, the classical economists recommended *minimum range of operations* for fiscal policy. According to them, the government should tax the least and spend the least, which meant a small-sized budget for the government. The revenue raising as well as the spending activities of the government should be reduced to the minimum in the view of the classical economists. They stood not only for a small budget, but also balanced budget. What this implied was that the current revenue and current expenditure of the government should balance the budget. The principle of balanced budget was an integral part of doctrine of sound finance which was so dear to the classical economists. They missed no opportunity to stress its importance in the fiscal operations of the government.

A "balanced budget" was an article of faith with the classical economists on several grounds : *Firstly,* an unbalanced budget leads to public borrowings which naturally reduce the amount of loanable funds available to private entrepreneurs for productive purposes. *Secondly,* governmental borrowings consequent upon an unbalanced budget cause the market rate of interest to rise upwards, which, in turn, adversely affects private investment activity in the economy. *Thirdly,* unbalanced budgets cause a continual increase in the burden of public debt. At the time of maturity, the government has to find the necessary financial resources through additional taxation to repay the public debt. This additional taxation again has the effect of adversely affecting the saving capacity of the people, besides dampening their incentive to work. *Fourthly,* unbalanced budgets have the effect of generating inflationary pressures in the economy on account of excessive public expenditure, mostly of an unproductive variety. *Fifthly,* unbalanced budgets lead to an unnecessary extension of the activities of the State into fields not meant for it or meant only for private enterprise. It is on these grounds that the classical economists advocated not only a balanced but also *small-sized budget*. According to the classical economists, that government was the best government which resorted to the minimum range of fiscal operations, both on the revenue as well as the expenditure sides.

2. Neo-classical View

The neo-classical view of fiscal policy is represented by Marshall and Pigou. Both of them held the firm belief that *laissez-faire* capitalism produced the socially most undesirable effects on the economic system. It led to the accentuation and perpetuation of social inequalities in the economic system. In a *laissez-faire* capitalistic economy, the principle of maximum social welfare could not be realized with the State pursuing the policy of non-intervention in economic affairs. It was, therefore, necessary on the part of the State to give up the policy of *laissez-faire* and pursue an active policy of State intervention in economic affairs to maximize social welfare. Both Marshall and Pigou, it should be remembered, were welfare economists. Maximization of economic welfare was the objective of their thinking. Now this objective could hardly be realized with the State following a policy of *laissez-faire* in economic matters. The State should, in their view, actively intervene to correct undesirable trends in the economy. The State should, for example, discourage investment in undesirable sectors through fiscal measures and encourage investment in productive channels through grant of subsidies. The State should not only encourage production, but should also take appropriate measures to eliminate or to minimize socio-economic inequalities in the economy. Marshall and Pigou, therefore, envisaged an enlarged and a more active role for the State in economic affairs. But this could not be made possible without enlarging, at the same time, the range of fiscal operations in the economy. They, therefore, advocated an *enlarged budget*–more revenue and more expenditure–to attain maximum welfare in the economy.

3. Keynesian View

Fiscal policy underwent a complete transformation with the publication of Keynes' General Theory in 1936. The Keynesian Economics constituted almost a complete break with the old, classical traditions. Classicism, as is well-known, was based on Say's *Law of Markets*. According to J.B. Say, every supply creates its own demand and that there is no possibility of overproduction and consequent unemployment in a *lassez-faire* capitalistic economy. J.M. Keynes challenged Say's *Law of Markets* to prove that every supply does not create its own demand and that there is every possibility of overproduction and unemployment in a capitalistic society. The entire Keynesian theory of employment is based on the concept of *deficient aggregate demand* in the economy. It is the existence of this deficient aggregate demand which led to overproduction and consequent unemployment in the economy. If somehow this deficiency of aggregate demand could be tackled, there would neither be overproduction nor unemployment in the economy. According to Keynes, there were, broadly speaking, two methods of tackling this deficient aggregate demand–(i) by increasing consumption expenditure, and (ii) by increasing investment expenditure. There was little scope for increasing consumption expenditure in the short period, because the prospensity to consume was stable in that period. So the burden of tackling with the deficient aggregate demand naturally fell on the second method, namely, on increase in the investment expenditure. But due to depressed conditions in industry and trade, there was hardly any scope for bringing about any worthwhile increase in *private* investment expenditure, even though attempts could be made to encourage it by following a cheap money policy at a time of depression. The main burden of tackling with the deficient aggregate demand (and of promoting the volume of employment) thus fell on the second component of investment, namely public investment expenditure. In order to increase the volume of employment, the State should step up investment expenditure on public works projects, such as, roads, irrigation works, public buildings, etc., on a large scale. To be concrete, Keynes advocated at such times a policy of *unbalanced budget* by the government. The deficit, in the budget, he further suggested, should be met through *deficit financing* or by putting the printing press into motion. An *unbalanced* budget, according to Keynes, was the only way to deal with a deflationary situation accompanied by mass unemployment in a developed economy.

Lerner's Concept of Functional Fiscal Policy

The latest trend in the developed capitalist countries of the West is represented by the concept of *Functional Finance*. This concept, though based almost wholly on Keynesian ideology, has been developed and refined by A.P. Lerner in recent years. Modern governments in the capitalist countries of the West now stand committed to the new concept of functional finance. According to Lerner, the fiscal policy should be *contra-cyclical* in nature to used as an instrument to bring about economic *stabiization* in the economy. The budget of the government, according to this principle, should never be a balanced one. It should be *deficit budget* during depression and unemploymnet, and a surplus budget at a time of boom and overfull employment. At a time of depression and unemployment, the government should spend more than its revenue and thus incur a deficit in the budget. The deficit incurred in the budget should be met by resorting to the printing press i.e., by printing more paper currency. This policy of monetary expansion would help to remove depression and unemployment in the economy. The injection of more money supply into circulation would stimulate the economy and help in gradually raising the price-level in the country.

On the contrary, if the economy is confronted with inflation and overfull employment, the government may resort to the policy of *surplus-budgeting* to deal with the situation. The government should resort to heavy taxation, both personal as well as commodity taxation, to withdraw the excess purchasing power from the hands of the public. The government should also undertake extensive borrowing programmes to neutralize the excess purchasing power in the economy. The government should also apply a drastic cut in its overall expenditure to deal with the inflationary forces. All these measures would result in a surplus budget which would act as an antidote to inflation in the economy. The concept of functional finance, thus, involves the alternative application of the policies of deficit budgeting and surplus budgeting to achieve economic stabilization in the economy. In short, functional finance deliberately aims at unbalancing the governmental budget with a view to achieving and maintaining economic stability in a developed country. But the concept of functional finance may have to be modified slightly in the context of the peculiar situation prevailing in an underdeveloped economy. The problem in an underdeveloped country is not one of full employment, but is one of achieving speedy economic development. It is in this context that the concept of functional finance may have to be modified to include deficit-budgeting as an instrument of economic growth. Deficit financing is restored to, as part of the concept of functional finance, in a developed country to tackle with the problem of depression and unemployment. In an underdeveloped country, however, deficit financing may be used as an instrument to promote economic growth.

Objective of Fiscal Policy

Fiscal policy, in modern era, subscribes to the following major macro-economic goals:

(a) Full employment.

(b) Economic stabilisation.

(c) Economic growth.

(d) Social justice or equity in the distribution of income and wealth.

Fiscal Policy for Full Employment

Keynes regarded public finance as compensatory finance ordained to attain and maintain full employment in the economy. To pursue this goal, Keynes suggested that :

(a) Taxation should be devised to promote and sustain consumption and investment.

(b) To raise the level of effective demand and to overcome depressionary forces, budget should be in deficit and it should have deficit financing.

(c) Public expenditure has to be compensatory one. It has to be in a planned way to finance public works programmes and provide social security measures.

(d) Direct taxes should be lowered to encourage savings and investments directed towards creation of more employment opportunities.

(e) Public expenditure should be meant for uplifting the level of aggregate demand, investment and employment.

(f) Public borrowings should be on a large scale to finance productive public expenditure.

Once full employment level is reached, it has to be constantly maintained by adopting appropriate fiscal measures from time to time.

In a developing economy, fiscal policy has also to solve the problem of disguised unemployment. Hence, public works programmes have to be undertaken at village level to provide alternative employment opportunities.

Fiscal Policy and Economic Stabilisation

Economic stability is another prime aim of a sound fiscal policy. This goal implies maintenance of full employment with relative price stabilisation. Price stability here means relative price stability. Inflation should be curbed and deflation should be avoided. In short, economic growth and stability are the twin objectives jointly pursued by a developing country's fiscal policy. The forces stimulating growth process should be given a boost at a time while inflationary pressures are to be curbed

In a growing economy, when huge investment is undertaken to construct social overhead capital, infrastructures of the economy and development of heavy industries, on account of long gestation period, returns are not immediate, as scarcity of consumption goods is felt. This leads to a rising price spiral. A demand pull inflation thereby causes wages etc. to go up and a cost-push inflation is provoked. The vicious circle of inflation has to be checked through appropriate fiscal measures.

Fiscal Policy and Economic Growth

Poor countries are entangled in the vicious circle of poverty. It should be broken. Thus, rapid economic growth is the fundamental objective of fiscal policy in a developing economy.

Fiscal policy as a means of encouraging growth process has the following objectives.

1. To realise and mobilise potential resources into the productive channels. For this fiscal policy should aim at improving marginal propensity to save and the consequent incremental saving ratio. The following methods have been suggested by Prof. Tripathy for raising the incremental saving ratio :

   (a) Imposition of additional taxes.

   (b) Direct physical control.

   (c) Revenue of public enterprises.

   (d) Increase in the rates of taxation.

(e) Public debt.

(f) Deficit financing.

2. To accelerate the rate of economic growth. In this regard, fiscal measure must be conducive to growth process. In no way should fiscal means adversely affect the ability and willingness to work hard, save more and invest.
3. To induce and stimulate private sector investment.
4. To promote investment into socially desirable channels.
5. To alter the pattern of investment and production in such a way as to improve the general economic welfare and sustain egalitarian goals like equity in distribution and eradication of poverty.

Fiscal Policy and Social Justice

A welfare state should provide social justice by giving equitable distribution of income and wealth. Fiscal policy can serve as an effective means of achieving this much desired goal of socialism in developed as well as developing countries. Progressive tax system can be of much use in realising this objective. Moreover, public expenditure helps in redistributing income from the rich to the poor section of the society.

Thus, fiscal policy insists that in a budget, growing allocation should be made for programmes like free medical care, free education, subsidised housing, subsidised essential commodities like milk, etc.

From the above discussion, it follows that the objectives of fiscal policy are not conflicting but complementary to each other.

Fiscal Policy and Under Developed Countries

The Keynesian analysis of fiscal policy is applicable to advanced economies. The role of fiscal policy in advanced economies is to maintain the condition of full employment, economic stability and to stabilise the rate of growth. While in an under-developed economy, the role of fiscal policy is to accelerate the rate of capital formation and investment, so that the productive capacity of the economy is developed and economic growth becomes possible. Thus, it is designed as an instrument of economic development. Besides, fiscal policy may also aim at influencing the pattern of production, the general price level and bring about equitable distribution of wealth and incomes.

Objectives of Fiscal Policy in Under Developed Economies

The role of fiscal policy as an instrument of economic development implies the rejection of what Prof. Benjamin Higgins calls "gradualism" as an approach to development policy and, in its place a policy of "big push" through government intervention has been advocated by him. Public finance for promoting the economic development of under-developed countries; operating within the framework of a mixed economy, may have four important dimensions.

(a) to promote and accelerate the growth of productive investment in the economy both in the public and private sectors.

(b) to mobilise the maximum volume of real and financial resources for the investment plans of the public sector, keeping in view the expanding demand for real and financial resources of the private sector.

(c) to promote the maintenance of a reasonable measure of monetary stability in keeping with the maximum rate of growth of the economy.

(d) to redistribute the growing national output.

Thus, the fiscal operations of the government for promoting the economic development of the under-developed countries are as an invested, as a stabiliser, as a saver and as an income redistributor.

The Report of the Sub-commission, appointed by the United Nations, also emphasised the following objectives of fiscal policy in under-developed countries :

(a) to correct excessive or harmful inequalities in the distribution of income and wealth, and in doing so to expand internal markets and reduce unessential imports.

(b) to contract the inflation which might result from economic developments.

(c) to provide incentives for desirable types of development and thus help to encourage development into desirable directions.

(d) to increase the total volume of saving available for economic development.

Prof. R.N. Tripathy, in this context, has rightly pointed out that these objectives of fiscal policy may come in conflict with one another. The achievement of a high rate of economic growth as the end of fiscal policy may come in conflict with its redistributive objective. Too much emphasis on redistributive objective is bound to produce an adverse effect on incentives and thus to retard the rate of economic growth. Thus, a reconciliation has to be achieved between these conflicting ends of fiscal policy by imparting selective overtones to it.

How an underdeveloped country would achieve a reconciliation between them would depend upon the role it assigns to the private sector in the process of growth, the economic and social philosophy it pursues and the condition of its economy as well as the rate of growth it desires to achieve. In some of the countries of Asia and Latin America, where there exist large inequalities in the distribution of income and wealth, the redistribution role of fiscal policy becomes important. But this role is much less important under conditions such as those of tropical Africa because of the absence of large private fortunes.

However, fiscal policy as a means of promoting economic development of under developed countries may have to play the following role.

1. Mobilisation of Resources

The national income and percapita income of underdeveloped countries being low, hence, the volume of voluntary saving is also low. Therefore, financing of development plan poses a very difficult problem for the government of an underdeveloped country. It is of utmost importance to increase the rate of investment and capital formation, so as to accelerate the rate of economic growth in underdeveloped countries. Hence, the governments of underdeveloped countries are compelled to resort to the device of forced savings for mobilising an adequate volume of resources.

Ragnar Nurkse considered the maximisation of the "incremental saving ratio–the marginal propensity to save" as one of the most important determinant of economic growth. Prof. R.N. Tripathy suggests the following methods to raise the incremental saving ratio so as to provide the required finances for development plans :

(a) Direct Physical Control.

(b) Increase in the rates of existing taxes.

(c) Imposition of new taxes.

(d) Surplus from public enterprises.

(e) Public borrowing of a non-inflatinary nature.

(f) Deficit financing.

The process of development is inherently inflationary in nature as it generates additional effective demand without an immediate and corresponding increase in the output of consumption goods. Thus, the direct curtailment of consumption and socially unproductive investment may be helpful for the mobilisation of resources and to check the inflationary trend. But direct physical controls may be difficult to administer as the level of consumption being low in an underdeveloped country.

However, some amount of direct physical control has been considered necessary for an adequate mobilisation of resources.

Progressive income-tax, heavy duties on luxury imports, ban on the manufacture of luxury goods and heavy excise duties on the manufacture of luxury goods are the measures, which curtail consumption and help in the mobilisation of resources. Taxation thus, serves as an important instrument for development finance. Hence, progressive income taxes, on windfalls, on unearned incomes, on capital gains, on expenditure and real estates etc., should be levied for financing development plans as they do not adversely affect production and consumption, but help in equitable distribution.

The revenue from public enterprises in under-developed countries does not form an important source of development finance, as the cost of production of these enterprises in the initial stages of development remains high, which affects the profits and hence the revenue of the government. Moreover, there are not so many public enterprises as to warrant a surplus, and there is no profit motive.

Public borrowing of non-inflationary nature may not always be very certain, as the response of the government bonds floated in the capital market depends on a large number of factors such as the relative yield on various kinds of profit-yielding assets, confidence in the government policy and psychological behaviour of the capital market, and some factors are outside the control of the public policy. Moreover, the resources, mobilised from public borrowing, may not be adequate.

Though, deficit financing is an important source for financing development plans in under-developed countries, but as it leads to inflationary tendencies and hence, it has a limited scope.

Thus, taxation is the most important source for raising revenues to finance development programmes in the absence of adequate voluntary saving. The requirement of public sector is largely for non-profit making capital and this constitutes a special argument in favour of an extended use of taxation as the method of compulsory saving. It has also the advantage that implementation of large scale investment programme leads to inflationary pressures in under-developed countries, but taxation helps in achieving growth with stability.

2. To Accelerate the Rate of Economic Growth

The fiscal means such as taxation, public borrowing and deficit financing etc. should be used in such a combination so that the production, consumption and distribution are nor adversely affected, but the economy as a whole should develop so as to increase the national income and per capita income rapidly. It is possible only when more opportunities and incentives are provided by the government to save and invest.

Pattern of growth—It is now considered of utmost importance that interdependent sectors, such as agriculture and industry, should grow simultaneously. The development of agriculture depends on industrial development as the demand for agriculture products comes from industrial sector. Similarly, the development of industrial sector depends upon the development of agricultural sector as the raw material is supplied by the agriculture, and the demand for industrial products comes from agricultural sector. *Thus, Prof. Raja J. Chelliah, rightly said that "the most fruitful line of advance lies along the path of a balanced development of agriculture and industry."*

3. To Encourage Investment into Socially Desirable Channels

Fiscal policy should encourage investment into those channels which are judged to be most desirable from the point of view of the society. It would be possible if inducement to make investment are increased by providing various incentives to private entrepreneurs such as development rebates, subsidies, tax concessions etc., into those sectors of the economy which are considered useful to the society. In short, fiscal policy should aim at rapid economic development and must induce a flow of economic resources into those sectors of the economy, which are considered essential for rapid economic development and socially desirable. Besides, the unproductive investment, such as speculative investment in land or in gold, should be subject to heavy taxation, so as to divert the resources, from unproductive channels to productive and socially desirable channels.

4. Inducement to Investments

It is not enough to grant rebates, subsidies, tax concessions to induce investment in private sector and subjecting unproductive investment to heavy taxes to divert resources into productive channels. But, in the early stages of development the government must try to build up economic and social overheads like transport and communication facilities, flood control, irrigation facilities, power installation, ports, facilities for technical training, education and health facilities, schools, hospitals etc., so as to provide external economies to induce investment in agriculture and industry and the economy as a whole to achieve rapid economic development. These economic and social overheads are helpful for widening the size of market, reducing the cost of production, and increasing the social marginal productivity of investment, hence they provide incentives to investment in private sector. The government may also undertake production in strategic industries and services of public utility. Moreover, the government may induce investment in private sector by providing assistance to new industries to introduce modern techniques of production in industries and agriculture both.

5. The Pattern of Investment

The optimum pattern of investment for an underdeveloped country will depend, among other things, on the fruitful lines of development open to the country concerned, and on the social marginal productivity of different lines of investment. This implies that only those investment projects should be selected, the social marginal productivity of which is the highest. But the application of the principle of social marginal productivity in the context of planned allocation of resources may present a number of difficulties. Economic development is a dynamic process which involves changes in the size and quality of population, tastes, which also involves knowledge and social and institutional factors whereas the criterion of social marginal productivity assumes a static setting. In view of this, "the criterion of social marginal productivity must, therefore, be interpreted within the usual dynamic complex."[1] Thus, in short, if the marginal productivity in socially desirable projects is low, the objective of fiscal policy should be to increase the social marginal productivity and, to divert resources to those projects where the social marginal productivity is highest.

6. Fiscal Policy and Price Stability

The objective of economic growth and that of price stability have sometimes been regarded as antithetical. But this is a highly over–simplified view and it distorts the issue. At present there is a general agreement that economic growth and stability are joint objectives for under-developed countries to pursue. Stagnation is regarded as too heavy and unacceptable a price to pay for the achievement of stability. At the same time, the evils of inflation are such that no one would today recommend large scale inflation as a means for promoting the economic development of underdeveloped countries. Though some economists have favoured gentle rising of prices as an incentive for capital formation, they have emphasised that large scale inflation would retard economic growth. In fact the debate today is "not over the desirability of economic growth and stability, but only over the inter-relationships between them and over the policies necessary to achieve them".

Thus, fiscal policy should, aim at curbing inflationary pressures inherent in a developing economy. In such an economy there is always an imbalance between the demand for and supply of real resources. Because of large scale investment and repeated push of investment expenditure into capital goods industries demands rises, but supply remains relatively inelastic due to structural rigidities, market imperfections and bottle-necks, which impede the supply of essential goods. This leads to inflationary rise in prices. A rise of the prices of basic commodities tends to generate a demand for higher wages and the rise in the level of wage-price spiral. Thus, a demand pull inflation tends to generate into a cost push inflation in a developing economy.

The fiscal measures that can be taken to check the inflationary tendencies are taxation and borrowing, as these measures remove purchasing power form circulation. However, fiscal measure must be supplemented with monetary measure to make them more effective. Besides, the efforts must be made to increase production especially of essential commodities.

Though, deflationary trend is not so common a characteristic of developing economies as that of rising prices, but if such a situation occurs, fiscal policy along with other instruments of economic policy must operate in co-ordination with each other.

Fiscal role of the government should also include the removal of bottlenecks and structural rigidities, planned development of the various sectors of the economy, physical controls of essential products, their purchase and sale by the government and granting of subsidies and protection to essential consumer goods industries in the economy to maintain stability in the general price level.

7. Fiscal Policy and Distribution

It is needless to emphasise the importance of distributional effects of the rising national product. A mere increase in per capita income does not necessarily lead to an increase in the welfare of all sections of the people, unless an equitable distribution of the rising national product is assured. An equitable distribution is usually taken to mean a reduction in the existing inequalities of income and wealth. The existence of extreme inequalities in income and wealth distribution may have adverse effects on the economic development of under-developed countries. It has rightly been pointed out by some economists that extreme inequalities in the distribution of income and wealth are detrimental to economic development in so far as they reduce the nutritional, health and living standards of the people, create in excessive demand for imported luxury consumption goods, further an excessive transfer of funds to abroad may prevent the growth of internal markers, where such conditions exist, fiscal methods are appropriate to bring about more equitable distribution of incomes and channel additional resources into economic development.

Besides, extreme inequalities create political and social discontent, generate economic instability and hence, the removal of inequalities of income and wealth is of great importance for economic development.

The problem of reducing inequalities of income and wealth may be solved through redistributive public expenditure and redistributive tax policy. The government to reduce inequalities, should direct its expenditure on those activities which benefit low income groups in increasing the standard of living and which are helpful in improving their productivity and technology. The programme of planned development, which removes regional imbalances also help in equitable distribution of income and wealth. Thus, redistributive expenditure helps economic development and economic development helps redistribution. In this context, W.W. Heller rightly pointed out "Redistributive finance appears to offer greater gains and involves less cost to under-developed than to developed countries."

A redistributive tax policy should aim at imposing heavy taxation on rich and exempting poorer section of the community that is, the tax system should be steeply progressive. It should discourage commodity taxation as they are regressive in effect. However items of luxuries and those items which are consumed by the richer section of the society, may be subject to heavy taxation.

Tax policy as a redistributive instrument must be highly progressive. But a highly progressive tax structure may cut the roots of saving and investment in private sector and hence may go against the objectives of economic development. A via-media between these two conflicting aims has been suggested by some economists as "though functional inequality may be maintained to some extent, non-functional inequality should be eliminated." This implies stiff taxation of non-entrepreneurial incomes and non functional consumption, that is, functional inequality, in order to encourage saving and investment, may be allowed to some extent by granting concessions or light taxation on saving and investment but personal inequality (non-functional inequality) should be reduced through the taxation on expenditure at high levels.

Fiscal Policy in Nut-Shell

On the basis of the above discussion of fiscal policy contained in the foregoing pages and in the light of the currently accepted social goal of equitable distribution of the national income, the main objective that should government tax and budgetary policy in a country, such as India, may be stated as follows–

(a) To increase the rate of investment, and capital formation, so as to accelerate the rate of economic growth.

(b) To check the actual and potential consumption, so as to increase the rate of savings and investment in private sector.

(c) To encourage the flow of investment into those channels which are considered to be most desirable from the point of view of society.

(d) To regulate the flow of purchasing power in accordance with the overall pattern laid down in the plan of economic development, that is to achieve the objective of economic growth with price stability.

(e) To reduce the large inequalities of income and wealth in a manner and to the extent that are consistent with the best long term interests of the population as a whole.

(f) To remove the regional imbalance in the economy.

(g) To divert the investment and spendings from unproductive uses such as the production and consumption of intoxicants to productive channels.

(h) To raise the standard of living of the country as a whole and especially of poor section of the community.

Broadly speaking, all these objectives relate to increasing the overall flow of resources into investment. Secondly, they relate to socially optimum pattern of investment. Thirdly, they are relevant where the quantum as well as the pattern is centrally planned to some extent. In this case fiscal policy becomes an adjunct to investment policy. The fulfillment of all these objectives will lead to a rise in the national product.

Besides, these objectives also relate to the distribution of the rising national product. It is needless to canvas the importance of distributional considerations. A mere increase in per capita income does not necessarily lead to an increase in the welfare of all sections of people, unless an equitable distribution of the rising national product is assured. An equitable distribution is usually taken to mean a reduction in the existing inequalities of income and wealth. To what extent inequalities should be reduced is partly a matter of value judgement, partly a matter of economic system that is adopted and partly a matter of incentives within the system. Here, it can only be said that, reduction of inequalities is as important as the raising of national products. In other words, distribution and production are equally important.

Fiscal Instruments

Fiscal policy can seek to influence the economy, on the one hand by the amount of public income that is raised, and on the other by the amount and direction of public expenditure. As already stated, there are three important fiscal means by which resources can be raised for the public exchequer : taxation, borrowing from the public (other than commercial banks) and credit creation or deficit financing. These means must be used in harmonious combination so as to produce the best overall effects in such a term of economic progress with stability.

Of these three means, it is taxation that is the most important. If wisely conceived and skilfully used, it can become a very effective instrument of fiscal policy. As a part of a general programme of develop-ment, taxation may be used to accomplish the following objectives:

(a) To curtail consumption and thus, transfer resources from consumption to investment.

(b) To increase the incentives to save and invest.

(c) To transfer resources from the hands of the public to the hands of the state, so as to make public investment possible.

(d) To modify the pattern of investment in a socially desirable manner.

(e) To reduce economic inequalities and to make the equitable distribution of incomes and wealth in the society.

(f) To increase national output and income.

If should, however, be noted that taxation has a limited scope in an underdeveloped country, where the taxable capacity is relatively low on account of wide spread poverty and low per capita income. Moreover, excessive taxation may not have desirable effects on saving and investment as well as on consumption. Besides, commodity taxes are regressive in effects and generate inflationary pressures as they are generally included in price. But progressive taxation on incomes and wealth, and commodity taxation on items of luxuries, and on those items of consumption, which are used by rich people, may have desirable effects. In view of all these limitations and advantages, a properly devised tax policy will certainly help in achieving the objective of growth with stability and to reduce the economic inequalities and to make the distribution of income and wealth equitable, which are integral parts of the fiscal policy in underdeveloped countries.

Limitations of Fiscal Policy

Fiscal policy has the following limitations :

1. It is inappropriate to deal with problems that require structural adjustments.
2. It cannot adjust the distribution of money flows.
3. It has operational limitation due to the involvement of time lags. There may be delays in diagnosing recessions and inflations and then devising and pursuing appropriate fiscal measures.
4. It is also difficult to decide the magnitude of fiscal action and the optimum size of budget.
5. Theory of fiscal policy assumes operation of the multiplier effect. But, in reality, it cannot be easily estimated on account of many leakages involved.
6. Its efficiency depends on strict financial discipline on the part of government and its correct value judgement.

Deficit Financing

Deficit financing is an essential element in the fiscal policy of a developing economy.

Meaning

When domestic resource together with external assistance cannot meet adequately the expenditure of development, the State is forced to resort to deficit financing. The term deficit financing implies an action on the part of the State to cover the deficit in the budget. It is a recognized method of promoting economic development particularly in underdeveloped countries where incomes are low and propensity to consume high, on account of which savings are very low. Thus the responsibility of augmenting the resources for smooth growth of the economy devolves on the Government. The first report of the Indian Planning Commission explains the meaning and technique of deficit financing in the following words, "The term deficit financing is used to denote the direct addition to Gross National Expenditure through budget deficits, whether the deficits are on revenue or on capital account. The essence of such a policy lies in the Government spending in excess of the revenue it receives". The Government may cover the deficit either

(a) by running down its accumulated balances (withdrawing its cash balances),

(b) by borrowing from the central bank,

(c) by borrowing from the commercial banks, and

(d) by creating new money by resorting to the printing press.

Such a type of created money is not backed by any gold reserves, other than the promise of the Government to repay the amount. In other words, deficit financing means public expenditure in excess of public revenue. Deficit financing may also be called deficit spending.

Deficit financing is a pragmatic tool of economic development and has been used by the Indian Government to obtain the necessary resources to finance the Five-Year Plans. It is necessary to emphasize the fact that deficit financing does not create real resources that are nonexistent but it is only a device which helps in the transfer of resources to the Government. The real resources are equipment, materials, skill and labour. These cannot be created by printing money or by creating bank credit.

Purposes of Deficit Financing

Government generally resort to deficit financing for any of the following three purposes : (a) to finance war-expenditure ; (b) to lift the economy out of the depths of economic depression ; and (c) to promote the economic development of the country.

1. War - Finance

The historical origin of deficit financing lies in war finance. Modern wars, being total wars, are extremely expensive to fight by the belligerent nations. A nation may stake everything to fight the war to a successful end. So it resorts to all sorts of devices to raise the necessary funds for the successful prosecution of the war. The financial resources raised through taxation and public borrowings do not suffice to meet the cost of the war. Willy-nilly, therefore, the government of a country may resort to deficit financing to raise the necessary financial resources for the successful prosecution of the war. Deficit financing at such a time may assume any of the forms described above, namely, the government may borrow from the Central Bank, or it may run down its own cash reserves with the Central Bank, or it may print more paper notes and put them into circulation. Unlike taxation, the method of deficit financing, hardly arouses any public resistance worth the name. Nor does it put any financing burden on the government unlike public loans on which the government has to pay pre-determined interest rate. The method of deficit financing therefore, comes quite handy to a government at a time of war. Few governments have been able to resist the temptation of raising financial resources through deficit financing during wartime. During the First as well the Second World Wars, several governments resorted to deficit financing as a method of war-finance. It is clear that deficit financing during wartime cannot be productive in any sense of the term. The newly created money is *not* matched with any addition to the productive assets of the nation. What to talk of new assets, even the existing assets suffer destruction and devastation as a consequence of the war. The newly-created money is accompanied by dwindling physical assets. The result is the inflationary spiral which may play havoc with the country's economy and may ultimately lead to its complete ruination. Wartime deficit financing is, therefore, highly detrimental to the stability of the economic system. It was on account of this potential danger that the classical economists looked down upon deficit financing as a method of governmental finance. That their fears were not imaginary was fully borne out by the experience of the two World Wars.

2. Economic Depression

Lord Keynes advocated the use of deficit financing as a means to lift the economy out of the depths of economic depression, which is often accompanied by unemployment in the country. At such a time, private investment becomes slack on account of the all-round pessimism in the economy. Lord Keynes looked upon public investment as an effective antidote to declining private investment during depression. Since any public investment expenditure to the effective must be on a large scale, this naturally raises the question of finds. Obviously, there are there methods open to the government for financing the public investment.

The first can be *taxation*. Taxation, as a method of finance, should be considered to be the most unsatisfactory. Public investment, if it is to alleviate unemployment, must represent an altogether new expenditure. The use of taxation to finance public works does not represent new expenditure. It simply represents the transfer of purchasing power of money from the citizens to the State, money which was already being spent upon private consumption.

The second method can be *borrowings* or *loans*. As a method of financing public works, it is better than taxation in so far as it does not represent substitution of private expenditure by State expenditure. The money lent to the State represents only inactive balances which were not being spent by the citizens. There are, however, certain objections against borrowings as a method of finance. It is pointed out that public borrowing inflates public debt and the community has to bear the heavy burden of interest changes. Why should, it is argued, the community pay such heavy interest charges to commercial banks and other institutions ? Why cannot the government itself issue new money (i.e., resort to deficit financing) to finance public investment programme. The government has simply to put the printing press in motion to secure the requisite supply of money to put idle resources to work. Some writers have, however, raised objection to monetary expansion (i.e., deficit financing) as a method of financing public investment on the ground that such a method would lead directly to inflation, placing the economy in a difficult and even dangerous position. The Keynesians, however, argue that so long as there are idle or unemployed resources present in the economy, deficit financing is not going to produce inflationary symptoms. Rather, it would help in mobilizing the idle resources for the task of production and increasing employment opportunities. The trouble shall arise only if deficit financing continues even beyond the point of full employment. Then it shall lead to the emergence of inflationary trends in the economy. The question, however, arises : Why should deficit financing continue after full employment has been achieved ? There is clearly no place for it in the *post-full employment stage*. To the Keynesians, therefore, deficit financing is a perfectly legitimate means and there is absolutely no harm in having recourse to it in an economy, faced with depression and unemployment. "Thus that loose lady of the Fisc, the deficit-budget", in the words of Joseph S. Lawrence, "was touched by Keynes with the wand of a refreshing philosophy and made respectable".

3. Economic Development

Deficit financing is also being increasingly utilized by the developing countries for promoting their economic growth. A number of underdeveloped countries attained political freedom after the end of the Second World War. Naturally enough, most of them resorted to the technique of economic planning for the purpose of accelerating their economic growth. Their attempts in this direction, at least in the beginning, were frustrated on account of the general paucity of financial resources. Taxation, in these countries, had a very narrow base, on account of the universal poverty of the people. It hardly accounted for 8 to 10 percent of the total national income of the country concerned. Public borrowings, as a source of finance, had a limited scope on account of low incomes and high marginal propensity to consume of the people. The low saving capacity of the public sets limits to the amount that can be raised through public borrowings. Further, most of these newly independent countries had a democratic political set-up. There was, therefore, limited shops for additional taxation on political grounds. The governments of these countries therefore, found it more expedient to raise additional financial resources through deficit financing, i.e., by printing more paper currency. Deficit financing, as a method of finance, aroused little opposition from the public. As such, there were few developing countries which did not avail of the opportunity of raising additional funds through the technique of the deficit financing. In India, for example deficit financing constituted quite a sizeable source of finance for implementing the Five-Year Plans. There was hardly any Five-Year Plan which was not financed, in part, through deficit financing. Other developing countries were no exception. The technique of deficit financing, as a method of development finance has, therefore, come to stay.

Arguments in Favour of Deficit Financing

The following are the arguments in favour of deficit financing :

(a) ***Exploitation of Unutilized and underutilized resources***

It is well known that an underdeveloped country possesses large unutilized or underutilized natural resources. Without finance there is no way of developing these resources. With the created money these natural resources can be exploited, leading to capital formation.

(b) *More money supply necessary in a developing economy*

When an economy embarks on development planning the GNP increases. Expansion of money supply is absolutely necessary in a corresponding proportion : otherwise, prices may fall and cause hardship and create distortions in the economy.

(c) *Non-monetized sector shrinks, requiring more money supply*

In a traditional economy 70% to 90% of the people depend upon agricultural and primary activities. They adopt barter system; wages are paid in kind and most of the produce is consumed on the spot. There is a vast non-monetized sector which shrinks as economy develops under the impact of planning. Hence there is need for more money, even created money.

(d) *Improved living conditions need more money supply*

The purpose of all development is to increase output and thereby raise the per capita income. People can buy better food, more clothing, etc. When the standard of living goes up the demand for money increases. They wish to have more cash balances. Deficit financing helps in meeting the needs of the people for more money.

(e) *More money supply is needed to meet the import surplus*

When the economy gets foreign aid in large quantities, there is likely to be an import surplus. This results in a greater demand for money and the Government can meet this increased demand for money by resorting to deficit financing.

(f) *Deficit financing does not provoke the opposition of the public*

When planned expenditure is very high, it is difficult to raise resources by further increases in taxation due to public resentment and opposition. Again, there is a limit to the amount that can be raised through public borrowing. Deficit financing provides the Government with resources quickly and in a concealed manner without rousing public opposition.

Arguments Against Deficit Financing

Deficit financing is considered an evil or harbinger of sorrow for a number of reasons. Its use may end up in economic paralysis as it happened in Germany after World War I. The following are the arguments highlighting the adverse effects of deficit financing on the economy.

(a) *Deficit financing and inflation*

The most serious disadvantage of deficit financing is the inflationary rise of prices, followed by all the attendant consequences of inflation. When the total volume up of money supply in the country increases without an immediate increase in supply of goods and services, deficit financing leads to spiralling up of prices. The fixed income groups are the worst hit. Rising prices will lead to demand for increased wages, and increased wages push up further the cost of production. The vicious circle of prices and wages chasing each other and the vicious circle of more money chasing fewer goods will ultimately bring about the collapse of the monetary system. Some sections of the community no doubt are better off than others. For example, there is a redistribution of income in favour of the entrepreneurial classes at the cost of the fixed income groups. Prof. Higgins remarks "The destruction of the middle classes, impoverishment of the workers and enrichment of the speculators and the black marketeers intensify social conflict and permit radical parties of right or left to take over power. The underdeveloped countries prone to political instability cannot afford the added burdens of hyperinflation".

This argument is partially answered by stating that although there is a shortage of goods and services in the beginning, eventually production gathers momentum and checks the rise in prices. Further, the Government can adopt anti-inflationary measures like rationing and control of prices.

(b) *Change in the pattern of investment*

Investment caused by inflation may not be of the pattern sought under the Plans. The speculators and black marketers who benefit by inflation do not use their saving for productive investments. Inflation has a tendency to bring about the wrong type of investments like inventory holding, luxury urban construction, purchase of gold jewellery and even foreign assets. These are not the types of investments which would fit in with the pattern of economic development.

(c) *Forced Saving*

When inflation occurs, consumption declines due to rising prices and forced saving occurs. This argument of reduced consumption is only true of the fixed income groups. But it is not so in respect of the higher income groups. From the social point of view, the loss in the real consumption of the masses will exceed the gain in total savings of the community.

(d) *Uncertainty in future expectations*

On account of the rising prices due to inflation there is an uncertainty in future returns of investments to be made. As a result, investment decisions will be adversely affected.

(e) *Credit creation by banks*

Deficit financing means increase in Government spending without a corresponding decrease in private spending. This increases the bank deposits with the central bank. The commercial banks are in a position now to make extra advances as their liquidity has increased. There is a sort of boom in the economy with scope for speculative gains. There is a greater demand for bank credit which is freely satisfied. In this way, the inflationary forces started by deficit financing will get out of control resulting ultimately in the collapse of the economic system.

(f) *Self-defeating*

Due to inflation caused by deficit financing the cost of development project goes up and has to be revised upwards again and again. In other words, to achieve the same quantum of development more money will have to be raised. The profitability of the investments declines and investments may stop. This will lead to economic retardation and not economic development. For this reason it is said that deficit financing is self-defeating.

(g) *Balance of payments difficulties*

Rise in domestic incomes and prices due to inflation caused by deficit financing may encourage people to import more commodities from abroad. This leads to flight of capital from the country. Again when domestic prices are high as compared with foreign prices, exports become dearer and more difficult. Foreign investors are scared by the situation where costs are continuously rising and thus foreign inflow of investment is discouraged. Efforts to restrict imports may lead to greater rise in prices. Hence, deficit financing creates balance of payments difficulties as well as depletion of foreign exchange.

Safe Limits of Deficit Financing and Remedies

Deficit financing is an expansionist device of currency machine and is accompanied by inflation and has many adverse effects on the economy. The degree of inflation would depend upon both the magnitude as well as repeated use or continuity of deficit financing. And hence, it has to be used within limits of safety, so that the prices may rise or creep slowly and not gallop very fast. For this reason, deficit financing is a delicate instrument to be handled with care. It has also been compared to a drug marked in red 'Poison' which is prescribed for a certain purpose and has to be administered in small regulated doses. There should be proper checks and counterchecks. By the safe limit of deficit financing is meant the quantum of deficit financing which leads to capital formation without causing steep inflationary rise in prices. The following are the guidelines for determining the safe limits.

(1) *Growth rate of G.N.P.*

The first factor which determines the safe limit is the rate at which the G.N.P. is increasing. Suppose the growth rate is 5% per annum and the total supply of money in the economy is Rs. 10,000 crores, then the economy can absorb Rs. 500 crores annually. If money to this extent is not injected into the economy, there is more output in the economy, outstripping the supply of money, with the result that deflationary tendencies will appear.

(2) *Growth rate of monetized sector*

In an underdeveloped economy there exists a large non-monetized sector. As the economy develops, this sector gradually is converted into monetized sector requiring additional supply of money. Thus the safe limit for deficit financing could be increased to the extent by which the non-monetized sector is transformed into the monetized sector.

(3) *Growth rate of savings*

A third factor which will increase the safe limit is the rate at which production, employment and income of the people grow. These increases will make a greater demand on money with the result that cash balances of the people tend to increase. During periods of war, the increased production is used for war purposes, and does not go into the hands of the people. When deficit financing is adopted for development purposes the people are assured of steady supplies of the essential commodities. Hence, when credit expands with a simultaneous increase in production, people consume more, export more and save more. This brings in foreign exchange as well as increases savings which can be mopped up in the form of loans and taxes. To the extent production, employment and savings increase, the safe limits for deficit financing could be increased. As Prof. W.A. Lewis says, "If the Government wishes the inflation to peter out as soon as possible by maintaining its new higher levels of expenditure (in real terms) and if it cannot rely on the savers hoarding their savings, then, it must get hold of the savings in some other way either by taxing them away or by offering favourable terms for Government bonds".

(4) *Multifarious controls*

The safe limit for deficit financing can be increased to the extent inflation could be checked by adopting multiple controls. The following physical and financial controls have been suggested :

(*i*) Basic commodities like cloth, sugar and wheat should be made available in sufficient quantities by efficient regulation of prices and distribution. The impact of more money due to deficit financing will shift to other commodities and services which are unimportant from the point of view of cost of living.

(*ii*) The Government should adopt a scientific policy of credit regulation and credit curb through the central bank. The Indian Planning Commission stresses this point in the following words : "Without a firm and clear policy regarding controls and without also assurance of continuity in that policy over a period of time, not only does the scope for deficit financing become limited but there is a perpetual danger of even relatively small budgetary deficits generating inflationary pressures. In this sense therefore it is not finance as such which limits the scale of investment effort but the limitation of policy and administration regarding the supply and distribution of foodgrains and other essential commodities.

(*iii*) Added to this there should be control of the wages. Generally the people have an aversion to controls. They must know that controls are unavoidable. It is very aptly stated in the following words : "To ask for deficit financing and, at the same time, object to economic controls is a contradiction in terms; and the sooner this is recognized, the greater will be the chances of successful economic planning". Better that people suffer controls rather than curtail planning.

(5) *Creation of import surplus*

The inflationary character of deficit financing is reduced to the extent that the Government can create import surplus. This can be achieved by obtaining foreign exchange from the central bank against its cash balances for importing capital equipment, industrial raw materials and foodgrains.

(6) *Increase in supply of goods*

It is well known that inflation is caused by too much money chasing too few goods. Usually, there is a timelag between investments made through deficit financing and resulting increase in output. This is the crucial period when money in circulation is more and consumption level is low. It is therefore of prime importance to bridge the gap between money supply and goods supply. For this purpose, the planner should invest in projects which could quickly increase the supply of goods such as DPA and not SOC.

(7) *Spirit of sacrifice*

A long with the above factors determining the safe limit, the most important factors are the discipline of the planning authorities and the spirit of sacrifice of the people. Dr. V.K.R.V. Rao has pointed out to this aspect when he writes, "I would like to emphasize the role of public understanding and public co-operation as a positive factors intending to diminish the price effect of deficit financing".

Conclusion

In conclusion, we may say that though fiscal policy is the most important and potent weapon in the hands of the state to secure economic development of the underdeveloped countries but it has its own limitations and therefore, it must be supplemented by appropriate monetary policy. Besides, suitable economic, social and political environment conducive to economic growth is necessary for the successful implementation of fiscal policy.

Questions for Discussion

1. Comment upon the role of fiscal policy for economic growth.
2. Suggest a suitable fiscal policy for under-developed countries.
3. Give a critical estimate of main fiscal instruments.
4. Write a critical note on the effectiveness of fiscal policy in underdeveloped countries.
5. What is deficit financing ? How does it assist in accelerating economic development ? What are its limitations.

BIBLIOGRAPHY

1. Day, A.C.L., Out Line of Monetary Economics.
2. Basu, A.K., Fundamentals of Banking Theory and Practice.
3. De Cock, M.H., Central Banking.
4. Hansen, J.L., Monetary Theory and Practice.
5. Sayers, R.S., Modern Banking.
6. Whittlesey, C.R., Principles and Practices of Money and Banking.
7. Fredericc, A. Bradford, Money and Banking.
8. Sheldon, H.P., Practice and Law of Banking.
9. Ghosh, Alak, Indian Economy.
10. Mehta N.C and Panandikar, Rural Banking.
11. Reserve Bank, Functions and Working of RBI.
12. World Bank, Principles and Policies.
13. Gupta S.B., Monetary Economics.
14. Chandler, L.V., The Economics of Money and Banking.
15. Kent, R. P., Money and Banking.
16. S.K. Misra, V.K. Puri, Indian Economy.
17. T.N. Chhabra, Banking Theory and Practice.
18. K.C. Shekhar, Banking Theory and Practice.
19. Halm, George A., Monetary Theory.
20. Ne. Thi. Somashekat, Vanijya Nyaya.
21. M.S. Rao & S.N. Sen, Money, Banking, Trade and Finance.
22. P.K. Srivastava, Banking Theory and Practice.
23. M.L. Seth, Monetary Economics.
24. A.N. Agarawal, Indian Economy.
25. Holden, J. Milness, The Law and Practice of Banking.

26. Tokhi, M.R. and Sharma, D.P., Rural Bank of India.
27. Ne.Thi. Somashekar, Banking Theory and Practice.
28. Ne.Thi. Somashekar, Development and Environmental Economics.

Annual Reports

1. Reserve Bank of India.
2. State Bank of India.
3. World Bank.
4. Deposit Insurance Corporation.

Periodicals

1. Reserve Bank of India Monthly Bulletin.
2. State Bank of India Monthly Review.
3. The Journal of the Institute of Bankers.
4. Commerce.
5. Capital.